Economic Report of the President

Transmitted to the Congress
February 1983

TOGETHER WITH

THE ANNUAL REPORT

OF THE

COUNCIL OF ECONOMIC ADVISERS

UNITED STATES GOVERNMENT PRINTING OFFICE
WASHINGTON : 1983

For sale by the Superintendent of Documents, U.S. Government Printing Office
Washington, D.C. 20402

CONTENTS

*For a detailed table of contents of the Council's Report, see page 13.

ECONOMIC REPORT OF THE PRESIDENT

ECONOMIC REPORT OF THE PRESIDENT

To the Congress of the United States:

Two years ago, I came to Washington with a deep personal commitment to change America's economic future. For more than a decade, the economy had suffered from low productivity growth and a rising rate of inflation. Government spending absorbed an increasing share of national income. A shortsighted view of economic priorities was destroying our prospects for long-term prosperity.

The economic program that I proposed shortly after I took office emphasized economic growth and a return to price stability. My tax proposals were designed to encourage private initiative and to stimulate saving and productive investment. I have supported and encouraged the Federal Reserve Board in its pursuit of price stability through sound monetary policy. My Administration has slowed the growth of Federal regulation, strengthening the forces of competition in a number of economic sectors. And I have worked with the Congress to enact legislation that has reversed or limited the growth of government programs that have become too large or outlasted their usefulness.

Although the full effect of these changes in government policy will take time to develop, some of the benefits have already become apparent. The rate of consumer price inflation between December 1981 and December 1982 was only 3.9 percent, about one-third of the rate in the year before I took office. Interest rates are now lower than when I took office, and have fallen rapidly during the last 6 months.

The Administration will propose many additional measures over the next several years to strengthen economic incentives, reduce burdensome regulations, increase capital formation, and raise our standard of living. It is easy to lose sight of these long-term goals in a year, like 1982, when the economy was in an extended recession. I am deeply troubled by the current level of unemployment in the United States and by the suffering and anxiety that it entails for millions of Americans. The unemployment that many of our citizens are experiencing is a consequence of the disinflation that must necessarily follow the accelerating inflation of the last decade. Allowing the upward trend of inflation to continue would have risked even greater increases in unemployment in the future. In spite of the present high unemployment rate and the accompanying hardships, it is essential that we maintain the gains against inflation that we have recently achieved at substantial cost. Continuing success in restraining inflation will provide a stronger foundation for economic recovery in 1983 and beyond.

Reducing Unemployment

The Federal Government can play an important role in reducing unemployment. I believe, however, that the government should focus its attention on those groups that will continue to face high unemployment rates even after the recovery has begun. By helping them to develop their job-related skills, we will foster productive careers in the private sector rather than dead-end jobs. This emphasis on training and private sector employment is the focus of the Jobs Training Partnership Act that I supported and signed into law in 1982. I am proposing additional steps this year to strengthen Federal training and retraining programs and to help the structurally unemployed find lasting jobs.

It is understandable that many well-meaning members of the Congress have responded to the current high unemployment rate by proposing various public works and employment programs. However, I am convinced that such programs would only shift unemployment from one industry to another at the cost of increasing the Federal budget deficit.

Although programs to help the structurally unemployed are important, only a balanced and lasting recovery can achieve a substantial reduction in unemployment. There are now over four million more unemployed people than there were at the peak of the last business cycle. Nine million new workers are expected to join the labor force by 1988. Only a healthy and growing economy can provide the more than 13 million jobs needed to achieve a progressively lower level of unemployment over the next 5 years.

The Prospects for Economic Recovery

There are now signs that an economic recovery will begin soon. By December 1982 the index of leading economic indicators had risen in 7 of the last 8 months. Housing starts have risen substantially over the last year, and by December 1982 were 39 percent higher than 12 months earlier. Inventory levels have fallen sharply, so that increased sales should translate quickly into increased production and employment. Both long-term and short-term interest rates have fallen substantially. The Administration's economic forecast predicts that the gross national product will begin to rise in the first quarter of 1983 and will then rise more quickly as the year continues. Most private forecasters also predict a recovery in 1983.

Monetary policy will play a critical role in achieving a sound and sustainable economic recovery. If the monetary aggregates grow too slowly, the economy will lack the level of financial resources needed for continued economic growth. But if these aggregates are allowed to expand too rapidly, an increase in inflation and a short-lived recovery will result. I recognize the difficulties that the Federal Reserve has faced and will continue to face in guiding the growth of the money supply at a time when major regulatory changes have made it difficult to rely on old guidelines. I expect that in 1983 the Federal Reserve will expand the money supply at a moderate rate consistent with both a sustained recovery and continued progress against inflation.

Investment and Economic Growth

An economic recovery beginning in 1983 should bring not only a reduction in unemployment but also an increase in business investment over the next several years. A higher level of investment is an important ingredient in raising productivity and economic growth. The Accelerated Cost Recovery System that I proposed and that the Congress enacted in 1981 was designed to encourage a substantial expansion of business investment above the relatively low levels of the 1970s. Since that time the adverse effects of the recession have outweighed the positive effects of the new tax rules. As the economy turns from recession to recovery, however, incentives to invest will become more powerful. But business investment may not grow rapidly unless measures proposed by the Administration to reduce potentially large Federal budget deficits are enacted.

Federal borrowing competes with private investment for available savings. If the government continues to borrow large amounts to finance its deficit, the real interest rate will remain high and discourage private investment. This process of "crowding out" will tend to depress private investment in the years ahead unless the budget deficit is progressively reduced.

Fiscal Year 1984 Budget Proposals

It is important to distinguish the cyclical part of the budget deficit from the structural part, which would remain even at the peak of the business cycle. Approximately one-half of the 1983 budget deficit is due to the depressed state of the economy. With earnings and profits reduced, tax receipts have significantly decreased, and expenditures have increased. As the economy recovers, the cyclical part of the deficit will shrink. But cyclical recovery alone will not bring the deficit down to an acceptable size.

In the budget I am now submitting to the Congress, I am proposing the dramatic steps needed to reduce Federal budget deficits in future years. My budget proposals are designed to reduce the deficit by dealing directly with the rapid growth of the domestic spending programs (apart from interest payments) of the Federal Government. In 1970 these programs accounted for 10 percent of the gross national product and 48 percent of Federal spending. By 1980 these programs had grown to 14 percent of gross national product and 63 percent of the budget. I remain committed to the idea that we can reduce budget deficits without increasing the burden on the poor, without weakening our national defense, and without destroying economic incentives by counterproductive tax increases.

Rapid congressional enactment of the budget would provide clear and credible evidence that the Federal Government intends not to place heavy burdens on the capital markets in future years. Such reassurance should hasten the decline in interest rates, especially long-term interest rates on bonds and residential mortgages, and improve prospects for the recovery of the housing, automobile, and capital investment sectors of the economy.

I recognize the special importance of protecting the social security and medicare programs for aged retirees and their dependents. These programs now face very serious financial problems. The bipartisan National Commission on Social Security Reform has recently recommended a series of measures, which I have endorsed, to eliminate the cumulative deficiency of $150 billion to $200 billion projected for the social security system in the years 1983 through 1989. It is critically important at this time to make changes in the social security programs that will protect their solvency and financial viability for the years to come.

The Remaining Burden of Federal Economic Regulation

For many decades, the Federal Government has regulated the price and entry conditions affecting several sectors of the American economy. Much of this regulation is no longer appropriate to the conditions of the contemporary economy. Over time, most of this regulation—by restraining competition and the development of new services and technologies—has not served the interests of either consumers or producers. Since deregulation of some markets began several years ago, the experience has been almost uniformly encouraging. My Administration has supported these step-by-step efforts to reduce these regulations in markets that would otherwise be competitive. It is now time to consider broad measures to eliminate many of these economic regulations especially as they affect the natural gas, transportation, communications, and financial markets.

Interest Rates and the U.S. Trade Deficit

The very high levels of real interest rates over the last several years are a principal cause of the sharp rise in the exchange value of the dollar relative to foreign currencies. This rise has reduced the ability of American exporters to compete in foreign markets and increased the competitiveness of imports in the domestic market. Largely as a result, the U.S. merchandise trade balance showed a substantial deficit in 1982.

Our current trade deficit is a reminder of the importance of international trade to the American economy. The export share of U.S. gross national product has more than doubled over the last three decades. American workers, businesses, and farmers suffer when foreign governments prevent American products from entering their markets, thus reducing U.S. export levels. While the United States may be forced to respond to the trade distorting practices of foreign governments through the use of strategic measures, such practices do not warrant indiscriminate protectionist actions, such as domestic content rules for automobiles sold in the United States. Widespread protectionist policies would hurt American consumers by raising prices of the products they buy, and by removing some of the pressures for cost control and quality improvement that result from international competition. Moreover, protectionism at home could hurt the workers, farmers, and firms in the United States that produce goods and services for export, since it would almost inevitably lead to increased protectionism by governments abroad. I am committed to a policy of preventing the enactment of protectionist measures in the United States, and I will continue working to persuade the other nations of the world to eliminate trade distorting practices that threaten the viability of the international trading system upon which world prosperity depends.

Trade in goods and services is only one aspect of our economic relations with the rest of the world. The international flow of capital into the United States and from the United States to other countries is also of great importance. The United States should play a primary role in preserving the vitality of the international capital market. Severe strains on that market developed in 1982 as several nations found it difficult to service their overseas debt obligations. In 1982, the Federal Government worked closely with debtor and creditor nations and the major international lending agencies to prevent a disruption in the functioning of world capital markets. Now, with the cooperation of a wide variety of creditors, countries with especially severe debt-servicing difficulties are establishing economic and financial programs that will permit them to meet their international obligations.

The Years Ahead

We are now at a critical juncture for the American economy. The recession has led to strong pressures from some members of the Congress and from others to abandon our commitment to a policy that is aimed at long-term economic growth, capital accumulation, and price stability. There are many who urge new government spending programs and forcing the Federal Reserve to raise monetary growth rates to levels that would rekindle inflation.

I am convinced that such policies would prove detrimental to the long-run interests of the American people. Our economy, despite the recession, is extraordinarily resilient and is now on the road to a healthy recovery. It is essential in the year ahead that the Administration and the Congress work together, take a long-term perspective, and pursue economic policies that lead to sustained economic growth and to greater prosperity for all Americans.

Ronald Reagan

February 2, 1983

THE ANNUAL REPORT
OF THE
COUNCIL OF ECONOMIC ADVISERS

LETTER OF TRANSMITTAL

COUNCIL OF ECONOMIC ADVISERS,
Washington, D.C., January 31, 1983.

MR. PRESIDENT:

The Council of Economic Advisers herewith submits its 1983 Annual Report in accordance with the provisions of the Employment Act of 1946 as amended by the Full Employment and Balanced Growth Act of 1978.

Sincerely,

Martin Feldstein
CHAIRMAN

William A. Niskanen

William Poole

CONTENTS

384-041 O - 83 - 2 : QL 3

List of Tables and Charts

Tables

Tables

Charts

CHAPTER 1

From Recession to Recovery and Growth

THE MAJOR ECONOMIC ACHIEVEMENT OF 1982 was a dramatic reduction of inflation to its lowest rate in a decade. The 4.6 percent increase in the gross national product (GNP) implicit price deflator between the fourth quarters of 1981 and 1982 was less than half the 10.2 percent rate of increase between the fourth quarters of 1979 and 1980. This decline in inflation has moderated the earlier widespread fears that inflation would accelerate. While some of this improvement in inflation was transitory, reflecting such special factors as the appreciation of the exchange value of the dollar, the largest share was almost certainly due to a decline in the underlying rate of inflation. The reduced rate of inflation is a major step toward the Administration's goals of full employment, healthy economic growth, and price stability.

The progress made in reducing inflation, however, was accompanied by a painful slowdown of the economy. Beginning in July 1981, the Nation suffered the second of two back-to-back recessions that brought the unemployment rate to 10.8 percent in December 1982. At that time, approximately 5 million more people were unemployed than in January 1980, when the first of the two recessions began.

The increase in long-term unemployment poses a particularly severe problem. In January 1980, about 550,000 people had been unemployed for more than 6 months. In December 1982 there were more than four times as many. Long-term unemployment is particularly serious in that it causes substantial financial hardship and is associated with a loss of job skills that may reduce future income significantly.

Some temporary decline in real economic activity was probably unavoidable in the process of reversing the upward trend of inflation. The United States entered the 1980s with a high rate of inflation and with widespread public expectations that the rate would remain high, and perhaps increase. As high inflation persisted, it became embedded in the plans and contracts of firms and workers, and lowering it involved a painful process. The decline of real GNP since early 1981 was in large part the price the United States paid for failing to control inflation in the late 1970s.

LEGACIES OF THE 1970s

In the 1960s, many economists believed that the Federal Government could keep unemployment down permanently by accepting a higher rate of inflation. Steady rises in productivity and living standards were taken for granted. During the 1970s these views proved to be incorrect. By the closing years of the 1970s, both the unemployment rate and the inflation rate were higher than they had been in the 1960s, and the rate of productivity growth was lower.

Why did unemployment, productivity growth, and inflation all worsen in the 1970s? These developments occurred in part because of factors outside the government's control, such as changes in the size and composition of the work force and rising world energy prices. But the economy also suffered from long-standing government policies that exacerbated inflation and distorted the incentives to work, save, and invest.

RISING UNEMPLOYMENT

Total employment grew rapidly in the 1970s but so did the rate of unemployment. The civilian labor force participation rate rose from 60.4 percent of the population in 1970 to 63.8 percent in 1980. The unemployment rate averaged 5.4 percent in the first half of the 1970s, greater than the 4.8 percent average of the 1960s. The recession of 1975 took the unemployment rate to a monthly high of 9.0 percent. Unemployment then declined to a monthly low of 5.6 percent in 1979, only to begin rising again to a peak of 7.8 percent in July 1980.

In addition to cyclical fluctuations in the economy, a number of structural factors contributed to the rise in the unemployment rate over the decade. These included the changing demographic structure of the labor force, the increased number of workers dislocated by changes in technology and international competitiveness, and the work registration requirements in a number of government welfare programs.

A more detailed analysis of unemployment and the labor market consequences of macroeconomic policy is presented in Chapter 2.

DECLINING PRODUCTIVITY GROWTH

From 1960 to 1970, real output per hour in the private sector rose at an annual rate of 3.0 percent; from 1970 to 1980 it rose at a rate of only 1.4 percent. Labor productivity growth would probably have slowed somewhat in the 1970s regardless of the policies adopted. The sharp increases in the price of oil caused by supply disruptions in 1974 and 1979 reduced productivity growth as firms substituted capital and labor for energy. Furthermore, as the post-World War II baby-boom generation entered the labor force and the percentage of working-age women seeking employment rose, the proportion of less experienced workers increased, further depressing productivity.

The slowdown in productivity growth was, however, exacerbated by a decline in rates of capital formation. Net investment in fixed business capital fell from 3.5 percent of GNP in the 1960s to 3.0 percent in the 1970s, and the rate of growth of capital per worker fell even more sharply, from 3.2 percent per year in the 1960s to only 1.3 percent in the 1970s. The interaction of the tax system with inflation played an important role in reducing the rate of capital formation.

Another cause of slow productivity growth was an increase in government regulation. In some sectors of the economy, Federal regulations directly reduced labor productivity; in others, they diverted capital investment away from the improvement of productivity into the satisfaction of regulatory requirements. Some of these regulations served useful purposes, but some imposed economic costs that exceeded their economic benefits.

The tax changes proposed by the Administration and enacted by the Congress in 1981 and 1982 were designed to lead to faster growth and higher productivity by stimulating saving, investment, and individual effort. In addition, the Administration's policy of reducing government regulation is intended to enhance the efficiency of individual markets and thereby increase total production.

RISING INFLATION

Of all the economic problems that this Administration inherited when it came to office in 1981, the most urgent was the problem of rising prices. Double-digit inflation had created serious economic distortions. An equally serious concern was that the trend rate of inflation was rising over time.

From 1960 to 1970, the GNP deflator rose at an average rate of 3.0 percent per year. Between 1970 and 1973, the average rate of inflation by this measure was 5.3 percent. Then, aggravated by the sharp jump in world oil prices and other special factors, inflation reached 10.2 percent during 1974, but by 1976 it was down to 4.7 percent. In the next 4 years, which included the second oil price shock in 1979, inflation increased continually until it reached 10.2 percent again in 1980.

Over short periods of time a variety of factors influence the rate of inflation. One important factor in the 1970s was supply-determined changes in commodity prices resulting from fluctuations in harvests and disruptions in the supply of foreign oil. Another important factor was the increasing level of expected inflation. Once the expectation of continuing inflation has become firmly entrenched, prices and wages may continue to rise even in the face of declining demand, and the cost of reducing inflation may increase.

These factors, however, only affect the rate of inflation for a limited time. The popular axiom that attributes inflation to "too much money chasing too few goods" reflects a basic truth: it is difficult to imagine a sustained inflation that is not supported by excessive money growth. Over long periods of time, an additional percentage point in the rate of growth of the money stock will tend to produce an additional percentage point of growth of nominal GNP, that is, GNP measured at current prices. If the rate of real GNP growth does not change, the entire increase in nominal GNP growth will take the form of increased inflation. Although the relations between money growth, nominal GNP growth, and inflation are considerably more variable over shorter periods than they are in the long run, the impact of money growth on nominal income and inflation remains powerful even in the short run.

THE RECESSION

The substantial decline in the rate of growth of the M1 measure of money that occurred between the end of 1980 and the end of 1981 was a principal contributor to the decline in nominal income growth in 1982, a decline compounded by a marked change in the velocity of money. Part of the slowdown in nominal GNP growth took the form of lower inflation, and part of it took the form of a decline in real economic activity.

The adverse short-run effect of a slowdown in nominal GNP on real economic activity is a basic feature of our economy that reflects the stickiness of wages and prices in most markets. If prices and wages were perfectly flexible, reduced nominal GNP growth would translate immediately and painlessly into reduced inflation. However, not all wages and prices are flexible. When expectations of future inflation are deeply embedded, prices and wages may continue to rise for some time despite excess supplies of goods and labor. A change in inflationary expectations, together with the direct pressures exerted by excess supplies, eventually causes prices and wages to adjust to new market-clearing levels. But until that occurs a slowdown in nominal GNP growth is reflected in a slowing of real growth as well as in a slowing of inflation.

The severity of the recession in 1982 reflected a combination of circumstances which caused a very sharp decline in nominal GNP growth between 1981 and 1982. Between the fourth quarter of 1980 and the fourth quarter of 1981, nominal GNP grew at a rate of 9.6 percent; in contrast, nominal GNP rose only 3.3 percent last year. About one-third of the 6.3 percentage point drop in nominal GNP growth between 1981 and 1982 was reflected in a 1.9 percentage point decline in the real GNP growth rate—from an increase of 0.7 percent in 1981 to a decline of 1.2 percent in 1982. The reduction in inflation accounted for the remaining two-thirds of the drop in nominal GNP.

Although some slowdown in nominal GNP growth and in inflation in 1982 was a predictable effect of tighter monetary policies, the very sharp decline actually experienced did not reflect a decrease in the growth of the monetary aggregates. Rather the exceptional severity of the slowdown in nominal GNP growth can be traced to a combination of factors that led to an unusually sharp decline in the velocity of money, that is, in the ratio of GNP to the money stock.

THE DECLINE IN VELOCITY

The 1982 decline in the velocity of money—as measured by the velocity of either the M1 or M2 monetary aggregates—was historically atypical. Between 1961 and 1981, M1 velocity rose at an average annual rate of 3.2 percent, while the velocity of M2 remained essentially constant, rising at an average annual rate of 0.2 percent. In contrast, in 1982 the velocity of M1 fell 4.9 percent and M2 velocity fell 6.0 percent on a fourth quarter to fourth quarter basis. By either measure, the growth of nominal GNP was well below the rate that would have prevailed if the M1 or M2 measures of velocity had grown at their average historic rates. These velocity declines were the largest since 1959, the earliest year for which the Federal Reserve has published data on the monetary aggregates under the definitions currently in use.

If these velocity shifts had not occurred, the rise in nominal GNP in 1982 would have been between 10 and 12 percent. While it is uncertain how this hypothetical change would have been distributed between real activity and inflation, it is likely that real GNP would have increased enough to have ended the recession sometime before the final quarter of 1982.

Although the cause of the large velocity shift that occurred in 1982 is not fully understood, it is likely that major changes in asset demands of individuals and businesses played an important role. More precisely, an increase in the demand for M1 or M2 at any income level decreases the corresponding velocity of money. Such shifts may occur because of regulatory changes that provide new financial opportunities—like the introduction of nationwide interest-bearing negotiable order of withdrawal (NOW) accounts—or because of changes in asset preferences—like the increased demand for money market mutual funds instead of long-term securities.

The uncertain cause of the recent decline in velocity is characteristic of the problems that the Federal Reserve has encountered in applying the new monetary control procedures that it adopted in October 1979. Changes in banking regulations and the development of new financial instruments by the private sector have compelled the Federal Reserve to make frequent revisions to the definitions of the monetary aggregates and reassessments of their economic impacts. In 1980 a complete revision of the definitions of the monetary aggregates was introduced. In the next year, a "shift adjusted" M1-B was defined in an effort to adjust for shifts from savings deposits to NOW accounts. Most recently, in 1982 and early 1983, definitional changes in M1 and M2 were required to deal with the advent of the new money market deposit account—which was added to M2—and the new super NOW account—which was added to M1.

The Federal Reserve was aware throughout 1981 and 1982 that the relationship between the monetary aggregates and economic activity was in a state of flux, and that future velocity trends were uncertain. While sustained but unanticipated shifts in velocity growth can be identified in hindsight, it is nearly impossible to know at the time they occur whether unusual quarter-to-quarter changes in velocity will continue or reverse themselves. The presumption, on the basis of past experience, is that most velocity changes are temporary. Thus, increasing the rate of money growth in response to temporary declines in velocity runs the risk of providing excessive liquidity and increasing inflation, while a failure to recognize a continuing shift in liquidity preference or velocity runs the risk of providing inadequate liquidity and reducing real GNP. Given the circumstances of 1982, the somewhat greater growth in the monetary aggregates than initially intended by the Federal Reserve appeared to be an appropriate way to balance those risks.

ECONOMIC RECOVERY

The Administration believes that the American economy will soon recover from the recession that began in July 1981. The forecast presented in Chapter 6 projects that economic recovery will begin in 1983, marking the start of a long period of sustained growth with low inflation. More specifically, the Administration forecasts that real GNP will rise 3.1 percent from the fourth quarter of 1982 to the fourth quarter of 1983, and that nominal GNP will rise 8.8 percent. Realization of the economic forecast and steady noninflationary growth in subsequent years will depend upon the implementation of appropriate monetary and fiscal policies.

IMPLEMENTING A STABLE MONETARY POLICY

The Administration has repeatedly indicated that the fundamental guiding principle of monetary policy in an inflationary economy should be a gradual reduction in the rate of growth of the money stock until the rate is consistent with price stability. This principle is consistent with the general approach enunciated in recent years by the independent Federal Reserve.

The basic challenge for monetary policy at present is to balance the principle of stable money growth with the need to take account of changing asset preferences that may alter the velocity of money. While maintaining the approach of setting specified target ranges for money growth, the Federal Reserve will also need to use its judgment to adjust money growth rates and the corresponding targets to reflect lasting changes in asset demands.

The extent to which a policy of predetermined money growth rates is appropriate depends on the stability and predictability of the velocity of money. Strictly speaking, inflexible monetary growth rates are appropriate only if the trend in income velocity is constant or has purely random disturbances. The advisability of a strict policy rule depends on the degree of predictability of velocity disturbances. The more predictable velocity disturbances are, the more they can be offset by countervailing shifts in the money stock. The less predictable they are, the more likely it is that any attempt at countervailing shifts in the money stock will add to the overall volatility of nominal GNP.

The task of making appropriate adjustments to the monetary targets is enormously difficult. An excessive increase in the money stock will cause a period of increased inflation while an insufficient increase in the money stock will not provide adequate liquidity for the needs of an expanding economy. Eventually such deviations are self-correcting, but only after a period of accelerating inflation or weak economic performance.

One possible way to avoid such periods is to use the observed behavior of nominal GNP to guide a gradual recalibration of the monetary growth targets, recognizing that there are uncertain lags between money stock changes and the resulting changes in nominal GNP. Basing the recalibration of monetary targets on nominal GNP is consistent with the basic principle of pursuing a stable monetary policy. Indeed, it is the relatively stable long-run relationship between the monetary aggregates and nominal GNP that justifies the Federal Reserve's policy of setting targets for the growth of M1 and M2. This implies that caution in revising these targets is appropriate. The principle of targeting money growth rates is not an end in itself but only a means of achieving control of nominal GNP.

Disadvantages of Interest Rate Targeting

From World War II until the mid-1970s the Federal Reserve, like most central banks, conducted monetary policy by focusing on interest rates and money market conditions. Over the 1970s, increasing emphasis was given to targeting monetary aggregates. More recently, under new procedures first adopted in October 1979, the Federal Reserve has given greater emphasis to keeping the growth of the monetary aggregates within pre-announced target ranges, even though it was recognized that this could result in greater variations in interest rates.

Since 1979 both long-term and short-term interest rates have proven more variable than in the past. Many critics attribute this change to the increased emphasis on monetary targets and the level of bank reserves as the operational basis for monetary policy. Although some have argued that the Federal Reserve should drop monetary targeting in favor of targeting interest rates, the Administration believes strongly that targeting interest rates, either nominal or real, would prove to be a serious error.

The *nominal* rate of interest is a very unreliable indicator of the thrust of monetary policy. The financial variable important to borrowers and lenders is not the *nominal* interest rate but a *real* interest rate determined by subtracting the rate of inflation from the nominal interest rate. Borrowers and lenders take into account the fact that the dollars repaid when a loan matures do not have the same purchasing power as the dollars originally borrowed. When inflation is expected, lenders insist that the nominal rate of interest include a premium to compensate them for the declining purchasing power of the dollar, and borrowers are willing to pay such a premium.

Although the real interest rate is more closely linked to borrowing and lending decisions than the nominal interest rate, the real interest rate is also not an appropriate target for monetary policy. There are several basic reasons for rejecting the policy of real interest rate targeting.

First, real interest rate targeting might well lead to an inflationary monetary policy. Any given real interest rate is compatible with a wide range of inflation rates. For example, a real interest rate of 2 percent could occur with a 5 percent nominal rate and a 3 percent inflation rate, or with a 12 percent nominal rate and a 10 percent inflation rate. Thus, achieving a real interest rate target would provide no assurance of price stability.

Second, the real interest rate that governs economic behavior is the difference between the nominal interest rate and the *expected* rate of inflation. Since expectations of inflation are not observable, the monetary authorities cannot as a practical matter measure or target the expected real interest rate.

A third reason why real interest rate targeting is not feasible is that the relevant interest rate is not merely the real rate but the real net-of-tax interest rate. Because net-of-tax rates of interest vary among individuals and businesses in different tax positions, there is no way for the monetary authorities to determine the relevant average real net-of-tax interest rate in financial markets. Compounding the problem further, different rates of inflation can result in very different net-of-tax real interest rates corresponding to the same pretax real interest rate, even for a particular taxpayer. For example, a taxpayer with a marginal tax rate of 40 percent earns a real net-of-tax return of 1 percent if he receives a nominal rate of 10 percent and there is 5 percent inflation; that same taxpayer earns a real net-of-tax return of −2 percent if he receives the same real return of 5 percent but there is zero inflation. Similarly, the real interest rate and the real net-of-tax interest rate can easily move in opposite directions when the inflation rate changes.

There is a final and even more fundamental reason for rejecting real interest rate targeting. Even if the expected real interest rate were measurable, there would remain the virtually impossible task of determining what level of that interest rate is actually compatible with noninflationary growth. The problem of identifying the equilibrium interest rate is made even more difficult by the interaction of tax rules and inflation.

Monetary Rules and Discretion

There is no simple solution to the problem of guiding monetary policy in a time of rapid institutional change. Interest rate targeting, as shown above, is not a desirable approach. Instead, the monetary authorities should be guided by the principle of keeping money growth within a prespecified target range while adjusting those targets when a careful consideration of the evidence indicates that sustained shifts in asset demands have occurred.

The combination of monetary rules and discretion must be applied with great care and judgment. The observance of rules must not become a doctrinaire attachment to arbitrary standards, and the exercise of discretion must not degenerate into unprincipled fine tuning. Instead, the monetary rules must be understood as a way of achieving an appropriate long-run path for the economy. The exercise of discretion in recalibrating monetary targets must be subject to the discipline that such revisions are ultimately compatible with the desired long-run path of nominal GNP. With rules and discretion balanced in this way, monetary policy can support a sound recovery that leads to sustained and noninflationary growth.

THE BUDGET DEFICIT

The Federal budget deficit has become a major problem for the American economy. Without the savings proposed by the Administration in its budget plan for the years 1984 through 1988, the United States is forecasted to experience a series of deficits that would consume more than 6 percent of GNP in each of the next 6 years. Although budget deficits have been a nearly constant feature of our Nation's economic life for the past two decades, the prospective budget deficits that would result if no legislative actions were taken to reduce them would be far larger than those previously experienced in the postwar period. The economic effects of such deficits are beyond our previous experience.

The fiscal 1983 deficit is partially a result of the recession. Any recession reduces tax collections and increases outlays for unemployment benefits, retirement benefits, and certain other activities. A reasonable approximation is that the change in economic output associated with a percentage point change in the unemployment rate would raise the fiscal 1983 deficit by about $25 billion. The Administration forecasts that the unemployment rate for fiscal 1983 will average 10.7 percent. If the unemployment rate were 6.5 percent instead, the budget deficit would be about half the $208 billion now forecast for fiscal 1983. The cyclical component represents a similarly large share of the fiscal 1984 deficit.

Economic recovery and growth in the years ahead will reduce the cyclical component of the deficit. The Administration's forecast projects a decline in the unemployment rate by 4 percentage points between fiscal 1983 and fiscal 1988, leaving only a negligible cyclical component in the fiscal 1988 budget. Unless the Administration's proposals are enacted, a current services budget deficit of $300 billion is forecasted to materialize.

To see the origin of these large deficits, it is useful to compare the components of the 1988 current services budget with the same components for 1970. Between those years, taxes decline very slightly as a percentage of GNP, from 19.9 percent in 1970 to 18.9 percent in 1988. The defense share of GNP remains unchanged at 8.1 percent of GNP in both years. By contrast, nondefense activities excluding interest rise from 10.6 percent of GNP in 1970 to 13.6 percent in

1988, an increase of about one-fourth. In addition, the accumulation of previous deficits raise the net interest component of the budget deficit from 1.5 percent of GNP to 3.4 percent of GNP.

Deficits and Long-Term Growth

A succession of large budget deficits is likely to reduce substantially the rate of capital formation. The government's borrowing to finance such deficits would compete directly with borrowing by private businesses and households. With a limited amount of savings available for borrowing, high budget deficits would cause interest rates to rise until private demand for funds was reduced to the amount that remained after the government's borrowing needs were satisfied.

The magnitude of the potential crowding out of private investment is immense. During the past two decades, the net saving of households and businesses totaled only about 7 percent of GNP. Prospective deficits of more than 6 percent of GNP would represent virtually all of current net saving. Even though existing saving would be augmented by borrowing from abroad and by some increase in the private saving rate, the reduced rate of capital formation would be very substantial.

A lower rate of capital formation would have adverse consequences because the accumulation of capital is a key determinant of future increases in productivity and economic growth and therefore of higher real wages and standards of living. Further reductions in the rate of capital formation would be particularly unfortunate because, as Chapter 4 discusses in detail, the U.S. rate of capital formation has been undesirably low for several decades. In the years since 1960, net private investment has averaged only 6 percent of GNP, significantly less than the rate in most major industrial countries. Moreover, since half of this 6 percent has gone into housing, only about 3 percent of GNP has been available for productivity-increasing investments in plant and equipment. Deficits of the level implied by the current services budget could reduce the rate of net investment in plant and equipment enough to preclude any increase in the amount of capital per worker. If this occurred, the process of increasing capital intensity would cease to contribute to rising productivity and real wages.

Deficits and the Recovery

The adverse effects of large budget deficits are not limited to the distant future. The deficits that would occur without the budget actions proposed by the Administration could seriously affect the degree to which various economic sectors share in the benefits of recovery from the current recession. The crowding out of private investment which would accompany large deficits could depress the level of output in the construction industries, the steel industry, the machinery and equipment industries, and industries that produce other durable goods.

In addition, large budget deficits raise the exchange value of the dollar relative to foreign currencies by attracting foreign capital to the United States. This weakens the competitive position of U.S. exports in the world economy and hurts those domestic industries that compete with imports from abroad. The nature and magnitude of this effect are discussed in Chapter 3 of this *Report.*

A "lopsided" recovery in which some sectors remained relatively depressed might prove more fragile than a recovery which was broadly based. An increase in economic activity limited to some sectors and regions might result in greater upward pressure on prices and wages at any given level of total output and employment than would be the case if there were balanced expansion among industries. In addition, an unbalanced recovery would produce more inflation and less real growth, regardless of the rate of expansion of nominal GNP.

The prospect of large budget deficits in the second half of this decade may also have an adverse effect on the prospects for recovery in 1983. If the financial markets respond to expected future deficits by keeping real long-term interest rates higher in 1983 than they would otherwise be, the level of spending in 1983 on interest-sensitive purchases may remain depressed. Clear evidence of the willingness of the Administration and the Congress to reduce Federal budget deficits substantially in the second half of the 1980s can play an important part in ensuring a healthy and balanced economic recovery in the more immediate future.

CHAPTER 2

The Dual Problems of Structural and Cyclical Unemployment

UNEMPLOYMENT IS THE MOST SERIOUS ECONOMIC PROBLEM now facing the United States. By December 1982 the number of unemployed had risen by more than 4 million since the beginning of the recession in July 1981. The unemployment rate was higher in December 1982 than at any point since the Depression, with over 12 million persons counted as unemployed. Even after the economy recovers from the recent recession, it is likely that the unemployment rate will reach a plateau between 6 and 7 percent.

This chapter analyzes the two major types of unemployment: cyclical and structural. The high level of cyclical unemployment now prevailing in the United States is a major problem, but it should prove transitory. Only a healthy and sustained recovery from the recent recession can effectively diminish cyclical unemployment. Even after full recovery, however, a serious structural unemployment problem will remain unless measures are taken to improve the functioning of labor markets. Reducing structural unemployment will require attacking the special problems of young people and the long-term adult unemployed.

This chapter begins by describing the dimensions of the cyclical and structural unemployment problems. It then examines the potential of public employment programs and macroeconomic policies to lower cyclical unemployment. Finally, policies for reducing structural unemployment are considered.

THE RECENT RECESSION

The unemployment rate in December 1982 stood at 10.8 percent of the civilian labor force. Since the recent period of economic slack that began in January 1980, the unemployment rate has risen by 4.5 percentage points. During the recent recession, which began in July 1981, the unemployment rate rose by 3.6 percentage points. Historical experience suggests that the unemployment rate tends to increase for several months after the level of production bottoms out

384-041 O - 83 - 3 : QL 3

and it is possible that the unemployment rate will reach 11 percent at some point during 1983.

Beyond those officially counted as unemployed, the recent recession has prevented many Americans from working as much as they would like. In December 1982 there were over two million persons involuntarily working part time. The Bureau of Labor Statistics also reported that there were over 1.8 million discouraged workers in December. These are individuals who have given up looking for work because they believe they cannot find jobs.

Unemployment is often linked to economic hardship. While many of the unemployed receive unemployment insurance and live in families that have other members who work, many unemployed individuals and their families suffer economic distress. Table 2–1 presents information on the incomes of families in which the husband, wife, or head of household experienced unemployment during 1981. (Data for 1982 are not yet available.) Three types of families are distinguished: (1) families in which both husband and wife worked, (2) families in which only the husband or male head worked, and (3) families in which only the wife or female head worked. For all of the family types, unemployment experienced by husband, wife, or head of household significantly lowered median family income. For example, single-earner families in which the husband (or male head) was never unemployed had a median income in 1981 of $25,000. In contrast, the median income of similar families in which the male head experienced 1 to 26 weeks of unemployment was $16,500. Families in which the male head was unemployed for more than 26 weeks had a median family income of $10,200.

TABLE 2–1.—*Median family income by unemployment and family status, 1981 (current dollars)*

Family status	Unemployment status of husband, wife, or head of household		
	Person never unemployed	Person unemployed less than 26 weeks	Person unemployed more than 26 weeks
Husband and wife both work	$31,600	$23,000	$17,900
Only husband or male head works	25,000	16,500	10,200
Only wife or female head works	18,900	15,200	11,200

Source: Department of Labor, Bureau of Labor Statistics.

The financial losses of the unemployed are not the only costs of a prolonged economic decline. Considerable anxiety and emotional distress is experienced by those who have lost their jobs or who fear that they might lose their jobs in an economy with a declining number of employment opportunities. Protracted unemployment is frequently associated with poor health, psychological problems, and gradual erosion of job-related skills.

THE COMPOSITION OF CYCLICAL AND STRUCTURAL UNEMPLOYMENT

The unemployment problem can be divided into two components, cyclical and structural unemployment. The term *cyclical unemployment* is used to refer to the unemployment associated with cyclical downturns in aggregate economic activity. The incremental unemployment associated with the recent recession would fall into this category. The term *structural unemployment* is used to refer to the unemployment that remains even after cyclical recoveries in aggregate economic activity.

In large part, structural unemployment is a natural concomitant of a dynamic economy with constantly changing patterns of demand. Labor markets are in constant flux, with people entering and leaving the labor force, losing or quitting old jobs, and looking for and acquiring new jobs. Some amount of structural unemployment is an inevitable aspect of a large modern industrial economy such as ours. It is important to realize that although expansionary macroeconomic policies cannot reduce structural unemployment permanently, certain microeconomic policy interventions can affect the ease and speed of the process that matches workers with jobs.

Some insight into the differences between cyclical and structural unemployment can be obtained by comparing the characteristics of the unemployed in 1982 and in a period of low cyclical unemployment. Since the unemployment rate in 1978 was 6.1 percent, close to most observers' estimates of full employment, data from that year will be used to illustrate the characteristics of structural unemployment. The next two sections examine the composition of the unemployed population in 1978 and 1982 in terms of demographic composition and reasons for unemployment. A third section analyzes the dynamics of unemployment.

DEMOGRAPHIC COMPOSITION

Chart 2-1 provides information on the demographic composition of the unemployed population in 1978 and in 1982. The chart shows that young people under age 24 account for a substantial fraction of unemployment both when the economy is weak and when it is strong. Persons under 24 accounted for 49 percent of total unemployment during 1978 and 41 percent of unemployment in 1982. The decline in the share of youth unemployment reflected the large increase in unemployment among adult males in cyclically sensitive sectors of the economy, such as manufacturing.

Chart 2–1

Distribution of Unemployment by Age and Sex

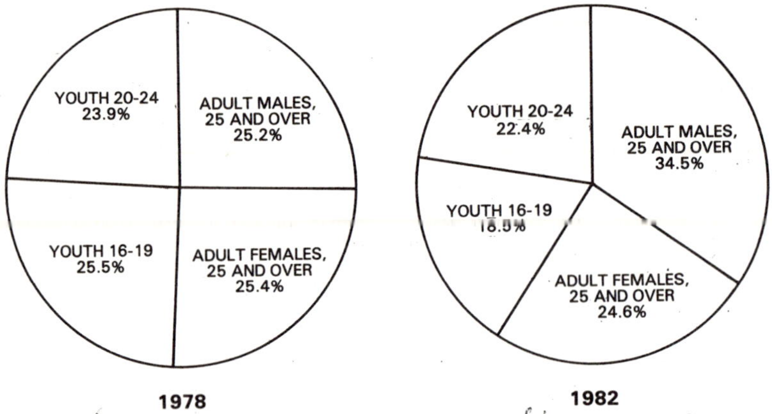

(peak year) (see p. 31)

(trough year)

NOTE.—DATA RELATE TO PERSONS 16 YEARS AND OVER.

SOURCE: DEPARTMENT OF LABOR.

A pattern that appears in Chart 2–2 is the cyclical sensitivity of unemployment among those who provide the primary financial support for a family. The share of unemployment among husbands, wives, and family heads in families without a working spouse rose from 20 percent in 1978 to 24 percent in 1982. Because unemployment undoubtedly imposes its greatest hardship when it hits a worker upon whom others depend for their sole support, this increase is particularly distressing.

A continuing tragedy in both good and bad times is the very high rates of unemployment of blacks and other minorities. This group accounts for a share of unemployment that is greatly disproportionate to its share of the labor force. While blacks and other minorities comprised 13 percent of the labor force in 1982, they comprised approximately 23 percent of the unemployed. Chart 2–3, shows that the recent recession raised the unemployment rate of blacks and other minorities proportionally less than that of the rest of the population.

However, black and other minority unemployment rates increased sharply during the recession and continue to greatly exceed those of the entire population. The unemployment rate for black and other minority adult males was 16.2 percent in 1982, compared to 7.8 percent for white males. For black and other minority teenagers the unemployment rate was 43.9 percent, compared to 20.4 percent for white teenagers.

Chart 2–2

Distribution of Unemployment by Family Status

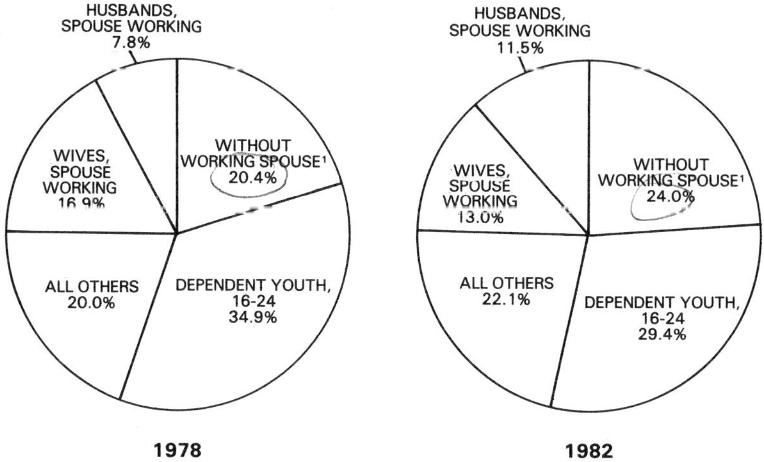

[1]HUSBANDS AND WIVES WHOSE SPOUSE DOES NOT WORK AND PERSONS WHO MAINTAIN FAMILIES.

NOTE.—DATA RELATE TO PERSONS 16 YEARS AND OVER.

SOURCE: DEPARTMENT OF LABOR.

REASONS FOR UNEMPLOYMENT

Analyzing the problem of unemployment requires understanding the process by which people become unemployed. The unemployed are often described in stereotyped terms as the victims of permanent layoffs by firms that are either partially or fully shutting down. Even during the recent recession, however, this characterization applied to less than half of the unemployed.

As part of the monthly Current Population Survey, the unemployed are asked a number of questions designed to elicit the reasons for their unemployment. The answers to these questions permit a breakdown of the unemployed into five groups: (1) persons laid off who can expect to return to the same job; (2) persons who have lost jobs to which they cannot expect to return; (3) persons who have quit their jobs; (4) reentrants who are returning to the labor force after a spell of neither working nor looking for work; and (5) new entrants who have never worked at a full-time job before but are now seeking employment.

Chart 2–4 shows that the distribution of the unemployed among these categories is very sensitive to cyclical conditions. The share of persons who have lost their jobs, either temporarily or permanently,

Chart 2–3

Distribution of Unemployment by Race

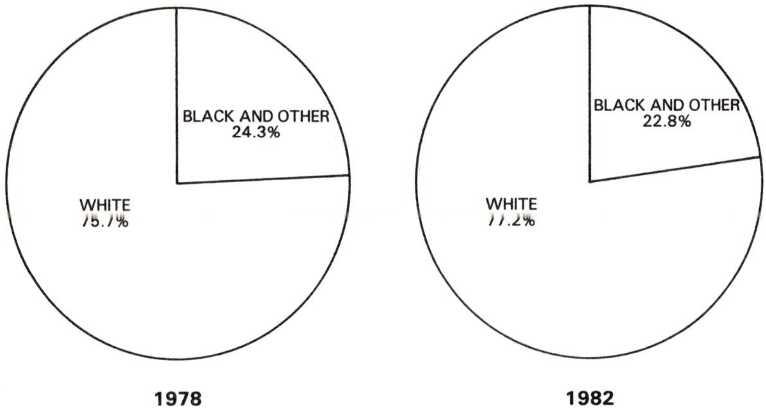

NOTE.—DATA RELATE TO PERSONS 16 YEARS AND OVER.
SOURCE: DEPARTMENT OF LABOR.

is particularly sensitive, rising from 42 percent in 1978 to 59 percent in 1982. Over this period the number of job losers on temporary layoff tripled and the number of permanent job losers more than doubled. The decline in alternative employment opportunities resulted in a decline in the share of unemployment traceable to workers leaving their jobs voluntarily during the recession—from 14 percent in 1978 to 8 percent in 1982. Finally, because the number of labor force entrants and reentrants is relatively constant, their share in total unemployment declined somewhat during the recession.

The data on reasons for unemployment indicate a major difference between cyclical and structural unemployment. Almost 90 percent of the increase in unemployment during cyclical downturns involves increases in job losses and layoffs, as firms respond to declines in demand for their products. On the other hand, almost 60 percent of structural unemployment is comprised of voluntary job leavers, labor force entrants, and reentrants. The remainder are job losers. As described below, the very different causes of cyclical and structural unemployment suggest that different policy responses are appropriate.

Chart 2–4

Distribution of Unemployment By Reason

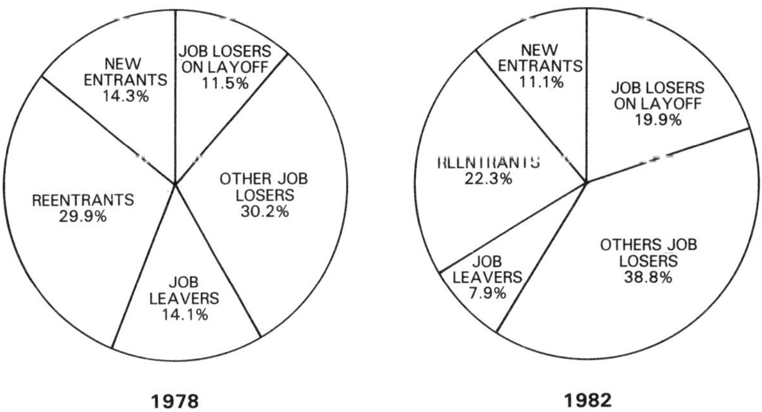

NOTE.—DATA RELATE TO PERSONS 16 YEARS AND OVER.

SOURCE: DEPARTMENT OF LABOR.

THE DYNAMICS OF UNEMPLOYMENT

An essential feature of the unemployment problem is its dynamic character. The appropriate design of policies to reduce unemployment depends on whether most of the unemployed are out of work for a long time and must wait for an economic upturn to find jobs or whether they are a group whose membership changes rapidly, even during recessions.

The principal source of information on the duration of unemployment is the monthly Current Population Survey, which asks persons who report themselves as unemployed to report how long they have been unemployed. Chart 2–5 presents information on the duration of unemployment in 1978 and 1982. The clearest difference between cyclical and structural unemployment emerges in the incidence of long-term unemployment. In 1982 the number of unemployed individuals who reported that they had been out of work for 6 or more months was almost three times the corresponding number in 1978, when the economy was operating without significant cyclical unemployment.

While the incidence of long-term unemployment increases sharply during recessions, it is important to recognize that many of the un-

Chart 2–5

Distribution of Unemployment by Duration

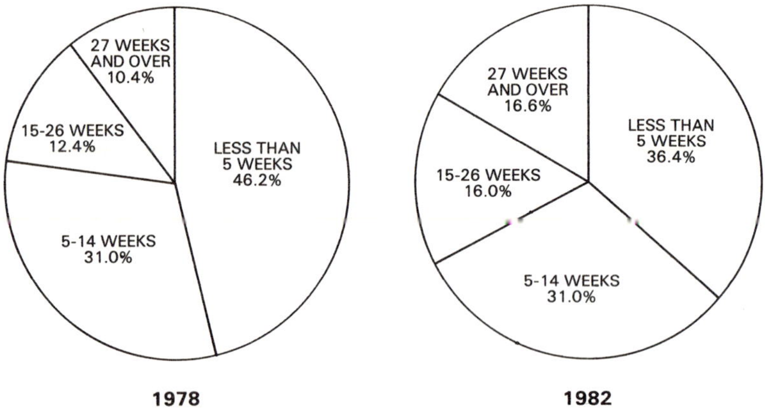

NOTE.—DATA RELATE TO PERSONS 16 YEARS AND OVER.
SOURCE: DEPARTMENT OF LABOR.

employed find jobs or withdraw from the labor force relatively quickly. Of all the persons who became unemployed in September 1982, over 45 percent were no longer unemployed by October, and over 65 percent were no longer unemployed by November. However, evidence on the duration of unemployment is not purely indicative of the ease or difficulty with which persons find jobs since almost half the unemployed leave the labor force without finding jobs.

While most persons who become unemployed look for work only briefly, this group does not comprise a large part of the unemployment problem. It is long-term unemployment that is of special concern. A recent study found that in 1978, more than 40 percent of total unemployment was due to the 15 percent of the unemployed population who were out of work a total of 6 months or longer during the year. This concentration of long-term unemployment among a relatively small group of the unemployed is particularly pronounced during cyclical downturns. Data on this subject are not yet available for 1982. During 1975, however, when the unemployment rate was 8.5 percent, an estimated 52 percent of unemployment was due to the 22 percent of the unemployed population who were out of work more than 6 months.

These findings suggest several conclusions. First, even during recessions, most persons who become unemployed either find jobs or leave the labor force relatively quickly. Second, the unemployment problem is most serious for those who are unemployed for prolonged stretches. Third, the incidence of long-term unemployment is very sensitive to cyclical conditions, which suggests that it will diminish as the economy recovers. Even after a recovery is well underway, however, a sizable fraction of total unemployment will involve protracted joblessness. The needs of the long-term unemployed deserve special recognition in the designing of policies to attack structural unemployment.

COMBATING CYCLICAL UNEMPLOYMENT

High rates of cyclical unemployment, which the American economy is now experiencing, are largely a consequence of fluctuations in aggregate demand caused by macroeconomic policies and shocks to the economy. As described in Chapter 1, the historical experience of the United States and other countries suggests that disinflation is generally associated with lost output and increased unemployment. During periods of disinflation and recession, the measures available to reduce the pain of the transition from accelerating inflation to price stability are limited. Greater fiscal or monetary stimulus might increase employment, but only at the risk of igniting inflation. Chapter 1 describes the principles that the Administration feels govern sound macroeconomic policies.

THE LIMITS OF MACROECONOMIC POLICY

The only way to reduce current high levels of cyclical unemployment is for the United States to achieve a sound recovery from the recent recession. Avoiding future recurrences of high cyclical unemployment requires avoiding an expansion so rapid as to lead to rapidly increasing inflation. Historical experience suggests that the change in the rate of inflation depends both on the rate at which economic activity is expanding and on the level of economic slack. If the slack in the economy declines too rapidly, or capacity utilization is held at too high a level, inflation will tend to increase. The lower limit on unemployment below which inflation will tend to increase is referred to as the *inflation threshold* unemployment rate.

While it is not easy to pinpoint the inflation threshold unemployment rate precisely, it probably lies between 6 and 7 percent. Econometric studies of historical data suggest that when unemployment is close to 6 percent, the rate of inflation tends to accelerate. For example, during 1978 when the unemployment rate was 6.1 percent, inflation as measured by percentage changes in the gross national product (GNP) deflator rose to 7.4 percent from 5.8 percent in 1977. An even larger increase occurred in 1979 when the unemployment rate averaged 5.8 percent.

The Effect of Demographic Factors

There are a number of reasons to believe that the inflation threshold unemployment rate increased during the 1960s and 1970s. Many economists believe that demographic factors may have contributed to the increase. Persons with little labor market experience tend to have high rates of unemployment as they move from job to job in an effort to obtain a desirable career position. In the last 15 years, the children of the baby boom have reached maturity thus raising substantially the share of inexperienced workers in the labor force. In addition, women with little recent labor market experience have entered the labor force at an unprecedented rate during the last 15 years. It has been estimated that if the labor force had the same demographic composition today as it had in 1958, the unemployment rate would have been about three-quarters of a percentage point lower in 1982. The share of young people in the labor force will decline sharply over the next decade due to a dramatic reduction in the birth rate throughout the late 1960s and the 1970s. This provides grounds for cautious optimism that the inflation threshold unemployment rate will decline.

Social Insurance Programs

Other factors which have increased the inflation threshold unemployment rate in recent years are less likely to be reversed in the next decade. These include the effects of social programs. While providing important financial support to their recipients, these programs also have both behavioral and reporting effects on the measured unemployment rate.

Behavioral effects of social insurance programs such as unemployment insurance include the encouragement of firms to lay off workers and the inducement of persons to prolong their spells of unemployment. These effects are discussed in more detail below. Reporting effects occur when programs induce persons to change reporting of their labor force status, without changing their behavior. For example, some experts believe that the Federal Supplemental Benefits program instituted during the 1975 recession caused persons who otherwise would have withdrawn from the labor force to report that they were unemployed because of job search requirements. There is some evidence to suggest that the work registration requirements in the food stamp and AFDC programs have had a similar effect.

Wage Rigidity

A number of studies show that wages and prices are much more rigid now than prior to World War II, and that rigidity has increased within the post-War period. Increased wage rigidity is likely to raise the economy's inflation threshold level of unemployment, since less flexible wages increase the inevitable unemployment associated with the sectoral shocks which buffet the economy.

The reasons for this change are not well understood. A side effect of the provision of a "safety net" program is that employees may become more resistant to wage reductions, leading to increases in wage and price rigidity. To the extent that the two-earner family is a form of private "safety net" against the financial losses of unemployment, the recent growth in the number of two-earner families may also have contributed to increasing wage rigidity in the United States over time.

Increasing Structural Change

A final factor that may have contributed to a rising inflation threshold unemployment rate is the increasing rapidity of structural change in the economy. This acceleration, which is in part caused by the economy's increasing sensitivity to events in the world economy, is evidenced by increasing dispersion across industries and localities in rates of unemployment. Because transfers of human and physical resources are costly and take time, increased unemployment is a concomitant of structural change.

While the separate impacts of these factors—changing demographic composition, larger social insurance programs, increased wage rigidity, and increased structural change—are difficult to quantify, it is reasonable to conclude that together they may have significantly increased the inflation threshold unemployment rate. Expansionary macroeconomic policies are unlikely to reverse the effects of these changes.

PUBLIC WORKS EMPLOYMENT PROGRAMS

Direct provision of public works jobs by the government is a politically popular response to cyclical unemployment during recessions. Available evidence suggests, however, that public works programs adopted in past recessions proved counterproductive, and that the inherent capability of public works programs to combat cyclical unemployment is limited.

The Timing of Public Works Expenditures

Public employment programs that produce useful goods or services generally take time to plan and implement. Therefore, such programs often have their greatest effects on public employment long after an economic recovery has begun. For this reason, public employment programs have sometimes exacerbated rather than mitigated cyclical fluctuations in aggregate demand. A study of the Accelerated Public Works program enacted in September 1962 by the Congress to combat the high unemployment rate of the early 1960s found that the number of jobs created by the program peaked in June 1964, 37 months after the bottom of the recession. More recent experience also confirms that lags in implementation are long. A recent study by the Office of Management and Budget found that 90 percent of the outlays for local public works projects designed to stimulate recovery from the 1974–75 recession occurred more than 2½ years after the trough of the recession. The lags in implementing public works programs result in their having destabilizing effects, since a large share of the resulting spending occurs during periods of economic expansion.

The Effect of Federal Funding of Public Works on State Expenditures

Even when spending for these programs begins immediately after they are enacted, many public works projects do not yield a net increase in employment. Because of the long planning and implementation lags, most of the projects available for immediate funding are those that were planned before the recession began. Thus, Federal expenditures on these projects often substitute for outlays that would have taken place anyway.

A major effect of Federal public works expenditures may be to alter the timing of public works projects. The expectation of new public works programs may induce State and local governments to delay making outlays during the early stages of economic downturns in the hope that they will receive Federal funds for projects they have "on the shelf." The importance of this possibility is suggested by experiences with the Local Public Works Capital Development and Investment Act of 1976 and the Public Works Employment Act of 1977, programs intended to spur recovery from the 1975 recession. Three characteristics of these programs may have created incentives for local governments to delay their own discretionary spending until they could see whether the Federal Government would pay their entire bill: (1) projects were financed fully by the Federal Government; (2) grants were limited to quick-starting projects; and (3) there was considerable uncertainty and lengthy delays in the process of awarding money to State and local governments. One study found that State and local public works expenditures fell substantially in mid-1976 and decreased further between 1976 and 1977. It suggested that this may have occurred because States and local governments delayed projects in anticipation of funds becoming available under the 1976 and 1977 public works programs. The study also suggested that these measures may have caused the postponement of as much as $22 billion in total government spending.

Crowding Out of Private Sector Employment

Another reason for discounting the efficacy of public works measures is their adverse side effects on private employment. If public works outlays are financed by additional taxes, the income and spending of consumers are reduced, decreasing the number of jobs in the private economy. Alternatively, insofar as public works outlays are financed by borrowing from the public, interest rates are raised, crowding out some forms of private spending and reducing private employment. The higher interest rates resulting from increased Federal borrowing also discourage capital investments that help create future employment.

Benefits to Workers

An additional reason to discount the efficacy of accelerated public works projects is their limited value to participants. Most jobs in countercyclical public works projects are of extremely short duration and are unlikely to provide participants with lasting job skills. Under the Public Works Impact Program, initiated in fiscal year 1972, the average duration of employment amounted to only 4.1 weeks. Almost 60 percent of all employees worked 2 weeks or less. Data for the local public works programs initiated in 1976 and 1977 and described above, indicate that the average job lasted only 3.5 weeks.

Although public works programs are motivated by a desire to provide jobs for the unemployed, very few jobs are actually filled by unemployed workers. Under the Public Works Impact Program, only 27 percent of all jobs were filled by the previously unemployed. Under the more recent public works programs of 1976 and 1977, it has been estimated that only 12 percent of all jobs were filled by previously unemployed workers.

COMBATING STRUCTURAL UNEMPLOYMENT

The preceding analysis suggests that it would be imprudent to use macroeconomic policies to reduce the unemployment rate below its inflation threshold level of 6 to 7 percent. Such an effort would increase inflation, and ultimately prove counterproductive as increased inflation was followed by recession. This does not mean that unemployment rates in the 6 to 7 percent range are either inevitable or desirable. The inflation threshold level of unemployment can be reduced by policies that consider the special problems of two groups of workers: (1) young people, and (2) adults experiencing long-term unemployment. It can also be reduced by reforms of the unemployment insurance system, which, while providing valuable insurance, may increase the incidence of unemployment.

THE PROBLEM OF YOUTH UNEMPLOYMENT

At times of low cyclical unemployment, about half the unemployed are young people between the ages of 16 and 24. Close to one-fourth of all the unemployed are teenagers aged 16 to 19. While unemployment clearly imposes hardships on youths, it has very different economic impacts than it does for adults. Many unemployed youths are in school and looking for part-time work. Most of this group, and many other young people who have left school, are not economically independent, but rather live at home and rely on their parents for financial support. Many other young people experience only brief periods of unemployment as they move from one job to the next.

Table 2-2 provides information on the labor market activities of young men and women aged 16 to 19 in October 1981, when the teenage unemployment rate was 24.1 percent. Data for 1982 are not yet available. As the table reveals, only 5 percent of all teenagers were out of school and measured as unemployed (because they were looking for work). A striking feature of the youth labor market is the large fraction of young people who are out of school but are neither working nor looking for work. Over 30 percent of female and 14 percent of male out-of-school teenagers were not in the labor force. The factors underlying this labor force withdrawal by young people are not well understood. In some cases, young people may withdraw from the labor force because they are discouraged about their prospects for finding suitable employment. In other cases, labor force withdrawal may reflect a desire for leisure.

The observations about the dynamic character of unemployment made elsewhere in this chapter are especially true of young people.

TABLE 2-2.—*Educational and labor market activities of youth aged 16 to 19, by sex, October 1981*

Item	Number (thousands)	Percent of subgroup	Percent of population	Number (thousands)	Percent of subgroup	Percent of population
	Males			Females		
Total population	8,036		100.0	8,059		100.0
Enrolled in school	5,683	100.0	70.7	5,526	100.0	68.6
Employed	2,024	35.6	25.2	1,829	33.1	22.7
Unemployed	424	7.5	5.3	429	7.8	5.3
Not in labor force	3,235	56.9	40.3	3,268	59.1	40.6
Unemployment rate (percent)	17.3			19.0		
Not enrolled in school	2,353	100.0	29.3	2,533	100.0	31.4
Employed	1,585	67.4	19.7	1,340	52.9	16.6
Unemployed	434	18.4	5.4	417	16.5	5.2
Not in labor force	334	14.2	4.2	776	30.6	9.6
Unemployment rate (percent)	21.5			23.7		

Source: Department of Labor, Bureau of Labor Statistics.

Most young people find jobs or leave the labor force fairly quickly. It was recently estimated that of those male teenagers who become unemployed in a given month only 42 percent remain unemployed in the next month.

Youth unemployment is nevertheless a critical economic problem. A large part of the youth unemployment problem is traceable to the small group of teenagers who experience extensive unemployment. More than 52 percent of all unemployment experienced by teenage males aged 16 to 19 in 1981 was due to the 4.4 percent of the male teenage population of this group who were out of work for more than 6 months during that year.

Evidence also suggests that certain teenagers who suffer extensive unemployment earn lower wages later in life. The direction of causation is very difficult to establish since persons with low skills may simply fare poorly both early and late in life. However, the best evidence available suggests that poor labor market experiences early in life cause reduced wages during adulthood. This suggests the importance of developing policies to improve employment opportunities for the long-term unemployed and to reduce job turnover.

Training, Unemployment, and the Minimum Wage

A major problem in the youth labor market is the dearth of "career-oriented" employment opportunities. While people who participate in post-secondary schooling are generally subsidized by the public sector, public support of equivalent magnitude has not been available for the post-high school training of youth who choose to enter the labor force after high school.

Employers may find it very difficult to offer such training because of the constraints imposed by minimum wage legislation. These laws discourage employers from hiring unskilled workers at very low wages and compensating them further by providing training. This may help explain very high job turnover among youths as they move rapidly in and out of "dead-end" jobs. Another consequence of minimum wage laws is that they prevent some young people from acquiring the training that would permit them to find steady, well-paying employment as adults. Statistical studies provide evidence that minimum wages significantly depress the accumulation of valuable skills and resulting growth in earnings among youths who are paid the minimum wage. There is also evidence that the negative effects of the minimum wage on employment and training are concentrated disproportionately among youths with the fewest labor market skills. Thus, although the stated purpose of the minimum wage is to reduce poverty, experience suggests that it may actually decrease the lifetime earnings of some of the poor and thereby increase income inequality.

POLICIES TO REDUCE YOUTH UNEMPLOYMENT

Almost all observers agree that mitigating the problems of instability and high unemployment in the youth labor market requires increasing the availability of career-oriented employment and training. This can be accomplished through public support of training, minimum wage reforms, and employment tax credits.

The Job Training Partnership Act

The Job Training Partnership Act (JTPA) of 1982 represents a major Federal initiative to reduce structural unemployment among youth and adults. The JTPA departs from previous Federal employment training programs by establishing a formal partnership between private industry, the public sector, and vocational training institutions for the purposes of planning, designing, and providing federally financed training. Federal resources are targeted to individuals identified as most in need: economically disadvantaged youth, low-skilled and chronically unemployed adults, and skilled workers who have lost jobs in declining industries and regions. The problems faced by the latter group are discussed more fully later in this chapter.

The JTPA is intended to fill an important niche in the national employment and training system by serving individuals who are unable to make use of job training provided by more traditional institutions: high schools, vocational-technical schools, community colleges, universities, and employers. Federally funded training programs such as JTPA provide a second chance to youth and adults experiencing trouble in the labor market. The JTPA is administered at the State and local level. This allows training programs to be tailored to the particular needs of workers and employers in local labor markets.

Minimum Wage Reforms

The Administration will propose a summertime differential minimum wage for young people under the age of 22. Between May 1 and September 30 of each year the minimum wage for this group would be reduced to $2.50 from $3.35. This measure would encourage firms to hire young people, just out of school, and give them the experience needed to compete effectively in the labor market. It will also encourage employers to provide youth who remain in school with valuable work experience during the summer months.

The Targeted Jobs Tax Credit

An alternative policy avenue for encouraging employment and training of young people is to provide tax credits or wage subsidies to employers who hire youths. Tax credits are currently provided to firms that employ economically disadvantaged youths, aged 18 to 24, under the Targeted Jobs Tax Credit program. The credits are also targeted to welfare recipients, and economically disadvantaged Vietnam veterans, cooperative education students, handicapped persons, and ex-convicts.

The tax credit lasts for up to 2 full years. In the first year it is equal to 50 percent of an individual's earnings, up to a maximum credit of $3,000. In the second year it is equal to 25 percent of earnings, up to a maximum credit of $1,500. Participation in the program has been limited since its inception in 1979. This is an apparent consequence of administrative problems encountered by the agencies responsible for determining program eligibility (especially the Job Service), reluctance on the part of eligible recipients to use the tax credit as a self-marketing tool, and employers' reluctance to let government programs influence hiring decisions.

Recent legislation added a second component to the tax credit program by providing a tax credit for summer employment targeted at economically disadvantaged youths aged 16 and 17. The tax credit for this group is quite large, equaling 85 percent of wages, up to a total summer income of $3,000. The summer Targeted Jobs Tax Credit program, in effect, allows employers to hire eligible youths, who are paid the minimum wage for a net cost to the firms of 50 cents an hour. The program will be in place for the first time during the summer of 1983.

A virtue of measures which subsidize employment and on-the-job training for youth is that they counteract the large bias toward formal schooling over on-the-job training inherent in current policies. In part because of large public subsidies to higher education during the last two decades, the percentage of young people, aged 18 to 24, enrolled in higher education rose very sharply from 26 percent in 1963 to 41 percent in 1975. This shift toward increased formal schooling was accompanied by a decline in the relative wages of college graduates and high school graduates. The ratio of the average annual incomes of college graduates to that of high school graduates, aged 25 and over, fell from 1.53 in 1968 to 1.38 in 1978.

LONG-TERM UNEMPLOYMENT AND STRUCTURAL CHANGE

An especially visible and serious component of the unemployment problem is composed of adults suffering protracted unemployment. At present, most long-term unemployment is a consequence of the recession and the resulting reduction in the demand for labor. But as discussed earlier in the chapter, long-term unemployment will remain a significant problem even after the economy recovers.

384-041 0 - 83 - 4 : QL 3

Structural Change and Economic Adjustment

A large part of long-term unemployment among adults can be traced to structural changes in the economy. An increasingly important source of structural change is the growing interdependence of the U.S. economy with that of the rest of the world. The share of export and import-competing industries in GNP has increased over the last several decades, and many industries have consequently felt the cold winds of economic change. By December 1982 the unemployment rate had reached 23.2 percent in the motor vehicle industry and 29.2 percent in the primary metals industry. Other industries, including mining, construction, and lumber, have also contracted rapidly, leaving behind a significant number of long-term unemployed. These figures reflect both changes resulting from foreign competition and the sharp declines in the demand for manufactured goods caused by the recent recession. The gradual decline of the dollar in foreign exchange markets to historically prevailing levels, a drop in real interest rates, and general economic recovery would contribute to easing the problems of troubled industries, as explained in Chapter 3. However, most observers believe that foreign competition will present persistent problems in some domestic industries even in the long run.

In a number of these industries, significant adjustments will need to take place. If foreign firms can continue to produce goods at lower costs than U.S. firms, either domestic production will contract, forcing workers to leave the affected industries, or workers will have to accept constant or even declining real wages. The former option is particularly painful in industries like automobiles and steel, where workers have become accustomed to high standards of living. Because wages in these industries are substantially greater than wages in other manufacturing industries, workers find it difficult to locate suitable alternative jobs.

Programs which inhibit the transition of workers from declining industries to growing industries would raise the level of structural unemployment in the economy. Included in this group are programs which would provide financial assistance to industries without providing incentives for employee relocation or wage and price flexibility. In a dynamic economy subject to the pressures of domestic and foreign competition, our economic health depends critically on the ability of workers and firms to respond quickly to changing economic conditions.

Policies to Alleviate Long-term Unemployment

The centerpiece of Federal policy to alleviate long-term unemployment is Title III of the new Job Training Partnership Act discussed earlier in the chapter. Title III established State-administered programs of employment and training assistance for dislocated workers, defined broadly to include individuals who have become unemployed as a result of plant closures, laid-off workers who are unlikely to return to their previous industry or occupation, and individuals experiencing long-term unemployment in occupations with limited employment opportunities. Matching grants are provided to States on the basis of their unemployment conditions. Title III authorizes States to establish a wide variety of employment and training activities, including job search assistance, job training, relocation assistance, and employment counseling. Individuals receiving Title III assistance may also receive unemployment compensation, if they are eligible.

The Administration in its 1984 budget has introduced two new approaches to the problem of reducing long-term unemployment. First, it has proposed that Federal unemployment laws be amended to permit States to use a portion of the unemployment insurance taxes they collect to support retraining and job search assistance for their unemployed workers. Second, the Administration has proposed that the Federal Supplemental Compensation program be replaced when it expires with a new temporary program that provides incentives for work as well as compensation for long-term unemployment. As an alternative to added weeks of unemployment compensation, this program would give recipients the option of receiving assistance in securing work through a system of tax credits to employers. This will give employers a significant incentive to hire the long-term unemployed.

THE EFFECTS OF UNEMPLOYMENT COMPENSATION

For more than 40 years, unemployment compensation has given valuable support to millions of unemployed workers and has provided an important source of security to millions more who are employed. Along with these beneficial consequences, however, the present structure of the unemployment insurance system has altered the incentives faced by employers in hiring and firing decisions and the incentives of unemployed workers to accept new employment opportunities. As a result, unemployment compensation seems to have increased the incidence and duration of unemployment.

The current system of unemployment compensation produces two distinct but related adverse incentive effects. First, for those who are unemployed it reduces the cost of unemployment, providing an incentive for longer durations of unemployment. Second, current methods of financing unemployment insurance increase the incidence of unemployment by increasing the size of seasonal and cyclical fluctuations in unemployment and by making temporary jobs more common.

Incentives to Prolong Unemployment

Payments to the unemployed clearly raise the level of household expenditures that can be maintained when one or more family members are not working. Such payments reduce the economic pressure to find work immediately, encouraging a longer period of job search during which the unemployed worker hopes to find a more attractive job than might otherwise be found. For some workers unemployment insurance replaces more than 70 percent of after-tax wages during periods of unemployment. Economic research indicates that there is a positive relationship between duration of job search and the level of unemployment benefits.

Workers who take longer to find jobs because of unemployment compensation are in no sense "loafing" or "cheating." An unemployed person who does not expect to be recalled by his previous employer can expect, on average, to find a better job the longer and more carefully he looks. Unemployment insurance, by reducing the cost of additional weeks without work, encourages unemployed workers to continue searching for better employment opportunities.

Incentives for More Unstable Employment

A second avenue through which the unemployment insurance system, as currently financed, tends to increase the economy's rate of structural unemployment is by increasing seasonal and cyclical fluctuations in the demand for labor and the relative number of short-lived, casual jobs.

The effect of unemployment compensation is to offset the market forces that would otherwise decrease, at least somewhat, the amount of unstable employment in the economy. Insofar as unemployment compensation provides a subsidy to unstable employment practices, it reduces the wage differential required to attract workers to seasonal, cyclical, and temporary jobs. And because employers pay a relatively small premium for unstable employment practices under current methods of financing unemployment insurance, they have little incentive to reduce this instability.

The current subsidy to unstable employment patterns would be reduced if unemployment insurance were financed through a more completely experience-rated employer tax that more accurately reflected the expected level of unemployment benefits to a firm's laid-off workers in the future. The theory of experience rating is clear: if an employer pays the full cost of the unemployment benefits that his former employees receive, he will not have an incentive to make excessive use of unstable employment practices. Recent statistical research demonstrates that there is, in fact, a strong positive relationship between incomplete experience rating and employment instability.

Most States use experience rating to some extent, in that some employers contribute to the State unemployment compensation fund partially on the basis of the unemployment experience of their own employees. The degree of experience rating is highly imperfect, however, for two reasons.

First, a significant share of benefits paid are not directly charged to firms, but rather, are spread across all the firms in a State. These include benefits paid to job leavers, benefits to employees of firms no longer doing business in a State, and allowances for dependents. Extended benefits, which are available in high unemployment States to workers who have exhausted their regular unemployment insurance, are also not directly charged to employers.

Second, employer contributions are limited by minimum and maximum tax rates. Firms stuck at the maximum or minimum tax rates will find that their tax rates do not change even if the unemployment experience of their workers is altered. As a consequence they face reduced economic incentives to smooth employment fluctuations.

One measure of the extent of experience rating is the proportion of benefits received that are not effectively charged to the former employer. A value of 100 percent represents perfect experience rating. A recent study of nine States over the period 1971–1978 found that on average, less than 60 percent of total benefits were experience rated, by this definition. The degee of experience rating fell to 47.5 percent during the 1975 recession and reached a high of 62.6 percent in 1978, a year with relatively low unemployment.

The problem of imperfect experience rating has been partially remedied by a provision of the Tax Equity and Fiscal Responsibility Act of 1982 which raised the federally proscribed lower bound on State maximum unemployment insurance tax rates from 2.7 percent to 5.4 percent of employers' taxable payroll. Because of this change, fewer firms are likely to face the maximum tax rate.

CONCLUSIONS

The dual problems of cyclical and structural unemployment are both extremely serious. Increased unemployment during cyclical downturns, and the high levels of unemployment that prevail even after the economy recovers, impose large costs on the unemployed and the economy as a whole. Fortunately, both can be ameliorated by prudent public policy. Sound macroeconomic policies will avoid recurrences of the rising inflation of the 1970s and subsequent increases in cyclical unemployment. Policies directed at young people and the long-term unemployed, and reform of the unemployment insurance system, can significantly reduce the level of structural unemployment.

CHAPTER 3

The United States in the World Economy: Strains on the System

DURING THE 1970s the world's market economies became more integrated with each other than ever before. Exports and imports as a share of gross national product (GNP) reached record levels for most industrial countries, while international lending and direct foreign investment grew even faster than world trade. This closer linkage of economies was mutually beneficial. It allowed producers in each country to take greater advantage of their country's special resources and knowledge, and to take advantage of economies of scale. At the same time, it allowed each country to consume a wider variety of products, at lower costs, than it could produce itself.

Underlying the growth in world trade and investment was a progressive reduction of barriers to trade. The postwar period was marked by a series of agreements to liberalize trade: both multilateral, like the Kennedy Round, and bilateral, like the Canada-U.S. auto pact.

In spite of its huge benefits, however, this liberalized trading system is now in serious danger. Within the United States, demands for protection against imports and for export subsidies have grown as a combination of structural changes, sectoral problems, and short-run macroeconomic developments has led to a perception that we are becoming uncompetitive in world markets. In Europe, a growing structural unemployment problem, aggravated by the recession, has increased protectionist pressures. In the developing countries a financial crisis threatens the integration of capital markets and is pushing many countries back toward the exchange controls and import restrictions they had begun to dismantle.

These problems must not be allowed to disrupt world trade. If the system comes apart—if the world's nations allow themselves to be caught up in a spiral of retaliatory trade restrictions—a long time may pass before the pieces are put back together.

This chapter reviews the strains on the international economic system and the policies by which the United States is attempting to overcome them. It is divided into four sections. The first section discusses long-term changes in U.S. competitiveness. The correction of widespread misconceptions about the competitive position of the United States is essential if we are to get through the difficult period ahead without making major policy mistakes. The second section of the chapter is devoted to financial developments and their effects on trade, especially the appreciation of the dollar and its likely effects on the U.S. trade balance. Two final sections examine macroeconomic and financial problems in Europe and the developing countries.

LONG-RUN TRENDS IN U.S. COMPETITIVENESS: PERCEPTIONS AND REALITIES

Concern over the international competitiveness of the United States is as high as it has ever been. It is argued with increasing frequency that U.S. business has steadily lost ground in the international marketplace. This alleged poor performance is often attributed both to failures of management in the United States and to the support given to foreign businesses by their home governments. Feeding the perception of declining competitiveness is the persistent U.S. deficit in merchandise trade, especially the imbalance in trade with Japan.

Changes in U.S. trade performance must, however, be put into the context of changes in the U.S. role in the world economy. This wider approach reveals that much of the concern about long-run competitiveness is based on misperceptions. Although the recent appreciation of the dollar has created a temporary loss of competitiveness, the United States has not experienced a persistent loss of ability to sell its products on international markets; in fact, in the 1970s the United States held its own in terms of output, exports, and employment. Changes in the relationship of the United States to the world economy, however, have made the United States look less competitive by some traditional measures.

AGGREGATE PERFORMANCE OF THE UNITED STATES AND OTHER DEVELOPED COUNTRIES

Discussion of U.S. competitiveness often gives the misleading impression that the United States has consistently performed poorly relative to other industrial countries. The U.S. share of world trade and world GNP did in fact decline throughout the 1950s and 1960s, reflecting the recovery of the rest of the world from World War II, together with the narrowing of the huge and unsustainable U.S. technological lead. In the 1970s, however, this long decline leveled off.

- From 1973 to 1980, real gross domestic product (GDP) in the United States grew at an annual rate of 2.3 percent, compared with 2.6 percent in the other Organization for Economic Cooperation and Development (OECD) countries.

- From 1973 to 1980 the U.S. share of OECD exports remained nearly constant, declining from 17.6 to 17.2 percent.
- Over the same period, employment in the United States grew at 2.1 percent a year, compared with only 0.5 percent in the rest of the OECD countries.

The United States, in part as a side effect of its relatively rapid growth in employment, did do poorly by comparison in one respect, productivity growth. Output per worker grew at only 0.2 percent in the United States, compared with 2.2 percent a year in the rest of the OECD countries. Productivity is, of course, crucial to living standards; ultimately, the level of consumption per capita depends on the level of output per worker. But there is no necessary relation between productivity and competition in international markets. Slow growth in productivity only hampers a country's international competitiveness if it is not offset by correspondingly slow growth in real wages. If U.S. workers, for example, were to receive real wage increases equal to those granted in other countries while their productivity failed to increase at a comparable rate, U.S. industry would find itself increasingly uncompetitive. The fact is, however, that this did not occur, as the comparative experience of the United States and the European Economic Community illustrates. From 1973 to 1980 output per manufacturing worker in the European Economic Community rose at an annual rate of 2.7 percent, but real compensation rose at an annual rate of 4.1 percent. By contrast, output per worker in the United States rose 1.1 percent annually, while real compensation rose only 1.8 percent annually. In fact, until the recent rise in the dollar's exchange rate, it was workers in the European Economic Community, rather than those in the United States, who were probably pricing themselves out of the world market in spite of their relatively good productivity performance.

The overall performance of the United States, then, does not suggest a long-term problem of competitiveness. The shift from persistent trade surplus to persistent deficit which occurred over the last decade is, however, often misinterpreted as a sign of an inability to compete. In fact, changes in the structure of the U.S. balance of payments are more the result of changes in the U.S. saving and investment position than of slow productivity growth.

THE CHANGING STRUCTURE OF THE U.S. BALANCE OF PAYMENTS

In the 1950s and early 1960s the United States normally had a trade surplus and invested heavily in other countries. In the years after 1973, however, the United States normally had a trade deficit, and annual investment by foreigners in the United States began to approach annual U.S. investment abroad. The shift in the U.S. trade balance was closely connected with the shift in investment flows.

Taken as a whole, U.S. international transactions always balance. Any force tending to increase or decrease the balance in one category of transactions sets in motion a process leading to exactly offsetting changes in balances in other categories. For example, an increase in foreign demand for U.S. exports tends directly to improve the trade balance, but this improvement leads to a rise in the dollar's exchange rate against foreign currencies. The exchange-rate appreciation in turn leads to increases in imports, a worsened balance on services, and so on. Similarly, an increased desire by foreign residents to invest in the United States is reflected in an increase in the capital account but leads to an appreciation of the dollar and an offsetting decline in other parts of the balance of payments.

The shift in the U.S. trade balance from persistent surplus to persistent deficit was largely an offset to changes in the U.S. capital account. In the 1950s and the first half of the 1960s, rates of return on capital were lower and wage rates were higher in the United States than in other industrial countries. Since the United States suffered no war damage, its capital stock was intact, and the diffusion of U.S. technology abroad created a demand for new capital investment in the recipient countries. The result was that returns to investment were higher abroad than in the United States, and the United States was a heavy net foreign investor. The counterpart to this foreign investment was a persistent surplus on current transactions, including merchandise trade.

By the 1970s the other industrial countries had narrowed or eliminated these differences in capital and labor costs. The result was that the demand for new capital abroad was no longer a great deal larger than it was in the United States. At the same time, the supply of savings in the United States was restricted by a low national saving rate (the lowest among the major industrial countries). Thus the United States ceased to be a major net exporter of capital, and the current account of the balance of payments moved from surplus to rough balance. Meanwhile, the U.S. balance on items other than merchandise trade improved: the deficit in military transactions fell, the surplus in services rose, and, in particular, the accumulation of past foreign investments began to yield increasing income. This meant that a balanced current account was associated with a deficit in merchandise trade.

Table 3-1 and Chart 3-1 show how the structure of the U.S. current account has changed, measuring its components as percentages of GNP.

TABLE 3-1.—*Structure of the U.S. balance of payments, as percent of GNP, 1960–80*

Type of balance	Percent of GNP		Change, percentage points
	1960–66	1974–80	
Merchandise trade	0.86	−0.80	−1.66
Investment income	.74	1.06	.32
Military transactions	−.41	−.03	.38
Travel and services	−.04	.12	.16
Remittances	−.44	−.30	.15
Current account	.70	.06	−.64

Source: Department of Commerce, Bureau of Economic Analysis.

Chart 3–1

Structural Changes in the Current Account Balance

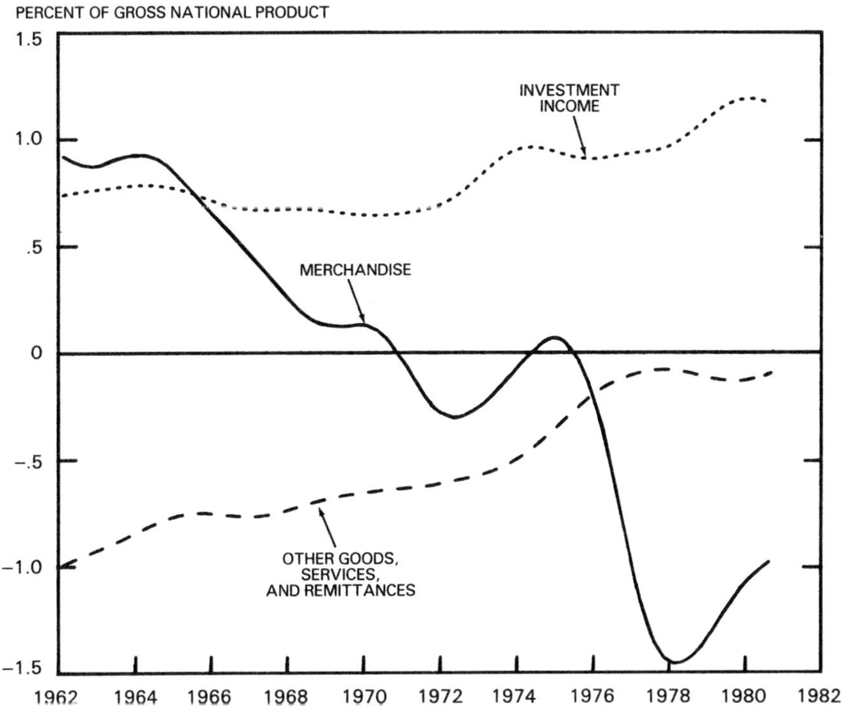

NOTE.—DATA ARE 16–QUARTER WEIGHTED CENTERED MOVING AVERAGES.

SOURCE: DEPARTMENT OF COMMERCE.

The perception of diminished U.S. competitiveness stems not only from the U.S. trade deficit but from an impression that U.S. trade performance compares poorly with that of other countries, especially that of Japan. Japan runs a huge surplus in its manufactures trade, while the United States runs only a small one, and Japan also has a large surplus in its bilateral trade with the United States. These facts are often attributed to Japanese trade restrictions. Japan does maintain restrictions which seriously hurt U.S. businesses. Trade restrictions, however, do not in the long run improve the Japanese trade balance; as discussed more fully below, they lead to offsetting increases in other imports or declines in exports. The main explanation of Japan's surplus in manufactures trade and in trade with the United States is that Japan, with few natural resources, incurs huge deficits in its trade in primary products, especially oil, and with primary producers, especially the Organization of Petroleum Exporting Countries (OPEC). The surpluses in the rest of Japan's trade offset these deficits.

Table 3–2 and Chart 3–2 show the differences in the structure of the Japanese, European, and U.S. trade accounts. They show clearly how the huge Japanese surplus in manufactures offsets large deficits in primary products.

Corresponding to the Japanese sectoral deficit in primary products, especially oil, is a regional deficit with OPEC. Japan makes up for its deficit with OPEC by running surpluses in its trade with other regions. The extent of this regional imbalance—and its contrast with the U.S. position—is shown in Table 3–3. The point here is similar to that already made with respect to the overall U.S. trade balance: looking at Japanese-U.S. trade in isolation is misleading. The Japanese surplus in trade with the United States is largely a response to the rise of OPEC.

Although Japanese trade policy does not play a central role in causing the bilateral trade imbalance with the United States, Japanese import restrictions remain a major source of friction. Japan maintains a variety of nontariff barriers against imports. These include import quotas for a number of agricultural products and "red tape" barriers against manufactured goods, such as stringent inspection requirements applied against imported goods but not against Japanese products. These trade restrictions probably do not lead to a larger overall Japanese trade surplus. If they were removed, the yen would depreciate and increased Japanese imports in the currently protected sectors would be offset by reduced deficits or increased surpluses elsewhere. Japanese trade restrictions do, however, distort the composition of U.S. trade with Japan, imposing serious costs on some U.S. produc-

TABLE 3-2.—*Trade balances by commodity group as percent of GDP, United States, Japan, and the European Economic Community, 1980*

[Percent of GDP]

Commodity group	United States	Japan	European Economic Community
Total	−1.45	−0.99	−2.23
Primary products	−1.93	−10.11	−5.41
Food, beverages, and tobacco	.40	−1.26	−.41
Crude materials excluding petroleum	.54	−2.15	−1.23
Mineral fuels	−2.87	−6.71	−3.77
Manufactures	.48	9.12	3.18
Machinery and transport equipment	−.42	3.09	.88
Other manufactured goods	.90	6.02	2.30

Source: Organization for Economic Cooperation and Development.

Chart 3–2

Composition of Trade, 1980

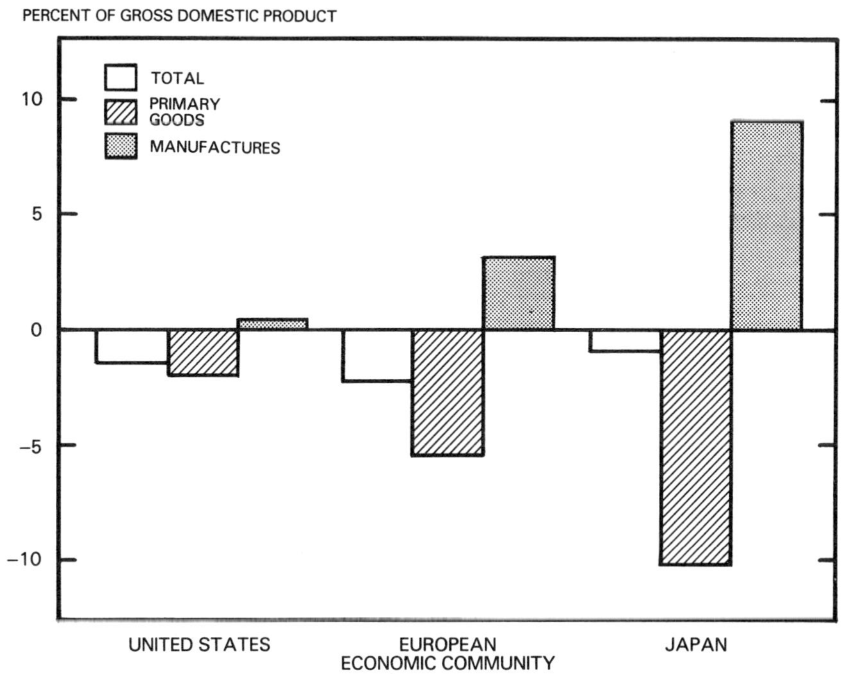

SOURCE: ORGANIZATION FOR ECONOMIC COOPERATION AND DEVELOPMENT.

ers. As the fastest growing and second largest market economy, Japan has a responsibility to help sustain the open trading system. A major trade liberalization by Japan would do much to relieve the political strains on that system, while the failure of Japan to make more than token concessions would intensify them.

TABLE 3–3.—*Trade balances by region as percent of GDP, United States and Japan, 1980*

[Percent of GDP]

Region	United States	Japan
Industrial countries	0.23	1.92
Oil-exporting countries	−1.45	−3.20
Non-oil developing countries	.50	1.40

Source: International Monetary Fund.

THE PROBLEM OF UNCOMPETITIVE SECTORS

Analysis of the overall U.S. trade deficit and the bilateral deficit with Japan suggests that worries about U.S. competitiveness are based in part on a misunderstanding of the situation. There is no question, however, that increased foreign competition has forced some sectors of the U.S. economy to contract.

This is partly a consequence of the fact that trade has become more important to the U.S. economy. Specialization by nations is the reason for international trade. If the United States is to expand its trade, the U.S. economy must become more specialized. This means that some sectors will grow and others will shrink. During the 1970s the United States developed increasing surpluses in areas in which it already enjoyed a comparative advantage and developed increasing deficits in sectors in which it was at a disadvantage. Some illustrative numbers are given in Table 3–4.

TABLE 3–4.—*U.S. trade balances by sector as percent of GDP, 1972–79*

[Percent of GDP]

Item	1972	1979
U.S. comparative advantage:		
Research-intensive manufactures	0.93	1.63
Resource-intensive products, other than fuels	.06	.67
Invisibles (services and investment income)	.40	1.44
U.S. comparative disadvantage:		
Nonresearch-intensive manufactures	−1.27	−1.44
Fuels	−.27	−2.41

Sources: International Monetary Fund, National Science Board, and Organization for Economic Cooperation and Development.

Specialization of this kind is desirable both for the United States and for its trading partners. Specialization and trade raise the efficiency of the world economy as a whole by allowing each country to concentrate on doing what it does relatively well, and by allowing increased economies of scale. But greater specialization can leave those involved in the contracting sectors worse off, at least temporarily. Attempts to prevent adjustment through trade barriers or subsidies, however, impose severe costs on unprotected sectors.

Some sectoral reallocation of resources, then, is a normal consequence of the increasing U.S. integration into the world economy. This is not the whole story, however. Some sectors of the U.S. economy are confronted by a problem that is not simply the result of market forces. Broadly speaking, these sectors fall into two groups. In one group are sectors where firms or their workers, accustomed to having substantial market power, now find that they have priced themselves out of the world market. In the other group are sectors which are hurt by foreign protectionism or export subsidies.

Market Power and Competitiveness

The "problem" of diminished market power in some sectors actually derives from a desirable aspect of trade: the fact that trade increases competition. One of the major benefits of an increasingly open U.S. economy is that it reduces the problems of monopoly and market power, thus increasing efficiency and helping consumers. But the transition to more competitive markets can prove painful. When an industry accustomed to having domestic market power encounters international competition, it must accept a reduction in the premium in prices and wages it previously commanded over other sectors of the economy. Both firms and workers may be reluctant to accept this implication of increased competition, and idle capacity and unemployment may result. Prices and wages in some U.S. heavy industries are probably too high to be sustainable in an integrated world economy.

Policies of Foreign Governments

A different problem is posed when foreign governments engage in protective or export promotion measures that harm U.S. producers. U.S. trade negotiators have emphasized four particular areas of concern:

1. *Agriculture:* Japan and the European Economic Community have high protective barriers against U.S. agricultural products. Further, the European Economic Community now engages in massive subsidized export of agricultural products to dispose of the surpluses created by its price-support program. These measures depress world prices of agricultural products, imposing substantial costs on U.S. producers in a sector where the United States holds a clear comparative advantage.

2. *High technology:* In recent years, many countries have come to view the high-technology industries as vehicles for economic growth and have sought to promote them through a complex mix of policies—outright subsidies, export credit subsidies, research subsidies, preferential procurement by State-owned enterprises, and so on. The United States holds a comparative advantage in high-technology products, and the U.S. export market share has remained roughly constant since 1973. Nevertheless, there is concern that in some specific areas, especially aircraft, foreign subsidies are threatening the position of U.S. producers.

3. *Services:* The United States has developed an increasingly strong net export position in services. Services, however, have never been recognized as being under the rules of the international trading system, and trade in services is limited by a maze of foreign government regulations.

4. *Investment:* Many countries impose "investment performance requirements" on foreign investors in exchange for the right to invest or to receive investment incentives. Many of those performance requirements are trade-related, requiring foreign companies to export more, reach a specified level of local content, or reduce imports.

CHALLENGES TO U.S. TRADE POLICY

The next few years are critical for the international trading system. Accumulating structural problems have combined with short-run macroeconomic stresses to produce a resurgence of protectionist pressures. The Administration's aim, nonetheless, is to preserve and extend the benefits of freer trade. To do this will require resisting protectionist pressures at home while continuing to urge foreign governments to eliminate their more objectionable trade-distorting policies.

Responding to Foreign Actions

The practices of foreign governments pose extremely difficult issues for U.S. trade policy. The United States customarily seeks to induce other nations to move in the direction of freer trade. The dilemma is how to do this without imposing costs on ourselves that exceed the benefits from changes in other countries' policies.

Trade-distorting measures, whether they take the form of protection against imports or the promotion of exports, hurt the country which adopts them as well as other countries, even when they are a response to foreign trade-distorting practices. If foreign governments limit imports from the United States and we respond in kind, the initial results will be further reductions in economic efficiency at home and higher domestic prices. If foreign governments subsidize exports, depressing world prices for U.S. products, a countersubsidy by the United States will depress prices still further. The belief that departures from free trade are automatically called for if other countries do not play by the rules is a fallacy.

Intervention in international trade by the U.S. Government, even though costly to the U.S. economy in the short run, may, however, be justified if it serves the *strategic* purpose of increasing the cost of interventionist policies by foreign governments. Thus, there is a potential role for carefully targeted measures, explicitly temporary, aimed at convincing other countries to reduce their trade distortions.

There are obvious risks in such a course of action. Instead of inducing other countries to move toward freer trade, U.S. pressure might set off a cycle of retaliation which would leave everyone worse off. There are also domestic political risks. Trade measures intended to be temporary may end up permanent and institutionalized. The need to balance the strategic objective of reducing foreign trade barriers against the harm which might be caused by U.S. retaliatory measures explains the U.S policy of negotiating for freer trade while holding open the possibility of more direct action as a last resort.

Responding to Problem Industries

The problems of industries which have recently lost their traditional market power also pose a serious policy dilemma. There is strong pressure to give these industries at least temporary relief from imports, in the hope that lower wage and price increases and improved productivity will eventually make them competitive again. On the other hand, protection reduces the incentives for both firms and workers to make these changes. Furthermore, protectionist measures, however temporary they are supposed to be, tend to become permanent. The limitation of protection for these problem industries is a central goal of U.S. economic policy.

EXCHANGE RATES AND THE BALANCE OF PAYMENTS

During 1982 the dollar rose against other major currencies to its highest level since the beginning of floating exchange rates in 1973. The strength of the dollar provided some benefits to the U.S. economy by reducing import prices and thus accelerating progress against inflation. On the other hand, the strong dollar caused severe problems by decreasing the cost competitiveness of exported U.S. goods.

CAUSES OF THE DOLLAR'S STRENGTH

Exchange-rate movements are not well understood. Econometric models of exchange-rate determination proposed in the past decade have not shown any consistent ability to track past exchange-rate movements, let alone predict future changes. Nevertheless, careful

384-041 0 - 83 - 5 : QL 3

analysis can narrow the range of plausible explanations of the dollar's rise.

The recent appreciation of the dollar, unlike many earlier exchange-rate movements, did not simply reflect contemporaneous changes in relative price levels. The well-known theory of purchasing power parity suggests that the rate of change in the exchange rate should equal the difference between the foreign and domestic inflation rates. Over the very long run, or in situations of very large differences in inflation rates, the purchasing power parity theory has proved to be a useful guide. But the theory has little or no power to explain the recent rise of the dollar. Price increases over the past 2 years in Germany and Japan, for instance, were lower than in the United States. Yet the dollar appreciated dramatically during that period against both the mark and the yen. Stated differently, the rise of the dollar was not simply a nominal but also a real appreciation, as illustrated in Chart 3–3.

Large exchange-rate movements may also occur because of shifts in world demand for a country's exports or changes in a country's demand for imports. An example of such an event was Great Britain's discovery of oil in the North Sea, which has played at least some role in the high level of Great Britain's real exchange rate relative to other European currencies.

No comparable event accounts for the appreciation of the dollar, although U.S. oil imports have declined sharply. The rise of the dollar was not initially accompanied by a deterioration of the trade balance, a fact which might seem to suggest that there was an increase in demand for U.S. goods. The initial lack of deterioration, however, stemmed from lags in the effect of the exchange rate on the trade balance rather than from a shift in either export or import demand, and the U.S. trade deficit grew rapidly in the second half of 1982.

What the rise of the dollar seems clearly to reflect is a rise not in the demand for U.S. goods, but in the demand for U.S. assets. The reasons for the increased attractiveness of investment in the United States are somewhat controversial, but the effects are not. In order to buy U.S. assets, foreigners must first acquire dollars. The increased demand for dollars drives up the exchange rate.

One important factor in the increased demand for U.S. assets was that real interest rates in the United States were high relative to real interest rates elsewhere. Real interest rates are not directly measurable, since they equal the nominal rate minus *expected* inflation. But some rough measure is attainable by computing the nominal rate minus *actual* inflation. Chart 3–4 shows the differential in real interest rates computed in this way between the United States and other

Chart 3–3

Real Exchange Rates Of Major Currencies Against The Dollar

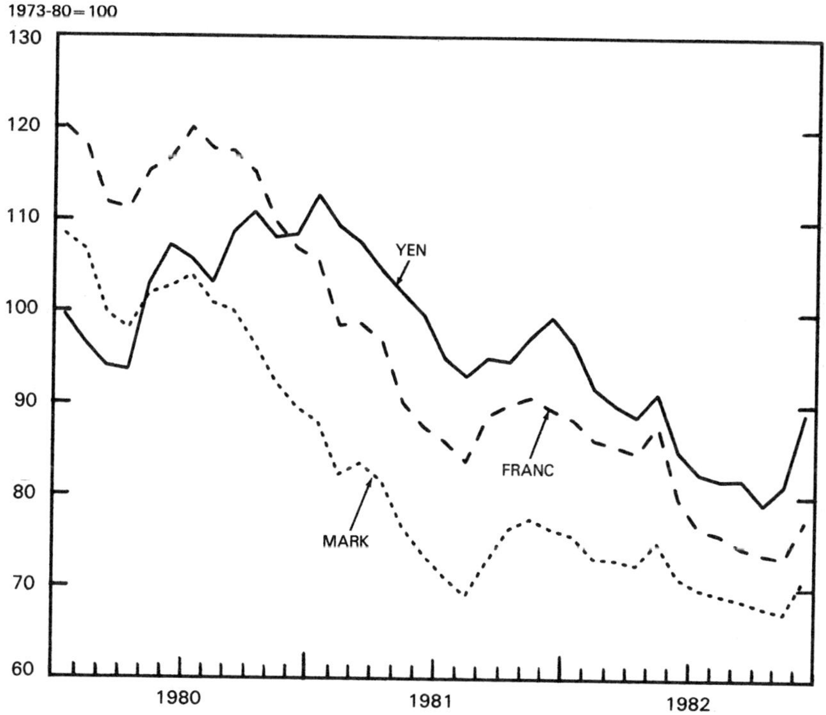

NOTE.—CONSUMER PRICES USED AS DEFLATOR.
SOURCE: INTERNATIONAL MONETARY FUND.

industrial countries. The chart suggests that the real interest rate in the United States was substantially higher than foreign rates in recent years.

But events in the fall of 1982 cast some doubt on whether real interest rates alone can explain the dollar's strength. As U.S. short-term interest rates fell sharply, the differential between short-term interest rates in the United States and other countries was greatly reduced. Yet the dollar continued to rise. The explanation for this may lie in the difference between short- and long-term rates. Most exchange-rate models suggest that long-term real rates, and not short-term ones, are what affect the real exchange rate. A notable feature of the U.S. financial scene in the fall of 1982 was that long-term rates

Chart 3–4

International Real Short-Term Interest Rate Differentials

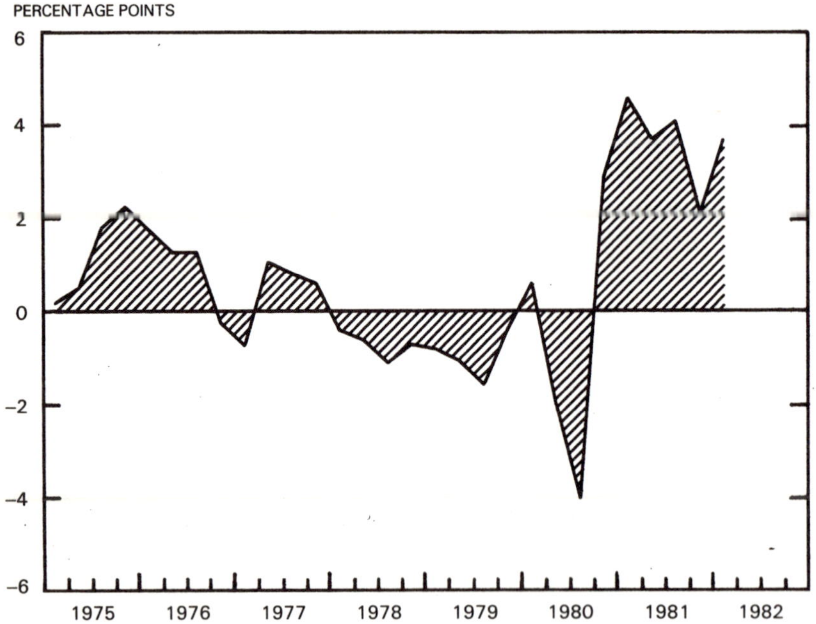

NOTE.—DATA ARE U.S. RATE MINUS AVERAGE OF RATES FOR MAJOR INDUSTRIAL COUNTRIES WEIGHTED BY GNP, ADJUSTED FOR DIFFERENCES IN CONSUMER PRICE INFLATION.

SOURCE: INTERNATIONAL MONETARY FUND.

did not fall nearly as much as short-term rates. At the same time, long-run inflation expectations may have declined, so that it is unclear how much long-term real interest rates actually fell.

Many observers believe that other factors besides real interest rates help explain the dollar's strength. In particular, the unsettled state of the world economy—particularly the problems in Europe and Latin America described later in this chapter—may have created a desire on the part of investors for a safe haven for their funds. The United States, according to this argument, is still regarded as the most politically and economically stable of the market economies and has become a financial refuge in troubled times. While the importance of this factor is hard to assess, the worldwide search for financial security may partially explain this country's rising capital account surplus and its growing current account deficit.

AN UNDERVALUED YEN?

The explanations of the strong dollar discussed so far leave out a view which has received considerable attention—that the strength of the dollar reflects deliberate undervaluation of their currencies by our competitors, especially Japan. This view is important enough in its implications for U.S. international economic policy to deserve separate treatment.

Arguments that the yen is undervalued are of two types, which are basically independent of one another. One argument is that the Japanese government has persistently kept the yen undervalued. The other is that the Japanese have only recently engineered a decline in the yen to gain competitive advantage. Neither of these views appears correct in light of the actual behavior of Japan's balance of payments and exchange rate.

If the first allegation—that the yen has been persistently undervalued—was correct, Japan would run persistent current account surpluses in excess of what seems justified. We would also expect Japan to have experienced exceptionally rapid growth in its foreign exchange reserves. Neither of these was the case:

- From the beginning of floating exchange rates in 1973 through 1981, Japan had an average surplus in its current account of only 0.15 percent of GNP. This was not much more than the U.S. figure for the same period (0.11 percent), considerably less than that of Germany (0.47 percent), and much less than the U.S. surplus of the early 1960s (0.70 percent).
- From the beginning of floating exchange rates in 1973 to the third quarter of 1982, Japan's reserves minus gold grew at an annual rate of 4.8 percent, far less than the 9.7 percent rate of reserve growth for all non-OPEC countries.

These facts contradict the view that the yen was persistently undervalued. There remains the possibility that the yen's weakness during much of 1982 was excessive in some sense. A natural question is whether, after adjustment for purchasing power parity, the yen fell more against the dollar than other currencies. The answer to this question depends on the base period used for comparison. For most base periods, however, the real depreciation of the yen against the dollar appears smaller than that of the French franc and the German mark. Table 3-5 shows an illustrative set of numbers. As the table shows, only for a few base periods does the yen appear more "undervalued" than the other two currencies.

The actual behavior of the Japanese balance of payments and exchange rate thus do not support the view that there is any special undervaluation of the yen—that is, they suggest that exchange-rate

TABLE 3-5.—*Real appreciation of the dollar against major currencies to August 1982*

[Percent change from base year to August 1982[1]]

Base year	French franc	German mark	Japanese yen
1971	-1.0	-2.1	-25.3
1972	11.8	9.5	-13.1
1973	27.9	31.4	2.0
1974	21.4	31.0	6.4
1975	39.5	33.7	7.3
1976	29.6	28.8	10.9
1977	29.4	35.9	24.3
1978	43.0	50.1	[2]53.1
1979	50.8	53.8	36.8
1980	51.6	44.2	25.9
1981	21.1	11.3	[2]22.9

[1]Percent change in the price of the dollar in each currency, adjusted for differences in consumer price inflation.
[2]Indicates a base year relative to which the August 1982 exchange rate of the yen looks lower than that of the other currencies.

Source: Board of Governors of the Federal Reserve System.

movements over the last several years stemmed from a strong dollar rather than a weak yen. An examination of Japanese policy by the U.S. Treasury supports this conclusion. This study found that Japan has attempted to isolate its domestic capital market from world capital markets, but that this has tended to limit capital outflow rather than inflow, supporting rather than weakening the yen. Japanese capital controls have been relaxed in recent years, a move which the United States supports even though the result will be a weaker yen and an increase in Japan's current account surplus. In the 1980s, Japan may well become more of a capital exporter than it was in the 1970s, and thus have larger current account surpluses. These surpluses, if they materialize, will result from Japan's high domestic saving rate, which gives Japan a natural role as an exporter of capital to the rest of the world.

To show that there is no special yen issue is not to deny that a substantial deterioration has occurred in the relative cost position of U.S. firms. This deterioration was actually larger relative to other industrial countries, but since Japan is the United States' most important competitor, the depreciation of the yen worries U.S. firms more. There is no special yen issue, but the strong dollar does pose genuine problems.

EFFECTS OF A STRONG DOLLAR ON U.S. TRADE

The rise of the dollar was associated with a large rise in the production costs of U.S. firms relative to those of foreign competitors. To take one measure, unit labor costs in U.S. manufacturing rose 32 percent relative to those of a weighted average of other industrial countries from their low point in the third quarter of 1980 to the second quarter of 1982. This rise in relative costs has at least temporarily reduced the international competitiveness of U.S. industry dramatically. Other U.S. exporting and import-competing sectors, especially agriculture, have also been squeezed.

Despite this deterioration in competitive position, it was only in the third quarter of 1982 that the U.S. trade deficit began to show a significant increase. This delay was in line with previous experience of the effect of exchange rates on trade. The full effect of changes in exchange rates on the volume of exports and imports is felt only after some time has passed, because some trade takes place under contracts signed in advance and because customers do not always change suppliers immediately when relative prices change. The short-term effect of a rise in the dollar is to reduce import prices, which actually tends to *improve* the trade balance. Although the negative effects eventually dominate, some econometric estimates suggest that the full negative effect is not felt for more than 2 years.

As the effects of the strong dollar are increasingly reflected in U.S. trade, the trade deficit will widen. Economic developments elsewhere in the world will also contribute to a widening trade deficit. The recession in other industrial countries will depress the demand for U.S. exports, and financial constraints in developing countries will lead them to import less. Both developments will have negative consequences for U.S. exports. Record trade and current account deficits in 1983 will almost surely result.

Whether the trade and current account deficits persist will largely depend on U.S. macroeconomic policies, particularly on the fiscal side. If large budget deficits are allowed to continue to depress the U.S. national saving rate, real interest rates may rise again, sustaining or even increasing the high real exchange rate of the dollar. In this case the trade deficit could remain high for several years.

A large and sustained trade deficit would result in an economic recovery which would be "lopsided" in the sense that exporting and import-competing sectors would not share in the gains. Should this occur, government, business, and labor officials must bear in mind that even though protectionist foreign trade practices distort the composition of world trade and reduce economic efficiency both in the United States and abroad, large trade deficits are not the result of unfair foreign competition. Large projected U.S. trade deficits are a result of macroeconomic forces, particularly large budget deficits. The main sources of the U.S. trade deficit are to be found not in Paris or in Tokyo, but in Washington.

RESPONSES TO THE STRONG DOLLAR

The temporary adverse effects of a strong dollar create pressure to do something for the exporting and import-competing sectors. Three kinds of policies might be used: microeconomic intervention in the form of protection or export subsidies, direct intervention in the foreign exchange market, and changes in monetary and fiscal policy.

Protection and Export Promotion

The negative effect of the strong dollar on the competitiveness of many U.S. firms has fueled pressures for an interventionist trade policy. These pressures must be resisted. Protecting import-competing industries or subsidizing exports is not just a harmful long-run policy. With a floating exchange rate, such policies would fail to improve the trade balance or create employment even in the short run.

The exchange rate always moves to clear the market. An increase in exports or a reduction in imports would lead to an increased demand for or reduced supply of dollars on the world market, raising the exchange rate. This would lead to a further loss of competitiveness in the sectors not protected or promoted. An export subsidy for agricultural products would worsen the situation of the auto industry, an import quota on steel would hurt the competitiveness of the aircraft industry, and so on. Although these indirect effects may seem of doubtful importance in the real world, they are not. That governments cannot simultaneously protect everyone is a basic principle of international trade.

Instead of creating additional employment and output, the distortion of trade through protectionist policies or export promotion would probably reduce them. Market-distorting policies reduce the efficiency of the economy. Thus, a turn to protectionism could create a "supply-side" shock that might have the same kind of stagflationary effects as an oil price increase. The effects would prove still worse if, as is likely, U.S. actions were to provoke foreign retaliation.

Although protectionism and export subsidies provide no answer to the problems caused by a strong dollar, the pressure to use them is increasing. Many of the exporting sectors, which make up the traditional constituency for freer trade, appear to have become convinced by the strength of the dollar and the resulting loss of U.S. competitiveness that a more interventionist policy is needed.

Exchange-Market Intervention

Since March 1981 the United States has abstained as much as possible from direct intervention in the foreign exchange market. This unwillingness to intervene is based on doubts about whether exchange-market intervention is effective or desirable. As long as the Federal Reserve continues to pursue a policy of targeting monetary aggregates, any U.S. intervention on the foreign exchange market must be *sterilized*—that is, offset by other transactions on domestic financial markets. These transactions are likely to wipe out most of the effect of the initial exchange-market intervention.

The process of sterilization is straightforward. If the U.S. Government attempted to drive up the price of foreign exchange and weaken the dollar by buying foreign securities, the Federal Reserve would issue dollars to pay for the foreign assets. In order to prevent these dollars from increasing the U.S. money stock, however, the Federal Reserve would then have to withdraw an equal number of dollars from the market by selling Treasury bills. The only net result would be that the world's supply of dollar-denominated assets would increase, while its supply of assets denominated in other currencies would fall.

The increase in the level of dollar-denominated assets would probably have little effect on the exchange rate because of the sheer size of world financial markets. The world market in dollar-denominated securities includes not only the dollar assets actually owned abroad—foreign deposits in U.S. banks, foreign holdings of Treasury bills, Eurodollar deposits, and the like—but also all those dollar assets which are potentially tradeable. Thus, the total pool of internationally mobile dollar assets is probably in the trillions of dollars. This makes it questionable whether even very large interventions in the exchange market can have much effect on the exchange rate.

Macroeconomic Policies

Although the government cannot significantly affect exchange rates through direct intervention, monetary and fiscal policies do indirectly affect the exchange rate. A feasible strategy for bringing the dollar down would involve looser monetary policies and tighter fiscal policies. Both of these changes would tend to lower real interest rates (at least in the short run), making capital movement into the United States less attractive and thus driving down the value of the dollar.

Despite its unfortunate effects on the U.S. balance of trade, however, monetary restraint is the prime weapon in the fight against inflation. Disinflation, as we have learned, unfortunately involves substantial costs. Under fixed exchange rates the heaviest costs of monetary contraction and disinflation fell on the interest-sensitive sectors of the economy, such as construction and consumer durables. With floating exchange rates, however, much of the burden also falls on exporting and import-competing sectors, which are injured by the rise in the value of the dollar.

A tighter fiscal policy would also lower real interest rates and lead to a lower dollar. Under fixed exchange rates, budget deficits crowded out domestic investment. With a floating exchange rate they crowd out exporting and import-competing products as well. A reduction in deficits would lead—with some lag—to an improvement in the trade balance as well as higher investment.

The strength of the dollar has put considerable strain on the resolve of the United States to remain committed to free trade. This strain is not unique to the international sector. The recession and high interest rates have also put a strain on the resolve to let other types of markets, from housing to labor markets, operate freely. If there is special reason for concern about the international side, it is because of the danger that mistakes in U.S. policy could set off a spiral of retaliation among all the major trading nations.

The competitiveness of U.S. business as a whole—as opposed to that of particular sectors—and the balance of payments are macroeconomic phenomena. Microeconomic interventions cannot cure macroeconomic problems; they can only make one sector better off by hurting other sectors even more. The most effective strategy the United States can pursue for its exporting and import-competing sectors is to get its overall economic house in order—above all, by bringing budget deficits and real interest rates under control.

MACROECONOMIC PROBLEMS IN EUROPE

More than 90 percent of the output of the industrial countries, and more than 70 percent of the output of the world's market economies, is produced by the United States, Japan, and the European Economic Community. Table 3–6 shows some comparative figures for the three. The most striking feature of the table is the favorable performance of Japan by all measures. The United States and the European Economic Community look rather similar in their less favorable performances. They experienced nearly the same growth rates before 1979, have suffered nearly equal decelerations of growth since then, and had roughly the same unemployment rate in 1981. The U.S. inflation rate was lower than that in Europe, but the United States also showed lower productivity growth.

Behind the similarity of U.S. and European experience, however, lies a major difference. The U.S. economy, whatever its other difficulties, has provided employment opportunities for a rapidly growing labor force. The current high unemployment rate is a cyclical problem, not the result of a persistent failure of employment to expand. In Europe, by contrast, employment was virtually stationary over the last decade, and unemployment has risen in every year since 1973. This is a worrisome aspect of the European situation.

For a given rate of unemployment, the strains on society are probably greater if employment is stagnant than if it is growing. Growing employment means that more new jobs are always opening up, offer-

TABLE 3-6.—*Economic performance by major industrial countries, 1973-82*

[Percent]

Item	United States	Four large European countries [1]	Japan
Growth rate in:			
Real gross domestic product (GDP), 1973-80	2.3	2.2	3.7
Real GDP per employed person, 1973-80	.2	2.2	3.0
Real GDP, 1980:I-1981:IV	-.2	.1	2.3
Level:			
Consumer price inflation, year ending 1982:II	6.8	10.2	2.4
Unemployment rate, 1981	7.6	7.4	2.3

[1] France, Germany, Italy, and United Kingdom.

Sources: International Monetary Fund and Organization for Economic Cooperation and Development.

ing job losers a chance for reemployment and new entrants to the labor market a chance to get their first job. If employment is stationary, workers who have lost their jobs may stay unemployed for a long time, and young people may never find jobs. The results of near-zero employment growth are painfully visible in Europe, where long-term unemployment (more than 6 months) is several times higher than in the United States, and where the share of youth unemployment in the total pool of unemployed has risen steadily since 1973.

How did the problem arise? The causes of structural unemployment are always controversial, but a key element in the European employment problem was probably rapid increases in real labor costs in the first half of the 1970s in the face of declining productivity growth and rising oil prices. These increases in labor costs—which stemmed at least in part from increases in social insurance payments—squeezed profitability. Firms closed their marginal plants and invested in increasingly capital-intensive techniques, which helped to sustain the rate of productivity growth but also led to employment stagnation.

The unemployment problem in Europe is not caused solely by excessive labor costs. The periods of rapid increase in European unemployment, in 1973-76 and since 1979, came during business cycle contractions (Table 3-7). The most recent rise in unemployment is probably mostly due to restrictive monetary and fiscal policies adopted by the European countries following the oil price shock of 1979. These policies were adopted out of concern that the rise in import prices resulting from that shock—and, later, the further rise in import prices resulting from the appreciation of the dollar—would lead to an uncontrollable inflationary spiral. Thus, recent developments in the European economy are to some extent similar in character to those in the United States, which have also resulted largely from disinflationary policies. The European situation is more serious, however, because the current recession comes on top of a steadily growing structural unemployment problem.

TABLE 3-7.—*Employment and unemployment in the European Economic Community, 1973–80*

[Percent]

Year	Increase in employment	Unemployment rate
1973	1.1	2.8
1974	.1	3.0
1975	−1.1	4.2
1976	−.1	4.9
1977	.4	5.2
1978	.6	5.3
1979	.8	5.3
1980	.2	5.7

Source: Organization for Economic Cooperation and Development.

The United States has a major stake in the success of the European countries in dealing with their macroeconomic problems. The stake is not simply due to the fact that the major European countries are also allies of the United States, nor is it simply due to the fact that roughly one-quarter of U.S. exports go to Western Europe. More than this, Europe is a key part of the world economy, with an aggregate GNP as large as that of the United States itself. If European countries remain mired in economic stagnation and turn toward increased protectionism as a consequence, little chance will remain of saving the open trading system.

THE INTERNATIONAL DEBT PROBLEM

Different problems from those facing the United States and Europe afflict the economies of the developing nations. The problems of these economies have accumulated over the last several years and are products of both domestic policy mistakes and external developments, such as oil price increases, the recession in industrial countries, and high real interest rates. In the summer and fall of 1982 the problems came to a head in the form of a sharp reduction in international lending to the developing countries.

DEBT-FINANCED GROWTH IN THE 1970s

Until recently, the growth of such middle income developing countries as Brazil, South Korea, and Taiwan was widely viewed as one of the great success stories of the 1970s. Particularly notable was their success in expanding exports of manufactured goods. While the growth of these exports did give rise to some adjustment problems in industrial countries, the successes of some middle income countries were undoubtedly a highly favorable development for the United States. Such success provided a dramatic demonstration to other countries of the potential of market-oriented economic policies.

An important aspect of growth in the developing world, however, was heavy borrowing from foreign sources. There is nothing inherently wrong in external borrowing to finance growth. Some of the developed countries, including the United States, relied heavily on foreign capital during earlier periods of industrialization. But some developing nations borrowed too much, investing in projects of doubtful productivity. When overly optimistic expectations about export earnings and interest rates turned out to have been wrong, these countries found themselves in serious financial difficulty.

From 1973 to 1981 the medium- and long-term external debt of non-oil developing countries rose at an annual rate of more than 20 percent. Lenders might have viewed this rate of increase as more alarming than they did, were it not for several factors which appeared to indicate that the eventual repayment of the debt would not impose a severe burden on borrowing countries. These factors included:

- *A rapid growth in the ability of these countries to service their debt.* Exports of the non-oil developing countries grew at an annual rate of 18 percent.
- *Very low real interest rates.* From 1973 to 1979 Eurodollar rates in London, which set the basis for most international lending, averaged 8.5 percent, while U.S. wholesale prices rose at an annual rate of 9.8 percent. Even allowing for the fact that third-world borrowers paid small spreads over the Euromarket rate, the real interest rates they paid were still negative.
- *Special factors which appeared to ensure rising export earnings in the future.* The most important of these was oil reserves, which were essentially treated as an asset against which countries could safely borrow.

CAUSES OF THE LIQUIDITY PROBLEM

Excessive borrowing by some developing countries made an eventual financial problem inevitable. The proximate factor which brought the era of debt-financed growth to a halt was, however, a sharp deterioration in the world economy. The rise in oil prices in 1979 was a blow to many debtor countries, and further strains resulted from disinflation in the United States and other industrial countries. The factors which led to a loss of lender confidence in the developing countries included:

- *The effects of the world recession on export demand.* The rapid export growth of the 1970s came to an abrupt end in the early 1980s. Exports of the non-oil developing countries actually fell by 7.5

percent from the first half of 1981 to the first half of 1982. Exporters of primary products were hit particularly hard: real commodity prices fell by 25 percent from the fourth quarter of 1980 to the second quarter of 1982.

- *High real interest rates.* In 1981 and the first half of 1982, Euromarket interest rates averaged 16 percent, while wholesale prices in the United States rose at an annual rate of only 4.5 percent.
- *The appreciation of the dollar.* Since most international debt is denominated in dollars, while commodity prices tend to follow a weighted average of industrial country currencies, the effect of the rise in the value of the dollar was a sudden increase in the size of developing country debt relative to prospective export earnings.

The result of these developments was that banks, which had been willing to lend large amounts to developing countries throughout the 1970s, lost confidence that the loans would be promptly repaid. The debtor countries were highly vulnerable to such a loss of confidence. Much of their debt was of short maturity, so that a large fraction of their debt required refinancing each year. Argentina, Brazil, and Mexico, for example, must make annual payments of principal and interest which exceed their total exports of goods and services. During the 1970s these large financing needs did not pose a problem, since countries were able to roll over their debt as it came due. In the summer and fall of 1982, however, banks became reluctant to make new loans and roll over old ones, first to Mexico and then to other countries. The result was a quick exhaustion of the foreign exchange reserves of the major debtors.

IMPLICATIONS OF THE DEBT PROBLEM

The debt situation of the developing countries poses two problems for the world economy. Although quite unlikely, failure to resolve the debt situation in an orderly way could lead to major financial market disruptions. More likely—indeed, it has already happened to a considerable extent—is a situation of forced austerity in debtor countries, with adverse effects on world trade and output.

Risks to Financial Markets

The threat of a financial disruption arises from the possibility that debtor countries will be unable to live within their new financial constraints. The unwillingness of banks to lend as much as in the recent past means that debtor countries will need to cut their imports or expand their exports. In the case of the most heavily indebted countries, this will almost certainly mean achieving substantial trade surpluses in spite of depressed demand for their exports. The concern of lenders that some debtors will not be able to achieve the required adjustment is precisely what makes them reluctant to lend.

Fortunately, a serious financial disruption is unlikely. The debtor countries and the banks which are their major creditors share a strong interest in an orderly resolution of the debt problem. For the debtor countries, maintaining good financial standing is essential if they are to maintain access both to world capital markets and to their export markets. At the same time, banks realize that demanding too rapid a repayment from debtor countries could prove counterproductive, and they are probably willing to provide enough financing so that debtor countries can more easily handle the financial squeeze. Although banks find themselves in somewhat of a "prisoner's dilemma" situation, in which no one bank will want to lend if it believes that the loans will only go to repay other banks, this problem should not prove insoluble. The banking community should be able to work with the International Monetary Fund (IMF) in negotiating agreements which balance an adequate degree of new lending to the debtor countries with realistic economic adjustment plans. To aid in this process, the Administration and representatives of other industrial nations recently agreed in principle to an enlargement of the IMF's resources.

Perhaps the most important safeguard against a financial crisis is the ability of the governments and central banks of the major industrial countries to provide a safety net for the international financial system. Central banks act as lenders of last resort for commercial banks, providing effective protection against banking panics. At the same time, industrial country governments have demonstrated their willingness to help provide temporary financing for developing countries in order to bridge the interval until agreements can be reached with the IMF. (The IMF recently concluded agreements with Mexico, Argentina, and Brazil.)

Effects on World Trade

Although a serious disruption of the international financial system is unlikely, for all of the reasons cited, serious problems still exist. Even under optimistic assumptions, those developing countries with high ratios of debt to exports will be forced to improve their trade balances substantially in order to pay the interest on their debt. Much of this trade balance improvement will probably come through reductions in imports, involving painful reductions in output and real wages in the debtor countries. This will also depress demand for the products of industrial countries—particularly the United States, which has especially close trading relations with some of the major Latin American debtors. The debt problem of the developing countries may worsen the U.S. trade balance by $10 to $20 billion and reduce U.S. GNP by one-half percentage point or more from the level it would otherwise reach.

The Outlook for Debtor Nations

The problems of the developing countries are not insoluble. If growth in the world economy resumes and real interest rates fall to historical levels, the debt burden of even the most heavily indebted countries will become much more manageable. Mexico and Brazil, among the most heavily indebted countries, both have debts well below half their GNPs. At a historically typical real interest rate of 2 percent, the real burden of debt service would fall to less than 1 percent of GNP—a fully manageable level in a growing economy.

The key to recovery from the debt problem, however, lies in increased exports from the debtor countries. Import restrictions by the developing countries can only accomplish so much in improving their trade balances. Imports have already fallen considerably in high debt countries in the last year, leaving limited room for further cuts. As growth resumes among the debtor countries, they will tend to import more, and will need to export more to pay for the imports. They will not be able to do this if the industrial countries, including the United States, institute new protectionist measures. Yet as developing countries attempt to increase their exports, strong political pressures will develop in the industrial countries to stop them. Leaders in the industrial countries must realize that shutting out imports from the developing world will not only incur the usual costs of protection—higher prices to consumers and jobs lost in unprotected sectors—but also will threaten the basic stability of the world financial system.

CHAPTER 4

Increasing Capital Formation

ATTAINING AN ADEQUATE RATE OF CAPITAL FORMATION in the United States is a crucial challenge for economic policy during the 1980s. Devoting a larger share of national output to investment would help restore rapid productivity growth and rising living standards. During the past two decades, fiscal, monetary, and regulatory policies contributed to the low rate of net investment in plant and equipment; the share of gross national product (GNP) devoted to capital formation was below the levels achieved by most other industrialized nations.

The Administration and the Congress have instituted a set of tax and regulatory policies designed to increase the share of output devoted to capital formation. The noninflationary monetary policies followed by the Federal Reserve, with the Administration's support, should also contribute in the long run to increased capital formation and improved efficiency in the allocation of the capital stock. This chapter examines the linkages between economic policy and capital formation, and discusses the rationale for the Administration's initiatives in this area.

Many forms of investment contribute to productivity growth. Research and development expenditures provide the basis for the technological change that is a wellspring of productivity growth. Another major source of productivity growth is investment in education and training that promotes the accumulation of valuable human capital. Public sector infrastructure investments may also have an important role to play. This chapter, however, focuses on nonresidential plant and equipment investment. Past public policies probably discriminated most heavily against this form of investment. Plant and equipment investment is also more amenable to quantitative analysis than other forms of capital investment because of the difficulties involved in measuring intangible capital.

By late 1982, investment and capacity utilization rates in the United States had fallen to very low levels. Even after the recovery from the recession begins, capacity utilization will increase only gradually, and it will take time for new policies to increase the share of national output devoted to saving and investment. Hence, levels of

384-041 O - 83 - 6 : QL 3

investment may prove disappointing over the next several years despite the beneficial long-run impact of policies recently put in place. This should not cause us to lose sight of the importance of sound long-run policy and the need to increase net capital formation in the years and decades ahead.

THE HISTORICAL RECORD

Although gross private domestic investment, which includes residential and inventory investment, accounted for 16.1 percent of GNP between 1971 and 1980, gross investment in structures and equipment averaged only 10.8 percent of GNP during this period. Of this gross structure and equipment investment, more than two-thirds was devoted to replacing depreciated capital, leaving only 3.0 percent of GNP for new structures and equipment.

It is useful to place the patterns of investment in the United States during the last decade in historical and geographic perspective. Table 4-1 displays the behavior of alternative measures of capital accumulation. The data show that the rate of net nonresidential fixed investment as a fraction of GNP declined by 27.5 percent between the late 1960s and the late 1970s. The share of output devoted to net nonresidential fixed investment in the late 1970s was slightly lower than the average rate during the entire 1950–80 period.

Some analysts, examining only the data on gross investment, have concluded that investment performance was satisfactory during the 1970s. This procedure ignores the fact that depreciation as a share of GNP was greater during this period than in the 1960s because of a general shift in net investment from long-lived assets, such as structures, toward assets with shorter lives, and because of a higher ratio of capital to GNP. The appropriate focus in examining data on investment is the total stock of capital. Therefore, net investment, which measures the change in the total capital stock, is the most appropriate indicator of the adequacy of capital formation.

An alternative way to evaluate changes in the level of capital formation is to examine trends in the capital-labor ratio. Measures of capital per hour and capital per worker, displayed in Table 4–1 and Chart 4–1, both show a large decline in the growth rate of the capital stock relative to the growth in the supply of labor. Capital per hour increased at only a 0.9 percent annual rate between 1976 and 1980, compared to a 3.5 percent rate during the 1951–75 interval. Although this dramatic decline was in part due to the low rate of net investment during the late 1970s, it was primarily a consequence of the rapid growth of the labor force. To maintain the pre-1975 growth in the capital-labor ratio, a sharp increase in the post-1975 rate of net investment was required, instead of the decline which actually occurred.

TABLE 4-1.—*Alternative measures of capital formation, 1951-82*

[Percent]

Period	Net private domestic investment as percent of GNP		Growth rate of net capital stock [1]	
	Total investment	Nonresidential fixed investment	Per worker [2]	Per hour [2]
1951-55	7.2	2.9	3.1	3.5
1956-60	6.1	2.6	3.5	4.1
1961-65	6.7	2.9	2.5	2.4
1966-70	7.1	4.0	3.9	4.9
1971-75	6.4	3.1	2.2	2.6
1976-80	6.0	2.9	.4	.9
1951-80	6.6	3.1	2.6	3.0
1981	4.8	2.8	3.3	4.5
1982 [3]	2.1	2.0	(4)	(4)

[1] Real net private nonresidential fixed capital stock at year-end.
[2] All persons in private business sector. Year-end obtained by averaging fourth quarter value with value for first quarter of subsequent year.
[3] Preliminary.
[4] Not available.

Sources: Department of Commerce (Bureau of Economic Analysis), Department of Labor (Bureau of Labor Statistics), and Council of Economic Advisers.

Properly measured, the decline in the growth rate of the capital stock is understated by the net investment figures in Table 4-1. The energy price shocks of 1973 and 1979 hastened the obsolescence of a variety of past investments, which implies that actual depreciation was greater than the official statistics suggest. One estimate placed the premature obsolescence of capital during the late 1970s at an average of 0.5 percent of GNP per year. Other studies have obtained much larger estimates using data on the market valuation of capital. In addition, it is important to recall that much of the investment of the 1970s took place in the energy-producing sector. The share of GNP devoted to net fixed nonresidential investment outside the energy sector averaged only 1.8 percent between 1975 and 1980.

Unfortunately, the combined effects of the recent economic recession and large Federal budget deficits will hold down the rate of capital formation, as currently forecasted, over the next several years. Between 1981 and 1985, net investment in plant and equipment may prove disappointing even by the standard of the late 1970s. The capital-labor ratio will grow only slowly and may even decline. While the low forecasted rate of net investment over the next several years is due primarily to cyclical conditions, it does not negate the importance of developing permanent policies to encourage capital formation. In light of the depth of the recent recession, it is reasonable to expect that investment performance probably would have proven

Chart 4–1

Measures of Capital Formation

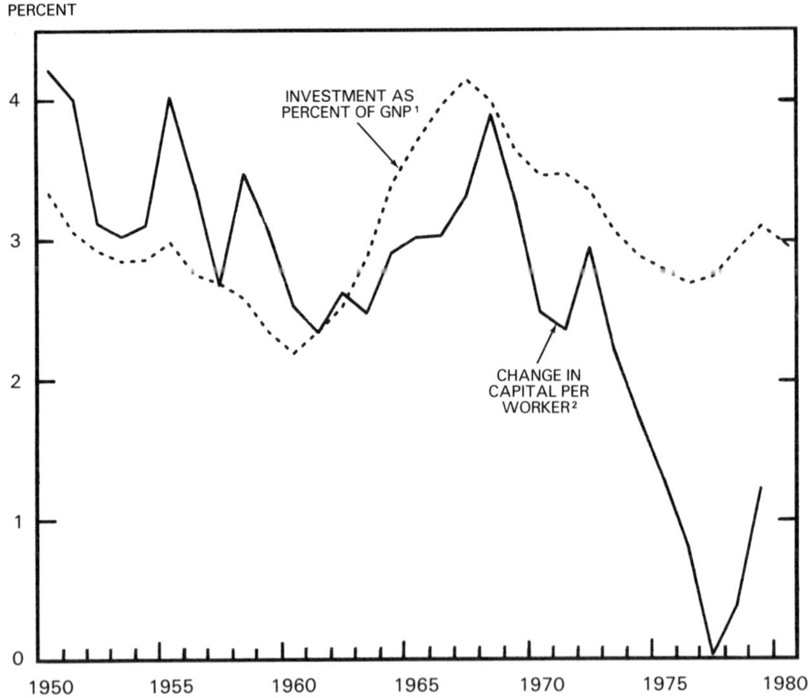

[1] NET PRIVATE NONRESIDENTIAL FIXED INVESTMENT AS PERCENT OF GNP; FIVE-YEAR CENTERED MOVING AVERAGES.
[2] PERCENT CHANGE IN REAL NET PRIVATE NONRESIDENTIAL FIXED CAPITAL STOCK PER WORKER IN THE BUSINESS SECTOR; FIVE-YEAR CENTERED MOVING AVERAGES.

SOURCES: DEPARTMENT OF COMMERCE, DEPARTMENT OF LABOR, AND COUNCIL OF ECONOMIC ADVISERS.

worse if the Congress and the Administration had not enacted tax measures to spur capital formation. These laws, and the proposals incorporated in the President's fiscal 1984 budget, are designed to raise the share of net investment to a high level by historical standards in the late 1980s or before.

AN INTERNATIONAL PERSPECTIVE

Table 4–2 shows that the United States falls behind other major industrial nations in several key measures of net capital formation. The share of U.S. gross domestic product (GDP) devoted to net fixed investment during the last decade was only 34 percent of the comparable share in Japan and 56 percent of the comparable share in West Germany. No other major industrial nation devotes as small a fraction of total output to new investment as does the United States.

TABLE 4–2.—*Comparison of capital formation in six OECD countries, 1971–80*

[Percent]

Country	Investment as percent of GDP			Growth rate of output per hour in manufacturing
	Gross investment	Gross fixed investment	Net fixed investment	
France	24.2	22.9	12.2	4.8
Germany	23.7	22.8	11.8	4.9
Italy	22.4	20.1	10.7	4.9
Japan	34.0	32.9	19.5	7.4
United Kingdom	19.2	18.7	8.1	2.9
United States	19.1	18.4	6.6	2.5

Source: Organization for Economic Cooperation and Development.

It is instructive to compare the growth rates of productivity for different countries with their shares of output devoted to new investment. Although productivity growth and investment rates are simultaneously determined by a multitude of factors, it is striking that a strong positive relationship emerges. As shown in Chart 4-2, Japan has both the highest investment share and the highest growth rate of productivity, while the United States has the worst investment performance and the lowest growth rate of productivity.

While the reasons for these large international differences in rates of capital formation are not precisely understood, some evidence suggests that the roots may lie in different public policies. After World War II, rebuilding of the capital stock was a primary goal of economic policy in continental Europe and Japan. Governments in those countries encouraged saving and investment and disregarded the early Keynesian fear that oversaving could reduce aggregate demand and depress real economic activity.

In contrast, officials in the United States feared a postwar relapse into depression and avoided policies which would encourage saving. For example, some economists advocated sustained budget deficits as a means of absorbing excess private savings.

It is now clear—on the basis of four decades of economic experience since the end of the Great Depression—that fears of secular stagnation caused by a high and rising saving rate are unwarranted. The much greater risk is that productivity growth in the United States will continue to stagnate at low levels, and that American workers will have to accept a lower growth rate in their standard of

Chart 4-2

International Comparison of Investment and Productivity Growth, 1971-80

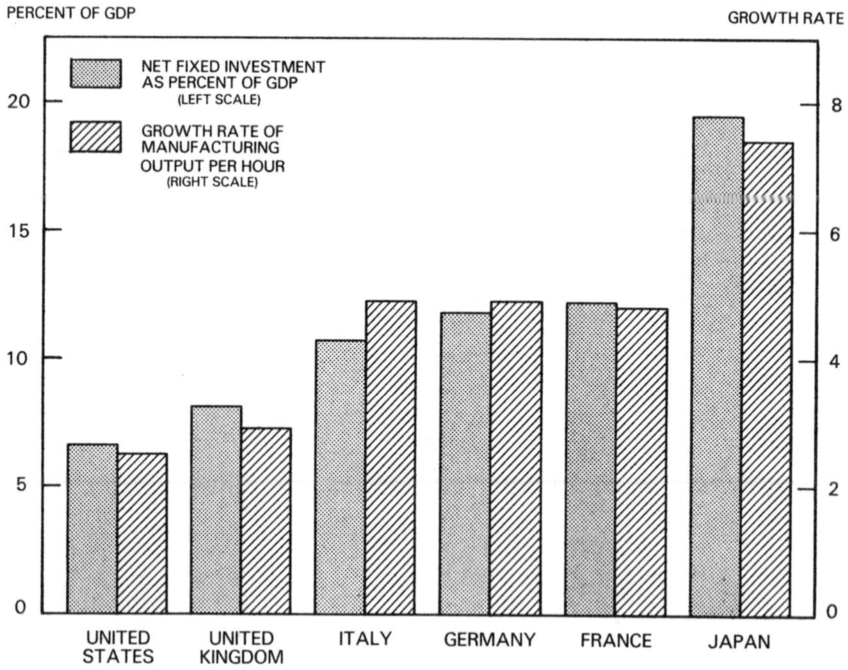

SOURCE: ORGANIZATION FOR ECONOMIC COOPERATION AND DEVELOPMENT.

living than their foreign counterparts. Otherwise, American goods could cease to be competitive on world markets.

THE IMPORTANCE OF CAPITAL FORMATION

The case for increasing the rate of capital formation ultimately rests on three justifications. First, increased capital formation can reverse part of the productivity slowdown that the United States has suffered during the last decade. Second, government policies have discriminated in favor of consumption and against saving and investment. Third, as a result of tax policies, the pretax return to capital investment exceeds the after-tax return that any individuals are able to capture privately, leading to an inappropriately low level of capital formation.

During the 1970s, productivity growth in the United States decelerated rapidly. Between 1948 and 1967 the growth rate of productivity (as measured by output per hour in the private business economy) was 3.1 percent, compared to 2.3 percent between 1967 and 1973 and only 0.8 percent between 1973 and 1981.

The consequences of reduced productivity growth for our standard of living over the long run are greater than those of any other current economic problem. In 1981 the American economy produced approximately $12,780 worth of output per capita. Had productivity growth continued at the 1948–67 rate during the 14 years subsequent to 1967, output per capita would have reached $16,128 in 1981, 26 percent higher than the actual value. As a standard of comparison, the recent recession reduced per capita output by only 4 percent between the third quarter of 1981 and the fourth quarter of 1982, less than one-fifth the reduction attributable to the productivity shortfall. As time passes, the consequences of reduced productivity growth are compounded. Increasing the productivity growth rate by 2 percentage points annually would more than double our material standard of living by 2020, compared to the level it would reach otherwise.

The productivity slowdown is not reliably attributable to any single cause or combination of causes. Various analysts have suggested that higher energy prices, regulatory changes, reduced research and development spending, reduced opportunities for technical innovation, the changing composition of the labor force, and changing worker attitudes, as well as reduced capital formation, are responsible for the productivity slowdown. An accurate accounting of the sources of the slowdown is probably impossible in light of the multitude of competing explanations and the statistical difficulties associated with distinguishing between their relative effects precisely.

Many of the possible causes of the productivity slowdown are probably not reversible through public policy. There is relatively little the Federal Government could have done to offset the negative effect of sharp increases in oil prices or, for that matter, to influence changing cultural attitudes toward work. Changing the rate of capital formation, however, is a principal way in which Federal economic policy can affect productivity growth.

Increasing the rate of capital formation will raise productivity growth in several ways. More rapid capital formation results, on average, in workers having more equipment at their disposal. In addition, increases in investment reduce the average age of the capital stock, permitting physical assets to embody more recent technological innovations. Technological development and the level of capital formation are intertwined, because the development of more efficient and sophisticated capital goods occurs when the demand for new capital goods increases.

The legacy of past policies, which have artificially depressed saving and investment, provides a second reason for increasing the rate of capital formation. As described below, this discrimination against capital formation has taken many forms, including tax policy, monetary policy and recurring Federal budget deficits. Although there exist instances of market failure, a market economy can generally be expected to allocate resources in an efficient way. When public policies systematically discriminate against one type of spending, however, there is a strong presumption that too little of it will take place.

A related and final justification for increased capital formation comes from a comparison of the total pretax return to investment with the return received by private investors. Estimates suggest that the total pretax return to investment in corporate capital, as measured by its pretax marginal product, is about 11 percent. This means that $1.00 invested today yields society $1.11 next year, or alternatively a permanent yield of 11 cents. While the total pretax return fluctuates from year to year with cyclical conditions, studies have tended to find that it has stayed within the range of 8 to 15 percent throughout the postwar period.

In contrast, private investors have earned much smaller rates of return over the last several decades, with many investors earning negative real after-tax returns over much of that period. Even leaving aside the effects of personal taxes, the real return on short-term debt instruments averaged less than 1 percent during the 1950–81 interval. While equity investments have yielded a higher average return, they carry with them a large amount of risk. The average real return on common stock before personal taxes was 6 percent over the 1950–81 period, but investors lost money in real terms in 12 of those years and over periods as long as 17 years.

This large spread between the total and private returns to investment is a consequence of the tax system, which extracts a portion of the total return to investment before it reaches private investors. Capital market returns are reduced because the corporate income tax reduces the return that corporations can pay out to investors. As a consequence of this tax-induced divergence between the private and total return to investment, too little investment takes place. This suggests the desirability of measures both to reduce tax distortions and to increase incentives to save and invest.

Domestic saving is an important determinant of a nation's level of investment. Economic output is either invested in capital assets, which help produce future output, or consumed privately or publicly. Only by forgoing consumption does it become possible for a nation to invest in a sustained way. While funds from abroad are available to finance some investment, experience suggests that most mature economies have financed investment through domestic saving. Increasing the rate of capital formation in the United States without increasing obligations to foreigners therefore probably requires increased national saving.

Table 4-3 provides information on net national saving as reported in the national income and product accounts. On average, from 1951 to 1981, the United States saved 6.7 percent of total output beyond that necessary to replace depreciated capital. Private saving, comprising personal saving and corporate retained earnings, totaled 7.3 percent of GNP. Federal Government dissaving through budget deficits averaged 0.9 percent of GNP, while the sum of State and local government surpluses averaged 0.3 percent of GNP.

TABLE 4-3.—*Net saving as percent of GNP, 1951-81*

[Percent]

Period	Total	Not adjusted for inflation			Adjusted for inflation [2]		
		Federal	State and local	Private [1]	Federal	State and local	Private
1951-55	6.7	−0.3	−0.1	7.2	0.9	−0.1	5.9
1956-60	6.9	.0	−.2	7.1	1.1	−.1	5.9
1961-65	7.4	−.4	.0	7.8	.2	.2	7.0
1966-70	7.5	−.6	.1	8.0	.6	.4	6.5
1971-75	6.4	−1.8	.6	7.6	−.3	1.1	5.6
1976-80	5.8	−1.9	1.2	6.5	−.2	1.6	4.4
1981	5.0	−2.0	1.1	5.9	.0	1.5	3.6
1951-81	6.7	−.9	.3	7.3	.4	.6	5.8

[1] Private saving less capital consumption allowances with capital consumption adjustment.
[2] Adjusted by GNP implicit price deflator.

Sources: Department of Commerce (Bureau of Economic Analysis), Board of Governors of the Federal Reserve System, and Council of Economic Advisers.

While the total saving rate can be measured unambiguously, there are serious conceptual problems in measuring its various components during an inflationary period. Inflation erodes the real value of the national debt. Interest rates incorporate inflation premiums and these premiums compensate lenders for the fact that they are repaid in cheaper dollars. Thus, they do not really represent income to borrowers or costs to lenders. This principle is recognized by the Financial Accounting Standards Board and is often applied in the private sector. Table 4-3 therefore also presents a breakdown between private, Federal, and State and local government saving that is adjusted for the effects of inflation.

BUDGET DEFICITS AND SAVING

Unacceptably large Federal budget deficits are likely in the next several years unless legislative changes are made. These deficits could significantly reduce investment during the economic recovery. Increased public consumption with no reduction in private consumption leaves fewer resources available for investment. When the Federal Government must compete with private borrowers for savings, real interest rates are bid up, discouraging investment.

Federal dissaving would not represent a serious problem if it automatically called forth more private saving. While increased deficits do not induce an equal increase in private saving, they also do not crowd out investment expenditure dollar for dollar. Increases in the real rate of return caused by Federal deficits raise the yield savers receive and may call forth some additional private saving. Higher real interest rates also discourage spending on consumer durables, housing, and construction by State and local governments. Finally, by contributing to increases in real interest rates, budget deficits encourage capital inflows from abroad. These factors imply that deficits do not completely crowd out private investment; rather, a reasonable estimate is that funds available for private investment are reduced by perhaps one-half to three-fourths of the budget deficit.

The possibility that Federal budget deficits crowd out private investment takes on greater importance in light of the large deficits that will occur over the next 5 years unless actions are taken. The fiscal 1982 budget deficit of $110.7 billion absorbed 3.65 percent of GNP. Projections now suggest the 1983 deficit will equal $207.7 billion or 6.5 percent of GNP. Unless significant actions are taken, deficits of this magnitude or larger may continue even as the economy recovers from the recent recession. If such deficits materialize, the consequences for capital formation could prove very serious unless a dramatic increase in private saving also takes place. A budget deficit of 5 percent of GNP would likely reduce net investment by an amount equal to about one-half its historical level, relative to a balanced budget. With large deficits, significant improvements in labor productivity and the quality and quantity of housing would be less likely in the years ahead.

TAX RULES AND PERSONAL SAVING

Many economists believe that tax rules in the United States encourage consumer borrowing and discourage private saving. During the 1970s the combination of tax rules and inflation produced a dramatic decline in the private return to saving and a large reduction in the cost of borrowing.

During the 1960s, nominal interest rates on 3-month Treasury bills averaged 4.0 percent, and the consumer price inflation rate averaged 2.3 percent. On a pretax basis, this left savers with an average real return of 1.7 percent. For a saver in the 30 percent marginal tax bracket, the real after-tax return was only 0.5 percent.

The return to saving fell significantly below this level during the 1970s. While the average inflation rate rose to 7.1 percent, the average interest rate increased to only 6.3 percent. This caused a decline in the real interest rate measured on a pretax basis and a larger decline in the average after-tax rate (for a person in the 30 percent bracket) from 0.5 percent to −2.7 percent.

The return to saving has fallen because of corporate taxes as well as individual taxes. Corporate income taxes decrease the returns corporations can afford to pay to the holders of their securities. As described below, these tax burdens also increased substantially during the 1970s. In addition, corporate taxes reduce the amount of funds that corporations can retain for reinvestment.

At the same time that tax rules have reduced the return on savings, they have encouraged dissaving through borrowing. Because consumer interest payments are tax deductible, taxpayers who itemize their deductions are encouraged to use credit to finance their purchases of consumer durables and other goods. As inflation increased during the 1970s, the real after-tax cost of borrowing declined and eventually became negative. Indeed, in the first quarter of 1980 the real after-tax cost of borrowing for a taxpayer in the 30 percent bracket was −1.2 percent. The encouragement of borrowing to finance purchases of durable goods probably reduced the aggregate saving rate substantially during the 1970s.

The tax reforms supported by the President in 1981 and enacted by the Congress were designed to increase saving. Reductions in marginal tax rates raise the after-tax return to saving and the after-tax cost of borrowing. The Economic Recovery Tax Act of 1981 will reduce the marginal tax rate facing a median income family in 1984 from 28 percent, which would have occurred under pre-1981 law, to 22 percent. The act immediately reduced the marginal tax rate on high income taxpayers, who account for a large fraction of personal saving, from 70 to 50 percent.

The Economic Recovery Tax Act of 1981 also contained several other provisions directed specifically at encouraging private saving. The Individual Retirement Account (IRA) provisions in the tax code were extended to cover the entire working population. Working individuals are now permitted to make a yearly tax deductible contribution of $2,000 to finance consumption during retirement. Taxes are only paid when the funds plus accumulated interest are withdrawn from the IRA. Private estimates suggest a substantial response to this legislation, with about $10 billion placed in IRAs during 1982. A crucial issue in evaluating the efficiency of IRAs is their effectiveness in raising saving incentives on the margin. Some critics have argued that IRAs do not provide an incremental incentive for saving because contributors can simply transfer funds from other sources without increasing total savings. While this occurs to some extent, it is certainly not universal and will decrease in the future as contributors exhaust their funds available from other sources. The fragmentary evidence available from private sources suggests that more than half of all IRA contributors contribute less than the maximum amount allowable, indicating that they do face increased saving incentives on the margin.

The 1981 tax legislation also provided for an interest exclusion starting in 1985, allowing individuals to exclude 15 percent of their net interest income up to a limit of $3,000. This will also raise the return to savings and spur capital formation. Extending the exclusion to dividends as well as interest payments would reduce the tax bias favoring debt over equity as a source of corporate finance.

The 1981 tax act also raised the return to saving by reducing the top marginal rate on capital gains from 28 percent to 20 percent. This reform partially compensates for the serious distorting effect of inflation on the measurement of capital gains. Because of inflation, an owner of an asset that experiences no real appreciation will nevertheless become liable, at the time of sale, for taxes on the nominal appreciation of the asset. Complete elimination of this distortion would require indexation for inflation in the measurement of capital gains.

In recent years support has grown among economists and other tax experts for moving the tax system toward taxation of consumption and away from taxation of income. This change might entail expanding the existing exclusions of interest and dividend income and those mechanisms, such as IRAs, which permit tax-deferred accumulation of savings. It might also involve limiting the deduction of interest expenses for consumer borrowing. Movement toward taxation of consumption is supported by some advocates on the grounds that taxing individuals on what they take from the economy is "more fair" than taxing what they contribute to the economy. A tax system based on consumption taxation might also prove easier to administer than the current system because it would eliminate many of the problems involved in measuring certain types of capital income.

FINANCIAL REGULATION AND PRIVATE SAVING

An additional set of public policies that has probably discouraged private saving over the last several decades is the regulation of financial institutions. As Chart 4–3 shows, small savers holding savings accounts subject to Regulation Q have received below market rates of interest, and holders of checking accounts have received even lower rates of interest. These low returns are largely consequences of regulations limiting the interest rates financial institutions may pay on customer deposits. As late as 1980, the spread between Treasury bill rates and the yield on savings deposits subject to Regulation Q was as great as 8 percent.

The adverse effects of financial regulations on personal saving have probably lessened considerably in recent years, due to both private and public actions. In the private sector, the development and explosive growth of money market funds has made it possible for most high and middle income savers to receive market rates of interest. Legislation adopted in 1982 with Administration support has allowed commercial banks and thrift institutions to offer financial instruments with competitive interest rates to a wide range of depositors.

The Administration has strongly supported removal of the many unnecessary regulations that have impeded competition in the financial services industry. As discussed in more detail in Chapter 5, the Depository Institutions Deregulation and Monetary Control Act of 1980 and the Depository Institutions Act of 1982 have played important roles in beginning this process of deregulation. Banks and thrift institutions can now offer insured accounts that are competitive with money market funds in terms of both the interest rates they pay and the services they provide, thereby increasing incentives for saving.

A related development has occurred in the Federal Government's policies regarding U.S. Savings Bonds. Savings bonds have historically paid low rates of return. In 1980, 10-year Treasury bonds paid 11.5 percent, while Series EE Savings Bonds paid an annual yield of only 7 percent from issue to maturity 11 years later. Because of legislation recently proposed by the President and passed by the Congress, the return on savings bonds is now based on market rates. Between November 1, 1982, and April 30, 1983, for example, U.S. Savings Bonds will earn 11.09 percent if they are held at least 5 years. Apart from making saving more attractive to savings bond purchas-

Chart 4–3

Three-Month Treasury Bill Rate and Regulation Q Maximum Rate on Savings Accounts

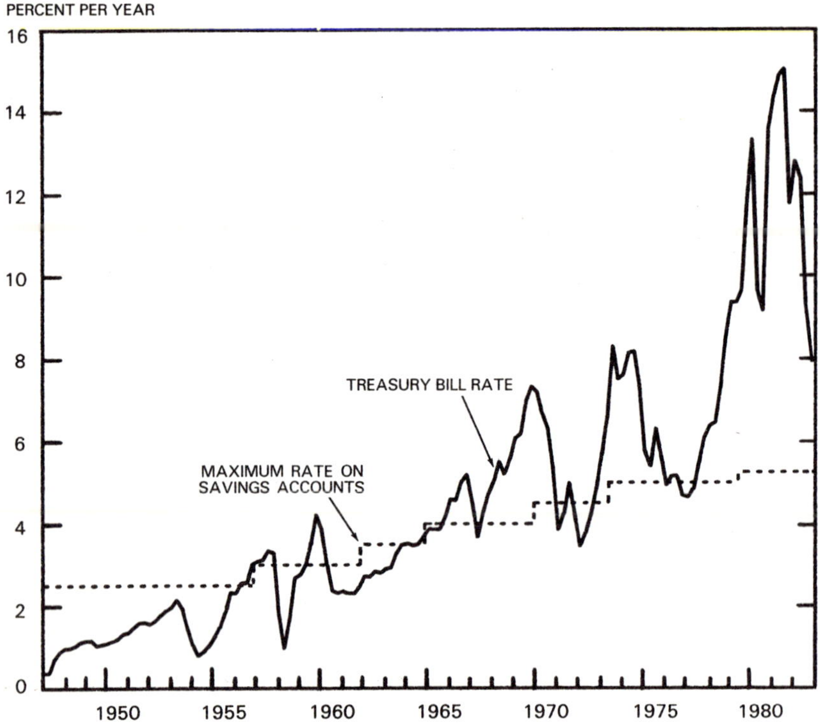

SOURCE: BOARD OF GOVERNORS OF THE FEDERAL RESERVE SYSTEM.

ers, the new rates on Series EE bonds are desirable on equity grounds because small savers can now obtain yields close to those received by their higher income counterparts.

THE ROLE OF INTERNATIONAL CAPITAL FLOWS

It is likely that budget deficits, tax policies, and ceilings on bank interest rates have contributed to the lower net saving rates which the United States has experienced in recent years. In theory, however, this low level of saving need not have strictly limited the level of funds available for investment. Funds from abroad can also finance investment in the United States. The link between domestic investment and domestic saving is not absolute.

Nevertheless, a number of economic studies cast doubt on the proposition that the United States could offset low domestic saving rates through sustained borrowing from abroad. These studies have found a consistently high correlation between rates of domestic investment and domestic saving in the major industrialized countries. While the reasons for these results are not well understood, they may reflect the high information costs and serious monitoring difficulties associated with holding foreign investments. Whatever the exact reason for the historically high correlation between domestic saving and investment, it suggests that increasing the rate of investment in the United States significantly will probably require policy measures which increase domestic saving.

Insofar as savings from abroad are available for investment in the United States, it is not clear that they provide a desirable substitute for domestic saving. Throughout most of the postwar period, the United States was a net exporter of capital. However, the United States has recently experienced a large surplus in its capital account and incurred a large offsetting deficit in its current account. This has entailed large merchandise trade deficits, with deleterious impacts on U.S. export industries and those domestic industries which compete with imports.

THE ALLOCATION OF CAPITAL

With only a relatively small fraction of GNP available to finance investment, and with large budget deficits looming over the next few years, the allocation of capital in the United States among alternative uses takes on added importance. In addition to holding down the rate of national saving, previous fiscal and monetary policies have tended to alter the allocation of capital investment, favoring housing, consumer durables, and State and local construction at the expense of business investment. Inflation, caused by overly expansionary monetary policies, and taxes interact to affect the incentives on different kinds of investments. While a sound economic recovery will boost saving sufficiently to provide for increases in all forms of investment, eliminating tax-induced distortions in the allocation of capital would also aid in regaining a rapidly rising standard of living.

It is useful to examine how the tax structure has very different effects on alternative forms of investment. The income from investments by corporations is taxed at both the individual and the corporate level. Corporate profits are taxed as they are earned. When these profits are received by shareholders in the form of either dividends or capital gains, they are taxed again. By contrast, the implicit returns from most other forms of investment remain untaxed. The services to investors in owner-occupied housing and consumer durables are largely untaxed.

The bias in our tax system against corporate capital investment was exacerbated during the 1970s by the effects of inflation. Corporations are permitted to take depreciation allowances based on historic rather than replacement costs for tax purposes. Thus, as the rate of inflation increases, the real value of depreciation allowances decreases, and the tax burden as a share of real profits rises. Another source of inflation-induced corporate tax increases is that inflation causes "phantom" gains in the value of inventories, raising taxes for firms using the first-in, first-out method of inventory valuation. One study estimated that the tax law's use of historic costs rather than replacement costs for depreciation purposes raised corporate tax payments by $19.1 billion in 1977, and raised tax burdens for corporations using first-in, first-out inventory accounting by $7.0 billion. Although these tax increases were partially offset because corporations deduct nominal rather than real interest payments in calculating their taxable income, the gains at the corporate level from the deductibility of nominal interest are offset to some extent by losses from taxation of the inflation component of interest rates at the individual level.

The effects of the interaction of taxes and inflation reached dramatic proportions during the 1970s. Increased taxation led to large market revaluations of corporate and noncorporate capital assets. The "q ratio," which measures the market value of capital in the nonfinancial corporate sector relative to its reproduction cost, fell from 1.09 in 1970 to .67 in 1980. The price of single-family nonfarm dwellings relative to the price of consumption goods rose by 29 percent during the same period. During the last 2 years of falling inflation, however, the q ratio rose to about .80 in the fourth quarter of 1982, and the relative price of single-family nonfarm dwellings fell by 5.3 percent.

The supply of different types of capital goods ultimately depends on their relative prices. The observation that reductions in inflation are associated with changes in the relative prices of different capital goods suggests that the reductions in inflation are likely to cause a reallocation of capital toward plant and equipment investment and away from investments in consumer durables and housing. These shifts simply reflect the reduced magnitude of the biases caused by our current tax system in periods of inflation.

TAX POLICY AND INVESTMENT

In 1981 the Congress instituted the accelerated cost recovery system as part of the Economic Recovery Tax Act. This tax legislation permitted businesses to depreciate most purchases of equipment according to an accelerated 5-year schedule. It also permitted businesses to depreciate structures over 15 years using a 175 percent declining balance schedule. The Economic Recovery Tax Act preserved the investment tax credit on equipment and called for further accelerations in depreciation schedules in 1985 and 1986.

The 1982 Tax Equity and Fiscal Responsibility Act altered the provisions of the Economic Recovery Tax Act by instituting a half-basis adjustment for investment tax credits in calculating depreciation and by eliminating the planned further accelerations in depreciation schedules. Table 4–4 shows the present value of the depreciation deductions and investment tax credits received by a corporation under the old accelerated depreciation system, Economic Recovery Tax Act (ERTA) rules and Tax Equity and Fiscal Responsibility Act (TEFRA) rules. The present value is calculated for a variety of hypothetical combinations of discount and inflation rates.

TABLE 4–4.—*Investment incentives* [1] *under different tax laws*

[5-year property]

Real interest rate	Tax law	Inflation rate (percent)			
		4	6	8	10
1 percent	Pre-ERTA [2]	.495	.473	.454	.436
	ERTA	.516	.500	.486	.472
	TEFRA	.495	.480	.466	.454
4 percent	Pre-ERTA [2]	.462	.444	.427	.412
	ERTA	.492	.478	.465	.452
	TEFRA	.472	.459	.446	.435
7 percent	Pre-ERTA [2]	.435	.419	.404	.390
	ERTA	.471	.458	.446	.434
	TEFRA	.452	.440	.428	.418
10 percent	Pre-ERTA [2]	.412	.397	.384	.372
	ERTA	.452	.440	.429	.418
	TEFRA	.435	.423	.412	.402

[1] Present value of depreciation deductions and investment tax credits per dollar of investment.
[2] Assumes depreciation over 9.5 years using double-declining balance switching to sum of years digits.
Source: Council of Economic Advisers.

Three qualitative conclusions emerge from these calculations. First, current tax laws provide significantly more stimulus to most categories of investment than did the pre-1981 law. Second, the reduction in inflation that has occurred during the past 2 years has also increased substantially the value of the depreciation allowances. Third, even with a relatively short 5-year cost recovery period, the value of the investment incentives remains quite sensitive to the anticipated rate of inflation.

In considering the economic effects of tax policies on investment, it is crucial to distinguish between measures which apply only to new investment, such as accelerated depreciation and the investment tax credit, and measures which reduce the tax burden on all kinds of

384-041 0 - 83 - 7 : QL 3

capital income, such as corporate rate reductions. These two types of investment incentives produce very different economic effects. Measures which apply only to new investments affect only marginal investment decisions; no tax benefit is conferred on the owners of existing capital. Therefore, in the short term more investment is stimulated per dollar of immediate revenue loss than would prove the case if the tax benefit were conferred on all capital. The tax legislation enacted in 1981 relied on tax incentives for new investments.

Incentives for new investment are viewed by some observers as benefiting primarily large wealthholders, but the reality may be different. Since measures like the accelerated cost recovery system reduce the effective cost of purchasing new capital goods, they are likely to reduce the value of the old capital goods with which they compete. For example, a subsidy for the purchase of new cars will reduce the value of used cars. Likewise, reduced taxation of new investment may temporarily reduce the level of stock market prices, which in part reflects the market's valuation of existing capital. Thus, investment incentives like those recently enacted, while raising the rate of return on new investments, may actually hurt holders of existing wealth. Workers should benefit as greater capital accumulation raises their productivity and wages. The effect on the distribution of income is ambiguous and might even prove progressive.

Beginning with the enactment of the accelerated depreciation provisions in 1954, policy has tended to rely on investment incentives that stimulate new investment and do not benefit existing investments. This continued reliance on measures that benefit new capital at the expense of existing capital carries a subtle but real risk. As investors come to anticipate this pattern of public policy, they may take into account expected future changes in tax laws as they make investment decisions. This might have an unintended effect. Investors who expect capital losses are less likely to invest. Stated differently, if the effective purchase price of new capital goods is expected to decline because of tax reforms, there will be a tendency to defer investments. This suggests that in designing future reforms it may be desirable to consider reducing taxes on existing as well as new capital.

While current tax law provides significantly more stimulus to investment than did earlier law, there is room for further reform. The value of depreciation allowances is still dependent on the rate of inflation, increasing the uncertainty of investment decisions. The acceleration of depreciation allowances has substantially reduced the burden of the corporate income tax, but investment in plant and equipment is still discouraged by taxes on dividends and capital gains.

A final problem under current tax law is the treatment of corporate losses. Because of low profits due to cyclical conditions, or large depreciation write-offs, many corporations do not have taxable income in some years, reducing the efficacy of investment incentives during those periods.

CONCLUSIONS

The tax programs put in place in the last 2 years should play an important role in increasing capital formation in the United States. Yet, much more can be done to ensure a rapidly growing standard of living in coming years. It is crucial that we take action to reduce large Federal deficits and to further stimulate private saving and investment.

In considering the issue of capital formation, policymakers should take a long view. The reasons for increasing capital formation primarily involve long-run growth rather than current economic conditions. We should not allow the poor performance of investment during a period of recession and high deficits to blind us to the importance of policies that can help us achieve sustained and rapid economic growth in the years to come.

CHAPTER 5

The Burden of Economic Regulation

FOR MANY DECADES, the Federal Government has regulated the prices and the conditions for entry in certain sectors of the U.S. economy. This type of regulation, often called "economic regulation," was broadly applied to the transportation, communications, and financial sectors of the economy. Whatever historical purposes were served by economic regulation, there is an increasing consensus that much of this Federal regulation no longer serves the interests of the contemporary economy. Indeed, over the last several years a substantial part of this economic regulation has been relaxed or eliminated.

A second form of regulation, "social regulation," is addressed to situations where unregulated activity may pose significant threats to public health, safety, or the environment. Although there is an increasing consensus that economic regulation should be substantially reduced, no such consensus exists concerning social regulation. Also, unlike economic regulation, the magnitude of social regulation has grown rapidly since the mid-1960s with the passage of extensive environmental and safety legislation.

Economic regulation has diminished in recent years due to a variety of deregulation measures. Substantial evidence is now available concerning the performance of industries that have experienced full or partial deregulation. This chapter summarizes the history of Federal economic regulation, its rationale, its impacts, and the effects of recent laws designed to ease economic regulation. The chapter also identifies some opportunities for further deregulation. Special attention is given to the economic regulation of energy, transportation, communications, and financial markets.

A BRIEF HISTORY OF ECONOMIC REGULATION

The first broad body of Federal economic regulation was established in 1887, when the Congress created the Interstate Commerce Commission (ICC) to resolve the increasing controversies between the railroads and shippers. Most of the regulation of other sectors, except for energy, was established by the end of the 1930s and reflected efforts to deal with problems similar to those that led to the creation of the ICC. The agencies created in the 1930s tended to operate in much the same way as the ICC, and the outcome was much the same.

Economic regulation often evolved from a dispute among several groups. For example, the Federal Communications Commission (FCC) was created to resolve disputes among users of the broadcast spectrum. The Civil Aeronautics Board (CAB) was created to resolve a dispute among several Federal agencies concerning the administration of airmail contracts.

Congress delegated direct resolution of these disputes to an independent agency with very general authority. The typical "public convenience and necessity" standard cited in the enabling legislation provides no direct guidance about how the regulatory agencies should resolve disputes. The independent commissions are essentially quasi-judicial institutions that have developed their own bodies of administrative law.

The initial regulations of the independent agencies often served the interests of the regulated industry. For example, some scholars contend that the ICC, by initially reinforcing the railroad cartels, caused higher average prices and reduced the variance of prices. For a long time, both the CAB and the FCC restricted entry to the number of firms operating at the time these commissions were created.

The initial regulation led to more regulation that served to protect the interests of the initially regulated firms. For example, ICC regulation was extended to trucks, buses, freight-forwarders, and barges, thus restraining the developing competition to the railroads. FCC regulation was extended to cable television, protecting broadcasters using the frequency spectrum.

Over the long run, many economic regulations have not served the interests of either producers or consumers. The development of excess capacity, relatively high wages, restraints on technological improvements and operating practices, and competition outside the regulated environment led to the lower-than-average rates of return in many of the regulated industries. Consumers have often been adversely affected by higher prices and restrictions on service.

One other pattern of economic regulation was introduced in the 1930s. A belief that the depression was caused by excessive competition provided a rationale for many laws and regulations that directly restricted entry, output, and competition. The broadest such law, the National Industrial Recovery Act, was declared unconstitutional; other similar legislation, such as the Agricultural Adjustment Act of 1938, is still in force. One might argue that the several regulatory commissions and laws approved in the 1930s achieved their intended effect of raising prices. A later generation questioned whether this effect was desirable.

THE TRADITIONAL RATIONALE FOR ECONOMIC REGULATION

The two traditional justifications for economic regulation have been to preserve the potential economic efficiencies associated with natural monopoly in some industries and to eliminate the inefficiencies thought to be associated with excessive competition in others.

Natural Monopoly

A *natural monopoly* exists when the entire relevant demand for a good or service can be satisfied at the least total cost by a single firm. At the local level it is probably wasteful to have duplicate distribution systems to provide telephone, electric, gas, and water services. Among industries regulated at the Federal level, major gas pipelines and high-voltage electric lines are often considered natural monopolies. Long-distance telephone transmission may also be a natural monopoly in areas of low density. Railroads are a potential natural monopoly only for that declining share of rail traffic for which the shipper does not have an effective choice of carrier or mode of transport.

Such industries present a dilemma. Competition may result in unnecessarily high production costs through duplication of facilities, but an unregulated monopoly may not act in the public interest. Without regulation, a monopoly would probably set prices too high and produce too little, with consumers willing to pay more for additional output than the cost of supplying that output. A typical solution to this dilemma is maximum price regulation. The primary objective of price regulation is to set the monopoly's price as close as possible to incremental cost while still assuring the monopoly a market rate of return on its investment.

The growth of demand or the introduction of substitutes for a product can often transform a natural monopoly into what—in the absence of regulation—could become an effectively competitive industry. Oil pipelines, for example, are often assumed to be natural monopolies. However, these pipelines now face competition from other pipelines and other modes of transportation. Regrettably, price regulation often continues long after it is efficient, restricting the emergence of a competitive market. The history of the railroads provides a compelling illustration. In many parts of the country rail lines were few and far between in the 19th century. But as the market for transportation services grew, and as technology developed, automobiles, buses, and airplanes provided increasing competition for passenger traffic, and trucks, barges, and pipelines provided increasing competition for freight. The natural monopoly justification for regulation was probably not applicable in most rail markets by the middle of the 20th century.

Even in markets where elements of natural monopoly still exist, government intervention will not necessarily produce a more efficient use of resources. Increasingly, analysts are coming to recognize that, just as there are market imperfections, there are also government imperfections that must be considered in making public policy choices. The relevant tradeoffs are not between imperfect markets and flawless government regulation, but rather between markets with imperfections and regulation which is imprecise and sometimes counterproductive.

Excessive Competition

The second traditional justification for economic regulation is that unfettered markets result in *excessive competition.* This justification was used for regulating railroads in the late 19th century and other industries in the 1930s. A common element in early discussions of excessive competition was that without regulation, unrestrained rivalry among firms would result in losses for some or all of them and that adequate production of an otherwise viable product would prove unsustainable. This argument, which was often rather vague, failed to note that business losses are not a sufficient basis for government intervention. Losses and business failures are a normal part of the operation of competitive markets; they act to eliminate inefficient firms and to shift production to meet changes in consumer demands.

While the concept of excessive competition was not generally well defined, it has now come to refer to at least four possible sources of market imperfection: natural monopoly, cyclical demand with imperfect capital markets, predatory pricing, and suboptimal product quality.

As explained earlier, where natural monopoly conditions exist, competition among several firms can lead to higher costs because of wasteful duplication.

A second interpretation of excessive competition is based on the argument that certain industries, particularly those with cyclical demand and heavy fixed investment, are prone to excessive price fluctuations. According to this argument, firms are forced to close down during recessions and then unnecessarily incur large start-up costs during recovery because of alleged imperfections in capital markets. These wasteful shutdown and start-up costs are avoidable, it is argued, if government regulation sets minimum prices or allows firms to do so.

A third definition of excessive competition focuses on the concept of predatory pricing. Unregulated competition in some markets is alleged to result in monopolization by a firm that engages in predatory pricing—setting prices below cost in order to drive out competitors. To succeed, a predator must outlast its rivals and barriers must exist to prevent the entry of new competitors once the predator raises prices. Regulation to prevent firms from charging excessively low prices is intended to prevent such predatory practices and hence the higher monopolistic prices that would prevail once the predator has eliminated its competitors. No consensus exists among economists that such predatory tactics are effective. Indeed, many economists believe that apparently "predatory" behavior, if ever successful, is a manifestation of cost advantages or an enhanced ability to bear risk.

A fourth interpretation concerns the alleged tendency of certain competitive markets to produce goods or services of inadequate quality, safety, or reliability if consumers are imperfectly informed about those characteristics. For example, it has been argued that under competitive pressure banks might choose excessively risky investments in order to offer their customers high rates of interest on deposits. Similarly, some have claimed that airlines may skimp on safety in a highly competitive market. Even if such claims were true, it does not follow that restricting competition will necessarily improve quality or safety. Moreover, there are more direct ways of addressing these potential market defects, such as Federal Aviation Administration airplane safety inspections and Federal Deposit Insurance Corporation guarantees.

PROBLEMS OF ECONOMIC REGULATION

Most economists agree that the regulation of price and entry in markets that would otherwise be competitive is inefficient. Regulation of transportation, for example, has generally resulted in higher prices, higher production costs, and slower technological growth. Regulation of oil and gas prices has occasionally kept prices too low, causing shortages and inefficient choices among competing fuels.

Deregulation usually leads to a reduction in cost to the marginal user, whether the discarded regulations established maximum or minimum prices. A price kept below the market price by regulation has the effect of creating a system of nonprice rationing in which excluded consumers are forced to pay higher prices for substitutes. The elimination of maximum price ceilings may lead to higher average prices but lower prices to the marginal consumer. Exceptions to this conclusion are where natural monopoly conditions exist or where regulations lead to some cross-subsidy among consumers.

In some cases, price regulation leads to an excessively high level of some service characteristic, because firms are prevented from competing on price. Because of price regulation of airlines by the Civil

Aeronautics Board, for example, the airlines competed primarily through frequency of flights, which led to low load factors and considerable excess capacity.

Direct economic inefficiencies are not the only costs of rate and entry regulation in inherently competitive industries. Some additional resources are used to lobby politicians and regulators for favorable regulatory actions. The greater the benefits to groups created by regulation, the more such groups have an incentive to spend to block deregulation. The magnitude of the benefits defended are often substantial. Trucking firms have sold operating rights, initially granted them by the ICC, for over $20 million, and the broadcast rights of individual television stations have sold for substantially more.

The argument that full deregulation is the appropriate policy for industries with competitive market structures applies strictly only in the long run. To minimize the risk of adverse short-run consequences from deregulation, most deregulatory initiatives have called for either partial deregulation or a gradual transition to full deregulation. The Civil Aeronautics Board was not immediately abolished by the Congress, and it retained some temporary domestic authority through 1982. The Staggers Rail Act provided railroads with greater price flexibility but did not provide for eventual elimination of all price and entry controls. The Natural Gas Policy Act provides for only partial deregulation of natural gas prices.

It is not clear how much information about the long-run benefits of deregulation can be obtained by observing the process of gradual or partial deregulation. For example, minimum price regulation may cause excess capacity in an industry. When deregulation occurs, some firms in the industry may go bankrupt. This may lead some to consider deregulation a failure and to propose re-regulation. Once the excess capacity is eliminated, however, the industry may operate profitably without any regulation.

Economists can offer one important piece of advice on partial deregulation: relaxing price restrictions without also relaxing entry restrictions may cause problems, such as developed in the air freight market. Eliminating minimum price constraints while barring entry may result in predation. Eliminating maxium price restrictions without allowing free entry may result in monopoly pricing.

Competitive economic forces, while powerful, are not the only means available to consumers of products from deregulated industries to defend themselves. Antitrust policies may also be used to protect consumers against the abuses regulation is sometimes claimed to prevent. The antitrust laws prohibit anticompetitive behavior. Since regulated industries have often enjoyed broad exemptions from the antitrust laws, a review of the antitrust policies pertaining to these industries should accompany the deregulation process. At the same time, however, it is important to avoid misusing the antitrust laws to maintain inappropriate types of regulation.

ENERGY POLICY

The pricing and allocation of energy resources was a frequent focus of public policies over the last decade. Many of these policies reduced the long-run supply of these important resources. In the last few years, several measures have been taken to remove the inefficiencies and uncertainty caused by these policies.

STEPS TOWARD A MARKET-ORIENTED OIL POLICY

In January 1981, President Reagan ended the petroleum price and allocation controls that were previously scheduled to expire in September 1981. Oil prices were first directly controlled as part of the general system of wage and price guidelines imposed in 1971. The data on subsequent production, drilling, consumption, imports, and the energy/gross national product (GNP) ratio suggest that oil price deregulation has had many beneficial effects.

Despite the disincentives provided by the "windfall profits" (excise) tax on crude oil, the data suggest that decontrol has reversed the steady decline in production (exclusive of Alaska) observed during the period of price controls. As of October 1982, there were seven consecutive monthly production increases over year-earlier levels, a series of increases not observed in the United States for 10 years. Reported oil well completions in 1982 were 49 percent higher than in 1980, despite the recent decline in real oil prices.

Since full decontrol, U.S. consumption has decreased by almost 11 percent. While part of this decline is due to the recession, a major cause is the continuing adjustment to the price increases of the 1970s. Since decontrol, the energy/GNP ratio has declined by over 5 percent and imports (net of additions to the Strategic Petroleum Reserve) have declined by about 34 percent. The elimination of the regulatory framework for petroleum prices removed the artificial incentives to import crude oil and residual fuel oil. The weakening of oil prices has contributed to a stronger dollar and, thus, to lower prices on all imported products.

NATURAL GAS PRICING AND ALLOCATION

Following the 1954 Supreme Court decision in *Phillips Petroleum Co. v. Wisconsin,* the wellhead prices of natural gas sold in interstate commerce were regulated by the Federal Power Commission (FPC). Since intrastate gas prices were not subject to regulation, a two-market system resulted. Price controls, when effective, led to shortages in the interstate market both because the interstate pipelines could not compete effectively against intrastate pipelines for gas supplies, and because artificially low prices encouraged consumers to demand more natural gas than they would have otherwise.

Rising oil prices in the 1970s triggered occasional gas shortages in interstate markets. Industrial use of gas was curtailed during periods of shortages, and many potential users of gas, both at the industrial and residential level, were proscribed from using gas. The abnormally cold winter of 1977 produced a severe interstate gas shortage, resulting in numerous factory shutdowns, thousands of layoffs, and other serious problems. It was evident by the mid-1970s that the existing system of wellhead price controls produced serious inefficiencies causing the underproduction of gas for the interstate market and the misallocation of gas between the interstate and intrastate markets and among different users within the interstate markets.

The Natural Gas Policy Act of 1978

The natural gas regulatory environment was changed substantially by passage of the Natural Gas Policy Act (NGPA) in 1978. This act was intended to encourage production by deregulating the prices of newly discovered gas while restraining the growth of average gas prices through permanent controls on the price of older gas. The Federal Energy Regulatory Commission replaced the Federal Power Commission, and price controls were extended to gas sold in intrastate markets. Over twenty regulated categories of gas were created, each with its own initial ceiling price and rules for price escalation over time.

The NGPA provides for the phased deregulation of the wellhead price of most gas discovered after 1977, which should account for 40 to 60 percent of all gas in January 1985, while a smaller volume of gas is scheduled for deregulation in July 1987. A small amount of high-cost new gas was deregulated under the NGPA in 1979. Most gas to be deregulated in 1985 or 1987 is fixed until those dates at a price, in inflation-adjusted dollars, leading to the oil equivalent price level existing in 1978. The NGPA also includes "incremental pricing" provisions intended to allocate high-priced gas to industrial users, thus preserving lower prices for other users. Along with the NGPA, the Congress passed the Powerplant and Industrial Fuel Use Act; this law authorizes nonprice rationing of gas to counter the problems inherent in continued price controls.

As with many efforts to regulate prices, the NGPA has created numerous problems. Instead of producing the lowest cost gas supplies first and moving successively to higher cost sources, producers are induced by the different price categories to produce high-cost gas first in many cases, and generally to shift production efforts away from cost-minimizing alternatives. The initial boom in the production of deep gas illustrated this effect.

Further problems arise from the control of the prices of new gas until those prices are decontrolled in 1985 and 1987. Since oil prices have risen substantially since 1978, partial decontrol will generate a continued increase in delivered gas prices in 1985 as consumers bid up gas prices to levels equivalent with those of close substitutes such as oil. Although real gas prices have risen and real oil prices have fallen in the last year, average real domestic wellhead prices of gas will rise by about 28 percent between 1983 and 1985 if there is no change in the NGPA according to a preliminary Department of Energy estimate.

The price of decontrolled gas is averaged with the price of controlled gas in determining the price to gas users and the demand for gas is affected by prices for fuel substitutes. This is reflected in preliminary Department of Energy estimates which indicate that the average 1985 prices of gas under the NGPA are not likely to differ greatly from those that would evolve under full decontrol. Under the partial decontrol authorized by NGPA, the prices of decontrolled gas are bid up somewhat above the levels that would be observed in a fully decontrolled market. Indeed, even now decontrolled deep gas is being sold at the wellhead for over $7.00 per million cubic feet. The preliminary Department of Energy estimates suggest that the average 1985 price under full decontrol will be $3.78 per million cubic feet (both in 1982 dollars).

The higher prices to be paid for decontrolled gas in 1985 and thereafter suggest that the average gas consumer will not benefit from the remaining controls, and that the primary beneficiaries will be the producers of decontrolled gas. Under the NGPA, however, different groups of consumers will fare differently. Pipelines with access to substantial quantities of price-controlled gas will be able to bid deregulated gas away from other pipelines. This is because the higher prices on decontrolled gas can be averaged with the lower prices paid for gas still subject to controls.

This means, for some period, that consumers in different regions may face different average prices, and that some gas will be reallocated artifically because of differential access to controlled gas. In particular, the intrastate pipelines will have relatively little access to controlled gas, and so some amount of gas will shift out of the intrastate market into the interstate market. Interstate pipelines also will vary in their ability to bid for decontrolled gas, depending on their access to controlled gas and the actions of local regulatory authorities. In summary, in addition to the waste in gas production caused by the

NGPA, both controlled and decontrolled gas will be allocated inefficiently among pipelines. The preliminary Department of Energy estimate of the present value of the efficiency gain that would accrue to the economy from full gas decontrol in 1983, relative to the partial deregulation authorized by the NGPA, is about $4.2 billion (in 1982 dollars).

The prospect of a price increase in 1985 may provide an impetus toward extension of the NGPA price controls beyond 1985. Such an extension would sustain the inefficiencies experienced as a result of the NGPA. The preliminary Department of Energy estimate of the present value of the efficiency gain of full decontrol in 1983, relative to extension to 1995 of price controls now imposed by the NGPA, is about $27 billion (in 1982 dollars). Because gas production would be reduced by extension of controls, oil consumption would probably increase. The preliminary Department of Energy estimate is that extension of gas price controls would increase oil import levels by about 288,000 barrels per day between 1983 and 1995.

Reported gas well completions in 1982 increased 21 percent over 1980, while under full decontrol, reported oil well completions increased by 49 percent in the same period. Total proved gas reserves (excluding Prudhoe Bay) declined over one-third during the 1970s. The extension of controls thus would have very serious implications for future domestic gas reserves.

Recent Natural Gas Price Developments

Natural gas prices have risen sharply in recent months because gas controlled at relatively low prices is gradually becoming a smaller component of total production and because some contracts fixing very low prices have expired. Moreover, the NGPA allows price increases for some gas beyond a simple inflation adjustment. While it appears that gas prices in some regions have reached short-term market clearing levels, that is not true for other regions. On average, gas prices are still apparently below market clearing levels—hence, the expected price increase in 1985 under the path outlined by the NGPA.

Some observers have noted that pipelines are buying expensive gas while gas subject to lower price ceilings remains unsold. They have concluded from this that gas markets are "irrational," and that full price decontrol would not work effectively. This analysis is questionable. Under "take-or-pay" contracts, pipelines agree to pay for a given volume of gas whether or not they resell ("take") it. Since price controls have prevented pipelines from competing for gas on the basis of price, they compete on the basis of contract terms. Increased "take-or-pay" contractual requirements are one form of such nonprice competition. This behavior is a rational response to the artificial constraints imposed by price controls and the general expectation of future shortages. In essence, increased "take-or-pay" requirements are a way for pipelines (and implicitly their customers) to buy insurance against future shortages. Pipelines with high levels of "take-or-pay" commitments must now take and pay for relatively expensive gas, even though "cheaper" gas is available. This is "irrational" only in hindsight since surpluses of gas exist. If shortages had developed instead, the use of "take-or-pay" commitments would look quite rational and "farsighted."

EMERGENCY PREPAREDNESS

Conditions in the world oil market and preceptions about the effects of supply disruptions have both changed substantially in the last several years. Trends in world oil production and consumption are similar to those of the United States. World (non-Communist) consumption fell from 51.5 million barrels per day (mmbd) in 1978 to 45.5 mmbd in 1982. Production outside of the Organization of Petroleum Exporting Countries (including Communist nations) increased from 30.3 mmbd in 1978 to 34.3 mmbd in 1982 (for the first 10 months). Furthermore, excess production capacity in OPEC has increased to at least 8.5 mmbd. It is likely that a future oil supply disruption, should one occur, would have smaller proportionate price effects than those caused by disruptions during the 1970's. Both the increasing geographic diversification of production and the presence of substantial excess production capacity would mitigate the effect of future disruptions.

The threat to use oil production as a political weapon may be less effective then was previously perceived. It is very difficult to "target" individual nations with such a weapon because the international oil transport industry has substantial capacity to transfer oil among nations. This is why the United States and the Netherlands, despite their status as the intended targets of the 1973 embargo, faced the same prices for imported oil as other oil-importing nations. Gasoline lines in the United States were caused by the U.S. regulations. Equally important, oil producers cannot impose large penalties upon others without imposing substantial revenue losses upon themselves.

The policies of this Administration reflect the view that preparation for disruptions in energy supplies can best take place through the operation of market forces, and that price adjustments present the most effective mechanism for dealing with such disruptions when they occur. Minimizing the aggregate adverse effects of energy supply disruptions is most efficiently accomplished by allowing prices to allocate available supplies to their most productive uses and by encouraging market forces to increase production of substitute fuels.

Price and allocation controls only redistribute some of the adverse effects of the disruption away from politically favored groups, therefore making matters worse for other groups. In the aggregate, price and allocation controls would exacerbate the adverse effects of the disruption.

Standby controls, even if never implemented, are harmful because they increase the perceived likelihood that controls will be imposed and thereby deter private preparedness. This is why the President vetoed the standby controls legislation in March 1982.

Present policies also reflect a recognition that firms may have insufficient incentives to prepare for energy supply disruptions, in substantial part because of past government policy. Previous price and allocation controls had the effect of penalizing those who had prepared for disruptions and subsidizing those who had not. Because of governmental responses to energy supply disruptions in the past, and the recent congressional proposal to establish standby price and allocation controls, firms must regard as substantial the likelihood that controls would be imposed once again, despite this Administration's firm commitment to avoid such policies. This expectation discourages both those who expect to benefit from controls and those who expect to have their supplies appropriated from preparing sufficiently for a disruption beforehand.

In recognition of this perverse effect of past policy, the Administration is striving to build up crude oil stocks in the Strategic Petroleum Reserve (SPR) at an efficient rate. Built up to only slightly more than 100 million barrels from 1977 until early 1981, the SPR now contains over 290 million barrels and is growing steadily toward the planned level of 750 million barrels. The SPR is intended to supplement, not substitute for, private sector stocks; accordingly, it would be used only in the event of a severe disruption. Once a decision was made to use SPR crude oil, it would be sold at market-clearing prices to whomever wished to purchase it. The Strategic Petroleum Reserve Plan submitted to the Congress in December 1982 contains a provision allowing the Secretary of Energy to reserve for special groups faced with extraordinary circumstances up to 10 percent of a given period's drawdown; oil allocated under this provision would be priced at the level established in the most recent competitive auction of SPR crude oil. This provision is not intended as a subsidy for particular groups. The policy of this Administration to fill the SPR at a steady rate will move energy security preparedness in the United States toward a more optimal level. To the extent that the availability of SPR crude oil, combined with other energy policies and programs, enables future Administrations to resist pressures for price and allocation controls during a disruption, the SPR may enhance private sector preparation as well.

Except to the extent that use of foreign energy supplies is increased artificially by price controls and other adverse policies, it is not the policy of this Administration to reduce dependence on foreign energy suppliers beyond the level determined by market forces. In a world with relatively free trade and substantial capacity for reallocation of supplies, the allocative effects of a change in oil prices (other than those operating through the exchange rate) are independent of whether a given nation's use of foreign supplies is great or small. A disruption would raise prices and thus reallocate all available supplies whether foreign or domestic. Thus, a nation totally self-sufficient in energy supplies still would face the same oil prices as a nation totally dependent on foreign sources. It is the policy of this Administration to facilitate free trade while preparing for future contingencies through primary reliance on market adjustments and judicious use of the Strategic Petroleum Reserve.

TRANSPORTATION AND COMMUNICATIONS

The transportation and communications industries serve vital linkage functions in our Nation's economy. Until recently, these industries were broadly subject to traditional rate and entry regulation.

Regulation of most transportation sectors is probably not efficient under contemporary market conditions. Most transportation markets, due to the mobility of most of the capital assets of the firms in those markets, are highly contestable. That is, with nearly costless entry and exit, new firms can enter markets which have excessive prices and can take advantage of the profitable opportunities that they provide. Thus, even with significant economies of scale in a transportation market, the threat of entry by new rivals should result in near-competitive pricing of transportation services. Additionally, most transportation firms face significant intermodal competition. They are also disciplined indirectly in some cases by competitive conditions in the national or international markets in which the commodities they transport are sold. The only segments of the interstate transportation system for which regulation on a natural monopoly basis may be justifiable are the major gas pipelines, long-distance electric transmission lines, and those sections of the rail system where shippers do not have an effective choice of carrier or mode of transport.

Telecommunications, due to a high rate of technological development, is one of the most rapidly changing sectors of the U.S. economy. The Federal Government plays an active role in the telecommunications industries through the regulation of common carriers and broadcasters. Several important steps toward deregulation of these industries were initiated in 1982. The government can enhance the development of these industries through continued deregulation.

EFFECTS OF AVIATION DEREGULATION

Until the late 1970s the Civil Aeronautics Board (CAB) regulated the airline industry extensively. It allocated interstate routes among the airlines and controlled airline fares on those routes. Through its control of air routes, the CAB restrained entry into the airline industry. From its inception in 1938 until the late 1970s, the CAB did not allow any new airline to enter the interstate trunk market. Largely as a consequence, air fares were higher on most interstate routes than if price competition and freedom of entry were permitted. This was reflected by the differences in fares between intrastate city-pairs that were not subject to CAB regulation, such as Los Angeles-San Francisco, and comparable interstate city-pairs that were. The latter often had fares that were as much as 60 percent higher than the former.

In 1977 the CAB began to ease restrictions on fares and entry. In 1978 the Congress affirmed and extended the CAB's measures by passing the Airline Deregulation Act. This act provided for the gradual deregulation of the airlines, with the termination of CAB domestic route authority in 1981, the termination of CAB domestic pricing authority in 1983, and the elimination of the CAB itself in 1985. Subsequent steps were taken to increase potential competition in international aviation. In July 1982 the U.S. Government entered a multilateral agreement with several European governments that permits greater flexibility in airline fares for trans-Atlantic flights than was previously allowed.

While rising aviation fuel costs, the weak economy, and the 1981 air traffic controllers strike complicate assessment of the effects of gradual deregulation, route and fare competition have increased substantially since 1977. From 1978 to 1981, the number of U.S. certificated airlines more than doubled (from 36 to 86). The market share of the major trunk airlines declined from 87.3 to 80.4 percent in the past 3 years while, during this same period, the market share of the local, intrastate, and new airlines increased from 11.5 to 16.4 percent. Aircraft departures from large, medium, small, and nonhub airports increased substantially over the 2 years immediately following airline deregulation. The percentage of domestic markets with four or more carriers grew from 13 in May 1978 to 73 in May 1981. In April 1982, 77 percent of the domestic coach traffic of the major airlines moved on discount fares, compared to 46 percent in April 1978. And while operating expenses per available seat mile rose by

384-041 0 - 83 - 8 : QL 3

73 percent from 1976 to 1981, airline revenue per available seat mile rose by only 58 percent in this same period.

Deregulation has also led to increases in operating efficiency. Airline labor cost increases have slowed and have actually declined relative to inflation. The established airlines have been forced to control their labor costs in order to compete effectively with the new entrants, many of which pay substantially lower wages. Load factors (the ratio of revenue passenger miles to available seat miles) rose from an average of less than 55 percent between 1973 and 1977 to more than 59 percent between 1978 and 1982. Airlines are now using a wider variety of airplanes to serve their diverse markets. Small markets are more likely to be served by smaller airplanes.

There is little need to fear monopoly in airline markets when the CAB expires. Several studies have demonstrated that no system-wide economies of scale exist. Since airplanes are easily transferable from one market to another, airline markets are readily contestable. The prospect of potential entry by rival carriers creates pressures for close-to-competitive fares even in markets served by only one airline.

Deregulation of airlines has established a competitive and more efficient airline industry. As air travel in the United States increases over this decade and as the busiest airports become even more congested, the new competitive structure may be challenged. Allowing competition and the full transferability of the right to land and take off at these airports may be necessary to sustain this competitive structure. Additionally, the maintenance and future development of a safe and effective national airway system is important to ensure that consumers are well served.

EFFECTS OF PARTIAL DEREGULATION IN SURFACE TRANSPORTATION

The traditional rate and entry regulation of the trucking, freight-forwarder, intercity bus, barge, and maritime industries is now largely out of date. Many studies have demonstrated the absence of significant economies of scale in these industries, weakening the "natural monopoly" rationale for entry restrictions. The high degree of capital mobility in these industries implies that individual city-pair and port-pair markets are highly contestable. The existence of intermodal sources of competition and competitive international output markets for transported commodities further reduces any misallocations resulting from monoply behavior. Additionally, the high rate of technological development in the transportation sector renders many regulations inapplicable. The experience since the recent deregulation of airlines and the partial deregulation of surface transportation indicates that a competitive industry structure would not reduce the financial viability of firms in these industries.

Several major pieces of legislation were enacted in the last few years to reduce the degree of regulation in the surface transportation industries, including the Railroad Revitalization and Regulatory Reform Act of 1976, the Motor Carrier Act of 1980, the Staggers Rail Act of 1980, and the Bus Regulatory Reform Act of 1982.

The effects of the partial deregulation of trucking—initiated by the Interstate Commerce Commission and affirmed by the Motor Carrier Act of 1980—have proven very encouraging. Published trucking rates are now subject to large and widely available discounts. Shippers appear to be overwhelmingly satisfied with the rates, service options, and competition for their business. Service to small communities has not deteriorated, as was originally predicted by the opponents of deregulation, and most shippers in small communities also appear to support deregulation. Both the number of new firms and failing firms have increased substantially, the latter due in part to the recession. Concerns have been expressed over the last year that the Interstate Commerce Commission may be slowing the deregulatory process. For example, the percentage of applications for grants of operating authority approved by the ICC declined slightly in both fiscal years since the passage of the Motor Carrier Act. On net, however, the ICC has facilitated increased competition in the trucking industry. The chaos predicted by the opponents of deregulation has not materialized, even during a sustained recession. The experience to date clearly supports the case for more general deregulation of surface transport.

The experience since the partial deregulation of railroads is similar. Although direct evidence on rail rates is not available, the number of contracts negotiated between rail carriers and shippers (a measure of the operating flexibility granted by the Staggers Rail Act) increased from 580 in fiscal 1980 to 2907 in fiscal 1982. Railroads have increased their share of total freight traffic and have substantially increased their shipments of some commodities, such as fruits and vegetables, that were previously carried almost exclusively by trucks. Railroad profits remained essentially steady despite the sustained recession.

While recent partial deregulation of the surface transportation industries has increased the competitiveness of these industries, the opportunity remains for significant gains from further deregulation. There seems to be little danger that further deregulation would enhance the monopoly power of carriers. The high degree of capital mobility in the trucking, bus, barge, and maritime industries should prevent monopoly pricing over a sustained period, even where there is only one carrier on a route.

For many decades, both carriers and shippers have made decisions based on expectations that the general regulatory system would continue. As a consequence, the transition to deregulation can be disruptive. The major conceptual problems of further deregulation involve the following four issues: (1) the antitrust status of the rate bureaus, (2) the vulnerability of shippers who do not have an effective choice of carrier or mode, (3) the restrictions on multimodal ownership, and (4) the restrictions on route abandonment.

As suggested below, these problems especially affect the prospects for further deregulation of the railroads.

Antitrust Status of Rate Bureaus

For many years the regional rate bureaus (composed of transportation firms) have performed the normal functions of a trade association and have provided the forum for multilateral agreements on both single-line and interline rates. These rate bureaus were exempted from the antitrust laws, and their proposed rates were generally endorsed by the ICC. The Motor Carrier Act of 1980 removed the antitrust immunity of the truck rate bureaus for single-line rates beginning in mid-1984, and established the Motor Carrier Ratemaking Study Commission to study whether the antitrust immunity for multilateral agreements on interline rates should be maintained. In testimony to this commission, the Administration supported elimination of the antitrust immunity of the truck rate bureaus. Members of the commission, which was scheduled to complete its study by the end of 1982, were equally divided on this issue at that time. Additionally, following the Railroad Revitalization and Regulatory Reform Act of 1976, the ICC restricted the authority of the rail rate bureaus to address single-line rates and restricted the carriers that could participate in an agreement on interline rates.

There remains a legitimate dispute about whether the rail rate bureaus should retain antitrust immunity when setting interline rates. The general view of economists is that further deregulation should be accompanied by the elimination of antitrust immunity. This approach would prevent the adverse effects of a carrier cartel and permit interline agreements to be treated as a joint venture. Some clarification of the application of the Sherman Act would also be appropriate to provide a stable legal environment for these interline agreements. The contrary view is that the antitrust immunity should be maintained as long as no carrier is bound by any bureau rates to which it did not agree. A multilateral agreement on interline rates may have substantially lower transactions costs on small shipments than the alternative pattern of bilateral joint ventures, and any attempt to set cartel rates would be disciplined by the freedom of any carrier to set other rates. (This issue is less important for trucks, because interline traffic is now less than 15 percent of total truck traffic, and complete freedom of routes would further reduce such interline traffic. Interline rail traffic, however, is 48 percent of total rail traffic, and it is more important to maintain a process that economizes on the contracting costs for small interline shipments.) The alternative may be an undesirable situation in which rail carriers refuse small interline shipments, use trucks for shipments to points beyond their routes, or face an artificial incentive for mergers.

The "Captive Shipper Problem"

The "captive shipper problem" is what initially led to rail rate regulation. This problem was substantially reduced by the development of alternative carriers and modes but has not been eliminated. Two dimensions of this problem, however, have sometimes been misunderstood. This relation is a bilateral monopoly. Both the rail carrier and the shipper have substantial bargaining power, and it is not clear that this relation leads to rates that are generally "too high." Second, this relation does not lead to any long-term misallocation of resources as long as the price of the shipped commodity is determined in a competitive market. In any case, the sum of the rents on rail and shipper property is constant. This inherent tension suggests that it is important to avoid any effective restraint on the common ownership of rail carriers and major shippers. One alternative may be to require joint track use by competing carriers. Another alternative would be to index the rate bands now authorized for, say, another decade and to terminate these bands at that time. Unless this problem is resolved, however, some form of maximum rate regulation is likely to be maintained in the rail industry.

Restrictions on Multimodal Ownership

There no longer appears to be any case for restrictions on multimodal ownership. It is especially important to allow rail carriers to own trucking operations to facilitate container and piggyback traffic. A change in the law would be required to allow rail carriers to own barge lines. A change in the law would also be required to allow freight-forwarders to own trucks, even though trucking companies are now allowed to own freight-forwarders. The Bus Regulatory Reform Act of 1982 provides a substantially streamlined process for approving intermodal mergers not prohibited by law.

Restrictions on Route Abandonment

The primary problem of the railroads is excess route capacity, a problem that reflects a combination of increased truck competition and ICC restrictions on route abandonment. Some studies have indicated that less than half of the existing rail mileage generates enough traffic to cover total costs. The Staggers Rail Act provides for more flexible procedures to resolve disputes on route abandonment. Recent highway legislation, by increasing allowable truck size, is expected to make trucks more competitive with railroads in moving low density freight. A better resolution of the route abandonment issue is probably necessary for a healthy railroad industry and an efficient distribution of freight traffic across modes.

In summary, pending a resolution of these four issues as they affect railroads, it is probably appropriate to focus any near-term legislative proposals on the other modes of surface transport and for the ICC to pursue selective rail deregulation within its existing authority. Additionally, the government should continue, through the appropriate application of user fees, to ensure that each mode of transport bears the entire costs of its operations when utilizing public facilities.

COMMON CARRIER TELECOMMUNICATIONS

Economies of scale provided the original rationale for making long-distance telecommunications a regulated monopoly. But rapid technological change has reduced the industry's natural monopoly characteristics and has paved the way for a more competitive industry structure. The growth of the market for telecommunications, due largely to the convergence of data processing and telecommunications technology, has further reduced the natural monopoly characteristics of the industry. These rapid developments in both demand and supply conditions have probably made the inherited regulatory framework inappropriate.

Major legal changes were made recently to allow increased competition. In 1982 a U.S. district judge gave final approval to a settlement between the American Telephone and Telegraph Company (AT&T) and the Department of Justice, transforming long-distance telecommunications services into a competitive market with a greater number of companies and less regulation.

In conjunction with other deregulatory steps by the Federal Communications Commission, the settlement is expected to have major benefits for both the telecommunications industry and its customers. Equal access to local facilities, which is the cornerstone of the settlement, should allow competition to act as an adequate substitute for regulation of interstate services. While the transition to equal access will take a few years, individual telephone customers will have progressively increased opportunities to make their own arrangements with AT&T's competitors in long-distance services. Meanwhile, AT&T will be allowed to develop its data processing subsidiary, American Bell Inc. While AT&T is prohibited from offering home computer information and advertising services via its long-distance lines for 7 years, it is likely to become a vigorous competitor in other fields, such as cellular mobile radio technology. It is also likely to face increasing competition in these areas.

In 1982 an appeals court affirmed the Federal Communication Commission's power to deregulate where technological change makes regulation outmoded. Developments in data processing and transmission have tended to make many Federal and State regulations unnecessary, inappropriate, or unworkable.

BROADCASTING

The FCC regulates the radio and television industries through issuance and renewal of broadcast licenses. It promulgates guidelines on the amount of news and public affairs programming that stations must broadcast, the maximum number of commercials permissible in any time period, the recording of broadcast materials, and the ascertainment and fulfillment of community needs. As a result, broadcasters are prevented in some cases from carrying programming that listeners and viewers would prefer.

The original purpose of FCC regulation was to allocate broadcast spectrum space. The FCC allocated these valuable spectrum rights in exchange for commitments on program content. Whatever the merits of this argument 50 years ago, it may be appropriate to review this form of regulation to reflect the rapidly developing competition from cable television, pay television, and direct satellite transmission.

Recently, the FCC has made several moves toward deregulation. In 1981 the Commission deregulated most commercial radio broadcasting and attempted, subject to legal challenge, to simplify the application renewal process. The FCC is in the process of repeating this deregulatory initiative for the television industry. It will soon attempt to amend the renewal process by eliminating the following criteria for renewal: nonentertainment content, ascertainment of community needs, advertising concentration, and recording. The last Congress also considered bills to repeal many requirements, such as the "reasonable access," "equal time," and "fairness" doctrines that are costly to broadcasters and unevenly applied to the mass media. These steps would partially remove the government from the determination of broadcast content.

DEREGULATION OF FINANCIAL MARKETS

The financial service sector has been among the most heavily regulated areas of the economy. Price regulation, entry restrictions, and portfolio regulation were pervasive in both the banking and securities industries. Substantial and numerous innovations in the financial sectors in the last decade largely preceded and were later facilitated by recent partial deregulation.

DEPOSITORY INSTITUTIONS

The present structure of regulatory restraints on commercial banks and other depository institutions was imposed primarily in response to the collapse of the banking system in the 1930s. A common interpretation of the events at that time is that the banking collapse was the result of an unsound banking structure which caused too much competition. Competition among banks was thought to force them into paying high interest rates for deposits, which in turn led them to seek out high-yielding but risky—and ultimately unsound—investments in the stock, bond, and real estate markets.

Legislative remedies in the Banking Acts of 1933 and 1935, and various revisions of the Federal Reserve Act, focused on limiting price competition between banks, separating banking from securities market activity, supervising banking and financial markets more closely, and restoring public confidence in the financial system.

Reflecting a general concern about excessive competition, the payment of interest on demand deposits was prohibited by law. In addition, the Federal Reserve Board and the Federal Deposit Insurance Corporation were given the power to place interest rate ceilings on the passbook and time deposits of commercial banks. Interest rate ceilings were extended to the deposits of mutual savings banks and savings and loan associations in 1966.

The type and quality of assets held by banks were closely monitored. Commercial banks were not permitted to hold securities of a speculative nature in their portfolios, and thrift institutions were subject to even greater limits on their asset acquisition powers. In addition, most securities activities were divorced from commercial banking by the Glass-Steagall sections of the Banking Act of 1933, and entry into banking became more closely controlled. To maintain the confidence of the public in the banking system, deposits were insured by the Federal Deposit Insurance Corporation and the Federal Savings and Loan Insurance Corporation. With the introduction of deposit insurance, the other regulations served mainly to limit the exposure of the insurance funds rather than to protect depositors. Nevertheless, recent studies suggest that the web of regulatory restraints was generally greater than required for this purpose.

Moreover, this extensive regulatory framework for financial institutions has adapted slowly to the economic changes of the last two decades. High inflation rates and consequent high nominal interest rates, combined with reduced transactions costs from the application of computer technology to the payments system, have created serious distortions in financial markets. As market interest rates rose above Regulation Q ceilings, inflows of funds to depository institutions were curtailed, and new nonregulated instruments (especially money market mutual funds) were created. The allocation of savings to various sectors of the capital market—particularly housing vis-a-vis other sectors—was altered, and small and less informed savers suffered declines in the real rate of return on their savings. In addition, Regulation Q generated a considerable amount of nonprice competition between financial institutions, such as an excessive number of branch offices, with resulting adverse effects on efficiency. Interest rate ceilings on selected deposits were removed progressively beginning in 1978.

The Administration continues to support the removal of unnecessary and excessive regulatory constraints on depository institutions. It is now widely asserted that the length and severity of the banking collapse of the 1930s was not the result of overly risky bank portfolios. Rather, many economists argue that these failures became widespread, initially, because of the reluctance of the Federal Reserve System to engage in aggressive open market operations to counter the conversion of deposits to currency and, later, because of the Federal Reserve's failure to assure adequate liquidity to banks experiencing runs on their deposits. As banks scrambled to liquidate their assets to meet the demands of their depositors for currency, their asset values fell, thus creating insolvencies. The provision of adequate liquidity by a lender of last resort has long been recognized as a primary responsibility of the Federal Reserve System.

Partial deregulation of depository institutions is now proceeding under provisions of the Depository Institutions Deregulation and Monetary Control Act of 1980 and the Garn-St Germain Depository Institutions Act of 1982. Under the 1980 act, interest rate ceilings on time and savings deposits are to be phased out over a period of 6 years. The same law permits depository institutions to offer negotiable order of withdrawal (NOW) accounts and preempted certain State usury ceilings. This act also created the Depository Institutions Deregulation Committee (DIDC) to administer the phaseout of interest rate ceilings at banks and thrifts.

In March 1982, the DIDC adopted a deregulation schedule that phases out interest rate ceilings, beginning with longer term time deposits. With the deregulation schedule in place, the focus of the DIDC turned to short-term deposit instruments. Prevailing high interest rates had caused a continued erosion of low-cost deposits at banks and thrifts, as depositors sought market rates elsewhere, particularly through money market mutual funds. The DIDC addressed this problem by authorizing, effective May 1, 1982, a 91-day time deposit with a $7,500 minimum denomination indexed to the 91-day Treasury bill rate, and establishing, effective September 1, 1982, a 7- to 31-day deposit account with a $20,000 minimum denomination, also indexed to the 91-day Treasury bill rate.

Following the directions given by the Garn-St Germain Act, the DIDC authorized, effective December 14, 1982, a new money market deposit account that can be offered by commercial banks, savings and loan associations, and mutual savings banks. In addition, the DIDC authorized a new super NOW account, effective January 5, 1983. Neither account is subject to interest rate ceilings when account balances exceed $2,500. The DIDC also reduced to $2,500 the minimum denomination required on the 6-month money market deposits, the 91-day time deposits, and the 7- to 31-day time deposits.

The introduction of NOW accounts nationwide in 1981, the authorization of the new money market accounts at banks and thrifts, and the general phasing out of interest rate restrictions substantially increase the ability of depository institutions to compete for funds. Simultaneously, various actions have been taken to allow thrift institutions greater flexibility in the investment of funds. The Deregulation and Monetary Control Act expands the asset powers of saving and loan associations and mutual savings banks to include consumer, corporate, and business loans. This will lead to more diversified portfolios for these institutions. In addition, new regulations issued by the Comptroller of the Currency in 1981 and the Federal Home Loan Bank Board in 1982 permit depository institutions to offer variable rate mortgages. Finally, the Garn-St Germain Act provides for Federal preemption of State laws and judicial decisions that restrict the enforcement of due-on-sale clauses in real property loans.

The Garn-St Germain Act also deals with the problems of the savings and loan institutions discussed above. It provides capital assistance to depository institutions that have suffered earnings and capital losses resulting from regulatory restraints on their assets and liabilities. The assisted institutions issue capital investments, called "net worth certificates," which the insuring agencies purchase with promissory notes. This increase in net worth reduces the likelihood of insolvencies arising from losses created by holdings of old, fixed-rate mortgages. As market rates of interest fall, and the earnings of these depository institutions improve, the net worth certificates will be retired.

Legislation following the banking collapse of the 1930s tended to prevent competition among financial institutions and created a complex and often counterproductive labyrinth of financial regulations. Recent legislation and regulatory changes have begun to reverse this trend by widening the sources and uses of funds available to depository institutions, and by allowing for a far larger measure of price competition in the financial services industry. These actions should contribute to a stronger and more responsive financial system.

STOCK EXCHANGES

Much of the regulation of the Nation's stock exchanges began in the 1930s, largely in response to the crisis in the financial markets created by the Great Depression. This regulation was broad and diverse, and included mandatory and systematic disclosure of corporate records as well as rule-setting authority over stock exchanges. Over the last several years, much of this regulation has been relaxed.

Commission Rates

Prior to 1968, commissions paid to members of stock exchanges were fixed by those stock exchanges and approved by the Securities and Exchange Commission (SEC). After 1968, however, the fixed commission schedule was slowly dismantled in favor of negotiated commissions. Beginning in May 1975, commission rates on all security transactions were negotiated.

Negotiated commission rates were the product of a market-induced breakdown of the fixed-rate commission structure. From 1961 to 1966 the dollar volume and market share of the regional stock exchanges increased dramatically because of the fixed-rate system. Regional stock exchanges allowed customers dealing on those exchanges to "give up" or have transferred a portion of their fixed commission to a third party who supplied other services. The New York Stock Exchange (NYSE) stipulated that customers of that exchange could only give up commissions to other members of the NYSE. This constraint that the NYSE imposed on its customers encouraged many of those customers to turn to the regional exchanges, where competition had effectively driven down the cost of exchange services.

Faced with a declining share of stock transactions, the NYSE asked the SEC to force regional exchanges to eliminate the rules that were affording them a competitive advantage. Commenting on the NYSE proposal, the Department of Justice suggested that the broader issue of possible elimination of the fixed-rate commission structure should be examined. In defense of the fixed-rate commission structure, a NYSE study suggested that "destructive competition," reflected in a decline in the quality of broker services, could result from the absence of fixed commission rates.

Despite the objections of the NYSE, the Congress passed the Securities Acts Amendments of 1975. These reconfirmed that nonmember commission rates were fully negotiable and made exchange floor rates fully negotiable by May 1976. The deregulation of fixed commission rates illustrates the efficiency gains that follow deregulation. Since the total deregulation of commission rates, average commissions charged to customers have decreased. Services which were previously provided jointly whether customers used them or not, are now substantially unbundled.

Financial Disclosure

The Securities Exchange Act of 1933 required financial disclosure for corporations seeking to raise capital through the issuance of new securities. The Securities Exchange Act of 1934 required periodic financial disclosure for corporations with publicly traded securities. One of the motivations for this original legislation was a belief that corporations must be forced to disclose financial information in order to protect the interests of investors. In recent years there has been concern that these requirements have precluded new security issues thus inhibiting the efficiency of the capital market. Additionally, a growing body of scholarship has questioned whether these requirements have served the interests of investors. Recently, some of these stringent disclosure requirements were ended for certain types of corporations. Specifically, corporations with less than $3 million in assets and 500 stockholders are now exempt from the filing requirements of the Securities Exchange Act of 1934.

The SEC has also recently allowed, on an experimental basis, some firms issuing new securities to use "shelf registration" forms, thus eliminating the requirement to file for each new security issue. The initiation of shelf registration is expected to reduce the costs of raising equity capital, allowing firms to manage their risk more efficiently by entering the capital markets more often.

Industry Structure

Before 1980, stocks listed on stock exchanges could not be traded by members of those stock exchanges in any other markets. This barrier to entry was partially lifted in June 1980, when the SEC approved Rule 19c–3. This rule allows members of stock exchanges to trade securities in other markets that were listed on those stock exchanges after May 1979.

Stock exchange members are now also allowed to execute trades in the "19c–3 securities" in markets other than the stock exchanges. The market share of non-19c–3 stocks on the Over-the-Counter (OTC) markets is considerably less than the OTC market share for 19c–3 securities. This larger market share for the OTC in 19c–3 securities suggests that, for some exchange members, it is more efficient to execute orders on the OTC rather than on the stock exchanges. That is, members can arbitrage price differentials that may exist between the OTC market and the exchanges.

Futures Markets

The Commodity Futures Trading Commission (CFTC) has also been very active in deregulation. In January 1982, the CFTC eliminated the 03 report, which had obligated large traders in future contracts to report their market positions daily to the CFTC. This action reduced the filing costs of these large traders by around 50 percent. In an effort to lessen the burden of Federal regulation on the futures industry, the CFTC's new legislation eases the disclosure, registration, and rule approval process.

OPPORTUNITIES FOR FURTHER DEREGULATION IN THE FINANCIAL INDUSTRY

While the financial and securities markets of today operate relatively unencumbered by unnecessary regulations, owing to the deregulatory advances discussed above, several opportunities for further deregulation remain.

Geographic Restrictions in Banking

Federal laws, such as the McFadden Act of 1927 and the Douglas Amendment to the Bank Holding Company Act of 1956, continue to impose geographic restrictions on commercial banking activities. The former law subjects the branching activities of national banks to the limits imposed by the States; the latter law prohibits bank holding companies from engaging in interstate banking unless given specific State authorization to do so. Although these prohibitions may reduce the concentration of financial resources on a national scale, they may also increase market concentration and lessen competition in local banking markets.

Moreover, these restrictions are effective only insofar as they affect the taking of retail deposits. Loan production offices, Edge Act corporations, personal finance companies, mortgage lending companies, and bank holding companies have long been the means used by banks to conduct wholesale and retail business on an interstate basis. With the emergence of automatic teller machine networks, the electronic revolution is incorporating even retail deposit-taking into large-scale operations. This process would be enhanced by exempting automatic teller machines from the existing restrictions on the establishment of branch offices. It is time to reconsider these geographic restrictions because they are probably not in the best interests of consumers or the more efficient financial institutions.

Portfolio Restrictions in Banking

The prohibitions of the Glass-Steagall Act have been eroded in recent years as both banking organizations and securities firms have attempted, either directly or indirectly, to enter each others' traditional lines of business. Moreover, Glass-Steagall now makes no important contribution to the protection of the public against bank failure or undue concentrations of economic power. Other government measures, such as Federal deposit insurance and broadened and strengthened Federal supervision, appear to have been more effective in that role. The Administration has proposed an amendment to the Glass-Steagall Act that would authorize bank holding company subsidiaries to conduct two new activities immediately: (1) to underwrite and deal in municipal revenue bonds, and (2) to sponsor and underwrite shares of mutual funds. The Garn-St Germain Act authorizes a new account at banks and thrifts that is directly competitive with money market mutual funds. However, the act does not provide for the operation and sale of shares in mutual funds or the underwriting of municipal revenue bonds. Moreover, the act also extends the longstanding protection of insurance companies against bank competition.

Margin Requirements

Margin requirements presently exist in the stock, options, and futures markets. In futures trading, the margin is a performance bond intended to protect other participants from the consequences of a failure to make good on a contractual obligation. Each futures exchange determines the margin without Federal regulation or oversight. In stock and options exchanges, the Federal Reserve Board sets initial margin requirements, and the exchanges set maintenance margins subject to SEC oversight. Margin practices in the stock and options markets may be less efficient than in futures markets, since regulation constrains decisionmaking by participants. It is now appropriate to review these regulations.

CONCLUSIONS

Federal regulation of price and entry are products of an earlier era, when both economic conditions and perceptions of economic problems were very different than they are today. Federal regulation of railroads began nearly a century ago, when there was no significant competition from other transport modes and political debate reflected strong populist sentiment. Most other Federal economic regulations date from the 1930s, when the severe economic problems, now believed to be due to a collapse in aggregate demand, were perceived to be a consequence of excessive competition. The present structure of Federal regulation of the energy markets dates from the 1970s and primarily reflects an attempt to protect consumers from the effects of the large increase in oil prices originating abroad.

These policies may or may not have been appropriate to the period in which they were initiated. But both conditions and perceptions are now very different. Increasing demand and changing technology have substantially reduced the initial monopoly power of many regulated firms. Our perceptions have also changed, largely in response to developing conditions during the long history of regulation and the encouraging developments during the more recent period of partial deregulation. There is now a more general perception that the developments in regulated markets have largely outrun the present structure of economic regulation.

As we approach the 100th anniversary of the first broad body of Federal economic regulation, it is time for a comprehensive review of whether this form of regulation serves the interests of the contemporary economy. A resolution of this issue would then permit greater attention to the different and more complex issues affecting the recent Federal regulation of health, safety, and environmental conditions.

CHAPTER 6

Review of 1982 and the Economic Outlook

FOR THE U.S. ECONOMY, 1982 was a year of painful transition toward price stability. The momentum of high inflation, built up over the last 15 years, was broken and inflation was reduced to its lowest rate in a decade. Success in reducing inflation, however, was accompanied by a recession that began in mid-1981 and lingered through 1982. A drop in real exports, along with inventory adjustments, accounted for the decline in U.S. production. Despite the recession, final sales to domestic purchasers increased. Expenditures for some interest-sensitive goods, such as housing and consumer durable goods, registered their first rise in recent years.

Economic developments in 1982 clearly set the stage for a recovery in 1983. The sizable slowdown in inflation contributed to the sharp drop in interest rates in the summer of 1982. The inventory cycle that held down production in 1982 is expected to turn around sometime in 1983. This development, combined with recovery in housing and durable consumer goods and continuing gains in defense spending, is expected to bring a moderate sustainable economic recovery. Prospects are good that this recovery can be maintained through the 1980s without reigniting inflationary pressures.

OVERVIEW OF 1982

Real gross national product (GNP) in 1982 was no higher than in 1979. After a surge of economic growth in 1978, the economy stalled in 1979. Cyclically volatile types of spending, such as auto sales and housing starts, had peaked in 1978. Since 1978 the output of goods and services in the United States has followed a saw-tooth pattern of alternating periods of growth and decline. The recessions of 1980 and 1981-82 bracketed the shortest economic expansion in 50 years. Employment in 1982 was below its 1979 level.

Production and employment remained sluggish for 4 years while supplies of labor and capital continued to grow, so that by the end of 1982 the unemployment rate rose to nearly 11 percent—its highest level since the early 1940s—and the capacity utilization rate fell to its lowest point in the post-World War II period. With this high level of unused economic capacity, inflationary pressures subsided.

The inflation rate fell dramatically in 1982 to its lowest level in a decade. The upward trend in inflation from 1976 through 1980 strengthened the Federal Reserve's determination to slow the growth in the monetary aggregates and contributed to high interest rates for an extended period. By mid-1982, when evidence of progress against inflation and continued weakness in economic activity became clear, interest rates began to fall sharply. The ensuing decline reduced interest rates to their lowest levels in more than 2 years, as illustrated in Chart 6–1.

Chart 6–1

Interest Rates

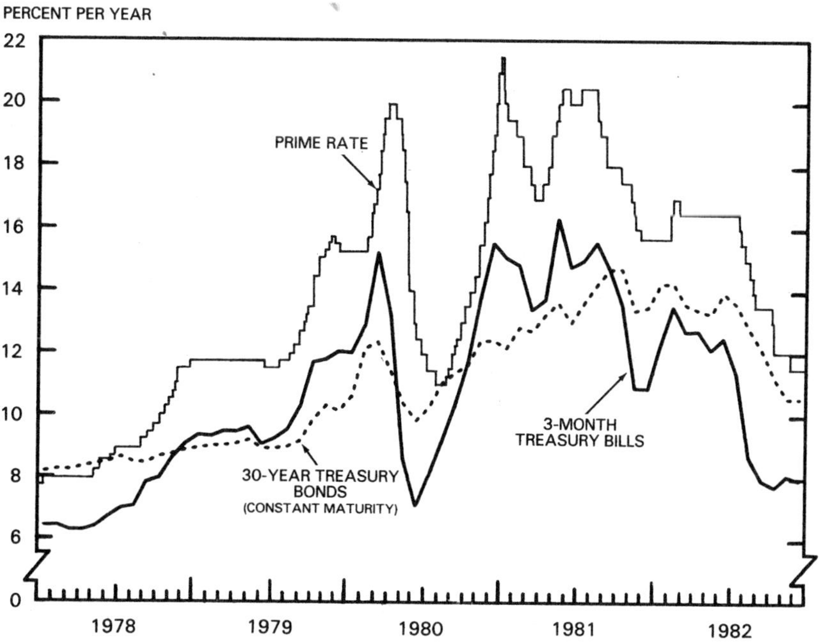

SOURCES: DEPARTMENT OF THE TREASURY AND BOARD OF GOVERNORS OF THE FEDERAL RESERVE SYSTEM.

The decline in interest rates brought much-needed relief to the interest-sensitive, cyclical sectors of the economy. By the end of 1982, clear progress toward recovery had been made, as reflected in continuing gains in the composite index of leading indicators of economic activity, as shown in Chart 6–2.

384-041 O - 83 - 9 : QL 3

Chart 6–2

Index of Leading Indicators and Real GNP

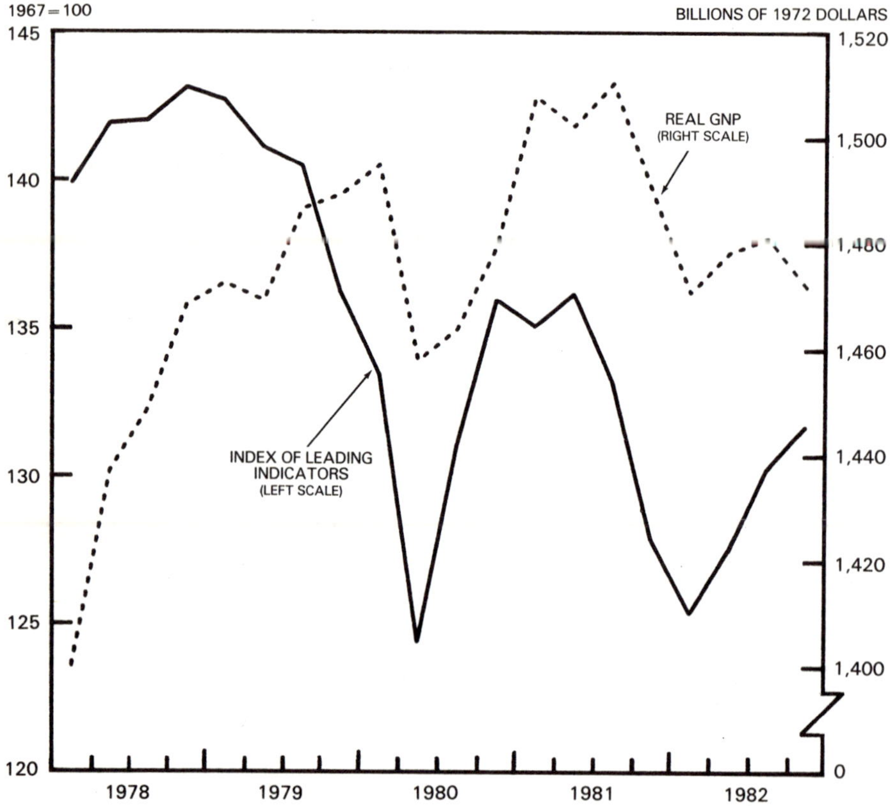

SOURCE: DEPARTMENT OF COMMERCE.

MAJOR SECTORS OF AGGREGATE DEMAND

Real output declined 1.2 percent from the fourth quarter of 1981 to the fourth quarter of 1982. This was the fourth consecutive year of little change in economic activity (Table 6–1). Businesses liquidated inventories in 1982, in contrast to the previous year when inventory levels increased. Another important factor in the decline was a sharp drop in U.S. exports that reflected both the strong dollar and the worldwide recession. Real final sales to domestic purchasers increased 1.3 percent in 1982, the largest increase in 3 years. Gains in personal consumption expenditures, residential investment, and Federal purchases dominated a large decline in business capital spending. Partly in response to the drop in interest rates, residential investment increased for the first time in 5 years, and consumer purchases of durable goods increased for the first time since 1978. State and local government purchases of goods and services were virtually unchanged over the year.

TABLE 6–1.—*Growth in major sectors of real GNP, 1978–82*

[Change, fourth quarter to fourth quarter and 5-year average]

Component	1978	1979	1980	1981	1982 [1]	5-year average [1,2]
Percent change:						
Real gross national product	5.8	1.4	−0.7	0.7	−1.2	1.5
Personal consumption expenditures	4.4	2.1	.3	.3	2.6	2.1
Consumer durables	5.7	−2.5	−4.6	−3.8	6.5	.1
Business fixed investment	12.8	3.5	−2.6	4.7	−8.4	3.3
Residential fixed investment	−.2	−8.3	−12.7	−19.4	4.5	−8.0
Government purchases of goods and services	2.3	1.3	.7	2.9	2.6	1.6
Federal	.6	1.0	1.4	10.7	6.6	2.9
Defense	2.6	3.0	2.1	9.3	6.8	3.8
State and local	3.4	1.4	.3	−1.7	.1	.7
Real final sales	5.4	2.6	−.4	.0	.3	1.8
Real final sales to domestic purchasers [3]	4.7	1.7	−.5	.6	1.3	1.7
Change in billions of 1972 dollars:						
Change in business inventories	5.1	−17.5	−3.9	11.0	−22.5	−4.4
Net exports of goods and services	11.2	14.9	1.4	−9.1	−15.4	1.7

[1] Preliminary.
[2] Based on annual data.
[3] Final sales less exports plus imports.
Source: Department of Commerce, Bureau of Economic Analysis.

PERSONAL CONSUMPTION EXPENDITURES

Despite declines in production, employment, and real wage and salary income, real disposable (after-tax) personal income increased in 1982, due in part to the reduction in personal income tax rates and an increase in transfer payments. The average effective Federal personal income tax rate fell from 12.5 percent to 11.4 percent between the third quarters of 1981 and 1982. Real personal consumption expenditures increased 2.6 percent in 1982 to reach their highest share of real GNP since 1949. Although real personal saving declined from its high level at the end of 1981, the personal saving rate in 1982 was higher than in any year since 1976, as shown in Table 6–2.

Consumer purchases of durable goods increased 6.5 percent in real terms in 1982, the first increase since 1978. The turnaround occurred early in the year, when auto sales rebounded from the depressed level of late 1981. Sales then languished until late in the year, when they again climbed, due in part to the decline in interest rates that produced lower financing costs. Nevertheless, domestic

TABLE 6-2.—*Real household income, consumption, saving, and residential investment, 1978-82*

[Percent change, fourth quarter to fourth quarter and 5-year average]

Item	1978	1979	1980	1981	1982 [1]	5-year average [1 2]
Income by type:						
Labor income [3]	4.7	1.2	−0.4	0.9	−1.9	1.6
Other income [4]	8.9	3.5	−1.0	8.8	.7	4.6
Net transfer payments [5]	−3.0	4.3	13.1	−.1	11.1	3.9
Personal income	4.9	2.0	.7	2.5	.0	2.4
Less: Federal tax payments	10.9	5.6	1.5	1.8	−5.5	3.6
Other tax and nontax payments [6]	5.4	1.8	.6	3.6	3.5	3.1
Disposable personal income	4.0	1.5	.5	2.6	.6	2.3
Personal consumption expenditures	4.4	2.1	.3	.3	2.6	2.1
Personal saving	−5.3	−11.4	9.3	39.8	−22.7	4.1
Personal saving rate [7]	6.1	5.9	5.8	6.4	6.5	6.1
Housing starts [8]	−1.7	−23.1	−4.3	−42.3	44.5	−11.6
Single family	−3.3	−29.2	−5.2	−45.0	48.0	−14.4
Multifamily	2.3	−7.9	−2.5	−37.3	38.9	−5.3
Mobile home shipments [8]	−7.5	−9.8	−6.7	−13.1	12.1	−2.8
Residential investment	−.2	−8.3	−12.7	−19.4	4.5	−8.0

[1] Preliminary.
[2] Based on annual data.
[3] Wage and salary disbursements and other labor income.
[4] Proprietors' income, rental income, personal dividend income, and personal interest income.
[5] Transfer payments less personal contributions for social insurance.
[6] State and local tax and nontax payments plus Federal nontax payments.
[7] Annual average.
[8] Units.

Note.—Income items, consumption, and saving deflated by the personal consumption deflator; residential investment deflated by the residential deflator.

Sources: Department of Commerce (Bureau of Economic Analysis and Bureau of the Census) and Council of Economic Advisers.

auto sales in 1982 for the entire year were lower than in any year since the early 1960s.

The extended period of weakness in durable goods sales accompanied a reduction in the burden of consumer debt. Consumer installment debt repayments relative to disposable personal income fell steadily from their 1978 peak to reach, by the third quarter of 1982, their lowest level since 1964, as illustrated in Chart 6-3. Total household debt has also fallen sharply relative to households' net worth.

RESIDENTIAL INVESTMENT

As indicated in Table 6-2, 1982 showed the first rise in housing activity in 5 years. By the fourth quarter of 1982, housing starts rose to 1.25 million at an annual rate, up nearly 45 percent from their trough of 865,000 units in the fourth quarter of 1981. Starts averaged less than one million units until mid-1982 as interest rates on mortgage commitments stayed around 17 percent. In August, mortgage interest rates began to fall, dropping below 14 percent by year-end. This drop encour-

Chart 6–3

Ratio of Consumer Installment Credit to Personal Income

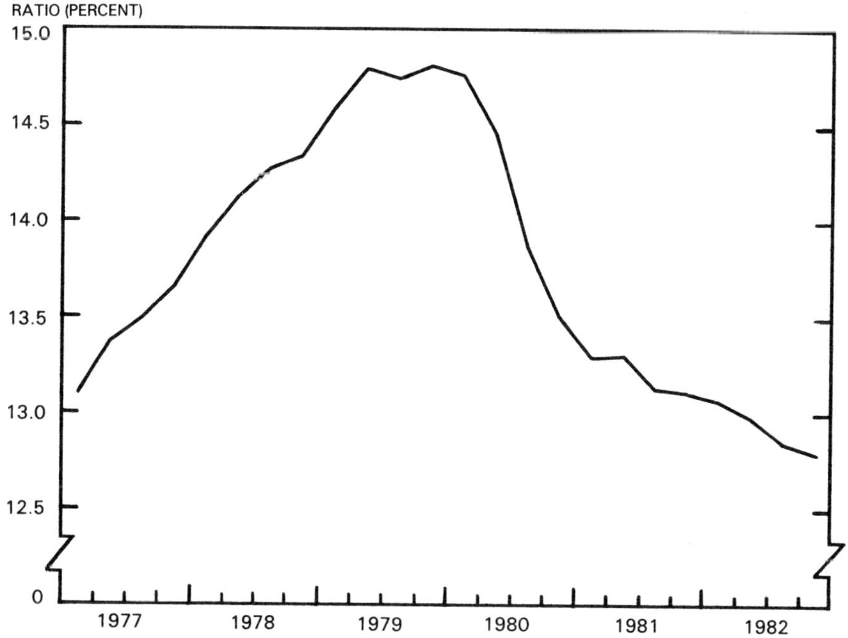

SOURCES: DEPARTMENT OF COMMERCE AND COUNCIL OF ECONOMIC ADVISERS.

aged the sale of houses, reduced the inventory of unsold new houses relative to current sales, and spurred new construction.

For the first time in recent years, house prices increased at a slower rate than general inflation. Moreover, the conventional measures of house price increases, which rose less than 3 percent, may well have overstated the 1982 rise because increased builder and seller financing at below market rates is not fully captured in the price data. Lower interest costs and more moderate house price increases helped to hold down mortgage payments and, thus, may favor a recovery in housing investment.

BUSINESS FIXED INVESTMENT

Real business fixed investment peaked in the last quarter of 1981, having grown at a 5.2 percent annual rate from 1977 to 1981. From its 1981 peak to the last quarter of 1982, real business fixed investment dropped 8.4 percent.

The 1982 decline in capital spending was broadly based, affecting even sectors that had fared well in previous years. Industrial and commercial construction declined about 1 percent in real terms from the fourth quarter of 1981 to the fourth quarter of 1982 having grown at an annual rate of more than 10 percent from 1977 to 1981. Computer, communications, and instrumentation equipment investment fell about 4 percent in 1982, a sharp contrast to over 9 percent annual rate of real growth from 1977 to 1981.

In the energy area, real investment in coal mine development continued to rise strongly in 1982. Real investment in oil field exploration and development dropped 15 percent between the fourth quarters of 1981 and 1982 as weak oil prices impaired cash flow in the petroleum industry. Reflecting the weakness in overall economic growth, investment in transportation equipment—autos, trucks, aircraft, ships, boats, and railroad equipment—continued to decline in 1982.

Business capital spending is likely to lag behind the recovery in the economy. Contracts and orders for new plant and equipment declined about 12 percent in real terms between the last quarters of 1981 and 1982. In addition, a Department of Commerce survey of business spending plans indicated that real nonfarm investment will decline about 5.2 percent in 1983.

INVENTORY INVESTMENT

Sluggish sales and high carrying costs encouraged business to pare inventories in 1982. A sharp drop in final sales in late 1981 triggered a swing to inventory liquidation in the first half of 1982. Even the more moderate sales forecasts for the second half of 1982 proved overly optimistic, and inventory-sales ratios climbed, prompting further cutbacks in production, employment, and inventories (Chart 6–4). Toward the end of the year, inventories were brought more in line with sales. Auto inventories, which accounted for about one-third of inventory liquidation in the final quarter of 1982, were especially lean, as the industry's aggressive pricing and marketing efforts helped to increase sales.

THE FARM ECONOMY

Total income per farm family in 1982 fell about 11 percent in real terms. Over two-thirds of farm family earnings came from off-farm sources as income from farm sources declined.

Net farm nominal income from farm operations declined from $25 billion in 1981 to about $19 billion in 1982. Relatively tight meat

Chart 6–4

Real Inventory/Sales Ratio and Industrial Production

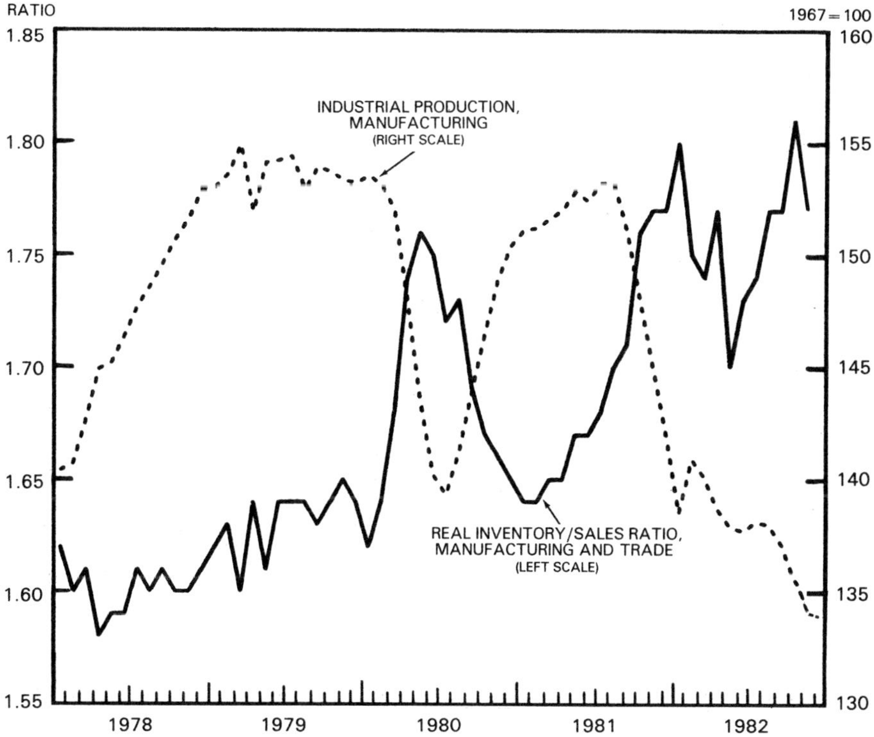

SOURCES: DEPARTMENT OF COMMERCE AND BOARD OF GOVERNORS OF THE FEDERAL RESERVE SYSTEM.

supplies and low feed prices in 1982 contributed to larger profit margins for most livestock producers. Many crop farmers, on the other hand, were hard hit by lower prices and increased production costs. Large domestic crops were only one of several factors contributing to lower prices. Livestock production declined, and domestic use of feedgrains and meals increased slowly. The value of agricultural exports in fiscal 1982 fell about 11 percent, primarily because of lower prices and reduced shipments of corn and grain sorghum. The weak export market reflected the world recession, a strong dollar, and an increase in world grain stocks. The U.S. share of world grain stocks is expected to continue its rapid growth of recent years and to reach over 50 percent in the 1982–83 crop year.

Lower crop prices, high mortgage rates, and lower inflation were the major factors leading to a decline in land values. Farm liabilities continued to increase and farmers' debt-to-asset ratio is estimated to have increased to about 20 percent, a significant rise from the 15 to 17 percent range typical of the late 1960s and 1970s.

U.S. agricultural policies have once again become a major factor in determining farm prices and incomes. Federal budget outlays for commodity price support and related programs soared to $12 billion in fiscal 1982 from $4 billion in the previous fiscal year. A program of voluntary acreage controls, including payments to those who restrict production in the 1983–84 crop year, was adopted in 1982 and supplemented by the addition of the "payment-in-kind" option in early 1983.

Food prices rose about 4 percent in 1982, with marketing costs rising at more than twice the rate of the farm value component of food prices.

FOREIGN TRADE

A reduction in U.S. trade was a key factor in the decline in aggregate demand in 1982. The main causes of the decline in net exports were the strength of the dollar and the worldwide recession. In December 1982 the trade-weighted value of the dollar was about 40 percent above its low point in 1980. Because exchange-rate appreciation lowers import prices and affects trade volume with a substantial lag, it initially tends to improve the trade balance. By the second half of 1982, however, the reduced cost competitiveness of U.S. firms began to overwhelm the short-term positive factors.

A secondary cause of the deteriorating trade balance was the international debt problem. Some heavily indebted developing countries, especially in Latin America, experienced difficulty in attracting capital inflows and were forced to cut imports sharply in 1982. Because several of the major high-debt developing countries have close trading ties with the United States, a large proportion of the import cuts came out of U.S. exports.

Cyclical factors had conflicting effects on the trade balance in 1982. On one side, the recession in the United States tended to reduce import demand, so that import volume fell more than 4 percent. On the other side, the recession in other industrial countries contributed to the 13 percent decline in real U.S. exports.

GOVERNMENT PURCHASES OF GOODS AND SERVICES

Real Federal, State, and local government purchases of goods and services increased 2.6 percent from the fourth quarter of 1981 to the fourth quarter of 1982. Much of the increase was attributable to a 6.8

percent increase in real defense purchases. Federal nondefense purchases rose in real terms, due to a large increase in real purchases of agricultural commodities by the Commodity Credit Corporation. State and local government purchases were virtually flat.

LABOR MARKET DEVELOPMENTS

Along with output, employment declined 1 percent in 1982, as shown in Table 6-3. At the end of the year, employment was 1.7 million persons below the peak level reached in the second quarter of 1981. The reduction in employment predominantly occurred among production workers and other blue-collar employees. Sales, clerical, and service workers' employment did not peak until September 1982.

TABLE 6-3.—*Labor market developments, 1978-82*

[Fourth quarter of indicated year]

Component	1978	1979	1980	1981	1982
	Percent change from year earlier[1]				
Change in civilian employment	3.8	2.3	−0.2	0.6	−1.0
Males 20 years and over	2.7	1.5	−.6	.2	−1.5
Females 20 years and over	5.6	4.0	1.6	2.8	.7
Both sexes 16-19 years	2.7	−.8	−6.6	−8.9	−8.0
White	3.3	2.2	−.1	.6	−1.2
Black and other	7.3	3.3	−.6	−.1	.4
	Percent[2]				
Unemployment rate[3]	5.9	5.9	7.4	8.3	10.7
Males 20 years and over	4.1	4.4	6.2	7.1	10.0
Females 20 years and over	5.8	5.7	6.7	7.2	9.0
Both sexes 16-19 years	16.4	16.3	18.3	21.2	24.3
White	5.1	5.2	6.5	7.3	9.5
Black and other	11.5	11.2	13.7	15.3	18.6
Participation rate[4]	63.5	63.8	63.7	63.8	64.1
Males 20 years and over	79.8	79.6	79.2	78.8	78.8
Females 20 years and over	50.1	51.0	51.5	52.3	52.9
Both sexes 16-19 years	58.2	57.9	56.3	54.6	54.1
White	63.6	64.0	64.0	64.2	64.5
Black and other	62.4	62.3	61.8	61.4	62.0

[1] 1978 data adjusted to reflect changes in sample and estimation procedures, which increased employment and labor force by 250,000 in January 1978.
[2] Seasonally adjusted.
[3] Unemployed as percent of civilian labor force.
[4] Civilian labor force as percent of civilian noninstitutional population.

Note.—Data relate to persons 16 years and over.

Source: Department of Labor, Bureau of Labor Statistics.

Generally speaking, the older the age cohort, the lower the unemployment rate. For example, the unemployment rate for the 55 and over age group was 5.7 percent in the final quarter of 1982. Young workers experienced the highest unemployment rate. Employment of the 16 to 19 year age group has dropped in every year since 1979. This decline was far faster than the decline in the number of persons in this age group. Women workers now have somewhat lower unemployment rates than men, a reversal of the historical relation.

The labor force participation rate—the ratio of the labor force to the population over 16 years of age—has experienced a modest upward drift as women workers continue to join the labor force. The growth in adult women's labor force participation has been strong in the past. Declining participation has occurred among workers less than 20 years of age and among workers, especially males, over 55—who are likely to have an income cushion provided by social security, private pension plans, and savings.

WAGES, PRODUCTIVITY, AND PRICES

In response to slack labor markets and lower rates of price inflation, wage increases slowed substantially in 1982. As shown in Table 6-4, the rate of increase in several measures of wages and compensation declined about 2 percentage points from 1981. The 5.9 percent increase in the hourly earnings index for private nonfarm workers was the smallest since 1973. As measured by the employment cost index, wages and salaries of private industry workers increased 6.9 percent between the third quarters of 1981 and 1982. The deceleration was about the same for union and nonunion workers. A survey of major collective bargaining settlements reached in private industry showed that in the first 9 months of 1982 the agreements provided wage adjustments that averaged 3.8 percent in the first contract year, exclusive of cost-of-living adjustments, compared with 8.3 percent when the same parties last bargained. Total labor compensation in the nonfarm business sector increased 6.7 percent, compared with

TABLE 6-4.—*Changes in wages and compensation, 1978–82*

[Percent change, fourth quarter to fourth quarter and 5-year average]

Measure	1978	1979	1980	1981	1982[1]	5-year average[1,2]
Adjusted hourly earnings index[3]	8.4	8.0	9.6	8.4	5.9	8.2
Employment cost index[4]	7.7	8.7	9.0	8.8	[5] 6.9	8.1
Union workers	8.0	9.0	10.9	9.6	[5] 7.4	8.8
Nonunion workers	7.6	8.5	8.0	8.5	[5] 6.6	7.8
Nonfarm business sector:[6]						
Compensation per hour	9.0	9.4	10.6	8.8	6.6	9.0
Real compensation per hour	.0	−2.9	−1.7	−.6	2.0	−.7

[1] Preliminary.
[2] Based on annual data.
[3] Private nonfarm employees.
[4] Wages and salaries, private nonfarm industry workers.
[5] Third quarter 1981 to third quarter 1982.
[6] All persons.

Sources: Department of Commerce (Bureau of Economic Analysis), Department of Labor (Bureau of Labor Statistics), and Council of Economic Advisers.

8.8 percent in 1981. These declines in wage inflation provide a basis for expecting that recent reductions in price inflation may be sustained.

Real compensation per hour rose 2.0 percent in 1982 as pay increased more rapidly than consumer prices. This was the first rise in this series since early 1978 and suggests that the historic trend of rising real wages and family incomes may resume.

Even though output declined for the third straight year, as shown in Table 6–5, labor productivity in the nonfarm business sector experienced its first substantial improvement since 1977. Lower rates of increase in hourly compensation and higher productivity growth together resulted in labor costs per unit of output increasing only 4.6 percent. This was less than half the rate of increase recorded in 1980, when labor productivity was weaker and hourly compensation rose at double-digit rates. The 4.6 percent increase in unit labor costs was associated with a rise of 4.3 percent in the nonfarm business sector price deflator.

TABLE 6–5.—*Productivity, costs, and prices in the nonfarm business sector, 1978–82*

[Percent change, fourth quarter to fourth quarter and 5-year average]

Item	1978	1979	1980	1981	1982 [1]	5-year average [1 2]
Output	5.6	0.2	−0.6	−0.2	−1.7	1.2
Output per hour	.3	−1.9	.3	−.1	1.9	.0
Compensation per hour	9.0	9.4	10.6	8.8	6.6	9.0
Unit labor cost	8.6	11.6	10.2	8.9	4.6	9.0
Implicit price deflator	8.2	8.5	10.7	9.6	4.3	8.3

[1] Preliminary.
[2] Based on annual data.
Note.—Data relate to all persons.
Source: Department of Labor, Bureau of Labor Statistics.

By all other measures as well, the rate of inflation declined significantly in 1982, as shown in Table 6–6. After increasing at double-digit rates in 1980 and by nearly 9 percent in 1981, the broadest measures of inflation—the GNP fixed-weight price index and the GNP implicit price deflator—increased nearly 5 percent in 1982. The all-urban consumer price index increased 4.5 percent, the slowest rate since 1972. Even when food and energy prices, which were especially weak, are excluded, consumer prices increased about 5 percent.

Beginning in 1983, the homeownership component of the consumer price index for all-urban consumers will be computed on a rental equivalence basis. On this conceptual basis, consumer prices increased about 5 percent in 1982.

Producer prices of finished goods increased only 3.6 percent in 1982, about the same as in 1972 and 1976. Price increases for both consumer finished goods and capital equipment showed a marked deceleration.

TABLE 6–6.—*Price changes, 1978–82*

[Percent change, fourth quarter to fourth quarter and 5-year average]

Item	1978	1979	1980	1981	1982 [1]	5-year average [1 2]
GNP price measures:						
Fixed-weighted index	8.9	9.3	10.3	8.9	5.0	8.6
Implicit deflator	8.5	8.2	10.2	8.9	4.6	8.2
Consumer prices: [3]						
All items	9.0	12.7	12.6	9.6	4.5	9.8
All items less food and energy	8.5	10.7	12.2	10.2	5.2	9.4
Producer prices—finished goods:						
Total	8.7	12.7	12.4	7.2	3.6	9.1
Consumer goods	9.0	13.9	12.6	6.8	3.4	9.2
Capital equipment	7.8	8.8	11.7	9.1	4.2	8.7

[1] Preliminary.
[2] Based on annual data.
[3] All urban consumers.
Source: Department of Commerce (Bureau of Economic Analysis) and Department of Labor (Bureau of Labor Statistics).

CREDIT MARKETS

During the first three quarters of 1982 the total amount of funds raised in U.S. credit markets averaged slightly more, at an annual rate, than the volume raised in 1981. As shown in Table 6–7, over the last 5 years the volume of funds raised by the nonfinancial sector has dropped from 18.6 percent to 13.6 percent of nominal GNP, a return to the cyclical lows recorded in 1974 and 1975.

TABLE 6–7.—*Funds raised by the nonfinancial sector of the economy, 1978–82*

[Billions of dollars, except as noted]

Sector	1978	1979	1980	1981	1982 [1]
Total funds raised	401.7	402.0	397.1	406.9	413.7
Households	169.3	176.5	117.5	120.4	87.0
Business	126.3	146.9	143.9	149.5	139.1
Federal Government	53.7	37.4	79.2	87.4	139.1
State and local government	19.1	20.2	27.3	22.3	37.2
Foreign	33.2	21.0	29.3	27.3	11.1
Funds raised as percent of GNP	18.6	16.6	15.1	13.9	13.6

[1] Average of first three quarters at seasonally adjusted annual rate.
Note.—Detail may not add to total due to rounding.
Sources: Department of Commerce (Bureau of Economic Analysis) and Board of Governors of the Federal Reserve System.

Different sectors of the credit market experienced widely different trends in 1982. High interest rates in the first half of the year and sluggish disposable income contributed to reduced borrowing for housing. Borrowing by the nonfinancial business sector also declined during the first three quarters of 1982. However, the easing of credit conditions in late summer encouraged an expansion in net corporate bond issues; the funds raised were used in part to pay off short-term debt.

Combined borrowing of State and local governments and the Federal Government rose approximately 60 percent in the first three quarters of 1982 from 1981 levels, as the growth of tax receipts slowed sharply relative to expenditures. For fiscal 1982, U.S. Treasury borrowing totaled $135.0 billion, of which $23.4 billion was used for making direct loans. Federally guaranteed loans declined sharply from 1981 levels, but borrowing by federally sponsored enterprises surged. Total Federal and federally assisted borrowing climbed to 48.9 percent of the funds raised in U.S. credit markets, surpassing the previous peacetime peak of 41 percent reached in 1976.

INTEREST RATES

As shown in Chart 6–1, interest rates rose in the first part of 1982 but began to decline sharply in the summer. The decline in interest rates partly reflected diminishing inflationary expectations that tend to be built into nominal interest rates.

The yield on 3-month Treasury bills, which had averaged just under 11 percent late in 1981, held in the 12 to 13 percent range until mid-1982 and then fell to less than 8 percent in the closing months of the year. The prime rate charged by commercial banks began the year at 15¾ percent, climbed to 17 percent in February, and then in July began a steady fall to 11½ percent by December. The corporate Aaa bond rate, which peaked at 15¼ percent in February, fell below 12 percent by November.

The expected real after-tax interest rate is the correct measure of the cost of credit to borrowers and lenders. It is approximately equal to the after-tax nominal interest rate less the anticipated rate of inflation. For example, with a 12 percent nominal interest rate, the after-tax cost of credit to a borrower in the 30 percent marginal tax bracket is 8.4 percent. If a 5 percent inflation rate is anticipated, the expected real after-tax cost of credit is 3.2 percent.

Because the tax brackets of borrowers differ widely and the expected rate of inflation cannot be observed directly, the realized real pretax interest rate—approximated by the nominal interest rate less the actual rate of inflation—is a more convenient measure of the cost of credit. The nominal 3-month Treasury bill rate and the corresponding realized real pretax rate are shown in Chart 6–5 for the period since 1955. The real pretax Treasury bill rate was abnormally low in 1972–73 and 1976–77, tending to increase aggregate demand.

It then moved to relatively high levels from 1980 through the first half of 1982, tending to reduce aggregate demand. By the end of 1982, however, the real pretax Treasury bill rate had fallen to about the same level as its highs in the 1950s and 1960s.

Chart 6–5

Nominal and Real 3-Month Treasury Bill Yield

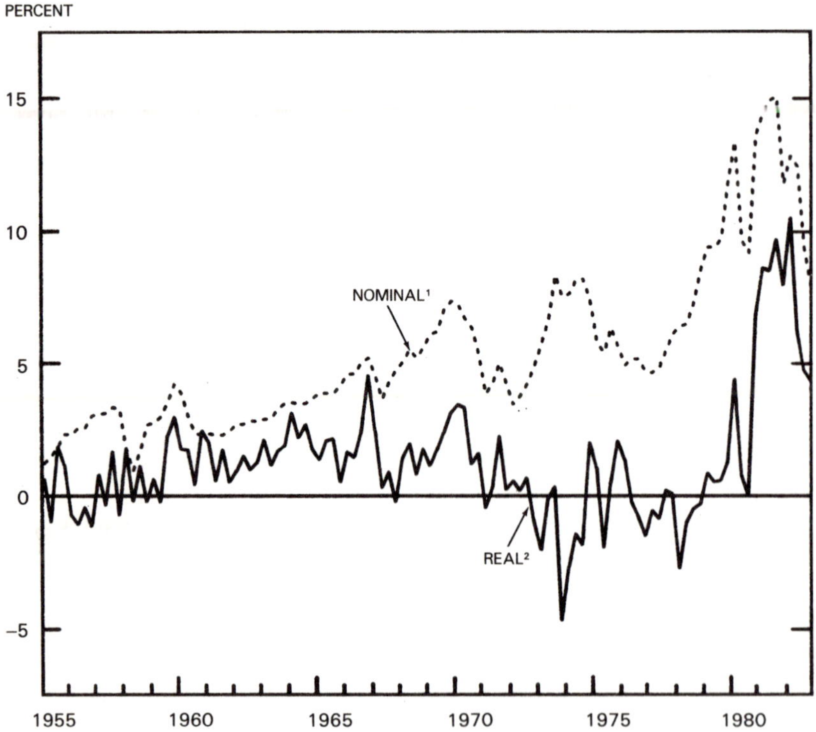

[1]CONVERTED TO EFFECTIVE ANNUAL YIELD FROM DISCOUNT BASIS.

[2]EQUALS NOMINAL YIELD LESS ACTUAL RATE OF INFLATION, DEFINED BY PERSONAL CONSUMPTION DEFLATOR, OVER THE PERIOD TO MATURITY. DEFLATOR FOR FIRST QUARTER 1983 FORECAST BY COUNCIL OF ECONOMIC ADVISERS.

SOURCES: DEPARTMENT OF COMMERCE, BOARD OF GOVERNORS OF THE FEDERAL RESERVE SYSTEM, AND COUNCIL OF ECONOMIC ADVISERS.

The sharp run-up and subsequent decline in real pretax rates during the 1980–82 period probably reflect in part the adjustment of credit markets to the decontrol of interest rates. During the late 1970s variable interest rate time and savings accounts were introduced by depository institutions, and the process of financial innovation speeded up the movement of funds out of regulated, fixed-rate accounts. In addition, the consumer has recently become a more vigorous competitor for credit as usury laws have been eliminated. As a result, the financial system now relies less on nonprice rationing of credit and may exhibit higher interest rates when credit is tight.

Even though real short-term rates have returned more nearly to the levels of the 1950s and 1960s, the equilibrium level of both long- and short-term rates may now be somewhat higher than before. To the extent that the accelerated cost recovery system in the Economic Recovery Tax Act of 1981 reduced the tax on earnings of depreciable property, it raised the real interest rate that business borrowers are willing to pay. In addition, large budget deficits in many countries have lowered national saving rates, tending to lead to higher real interest rates worldwide.

At the end of 1982, long-term interest rates were considerably higher than short-term interest rates, perhaps reflecting the concern that the inflation rate may be higher in the future than at present. To the extent that these inflationary expectations decline, further declines in nominal long-term interest rates can be anticipated.

MONETARY DEVELOPMENTS

The Administration's economic program includes support for a policy of gradual reduction in the rate of monetary growth in order to bring down inflation. Consistent with this policy, the Federal Reserve reduced the M1 target growth rate range from 3.5 to 6 percent in 1981 to 2.5 to 5.5 percent in 1982. The target range for M2 growth was kept at 6 to 9 percent.

In its February 1982 review of the tentative target ranges for 1982, established in July 1981, the Federal Open Market Committee recognized that the rapid increase of M1 in December 1981 and January 1982 had already placed it well above the top of its target range. Judging that the rapid money growth was temporary and that no basic change in the relation between the monetary aggregates and nominal GNP had occurred, the committee reaffirmed the tentative targets for 1982.

Consequently, the Federal Reserve slowed the growth of nonborrowed reserves during the first half of the year, with a view to gradually bringing M1 and M2 back into their target ranges. By June, M1 was within its target range, while M2 remained somewhat above the top of its range. Because M1 had shown virtually no growth since January, resumption of growth implied a step-up in the provision of bank reserves. After midyear, continued weakness in the economy, and a more ample supply of reserves and money contributed to a sharp drop in short-term interest rates. The 3-month Treasury bill rate fell from about 12 percent in July to 9 percent in August. A series of reductions in the Federal Reserve's discount rate followed, maintaining its alignment with short-term market rates and preventing sharp changes in the incentive for banks to borrow from the Federal Reserve.

Starting in August, M1 growth began to speed up. By the fourth quarter of 1982, M1 had risen 8.5 percent above its level in the fourth quarter of 1981, well above the upper end of the 1982 target range. Over the same period, M2 increased 9.8 percent, slightly more than the top of its target range. These increases in the monetary aggregates occurred against the background of an economy that was still in recession.

Part of the strength in M1 may be attributable to the effects of a large volume of All-Savers Certificates maturing in the fourth quarter of 1982, as the maturing funds moved through checking accounts or were temporarily "parked" there. Federal Reserve analysis suggested that an additional factor was an unusual demand for liquidity. Much of the increase in M1 was in interest-bearing negotiable order of withdrawal (NOW) accounts, which provide elements of both savings and transactions accounts. From the fourth quarter of 1981 to the fourth quarter of 1982, checkable deposits other than demand deposits grew about 35 percent. With market interest rates falling, these interest-bearing deposits, such as NOW accounts, provided a safe and convenient store of liquidity at a time of economic and financial uncertainty. Increased liquidity demand may also account for the above-target growth of M2.

As discussed in Chapter 1, the behavior of the "income velocity" measures—the ratios of GNP to the various monetary aggregates—was unusual in 1982. The velocity of M1 rose 3.2 percent a year on average over the 20 years ending in 1981, but in 1982 it declined 4.9 percent. While a tendency toward slower velocity is not unusual in the midst of a recession when interest rates generally are falling, the only other fourth quarter to fourth quarter decline in M1 velocity since the beginning of the current series in 1959 was a 0.1 percent fall in 1967. The velocity of M2, which historically has been relatively trendless, declined 6.0 percent in 1982; the largest previous decline was 3.8 percent in 1976. Without some accommodation of monetary growth—particularly for M1—to this drop in velocity, monetary policy would have been more restrictive than had been intended when the 1982 targets were established.

The number, size, and rapidity of recent changes in the financial sector may well have affected the behavior of velocity. As indicated in Table 6–8, checkable deposits other than ordinary demand deposits accounted for only 2.3 percent of M1 in December 1978. In December 1980, just before NOW accounts were authorized nationally, other checkable deposits were 6.5 percent of M1, but by December

1982 their share had risen to over 21 percent. Because these interest-bearing deposits may be regarded by their holders in part as savings rather than solely as transactions balances, the reported growth of M1 in 1981 and 1982 probably overstates the growth in transactions balances.

TABLE 6–8.—*Components of M1* and *M2,* 1978–82

[Averages of daily figures; billions of dollars; seasonally adjusted, except as noted]

Item	December				
	1978	1979	1980	1981	1982 [1]
Currency	97.4	106.1	116.1	123.1	132.6
Plus: Demand deposits [2]	257.4	265.9	271.4	240.7	244.6
Other checkable deposits	8.4	16.9	26.9	77.0	101.3
Equals: M1	363.2	389.0	414.5	440.9	478.5
Plus: Savings deposits [3]	479.9	421.7	398.9	343.6	400.3
Small time deposits	533.9	652.6	751.7	854.7	904.2
Overnight repurchase agreements (RPs) and overnight Eurodollars [4]	24.0	26.3	35.0	38.1	45.6
Money market mutual fund balances (excluding institution accounts) [4]	7.1	34.4	61.9	151.2	177.5
Equals: M2 [5]	1,403.9	1,518.9	1,656.2	1,822.7	1,999.1

[1] Preliminary.
[2] Includes travelers checks.
[3] Includes Money Market Deposit Account introduced December 14, 1982.
[4] Not seasonally adjusted.
[5] M2 will differ from the sum of components by a consolidation adjustment that represents the estimated amount of demand deposits and vault cash held by thrift institutions to service time and savings deposits.

Source: Board of Governors of the Federal Reserve System.

In general, the demand for any particular monetary aggregate—and hence its income velocity—depends in part on the difference between market rates of interest and the rates earned on the deposits in that aggregate. Consequently, the increased portion of M1 deposits that pay interest and the decline in market interest rates have combined to lower M1 velocity.

The rapid growth of general purpose and broker/dealer money market mutual fund balances, which are included in M2 but not in M1, has tended to raise M1 velocity and to lower M2 velocity. From December 1980 to December 1982 these money market mutual fund balances grew from $61.9 billion to $177.5 billion, which exceeded the growth in other checkable deposits by $41.2 billion. Although most money market mutual fund balances are subject to transfer by check, the average turnover of these accounts has been relatively low.

Interpretation of the macroeconomic significance of changes in the monetary aggregates became more difficult in late 1982 when the Depository Institutions Deregulation Committee authorized two new accounts. In mid-December, banks and thrift institutions introduced a Money Market Deposit Account with limited transactions capabilities and no interest rate ceiling. Within about 2 weeks, these accounts

384-041 0 - 83 - 10 : QL 3

had attracted an astonishing $87 billion. The Depository Institutions Deregulation Committee also authorized a new super NOW account effective January 1983, with no transactions limitations and no interest rate ceilings, having the same $2,500 minimum balance as the Money Market Deposit Account.

Financial deregulation and innovation favorably affect the efficiency of the U.S. financial system but also complicate the implementation of monetary policy. Large asset reallocations caused by changes in the financial and regulatory system can have large and unpredictable effects on M1 and M2 and on their relations to nominal GNP. In light of the particular difficulties with regard to M1, the Federal Open Market Committee has voted to place greater emphasis on M2 and M3 for an indefinite period. However, the broad framework of targeting the monetary aggregates has been retained, as have the reserve operating procedures, for implementing it.

PROSPECTS FOR 1983

Assuming that the Administration's 1984 budget proposals are enacted and that the monetary aggregates grow within the Federal Reserve's target ranges, the prospects for a moderate, sustainable economic recovery beginning early in 1983 are good (Table 6–9). As was true in the early stages of previous recoveries, the unemployment rate is likely to stabilize for several months before a downward trend becomes evident. A pattern of reduced inflation in 1982 is expected to continue in 1983. The sharp rise in the Federal budget deficit reflects reduced receipts because of lower inflation, as well as the effects of the 1981–82 recession.

The expectation of economic recovery is based on the view that continuing strength in household and defense spending will bring a turnaround in the inventory cycle. Cuts in production and increases in sales brought business inventories more in line with sales by the end of 1982. Future sales gains are thus likely to be met by increases in production, income, and employment, enhancing sales further. Once even a moderate but sustained increase in sales is underway, this sequence of events may lead to a temporary surge of above-average economic growth.

Increases in sales will come primarily from households whose income will be bolstered by the third stage of the personal income tax cut, whose debt burden has declined sharply relative to income and assets, and whose financial assets, in many cases, appreciated in rallies in the stock and bond markets. With continued moderate increases in food and oil prices, more income will become available for other consumer purchases. Because outlays on durable consumer

TABLE 6–9.—*Economic outlook for 1983*

Item	1982 [1]	1983 forecast
Percent change (fourth quarter to fourth quarter):		
Real gross national product	−1.2	3.1
Personal consumption expenditures	2.6	2.7
Nonresidential fixed investment	−8.4	−.3
Residential investment	4.5	27.6
Federal purchases	6.6	1.2
State and local purchases	.1	−2.0
GNP implicit price deflator	4.6	5.6
Compensation per hour [2]	6.6	6.0
Output per hour [2]	1.9	2.2
Level in fourth quarter: [3]		
Unemployment rate (percent) [4]	10.7	10.4
Housing starts (millions of units, annual rate)	1.3	1.5

[1] Preliminary.
[2] Nonfarm business, all persons.
[3] Seasonally adjusted.
[4] Actual rate for 1982 is percent of civilian labor force; forecast rate for 1983 is percent of total labor force including persons in the Armed Forces stationed in the United States.

Sources: Department of Commerce (Bureau of Economic Analysis and Bureau of the Census), Department of Labor (Bureau of Labor Statistics), and Council of Economic Advisers.

goods and houses have been depressed for the last 4 years, consumers are expected to devote increases in their income, and perhaps some of the recent gains in their financial wealth, to replenishing their holdings of durable goods. The sharp easing of credit terms and lower house price increases have already encouraged more households to consider buying houses. This uptrend is expected to intensify in 1983. New house purchases are invariably followed by a pickup in expenditures for furniture, appliances, and other housing-related goods.

The pace of the recovery in 1983 will probably be moderate by historical standards. Low capacity utilization rates and the need to rebuild corporate liquidity will restrain capital spending. The worldwide recession and the lagged effect of the appreciation of the dollar will curtail the growth of exports. Continued reductions in the nondefense public sector will limit it as a source of increased aggregate demand.

PROSPECTS AND POLICIES BEYOND 1983

Economic prospects for the rest of the 1980s depend greatly on the economic policies that are followed. The Administration believes that the four-point program it has pursued—reducing the growth of Federal outlays, taxes, regulation, and the money supply—constitutes the best approach for attaining and maintaining the economic goals set forth in the Full Employment and Balanced Growth Act of 1978.

The Full Employment and Balanced Growth Act calls for annual numerical goals for several key economic indicators over a 5-year period. The projections provided in Table 6–10 show gradual, steady progress toward our economic goals. These figures illustrate the Administration's belief, explained in Chapter 1, that policies based on consistent, long-term objectives can simultaneously achieve full employment, price stability, and sustained growth in real income. A major cause of our present economic ills was the inclination in the past to pursue one economic goal single-mindedly, without adequate attention to the longer run consequences for other economic objectives. This Administration remains determined to avoid the errors of past policies.

TABLE 6–10.—*Projections of economic goals, 1983–88*

[Calendar years, except as noted]

Item	1983	1984	1985	1986	1987	1988
	Level					
Employment (millions) [1]	101.5	104.2	107.0	109.6	112.3	114.9
Unemployment rate (percent) [2]	10.7	9.9	8.9	8.1	7.3	6.5
Federal budget outlays as percent of GNP (fiscal year basis)	25.2	24.3	24.1	23.9	23.5	23.0
	Percent change					
Consumer prices [3]	4.9	4.6	4.6	4.6	4.5	4.4
Real GNP	1.4	3.9	4.0	4.0	4.0	4.0
Real compensation per hour [4]	1.2	.8	1.1	1.4	1.6	1.6
Output per hour [4]	2.1	1.9	1.6	1.7	1.6	1.7

[1] Labor force series includes persons in the Armed Forces stationed in the United States.
[2] Unemployed as percent of total labor force. See footnote 1.
[3] Wage earners and clerical workers.
[4] Nonfarm business, all persons.
Source: Council of Economic Advisers.

A major prerequisite for achieving our economic goals is control of inflation. Marked progress toward this end has been made in the last 2 years. With continued moderate growth in the monetary aggregates, increased reliance on the private sector, and increased domestic and international economic competition, the prospects for sustaining and extending the progress against inflation are now quite favorable.

An important factor in achieving and sustaining high real economic growth is a high level of capital formation. Chapter 4 of this volume, which fulfills the legislative requirement for an annual Investment Policy Report, explains that lower inflation and the recently enacted tax incentives for saving and investment are the important first steps in fostering capital accumulation. Controlling the Federal deficit is now the single most important method of encouraging more capital formation.

A critical element in achieving healthy economic growth is maintaining a liberal worldwide trading system. As explained in detail in Chapter 3, the world's economies are now more integrated than ever before. This system has recently experienced severe strains. It is of utmost importance that these challenges be met in a manner consistent with an open, growing, balanced network of international tradc.

Just as an open worldwide trading system is crucial for the free world economies, a competitive free market system unfettered by unnecessary government regulation is essential for a strong domestic economy. As Chapter 5 points out, substantial progress toward reduction of traditional price and entry regulation has been made in recent years, but further opportunities for deregulation exist.

The year 1983 is expected to be the first of many years of sustained economic growth. Continued economic growth is the only way to sustain progress in reducing unemployment. But macroeconomic policies alone cannot reduce structural unemployment and achieve an acceptable level of employment. Chapter 2 describes some of the macroeconomic policies that, along with a sustained recovery, are necessary to achieve noninflationary full employment. These policies are designed ". . . to foster and promote free competitive enterprise . . ." as mandated in the Full Employment and Balanced Growth Act.

One major remaining threat to a sustainable, balanced recovery is the danger that large Federal budget deficits would preclude the continuing declines in real interest rates that are necessary for healthy growth in all sectors of the economy. The Administration's 1984 budget provides a plan which can lead to a steady decline in budget deficits and thus, ultimately, to a balanced Federal budget.

Appendix A
REPORT TO THE PRESIDENT ON THE ACTIVITIES OF THE COUNCIL OF ECONOMIC ADVISERS DURING 1982

LETTER OF TRANSMITTAL

COUNCIL OF ECONOMIC ADVISERS,
Washington, D.C., December 31, 1982.

MR. PRESIDENT:

The Council of Economic Advisers submits this report on its activities during the calendar year 1982 in accordance with the requirements of the Congress, as set forth in section 10(d) of the Employment Act of 1946 as amended by the Full Employment and Balanced Growth Act of 1978.

Sincerely,

MARTIN FELDSTEIN, *Chairman*

WILLIAM A. NISKANEN

WILLIAM POOLE

Council Members and their dates of service are listed below:

Name	Position	Oath of office date	Separation date
Edwin G. Nourse	Chairman	August 9, 1946	November 1, 1949.
Leon H. Keyserling	Vice Chairman	August 9, 1946	
	Acting Chairman	November 2, 1949	
	Chairman	May 10, 1950	January 20, 1953.
John D. Clark	Member	August 9, 1946	
	Vice Chairman	May 10, 1950	February 11, 1953.
Roy Blough	Member	June 29, 1950	August 20, 1952.
Robert C. Turner	Member	September 8, 1952	January 20, 1953.
Arthur F. Burns	Chairman	March 19, 1953	December 1, 1956.
Neil H. Jacoby	Member	September 15, 1953	February 9, 1955.
Walter W. Stewart	Member	December 2, 1953	April 29, 1955.
Raymond J. Saulnier	Member	April 4, 1955	
	Chairman	December 3, 1956	January 20, 1961.
Joseph S. Davis	Member	May 2, 1955	October 31, 1958.
Paul W. McCracken	Member	December 3, 1956	January 31, 1959.
Karl Brandt	Member	November 1, 1958	January 20, 1961.
Henry C. Wallich	Member	May 7, 1959	January 20, 1961.
Walter W. Heller	Chairman	January 29, 1961	November 15, 1964.
James Tobin	Member	January 29, 1961	July 31, 1962.
Kermit Gordon	Member	January 29, 1961	December 27, 1962.
Gardner Ackley	Member	August 3, 1962	
	Chairman	November 16, 1964	February 15, 1968.
John P. Lewis	Member	May 17, 1963	August 31, 1964.
Otto Eckstein	Member	September 2, 1964	February 1, 1966.
Arthur M. Okun	Member	November 16, 1964	
	Chairman	February 15, 1968	January 20, 1969.
James S. Duesenberry	Member	February 2, 1966	June 30, 1968.
Merton J. Peck	Member	February 15, 1968	January 20, 1969.
Warren L. Smith	Member	July 1, 1968	January 20, 1969.
Paul W. McCracken	Chairman	February 4, 1969	December 31, 1971.
Hendrik S. Houthakker	Member	February 4, 1969	July 15, 1971.
Herbert Stein	Member	February 4, 1969	
	Chairman	January 1, 1972	August 31, 1974.
Ezra Solomon	Member	September 9, 1971	March 26, 1973.
Marina v.N. Whitman	Member	March 13, 1972	August 15, 1973.
Gary L. Seevers	Member	July 23, 1973	April 15, 1975.
William J. Fellner	Member	October 31, 1973	February 25, 1975.
Alan Greenspan	Chairman	September 4, 1974	January 20, 1977.
Paul W. MacAvoy	Member	June 13, 1975	November 15, 1976.
Burton G. Malkiel	Member	July 22, 1975	January 20, 1977.
Charles L. Schultze	Chairman	January 22, 1977	January 20, 1981.
William D. Nordhaus	Member	March 18, 1977	February 4, 1979.
Lyle E. Gramley	Member	March 18, 1977	May 27, 1980.
George C. Eads	Member	June 6, 1979	January 20, 1981.
Stephen M. Goldfeld	Member	August 20, 1980	January 20, 1981.
Murray L. Weidenbaum	Chairman	February 27, 1981	August 25, 1982.
Jerry L. Jordan	Member	July 14, 1981	July 31, 1982.
William A. Niskanen	Member	June 12, 1981	
Martin Feldstein	Chairman	October 14, 1982	
William Poole	Member	December 10, 1982	

Report to the President on the Activities of the Council of Economic Advisers during 1982

The Employment Act of 1946 (P.L. 304–79th Congress), as amended, provides the statutory base for the activities of the Council of Economic Advisers. The Council, through the Chairman, provides advice to the President on a wide range of domestic and international economic policy issues.

Martin Feldstein became Chairman on October 14, 1982, succeeding Murray L. Weidenbaum, who returned to Washington University (St. Louis). The Chairman is on leave from Harvard University, where he is a Professor of Economics. On July 31, 1982, Jerry L. Jordan resigned to return to the University of New Mexico, where he is a Professor of Economics at the Anderson Schools of Management. On December 10, 1982, William Poole became a Member of the Council. Mr. Poole is on leave from Brown University where he is a Professor of Economics. William A. Niskanen continued to serve as a Member.

MACROECONOMIC POLICIES

As is its tradition, during 1982 the Council devoted much of its time to assisting the President in the formulation of broad economic policy objectives and the programs to carry them out. The development of economic assumptions and monitoring of current developments, under Council Member Jordan and subsequently Council Member Poole, were an area of major interest. Monetary policy developments received especially close attention.

Council Member Jordan and later Council Member Poole chaired the interagency subcabinet "Troika" forecasting group, consisting of representatives from the Department of the Treasury and the Office of Management and Budget, with participation by the Department of Commerce. The Chairman of the Council continued his responsibility for presenting to the President the economic assumptions developed with the Office of Management and Budget and the Department of the Treasury.

Council Members chaired or participated in numerous Cabinet Council working groups dealing with such issues as economic statistics, Federal credit programs, alternatives to Federal regulation, and Federal housing programs.

The Chairman actively participated during the early months of the year, and then during the late fall budget cycle, in Cabinet level reviews of agency budget requests and appeals.

MICROECONOMIC POLICIES

A wide variety of microeconomic issues received Council attention during the year. Council Member Niskanen chaired Cabinet Council working groups dealing with employee pension legislation and alternatives to Federal regulation. Trade issues were an area of continuing attention.

The Council assisted in the preparation of agency guidelines for implementing Executive Order 12291 dealing with Executive Office review of agency regulatory proposals, and worked closely with the Office of Management and Budget on selected regulatory issues.

PUBLIC INFORMATION

The Council's *Annual Report* is the principal medium through which the Council informs the public of its work and its views. It is also an important vehicle for presenting and explaining the Administration's domestic and international economic policies. Distribution of the *Report* in recent years has averaged about 50,000 copies. The Council also assumes primary responsibility for the monthly *Economic Indicators,* a publication prepared by the Council's Statistical Office, under the supervision of Catherine H. Furlong. The Joint Economic Committee issues the *Indicators,* which has a distribution of approximately 10,000 copies. Information is also provided to members of the public through speeches and other public appearances by the Chairman, Members, and staff economists of the Council.

ORGANIZATION AND STAFF OF THE COUNCIL

OFFICE OF THE CHAIRMAN

The Chairman is responsible for communicating the Council's views to the President. This function is carried out through direct consultation with the President and through written memoranda and reports on economic developments and on particular programs and proposals. The Chairman exercises ultimate responsibility for directing the work of the professional staff. He represents the Council at meetings of the full Cabinet and the various Cabinet Councils, and the Trade Policy Committee.

COUNCIL MEMBERS

The two Council Members are responsible for all subject matter covered by the Council, including direct supervision of the work of the professional staff. Members represent the Council at a wide variety of interagency and international meetings and assume major responsibility for selecting issues for Council attention.

In practice, the small size of the Council permits the Chairman and Council Members to work as a team in most circumstances. There was, however, an informal division of subject matter among them in 1982. Mr. Jordan and subsequently Mr. Poole, assumed primary responsibility for domestic and international macroeconomic analysis, economic projections, and monetary and financial issues. Mr. Niskanen is primarily responsible for microeconomic and sectoral analysis, international trade questions, and regulatory issues.

PROFESSIONAL STAFF

At the end of 1982 the professional staff consisted of the Special Assistant to the Chairman, who also acts as staff director, the Senior Statistician, a domestic policy economist, an international policy economist, 12 senior staff economists, 3 staff economists, and 6 junior staff economists.

The professional staff and their special fields at the end of 1982 were:

Eric I. Hemel	Special Assistant to the Chairman
Lawrence H. Summers	Domestic Policy Economist
Paul R. Krugman	International Policy Economist

Senior Staff Economists

Lincoln F. Anderson	Economic Forecasting
Geoffrey O. Carliner	International Trade
Daniel J. Frisch	Taxation and Social Insurance Programs
David R. Henderson	Health Policy and Social Insurance Programs
Thomas J. Kniesner	Labor and Employment Policy
Evan R. Kwerel	Regulatory Policies and Natural Resources
Thomas S. McCaleb	Taxation and Public Finance
Stephen K. McNees	Macroeconomic Policy
Glenn L. Nelson	Agricultural Policy
Adrian W. Throop	Monetary Policy and Financial Regulation
Robert S. Villanueva	Current Economic Conditions, Housing, and Economic Forecasting
Benjamin Zycher	Energy Policy and Regulation

Statistician

Catherine H. Furlong	Senior Statistician

Staff Economists

Lawrence B. Lindsey	Taxation and Public Finance
N. Gregory Mankiw	Macroeconomic Policy and Public Finance
Robert H. Meyer	Labor and Employment Policy

Junior Staff Economists

Christopher B. Ballinger	World Trade and International Finance
John H. Cochrane	Macroeconomic Analysis and Forecasting
John S. Earle	Public Finance and Labor Policy
Thomas W. Gilligan	Transportation and Regulatory Policy
David S. Reitman	Social Insurance Programs and General Budget Policy
Dan C. Roberts	Financial Institutions and Macroeconomic Policy

Catherine H. Furlong, Senior Statistician, continued to be in charge of the Council's Statistical Office. Mrs. Furlong has primary responsibility for managing the Council's statistical information system. She supervises the publication of *Economic Indicators* and the preparation of all statistical matter in the *Economic Report.* She also oversees the verification of statistics in memoranda, testimony, and speeches. Natalie V. Rentfro, Linda A. Reilly, and Barbara L. Sibel assist Mrs. Furlong.

Serving as consultants during the year were Stephen H. Brooks (consultant), Jose A. Gomez-Ibanez (Harvard University), and Robert A. Leone (Harvard University).

In preparing the Economic Report the Council relied upon the editorial services of John Phillip Sawicki.

SUPPORTING STAFF

The Administrative Office of the Council of Economic Advisers provides general support for the Council's activities. Serving in the Administrative Office were Elizabeth A. Kaminski, Staff Assistant to the Council, and Catherine Fibich, Administrative Assistant.

Members of the secretarial staff for the Chairman and Council Members during 1982 were Patricia A. Lee, Susan A. Lindsey, Georgia A. O'Connor, and Alice H. Williams. Secretaries for the professional staff were Carolyn L. Bazarnick, Bessie M. Lafakis, Rosemary M. Rogers, Margaret L. Snyder, and Lillie M. Sturniolo.

DEPARTURES

The Council's professional staff are in most cases on leave of absence from universities, other government agencies, or research institutions. Their tenure with the Council is usually limited to 1 or 2 years. Senior staff economists who resigned during the year and their subsequent affiliations were James B. Burnham (The World Bank), William D. Dobson (Purdue University), Michele U. Fratianni (Indiana University), Steven H. Hanke (Johns Hopkins University), Laurence J. Kotlikoff (Yale University), Michael J. McKee (Department of the Treasury), David C. Munro (General Motors), Susan C. Nelson (Department of the Treasury), Allen M. Parkman (University of New Mexico), Paul H. Rubin (Baruch College), and Elinor Y. Sachse (consultant).

Junior economists who resigned in 1982 were Robert G. Murphy (Massachusetts Institute of Technology), Chris P. Varvares (Washington University, St. Louis), and F. Katharine Warne (Yale University).

Appendix B

STATISTICAL TABLES RELATING TO INCOME, EMPLOYMENT, AND PRODUCTION

384-041 0 - 83 - 11 : QL 3

CONTENTS

NATIONAL INCOME OR EXPENDITURE:

POPULATION, EMPLOYMENT, WAGES, AND PRODUCTIVITY:

PRODUCTION AND BUSINESS ACTIVITY:

PRICES:

MONEY STOCK, CREDIT, AND FINANCE:

General Notes

Detail in these tables may not add to totals because of rounding.

Unless otherwise noted, all dollar figures are in current dollars.

Symbols used:

[p] Preliminary.

— —Not available (also, not applicable).

TABLE B–1.—*Gross national product, 1929–82*

[Billions of dollars, except as noted; quarterly data at seasonally adjusted annual rates]

Year or quarter	Gross national product	Personal consumption expenditures	Gross private domestic investment	Net exports of goods and services			Government purchases of goods and services					Final sales	Percent change from preceding period [1]	
				Net exports	Exports	Imports	Total	Federal			State and local		Gross national product	Final sales
								Total	National defense	Nondefense				
1929	103.4	77.3	16.2	1.1	7.0	5.9	8.8	1.4	....	....	7.4	101.7	6.6	....
1933	55.8	45.8	1.4	.4	2.4	2.0	8.2	2.1	....	....	6.1	57.4	−4.2	−5.6
1939	90.9	67.0	9.3	1.2	4.6	3.4	13.5	5.2	1.2	3.9	8.3	90.5	7.0	5.3
1940	100.0	71.0	13.1	1.8	5.4	3.6	14.2	6.1	2.2	3.9	8.1	97.8	10.0	8.1
1941	125.0	80.8	17.9	1.5	6.1	4.7	24.9	16.9	13.7	3.2	8.0	120.6	25.0	23.2
1942	158.5	88.6	9.9	.2	5.0	4.8	59.8	52.0	49.4	2.6	7.8	156.7	26.7	30.0
1943	192.1	99.4	5.8	−1.9	4.6	6.5	88.9	81.3	79.7	1.6	7.5	192.8	21.3	23.0
1944	210.6	108.2	7.2	−1.7	5.5	7.2	97.0	89.4	87.4	2.0	7.6	211.6	9.6	9.8
1945	212.4	119.5	10.6	−.5	7.4	7.9	82.8	74.6	73.5	1.1	8.2	213.5	.9	.9
1946	209.8	143.8	30.7	7.8	15.1	7.3	27.5	17.6	14.8	2.8	9.9	203.5	−1.2	−4.7
1947	233.1	161.7	34.0	11.9	20.2	8.3	25.5	12.7	9.0	3.7	12.8	233.5	11.1	14.8
1948	259.5	174.7	45.9	6.9	17.5	10.5	32.0	16.7	10.7	6.0	15.3	254.8	11.3	9.1
1949	258.3	178.1	35.3	6.5	16.3	9.8	38.4	20.4	13.2	7.2	18.0	261.4	−.5	2.6
1950	286.5	192.0	53.8	2.2	14.4	12.2	38.5	18.7	14.0	4.7	19.8	279.7	10.9	7.0
1951	330.8	207.1	59.2	4.4	19.7	15.3	60.1	38.3	33.5	4.8	21.8	320.5	15.5	14.6
1952	348.0	217.1	52.1	3.2	19.1	15.9	75.6	52.4	45.8	6.5	23.2	344.8	5.2	7.6
1953	366.8	229.7	53.3	1.3	18.0	16.7	82.5	57.5	48.6	8.9	25.0	366.3	5.4	6.2
1954	366.8	235.8	52.7	2.5	18.7	16.2	75.8	47.9	41.1	6.8	27.8	368.4	.0	.6
1955	400.0	253.7	68.4	3.0	21.0	18.0	75.0	44.5	38.4	6.0	30.6	394.1	9.0	7.0
1956	421.7	266.0	71.0	5.3	25.0	19.8	79.4	45.9	40.2	5.7	33.5	417.0	5.4	5.8
1957	444.0	280.4	69.2	7.3	28.1	20.8	87.1	50.0	44.0	5.9	37.1	442.6	5.3	6.1
1958	449.7	289.5	61.9	3.3	24.2	21.0	95.0	53.9	45.6	8.3	41.1	451.2	1.3	1.9
1959	487.9	310.8	78.1	1.4	24.8	23.4	97.6	53.9	45.6	8.3	43.7	482.2	8.5	6.9
1960	506.5	324.9	75.9	5.5	28.9	23.4	100.3	53.7	44.5	9.3	46.5	503.6	3.8	4.4
1961	524.6	335.0	74.8	6.6	29.9	23.3	108.2	57.4	47.0	10.4	50.8	522.2	3.6	3.7
1962	565.0	355.2	85.4	6.4	31.8	25.4	118.0	63.7	51.1	12.7	54.3	558.8	7.7	7.0
1963	596.7	374.6	90.9	7.6	34.2	26.6	123.7	64.6	50.3	14.3	59.0	590.7	5.6	5.7
1964	637.7	400.5	97.4	10.1	38.8	28.8	129.8	65.2	49.0	16.2	64.6	632.1	6.9	7.0
1965	691.1	430.4	113.5	8.8	41.1	32.3	138.4	67.3	49.4	17.8	71.1	681.2	8.4	7.8
1966	756.0	465.1	125.7	6.5	44.6	38.1	158.7	78.8	60.3	18.5	79.8	741.9	9.4	8.9
1967	799.6	490.3	122.8	6.3	47.3	41.0	180.2	90.9	71.5	19.5	89.3	789.3	5.8	6.4
1968	873.4	536.9	133.3	4.3	52.4	48.1	199.0	98.0	76.9	21.2	101.0	865.5	9.2	9.7
1969	944.0	581.8	149.3	4.2	57.5	53.3	208.8	97.6	76.3	21.2	111.2	934.2	8.1	7.9
1970	992.7	621.7	144.2	6.7	65.7	59.0	220.1	95.7	73.6	22.2	124.4	989.5	5.2	5.9
1971	1,077.6	672.2	166.4	4.1	68.8	64.7	234.9	96.2	70.2	26.0	138.7	1,070.0	8.6	8.1
1972	1,185.9	737.1	195.0	.7	77.5	76.7	253.1	101.7	73.1	28.5	151.4	1,175.7	10.1	9.9
1973	1,326.4	812.0	229.8	14.2	109.6	95.4	270.4	102.0	72.8	29.1	168.5	1,307.9	11.8	11.2
1974	1,434.2	888.1	228.7	13.4	146.2	132.8	304.1	111.0	77.0	33.9	193.1	1,420.1	8.1	8.6
1975	1,549.2	976.4	206.1	26.8	154.9	128.1	339.9	122.7	83.0	39.7	217.2	1,556.1	8.0	9.6
1976	1,718.0	1,084.3	257.9	13.8	170.9	157.1	362.1	129.2	86.0	43.2	232.9	1,706.2	10.9	9.6
1977	1,918.3	1,204.4	324.1	−4.0	182.7	186.7	393.8	143.4	92.8	50.6	250.4	1,895.3	11.7	11.1
1978	2,163.9	1,346.5	386.6	−1.1	218.7	219.8	431.9	153.6	100.3	53.3	278.3	2,137.4	12.8	12.8
1979	2,417.8	1,507.2	423.0	13.2	281.4	268.1	474.4	168.3	111.8	56.5	306.0	2,403.5	11.7	12.4
1980	2,633.1	1,667.2	402.3	25.2	339.2	314.0	538.4	197.2	131.4	65.8	341.2	2,643.1	8.9	10.0
1981	2,937.7	1,843.2	471.5	26.1	367.3	341.3	596.9	228.9	153.7	75.2	368.0	2,917.3	11.6	10.4
1982^p	3,057.5	1,972.0	421.9	16.5	349.7	333.2	647.1	257.3	178.5	78.8	389.8	3,078.9	4.1	5.5
1980:														
I	2,575.9	1,618.7	424.0	14.0	335.7	321.7	519.2	189.6	126.8	62.8	329.6	2,576.6	12.2	11.8
II	2,573.4	1,622.2	391.0	24.2	337.3	313.1	536.0	198.8	130.0	68.8	337.2	2,573.9	.1	.1
III	2,643.7	1,682.0	384.1	39.0	337.2	298.2	538.5	193.3	130.5	62.8	345.2	2,664.8	11.4	14.9
IV	2,739.4	1,745.8	410.3	23.5	346.7	323.2	559.8	207.0	138.1	68.9	352.8	2,757.1	15.3	14.6
1981:														
I	2,864.9	1,799.9	455.7	31.2	365.4	334.2	578.1	217.0	143.1	73.9	361.1	2,852.7	19.6	14.6
II	2,901.8	1,819.4	475.5	23.7	368.9	345.1	583.2	218.2	150.5	67.7	365.0	2,877.2	5.3	3.5
III	2,980.9	1,868.8	486.0	25.9	367.2	341.3	600.2	230.0	154.4	75.7	370.1	2,949.1	11.4	10.4
IV	3,003.2	1,884.5	468.9	23.5	367.9	344.4	626.3	250.5	166.9	83.6	375.7	2,989.9	3.0	5.7
1982:														
I	2,995.5	1,919.4	414.8	31.3	359.9	328.6	630.1	249.7	166.2	83.5	380.4	3,031.1	−1.0	5.6
II	3,045.2	1,947.8	431.5	34.9	365.8	330.9	630.9	244.3	176.2	68.2	386.6	3,061.4	6.8	4.1
III	3,088.2	1,986.3	443.3	6.9	349.5	342.5	651.7	259.0	182.7	76.3	392.7	3,083.5	5.8	2.9
IV^p	3,101.3	2,034.6	397.9	−6.9	323.7	330.6	675.7	276.1	188.9	87.2	399.6	3,139.8	1.7	7.5

[1] Changes are based on unrounded data and therefore may differ slightly from changes computed from data shown here.

Source: Department of Commerce, Bureau of Economic Analysis.

Table B-2.—*Gross national product in 1972 dollars, 1929–82*

[Billions of 1972 dollars, except as noted; quarterly data at seasonally adjusted annual rates]

Year or quarter	Gross national product	Personal consumption expenditures: Total	Personal consumption expenditures: Durable goods	Personal consumption expenditures: Nondurable goods	Personal consumption expenditures: Services	Gross private domestic investment: Total	Fixed investment: Total	Nonresidential: Total	Nonresidential: Structures	Nonresidential: Producers' durable equipment	Residential: Total	Residential: Nonfarm structures	Residential: Farm structures	Residential: Producers' durable equipment	Change in business inventories
1929	315.7	215.1	20.9	98.1	96.1	55.8	51.2	37.5	21.1	16.4	13.7	13.0	0.6	0.1	4.6
1933	222.1	170.5	10.7	82.9	76.9	8.4	13.2	10.4	5.0	5.5	2.8	2.5	.2	.1	−4.9
1939	319.8	219.8	18.6	115.1	86.1	33.6	32.0	20.9	8.7	12.1	11.1	10.4	.6	.1	1.6
1940	344.1	229.9	21.2	119.9	88.8	44.5	38.3	25.8	10.0	15.8	12.5	11.6	.8	.1	6.2
1941	400.4	243.6	24.2	127.6	91.8	55.8	43.8	30.4	12.0	18.5	13.3	12.3	.9	.2	12.0
1942	461.7	241.1	15.7	129.9	95.5	29.5	24.3	17.6	6.8	10.9	6.7	6.0	.6	.1	5.2
1943	531.6	248.2	14.0	134.0	100.2	18.1	18.0	14.0	4.2	9.8	4.0	3.5	.4	.0	.1
1944	569.1	255.2	13.0	139.4	102.8	19.7	22.0	18.7	5.5	13.2	3.4	3.0	.4	.0	−2.3
1945	560.4	270.9	14.4	150.3	106.3	27.7	31.4	27.6	8.3	19.2	3.8	3.4	.3	.1	−3.6
1946	478.3	301.0	25.4	158.9	116.7	70.9	58.7	42.1	18.9	23.2	16.6	15.3	1.1	.2	12.2
1947	470.3	305.8	30.1	154.8	120.9	70.0	70.2	48.9	17.4	31.5	21.3	19.7	1.3	.3	−.2
1948	489.8	312.2	32.5	155.0	124.7	82.1	76.6	51.1	18.4	32.6	25.6	23.8	1.5	.3	5.5
1949	492.2	319.3	35.5	157.4	126.5	65.4	69.8	46.0	17.9	28.1	23.8	22.1	1.4	.3	−4.4
1950	534.8	337.3	42.6	161.8	132.9	93.5	83.0	50.0	19.2	30.8	33.0	31.3	1.3	.3	10.6
1951	579.4	341.6	39.1	165.3	137.2	93.9	80.2	52.9	20.7	32.2	27.3	25.7	1.3	.3	13.7
1952	600.8	350.1	38.0	171.2	140.9	83.0	78.7	52.1	20.6	31.5	26.6	25.1	1.2	.3	4.3
1953	623.6	363.4	42.1	175.7	145.6	85.3	83.8	56.3	22.6	33.7	27.5	26.1	1.2	.3	1.5
1954	616.1	370.0	42.5	177.0	150.5	83.1	85.3	55.4	23.6	31.8	29.9	28.5	1.1	.3	−2.2
1955	657.5	394.1	51.1	185.4	157.6	103.8	96.1	61.3	25.4	35.9	34.8	33.5	.9	.4	7.7
1956	671.6	405.4	48.8	191.6	165.0	102.6	96.8	65.4	28.3	37.0	31.5	30.0	1.0	.4	5.8
1957	683.8	413.8	48.6	194.9	170.3	97.0	95.5	66.2	28.4	37.8	29.2	27.8	1.0	.4	1.5
1958	680.9	418.0	45.3	196.8	175.9	87.5	89.3	59.3	26.8	32.5	30.0	28.6	.9	.5	−1.8
1959	721.7	440.4	50.7	205.0	184.8	108.0	100.9	63.6	27.4	36.2	37.4	35.9	1.0	.6	7.0
1960	737.2	452.0	51.4	208.2	192.4	104.7	101.2	66.9	29.5	37.4	34.2	32.9	.8	.5	3.5
1961	756.6	461.4	49.3	211.9	200.2	103.9	100.9	66.7	30.2	36.5	34.3	32.8	1.0	.5	3.0
1962	800.3	482.0	54.7	218.5	208.8	117.6	109.7	72.0	31.6	40.4	37.7	36.3	.9	.6	7.8
1963	832.5	500.5	59.7	223.0	217.8	125.1	117.5	75.1	31.9	43.1	42.5	40.9	.9	.6	7.5
1964	876.4	528.0	64.8	233.3	229.8	133.0	125.9	82.7	34.4	48.3	43.1	41.5	.9	.7	7.1
1965	929.3	557.5	72.6	244.0	240.9	151.9	140.1	97.4	40.6	56.8	42.7	41.2	.8	.7	11.8
1966	984.8	585.7	78.4	255.5	251.8	163.0	146.2	108.0	43.4	64.5	38.2	36.6	.9	.8	16.8
1967	1,011.4	602.7	79.5	259.5	263.7	154.9	142.7	105.6	42.0	63.6	37.1	35.4	.9	.8	12.2
1968	1,058.1	634.4	88.3	270.5	275.6	161.6	152.6	109.5	42.8	66.8	43.1	41.3	.8	.9	9.0
1969	1,087.6	657.9	91.8	277.3	288.8	171.4	160.4	116.8	45.0	71.8	43.6	41.7	.9	1.1	11.1
1970	1,085.6	672.1	89.1	283.7	299.3	158.5	154.8	113.8	43.9	69.9	41.0	39.2	.6	1.1	3.8
1971	1,122.4	696.8	98.2	288.7	309.9	173.9	165.8	112.2	42.8	69.3	53.7	51.6	.7	1.3	8.1
1972	1,185.9	737.1	111.1	300.6	325.3	195.0	184.8	121.0	44.1	76.9	63.8	61.5	.7	1.5	10.2
1973	1,254.3	767.9	121.3	307.4	339.2	217.5	200.4	138.1	47.4	90.7	62.3	59.9	.6	1.7	17.2
1974	1,246.3	762.8	112.3	302.5	348.0	195.5	183.9	135.7	43.6	92.1	48.2	45.3	1.1	1.7	11.6
1975	1,231.6	779.4	112.7	307.5	359.3	154.8	161.5	119.3	38.3	81.1	42.2	39.8	.8	1.6	−6.7
1976	1,298.2	823.1	126.6	321.9	374.7	184.5	176.7	125.6	39.5	86.1	51.2	48.7	.8	1.7	7.8
1977	1,369.7	864.3	138.0	333.4	393.0	214.2	200.9	140.3	40.4	99.9	60.7	57.9	1.0	1.8	13.3
1978	1,438.6	903.2	146.8	344.4	412.0	236.7	220.7	158.3	44.6	113.7	62.4	59.5	1.0	1.9	16.0
1979	1,479.4	927.6	147.2	353.1	427.3	236.3	229.1	169.9	49.1	120.8	59.1	56.3	.8	2.0	7.3
1980	1,474.0	930.5	137.1	355.8	437.6	208.4	213.3	166.1	48.5	117.6	47.2	44.3	.8	2.0	−5.0
1981	1,502.6	947.6	140.0	362.4	445.2	225.8	216.9	172.0	51.6	120.4	44.9	42.1	.9	2.0	9.0
1982 p	1,475.5	957.1	138.7	365.2	453.2	196.9	205.4	165.4	53.2	112.2	40.0	37.1	1.0	1.9	−8.5
1980:															
I	1,494.9	937.0	145.4	357.8	433.9	222.7	225.3	171.9	51.1	120.8	53.4	49.9	1.4	2.1	−2.6
II	1,457.8	915.8	128.9	352.7	434.3	201.9	204.4	162.4	48.5	113.9	42.0	39.4	.6	2.0	−2.5
III	1,463.8	928.0	134.6	353.7	439.7	199.2	207.8	163.8	47.1	116.7	44.0	41.5	.5	2.0	−8.5
IV	1,479.4	941.0	139.5	359.0	442.5	209.6	215.9	166.4	47.5	118.9	49.5	46.6	.9	2.0	−6.2
1981:															
I	1,507.8	951.1	145.3	361.6	444.2	221.6	219.2	169.7	49.5	120.1	49.6	47.0	.6	2.0	2.4
II	1,502.2	944.6	138.6	361.7	444.3	229.5	217.4	170.1	51.0	119.1	47.3	44.6	.7	2.0	12.1
III	1,510.4	951.4	142.2	363.0	446.2	233.4	216.9	173.9	52.5	121.4	42.9	39.9	1.0	2.0	16.5
IV	1,490.1	943.4	134.1	363.1	446.2	218.9	214.1	174.2	53.3	120.9	39.9	36.7	1.2	2.0	4.8
1982:															
I	1,470.7	949.1	137.5	362.2	449.5	195.4	210.8	172.0	53.5	118.5	38.9	36.0	1.0	1.9	−15.4
II	1,478.4	955.0	138.3	364.5	452.2	202.3	206.7	166.7	53.7	113.0	40.1	37.0	1.1	1.9	−4.4
III	1,481.1	956.3	136.4	365.9	454.0	206.3	202.9	163.4	53.0	110.4	39.5	36.6	1.0	1.9	3.4
IV p	1,471.7	968.0	142.8	368.2	457.0	183.6	201.3	159.6	52.7	106.9	41.7	38.8	1.0	1.9	−17.7

See next page for continuation of table.

Table B-2.—*Gross national product in 1972 dollars, 1929–82*—Continued

[Billions of 1972 dollars, except as noted; quarterly data at seasonally adjusted annual rates]

Year or quarter	Net exports of goods and services			Government purchases of goods and services					Final sales	Percent change from preceding period [1]	
	Net exports	Exports	Imports	Total	Federal			State and local		Gross national product	Final sales
					Total	National defense	Nondefense				
1929	3.7	16.7	12.9	41.0	7.0	....	....	33.9	311.0	6.6	....
1933	.4	9.1	8.6	42.9	10.9	....	....	32.0	227.0	−2.2	−3.1
1939	3.4	14.3	10.9	63.0	22.8	....	....	40.3	318.2	7.8	6.3
1940	4.4	15.5	11.1	65.3	26.7	....	....	38.6	337.9	7.6	6.2
1941	3.2	16.4	13.2	97.8	61.0	....	....	36.8	388.4	16.3	14.9
1942	−.6	11.4	12.0	191.6	157.4	....	....	34.3	456.5	15.3	17.5
1943	−5.9	9.8	15.7	271.3	239.6	....	....	31.7	531.5	15.1	16.4
1944	−6.2	10.5	16.8	300.4	269.7	....	....	30.7	571.4	7.1	7.5
1945	−3.7	13.8	17.5	265.4	233.7	....	....	31.7	564.0	−1.5	−1.3
1946	13.2	27.3	14.0	93.1	58.2	....	....	34.9	466.1	−14.7	−17.4
1947	18.9	32.2	13.3	75.7	36.3	....	....	39.4	470.6	−1.7	1.0
1948	10.8	26.3	15.5	84.7	42.8	....	....	41.9	484.3	4.1	2.9
1949	10.7	25.8	15.2	96.8	49.2	....	....	47.5	496.6	.5	2.5
1950	5.9	23.6	17.7	98.1	47.3	....	....	50.8	524.2	8.7	5.6
1951	10.1	28.6	18.5	133.7	82.2	....	....	51.5	565.6	8.3	7.9
1952	7.9	27.9	20.0	159.8	107.2	....	....	52.7	596.5	3.7	5.5
1953	4.8	26.6	21.8	170.1	114.7	....	....	55.3	622.1	3.8	4.3
1954	6.9	27.8	20.9	156.0	96.1	....	....	59.9	618.2	−1.2	−.6
1955	7.3	30.7	23.4	152.3	88.2	....	....	64.1	649.8	6.7	5.1
1956	10.1	35.3	25.2	153.5	86.8	....	....	66.7	665.8	2.1	2.5
1957	11.8	38.0	26.1	161.2	90.6	....	....	70.6	682.2	1.8	2.5
1958	5.6	33.2	27.6	169.8	93.4	....	....	76.4	682.7	−.4	.1
1959	2.7	33.8	31.1	170.6	91.4	....	....	79.2	714.7	6.0	4.7
1960	7.7	38.4	30.7	172.8	90.4	....	....	82.4	733.7	2.2	2.7
1961	8.5	39.3	30.9	182.9	95.3	....	....	87.5	753.7	2.6	2.7
1962	7.5	41.8	34.3	193.2	102.8	....	....	90.4	792.4	5.8	5.1
1963	9.4	44.8	35.4	197.6	101.8	....	....	95.8	825.0	4.0	4.1
1964	12.8	50.3	37.5	202.6	100.2	....	....	102.4	869.3	5.3	5.4
1965	10.1	51.7	41.6	209.8	100.3	....	....	109.5	917.5	6.0	5.5
1966	6.5	54.4	47.9	229.7	112.6	....	....	117.1	968.0	6.0	5.5
1967	5.4	56.7	51.3	248.5	125.1	....	....	123.4	999.2	2.7	3.2
1968	1.9	61.2	59.3	260.2	128.1	....	....	132.1	1,049.1	4.6	5.0
1969	.9	65.0	64.1	257.4	121.8	....	....	135.6	1,076.6	2.8	2.6
1970	3.9	70.5	66.6	251.1	110.6	....	....	140.5	1,081.8	−.2	.5
1971	1.6	71.0	69.3	250.1	103.7	....	....	146.4	1,114.3	3.4	3.0
1972	.7	77.5	76.7	253.1	101.7	73.1	28.5	151.4	1,175.7	5.7	5.5
1973	15.5	97.3	81.8	253.3	95.9	68.3	27.6	157.4	1,237.1	5.8	5.2
1974	27.8	108.5	80.7	260.3	96.6	66.9	29.7	163.6	1,234.7	−.6	−.2
1975	32.2	103.5	71.4	265.2	97.4	66.4	31.0	167.8	1,238.4	−1.2	.3
1976	25.4	110.1	84.7	265.2	96.8	64.9	31.8	168.4	1,290.4	5.4	4.2
1977	22.0	112.9	90.9	269.2	100.4	65.4	35.0	168.8	1,356.4	5.5	5.1
1978	24.0	126.7	102.7	274.6	100.3	65.7	34.7	174.3	1,422.6	5.0	4.9
1979	37.2	146.2	109.0	278.3	102.1	67.4	34.8	176.2	1,472.2	2.8	3.5
1980	50.6	159.2	108.6	284.6	106.5	70.1	36.4	178.1	1,479.0	−.4	.5
1981	42.0	158.5	116.4	287.1	110.4	73.5	36.8	176.7	1,493.7	1.9	1.0
1982 p	30.3	147.5	117.2	291.2	116.1	78.7	37.4	175.0	1,484.0	−1.8	−.6
1980:											
I	50.5	164.4	113.9	284.7	106.4	70.3	36.1	178.3	1,497.5	1.5	1.6
II	53.2	161.2	108.0	286.9	109.1	70.4	38.7	177.8	1,460.3	−9.6	−9.6
III	53.1	155.9	102.8	283.4	105.5	70.0	35.5	177.9	1,472.3	1.6	3.3
IV	45.6	155.1	109.6	283.2	104.8	69.6	35.2	178.4	1,485.7	4.3	3.7
1981:											
I	48.2	159.3	111.1	286.8	107.9	71.0	36.9	179.0	1,505.4	7.9	5.4
II	44.2	159.7	115.5	283.9	107.0	72.9	34.1	176.9	1,490.1	−1.5	−4.0
III	39.2	157.8	118.7	286.4	110.7	74.3	36.5	175.7	1,493.9	2.2	1.0
IV	36.5	156.9	120.4	291.3	116.0	76.1	39.9	175.3	1,485.3	−5.3	−2.3
1982:											
I	36.9	151.7	114.7	289.2	114.4	74.5	39.8	174.9	1,486.1	−5.1	.2
II	35.7	154.4	118.7	285.3	110.3	78.2	32.1	175.0	1,482.7	2.1	−.9
III	27.5	147.5	120.0	291.1	116.2	80.6	35.5	174.9	1,477.8	.7	−1.3
IV p	21.1	136.4	115.3	299.0	123.7	81.3	42.4	175.4	1,489.3	−2.5	3.2

[1] Changes are based on unrounded data and therefore may differ slightly from changes computed from data shown here.

Source: Department of Commerce, Bureau of Economic Analysis.

TABLE B-3.—*Implicit price deflators for gross national product, 1929–82*

[Index numbers, 1972=100, except as noted; quarterly data seasonally adjusted]

Year or quarter	Gross national product[1]	Personal consumption expenditures				Gross private domestic investment[1]							
						Fixed investment							
							Nonresidential			Residential			
		Total	Durable goods	Non-durable goods	Services	Total	Total	Structures	Producers' durable equipment	Total	Nonfarm structures	Farm structures	Producers' durable equipment
1929	32.76	35.9	44.2	38.4	31.6	28.3	28.3	24.3	33.4	28.2	27.8	28.6	77.2
1933	25.13	26.9	32.5	26.8	26.1	22.4	22.9	19.2	26.2	20.7	19.8	19.5	58.8
1939	28.43	30.5	35.9	30.5	29.2	27.7	28.2	23.0	32.0	26.6	26.3	23.4	61.1
1940	29.06	30.9	36.7	30.9	29.5	28.5	29.1	23.4	32.8	27.4	27.2	23.6	59.6
1941	31.23	33.2	40.0	33.6	30.8	30.7	31.0	24.9	34.9	30.0	29.7	26.6	63.8
1942	34.32	36.7	43.7	39.1	32.4	33.5	33.9	28.4	37.3	32.4	31.8	30.7	71.3
1943	36.14	40.1	46.7	43.7	34.2	35.7	35.9	32.4	37.3	34.9	34.3	35.7	71.4
1944	37.01	42.4	51.3	46.2	36.1	37.0	36.8	33.8	38.0	38.1	37.3	40.8	75.0
1945	37.91	44.1	55.5	47.8	37.3	37.2	36.7	33.9	37.9	40.8	40.0	42.9	84.6
1946	43.88	47.8	62.1	52.1	38.8	41.3	40.0	36.6	42.8	44.6	43.9	46.6	95.2
1947	49.55	52.9	67.8	58.7	41.7	49.0	46.9	44.0	48.6	53.7	53.0	52.8	105.6
1948	52.98	56.0	70.3	62.3	44.4	53.7	51.5	48.8	53.0	58.1	57.5	57.3	111.5
1949	52.49	55.8	70.5	60.3	46.0	54.9	53.0	48.4	56.0	58.7	58.1	58.0	107.9
1950	53.56	56.9	72.2	60.7	47.4	56.7	54.5	49.3	57.8	60.0	59.5	59.4	107.4
1951	57.09	60.6	76.3	65.8	49.9	60.9	59.1	55.1	61.7	64.4	63.8	63.8	114.9
1952	57.92	62.0	76.7	66.5	52.6	62.3	60.1	56.3	62.6	66.4	65.8	65.7	114.6
1953	58.82	63.2	77.2	66.3	55.4	63.1	61.2	57.4	63.8	66.9	66.3	66.2	114.2
1954	59.55	63.7	75.0	66.6	57.2	63.6	61.7	56.5	65.5	67.1	66.6	66.5	112.4
1955	60.84	64.4	75.6	66.3	58.4	65.0	62.9	57.6	66.6	68.7	68.2	68.3	109.1
1956	62.79	65.6	77.7	67.3	60.1	68.5	67.3	62.4	71.1	71.0	70.5	70.6	104.3
1957	64.93	67.8	80.9	69.4	62.2	71.1	71.0	64.9	75.5	71.4	70.9	70.9	103.4
1958	66.04	69.2	81.3	71.0	64.1	71.0	70.9	63.9	76.6	71.2	70.7	70.8	101.9
1959	67.60	70.6	83.8	71.4	66.0	71.8	72.2	64.2	78.3	71.1	70.6	70.7	101.8
1960	68.70	71.9	83.8	72.6	67.9	72.1	72.5	63.7	79.4	71.4	70.9	71.1	100.8
1961	69.33	72.6	84.3	73.3	69.0	71.8	72.0	63.3	79.3	71.3	70.9	70.7	99.0
1962	70.61	73.7	85.4	73.9	70.4	72.2	72.5	63.6	79.4	71.5	71.1	71.2	96.8
1963	71.67	74.8	86.2	74.9	71.7	72.3	73.1	64.1	79.7	70.9	70.5	70.6	95.3
1964	72.77	75.9	87.1	75.8	72.7	72.9	73.8	64.9	80.1	71.2	70.8	70.9	94.3
1965	74.36	77.2	86.8	77.3	74.2	74.0	74.7	66.4	80.6	72.3	72.0	72.2	92.1
1966	76.76	79.4	86.7	80.1	76.4	76.3	76.9	69.2	82.1	74.6	74.3	74.2	90.8
1967	79.06	81.4	88.2	81.9	78.7	78.8	79.5	72.2	84.3	77.0	76.7	76.7	91.0
1968	82.54	84.6	91.1	85.3	81.9	82.2	82.8	75.8	87.2	80.7	80.5	80.6	93.5
1969	86.79	88.4	93.3	89.4	86.0	87.0	86.7	81.5	89.9	87.7	87.5	87.5	95.7
1970	91.45	92.5	95.7	93.6	90.5	91.1	91.3	88.2	93.2	90.5	90.3	90.6	97.8
1971	96.01	96.5	99.0	96.6	95.6	95.7	96.2	94.5	97.2	94.8	94.7	95.0	99.3
1972	100.00	100.0	100.0	100.0	100.0	100.0	100.0	100.0	100.0	100.0	100.0	100.0	100.0
1973	105.75	105.7	101.7	108.5	104.7	105.5	103.8	107.7	101.8	109.1	109.4	109.2	100.6
1974	115.08	116.4	108.2	123.4	113.0	116.7	115.4	128.2	109.3	120.3	120.8	120.5	106.8
1975	125.79	125.3	117.3	132.5	121.6	131.9	132.2	144.8	126.2	131.0	131.6	131.9	116.9
1976	132.34	131.7	123.9	137.2	129.6	139.2	138.6	149.0	133.9	140.7	141.3	140.7	122.7
1977	140.05	139.3	129.2	143.6	139.3	149.8	146.3	159.4	141.0	158.0	159.0	157.0	126.7
1978	150.42	149.1	136.4	153.4	150.0	163.2	157.2	176.4	149.7	178.3	179.8	180.0	132.6
1979	163.42	162.5	145.0	169.9	162.3	178.5	170.8	200.2	158.8	200.5	202.7	202.7	140.3
1980	178.64	179.2	156.3	188.4	178.8	193.3	186.1	227.7	169.0	218.5	221.7	218.8	149.2
1981	195.51	194.5	167.5	202.7	196.3	208.0	201.3	251.5	179.8	233.6	237.1	236.9	159.4
1982 p	207.23	206.0	174.9	208.9	213.3	215.8	210.1	266.4	183.4	239.3	242.8	242.6	168.3
1980:													
I	172.31	172.8	151.9	181.9	172.2	188.5	181.0	216.9	165.8	212.5	215.2	214.7	145.2
II	176.52	177.1	154.4	186.2	176.5	191.5	184.9	224.9	167.9	217.2	220.6	219.1	148.0
III	180.60	181.2	158.0	190.5	180.9	195.1	187.9	232.7	169.9	221.8	225.2	221.2	150.8
IV	185.16	185.5	161.1	195.1	185.4	198.3	190.8	237.2	172.3	223.4	226.4	224.3	153.0
1981:													
I	190.01	189.2	163.0	199.3	189.6	202.3	194.5	241.5	175.1	229.0	232.2	227.3	155.4
II	193.17	192.6	166.2	201.7	193.4	207.4	200.7	249.1	179.9	231.7	234.9	233.4	158.3
III	197.36	196.4	169.7	204.2	198.6	209.4	203.0	252.7	181.4	235.8	239.4	237.9	161.3
IV	201.55	199.8	171.3	205.6	203.6	212.9	206.8	261.9	182.5	239.2	243.3	242.7	162.8
1982:													
I	203.68	202.2	173.0	206.8	207.4	213.6	207.6	264.5	181.9	240.5	244.3	243.8	165.7
II	205.98	204.0	174.0	207.1	210.6	216.6	211.3	267.6	184.6	238.6	242.1	242.0	168.1
III	208.51	207.7	176.1	210.0	215.3	216.2	210.7	266.7	183.8	238.8	242.3	241.9	169.4
IV p	210.73	210.2	176.3	211.4	219.8	216.8	210.9	266.7	183.5	239.4	242.7	242.9	170.0

See next page for continuation of table.

TABLE B-3.—*Implicit price deflators for gross national product, 1929–82*—Continued

[Index numbers, 1972=100, except as noted; quarterly data seasonally adjusted]

Year or quarter	Exports and imports of goods and services [1]		Government purchases of goods and services					Final sales	Percent change from preceding period [2]	
	Exports	Imports	Total	Federal: Total	Federal: National defense	Federal: Non-defense	State and local		GNP implicit price deflator	Final sales implicit price deflator
1929	42.2	45.5	21.5	20.5	....	....	21.8	32.7	0.0	....
1933	26.5	23.6	19.2	19.4	....	....	19.1	25.3	−2.1	−2.6
1939	32.1	31.0	21.4	22.7	....	....	20.7	28.4	−.8	−.9
1940	34.9	32.8	21.7	22.7	....	....	20.9	29.0	2.2	1.8
1941	37.3	35.4	25.5	27.8	....	....	21.7	31.0	7.5	7.2
1942	43.6	40.0	31.2	33.0	....	....	22.8	34.3	9.9	10.6
1943	46.8	41.3	32.8	34.0	....	....	23.7	36.3	5.3	5.6
1944	51.9	42.7	32.3	33.1	....	....	24.8	37.0	2.4	2.1
1945	53.6	44.9	31.2	31.9	....	....	25.8	37.9	2.4	2.2
1946	55.4	51.8	29.6	30.2	....	....	28.5	43.7	15.7	15.3
1947	62.8	62.3	33.6	35.0	....	....	32.4	49.6	12.9	13.7
1948	66.5	67.8	37.7	39.0	....	....	36.4	52.6	6.9	6.0
1949	63.1	64.6	39.7	41.4	....	....	37.8	52.6	−.9	.1
1950	61.0	68.8	39.2	39.6	....	....	38.9	53.3	2.1	1.3
1951	68.8	82.6	45.0	46.6	....	....	42.3	56.7	6.6	6.2
1952	68.6	79.9	47.3	48.9	....	....	44.1	57.8	1.4	2.0
1953	67.5	76.7	48.5	50.1	....	....	45.2	58.9	1.6	1.9
1954	67.2	77.2	48.6	49.9	....	....	46.5	59.6	1.2	1.2
1955	68.5	77.1	49.2	50.4	....	....	47.6	60.6	2.2	1.8
1956	71.0	78.4	51.7	52.9	....	....	50.2	62.6	3.2	3.3
1957	74.0	79.6	54.0	55.1	....	....	52.6	64.9	3.4	3.6
1958	73.1	76.1	56.0	57.7	....	....	53.8	66.1	1.7	1.9
1959	73.5	75.2	57.2	59.0	....	....	55.1	67.5	2.4	2.1
1960	75.2	76.1	58.0	59.4	....	....	56.5	68.6	1.6	1.7
1961	76.1	75.5	59.1	60.2	....	....	58.0	69.3	.9	1.0
1962	76.0	74.2	61.1	62.0	....	....	60.1	70.5	1.8	1.8
1963	76.3	75.2	62.6	63.5	....	....	61.6	71.6	1.5	1.5
1964	77.2	76.8	64.1	65.1	....	....	63.1	72.7	1.5	1.5
1965	79.4	77.7	66.0	67.1	....	....	64.9	74.2	2.2	2.1
1966	81.9	79.4	69.1	70.0	....	....	68.2	76.6	3.2	3.2
1967	83.5	79.9	72.5	72.7	....	....	72.4	79.0	3.0	3.1
1968	85.5	81.1	76.5	76.5	....	....	76.4	82.5	4.4	4.4
1969	88.5	83.2	81.1	80.1	....	....	82.0	86.8	5.1	5.2
1970	93.2	88.6	87.7	86.6	....	....	88.6	91.5	5.4	5.4
1971	97.0	93.3	93.9	92.7	....	....	94.7	96.0	5.0	5.0
1972	100.0	100.0	100.0	100.0	100.0	100.0	100.0	100.0	4.2	4.1
1973	112.7	116.7	106.7	106.3	106.6	105.6	107.0	105.7	5.8	5.7
1974	134.8	164.6	116.8	114.9	115.1	114.2	118.0	115.0	8.8	8.8
1975	149.6	179.6	128.2	126.0	124.9	128.2	129.4	125.7	9.3	9.3
1976	155.3	185.6	136.6	133.5	132.4	135.7	138.3	132.2	5.2	5.2
1977	161.9	205.5	146.3	142.8	141.9	144.6	148.4	139.7	5.8	5.7
1978	172.6	214.1	157.3	153.1	152.7	153.8	159.7	150.3	7.4	7.5
1979	192.5	246.1	170.4	164.8	166.0	162.5	173.7	163.3	8.6	8.7
1980	213.1	289.3	189.2	185.2	187.4	181.0	191.6	178.7	9.3	9.5
1981	231.8	293.1	207.9	207.4	209.0	204.2	208.2	195.3	9.4	9.3
1982 *p*	237.1	284.3	222.3	221.6	226.9	210.4	222.7	207.5	6.0	6.2
1980:										
I	204.2	282.5	182.4	178.2	180.3	174.1	184.8	172.1	10.5	10.1
II	209.2	289.8	186.8	182.2	184.6	177.9	189.6	176.3	10.1	10.1
III	216.3	290.1	190.0	183.3	186.5	176.8	194.0	181.0	9.6	11.2
IV	223.5	294.9	197.7	197.5	198.4	195.7	197.8	185.6	10.5	10.5
1981:										
I	229.3	300.7	201.5	201.2	201.7	200.3	201.7	189.5	10.9	8.7
II	230.9	298.7	205.5	204.0	206.4	198.9	206.3	193.1	6.8	7.8
III	232.6	287.7	209.5	207.8	207.9	207.4	210.7	197.4	9.0	9.3
IV	234.5	286.1	215.0	216.0	219.5	209.4	214.3	201.3	8.8	8.1
1982:										
I	237.3	286.4	217.8	218.3	223.0	209.6	217.5	204.0	4.3	5.4
II	236.8	278.8	221.1	221.6	225.2	212.6	220.9	206.5	4.6	5.0
III	236.9	285.4	223.9	223.0	226.5	214.9	224.5	208.7	5.0	4.3
IV *p*	237.4	286.7	226.0	223.3	232.4	205.9	227.9	210.8	4.3	4.2

[1] Separate deflators are not calculated for gross private domestic investment, change in business inventories, and net exports of goods and services.

[2] Changes are based on unrounded data and therefore may differ slightly from changes computed from data shown here. Quarterly changes are at annual rates.

Source: Department of Commerce, Bureau of Economic Analysis.

TABLE B–4.—*Fixed-weighted price indexes for gross national product, 1972 weights, 1959–82*

[Index numbers, 1972=100, except as noted; quarterly data seasonally adjusted]

Year or quarter	Gross national product	Personal consumption expenditures	Gross private domestic investment[1]: Fixed investment: Total	Gross private domestic investment[1]: Fixed investment: Nonresidential	Gross private domestic investment[1]: Fixed investment: Residential	Exports and imports of goods and services[1]: Exports	Exports and imports of goods and services[1]: Imports	Government purchases of goods and services: Total	Government purchases of goods and services: Federal: Total	Government purchases of goods and services: Federal: National defense	Government purchases of goods and services: Federal: Nondefense	Government purchases of goods and services: State and local	Percent change from preceding period, gross national product fixed-weighted price index[2]
1959	69.8	73.1	74.4	74.1	74.9	73.4	75.0	56.9	58.5	....	....	55.8	....
1960	70.8	74.1	74.7	74.5	74.9	75.0	76.0	58.3	59.6	....	....	57.4	1.5
1961	71.6	74.8	74.4	74.3	74.7	76.0	75.2	59.5	60.5	....	....	58.9	1.1
1962	72.4	75.5	74.2	74.4	73.9	76.0	73.7	61.3	61.7	....	....	61.0	1.2
1963	73.2	76.3	74.0	74.7	72.6	76.3	74.7	62.8	63.3	....	....	62.5	1.1
1964	74.1	77.2	74.3	75.3	72.6	77.1	76.3	64.4	65.3	....	....	63.9	1.2
1965	75.3	78.2	75.2	76.1	73.5	79.4	77.1	66.2	67.1	....	....	65.6	1.7
1966	77.5	80.1	77.0	77.9	75.3	81.8	78.8	69.2	69.6	....	....	68.8	2.9
1967	79.8	82.0	79.3	80.3	77.5	83.3	79.3	72.4	71.5	....	....	73.1	3.0
1968	83.1	85.0	82.5	83.3	81.0	85.5	80.7	76.4	75.7	....	....	76.9	4.1
1969	87.3	88.7	87.3	87.0	87.8	88.5	83.0	81.3	79.8	....	....	82.3	5.0
1970	91.8	92.7	91.2	91.6	90.6	93.1	88.4	87.9	86.7	....	....	88.7	5.2
1971	96.2	96.6	95.8	96.3	94.9	97.0	93.3	94.0	92.9	....	....	94.8	4.8
1972	100.0	100.0	100.0	100.0	100.0	100.0	100.0	100.0	100.0	100.0	100.0	100.0	4.0
1973	106.0	106.1	105.8	104.0	109.2	112.6	116.7	106.9	106.7	106.9	106.1	107.0	6.0
1974	115.9	117.1	117.9	116.5	120.5	137.4	161.5	117.9	117.0	117.5	115.6	118.4	9.4
1975	126.4	126.3	132.3	132.9	131.2	151.8	175.1	129.2	128.0	127.9	128.3	130.0	9.1
1976	133.7	133.0	140.2	139.9	140.8	156.9	178.7	137.3	135.4	135.6	135.0	138.5	5.8
1977	142.2	141.2	151.8	148.5	158.0	164.0	195.0	147.0	145.0	145.5	143.6	148.4	6.3
1978	153.3	151.6	167.0	160.9	178.4	174.9	210.1	158.4	155.4	156.5	152.6	160.4	7.8
1979	167.8	166.3	185.4	177.2	200.8	197.2	244.5	173.2	169.5	171.7	164.0	175.7	9.5
1980	184.4	184.8	204.1	196.0	219.5	218.6	303.7	193.8	192.7	196.5	182.8	194.6	9.9
1981	202.0	202.1	220.9	213.5	235.0	239.3	319.0	212.2	214.7	219.7	201.7	210.6	9.6
1982 p	214.6	213.8	231.1	225.7	241.3	245.7	315.5	226.2	230.1	236.4	214.0	223.6	6.2
1980:													
I	177.8	178.2	197.1	188.7	213.2	210.4	291.0	186.6	184.9	188.2	176.4	187.7	10.5
II	182.1	182.7	202.5	194.2	218.4	214.3	300.6	191.4	189.5	193.7	178.7	192.7	10.0
III	186.3	187.0	207.5	199.2	223.0	221.2	309.8	195.1	191.9	196.1	181.4	197.2	9.4
IV	191.3	191.5	210.2	202.8	224.3	229.1	314.6	202.1	203.9	208.2	192.7	200.9	11.2
1981:													
I	195.9	196.6	215.0	207.1	229.9	235.4	322.6	206.0	208.1	211.6	199.1	204.6	10.0
II	199.9	200.2	219.0	211.7	233.0	238.4	323.4	210.3	212.2	217.4	198.8	209.0	8.4
III	204.2	203.9	223.2	215.6	237.5	241.1	316.3	213.6	214.5	219.6	201.6	212.9	8.9
IV	208.4	207.5	226.8	219.3	241.2	242.5	314.0	219.3	223.9	230.1	207.9	216.1	8.5
1982:													
I	210.8	209.9	229.2	222.0	242.7	245.6	319.1	222.4	227.1	233.4	211.0	219.2	4.8
II	213.0	211.6	230.4	225.0	240.7	246.3	313.6	224.5	228.4	234.6	212.6	221.9	4.1
III	216.0	215.4	232.0	227.4	240.7	245.2	313.6	227.2	230.1	236.3	214.2	225.2	5.9
IV p	218.8	218.4	233.0	228.7	241.1	245.5	315.3	231.0	234.9	241.4	218.2	228.3	5.2

[1] Separate deflators are not calculated for gross private domestic investment, change in business inventories, and net exports of goods and services.

[2] Quarterly changes are at annual rates.

Source: Department of Commerce, Bureau of Economic Analysis.

TABLE B-5.—*Changes in GNP and GNP price measures, 1929–82*

[Percent change from preceding period; quarterly data at seasonally adjusted annual rates]

Period	Gross national product					Personal consumption expenditures				
	Current dollars	Constant (1972) dollars	Implicit price deflator	Chain price index	Fixed-weighted price index (1972 weights)	Current dollars	Constant (1972) dollars	Implicit price deflator	Chain price index	Fixed-weighted price index (1972 weights)
1929	6.6	6.6	0.0							
1933	−4.2	−2.2	−2.1			−5.7	−2.0	−3.8		
1939	7.0	7.8	−.8			4.6	5.3	−.7		
1940	10.0	7.6	2.2			6.0	4.0	1.0		
1941	25.0	16.3	7.5			13.8	5.9	7.4		
1942	26.7	15.3	9.9			9.7	−1.0	10.8		
1943	21.3	15.1	5.3			12.2	2.9	9.0		
1944	9.6	7.1	2.4			8.8	2.8	5.8		
1945	.9	−1.5	2.4			10.5	6.2	4.1		
1946	−1.2	−14.7	15.7			20.3	11.1	8.3		
1947	11.1	−1.7	12.9			12.5	1.6	10.7		
1948	11.3	4.1	6.9			8.0	2.1	5.8		
1949	−.5	.5	−.9			1.9	2.3	−.3		
1950	10.9	8.7	2.1			7.8	5.6	2.0		
1951	15.5	8.3	6.6			7.9	1.3	6.5		
1952	5.2	3.7	1.4			4.8	2.5	2.3		
1953	5.4	3.8	1.6			5.8	3.8	1.9		
1954	.0	−1.2	1.2			2.7	1.8	.9		
1955	9.0	6.7	2.2			7.6	6.5	1.0		
1956	5.4	2.1	3.2			4.9	2.9	1.9		
1957	5.3	1.8	3.4			5.4	2.1	3.3		
1958	1.3	−.4	1.7			3.2	1.0	2.2		
1959	8.5	6.0	2.4			7.4	5.4	1.9		
1960	3.8	2.2	1.6	1.6	1.5	4.5	2.6	1.9	1.7	1.5
1961	3.6	2.6	.9	1.2	1.1	3.1	2.1	1.0	1.1	.9
1962	7.7	5.8	1.8	1.4	1.2	6.0	4.5	1.5	1.1	.9
1963	5.6	4.0	1.5	1.3	1.1	5.5	3.8	1.6	1.4	1.2
1964	6.9	5.3	1.5	1.4	1.2	6.9	5.5	1.4	1.2	1.1
1965	8.4	6.0	2.2	1.9	1.7	7.5	5.6	1.8	1.5	1.3
1966	9.4	6.0	3.2	3.1	2.9	8.1	5.1	2.9	2.7	2.4
1967	5.8	2.7	3.0	3.0	3.0	5.4	2.9	2.4	2.5	2.4
1968	9.2	4.6	4.4	4.3	4.1	9.5	5.3	4.0	3.8	3.6
1969	8.1	2.8	5.1	5.0	5.0	8.4	3.7	4.5	4.5	4.4
1970	5.2	−.2	5.4	5.3	5.2	6.9	2.2	4.6	4.6	4.5
1971	8.6	3.4	5.0	4.9	4.8	8.1	3.7	4.3	4.3	4.2
1972	10.1	5.7	4.2	4.1	4.0	9.6	5.8	3.7	3.6	3.5
1973	11.8	5.8	5.8	6.0	6.0	10.2	4.2	5.7	6.1	6.1
1974	8.1	−.6	8.8	9.1	9.4	9.4	−.7	10.1	10.4	10.4
1975	8.0	−1.2	9.3	9.2	9.1	9.9	2.2	7.6	7.7	7.8
1976	10.9	5.4	5.2	5.7	5.8	11.0	5.6	5.1	5.3	5.3
1977	11.7	5.5	5.8	6.1	6.3	11.1	5.0	5.8	6.0	6.2
1978	12.8	5.0	7.4	7.6	7.8	11.8	4.5	7.0	7.3	7.4
1979	11.7	2.8	8.6	8.9	9.5	11.9	2.7	9.0	9.3	9.7
1980	8.9	−.4	9.3	9.0	9.9	10.6	.3	10.3	10.7	11.2
1981	11.6	1.9	9.4	9.4	9.6	10.6	1.8	8.6	9.1	9.3
1982 [p]	4.1	−1.8	6.0	6.4	6.2	7.0	1.0	5.9	6.0	5.8
1980:										
I	12.2	1.5	10.5	9.0	10.5	10.7	−.7	11.5	12.6	13.4
II	−.4	−9.6	10.1	9.6	10.0	.9	−8.7	10.5	10.1	10.4
III	11.4	1.6	9.6	9.7	9.4	15.6	5.4	9.6	9.8	9.8
IV	15.3	4.3	10.5	11.0	11.2	16.1	5.7	9.8	10.0	10.1
1981:										
I	19.6	7.9	10.9	9.3	10.0	13.0	4.4	8.3	10.3	10.9
II	5.3	−1.5	6.8	8.2	8.4	4.4	−2.7	7.3	7.4	7.7
III	11.4	2.2	9.0	9.2	8.9	11.3	2.9	8.2	8.0	7.0
IV	3.0	−5.3	8.8	8.4	8.5	3.4	−3.3	7.0	7.2	7.1
1982:										
I	−1.0	−5.1	4.3	5.0	4.8	7.6	2.5	5.0	5.2	4.8
II	6.8	2.1	4.6	4.6	4.1	6.1	2.5	3.5	3.6	3.2
III	5.8	.7	5.0	6.0	5.9	8.1	.6	7.5	7.1	7.3
IV [p]	1.7	−2.5	4.3	5.2	5.2	10.1	5.0	4.9	5.6	5.7

Note.—Changes are based on unrounded data and may differ slightly from changes computed from data shown elsewhere in these tables.

Source: Department of Commerce, Bureau of Economic Analysis.

TABLE B–6.—*Gross national product by major type of product, 1929–82*

[Billions of dollars; quarterly data at seasonally adjusted annual rates]

Year or quarter	Gross national product	Final sales	Inventory change	Goods: Total: Total	Goods: Total: Final sales	Goods: Total: Inventory change	Goods: Durable goods: Final sales	Goods: Durable goods: Inventory change	Goods: Nondurable goods: Final sales	Goods: Nondurable goods: Inventory change	Services	Structures	Auto output
1929	103.4	101.7	1.7	56.1	54.4	1.7	16.1	1.4	38.3	0.3	35.9	11.4	....
1933	55.8	57.4	−1.6	27.0	28.6	−1.6	5.4	−.5	23.2	−1.1	25.9	2.9	....
1939	90.9	90.5	.4	49.0	48.6	.4	12.4	.3	36.2	.1	34.4	7.5	....
1940	100.0	97.8	2.2	56.0	53.8	2.2	15.4	1.2	38.4	1.0	35.7	8.3	....
1941	125.0	120.6	4.5	72.5	68.0	4.5	23.8	3.1	44.2	1.4	40.8	11.8	....
1942	158.5	156.7	1.8	93.7	91.9	1.8	34.5	1.0	57.4	.7	50.8	14.0	....
1943	192.1	192.8	−.6	120.4	121.0	−.6	54.2	.0	66.8	−.6	63.0	8.7	....
1944	210.6	211.6	−1.0	132.3	133.3	−1.0	58.5	−.6	74.8	−.3	72.3	6.1	....
1945	212.4	213.5	−1.0	128.9	129.9	−1.0	50.1	−1.3	79.8	.2	77.0	6.5	....
1946	209.8	203.5	6.4	125.3	118.9	6.4	31.8	5.3	87.1	1.1	68.8	15.7	....
1947	233.1	233.5	−.5	139.8	140.3	−.5	44.4	1.4	95.9	−1.9	71.6	21.7	7.2
1948	259.5	254.8	4.7	154.4	149.7	4.7	48.0	1.0	101.7	3.7	77.2	28.0	8.8
1949	258.3	261.4	−3.1	147.7	150.8	−3.1	50.0	−1.8	100.9	−1.3	82.2	28.4	11.9
1950	286.5	279.7	6.8	162.4	155.6	6.8	56.2	3.6	99.4	3.2	88.5	35.6	15.4
1951	330.8	320.5	10.3	189.5	179.2	10.3	66.4	6.1	112.8	4.2	103.5	37.8	13.3
1952	348.0	344.8	3.1	194.6	191.5	3.1	72.5	1.2	119.0	2.0	113.9	39.4	12.0
1953	366.8	366.3	.4	203.1	202.7	.4	77.8	1.5	124.9	−1.1	121.6	42.0	16.1
1954	366.8	368.4	−1.5	196.1	197.6	−1.5	73.9	−2.5	123.7	1.0	126.2	44.5	14.7
1955	400.0	394.1	6.0	214.5	208.5	6.0	81.4	3.4	127.1	2.6	136.1	49.5	21.2
1956	421.7	417.0	4.7	223.3	218.6	4.7	85.9	2.1	132.7	2.6	146.2	52.2	16.9
1957	444.0	442.6	1.3	232.3	231.0	1.3	91.3	.5	139.6	.8	158.7	53.0	19.4
1958	449.7	451.2	−1.5	228.2	229.7	−1.5	84.4	−2.8	145.3	1.3	167.7	53.8	14.4
1959	487.9	482.2	5.7	248.5	242.9	5.7	90.8	3.1	152.1	2.5	179.8	59.5	19.4
1960	506.5	503.6	3.0	254.2	251.3	3.0	93.3	1.6	158.0	1.3	193.8	58.5	21.3
1961	524.6	522.2	2.3	257.4	255.0	2.3	92.7	−.1	162.4	2.4	207.0	60.2	17.8
1962	565.0	558.8	6.3	278.5	272.2	6.3	102.9	3.4	169.3	2.8	222.0	64.5	22.5
1963	596.7	590.7	6.0	290.3	284.3	6.0	109.4	2.7	174.9	3.3	237.1	69.3	25.2
1964	637.7	632.1	5.6	309.8	304.2	5.6	118.9	4.0	185.3	1.6	255.0	72.9	25.9
1965	691.1	681.2	9.9	338.4	328.5	9.9	131.6	6.7	196.9	3.2	273.3	79.3	31.2
1966	756.0	741.9	14.1	375.0	360.9	14.1	147.0	10.2	213.9	3.9	299.0	82.0	30.4
1967	799.6	789.3	10.3	389.4	379.1	10.3	153.5	5.5	225.6	4.9	326.5	83.6	28.0
1968	873.4	865.5	7.9	421.3	413.4	7.9	167.9	4.7	245.5	3.1	358.2	94.0	35.1
1969	944.0	934.2	9.8	450.2	440.4	9.8	178.5	6.4	261.9	3.4	391.9	101.8	34.9
1970	992.7	989.5	3.2	459.9	456.6	3.2	179.2	−.1	277.5	3.3	429.9	102.9	28.7
1971	1,077.6	1,070.0	7.7	485.3	477.7	7.7	187.1	2.8	290.6	4.8	472.0	120.3	39.1
1972	1,185.9	1,175.7	10.2	529.6	519.4	10.2	207.4	7.2	312.0	3.0	519.0	137.3	41.6
1973	1,326.4	1,307.9	18.5	604.1	585.6	18.5	237.6	13.1	348.0	5.3	571.5	150.8	46.2
1974	1,434.2	1,420.1	14.1	646.7	632.5	14.1	250.7	12.0	381.8	2.2	636.1	151.4	39.2
1975	1,549.2	1,556.1	−6.9	694.0	700.9	−6.9	279.4	−8.4	421.5	1.5	705.2	150.0	40.7
1976	1,718.0	1,706.2	11.8	771.1	759.3	11.8	312.5	7.7	446.7	4.2	779.3	167.6	55.9
1977	1,918.3	1,895.3	23.0	855.0	832.0	23.0	354.9	10.4	477.2	12.6	867.2	196.1	65.1
1978	2,163.9	2,137.4	26.5	958.6	932.1	26.5	402.1	19.1	530.1	7.3	972.2	233.1	69.5
1979	2,417.8	2,403.5	14.3	1,065.6	1,051.3	14.3	454.3	10.5	597.0	3.8	1,089.7	262.5	68.0
1980	2,633.1	2,643.1	−10.0	1,141.9	1,151.9	−10.0	482.5	−5.2	669.4	−4.8	1,225.5	265.7	59.8
1981	2,937.7	2,917.3	20.5	1,289.2	1,268.7	20.5	519.4	8.7	749.4	11.7	1,364.3	284.2	69.2
1982 p	3,057.5	3,078.9	−21.4	1,280.6	1,302.0	−21.4	510.7	−15.5	791.3	−5.9	1,492.1	284.9	65.7
1980:													
I	2,575.9	2,576.6	−.7	1,125.2	1,125.8	−.7	488.1	−11.8	637.7	11.1	1,174.7	276.0	63.1
II	2,573.4	2,573.9	−.4	1,114.5	1,114.9	−.4	461.4	−.5	653.5	.0	1,207.2	251.8	51.9
III	2,643.7	2,664.8	−21.2	1,140.4	1,161.6	−21.2	481.2	−13.1	680.4	−8.1	1,243.3	259.9	56.8
IV	2,739.4	2,757.1	−17.7	1,187.4	1,205.1	−17.7	499.2	4.6	705.9	−22.3	1,277.0	275.1	67.5
1981:													
I	2,864.9	2,852.7	12.2	1,265.3	1,253.1	12.2	519.8	2.2	733.3	10.0	1,313.5	286.1	66.1
II	2,901.8	2,877.2	24.6	1,276.1	1,251.4	24.6	519.7	18.5	731.7	6.1	1,340.2	285.6	73.7
III	2,980.9	2,949.1	31.8	1,317.0	1,285.1	31.8	527.5	19.8	757.6	12.0	1,382.1	281.9	78.7
IV	3,003.2	2,989.9	13.2	1,298.4	1,285.2	13.2	510.5	−5.6	774.7	18.9	1,421.5	283.3	58.3
1982:													
I	2,995.5	3,031.1	−35.6	1,269.4	1,305.0	−35.6	513.2	−30.9	791.8	−4.8	1,444.4	281.7	53.5
II	3,045.2	3,061.4	−16.2	1,283.1	1,299.3	−16.2	512.6	−6.6	786.7	−9.6	1,476.7	285.3	69.9
III	3,088.2	3,083.5	4.7	1,295.5	1,290.7	4.7	506.8	10.1	783.9	−5.4	1,509.5	283.2	75.2
IV p	3,101.3	3,139.8	−38.5	1,274.5	1,313.0	−38.5	510.3	−34.7	802.7	−3.8	1,537.6	289.2	64.3

Source: Department of Commerce, Bureau of Economic Analysis.

TABLE B–7.—*Gross national product by major type of product in 1972 dollars, 1929–82*

[Billions of 1972 dollars; quarterly data at seasonally adjusted annual rates]

Year or quarter	Gross national product	Final sales	Inventory change	Goods							Services	Structures	Auto output
				Total			Durable goods		Nondurable goods				
				Total	Final sales	Inventory change	Final sales	Inventory change	Final sales	Inventory change			
1929	315.7	311.0	4.6	144.3	139.7	4.6	40.4	3.5	99.3	1.1	127.4	43.9	
1933	222.1	227.0	−4.9	97.5	102.3	−4.9	17.5	−2.1	84.9	−2.8	110.7	14.0	
1939	319.8	318.2	1.6	154.3	152.7	1.6	35.5	.7	117.2	.9	135.2	30.3	
1940	344.1	337.9	6.2	171.7	165.5	6.2	43.1	3.4	122.4	2.8	139.9	32.5	
1941	400.4	388.4	12.0	198.6	186.6	12.0	57.8	8.2	128.7	3.8	158.5	43.3	
1942	461.7	456.5	5.2	221.4	216.2	5.2	75.7	3.5	140.5	1.7	193.9	46.3	
1943	531.6	531.5	.1	263.3	263.3	.1	118.8	.7	144.4	−.6	242.0	26.2	
1944	569.1	571.4	−2.3	287.3	289.6	−2.3	135.9	−1.8	153.7	−.5	263.7	18.1	
1945	560.4	564.0	−3.6	278.5	282.2	−3.6	121.2	−3.7	161.0	.1	263.0	18.8	
1946	478.3	466.1	12.2	238.3	226.2	12.2	60.3	10.8	165.8	1.3	200.8	39.1	
1947	470.3	470.6	−.2	237.7	237.9	−.2	75.5	1.4	162.4	−1.6	188.1	44.6	12.3
1948	489.8	484.3	5.5	244.8	239.4	5.5	77.3	1.6	162.1	3.8	192.5	52.4	13.9
1949	492.2	496.6	−4.4	240.3	244.7	−4.4	78.3	−2.9	166.4	−1.5	198.3	53.6	18.0
1950	534.8	524.2	10.6	261.5	250.9	10.6	86.1	5.5	164.8	5.1	207.4	65.9	23.0
1951	579.4	565.6	13.7	283.7	270.0	13.7	98.2	9.0	171.8	4.7	231.3	64.3	19.3
1952	600.8	596.5	4.3	292.1	287.8	4.3	107.9	1.7	179.9	2.6	243.2	65.5	17.1
1953	623.6	622.1	1.5	306.8	305.3	1.5	116.2	2.3	189.1	−.8	247.5	69.3	22.6
1954	616.1	618.2	−2.2	292.7	294.9	−2.2	109.0	−3.7	185.9	1.5	249.1	74.3	21.6
1955	657.5	649.8	7.7	316.7	309.0	7.7	117.2	4.5	191.9	3.2	260.1	80.7	29.8
1956	671.6	665.8	5.8	320.9	315.1	5.8	117.8	2.9	197.2	2.9	270.2	80.5	23.0
1957	683.8	682.2	1.5	321.7	320.2	1.5	119.4	.9	200.8	.6	282.4	79.7	24.5
1958	680.9	682.7	−1.8	311.6	313.4	−1.8	109.2	−3.4	204.3	1.6	287.6	81.7	18.6
1959	721.7	714.7	7.0	332.5	325.5	7.0	113.6	3.9	211.9	3.1	299.4	89.8	23.2
1960	737.2	733.7	3.5	335.8	332.3	3.5	115.6	2.0	216.6	1.6	312.5	89.0	25.3
1961	756.6	753.7	3.0	338.0	335.0	3.0	114.7	−.1	220.3	3.0	326.9	91.7	21.2
1962	800.3	792.4	7.8	361.3	353.5	7.8	125.7	4.2	227.8	3.7	341.5	97.4	26.0
1963	832.5	825.0	7.5	372.2	364.7	7.5	132.5	3.4	232.2	4.2	356.2	104.1	28.7
1964	876.4	869.3	7.1	393.8	386.7	7.1	143.0	5.1	243.7	1.9	374.0	108.6	29.4
1965	929.3	917.5	11.8	422.6	410.8	11.8	157.2	8.2	253.6	3.6	390.7	116.0	35.7
1966	984.8	968.0	16.8	456.4	439.6	16.8	174.0	12.3	265.6	4.5	412.6	115.9	34.8
1967	1,011.4	999.2	12.2	463.4	451.2	12.2	178.3	6.6	272.9	5.6	434.1	113.9	31.8
1968	1,058.1	1,049.1	9.0	483.1	474.1	9.0	187.4	5.4	286.7	3.6	453.0	122.0	38.5
1969	1,087.6	1,076.6	11.1	496.0	484.9	11.1	193.0	7.2	291.9	3.9	469.2	122.5	37.4
1970	1,085.6	1,081.8	3.8	486.9	483.2	3.8	187.5	.0	295.7	3.7	482.4	116.3	29.8
1971	1,122.4	1,114.3	8.1	497.2	489.1	8.1	188.7	3.0	300.4	5.1	497.8	127.3	38.9
1972	1,185.9	1,175.7	10.2	529.6	519.4	10.2	207.4	7.2	312.0	3.0	519.0	137.3	41.6
1973	1,254.3	1,237.1	17.2	572.3	555.1	17.2	236.1	12.7	319.0	4.5	542.8	139.1	46.4
1974	1,246.3	1,234.7	11.6	562.5	550.9	11.6	234.1	9.4	316.8	2.2	562.8	121.0	37.1
1975	1,231.6	1,238.4	−6.7	547.4	554.2	−6.7	230.2	−6.4	324.0	−.3	575.9	108.3	35.7
1976	1,298.2	1,290.4	7.8	587.2	579.4	7.8	242.7	5.4	336.7	2.4	595.0	116.0	45.3
1977	1,369.7	1,356.4	13.3	628.1	614.8	13.3	264.7	6.9	350.1	6.3	617.3	124.4	50.7
1978	1,438.6	1,422.6	16.0	662.0	645.9	16.0	285.4	11.8	360.5	4.3	644.7	131.9	50.3
1979	1,479.4	1,472.2	7.3	677.7	670.4	7.3	299.1	6.2	371.3	1.1	670.7	131.0	47.0
1980	1,474.0	1,479.0	−5.0	667.9	672.9	−5.0	290.8	−2.6	382.1	−2.4	687.1	118.9	38.7
1981	1,502.6	1,493.7	9.0	689.5	680.5	9.0	289.3	3.8	391.2	5.1	695.6	117.6	41.5
1982 p	1,475.5	1,484.0	−8.5	661.1	669.6	−8.5	273.3	−6.5	396.3	−2.0	701.3	113.1	37.6
1980:													
I	1,494.9	1,497.5	−2.6	682.5	685.1	−2.6	304.2	−4.7	380.8	2.2	684.2	128.3	42.0
II	1,457.8	1,460.3	−2.5	658.2	660.7	−2.5	279.8	−1.2	380.9	−1.3	686.0	113.6	33.8
III	1,463.8	1,472.3	−8.5	659.5	668.0	−8.5	286.9	−6.2	381.1	−2.4	690.0	114.3	36.7
IV	1,479.4	1,485.7	−6.2	671.6	677.8	−6.2	292.4	1.8	385.5	−8.0	688.2	119.6	42.2
1981:													
I	1,507.8	1,505.4	2.4	692.8	690.4	2.4	298.9	.1	391.5	2.3	693.1	121.9	41.6
II	1,502.2	1,490.1	12.1	689.8	677.7	12.1	290.5	9.1	387.2	3.0	693.2	119.2	44.5
III	1,510.4	1,493.9	16.5	697.2	680.7	16.5	290.2	8.6	390.5	7.9	697.5	115.7	45.6
IV	1,490.1	1,485.3	4.8	678.0	673.2	4.8	277.6	−2.5	395.6	7.3	698.6	113.4	34.4
1982:													
I	1,470.7	1,486.1	−15.4	661.8	677.2	−15.4	278.7	−13.7	398.5	−1.7	697.0	111.9	31.3
II	1,478.4	1,482.7	−4.4	663.2	667.5	−4.4	274.9	−2.6	392.6	−1.7	702.2	113.0	39.7
III	1,481.1	1,477.8	3.4	665.1	661.7	3.4	269.2	4.8	392.5	−1.5	703.6	112.5	42.3
IV p	1,471.7	1,489.3	−17.7	654.5	672.1	−17.7	270.6	−14.7	401.5	−2.9	702.3	114.9	37.1

Source: Department of Commerce, Bureau of Economic Analysis.

Table B–8.—*Gross national product by sector, 1929–82*

[Billions of dollars, except as noted; quarterly data at seasonally adjusted annual rates]

Year or quarter	Gross national product	Gross domestic product									Rest of the world	Percent change from preceding period, gross national product [3]
		Total [1]	Business [1]				Households and institutions	Government [2]				
			Total	Nonfarm [1]	Farm	Statistical discrepancy		Total	Federal	State and local		
1929	103.4	102.6	95.4	84.7	9.7	1.1	2.9	4.3	0.9	3.5	0.8	6.6
1933	55.8	55.5	49.1	43.8	4.6	.7	1.7	4.7	1.2	3.5	.3	−4.2
1939	90.9	90.5	80.6	72.9	6.3	1.4	2.3	7.6	3.4	4.2	.5	7.0
1940	100.0	99.6	89.4	81.8	6.4	1.1	2.4	7.8	3.5	4.3	.4	10.0
1941	125.0	124.5	112.6	103.1	8.9	.6	2.5	9.4	5.0	4.4	.5	25.0
1942	158.5	157.9	139.9	127.7	12.0	.8	2.0	16.1	10.0	4.5	.5	26.7
1943	192.1	191.6	162.8	149.3	15.3	−1.8	3.2	25.6	20.9	4.7	.5	21.3
1944	210.6	210.1	174.2	156.2	15.3	2.7	3.7	32.2	27.2	4.9	.5	9.6
1945	212.4	212.0	172.8	152.7	16.0	4.1	4.1	35.2	29.8	5.4	.4	.9
1946	209.8	209.0	183.8	164.4	18.8	.5	4.5	20.8	14.6	6.2	.8	−1.2
1947	233.1	231.8	210.0	188.2	20.2	1.5	5.1	16.7	9.4	7.3	1.2	11.1
1948	259.5	257.9	234.9	213.1	23.3	−1.6	5.6	17.4	8.9	8.5	1.6	11.3
1949	258.3	256.9	231.5	212.2	18.8	.6	5.9	19.4	10.0	9.4	1.4	−.5
1950	286.5	284.8	257.5	236.3	20.0	1.3	6.4	20.9	10.7	10.1	1.6	10.9
1951	330.8	328.7	294.4	268.3	22.9	3.2	6.9	27.4	16.2	11.2	2.1	15.5
1952	348.0	345.7	307.3	283.4	22.2	1.7	7.2	31.2	18.9	12.3	2.3	5.2
1953	366.8	364.6	324.9	302.3	20.3	2.3	7.8	31.9	18.6	13.3	2.2	5.4
1954	366.8	364.5	323.9	302.3	19.7	2.0	8.1	32.5	17.8	14.7	2.3	.0
1955	400.0	397.3	354.0	333.9	18.8	1.3	9.1	34.2	18.4	15.8	2.8	9.0
1956	421.7	418.5	372.1	355.7	18.6	−2.1	9.8	36.6	19.0	17.6	3.2	5.4
1957	444.0	440.5	390.8	373.7	18.4	−1.2	10.5	39.1	19.6	19.6	3.5	5.3
1958	449.7	446.6	393.1	372.2	20.7	.2	11.4	42.1	20.5	21.6	3.0	1.3
1959	487.9	484.6	428.3	410.6	19.0	−1.3	12.3	44.0	20.9	23.1	3.3	8.5
1960	506.5	502.9	442.0	424.2	20.2	−2.4	13.8	47.1	21.7	25.5	3.6	3.8
1961	524.6	520.7	455.7	435.7	20.2	−.1	14.4	50.5	22.6	27.9	3.9	3.6
1962	565.0	560.5	490.6	468.1	20.4	2.1	15.5	54.3	24.1	30.2	4.6	7.7
1963	596.7	591.8	517.2	495.0	20.5	1.7	16.6	58.0	25.2	32.9	4.9	5.6
1964	637.7	632.3	551.6	532.2	19.3	.1	17.8	62.9	27.0	35.9	5.5	6.9
1965	691.1	685.2	598.4	577.7	21.9	−1.2	19.2	67.6	28.3	39.3	5.9	8.4
1966	756.0	750.3	652.6	628.4	22.8	1.4	21.1	76.5	32.4	44.1	5.6	9.4
1967	799.6	793.7	685.1	663.3	22.1	−.3	23.4	85.1	35.6	49.5	5.9	5.8
1968	873.4	866.7	745.4	725.0	22.6	−2.1	26.1	95.2	39.3	55.9	6.7	9.2
1969	944.0	937.1	803.2	782.1	25.1	−3.9	29.4	104.5	41.9	62.6	6.9	8.1
1970	992.7	985.4	837.3	813.1	25.8	−1.5	32.3	115.8	44.8	71.1	7.3	5.2
1971	1,077.6	1,068.5	907.1	875.4	27.6	4.1	35.4	126.0	46.8	79.3	9.2	8.6
1972	1,185.9	1,175.0	998.6	963.4	31.9	3.3	38.6	137.8	50.1	87.7	10.9	10.1
1973	1,326.4	1,310.4	1,118.7	1,068.0	49.9	.8	42.1	149.6	51.9	97.7	16.0	11.8
1974	1,434.2	1,414.4	1,206.4	1,155.0	47.7	3.7	45.8	162.2	54.9	107.3	19.8	8.1
1975	1,549.2	1,531.9	1,301.7	1,247.3	48.9	5.5	50.6	179.6	59.0	120.6	17.3	8.0
1976	1,718.0	1,697.5	1,447.3	1,396.3	45.9	5.1	55.6	194.6	62.4	132.3	20.5	10.9
1977	1,918.3	1,894.9	1,624.0	1,574.2	48.4	1.4	60.5	210.3	66.3	144.0	23.5	11.7
1978	2,163.9	2,134.3	1,837.2	1,781.0	58.7	−2.6	67.8	229.3	71.7	157.6	29.6	12.8
1979	2,417.8	2,375.2	2,052.1	1,982.1	71.6	−1.5	75.6	247.4	75.7	171.8	42.6	11.7
1980	2,633.1	2,587.0	2,228.8	2,159.5	65.4	3.9	85.4	272.8	82.9	189.9	46.1	8.9
1981	2,937.7	2,888.5	2,492.4	2,418.5	75.8	−1.9	96.4	299.7	92.3	207.4	49.2	11.6
1982 [p]	3,057.5	3,011.9	2,582.5	2,507.6	74.8	.1	106.7	322.7	99.8	222.9	45.7	4.1
1980:												
I	2,575.9	2,527.2	2,183.3	2,106.4	66.3	10.5	81.5	262.4	79.8	182.7	48.7	12.2
II	2,573.4	2,526.6	2,173.7	2,108.6	61.2	3.8	84.0	269.0	81.4	187.6	46.8	−.4
III	2,643.7	2,597.8	2,237.2	2,168.0	67.0	2.2	86.5	274.0	81.6	192.4	45.9	11.4
IV	2,739.4	2,696.5	2,321.1	2,255.2	66.9	−1.0	89.7	285.8	88.7	197.0	42.9	15.3
1981:												
I	2,864.9	2,817.9	2,433.4	2,357.5	70.8	5.1	92.9	291.6	89.9	201.7	47.1	19.6
II	2,901.8	2,855.2	2,463.9	2,394.6	73.9	−4.6	95.2	296.2	90.5	205.6	46.6	5.3
III	2,980.9	2,931.2	2,533.9	2,454.7	80.1	−.8	97.1	300.1	91.0	209.2	49.7	11.4
IV	3,003.2	2,949.8	2,538.6	2,467.4	78.4	−7.2	100.3	310.9	97.9	213.0	53.3	3.0
1982:												
I	2,995.5	2,949.6	2,530.6	2,465.1	72.9	−7.5	103.3	315.8	98.6	217.1	45.8	−1.0
II	3,045.2	2,995.7	2,570.1	2,494.4	74.8	.8	105.3	320.3	98.9	221.4	49.5	6.8
III	3,088.2	3,041.6	2,610.0	2,530.2	76.1	3.6	107.9	323.8	99.1	224.7	46.6	5.8
IV [p]	3,101.3	3,060.5	2,619.3	2,540.6	75.2	3.6	110.4	330.8	102.4	228.4	40.8	1.7

[1] Includes compensation of employees in government enterprises.
[2] Compensation of government employees.
[3] Changes are based on unrounded data and therefore may differ slightly from changes computed from data shown here.

Source: Department of Commerce, Bureau of Economic Analysis.

TABLE B-9.—*Gross national product by sector in 1972 dollars, 1929–82*

[Billions of 1972 dollars, except as noted; quarterly data at seasonally adjusted annual rates]

Year or quarter	Gross national product	Gross domestic product									Rest of the world	Percent change from preceding period, gross national product [3]
		Total	Business [1]				Households and institutions	Government [2]				
			Total [1]	Nonfarm [1]	Farm	Statistical discrepancy		Total	Federal	State and local		
1929	315.7	313.2	271.5	244.7	23.6	3.1	15.6	26.2	5.2	21.0	2.4	6.6
1933	222.1	220.9	180.0	152.5	24.9	2.6	12.2	28.8	6.6	22.1	1.3	−2.2
1939	319.8	318.2	261.0	231.3	25.2	4.6	15.1	42.1	10.9	25.2	1.0	7.0
1940	344.1	342.8	282.7	254.6	24.5	3.6	16.1	44.0	18.6	25.4	1.4	7.6
1941	400.4	398.7	327.6	299.8	26.2	1.6	15.9	55.2	29.6	25.6	1.7	16.3
1942	461.7	460.1	361.8	335.3	28.6	−2.1	16.4	81.9	56.7	25.2	1.5	15.3
1943	531.6	530.3	385.6	362.1	27.7	−4.2	15.2	129.4	105.0	24.5	1.3	15.1
1944	569.1	567.7	403.6	370.1	27.1	6.4	15.1	149.1	125.2	23.9	1.4	7.1
1945	560.4	559.3	397.9	362.8	25.6	9.4	15.0	146.4	121.8	24.6	1.1	−1.5
1946	478.3	476.4	385.5	358.6	25.8	1.1	15.1	75.9	49.7	26.2	1.8	−14.7
1947	470.3	467.8	393.8	367.0	24.0	2.9	16.0	58.0	29.8	28.2	2.5	−1.7
1948	489.8	486.8	412.0	389.0	25.8	−2.8	16.7	58.1	29.2	29.0	3.0	4.1
1949	492.2	489.4	409.8	383.4	25.6	.8	17.3	62.3	31.3	31.0	2.7	.5
1950	534.8	531.8	448.7	419.4	27.0	2.4	18.3	64.7	32.7	32.0	3.0	8.7
1951	579.4	575.6	478.0	447.2	25.8	5.0	18.7	79.0	46.2	32.8	3.7	8.3
1952	600.8	596.9	492.8	463.7	26.4	2.6	18.6	85.5	51.6	33.9	3.9	3.7
1953	623.6	619.8	515.6	484.3	27.7	3.6	19.3	85.0	49.6	35.4	3.7	3.8
1954	616.1	612.1	508.5	477.0	28.4	3.1	19.4	84.1	47.2	36.9	4.0	−1.2
1955	657.5	653.0	547.0	516.0	29.3	1.8	21.4	84.6	45.9	38.6	4.5	6.7
1956	671.6	666.5	557.4	531.5	28.9	−3.0	22.5	86.7	45.6	41.0	5.1	2.1
1957	683.8	678.3	566.1	539.5	28.2	−1.7	23.1	89.1	45.8	43.3	5.5	1.8
1958	680.9	676.2	561.7	532.0	29.3	.3	24.2	90.3	44.5	45.8	4.6	−.4
1959	721.7	716.8	600.0	574.0	27.8	−1.9	24.7	92.2	44.5	47.7	4.9	6.0
1960	737.2	732.0	610.1	584.2	29.2	−3.3	26.6	95.3	45.2	50.1	5.2	2.2
1961	756.6	751.0	625.1	596.3	28.9	−.2	27.0	98.9	46.2	52.7	5.7	2.6
1962	800.3	793.8	663.2	631.5	28.8	2.9	28.1	102.5	48.3	54.3	6.5	5.8
1963	832.5	825.6	691.6	659.7	29.6	2.3	28.9	105.2	48.2	57.0	6.9	4.0
1964	876.4	868.9	730.3	701.3	28.8	.2	29.8	108.8	48.5	60.4	7.5	5.3
1965	929.3	921.4	777.7	749.6	29.8	−1.6	30.9	112.7	48.7	64.0	7.9	6.0
1966	984.8	977.5	824.0	794.1	28.2	1.7	32.6	120.8	53.0	67.9	7.4	6.0
1967	1,011.4	1,003.9	842.0	812.8	29.5	−.3	34.3	127.7	57.2	70.5	7.5	2.7
1968	1,058.1	1,050.0	882.1	855.6	29.0	−2.5	35.4	132.4	58.0	74.4	8.2	4.6
1969	1,087.6	1,079.7	907.1	881.9	29.5	−4.4	37.0	135.7	58.2	77.4	7.9	2.8
1970	1,085.6	1,077.6	904.8	875.4	31.1	−1.7	36.7	136.1	55.2	80.9	8.0	−.2
1971	1,122.4	1,112.8	938.6	901.7	32.6	4.2	37.6	136.7	52.5	84.2	9.5	3.4
1972	1,185.9	1,175.0	998.6	963.4	31.9	3.3	38.6	137.8	50.1	87.7	10.9	5.7
1973	1,254.3	1,239.2	1,060.7	1,028.4	31.6	.7	39.4	139.1	48.2	90.8	15.1	5.8
1974	1,246.3	1.229.0	1,047.4	1,012.4	31.8	3.2	39.3	142.3	48.5	93.8	17.3	−.6
1975	1,231.6	1,217.8	1,032.4	994.5	33.6	4.4	40.5	144.9	48.4	96.5	13.8	−1.2
1976	1,298.2	1.282.6	1,095.4	1,059.5	32.1	3.8	40.9	146.3	48.5	97.8	15.6	5.4
1977	1,369.7	1,352.8	1,163.7	1,129.5	33.1	1.0	41.5	147.7	48.6	99.1	16.9	5.5
1978	1,438.6	1,418.7	1,224.3	1,193.5	32.6	−1.8	43.3	151.2	49.3	101.9	19.9	5.0
1979	1,479.4	1,453.2	1,255.6	1,222.4	34.2	−1.0	44.6	153.0	49.0	104.1	26.3	2.8
1980	1,474.0	1,447.9	1,246.7	1,210.3	34.2	2.2	45.8	155.4	49.5	105.9	26.1	−.4
1981	1,502.6	1,477.2	1,274.3	1,236.8	38.4	−.9	46.9	156.0	49.7	106.3	25.4	1.9
1982 ᵖ	1,475.5	1,453.2	1,249.7	1,210.1	39.6	.0	48.1	155.4	49.8	105.6	22.2	−1.8
1980:												
I	1,494.9	1,466.4	1,266.6	1,224.9	35.6	6.1	45.3	154.4	49.0	105.4	28.6	1.5
II	1,457.8	1,431.0	1,230.0	1,192.6	35.3	2.1	45.4	155.6	49.8	105.8	26.8	−9.6
III	1,463.8	1,438.1	1,236.2	1,200.9	34.0	1.2	46.0	155.9	49.8	106.1	25.7	1.6
IV	1,479.4	1,456.0	1,254.0	1,222.6	32.0	−.5	46.4	155.7	49.4	106.3	23.4	4.3
1981:												
I	1,507.8	1,482.8	1,279.7	1,242.9	34.1	2.7	46.8	156.3	49.6	106.8	25.0	7.9
II	1,502.2	1,477.8	1,274.8	1,240.9	36.3	−2.4	46.7	156.2	49.7	106.5	24.4	−1.5
III	1,510.4	1,485.0	1,282.4	1,241.9	40.9	−.4	46.7	155.9	49.8	106.1	25.4	2.2
IV	1,490.1	1,463.3	1,260.2	1,221.5	42.3	−3.6	47.4	155.8	49.8	106.0	26.7	−5.3
1982:												
I	1,470.7	1,448.0	1,244.4	1,210.0	38.1	−3.7	47.8	155.7	49.8	106.0	22.7	−5.1
II	1,478.4	1,454.1	1,250.5	1,212.2	38.0	.4	47.9	155.7	49.8	105.9	24.2	2.1
III	1,481.1	1,458.6	1,255.4	1,214.4	39.3	1.7	48.0	155.2	49.8	105.4	22.5	.7
IV ᵖ	1,471.7	1,452.2	1,248.4	1,204.0	42.8	1.7	48.6	155.1	49.9	105.3	19.5	−2.5

[1] Includes compensation of employees in government enterprises.
[2] Compensation of government employees.
[3] Changes are based on unrounded data and therefore may differ slightly from changes computed from data shown here.
Source: Department of Commerce, Bureau of Economic Analysis.

384-041 O - 83 - 12 : QL 3

TABLE B–10.—*Gross national product by industry, 1947–81*

[Billions of dollars]

Year	Gross national product	Gross domestic product												Rest of the world
		Agriculture, forestry, and fisheries	Mining	Construction	Manufacturing			Transportation and public utilities	Wholesale and retail trade	Finance, insurance, and real estate	Services	Government and government enterprises	Statistical discrepancy	
					Total	Durable goods	Nondurable goods							
1947	233.1	20.8	6.8	9.1	66.2	33.5	32.7	20.5	44.2	23.2	20.2	19.3	1.5	1.2
1948	259.5	24.0	9.4	11.5	74.7	38.1	36.5	23.1	48.4	26.2	21.9	20.2	−1.6	1.6
1949	258.3	19.5	8.1	11.5	72.1	37.1	35.0	23.4	48.0	28.6	22.6	22.5	.6	1.4
1950	286.5	20.8	9.3	13.0	83.7	45.8	37.9	25.7	51.3	31.9	24.0	23.8	1.3	1.6
1951	330.8	23.8	10.2	15.4	98.7	55.4	43.3	29.2	56.4	35.2	25.9	30.8	3.2	2.1
1952	348.0	23.1	10.1	16.6	103.0	58.9	44.1	31.0	58.5	38.7	27.5	35.3	1.7	2.3
1953	366.8	21.3	10.6	17.1	112.1	65.9	46.2	32.9	59.8	42.8	30.1	36.1	[illegible]	[illegible]
1954	366.8	20.7	10.9	17.2	106.4	60.8	45.6	32.6	60.8	46.5	30.5	36.9	2.0	2.3
1955	400.0	19.9	12.4	18.5	120.9	70.6	50.3	35.6	66.2	50.0	34.0	38.5	1.3	2.8
1956	421.7	19.7	13.4	20.6	126.8	73.7	53.2	38.3	70.4	53.5	37.3	40.7	−2.1	3.2
1957	444.0	19.5	13.5	21.4	131.4	77.7	53.7	40.2	73.9	57.6	40.2	44.0	−1.2	3.5
1958	449.7	21.9	12.4	21.0	123.8	69.7	54.1	40.4	75.2	62.4	42.3	47.1	.2	3.0
1959	487.9	20.2	12.3	22.8	141.3	81.2	60.0	43.7	81.9	67.3	46.3	50.0	−1.3	3.3
1960	506.5	21.4	12.6	23.2	143.8	82.1	61.7	45.8	84.2	71.6	49.2	53.4	−2.4	3.6
1961	524.6	21.5	12.7	24.0	144.4	81.3	63.1	47.4	86.3	75.4	52.3	56.7	−.1	3.9
1962	565.0	21.9	12.8	25.7	157.9	91.5	66.4	50.2	92.1	80.6	56.1	61.1	2.1	4.6
1963	596.7	22.0	13.1	27.4	167.4	97.6	69.8	53.0	96.1	85.3	60.0	65.9	1.7	4.9
1964	637.7	21.0	13.4	29.8	179.4	105.3	74.2	56.3	104.7	91.0	65.3	71.2	.1	5.5
1965	691.1	23.8	13.5	32.8	197.7	118.0	79.7	60.5	112.6	98.0	70.8	76.7	−1.2	5.9
1966	756.0	24.8	14.2	35.9	216.6	130.4	86.3	65.3	121.5	105.9	78.4	86.4	1.4	5.6
1967	799.6	24.2	14.6	37.5	222.3	133.6	88.7	68.6	130.1	114.2	86.1	96.3	−.3	5.9
1968	873.4	25.0	15.3	41.3	242.8	146.0	96.8	74.0	144.4	123.8	94.2	108.1	−2.1	6.7
1969	944.0	27.8	16.1	46.3	256.7	154.5	102.2	80.0	157.0	133.6	105.3	118.2	−3.9	6.9
1970	992.7	28.6	17.6	48.9	252.2	146.2	105.9	85.7	166.5	142.4	114.4	130.5	−1.5	7.3
1971	1,077.6	30.8	17.4	53.6	265.6	153.9	111.7	93.8	181.4	156.4	123.6	141.8	4.1	9.2
1972	1,185.9	35.4	19.0	59.4	292.5	173.2	119.3	104.3	199.5	169.8	136.5	155.4	3.3	10.9
1973	1,326.4	53.8	21.7	66.3	326.1	195.9	130.2	114.3	221.5	184.9	153.1	167.8	.8	16.0
1974	1,434.2	52.2	32.2	69.2	340.7	201.3	139.4	122.9	241.5	202.0	167.5	182.7	3.7	19.8
1975	1,549.2	53.3	38.8	69.9	358.2	207.6	150.6	135.7	266.2	216.2	186.2	202.0	5.5	17.3
1976	1,718.0	51.2	43.0	76.6	410.4	240.0	170.4	152.6	291.4	238.6	208.2	220.4	5.1	20.5
1977	1,918.3	54.6	47.4	86.6	464.8	277.7	187.1	170.9	322.3	275.5	234.3	237.2	1.4	23.5
1978	2,163.9	66.0	52.0	102.1	518.7	316.7	202.0	193.3	362.3	317.4	265.9	259.1	−2.6	29.6
1979	2,417.8	79.6	66.8	115.7	563.2	344.3	218.9	209.6	401.5	358.3	302.4	279.6	−1.5	42.6
1980	2,633.1	74.1	94.1	121.2	581.2	347.8	233.4	232.4	425.7	405.2	342.5	306.8	3.9	46.1
1981	2,937.7	85.6	127.2	127.2	644.0	388.4	255.6	261.9	472.7	448.2	386.9	336.7	−1.9	49.2

Note.—The industry classification is on an establishment basis and is based on the 1972 Standard Industrial Classification.

Source: Department of Commerce, Bureau of Economic Analysis.

TABLE B–11.—*Gross national product by industry in 1972 dollars, 1947–81*

[Billions of 1972 dollars]

Year	Gross national product	Gross domestic product														Rest of the world
		Agriculture, forestry, and fisheries	Mining	Construction	Manufacturing			Transportation and public utilities	Wholesale and retail trade	Finance, insurance, and real estate	Services	Government and government enterprises	Statistical discrepancy	Residual [1]		
					Total	Durable goods	Nondurable goods									
1947	470.3	26.3	10.8	22.9	114.9	68.5	46.4	42.3	75.9	54.7	55.9	68.7	2.9	−7.4		2.5
1948	489.8	28.2	11.3	26.5	121.4	72.0	49.4	42.1	78.0	56.6	57.5	69.2	−2.8	−1.2		3.0
1949	492.2	28.0	9.9	26.5	115.1	66.3	48.8	39.2	79.8	59.8	57.6	73.3	.8	−.6		2.7
1950	534.8	29.3	11.1	29.3	131.1	78.1	53.0	41.2	87.5	63.9	59.7	75.6	2.4	.8		3.0
1951	579.4	28.4	12.1	32.5	146.0	89.9	56.1	45.5	88.3	66.7	60.8	90.0	5.0	.2		3.7
1952	600.8	29.2	11.9	33.8	150.8	94.3	56.5	45.5	91.0	70.9	61.6	96.9	2.6	2.6		3.9
1953	623.6	30.5	12.2	34.8	161.1	102.6	58.5	46.6	93.9	73.9	62.7	96.3	3.6	4.1		3.7
1954	616.1	31.3	11.8	36.0	149.6	91.7	57.9	45.8	94.5	77.3	62.9	95.2	3.1	4.6		4.0
1955	657.5	32.1	13.2	38.2	165.7	103.4	62.3	49.7	103.1	81.8	67.6	95.7	1.8	4.2		4.5
1956	671.6	31.7	13.9	40.9	166.9	102.5	64.4	52.1	106.2	85.8	70.9	97.8	−3.0	3.4		5.1
1957	683.8	31.1	13.8	40.9	167.7	102.9	64.8	53.2	107.9	89.8	74.1	100.4	−1.7	.9		5.5
1958	680.9	32.2	12.7	42.1	153.3	88.8	64.5	51.9	107.8	93.4	76.2	101.7	.3	4.5		4.6
1959	721.7	30.6	13.3	45.5	171.2	100.9	70.3	55.4	115.4	98.5	80.8	104.0	−1.9	4.0		4.9
1960	737.2	32.1	13.5	46.1	171.8	101.0	70.8	57.5	117.5	102.7	83.5	107.7	−3.3	3.1		5.2
1961	756.6	31.8	13.6	46.7	172.0	99.5	72.5	58.6	118.7	107.3	86.6	111.6	−.2	4.4		5.7
1962	800.3	31.7	13.9	48.4	186.7	110.0	76.7	61.5	126.3	113.3	90.3	115.5	2.9	3.2		6.5
1963	832.5	32.5	14.5	49.9	202.2	119.5	82.8	65.0	131.1	116.8	94.0	118.7	2.3	−1.5		6.9
1964	876.4	31.8	15.1	52.2	216.7	129.8	86.8	68.1	139.1	122.1	98.8	123.1	.2	1.7		7.5
1965	929.3	32.8	15.7	54.4	236.7	144.6	92.0	73.4	148.2	128.5	103.1	127.8	−1.6	2.3		7.9
1966	984.8	31.3	16.5	54.6	254.9	157.3	97.6	79.4	156.3	133.9	109.0	136.9	1.7	3.0		7.4
1967	1,011.4	32.6	17.0	53.4	254.3	157.4	96.9	81.6	160.1	139.4	115.0	144.1	−.3	6.7		7.5
1968	1,058.1	32.1	17.6	56.9	268.2	165.5	102.7	88.2	169.9	145.7	118.8	148.9	−2.5	6.2		8.2
1969	1,087.6	32.7	18.2	55.8	277.2	170.3	106.8	92.6	173.6	152.9	124.0	152.5	−4.4	4.6		7.9
1970	1,085.6	34.4	18.9	53.4	261.2	155.2	106.0	94.9	176.4	155.8	126.7	152.9	−1.7	4.7		8.0
1971	1,122.4	35.9	18.4	57.9	266.8	156.4	110.4	97.9	185.5	162.6	128.4	153.9	4.2	1.2		9.5
1972	1,185.9	35.4	19.0	59.4	292.5	173.2	119.3	104.3	199.5	169.8	136.5	155.4	3.3	.0		10.9
1973	1,254.3	35.3	19.2	60.1	325.3	194.2	131.1	110.6	211.1	177.2	144.8	157.2	.7	−2.5		15.1
1974	1,246.3	35.8	19.2	53.3	311.7	186.3	125.3	111.9	207.0	184.5	147.9	161.2	3.2	−6.5		17.3
1975	1,231.6	37.1	18.9	48.3	289.6	168.8	120.8	113.5	209.7	187.9	148.5	164.3	4.4	−4.2		13.8
1976	1,298.2	35.8	19.1	52.8	317.4	187.2	130.1	118.6	220.2	194.8	154.7	165.7	3.8	−.2		15.6
1977	1,369.7	36.9	19.5	55.0	339.2	202.9	136.3	125.1	231.0	207.2	164.3	167.5	1.0	6.0		16.9
1978	1,438.6	37.0	20.1	58.8	357.2	217.4	139.8	134.2	244.6	217.8	174.2	171.7	−1.8	4.9		19.9
1979	1,479.4	38.9	20.8	58.2	367.0	223.4	143.6	140.0	250.7	229.4	183.0	174.3	−1.0	−8.1		26.3
1980	1,474.0	39.1	21.6	53.3	351.2	210.0	141.2	140.8	243.3	237.9	189.0	177.3	2.2	−7.7		26.1
1981	1,502.6	43.4	22.3	52.0	359.2	215.3	143.9	142.1	250.4	243.6	196.7	178.1	−.9	−9.7		25.4

[1] Equals GNP in constant dollars measured as the sum of incomes less GNP in constant dollars measured as the sum of gross product by industry.

Note.—The industry classification is on an establishment basis and is based on the 1972 Standard Industrial Classification.

Source: Department of Commerce, Bureau of Economic Analysis.

TABLE B-12.—*Gross domestic product of nonfinancial corporate business, 1929–82*

[Billions of dollars; quarterly data at seasonally adjusted annual rates]

Year or quarter	Gross domestic product of nonfinancial corporate business	Capital consumption allowances with capital consumption adjustment	Net domestic product												
			Total	Indirect business tax, etc.[1]	Domestic income										
					Total	Compensation of employees	Corporate profits with inventory valuation and capital consumption adjustments								Net interest
							Total	Profits					Inventory valuation adjustment	Capital consumption adjustment	
								Profits before tax	Profits tax liability	Profits after tax					
										Total	Dividends	Undistributed profits			
1929	50.1	5.5	44.5	3.4	41.2	32.3	7.5	8.4	1.2	7.3	5.1	2.2	0.5	−1.4	1.4
1933	24.4	4.3	20.2	3.8	16.3	16.7	−2.1	.6	.5	.1	2.0	−1.9	−2.1	−.6	1.7
1939	43.7	4.8	39.0	5.1	33.9	28.2	4.2	6.1	1.4	4.7	3.3	1.4	−.7	1.1	1.5
1940	50.4	4.9	45.4	5.5	40.0	31.2	7.4	8.8	2.7	6.1	3.5	2.6	−.2	−1.2	1.4
1941	65.6	5.4	60.2	6.4	53.8	39.8	12.7	16.4	7.5	9.0	3.9	5.0	−2.5	−1.3	1.3
1942	82.9	6.1	76.8	6.8	70.0	51.0	17.7	20.1	11.2	8.9	3.7	5.2	−1.2	−1.2	1.3
1943	98.7	6.2	92.4	7.3	85.2	62.2	21.8	23.6	13.8	9.8	3.9	5.8	−.8	−.9	1.1
1944	102.1	6.3	95.8	8.1	87.7	65.1	21.6	22.2	12.6	9.6	4.1	5.6	−.3	−.3	1.0
1945	95.3	6.5	88.8	8.9	79.9	61.9	17.1	17.8	10.2	7.6	4.1	3.5	−.6	−.2	1.0
1946	99.3	7.6	91.8	10.1	81.6	67.2	13.8	22.0	8.6	13.4	4.8	8.6	−5.3	−3.0	.7
1947	120.0	9.3	110.7	11.2	99.6	79.1	19.7	29.1	10.8	18.3	5.5	12.8	−5.9	−3.5	.8
1948	137.3	10.9	126.4	12.1	114.3	87.8	25.6	31.8	11.8	20.0	6.0	14.0	−2.2	−4.0	.9
1949	133.5	11.7	121.8	12.6	109.2	85.3	22.9	24.9	9.3	15.6	6.0	9.6	1.9	−3.9	1.0
1950	151.9	12.6	139.3	14.1	125.2	94.7	29.6	38.5	16.9	21.6	7.5	14.1	−5.0	−3.9	.9
1951	174.5	14.6	159.9	15.2	144.7	110.2	33.4	39.1	21.2	17.9	7.1	10.8	−1.2	−4.6	1.1
1952	182.3	15.8	166.6	16.8	149.7	118.3	30.2	33.8	17.8	16.0	7.1	8.8	1.0	−4.5	1.2
1953	195.0	16.8	178.2	18.2	160.0	128.7	30.0	34.9	18.5	16.4	7.3	9.1	−1.0	−3.9	1.3
1954	191.9	17.9	174.0	17.4	156.6	126.5	28.6	32.1	15.6	16.4	7.4	9.0	−.3	−3.2	1.5
1955	216.7	19.1	197.6	19.2	178.4	138.5	38.3	42.0	20.2	21.8	8.5	13.4	−1.7	−2.0	1.6
1956	231.6	21.8	209.8	20.8	189.0	151.4	35.9	41.8	20.1	21.8	9.0	12.7	−2.7	−3.2	1.7
1957	242.3	23.8	218.5	22.4	196.1	159.1	34.9	39.8	19.1	20.7	9.3	11.4	−1.5	−3.4	2.2
1958	236.3	24.8	211.6	22.8	188.8	155.9	30.2	33.7	16.2	17.5	9.3	8.2	−.3	−3.2	2.7
1959	266.0	25.8	240.2	25.4	214.8	171.6	40.1	43.1	20.7	22.4	10.0	12.4	−.3	−2.7	3.1
1960	277.0	26.8	250.2	28.3	221.9	181.1	37.4	39.7	19.2	20.5	10.6	9.9	−.2	−2.1	3.5
1961	285.0	27.5	257.5	30.1	227.3	185.1	38.3	39.5	19.5	20.1	10.6	9.5	.3	−1.5	3.9
1962	311.3	28.4	283.0	33.0	249.9	199.8	45.6	44.2	20.6	23.5	11.4	12.2	.0	1.4	4.5
1963	331.8	29.4	302.3	35.6	266.8	210.7	51.2	48.9	22.8	26.2	12.6	13.5	.1	2.3	4.8
1964	358.4	30.8	327.6	38.4	289.3	226.3	57.7	55.4	24.0	31.4	13.7	17.7	−.5	2.9	5.3
1965	393.6	32.7	360.9	41.1	319.8	246.1	67.7	65.2	27.2	38.0	15.6	22.4	−1.2	3.7	6.1
1966	431.5	35.6	395.9	42.9	353.0	273.5	72.2	70.3	29.5	40.8	16.8	24.0	−2.1	3.9	7.4
1967	454.1	38.9	415.2	45.8	369.5	291.9	68.8	66.3	27.7	38.6	17.5	21.2	−1.6	4.0	8.7
1968	500.2	42.6	457.6	51.5	406.1	322.8	73.3	72.9	33.4	39.5	19.1	20.4	−3.7	4.0	10.1
1969	544.1	47.1	497.0	58.0	439.1	358.5	67.5	69.4	33.1	36.2	19.1	17.1	−5.9	4.0	13.1
1970	563.7	52.2	511.4	63.4	448.1	378.4	52.7	56.8	27.0	29.8	18.5	11.3	−6.6	2.4	17.0
1971	609.9	57.3	552.6	70.5	482.1	402.0	62.1	65.4	29.8	35.6	18.5	17.1	−4.6	1.3	18.0
1972	678.0	62.6	615.5	76.7	538.7	447.0	72.7	76.6	33.6	43.0	20.1	22.9	−6.6	2.7	19.1
1973	759.4	67.9	691.6	83.7	607.9	506.2	78.6	96.0	40.0	56.0	21.1	35.0	−20.0	2.6	23.0
1974	818.9	79.5	739.4	89.7	649.7	556.5	63.6	105.3	42.0	63.3	21.4	41.9	−40.0	−1.8	29.6
1975	890.0	94.9	795.1	97.1	697.9	581.1	86.1	107.3	41.2	66.1	25.7	40.4	−11.6	−9.7	30.8
1976	1,001.3	104.8	896.5	105.3	791.2	654.4	107.3	135.0	52.6	82.3	30.1	52.2	−14.7	−13.0	29.5
1977	1,128.4	115.7	1,012.7	112.6	900.1	738.5	129.5	156.5	59.6	96.8	31.9	64.9	−16.2	−10.8	32.1
1978	1,276.2	130.9	1,145.3	122.0	1,023.3	844.3	142.1	178.4	66.9	111.5	37.7	73.8	−24.0	−12.3	36.9
1979	1,416.8	149.6	1,267.3	130.5	1,136.7	958.1	134.7	191.8	69.2	122.5	39.8	82.8	−43.1	−13.9	43.9
1980	1,537.7	172.0	1,365.7	148.6	1,217.1	1,041.7	123.0	183.0	64.8	118.2	42.4	75.8	−43.0	−17.0	52.4
1981	1,732.3	195.8	1,536.5	178.3	1,358.2	1,150.1	145.6	186.6	63.3	123.3	52.9	70.3	−24.6	−16.3	62.5
1982 p	1,779.3	213.7	1,565.6	182.0	1,383.6	1,189.2	121.9	136.5	40.6	95.9	61.0	34.9	−9.4	−5.2	72.5
1980:															
I	1,501.1	162.7	1,338.4	138.4	1,200.0	1,020.6	129.6	201.6	74.3	127.3	38.3	89.0	−57.2	−14.8	49.8
II	1,499.7	169.3	1,330.5	143.5	1,186.9	1,023.6	112.8	157.4	53.5	103.9	42.7	61.2	−28.2	−16.3	50.5
III	1,543.6	175.4	1,368.2	151.3	1,216.9	1,043.2	121.8	181.3	63.6	117.7	43.5	74.2	−41.1	−18.4	51.8
IV	1,606.5	180.8	1,425.7	161.0	1,264.7	1,079.6	127.7	191.6	67.8	123.8	44.9	78.9	−45.5	−18.4	57.5
1981:															
I	1,683.3	186.3	1,497.0	172.9	1,324.0	1,118.6	150.4	202.5	71.5	131.0	49.4	81.6	−35.5	−16.6	55.0
II	1,715.0	192.6	1,522.4	179.0	1,343.4	1,140.0	142.1	181.8	61.4	120.4	51.2	69.2	−22.8	−16.9	61.2
III	1,763.6	199.1	1,564.5	179.9	1,384.5	1,167.0	151.8	191.5	65.5	126.0	54.4	71.6	−23.0	−16.7	65.7
IV	1,767.2	205.1	1,562.0	181.3	1,380.8	1,174.5	138.2	170.5	54.8	115.7	56.7	58.9	−17.1	−15.1	68.1
1982:															
I	1,756.6	207.8	1,548.8	176.3	1,372.4	1,181.6	120.3	134.8	38.9	95.8	58.0	37.8	−4.4	−10.0	70.5
II	1,771.0	212.1	1,559.0	181.2	1,377.8	1,190.4	114.8	131.3	37.1	94.2	59.7	34.5	−9.4	−7.1	72.6
III	1,794.4	216.0	1,578.4	184.2	1,394.2	1,195.8	125.3	139.8	42.1	97.6	62.6	35.0	−10.3	−4.2	73.1
IV p	....	219.0	....	186.4	....	1,188.8	....	....	....	....	63.8	....	−13.4	.5	73.8

[1] Indirect business tax and nontax liability plus business transfer payments less subsidies.

Source: Department of Commerce, Bureau of Economic Analysis.

TABLE B–13.—*Output, costs, and profits of nonfinancial corporate business, 1948–82*

[Quarterly data at seasonally adjusted annual rates]

Year or quarter	Gross domestic product of nonfinancial corporate business (billions of dollars)		Current-dollar cost and profit per unit of output (dollars)[1]								Output per hour of all employees (1972 dollars)	Compensation per hour of all employees (dollars)
	Current dollars	1972 dollars	Total cost and profit[2]	Capital consumption allowances with capital consumption adjustment	Indirect business tax, etc.[3]	Compensation of employees	Corporate profits with inventory valuation and capital consumption adjustments: Total	Profits tax liability	Profits after tax[4]	Net interest		
1948	137.3	229.7	0.598	0.047	0.053	0.382	0.112	0.051	0.060	0.004		
1949	133.5	219.9	.607	.053	.057	.388	.104	.042	.062	.004		
1950	151.9	247.5	.614	.051	.057	.383	.120	.068	.051	.004		
1951	174.5	270.2	.646	.054	.056	.408	.124	.079	.045	.004		
1952	182.3	275.2	.663	.057	.061	.430	.110	.065	.045	.004		
1953	195.0	292.0	.668	.058	.062	.441	.103	.063	.040	.004		
1954	191.9	283.4	.677	.063	.061	.446	.101	.055	.046	.005		
1955	216.7	315.1	.688	.061	.061	.439	.122	.064	.057	.005		
1956	231.6	324.1	.715	.067	.064	.467	.111	.062	.049	.005		
1957	242.3	328.3	.738	.073	.068	.484	.106	.058	.048	.007		
1958	236.3	313.4	.754	.079	.073	.497	.097	.052	.045	.009	5.206	2.589
1959	266.0	347.4	.766	.074	.073	.494	.116	.060	.056	.009	5.433	2.684
1960	277.0	358.4	.773	.075	.079	.505	.104	.054	.051	.010	5.536	2.797
1961	285.0	367.2	.776	.075	.082	.504	.104	.053	.051	.011	5.727	2.887
1962	311.3	399.7	.779	.071	.083	.500	.114	.052	.062	.011	5.997	2.998
1963	331.8	426.3	.778	.069	.083	.494	.120	.053	.067	.011	6.248	3.089
1964	358.4	455.6	.787	.068	.084	.497	.127	.053	.074	.012	6.469	3.213
1965	393.6	495.2	.795	.066	.083	.497	.137	.055	.082	.012	6.673	3.316
1966	431.5	530.7	.813	.067	.081	.515	.136	.056	.080	.014	6.776	3.492
1967	454.1	543.0	.836	.072	.084	.538	.127	.051	.076	.016	6.847	3.680
1968	500.2	578.9	.864	.074	.089	.558	.127	.058	.069	.017	7.074	3.945
1969	544.1	604.0	.901	.078	.096	.594	.112	.055	.057	.022	7.092	4.209
1970	563.7	599.6	.940	.087	.106	.631	.088	.045	.043	.028	7.115	4.491
1971	609.9	626.8	.973	.091	.113	.641	.099	.047	.052	.029	7.450	4.778
1972	678.0	678.0	1.000	.092	.113	.659	.107	.049	.058	.028	7.664	5.052
1973	759.4	731.9	1.038	.093	.114	.692	.107	.055	.053	.031	7.849	5.429
1974	818.9	708.2	1.156	.112	.127	.786	.090	.059	.030	.042	7.555	5.937
1975	890.0	694.2	1.282	.137	.140	.837	.124	.059	.065	.044	7.774	6.507
1976	1,001.3	745.5	1.343	.141	.141	.878	.144	.071	.073	.040	8.002	7.024
1977	1,128.4	795.8	1.418	.145	.141	.928	.163	.075	.088	.040	8.144	7.558
1978	1,276.2	846.3	1.508	.155	.144	.998	.168	.079	.089	.044	8.217	8.199
1979	1,416.8	876.1	1.617	.171	.149	1.094	.154	.079	.075	.050	8.202	8.970
1980	1,537.7	860.3	1.787	.200	.173	1.211	.143	.075	.068	.061	8.169	9.891
1981	1,732.3	881.3	1.966	.222	.202	1.305	.165	.072	.093	.071	8.311	10.846
1982 *p*	1,779.3	856.4	2.078	.250	.213	1.389	.142	.047	.095	.085		
1980:												
I	1,501.1	874.1	1.717	.186	.158	1.168	.148	.085	.063	.057	8.164	9.533
II	1,499.7	847.3	1.770	.200	.169	1.208	.133	.063	.070	.060	8.089	9.771
III	1,543.6	852.5	1.811	.206	.178	1.224	.143	.075	.068	.061	8.192	10.024
IV	1,606.5	867.4	1.852	.208	.186	1.245	.147	.078	.069	.066	8.235	10.249
1981:												
I	1,683.3	883.0	1.906	.211	.196	1.267	.170	.081	.089	.062	8.328	10.551
II	1,715.0	884.2	1.940	.218	.202	1.289	.161	.069	.091	.069	8.320	10.727
III	1,763.6	887.5	1.987	.224	.203	1.315	.171	.074	.097	.074	8.324	10.947
IV	1,767.2	870.4	2.030	.236	.208	1.349	.159	.063	.096	.078	8.273	11.163
1982:												
I	1,756.6	858.8	2.045	.242	.205	1.376	.140	.045	.095	.082	8.279	11.391
II	1,771.0	857.9	2.064	.247	.211	1.388	.134	.043	.091	.085	8.334	11.564
III	1,794.4	859.3	2.088	.251	.214	1.392	.146	.049	.097	.085	8.429	11.730

[1] Output is measured by gross domestic product of nonfinancial corporate business in 1972 dollars.
[2] This is equal to the deflator for gross domestic product of nonfinancial corporate business with the decimal point shifted two places to the left.
[3] Indirect business tax and nontax liability plus business transfer payments less subsidies.
[4] With inventory valuation and capital consumption adjustments.

Sources: Department of Commerce (Bureau of Economic Analysis) and Department of Labor (Bureau of Labor Statistics).

Table B–14.—*Personal consumption expenditures, 1929–82*

[Billions of dollars; quarterly data at seasonally adjusted annual rates]

Year or quarter	Personal consumption expenditures	Durable goods	Nondurable goods	Services	Durable goods: Motor vehicles and parts	Durable goods: Furniture and household equipment	Durable goods: Other	Nondurable goods: Food	Nondurable goods: Clothing and shoes
1929	77.3	9.2	37.7	30.3	3.3	4.7	1.2	19.5	9.4
1933	45.8	3.5	22.3	20.1	1.1	1.9	.5	11.5	4.6
1939	67.0	6.7	35.1	25.2	2.3	3.4	1.0	19.1	7.1
1940	71.0	7.8	37.0	26.2	2.8	3.8	1.1	20.2	7.5
1941	80.8	9.7	42.9	28.2	3.5	4.8	1.3	23.4	8.8
1942	88.6	6.9	50.8	31.0	.7	4.6	1.6	28.4	11.0
1943	99.4	6.5	58.6	34.3	.0	3.0	1.9	33.2	13.4
1944	108.2	6.7	64.3	37.1	.8	3.8	2.1	36.7	14.6
1945	119.5	8.0	71.9	39.6	1.0	4.5	2.5	40.6	16.5
1946	143.8	15.8	82.7	45.3	4.1	8.4	3.2	47.4	18.2
1947	161.7	20.4	90.9	50.4	6.6	10.6	3.3	52.3	18.8
1948	174.7	22.9	96.6	55.3	8.0	11.5	3.4	54.2	20.1
1949	178.1	25.0	94.9	58.2	10.6	11.3	3.2	52.5	19.3
1950	192.0	30.8	98.2	63.0	13.7	13.7	3.3	53.9	19.6
1951	207.1	29.8	108.8	68.5	12.2	14.0	3.6	60.4	21.2
1952	217.1	29.1	113.9	74.0	11.3	14.0	3.9	63.4	21.9
1953	229.7	32.5	116.5	80.6	13.9	14.6	4.1	64.4	22.1
1954	235.8	31.8	118.0	86.1	13.0	14.6	4.2	65.4	22.1
1955	253.7	38.6	122.9	92.1	17.8	16.2	4.6	67.2	23.1
1956	266.0	37.9	128.9	99.2	15.8	17.1	5.0	69.9	24.1
1957	280.4	39.3	135.2	105.9	17.2	16.9	5.2	73.6	24.3
1958	289.5	36.8	139.8	112.8	14.8	16.6	5.4	76.4	24.7
1959	310.8	42.4	146.4	121.9	18.9	17.8	5.8	79.1	26.1
1960	324.9	43.1	151.1	130.7	19.7	17.7	5.8	81.1	26.7
1961	335.0	41.6	155.3	138.1	17.8	17.9	5.8	83.2	27.4
1962	355.2	46.7	161.6	147.0	21.5	18.9	6.3	85.5	28.7
1963	374.6	51.4	167.1	156.1	24.4	20.3	6.7	87.8	29.5
1964	400.5	56.4	176.9	167.1	26.1	22.8	7.6	92.7	31.9
1965	430.4	63.0	188.6	178.7	30.0	24.7	8.3	98.9	33.5
1966	465.1	68.0	204.7	192.4	30.4	27.7	9.9	106.6	36.6
1967	490.3	70.1	212.6	207.6	30.1	29.5	10.5	109.6	38.2
1968	536.9	80.5	230.6	225.8	36.3	32.3	11.8	118.7	42.1
1969	581.8	85.7	247.8	248.2	38.7	34.1	13.0	127.5	45.5
1970	621.7	85.2	265.7	270.8	36.2	35.2	13.9	138.9	46.8
1971	672.2	97.2	278.8	296.2	45.4	37.2	14.6	144.2	50.6
1972	737.1	111.1	300.6	325.3	52.4	41.7	16.9	154.9	55.4
1973	812.0	123.3	333.4	355.2	57.1	47.1	19.2	172.1	61.4
1974	888.1	121.5	373.4	393.2	50.4	50.6	20.5	193.7	64.8
1975	976.4	132.2	407.3	437.0	55.8	53.5	22.9	213.6	69.6
1976	1,084.3	156.8	441.7	485.7	72.6	59.1	25.2	230.6	75.3
1977	1,204.4	178.2	478.8	547.4	84.8	65.7	27.7	249.8	82.6
1978	1,346.5	200.2	528.2	618.0	95.7	72.8	31.7	275.9	92.4
1979	1,507.2	213.4	600.0	693.7	96.6	81.8	35.1	311.6	99.1
1980	1,667.2	214.3	670.4	782.5	89.7	86.3	38.3	343.7	104.7
1981	1,843.2	234.6	734.5	874.1	98.6	93.4	42.6	375.3	114.6
1982 [p]	1,972.0	242.7	762.7	966.6	106.2	92.7	43.7	397.8	118.6
1980:									
I	1,618.7	220.8	650.6	747.3	97.9	85.5	37.5	333.9	103.0
II	1,622.2	199.0	656.7	766.6	79.2	83.4	36.4	336.4	102.2
III	1,682.0	212.7	673.7	795.6	88.1	86.0	38.6	346.4	104.8
IV	1,745.8	224.7	700.5	820.6	93.7	90.4	40.6	358.0	108.9
1981:									
I	1,799.9	236.9	720.6	842.4	102.1	93.1	41.7	368.8	112.3
II	1,819.4	230.4	729.6	859.4	94.2	93.3	42.9	372.1	114.0
III	1,868.8	241.2	741.3	886.3	104.0	93.8	43.4	378.0	115.9
IV	1,884.5	229.6	746.5	908.3	93.9	93.3	42.4	382.3	116.0
1982:									
I	1,919.4	237.9	749.1	932.4	103.2	91.0	43.7	387.9	117.5
II	1,947.8	240.7	755.0	952.1	103.3	93.2	44.2	395.0	118.4
III	1,986.3	240.3	768.4	977.6	104.3	92.7	43.3	401.3	119.1
IV [p]	2,034.6	251.7	778.3	1,004.5	114.1	94.0	43.6	406.8	119.5

See next page for continuation of table.

Table B–14.—*Personal consumption expenditures, 1929–82*—Continued

[Billions of dollars; quarterly data at seasonally adjusted annual rates]

Year or quarter	Nondurable goods—cont'd			Services						
	Gasoline and oil	Fuel oil and coal	Other	Housing [1]	Household operation			Transportation	Other	
					Total	Electricity and gas	Other		Total	Medical care
1929	1.8	1.6	5.4	11.7	4.0	1.2	2.9	2.6	12.0	2.2
1933	1.5	1.2	3.5	8.1	2.8	1.1	1.7	1.5	7.7	1.5
1939	2.2	1.4	5.3	9.4	3.8	1.4	2.4	2.0	10.0	2.1
1940	2.3	1.5	5.8	9.7	4.0	1.5	2.6	2.1	10.3	2.2
1941	2.6	1.7	6.4	10.4	4.3	1.5	2.7	2.4	11.2	2.4
1942	2.1	1.9	7.5	11.2	4.8	1.6	3.2	2.7	12.2	2.6
1943	1.3	2.0	8.7	11.8	5.2	1.7	3.5	3.4	13.9	2.9
1944	1.4	2.0	9.6	12.3	5.9	1.8	4.1	3.7	15.2	3.3
1945	1.8	2.2	10.8	12.8	6.4	1.9	4.5	4.0	16.4	3.6
1946	3.4	2.5	11.3	14.2	6.8	2.1	4.7	5.0	19.4	4.5
1947	4.0	3.0	12.8	16.0	7.5	2.3	5.1	5.3	21.7	5.5
1948	4.8	3.4	14.1	17.9	8.1	2.6	5.4	5.8	23.6	6.3
1949	5.3	3.1	14.7	19.6	8.5	2.9	5.6	5.9	24.1	6.4
1950	5.5	3.4	15.8	21.7	9.5	3.3	6.2	6.2	25.6	6.9
1951	6.1	3.5	17.6	24.3	10.4	3.7	6.7	6.7	27.0	7.3
1952	6.8	3.4	18.3	27.0	11.1	4.1	7.0	7.1	28.8	8.0
1953	7.4	3.4	19.3	29.8	12.0	4.5	7.5	7.8	31.0	8.9
1954	7.8	3.5	19.2	32.2	12.6	5.0	7.6	7.9	33.3	9.7
1955	8.6	3.8	20.3	34.3	14.0	5.5	8.5	8.2	35.6	10.3
1956	9.4	3.9	21.6	36.7	15.2	6.1	9.2	8.6	38.7	11.0
1957	10.2	4.1	23.0	39.3	16.2	6.5	9.7	9.0	41.4	12.0
1958	10.6	4.2	24.0	42.0	17.3	7.1	10.2	9.3	44.3	13.1
1959	11.3	4.0	25.9	45.0	18.5	7.6	10.9	10.1	48.3	14.3
1960	12.0	3.8	27.5	48.1	20.1	8.3	11.8	10.7	51.7	15.4
1961	12.0	3.7	29.0	51.2	21.0	8.8	12.2	11.2	54.8	16.4
1962	12.6	3.7	31.1	54.7	22.2	9.4	12.8	11.7	58.3	18.0
1963	12.9	4.0	32.8	58.0	23.4	9.9	13.6	12.2	62.5	19.5
1964	13.5	4.1	34.6	61.4	24.8	10.4	14.4	12.8	68.1	22.3
1965	14.7	4.4	37.2	65.5	26.3	10.9	15.4	13.7	73.3	23.9
1966	16.0	4.7	40.9	69.5	28.0	11.5	16.5	15.0	79.9	26.0
1967	17.0	4.8	43.0	74.1	30.0	12.2	17.8	16.2	87.2	28.4
1968	18.6	4.7	46.5	79.8	32.2	13.1	19.2	17.6	96.2	31.4
1969	20.7	4.5	49.6	87.0	35.0	14.2	20.8	19.5	106.8	36.5
1970	22.4	4.4	53.2	93.9	37.7	15.4	22.2	22.0	117.2	41.0
1971	23.9	4.5	55.5	102.7	41.0	17.0	24.0	25.1	127.4	45.9
1972	25.4	5.0	59.8	112.5	45.2	18.8	26.4	27.5	140.1	51.4
1973	28.6	6.2	65.0	123.8	49.6	20.5	29.1	28.8	153.0	57.4
1974	36.6	7.7	70.5	137.4	55.2	24.0	31.2	30.9	169.8	64.5
1975	40.4	8.2	75.5	149.8	63.3	29.2	34.1	33.2	190.7	73.7
1976	44.0	9.8	82.1	166.5	71.6	32.9	38.7	38.6	209.0	83.3
1977	48.1	10.7	87.6	185.9	81.1	38.5	42.6	46.4	234.1	96.5
1978	51.2	11.9	96.9	209.6	90.1	42.9	47.2	51.2	267.1	108.4
1979	66.6	16.1	106.6	236.0	99.3	47.8	51.5	56.3	302.0	124.1
1980	87.0	19.0	116.0	266.0	111.7	56.6	55.1	62.9	341.9	143.5
1981	96.8	19.7	128.2	295.3	128.9	66.8	62.1	65.4	384.4	170.9
1982 [p]	93.9	17.6	134.8	324.7	144.1	75.2	68.9	70.3	427.6	194.7
1980:										
I	82.0	18.8	112.9	254.8	105.1	50.9	54.2	61.2	326.2	134.7
II	86.1	18.6	113.4	261.6	108.9	54.8	54.1	61.6	334.5	140.6
III	87.0	19.3	116.2	269.6	114.7	59.2	55.5	64.1	347.2	145.9
IV	92.8	19.2	121.6	278.1	118.2	61.4	56.8	64.6	359.8	152.9
1981:										
I	95.2	20.0	124.3	284.4	120.7	61.9	58.8	66.2	371.1	159.7
II	96.7	19.9	127.0	291.3	125.2	64.6	60.7	64.3	378.5	166.9
III	97.7	19.9	129.8	298.7	132.8	69.4	63.5	65.5	389.3	175.6
IV	97.5	19.2	131.5	307.0	136.9	71.2	65.7	65.7	398.7	181.5
1982:										
I	95.3	17.3	131.1	314.5	141.4	75.1	66.3	66.9	409.6	186.4
II	91.3	17.3	133.1	320.4	140.7	72.6	68.1	69.5	421.5	192.1
III	94.2	18.4	135.4	328.2	145.0	75.2	69.9	71.5	432.9	197.9
IV [p]	94.9	17.6	139.6	335.5	149.3	77.8	71.5	73.4	446.4	202.4

[1] Includes imputed rental value of owner-occupied housing.

Source: Department of Commerce, Bureau of Economic Analysis.

Table B–15.—*Gross private domestic investment, 1929–82*

[Billions of dollars; quarterly data at seasonally adjusted annual rates]

Year or quarter	Gross private domestic investment	Fixed investment								Change in business inventories	
		Total	Nonresidential			Residential					
			Total	Structures	Producers' durable equipment	Total	Nonfarm structures	Farm structures	Producers' durable equipment	Total	Nonfarm
1929	16.2	14.5	10.6	5.1	5.5	3.9	3.6	0.2	0.1	1.7	1.8
1933	1.4	3.0	2.4	1.0	1.4	.6	.5	.0	.0	−1.6	−1.4
1939	9.3	8.8	5.9	2.0	3.9	2.9	2.7	.1	.1	.4	.3
1940	13.1	10.9	7.5	2.3	5.2	3.4	3.2	.2	.1	2.2	1.9
1941	17.9	13.4	9.4	3.0	6.4	4.0	3.6	.2	.1	4.5	4.0
1942	9.9	8.1	6.0	1.9	4.1	2.2	1.9	.2	.1	1.8	.7
1943	5.8	6.4	5.0	1.4	3.7	1.4	1.2	.2	.0	−.6	−.6
1944	7.2	8.1	6.9	1.9	5.0	1.3	1.1	.1	.0	−1.0	−.6
1945	10.6	11.7	10.1	2.8	7.3	1.5	1.4	.1	.0	−1.0	−.6
1946	30.7	24.3	16.9	6.9	9.9	7.4	6.7	.5	.2	6.4	6.4
1947	34.0	34.4	23.0	7.7	15.3	11.4	10.4	.7	.3	−.5	1.3
1948	45.9	41.1	26.3	9.0	17.3	14.9	13.7	.9	.3	4.7	3.0
1949	35.3	38.4	24.4	8.7	15.7	13.9	12.8	.8	.3	−3.1	−2.2
1950	53.8	47.0	27.3	9.5	17.8	19.8	18.6	.8	.4	6.8	6.0
1951	59.2	48.9	31.3	11.4	19.9	17.6	16.4	.8	.4	10.3	9.1
1952	52.1	49.0	31.3	11.6	19.7	17.7	16.5	.8	.4	3.1	2.1
1953	53.3	52.9	34.5	12.9	21.5	18.4	17.3	.8	.4	.4	1.1
1954	52.7	54.3	34.2	13.4	20.8	20.1	19.0	.7	.4	−1.5	−2.1
1955	68.4	62.4	38.5	14.6	23.9	23.9	22.8	.6	.4	6.0	5.5
1956	71.0	66.3	44.0	17.7	26.3	22.3	21.2	.7	.5	4.7	5.1
1957	69.2	67.9	47.0	18.4	28.6	20.9	19.7	.7	.5	1.3	.8
1958	61.9	63.4	42.0	17.2	24.9	21.4	20.3	.7	.5	−1.5	−2.3
1959	78.1	72.5	45.9	17.6	28.3	26.6	25.3	.7	.6	5.7	5.7
1960	75.9	72.9	48.5	18.8	29.7	24.5	23.3	.6	.5	3.0	2.7
1961	74.8	72.5	48.0	19.1	28.9	24.5	23.2	.7	.5	2.3	2.0
1962	85.4	79.2	52.2	20.1	32.1	27.0	25.8	.6	.5	6.3	5.5
1963	90.9	84.9	54.8	20.5	34.4	30.1	28.9	.7	.6	6.0	5.2
1964	97.4	91.7	61.0	22.4	38.7	30.7	29.4	.7	.6	5.6	6.2
1965	113.5	103.7	72.7	27.0	45.8	30.9	29.6	.6	.7	9.9	8.9
1966	125.7	111.6	83.1	30.1	53.0	28.5	27.1	.7	.7	14.1	14.3
1967	122.8	112.5	83.9	30.3	53.7	28.6	27.2	.7	.7	10.3	9.6
1968	133.3	125.4	90.7	32.4	58.2	34.8	33.3	.6	.9	7.9	7.8
1969	149.3	139.5	101.3	36.7	64.6	38.2	36.5	.7	1.0	9.8	9.7
1970	144.2	141.0	103.9	38.7	65.2	37.1	35.4	.6	1.1	3.2	3.1
1971	166.4	158.8	107.9	40.5	67.4	50.9	48.9	.7	1.3	7.7	6.4
1972	195.0	184.8	121.0	44.1	76.9	63.8	61.5	.7	1.5	10.2	9.6
1973	229.8	211.3	143.3	51.0	92.3	68.0	65.6	.7	1.7	18.5	15.2
1974	228.7	214.5	156.6	55.9	100.7	57.9	54.8	1.3	1.8	14.1	16.0
1975	206.1	213.0	157.7	55.4	102.3	55.3	52.4	1.0	1.9	−6.9	−10.5
1976	257.9	246.0	174.1	58.8	115.3	72.0	68.8	1.1	2.1	11.8	13.9
1977	324.1	301.0	205.2	64.4	140.8	95.8	92.0	1.5	2.3	23.0	21.9
1978	386.6	360.1	248.9	78.7	170.2	111.2	107.0	1.7	2.5	26.5	25.4
1979	423.0	408.8	290.2	98.3	191.9	118.6	114.0	1.7	2.9	14.3	8.6
1980	402.3	412.4	309.2	110.5	198.6	103.2	98.3	1.9	3.0	−10.0	−5.7
1981	471.5	451.1	346.1	129.7	216.4	104.9	99.7	2.1	3.2	20.5	15.0
1982 ᵖ	421.9	443.3	347.5	141.7	205.8	95.8	90.1	2.5	3.2	−21.4	−21.6
1980:											
I	424.0	424.6	311.2	110.9	200.2	113.5	107.4	3.1	3.0	−.7	.7
II	391.0	391.4	300.2	109.1	191.2	91.2	86.9	1.4	2.9	−.4	4.0
III	384.1	405.3	307.8	109.5	198.2	97.6	93.5	1.0	3.0	−21.2	−15.4
IV	410.3	428.0	317.5	112.6	204.9	110.5	105.4	2.0	3.1	−17.7	−12.3
1981:											
I	455.7	443.5	330.0	119.6	210.4	113.6	109.1	1.3	3.2	12.2	10.0
II	475.5	450.9	341.3	127.0	214.3	109.5	104.7	1.6	3.2	24.6	19.3
III	486.0	454.2	353.0	132.7	220.2	101.2	95.6	2.4	3.2	31.8	24.6
IV	468.9	455.7	360.2	139.6	220.6	95.5	89.4	2.9	3.2	13.2	6.0
1982:											
I	414.8	450.4	357.0	141.4	215.6	93.4	87.9	2.4	3.1	−35.6	−36.0
II	431.5	447.7	352.2	143.6	208.6	95.5	89.6	2.8	3.2	−16.2	−15.0
III	443.3	438.6	344.2	141.3	203.0	94.3	88.7	2.4	3.2	4.7	3.7
IV ᵖ	397.9	436.4	336.6	140.4	196.2	99.8	94.1	2.4	3.2	−38.5	−39.0

Source: Department of Commerce, Bureau of Economic Analysis.

Table B–16.—*Gross and net private domestic investment, 1929–82*

[Billions of dollars]

Year	Gross private domestic investment	Less: Capital consumption allowances with capital consumption adjustment	Equals: Net private domestic investment									
			Total	Net fixed investment								Change in business inventories
				Total	Nonresidential			Residential				
					Total	Structures	Producers' durable equipment	Total	Nonfarm structures	Farm structures	Producers' durable equipment	
1929	16.2	9.7	6.5	4.8	3.1	1.7	1.4	1.7	1.7	−0.1	0.0	1.7
1933	1.4	7.4	−6.0	−4.5	−3.5	−1.6	−1.8	−1.0	−.9	−.1	−.0	−1.6
1939	9.3	8.7	.6	.1	−.6	−1.0	.3	.8	.8	−.0	.0	.4
1940	13.1	9.1	4.1	1.9	.7	−.7	1.4	1.2	1.1	.0	.0	2.2
1941	17.9	10.0	7.9	3.4	2.0	−.3	2.2	1.5	1.4	.0	.0	4.5
1942	9.9	11.2	−1.3	−3.0	−2.5	−1.7	−.7	−.6	−.5	−.1	−.0	1.8
1943	5.8	11.5	−5.7	−5.0	−3.5	−2.6	−.9	−1.6	−1.4	−.1	−.1	−.6
1944	7.2	11.7	−4.6	−3.6	−1.7	−2.0	.3	−1.9	−1.7	−.1	−.1	−1.0
1945	10.6	12.2	−1.6	−.6	1.3	−1.2	2.4	−1.8	−1.6	−.2	−.1	−1.0
1946	30.7	14.0	16.6	10.3	6.6	2.4	4.2	3.7	3.4	.2	.1	6.4
1947	34.0	17.3	16.6	17.1	10.2	2.1	8.2	6.8	6.4	.3	.2	−.5
1948	45.9	20.2	25.6	20.9	11.3	2.7	8.6	9.7	9.1	.4	.2	4.7
1949	35.3	21.8	13.5	16.6	8.1	2.3	5.8	8.5	7.9	.4	.1	−3.1
1950	53.8	23.5	30.3	23.5	9.6	2.9	6.7	13.9	13.4	.3	.2	6.8
1951	59.2	27.2	32.0	21.7	10.7	3.9	6.7	11.0	10.6	.3	.1	10.3
1952	52.1	29.3	22.8	19.7	9.1	3.8	5.3	10.6	10.3	.3	.1	3.1
1953	53.3	31.0	22.4	21.9	10.8	4.8	6.0	11.1	10.8	.3	.1	.4
1954	52.7	32.7	20.0	21.6	9.1	5.1	4.0	12.5	12.2	.2	.1	−1.5
1955	68.4	34.8	33.6	27.6	11.9	5.9	6.0	15.7	15.6	.0	.1	6.0
1956	71.0	38.7	32.3	27.6	13.9	7.9	6.0	13.7	13.4	.1	.1	4.7
1957	69.2	41.7	27.5	26.1	14.3	7.9	6.4	11.8	11.7	.1	.1	1.3
1958	61.9	43.5	18.4	19.9	8.1	6.4	1.8	11.8	11.6	.1	.1	1.5
1959	78.1	44.9	33.2	27.5	10.6	6.4	4.2	16.9	16.7	.1	.2	5.7
1960	75.9	46.3	29.6	26.7	12.3	7.3	5.0	14.4	14.3	−.0	.1	3.0
1961	74.8	47.5	27.3	24.9	10.9	7.3	3.6	14.0	13.9	.1	.1	2.3
1962	85.4	49.0	36.5	30.2	14.0	7.9	6.1	16.2	16.1	.0	.1	6.3
1963	90.9	50.6	40.3	34.4	15.3	7.8	7.5	19.0	18.8	.0	.1	6.0
1964	97.4	52.9	44.5	38.9	19.7	9.1	10.6	19.1	18.9	.0	.2	5.6
1965	113.5	56.0	57.5	47.6	28.9	12.9	16.0	18.7	18.6	−.0	.2	9.9
1966	125.7	60.7	65.0	50.9	35.4	14.8	20.6	15.5	15.3	.0	.2	14.1
1967	122.8	65.9	57.0	46.6	31.9	13.8	18.2	14.7	14.5	.0	.2	10.3
1968	133.3	72.1	61.2	53.3	33.6	14.5	19.1	19.8	19.6	−.1	.3	7.9
1969	149.3	80.0	69.3	59.5	38.1	16.6	21.5	21.3	21.0	−.0	.4	9.8
1970	144.2	88.1	56.2	52.9	33.9	16.3	17.6	19.0	18.9	−.2	.4	3.2
1971	166.4	96.5	69.9	62.3	31.1	15.6	15.5	31.2	30.9	−.2	.5	7.7
1972	195.0	106.4	88.6	78.4	37.0	16.6	20.4	41.3	40.9	−.2	.6	10.2
1973	229.8	116.5	113.3	94.8	51.9	20.7	31.2	42.9	42.5	−.4	.7	18.5
1974	228.7	136.0	92.7	78.5	49.2	18.9	30.3	29.3	28.4	.2	.7	14.1
1975	206.1	159.3	46.8	53.7	30.3	13.1	17.3	23.4	23.1	−.2	.5	−6.9
1976	257.9	175.0	82.8	71.0	34.3	14.1	20.2	36.8	36.5	−.2	.5	11.8
1977	324.1	195.2	128.9	105.9	50.7	16.0	34.7	55.2	54.5	.1	.6	23.0
1978	386.6	222.5	164.1	137.7	73.6	23.3	50.4	64.0	63.3	.1	.6	26.5
1979	423.0	256.0	167.0	152.7	89.0	33.7	55.3	63.7	63.2	−.2	.7	14.3
1980	402.3	293.2	109.1	119.1	77.3	36.0	41.3	41.8	41.4	−.2	.6	−10.0
1981	471.5	330.1	141.4	121.0	82.9	45.9	37.0	38.1	37.7	−.1	.5	20.5
1982 [p]	421.9	356.8	65.1	86.5	60.9	49.5	11.5	25.6	25.1	.2	.2	−21.4

Source: Department of Commerce, Bureau of Economic Analysis.

TABLE B-17.—*Inventories and final sales of business, 1946–82*

[Billions of dollars, except as noted; seasonally adjusted]

Year and quarter	Inventories[1]							Final sales[2]	Inventory—final sales ratio	
	Total	Farm	Nonfarm						Total	Nonfarm[3]
			Total	Manufacturing	Wholesale trade	Retail trade	Other			
Fourth quarter:										
1946	72.0	22.7	49.3	26.7	10.1	11.4	3.5	16.0	4.50	3.08
1947	82.6	25.1	57.5	29.3	10.5	13.1	4.6	18.3	4.51	3.14
1948	87.2	22.9	64.3	32.5	11.7	15.1	5.0	19.6	4.44	3.27
1949	78.7	19.8	59.0	28.9	11.8	14.0	4.3	19.5	4.03	3.02
1950	98.0	26.1	71.9	35.2	13.8	17.5	5.4	21.7	4.53	3.32
1951	110.5	28.3	82.2	43.4	14.6	18.0	6.1	24.6	4.49	3.34
1952	109.2	26.0	83.1	44.4	14.8	17.7	6.2	26.1	4.18	3.18
1953	110.1	24.6	85.5	46.4	15.0	18.3	6.0	27.2	4.05	3.15
1954	107.6	23.8	83.9	44.3	15.3	18.5	5.9	27.5	3.91	3.05
1955	114.8	22.5	92.2	48.8	16.6	20.9	6.0	29.7	3.86	3.10
1956	124.0	22.9	101.0	54.5	17.9	21.7	6.9	31.4	3.95	3.22
1957	127.6	24.3	103.3	54.8	18.2	22.9	7.3	32.7	3.90	3.16
1958	127.3	25.6	101.7	53.2	18.3	22.9	7.3	33.7	3.77	3.01
1959	132.0	24.4	107.6	55.7	20.0	23.9	8.0	35.6	3.71	3.02
1960	136.0	25.6	110.4	56.6	20.4	25.3	8.1	36.9	3.69	2.99
1961	137.9	25.9	112.1	57.7	20.9	24.9	8.7	38.8	3.55	2.89
1962	144.6	27.3	117.3	60.9	21.5	26.3	8.6	41.1	3.52	2.85
1963	150.4	27.6	122.7	62.9	23.1	27.6	9.2	43.7	3.44	2.81
1964	156.2	26.5	129.7	66.4	24.4	29.0	9.9	46.2	3.38	2.81
1965	170.5	29.9	140.6	71.5	26.3	31.9	10.9	51.0	3.34	2.76
1966	187.4	29.6	157.8	81.7	29.9	34.6	11.6	54.1	3.46	2.92
1967	199.4	29.5	169.9	88.7	32.4	35.3	13.5	57.6	3.46	2.95
1968	213.5	30.6	182.9	95.2	34.3	39.0	14.4	63.3	3.37	2.89
1969	234.6	33.3	201.3	104.8	37.7	42.8	16.0	67.4	3.48	2.99
1970	244.0	32.3	211.6	108.4	41.7	44.3	17.3	70.8	3.45	2.99
1971	260.8	36.7	224.1	109.9	44.9	50.5	18.8	77.2	3.38	2.90
1972	288.7	45.6	243.1	116.8	49.4	55.7	21.2	85.8	3.37	2.83
1973	357.7	66.6	291.2	141.1	60.2	64.8	25.0	94.5	3.79	3.08
1974	434.4	62.4	372.0	189.6	76.9	74.1	31.3	102.0	4.26	3.65
1975	439.4	64.5	374.9	189.8	77.3	74.6	33.3	113.6	3.87	3.30
1976	473.6	60.6	413.0	207.5	86.9	82.9	35.7	124.1	3.82	3.33
1977	519.5	59.9	459.6	224.7	98.7	93.7	42.5	138.9	3.74	3.31
1978	602.3	73.9	528.3	254.2	114.6	109.0	50.6	159.5	3.78	3.31
1979	705.0	81.9	623.1	306.6	135.7	121.0	59.8	176.9	3.99	3.52
1980	776.0	86.9	689.1	342.6	153.0	127.7	65.7	194.9	3.98	3.54
1981	822.4	81.8	740.5	366.4	163.0	140.7	70.5	210.4	3.91	3.52
1982 p	806.1	80.6	725.5	346.9	162.1	141.8	74.8	221.5	3.64	3.28
1980:										
I	724.1	79.0	645.1	321.0	140.5	121.3	62.2	182.0	3.98	3.54
II	737.2	81.1	656.1	328.1	144.0	122.4	61.5	181.2	4.07	3.62
III	757.3	86.2	671.1	333.2	148.5	126.1	63.4	188.2	4.02	3.57
IV	776.0	86.9	689.1	342.6	153.0	127.7	65.7	194.9	3.98	3.54
1981:										
I	791.6	85.9	705.7	352.6	156.5	129.0	67.6	201.8	3.92	3.50
II	804.2	86.5	717.7	357.2	158.1	134.2	68.3	203.3	3.96	3.53
III	814.3	81.5	732.8	365.1	159.5	139.1	69.1	208.5	3.91	3.51
IV	822.4	81.8	740.5	366.4	163.0	140.7	70.5	210.4	3.91	3.52
1982:										
I	809.7	84.5	725.2	358.1	158.4	137.6	71.1	213.8	3.79	3.39
II	812.5	86.4	726.1	352.7	160.8	140.2	72.4	215.5	3.77	3.37
III	816.0	83.5	732.5	351.3	161.9	145.6	73.7	217.1	3.76	3.37
IV p	806.1	80.6	725.5	346.9	162.1	141.8	74.8	221.5	3.64	3.28

[1] End of quarter.

[2] Quarterly totals at monthly rates. Business final sales equals final sales less gross product of households and institutions, government, and rest of the world, and includes a small amount of final sales by farms.

[3] Ratio based on total business final sales, which includes a small amount of final sales by farms.

Note.—The industry classification of inventories is on an establishment basis and is based on the 1972 Standard Industrial Classification (SIC) beginning 1948 and on the 1942 SIC prior to 1948.

Source: Department of Commerce, Bureau of Economic Analysis.

TABLE B-18.—*Inventories and final sales of business in 1972 dollars, 1947–82*

[Billions of 1972 dollars, except as noted; seasonally adjusted]

Year and quarter	Inventories[1]							Final sales[2]	Inventory—final sales ratio	
	Total	Farm	Nonfarm						Total	Nonfarm[3]
			Total	Manufacturing	Wholesale trade	Retail trade	Other			
Fourth quarter:										
1947	116.1	25.7	90.5	47.4	16.0	18.3	8.7	33.2	3.50	2.73
1948	121.6	26.7	94.8	48.8	17.2	20.3	8.6	34.4	3.53	2.76
1949	117.2	26.2	91.0	46.2	17.2	19.8	7.8	34.6	3.38	2.63
1950	127.7	27.5	100.2	49.3	19.2	23.0	8.7	36.9	3.46	2.72
1951	141.4	29.1	112.3	60.0	19.7	23.0	9.5	39.8	3.55	2.82
1952	145.7	30.4	115.4	62.7	20.1	23.0	9.6	41.6	3.51	2.78
1953	147.2	30.2	117.1	64.5	20.3	23.6	8.7	43.0	3.42	2.72
1954	145.0	31.1	114.0	60.9	20.6	23.7	8.8	43.1	3.36	2.64
1955	152.8	31.5	121.2	64.3	22.1	26.5	8.4	45.6	3.35	2.66
1956	158.6	30.7	127.8	69.1	22.8	26.8	9.2	46.5	3.41	2.75
1957	160.1	31.4	128.7	68.7	22.5	27.8	9.8	47.1	3.40	2.73
1958	158.3	32.4	125.9	66.1	22.5	27.5	9.8	48.1	3.29	2.62
1959	165.3	32.4	132.9	69.1	24.6	28.7	10.5	49.7	3.33	2.68
1960	168.8	32.8	136.1	69.9	25.1	30.3	10.7	50.7	3.33	2.68
1961	171.8	33.2	138.6	71.7	25.7	29.8	11.4	53.1	3.24	2.61
1962	179.7	34.5	145.2	75.6	26.6	31.6	11.4	55.3	3.25	2.62
1963	187.2	35.7	151.5	78.2	28.4	33.0	12.0	58.3	3.21	2.60
1964	194.3	35.1	159.2	82.0	29.9	34.5	12.8	60.9	3.19	2.61
1965	206.1	36.2	169.9	87.0	31.6	37.4	13.8	66.1	3.12	2.57
1966	222.9	36.0	186.8	97.2	35.3	40.0	14.3	67.5	3.30	2.77
1967	235.1	36.8	198.3	104.1	37.8	40.0	16.3	70.1	3.36	2.83
1968	244.1	37.0	207.0	108.4	38.9	43.0	16.8	73.8	3.31	2.81
1969	255.1	37.3	217.8	112.8	41.2	45.9	17.9	74.7	3.41	2.92
1970	258.9	37.7	221.2	112.9	44.0	46.1	18.2	75.2	3.44	2.94
1971	267.0	39.2	227.8	111.8	45.9	51.2	19.0	78.9	3.38	2.89
1972	277.2	39.8	237.4	114.4	47.9	54.6	20.5	84.7	3.27	2.80
1973	294.4	42.1	252.3	121.8	50.4	58.8	21.4	87.2	3.38	2.89
1974	306.0	41.8	264.2	130.9	54.1	58.3	20.9	85.0	3.60	3.11
1975	299.2	43.0	256.3	127.1	52.2	55.8	21.1	88.1	3.40	2.91
1976	307.0	41.1	265.9	130.9	55.5	58.8	20.8	92.2	3.33	2.88
1977	320.3	40.8	279.5	134.1	59.7	63.1	22.6	97.6	3.28	2.86
1978	336.3	40.8	295.5	139.8	63.5	67.3	24.9	103.0	3.27	2.87
1979	343.6	43.2	300.4	145.0	64.7	66.1	24.6	105.4	3.26	2.85
1980	338.6	41.1	297.5	145.9	65.0	63.0	23.6	105.0	3.22	2.83
1981	347.6	43.2	304.4	148.4	66.5	66.1	23.4	104.6	3.32	2.91
1982 p	339.1	43.3	295.7	141.0	65.7	65.4	23.6	105.5	3.21	2.80
1980:										
I	342.9	43.0	299.9	146.6	64.6	64.2	24.5	105.8	3.24	2.84
II	342.3	42.4	299.9	147.4	64.9	63.7	23.8	102.7	3.33	2.92
III	340.2	41.7	298.4	146.3	65.0	63.5	23.6	103.7	3.28	2.88
IV	338.6	41.1	297.5	145.9	65.0	63.0	23.6	105.0	3.22	2.83
1981:										
I	339.2	41.2	298.0	146.9	64.6	62.8	23.6	106.4	3.19	2.80
II	342.3	41.7	300.6	147.5	65.1	64.6	23.4	105.2	3.25	2.86
III	346.4	42.4	304.0	149.4	65.4	65.9	23.3	105.5	3.28	2.88
IV	347.6	43.2	304.4	148.4	66.5	66.1	23.4	104.6	3.32	2.91
1982:										
I	343.7	43.3	300.5	146.4	65.3	65.1	23.6	105.0	3.27	2.86
II	342.6	43.1	299.5	144.6	65.8	65.4	23.7	104.6	3.28	2.86
III	343.5	43.3	300.2	143.3	66.1	67.2	23.7	104.3	3.29	2.88
IV p	339.1	43.3	295.7	141.0	65.7	65.4	23.6	105.5	3.21	2.80

[1] End of quarter.

[2] Quarterly totals at monthly rates. Business final sales equals final sales less gross product of households and institutions, government, and rest of world, and includes a small amount of final sales by farms.

[3] Ratio based on total business final sales, which includes a small amount of final sales by farms.

Note.—The industry classification of inventories is on an establishment basis and is based on the 1972 Standard Industrial Classification (SIC) beginning 1948 and on the 1942 SIC prior to 1948.

Source: Department of Commerce, Bureau of Economic Analysis.

Table B–19.—*Relation of gross national product, net national product, and national income, 1929–82*

[Billions of dollars; quarterly data at seasonally adjusted annual rates]

Year or quarter	Gross national product	Less: Capital consumption allowances with capital consumption adjustment	Equals: Net national product	Less: Indirect business tax and nontax liability	Less: Business transfer payments	Less: Statistical discrepancy	Plus: Subsidies less current surplus of government enterprises	Equals: National income
1929	103.4	9.7	93.7	7.1	0.6	1.1	−0.2	84.8
1933	55.8	7.4	48.4	7.1	.7	.7	−.0	39.9
1939	90.9	8.7	82.2	9.4	.5	1.4	.4	71.4
1940	100.0	9.1	91.0	10.1	.4	1.1	.4	79.7
1941	125.0	10.0	115.0	11.3	.5	.6	.1	102.7
1942	158.5	11.2	147.3	11.8	.5	−.8	.1	135.9
1943	192.1	11.5	180.7	12.8	.5	−1.8	.1	169.3
1944	210.6	11.7	198.9	14.2	.5	2.7	.6	182.1
1945	212.4	12.2	200.2	15.5	.5	4.1	.7	180.7
1946	209.8	14.0	195.8	17.1	.5	.5	.9	178.6
1947	233.1	17.3	215.7	18.4	.6	1.5	−.2	194.9
1948	259.5	20.2	239.3	20.1	.7	−1.6	−.1	219.9
1949	258.3	21.8	236.5	21.3	.8	.6	−.3	213.6
1950	286.5	23.5	263.0	23.4	.8	1.3	.1	237.6
1951	330.8	27.2	303.6	25.3	.9	3.2	−.1	274.1
1952	348.0	29.3	318.7	27.7	1.0	1.7	−.3	287.9
1953	366.8	31.0	335.8	29.7	1.2	2.3	−.5	302.1
1954	366.8	32.7	334.1	29.6	1.1	2.0	−.3	301.1
1955	400.0	34.8	365.3	32.2	1.2	1.3	−.0	330.5
1956	421.7	38.7	383.0	35.1	1.4	−2.1	.7	349.4
1957	444.0	41.7	402.3	37.5	1.5	−1.2	.7	365.2
1958	449.7	43.5	406.2	38.7	1.6	.2	1.1	366.9
1959	487.9	44.9	443.0	41.8	1.8	−1.3	.1	400.8
1960	506.5	46.3	460.2	45.4	2.0	−2.4	.4	415.7
1961	524.6	47.5	477.0	48.0	2.0	−.1	1.7	428.8
1962	565.0	49.0	516.1	51.6	2.1	2.1	1.8	462.0
1963	596.7	50.6	546.1	54.6	2.4	1.7	1.1	488.5
1964	637.7	52.9	584.8	58.8	2.7	.1	1.7	524.9
1965	691.1	56.0	635.0	62.6	2.8	−1.2	1.6	572.4
1966	756.0	60.7	695.3	65.3	3.0	1.4	2.5	628.1
1967	799.6	65.9	733.7	70.2	3.1	−.3	1.6	662.2
1968	873.4	72.1	801.3	78.9	3.4	−2.1	1.4	722.5
1969	944.0	80.0	864.0	86.6	3.9	−3.9	1.9	779.3
1970	992.7	88.1	904.7	94.3	4.1	−1.5	2.9	810.7
1971	1,077.6	96.5	981.1	103.7	4.4	4.1	2.6	871.5
1972	1,185.9	106.4	1,079.5	111.5	4.9	3.3	3.8	963.6
1973	1,326.4	116.5	1,209.9	120.9	5.5	.8	3.4	1,086.2
1974	1,434.2	136.0	1,298.2	129.1	5.8	3.7	1.1	1,160.7
1975	1,549.2	159.3	1,389.9	140.1	7.4	5.5	2.4	1,239.4
1976	1,718.0	175.0	1,543.0	151.7	7.9	5.1	1.0	1,379.2
1977	1,918.3	195.2	1,723.2	165.7	8.6	1.4	3.1	1,550.5
1978	2,163.9	222.5	1,941.4	178.2	9.3	−2.6	3.7	1,760.3
1979	2,417.8	256.0	2,161.7	189.6	10.3	−1.5	3.4	1,966.7
1980	2,633.1	293.2	2,339.9	213.0	11.4	3.9	5.5	2,117.1
1981	2,937.7	330.1	2,607.6	251.3	12.4	−1.9	6.6	2,352.5
1982 p	3,057.5	356.8	2,700.8	258.8	13.7	.1	8.3	2,436.5
1980:								
I	2,575.9	278.4	2,297.5	200.1	11.0	10.5	3.8	2,079.7
II	2,573.4	289.2	2,284.3	206.7	11.3	3.8	4.7	2,067.2
III	2,643.7	298.6	2,345.0	216.3	11.5	2.2	7.4	2,122.3
IV	2,739.4	306.6	2,432.9	228.9	11.8	−1.0	6.0	2,199.2
1981:								
I	2,864.9	315.4	2,549.5	244.6	12.0	5.1	5.8	2,293.7
II	2,901.8	325.0	2,576.8	252.0	12.2	−4.6	7.2	2,324.4
III	2,980.9	335.2	2,645.8	253.3	12.5	−.8	6.5	2,387.3
IV	3,003.2	344.8	2,658.4	255.3	12.8	−7.2	7.0	2,404.5
1982:								
I	2,995.5	348.7	2,646.7	250.2	13.1	−7.5	6.0	2,396.9
II	3,045.2	353.9	2,691.2	256.7	13.5	.8	4.9	2,425.2
III	3,088.2	359.4	2,728.9	261.7	13.8	3.6	5.8	2,455.6
IV p	3,101.3	365.0	2,736.3	266.5	14.3	....	16.5	....

Source: Department of Commerce, Bureau of Economic Analysis.

TABLE B–20.—*Relation of national income and personal income, 1929–82*

[Billions of dollars; quarterly data at seasonally adjusted annual rates]

Year or quarter	National income	Less:				Plus:				Equals:
		Corporate profits with inventory valuation and capital consumption adjustments	Net interest	Contributions for social insurance	Wage accruals less disbursements	Government transfer payments to persons	Personal interest income	Personal dividend income	Business transfer payments	Personal income
1929	84.8	9.0	4.7	0.2	0.0	0.9	6.9	5.8	0.6	85.0
1933	39.9	−1.7	4.1	.3	.0	1.5	5.5	2.0	.7	47.0
1939	71.4	5.3	3.6	2.1	.0	2.5	5.4	3.8	.5	72.4
1940	79.7	8.6	3.3	2.3	.0	2.7	5.3	4.0	.4	77.9
1941	102.7	14.1	3.3	2.8	.0	2.6	5.3	4.4	.5	95.4
1942	135.9	19.3	3.1	3.5	.0	2.7	5.2	4.3	.5	122.6
1943	169.3	23.5	2.7	4.5	.2	2.5	5.1	4.4	.5	150.8
1944	182.1	23.6	2.4	5.2	−.2	3.1	5.2	4.6	.5	164.5
1945	180.7	19.0	2.2	6.1	.0	5.6	5.9	4.6	.5	170.0
1946	178.6	16.6	1.8	6.1	−.0	10.8	6.6	5.6	.5	177.6
1947	194.9	22.3	2.3	5.8	.0	11.2	7.6	6.3	.6	190.1
1948	219.9	29.4	2.4	5.4	.0	10.6	8.1	7.0	.7	209.0
1949	213.6	27.1	2.7	5.9	−.0	11.7	8.7	7.2	.8	206.4
1950	237.6	33.9	3.0	7.1	.0	14.4	9.7	8.8	.8	227.2
1951	274.1	38.7	3.5	8.5	.1	11.6	10.5	8.5	.9	254.9
1952	287.9	36.1	4.0	9.0	−.0	12.1	11.2	8.5	1.0	271.8
1953	302.1	36.3	4.4	9.1	−.1	12.9	12.5	8.8	1.2	287.7
1954	301.1	35.2	5.3	10.1	.0	15.1	13.7	9.1	1.1	289.6
1955	330.5	45.5	5.9	11.5	.0	16.2	14.9	10.3	1.2	310.3
1956	349.4	43.7	6.6	12.9	.0	17.3	16.7	11.1	1.4	332.6
1957	365.2	43.3	7.9	14.9	.0	20.1	18.8	11.5	1.5	351.0
1958	366.9	38.5	9.6	15.2	.0	24.3	20.3	11.3	1.6	361.1
1959	400.8	49.6	10.3	18.0	.0	25.2	22.5	12.2	1.8	384.4
1960	415.7	47.6	11.4	21.1	.0	27.0	25.0	12.9	2.0	402.3
1961	428.8	48.6	13.0	21.9	.0	30.8	26.4	13.3	2.0	417.8
1962	462.0	56.6	14.7	24.3	.0	31.6	29.0	14.4	2.1	443.6
1963	488.5	62.1	16.4	27.3	.0	33.4	32.2	15.5	2.4	466.2
1964	524.9	69.2	18.3	28.7	.0	34.8	35.6	17.3	2.7	499.2
1965	572.4	80.0	21.0	30.0	.0	37.6	39.7	19.1	2.8	540.7
1966	628.1	85.1	24.4	38.8	.0	41.6	44.4	19.4	3.0	588.2
1967	662.2	82.4	27.6	43.4	.0	49.5	48.3	20.2	3.1	630.0
1968	722.5	89.1	30.0	47.9	.0	56.4	53.4	21.9	3.4	690.6
1969	779.3	85.1	34.8	55.0	.0	62.8	61.1	22.4	3.9	754.7
1970	810.7	71.4	41.4	58.6	.0	76.1	69.4	22.2	4.1	811.1
1971	871.5	83.2	46.5	64.6	.6	90.0	74.8	22.6	4.4	868.4
1972	963.6	96.6	51.2	74.2	.0	99.8	80.9	24.1	4.9	951.4
1973	1,086.2	108.3	60.2	92.4	−.1	114.0	93.9	26.5	5.5	1,065.2
1974	1,160.7	94.9	76.1	104.3	−.5	135.4	112.4	29.1	5.8	1,168.6
1975	1,239.4	110.5	84.5	110.9	.0	170.9	123.2	29.9	7.4	1,265.0
1976	1,379.2	138.1	87.2	126.0	.0	186.4	132.5	36.5	7.9	1,391.2
1977	1,550.5	167.3	102.5	140.6	.0	199.3	152.8	39.6	8.6	1,540.4
1978	1,760.3	192.4	121.7	161.8	.2	214.6	179.4	45.3	9.3	1,732.7
1979	1,966.7	194.8	153.8	186.9	−.2	240.0	218.7	50.8	10.3	1,951.2
1980	2,117.1	181.6	187.7	204.0	−.0	285.8	263.4	55.9	11.4	2,160.4
1981	2,352.5	190.6	235.7	238.1	.0	323.9	329.0	62.5	12.4	2,415.8
1982 [p]	2,436.5	161.1	265.3	253.7	.0	360.8	371.8	67.0	13.7	2,569.7
1980:										
I	2,079.7	195.3	175.7	199.4	−.2	263.2	249.1	54.1	11.0	2,086.8
II	2,067.2	172.2	181.6	200.5	.0	271.9	258.0	55.7	11.3	2,109.6
III	2,122.3	177.8	190.4	204.6	.5	301.8	266.4	56.5	11.5	2,185.3
IV	2,199.2	181.2	203.0	211.3	−.5	306.5	280.2	57.4	11.8	2,260.0
1981:										
I	2,293.7	200.3	217.6	232.5	.0	310.8	304.7	59.2	12.0	2,330.0
II	2,324.4	185.1	231.6	236.2	.0	314.8	320.6	61.5	12.2	2,380.6
III	2,387.3	193.1	244.0	240.3	.2	332.3	339.6	64.1	12.5	2,458.2
IV	2,404.5	183.9	249.5	243.5	−.1	337.9	351.0	65.2	12.8	2,494.6
1982:										
I	2,396.9	157.1	258.7	250.8	−.2	341.4	359.7	65.8	13.1	2,510.5
II	2,425.2	155.4	267.5	253.0	.0	351.7	372.0	66.1	13.5	2,552.7
III	2,455.6	166.2	268.1	255.2	.0	367.2	378.2	67.2	13.8	2,592.5
IV [p]	....	....	267.0	255.8	.0	382.9	377.2	68.8	14.3	2,623.2

Source: Department of Commerce, Bureau of Economic Analysis.

TABLE B–21.—*National income by type of income, 1929–82*

[Billions of dollars; quarterly data at seasonally adjusted annual rates]

Year or quarter	National income [1]	Compensation of employees			Proprietors' income with inventory valuation and capital consumption adjustments							
						Farm			Nonfarm			
		Total	Wages and salaries	Supplements to wages and salaries [2]	Total	Total	Proprietors' income [3]	Capital consumption adjustment	Total	Proprietors' income [4]	Inventory valuation adjustment	Capital consumption adjustment
1929	84.8	51.1	50.5	0.6	15.0	6.1	6.3	−0.2	8.9	8.8	0.1	−0.1
1933	39.9	29.5	29.0	.5	5.9	2.5	2.6	−.0	3.3	3.9	−.5	.0
1939	71.4	48.1	46.0	2.1	11.8	4.4	4.5	−.1	7.4	7.6	−.2	−.0
1940	79.7	52.1	49.9	2.3	13.0	4.4	4.5	−.1	8.6	8.6	−.0	.0
1941	102.7	64.8	62.1	2.7	17.5	6.4	6.5	−.2	11.1	11.7	−.6	.0
1942	135.9	85.3	82.1	3.2	24.2	10.1	10.3	−.2	14.1	14.4	−.4	.1
1943	169.3	109.5	105.8	3.8	29.1	12.0	12.2	−.2	17.1	17.1	−.2	.2
1944	182.1	121.2	116.7	4.5	30.4	12.0	12.2	−.3	18.4	18.3	−.1	.2
1945	180.7	123.1	117.5	5.6	31.8	12.4	12.7	−.3	19.4	19.3	−.1	.2
1946	178.6	118.1	112.0	6.0	36.7	14.9	15.2	−.3	21.8	23.3	−1.7	.2
1947	194.9	129.2	123.1	6.1	35.9	15.1	15.7	−.5	20.8	21.8	−1.5	.5
1948	219.9	141.4	135.5	5.9	40.9	17.6	18.2	−.6	23.3	23.1	−.4	.6
1949	213.6	141.3	134.7	6.6	36.4	12.8	13.5	−.7	23.6	22.2	.5	.9
1950	237.6	154.8	147.0	7.8	38.7	13.7	14.4	−.7	25.0	25.1	−1.1	1.0
1951	274.1	181.0	171.3	9.7	43.2	16.1	16.9	−.8	27.2	26.4	−.3	1.0
1952	287.9	195.7	185.3	10.4	43.4	15.1	16.0	−.8	28.2	26.9	.2	1.1
1953	302.1	209.6	198.5	11.0	41.8	13.1	13.9	−.8	28.6	27.6	−.2	1.2
1954	301.1	208.4	196.8	11.6	41.2	12.5	13.3	−.8	28.7	27.6	−.0	1.2
1955	330.5	224.9	211.7	13.2	42.9	11.5	12.2	−.8	31.4	30.5	−.2	1.2
1956	349.4	243.5	228.3	15.2	43.9	11.2	12.1	−.9	32.7	31.8	−.5	1.4
1957	365.2	256.5	239.3	17.2	45.3	11.1	12.1	−.9	34.2	33.1	−.3	1.4
1958	366.9	258.2	240.5	17.7	47.7	13.2	14.1	−.9	34.5	33.2	−.1	1.4
1959	400.8	279.6	258.9	20.6	47.6	10.9	11.9	−1.0	36.7	35.3	−.0	1.4
1960	415.7	294.9	271.9	23.0	47.2	11.7	12.6	−.9	35.5	34.2	.0	1.3
1961	428.8	303.6	279.5	24.1	48.6	12.1	12.9	−.8	36.5	35.3	.0	1.2
1962	462.0	325.1	298.0	27.1	49.9	12.3	13.0	−.8	37.6	36.4	−.0	1.2
1963	488.5	342.9	313.4	29.5	50.5	12.0	12.8	−.7	38.5	37.2	−.0	1.4
1964	524.9	368.0	336.1	31.8	52.5	10.8	11.5	−.7	41.7	40.2	−.1	1.5
1965	572.4	396.5	362.0	34.5	56.9	13.1	13.8	−.7	43.8	42.7	−.2	1.3
1966	628.1	439.3	398.4	40.9	60.5	14.1	14.9	−.8	46.4	45.3	−.2	1.3
1967	662.2	471.4	427.0	44.4	61.2	12.6	13.5	−.9	48.6	47.5	−.2	1.3
1968	722.5	519.9	469.6	50.3	64.0	12.7	13.7	−1.0	51.3	50.6	−.4	1.1
1969	779.3	572.9	515.7	57.2	67.0	14.6	15.7	−1.2	52.5	51.9	−.5	1.1
1970	810.7	612.0	548.7	63.2	66.2	14.3	15.6	−1.3	51.9	51.7	−.5	.8
1971	871.5	652.2	581.5	70.7	69.4	15.0	16.4	−1.4	54.4	54.5	−.6	.4
1972	963.6	718.0	635.2	82.8	76.9	18.7	20.4	−1.6	58.1	58.1	−.7	.8
1973	1,086.2	801.3	702.6	98.7	93.8	32.8	34.6	−1.8	61.0	62.3	−2.0	.6
1974	1,160.7	877.5	765.2	112.3	88.7	26.5	29.0	−2.5	62.2	65.8	−3.7	.1
1975	1,239.4	931.4	806.4	125.0	90.0	24.6	28.0	−3.4	65.4	67.4	−1.2	−.8
1976	1,379.2	1,036.3	889.9	146.4	94.1	19.1	22.8	−3.7	75.0	77.1	−1.2	−.9
1977	1,550.5	1,152.1	983.2	168.9	103.9	19.1	23.3	−4.3	84.8	86.8	−1.2	−.8
1978	1,760.3	1,301.1	1,106.5	194.6	118.5	26.3	31.3	−5.0	92.2	94.9	−2.0	−.7
1979	1,966.7	1,458.1	1,237.4	220.7	132.1	31.9	37.8	−5.9	100.2	103.2	−2.9	−.1
1980	2,117.1	1,598.6	1,356.1	242.5	116.3	19.4	26.4	−7.0	96.9	99.9	−3.1	.1
1981	2,352.5	1,767.6	1,494.0	273.6	124.7	24.0	31.8	−7.9	100.7	100.3	−1.6	2.1
1982 [p]	2,436.5	1,855.9	1,560.1	295.8	120.1	18.6	26.8	−8.1	101.4	94.6	−.5	7.3
1980:												
I	2,079.7	1,555.2	1,319.5	235.7	122.7	22.1	28.7	−6.6	100.5	104.9	−4.3	.0
II	2,067.2	1,571.7	1,332.1	239.6	108.9	15.9	22.9	−7.0	93.0	95.1	−2.0	−.2
III	2,122.3	1,604.9	1,361.0	243.9	115.5	20.3	27.5	−7.2	95.1	98.2	−3.1	.0
IV	2,199.2	1,662.8	1,411.7	251.0	118.0	19.2	26.5	−7.3	98.8	101.4	−3.0	.5
1981:												
I	2,293.7	1,718.0	1,452.8	265.2	123.4	21.6	29.1	−7.5	101.8	103.2	−2.5	1.2
II	2,324.4	1,750.0	1,479.4	270.6	123.8	22.5	30.3	−7.8	101.2	100.9	−1.4	1.8
III	2,387.3	1,789.1	1,512.6	276.5	127.5	27.1	35.1	−8.0	100.4	99.3	−1.2	2.3
IV	2,404.5	1,813.4	1,531.1	282.3	124.1	24.6	32.8	−8.2	99.5	97.7	−1.2	3.0
1982:												
I	2,396.9	1,830.8	1,541.5	289.3	116.4	17.8	26.0	−8.2	98.6	93.8	.0	4.7
II	2,425.2	1,850.7	1,556.6	294.1	117.3	17.4	25.5	−8.1	99.9	94.5	−1.0	6.4
III	2,455.6	1,868.3	1,570.0	298.3	118.4	16.6	24.7	−8.1	101.7	94.4	−.5	7.9
IV [p]	....	1,873.7	1,572.3	301.4	128.1	22.6	30.8	−8.2	105.5	95.7	−.4	10.3

[1] National income is the total net income earned in production. It differs from gross national product mainly in that it excludes depreciation charges and other allowances for business and institutional consumption of durable capital goods and indirect business taxes. See Table B–19.

[2] Employer contributions for social insurance and to private pension, health, and welfare funds; workmen's compensation; directors' fees; and a few other minor items.

See next page for continuation of table.

Table B–21.—*National income by type of income, 1929–82*—Continued

[Billions of dollars; quarterly data at seasonally adjusted annual rates]

Year or quarter	Rental income of persons with capital consumption adjustment			Corporate profits with inventory valuation and capital consumption adjustments									Net interest
	Total	Rental income of persons	Capital consumption adjustment	Total	Profits with inventory valuation adjustment and without capital consumption adjustment							Capital consumption adjustment	
					Total	Profits					Inventory valuation adjustment		
						Profits before taxes	Profits tax liability	Profits after tax					
								Total	Dividends	Undistributed profits			
1929	4.9	5.7	-0.8	9.0	10.5	10.0	1.4	8.6	5.8	2.8	0.5	1.4	4.7
1933	2.2	2.3	-.1	-1.7	-1.2	1.0	.5	.4	2.0	-1.6	-2.1	-.6	4.1
1939	2.6	3.1	-.6	5.3	6.5	7.2	1.4	5.7	3.8	2.0	-.7	-1.1	3.6
1940	2.7	3.3	-.6	8.6	9.8	10.0	2.8	7.2	4.0	3.2	-.2	-1.2	3.3
1941	3.1	3.9	-.8	14.1	15.4	17.9	7.6	10.3	4.4	5.8	-2.5	-1.3	3.3
1942	4.0	5.0	-1.0	19.3	20.5	21.7	11.4	10.3	4.3	6.0	-1.2	-1.2	3.1
1943	4.4	5.6	-1.2	23.5	24.5	25.3	14.1	11.2	4.4	6.7	-.8	-1.0	2.7
1944	4.5	5.9	-1.4	23.6	24.0	24.2	12.9	11.3	4.6	6.7	-.3	-.3	2.4
1945	4.6	6.2	-1.6	19.0	19.3	19.8	10.7	9.1	4.6	4.5	-.6	-.2	2.2
1946	5.5	7.3	-1.8	16.6	19.6	24.8	9.1	15.7	5.6	10.2	-5.3	-3.0	1.8
1947	5.3	7.7	-2.5	22.3	25.9	31.8	11.3	20.5	6.3	14.2	-5.9	-3.6	2.3
1948	5.7	8.5	-2.8	29.4	33.4	35.6	12.4	23.2	7.0	16.2	-2.2	-4.0	2.4
1949	6.1	8.9	-2.8	27.1	31.1	29.2	10.2	19.0	7.2	11.8	1.9	-3.9	2.7
1950	7.1	10.0	-2.9	33.9	37.9	42.9	17.9	25.0	8.8	16.2	-5.0	-4.0	3.0
1951	7.7	11.0	-3.3	38.7	43.3	44.5	22.6	21.9	8.5	13.4	-1.2	-4.6	3.5
1952	8.8	12.2	-3.4	36.1	40.6	39.6	19.4	20.2	8.5	11.8	1.0	-4.5	4.0
1953	10.0	13.4	-3.4	36.3	40.2	41.2	20.3	20.9	8.8	12.1	-1.0	-3.9	4.4
1954	11.0	14.4	-3.3	35.2	38.4	38.7	17.6	21.1	9.1	11.9	-.3	-3.2	5.3
1955	11.3	14.8	-3.5	45.5	47.5	49.2	22.0	27.2	10.3	16.9	-1.7	-2.0	5.9
1956	11.6	15.2	-3.6	43.7	46.9	49.6	22.0	27.6	11.1	16.6	-2.7	-3.2	6.6
1957	12.2	15.9	-3.6	43.3	46.6	48.1	21.4	26.7	11.5	15.2	-1.5	-3.4	7.9
1958	12.9	16.7	-3.8	38.5	41.6	41.9	19.0	22.9	11.3	11.6	-.3	-3.2	9.6
1959	13.6	17.4	3.8	49.6	52.3	52.6	23.6	28.9	12.2	16.7	-.3	-2.7	10.3
1960	14.5	18.0	-3.5	47.6	49.7	49.8	22.7	27.1	12.9	14.3	-.2	-2.0	11.4
1961	15.0	18.4	-3.4	48.6	50.0	49.7	22.8	26.9	13.3	13.6	.3	-1.4	13.0
1962	15.8	19.1	-3.4	56.6	55.1	55.0	24.0	31.1	14.4	16.6	.0	1.5	14.7
1963	16.5	19.7	-3.2	62.1	59.7	59.6	26.2	33.4	15.5	17.9	.1	2.5	16.4
1964	17.1	20.2	-3.2	69.2	66.0	66.5	28.0	38.5	17.3	21.2	-.5	3.1	18.3
1965	18.0	21.2	-3.3	80.0	76.0	77.2	30.9	46.3	19.1	27.2	-1.2	4.0	21.0
1966	18.7	22.3	-3.6	85.1	80.9	83.0	33.7	49.4	19.4	29.9	-2.1	4.2	24.4
1967	19.7	23.6	-3.9	82.4	78.1	79.7	32.5	47.2	20.2	27.0	-1.6	4.3	27.6
1968	19.5	24.0	-4.5	89.1	84.9	88.5	39.2	49.4	22.0	27.3	-3.7	4.3	30.0
1969	19.6	25.2	-5.6	85.1	80.8	86.7	39.5	47.2	22.5	24.7	-5.9	4.3	34.8
1970	19.7	25.8	-6.1	71.4	68.9	75.4	34.2	41.3	22.5	18.8	-6.6	2.5	41.4
1971	20.2	27.1	-6.9	83.2	82.0	86.6	37.5	49.0	22.9	26.1	-4.6	1.3	46.5
1972	21.0	29.0	-8.0	96.6	94.0	100.6	41.6	58.9	24.4	34.5	-6.6	2.7	51.2
1973	22.6	32.1	-9.5	108.3	105.6	125.6	49.0	76.6	27.0	49.6	-20.0	2.7	60.2
1974	23.5	35.3	-11.8	94.9	96.7	136.7	51.6	85.1	29.9	55.2	-40.0	-1.8	76.1
1975	23.0	36.8	-13.8	110.5	120.6	132.1	50.6	81.5	30.8	50.7	-11.6	-10.1	84.5
1976	23.5	39.2	-15.6	138.1	151.6	166.3	63.8	102.5	37.4	65.1	-14.7	-13.5	87.2
1977	24.8	44.0	-19.1	167.3	178.5	194.7	72.7	122.0	40.8	81.2	-16.2	-11.3	102.5
1978	26.6	50.0	-23.4	192.4	205.1	229.1	83.2	145.9	47.0	98.9	-24.0	-12.7	121.7
1979	27.9	56.2	-28.3	194.8	209.6	252.7	87.6	165.1	52.7	112.4	-43.1	-14.8	153.8
1980	32.9	65.3	-32.4	181.6	199.4	242.4	84.7	157.8	58.1	99.7	-43.0	-17.8	187.7
1981	33.9	69.4	-35.5	190.6	207.5	232.1	81.2	150.9	65.1	85.8	-24.6	-16.8	235.7
1982 [p]	34.1	70.8	-36.7	161.1	166.0	175.4	58.8	116.6	70.3	46.3	-9.4	-4.9	265.3
1980:													
I	30.8	61.8	-31.0	195.3	211.0	268.2	95.3	172.9	56.2	116.7	-57.2	-15.7	175.7
II	32.7	64.8	-32.1	172.2	189.4	217.6	73.3	144.3	57.8	86.4	-28.2	-17.2	181.6
III	33.8	66.9	-33.1	177.8	197.0	238.1	82.2	155.9	58.7	97.3	-41.1	-19.3	190.4
IV	34.2	67.5	-33.3	181.2	200.4	245.9	87.8	158.1	59.6	98.5	-45.5	-19.2	203.0
1981:													
I	34.4	68.7	-34.3	200.3	217.6	253.1	91.5	161.6	61.5	100.1	-35.5	-17.3	217.6
II	34.0	68.9	-34.9	185.1	202.6	225.4	79.2	146.2	64.0	82.2	-22.8	-17.5	231.6
III	33.6	69.5	-35.9	193.1	210.3	233.3	82.4	150.8	66.8	84.0	-23.0	-17.1	244.0
IV	33.6	70.5	-36.9	183.9	199.4	216.5	71.6	144.9	68.1	76.9	-17.1	-15.5	249.5
1982:													
I	33.9	71.0	-37.1	157.1	167.2	171.6	56.7	115.0	68.8	46.1	-4.4	-10.1	258.7
II	34.2	70.7	-36.4	155.4	162.2	171.7	55.3	116.3	69.3	47.0	-9.4	-6.9	267.5
III	34.6	70.9	-36.3	166.2	170.0	180.3	60.9	119.4	70.5	48.8	-10.3	-3.8	268.1
IV [p]	33.9	70.9	-37.0	....	....	....	....	....	72.4	....	-13.4	1.2	267.0

[3] With inventory valuation adjustment and without capital consumption adjustment.
[4] Without inventory valuation and capital consumption adjustments.

Source: Department of Commerce, Bureau of Economic Analysis.

TABLE B–22.—*Sources of personal income, 1929–82*

[Billions of dollars; quarterly data at seasonally adjusted annual rates]

Year or quarter	Personal income	Wage and salary disbursements[1]: Total	Commodity-producing industries: Total	Commodity-producing industries: Manufacturing	Distributive industries	Service industries	Government and government enterprises	Other labor income[1]	Proprietors' income with inventory valuation and capital consumption adjustments: Farm	Proprietors' income: Nonfarm
1929	85.0	50.5	21.5	16.1	15.6	8.4	5.0	0.5	6.1	8.9
1933	47.0	29.0	9.8	7.8	8.8	5.2	5.2	.4	2.5	3.3
1939	72.4	46.0	17.4	13.6	13.3	7.1	8.2	.6	4.4	7.4
1940	77.9	49.9	19.7	15.6	14.2	7.5	8.5	.6	4.4	8.6
1941	95.4	62.1	27.5	21.7	16.3	8.1	10.2	.7	6.4	11.1
1942	122.6	82.1	39.1	30.9	18.0	9.0	16.0	.9	10.1	14.1
1943	150.8	105.6	49.0	40.9	20.1	9.9	26.6	1.1	12.0	17.1
1944	164.5	116.9	50.4	42.9	22.7	10.9	33.0	1.5	12.0	18.4
1945	170.0	117.5	45.9	38.2	24.8	11.9	34.9	1.8	12.4	19.4
1946	177.6	112.0	46.0	36.5	31.0	14.3	20.7	2.0	14.9	21.8
1947	190.1	123.1	54.2	42.5	35.2	16.1	17.5	2.4	15.1	20.8
1948	209.0	135.5	61.1	47.1	37.5	17.9	19.0	2.7	17.6	23.3
1949	206.4	134.8	57.8	44.6	37.7	18.5	20.8	2.9	12.8	23.6
1950	227.2	147.0	64.8	50.3	39.8	19.8	22.6	3.7	13.7	25.0
1951	254.9	171.3	76.3	59.3	44.3	21.5	29.2	4.6	16.1	27.2
1952	271.8	185.4	82.0	64.1	46.9	23.1	33.3	5.2	15.1	28.2
1953	287.7	198.6	89.6	71.2	49.7	24.9	34.4	5.9	13.1	28.6
1954	289.6	196.8	85.7	67.5	50.1	26.1	34.9	6.1	12.5	28.7
1955	310.3	211.7	93.1	73.8	53.4	28.6	36.6	7.0	11.5	31.4
1956	332.6	228.3	100.6	79.4	57.7	31.3	38.8	8.0	11.2	32.7
1957	351.0	239.3	104.2	82.4	60.5	33.6	41.0	9.0	11.1	34.2
1958	361.1	240.5	100.0	78.6	60.8	35.6	44.1	9.4	13.2	34.5
1959	384.4	258.9	109.6	86.8	64.8	38.5	46.0	10.6	10.9	36.7
1960	402.3	271.9	113.1	89.7	68.2	41.4	49.2	11.2	11.7	35.5
1961	417.8	279.5	113.7	89.8	69.3	44.1	52.4	11.8	12.1	36.5
1962	443.6	298.0	121.8	96.7	72.8	47.2	56.3	13.0	12.3	37.6
1963	466.2	313.4	126.9	100.6	76.3	50.2	60.0	14.0	12.0	38.5
1964	499.2	336.1	135.4	107.1	81.4	54.4	64.9	15.7	10.8	41.7
1965	540.7	362.0	146.0	115.5	87.2	58.9	69.9	17.8	13.1	43.8
1966	588.2	398.4	161.0	128.0	94.4	64.7	78.3	19.9	14.1	46.4
1967	630.0	427.0	168.3	134.1	100.9	71.3	86.4	21.7	12.6	48.6
1968	690.6	469.6	183.4	145.8	110.0	79.6	96.6	25.2	12.7	51.3
1969	754.7	515.7	199.6	157.5	120.8	89.7	105.5	28.5	14.6	52.5
1970	811.1	548.7	203.0	158.2	130.3	98.3	117.1	32.5	14.3	51.9
1971	868.4	580.9	208.3	160.3	139.4	106.7	126.5	36.7	15.0	54.4
1972	951.4	635.2	227.3	175.4	152.1	118.2	137.5	43.0	18.7	58.1
1973	1,065.2	702.7	254.3	196.2	168.3	131.3	148.7	48.8	32.8	61.0
1974	1,168.6	765.7	274.7	211.4	184.6	145.6	160.9	55.8	26.5	62.2
1975	1,265.0	806.4	275.0	211.0	195.6	159.7	176.1	64.5	24.6	65.4
1976	1,391.2	889.9	307.3	237.4	216.6	177.4	188.7	75.9	19.1	75.0
1977	1,540.4	983.2	343.6	266.0	239.5	197.7	202.4	89.4	19.1	84.8
1978	1,732.7	1,106.3	389.4	299.2	270.7	226.6	219.5	102.5	26.3	92.2
1979	1,951.2	1,237.6	438.4	333.9	303.4	259.7	236.2	114.9	31.9	100.2
1980	2,160.4	1,356.1	468.0	354.4	330.5	297.4	260.2	127.2	19.4	96.9
1981	2,415.8	1,493.9	510.8	386.4	361.4	338.6	283.1	140.4	24.0	100.7
1982 p	2,569.7	1,560.1	509.9	382.6	375.7	372.3	302.3	153.8	18.6	101.4
1980:										
I	2,086.8	1,319.7	462.7	350.3	323.2	283.4	250.4	123.2	22.1	100.5
II	2,109.6	1,332.1	458.6	347.0	324.9	292.0	256.6	125.9	15.9	93.0
III	2,185.3	1,360.5	465.6	352.8	331.9	301.4	261.6	128.4	20.3	95.1
IV	2,260.0	1,412.2	485.1	367.7	341.9	313.1	272.2	131.5	19.2	98.8
1981:										
I	2,330.0	1,452.8	499.2	377.0	352.1	325.2	276.2	135.3	21.6	101.8
II	2,380.6	1,479.4	507.2	386.9	358.7	333.7	279.8	138.4	22.5	101.2
III	2,458.2	1,512.3	519.3	392.9	366.5	342.8	283.8	142.2	27.1	100.4
IV	2,494.6	1,531.2	517.7	388.7	368.3	352.8	292.4	145.8	24.6	99.5
1982:										
I	2,510.5	1,541.6	514.3	385.1	371.4	359.5	296.5	149.1	17.8	98.6
II	2,552.7	1,556.6	513.6	385.6	375.4	367.6	300.0	152.5	17.4	99.9
III	2,592.5	1,570.0	510.2	383.8	378.4	377.8	303.5	155.5	16.6	101.7
IV p	2,623.2	1,572.3	501.4	375.8	377.4	384.3	309.1	157.9	22.6	105.5

[1] The total of wage and salary disbursements and other labor income differs from compensation of employees in Table B–21 in that it excludes employer contributions for social insurance and the excess of wage accruals over wage disbursements.

See next page for continuation of table.

Table B–22.—*Sources of personal income, 1929–82*—Continued

[Billions of dollars; quarterly data at seasonally adjusted annual rates]

Year or quarter	Rental income of persons with capital consumption adjustment	Personal dividend income	Personal interest income	Transfer payments: Total	Transfer payments: Old-age, survivors, disability, and health insurance benefits	Transfer payments: Government unemployment insurance benefits	Transfer payments: Veterans benefits	Transfer payments: Government employee retirement benefits	Transfer payments: Aid to families with dependent children (AFDC)	Transfer payments: Other	Less: Personal contributions for social insurance	Nonfarm personal income [2]
1929	4.9	5.8	6.9	1.5	....	....	0.6	0.1	0.8		0.1	....
1933	2.2	2.0	5.5	2.1	....	....	.6	.2	1.4		.2	....
1939	2.6	3.8	5.4	3.0	0.0	0.4	.5	.3	1.7		.6	....
1940	2.7	4.0	5.3	3.1	.0	.5	.5	.3	1.7		.7	....
1941	3.1	4.4	5.3	3.1	.1	.4	.5	.3	1.8		.8	....
1942	4.0	4.3	5.2	3.1	.1	.4	.5	.3	1.8		1.2	....
1943	4.4	4.4	5.1	3.0	.2	.1	.5	.4	1.8		1.8	....
1944	4.5	4.6	5.2	3.6	.2	.1	1.0	.4	2.0		2.2	....
1945	4.6	4.6	5.9	6.2	.3	.4	3.0	.5	2.0		2.3	....
1946	5.5	5.6	6.6	11.3	.4	1.1	7.0	.7	2.1		2.0	159.9
1947	5.3	6.3	7.6	11.7	.5	.8	7.0	.7	.3	2.5	2.1	171.9
1948	5.7	7.0	8.1	11.3	.6	.9	5.9	.7	.4	2.9	2.2	188.2
1949	6.1	7.2	8.7	12.5	.7	1.9	5.3	.9	.5	3.3	2.2	190.4
1950	7.1	8.8	9.7	15.2	1.0	1.5	7.7	1.0	.6	3.5	2.9	210.2
1951	7.7	8.5	10.5	12.6	1.9	.9	4.6	1.1	.6	3.6	3.4	235.4
1952	8.8	8.5	11.2	13.1	2.2	1.1	4.3	1.2	.5	3.8	3.8	253.1
1953	10.0	8.8	12.5	14.1	3.0	1.0	4.1	1.4	.5	4.1	4.0	271.3
1954	11.0	9.1	13.7	16.2	3.6	2.2	4.2	1.5	.6	4.1	4.6	273.9
1955	11.3	10.3	14.9	17.5	4.9	1.5	4.4	1.7	.6	4.3	5.2	295.5
1956	11.6	11.1	16.7	18.7	5.7	1.5	4.4	1.9	.6	4.5	5.8	318.0
1957	12.2	11.5	18.8	21.6	7.3	1.9	4.5	2.2	.7	4.9	6.7	336.6
1958	12.9	11.3	20.3	25.9	8.5	4.1	4.7	2.5	.8	5.3	6.9	344.4
1959	13.6	12.2	22.5	27.0	10.2	2.8	4.6	2.8	.9	5.8	7.9	369.8
1960	14.5	12.9	25.0	28.9	11.1	3.0	4.6	3.1	1.0	6.2	9.3	386.7
1961	15.0	13.3	26.4	32.8	12.6	4.3	5.0	3.4	1.1	6.4	9.7	401.6
1962	15.8	14.4	29.0	33.8	14.3	3.1	4.7	3.7	1.3	6.7	10.3	427.1
1963	16.5	15.5	32.2	35.8	15.2	3.0	4.8	4.2	1.4	7.3	11.8	449.7
1964	17.1	17.3	35.6	37.4	16.0	2.7	4.7	4.7	1.5	7.8	12.6	483.7
1965	18.0	19.1	39.7	40.4	18.1	2.3	4.9	5.2	1.7	8.3	13.3	522.6
1966	18.7	19.4	44.4	44.7	20.8	1.9	4.9	6.1	1.9	9.2	17.8	568.9
1967	19.7	20.2	48.3	52.6	25.5	2.2	5.6	6.9	2.3	10.2	20.6	611.9
1968	19.5	21.9	53.4	59.8	30.2	2.1	5.9	7.6	2.8	11.1	22.9	672.1
1969	19.6	22.4	61.1	66.7	32.9	2.2	6.7	8.7	3.5	12.5	26.2	733.9
1970	19.7	22.2	69.4	80.1	38.5	4.0	7.7	10.2	4.8	15.0	27.9	790.0
1971	20.2	22.6	74.8	94.4	44.5	5.8	8.8	11.8	6.2	17.4	30.7	846.5
1972	21.0	24.1	80.9	104.7	49.6	5.7	9.7	13.8	6.9	19.0	34.5	925.3
1973	22.6	26.5	93.9	119.5	60.4	4.4	10.4	16.0	7.2	21.1	42.6	1,023.7
1974	23.5	29.1	112.4	141.2	70.1	6.8	11.8	19.0	7.9	25.6	47.9	1,131.8
1975	23.0	29.9	123.2	178.3	81.4	17.6	14.5	22.7	9.2	32.8	50.4	1,229.1
1976	23.5	36.5	132.5	194.3	92.9	15.8	14.4	26.1	10.1	35.1	55.5	1,359.3
1977	24.8	39.6	152.8	207.9	104.9	12.7	13.8	29.0	10.6	36.9	61.1	1,506.5
1978	26.6	45.3	179.4	223.8	116.2	9.7	13.9	32.7	10.7	40.7	69.8	1,689.7
1979	27.9	50.8	218.7	250.3	131.8	9.8	14.4	36.9	11.0	46.3	81.1	1,899.3
1980	32.9	55.9	263.4	297.2	154.2	16.1	15.0	43.0	12.4	56.6	88.7	2,117.3
1981	33.9	62.5	329.0	336.3	182.0	15.4	16.1	49.2	13.4	60.3	104.9	2,364.1
1982 ^{p}	34.1	67.0	371.8	374.5	204.5	24.9	16.3	54.0	13.1	61.6	111.7	2,518.9
1980:												
I	30.8	54.1	249.1	274.2	142.1	11.8	14.8	40.1	11.7	53.6	86.9	2,042.2
II	32.7	55.7	258.0	283.2	144.7	15.9	14.6	42.3	12.1	53.5	86.9	2,070.3
III	33.8	56.5	266.4	313.4	163.4	18.7	14.9	43.4	12.8	60.2	89.1	2,140.9
IV	34.2	57.4	280.2	318.2	166.4	18.0	15.7	46.0	13.0	59.1	91.8	2,216.0
1981:												
I	34.4	59.2	304.7	322.8	171.0	15.7	16.0	47.2	13.1	59.8	102.5	2,282.5
II	34.0	61.5	320.6	327.0	173.7	15.1	15.9	49.1	13.4	59.8	104.1	2,330.9
III	33.6	64.1	339.6	344.8	190.6	14.1	16.0	49.6	13.5	61.0	106.1	2,402.6
IV	33.6	65.2	351.0	350.7	192.8	16.7	16.4	50.8	13.4	60.6	107.0	2,440.3
1982:												
I	33.9	65.8	359.7	354.6	194.7	18.7	16.3	51.5	13.2	60.1	110.6	2,461.6
II	34.2	66.1	372.0	365.2	197.5	23.5	16.1	54.4	13.2	60.6	111.4	2,503.2
III	34.6	67.2	378.2	381.0	209.2	25.5	16.3	54.9	13.0	62.1	112.4	2,543.3
IV ^{p}	33.9	68.8	377.2	397.2	216.6	31.8	16.6	55.3	13.1	63.8	112.4	2,567.6

[2] Personal income exclusive of farm proprietors' income, farm wages, farm other labor income, and farm net interest.

Note.—The industry classification of wage and salary disbursements and proprietors' income is on an establishment basis and is based on the 1972 Standard Industrial Classification (SIC) beginning 1948 and on the 1942 SIC prior to 1948.

Source: Department of Commerce, Bureau of Economic Analysis.

384-041 O - 83 - 13 : QL 3

Table B–23.—*Disposition of personal income, 1929–82*

[Billions of dollars, except as noted; quarterly data at seasonally adjusted annual rates]

Year or quarter	Personal income	Less: Personal tax and nontax payments	Equals: Disposable personal income	Less: Personal outlays				Equals: Personal saving	Percent of disposable personal income		
				Total	Personal consumption expenditures	Interest paid by consumers to business	Personal transfer payments to foreigners (net)		Personal outlays		Personal saving
									Total	Personal Consumption expenditures	
1929	85.0	2.6	82.4	79.1	77.3	1.5	0.3	3.3	96.0	93.8	4.0
1933	47.0	1.4	45.6	46.5	45.8	.5	.2	−0.9	102.0	100.5	−2.0
1939	72.4	2.4	70.0	67.8	67.0	.7	.2	2.2	96.9	95.6	3.1
1940	77.9	2.6	75.3	72.0	71.0	.8	.2	3.4	95.5	94.2	4.5
1941	95.4	3.3	92.2	81.8	80.8	.9	.2	10.3	88.8	87.6	11.2
1942	122.6	5.9	116.6	89.4	88.6	.7	.1	27.2	76.7	76.0	23.3
1943	150.8	17.8	133.0	100.1	99.4	.5	.2	32.9	75.3	74.7	24.7
1944	164.5	18.9	145.6	109.0	108.2	.5	.4	36.6	74.8	74.3	25.2
1945	170.0	20.8	149.1	120.4	119.5	.5	.5	28.7	80.8	80.1	19.2
1946	177.6	18.7	158.9	145.2	143.8	.7	.7	13.7	91.4	90.5	8.6
1947	190.1	21.4	168.7	163.5	161.7	1.0	.7	5.2	96.9	95.9	3.1
1948	209.0	21.0	188.0	176.9	174.7	1.4	.7	11.1	94.1	93.0	5.9
1949	206.4	18.5	187.9	180.4	178.1	1.7	.5	7.5	96.0	94.8	4.0
1950	227.2	20.6	206.6	194.7	192.0	2.3	.4	11.9	94.2	92.9	5.8
1951	254.9	28.9	226.0	210.0	207.1	2.5	.4	16.1	92.9	91.6	7.1
1952	271.8	34.0	237.7	220.4	217.1	2.9	.4	17.4	92.7	91.3	7.3
1953	287.7	35.5	252.2	233.7	229.7	3.6	.5	18.5	92.7	91.1	7.3
1954	289.6	32.5	257.1	240.1	235.8	3.8	.5	17.0	93.4	91.7	6.6
1955	310.3	35.4	275.0	258.5	253.7	4.4	.4	16.4	94.0	92.3	6.0
1956	332.6	39.7	292.9	271.6	266.0	5.1	.5	21.3	92.7	90.8	7.3
1957	351.0	42.4	308.6	286.4	280.4	5.5	.5	22.3	92.8	90.9	7.2
1958	361.1	42.1	319.0	295.4	289.5	5.6	.4	23.6	92.6	90.7	7.4
1959	384.4	46.0	338.4	317.3	310.8	6.1	.4	21.1	93.8	91.8	6.2
1960	402.3	50.4	352.0	332.3	324.9	7.0	.4	19.7	94.4	92.3	5.6
1961	417.8	52.1	365.8	342.7	335.0	7.3	.4	23.0	93.7	91.6	6.3
1962	443.6	56.8	386.8	363.5	355.2	7.8	.5	23.3	94.0	91.8	6.0
1963	466.2	60.3	405.9	384.0	374.6	8.8	.6	21.9	94.6	92.3	5.4
1964	499.2	58.6	440.6	411.0	400.5	9.9	.6	29.6	93.3	90.9	6.7
1965	540.7	64.9	475.8	442.1	430.4	11.1	.7	33.7	92.9	90.5	7.1
1966	588.2	74.5	513.7	477.7	465.1	12.0	.7	36.0	93.0	90.5	7.0
1967	630.0	82.1	547.9	503.6	490.3	12.5	.9	44.3	91.9	89.5	8.1
1968	690.6	97.2	593.4	551.5	536.9	13.8	.8	41.9	92.9	90.5	7.1
1969	754.7	115.7	638.9	598.3	581.8	15.6	.9	40.6	93.6	91.1	6.4
1970	811.1	115.8	695.3	639.5	621.7	16.7	1.1	55.8	92.0	89.4	8.0
1971	868.4	116.7	751.8	691.1	672.2	17.7	1.1	60.7	91.9	89.4	8.1
1972	951.4	141.0	810.3	757.7	737.1	19.5	1.1	52.6	93.5	91.0	6.5
1973	1,065.2	150.7	914.5	835.5	812.0	22.3	1.3	79.0	91.4	88.8	8.6
1974	1,168.6	170.2	998.3	913.2	888.1	24.1	1.0	85.1	91.5	89.0	8.5
1975	1,265.0	168.9	1,096.1	1,001.8	976.4	24.4	.9	94.3	91.4	89.1	8.6
1976	1,391.2	196.8	1,194.4	1,111.9	1,084.3	26.7	.9	82.5	93.1	90.8	6.9
1977	1,540.4	226.4	1,314.0	1,236.0	1,204.4	30.7	.9	78.0	94.1	91.7	5.9
1978	1,732.7	258.7	1,474.0	1,384.6	1,346.5	37.4	.8	89.4	93.9	91.3	6.1
1979	1,951.2	301.0	1,650.2	1,553.5	1,507.2	45.5	.8	96.7	94.1	91.3	5.9
1980	2,160.4	336.3	1,824.1	1,717.9	1,667.2	49.9	.8	106.2	94.2	91.4	5.8
1981	2,415.8	386.7	2,029.1	1,898.9	1,843.2	55.1	.6	130.2	93.6	90.8	6.4
1982 p	2,569.7	397.2	2,172.5	2,031.4	1,972.0	58.6	.9	141.1	93.5	90.8	6.5
1980:											
I	2,086.8	319.9	1,766.9	1,669.1	1,618.7	49.6	.7	97.9	94.5	91.6	5.5
II	2,109.6	328.6	1,781.0	1,672.4	1,622.2	49.4	.7	108.6	93.9	91.1	6.1
III	2,185.3	339.7	1,845.5	1,732.5	1,682.2	49.7	.8	113.1	93.9	91.1	6.1
IV	2,260.0	357.1	1,902.9	1,797.6	1,745.8	50.8	.9	105.3	94.5	91.7	5.5
1981:											
I	2,330.0	371.2	1,958.7	1,852.8	1,799.9	52.4	.5	105.9	94.6	91.9	5.4
II	2,380.6	384.2	1,996.5	1,874.5	1,819.4	54.4	.8	122.0	93.9	91.1	6.1
III	2,458.2	398.1	2,060.0	1,925.7	1,868.8	56.2	.7	134.4	93.5	90.7	6.5
IV	2,494.6	393.2	2,101.4	1,942.7	1,884.5	57.5	.7	158.6	92.5	89.7	7.5
1982:											
I	2,510.5	393.4	2,117.1	1,977.9	1,919.4	57.8	.8	139.1	93.4	90.7	6.6
II	2,552.7	401.2	2,151.5	2,007.2	1,947.8	58.4	.9	144.3	93.3	90.5	6.7
III	2,592.5	394.4	2,198.1	2,046.1	1,986.3	59.0	.8	152.0	93.1	90.4	6.9
IV p	2,623.2	399.7	2,223.5	2,094.6	2,034.6	59.1	.9	128.9	94.2	91.5	5.8

Source: Department of Commerce, Bureau of Economic Analysis.

TABLE B-24.—*Total and per capita disposable personal income and personal consumption expenditures in current and 1972 dollars, 1929–82*

[Quarterly data at seasonally adjusted annual rates, except as noted]

Year or quarter	Disposable personal income				Personal consumption expenditures				Population (thousands)[1]
	Total (billions of dollars)		Per capita (dollars)		Total (billions of dollars)		Per capita (dollars)		
	Current dollars	1972 dollars	Current dollars	1972 dollars	Current dollars	1972 dollars	Current dollars	1972 dollars	
1929	82.4	229.5	676	1,883	77.3	215.1	634	1,765	121,878
1933	45.6	169.6	363	1,349	45.8	170.5	364	1,356	125,690
1939	70.0	229.8	534	1,754	67.0	219.8	511	1,678	131,028
1940	75.3	244.0	570	1,847	71.0	229.9	537	1,740	132,122
1941	92.2	277.9	691	2,083	80.8	243.6	605	1,826	133,402
1942	116.6	317.5	865	2,354	88.6	241.1	657	1,788	134,860
1943	133.0	332.1	973	2,429	99.4	248.2	727	1,815	136,739
1944	145.6	343.6	1,052	2,483	108.2	255.2	781	1,844	138,397
1945	149.1	338.1	1,066	2,416	119.5	270.9	854	1,936	139,928
1946	158.9	332.7	1,124	2,353	143.8	301.0	1,017	2,129	141,389
1947	168.7	318.8	1,170	2,212	161.7	305.8	1,122	2,122	144,126
1948	188.0	335.8	1,282	2,290	174.7	312.2	1,192	2,129	146,631
1949	187.9	336.8	1,259	2,257	178.1	319.3	1,194	2,140	149,188
1950	206.6	362.8	1,362	2,392	192.0	337.3	1,266	2,224	151,684
1951	226.0	372.6	1,465	2,415	207.1	341.6	1,342	2,214	154,287
1952	237.7	383.2	1,515	2,441	217.1	350.1	1,383	2,230	156,954
1953	252.2	399.1	1,581	2,501	229.7	363.4	1,439	2,277	159,565
1954	257.1	403.2	1,583	2,483	235.8	370.0	1,452	2,278	162,391
1955	275.0	426.8	1,664	2,582	253.7	394.1	1,535	2,384	165,275
1956	292.9	446.2	1,741	2,653	266.0	405.4	1,581	2,410	168,221
1957	308.6	455.5	1,802	2,660	280.4	413.8	1,637	2,416	171,274
1958	319.0	460.7	1,832	2,645	289.5	418.0	1,662	2,400	174,141
1959	338.4	479.7	1,911	2,709	310.8	440.4	1,755	2,487	177,073
1960	352.0	489.7	1,947	2,709	324.9	452.0	1,797	2,501	180,760
1961	365.8	503.8	1,991	2,742	335.0	461.4	1,823	2,511	183,742
1962	386.8	524.9	2,073	2,813	355.2	482.0	1,904	2,583	186,590
1963	405.9	542.3	2,144	2,865	374.6	500.5	1,979	2,644	189,300
1964	440.6	580.8	2,296	3,026	400.5	528.0	2,087	2,751	191,927
1965	475.8	616.3	2,448	3,171	430.4	557.5	2,214	2,868	194,347
1966	513.7	646.8	2,613	3,290	465.1	585.7	2,366	2,979	196,599
1967	547.9	673.5	2,757	3,389	490.3	602.7	2,467	3,032	198,752
1968	593.4	701.3	2,956	3,493	536.9	634.4	2,674	3,160	200,745
1969	638.9	722.5	3,152	3,564	581.8	657.9	2,870	3,245	202,736
1970	695.3	751.6	3,390	3,665	621.7	672.1	3,031	3,277	205,089
1971	751.8	779.2	3,620	3,752	672.2	696.8	3,237	3,355	207,692
1972	810.3	810.3	3,860	3,860	737.1	737.1	3,511	3,511	209,924
1973	914.5	864.7	4,315	4,080	812.0	767.9	3,831	3,623	211,939
1974	998.3	857.5	4,667	4,009	888.1	762.8	4,152	3,566	213,898
1975	1,096.1	874.9	5,075	4,051	976.4	779.4	4,521	3,609	215,981
1976	1,194.4	906.8	5,477	4,158	1,084.3	823.1	4,972	3,774	218,086
1977	1,314.0	942.9	5,965	4,280	1,204.4	864.3	5,468	3,924	220,289
1978	1,474.0	988.8	6,621	4,441	1,346.5	903.2	6,048	4,057	222,629
1979	1,650.2	1,015.7	7,331	4,512	1,507.2	927.6	6,695	4,121	225,106
1980	1,824.1	1,018.0	8,012	4,472	1,667.2	930.5	7,323	4,087	227,654
1981	2,029.1	1,043.1	8,827	4,538	1,843.2	947.6	8,018	4,123	229,872
1982 p	2,172.5	1,054.5	9,362	4,544	1,972.0	957.1	8,498	4,125	232,050
1980:									
I	1,766.9	1,022.8	7,793	4,511	1,618.7	937.0	7,140	4,133	226,727
II	1,781.0	1,005.5	7,834	4,423	1,622.2	915.8	7,136	4,029	227,332
III	1,845.5	1,018.2	8,095	4,466	1,682.0	928.0	7,378	4,071	227,978
IV	1,902.9	1,025.7	8,325	4,487	1,745.8	941.0	7,638	4,117	228,579
1981:									
I	1,958.7	1,035.0	8,551	4,519	1,799.9	951.1	7,858	4,152	229,053
II	1,996.5	1,036.6	8,698	4,516	1,819.4	944.6	7,926	4,115	229,539
III	2,060.0	1,048.8	8,951	4,557	1,868.8	951.4	8,120	4,134	230,145
IV	2,101.4	1,051.9	9,107	4,559	1,884.5	943.4	8,167	4,088	230,751
1982:									
I	2,117.1	1,046.9	9,155	4,527	1,919.4	949.1	8,300	4,104	231,246
II	2,151.5	1,054.8	9,285	4,552	1,947.8	955.0	8,406	4,121	231,724
III	2,198.1	1,058.3	9,461	4,555	1,986.3	956.3	8,550	4,116	232,320
IV p	2,223.5	1,057.9	9,546	4,542	2,034.6	968.0	8,735	4,156	232,910

[1] Population of the United States including Armed Forces overseas; includes Alaska and Hawaii beginning 1960. Annual data are for July 1 through 1958 and are averages of quarterly data beginning 1960. Quarterly data are average for the period. Data beginning 1970 reflect results of the 1980 census of population.

Source: Department of Commerce (Bureau of Economic Analysis and Bureau of the Census).

Table B–25.—*Gross saving and investment, 1929–82*

[Billions of dollars; quarterly data at seasonally adjusted annual rates]

Year or quarter	Gross saving								Gross investment			Statistical discrepancy
	Total	Gross private saving			Government surplus or deficit (−), national income and product accounts			Capital grants received by the United States (net) [2]	Total	Gross private domestic investment	Net foreign investment [3]	
		Total	Personal saving	Gross business saving [1]	Total	Federal	State and local					
1929	15.9	14.9	3.3	11.6	1.0	1.2	−.2	....	17.0	16.2	0.8	1.1
1933	.9	2.2	−.9	3.1	−1.4	−1.3	−.1	....	1.6	1.4	.2	.7
1939	8.8	11.0	2.2	8.8	−2.2	−2.2	.0	....	10.3	9.3	1.0	1.4
1940	13.5	14.2	3.4	10.8	−.7	−1.3	.6	....	14.7	13.1	1.5	1.1
1941	18.6	22.4	10.3	12.1	−3.8	−5.1	1.3	....	19.2	17.9	1.3	.6
1942	10.7	42.0	27.2	14.8	−31.4	−33.1	1.8	....	9.8	9.9	−.1	−.8
1943	5.4	49.6	32.9	16.7	−44.1	−46.6	2.5	....	3.7	5.8	−2.1	−1.8
1944	2.4	54.2	36.6	17.6	−51.8	−54.5	2.7	....	5.2	7.2	−2.0	2.7
1945	5.2	44.7	28.7	16.0	−39.5	−42.1	2.6	....	9.3	10.6	−1.3	4.1
1946	35.1	29.6	13.7	15.9	5.4	3.5	1.9	....	35.6	30.7	4.9	.5
1947	41.7	27.3	5.2	22.1	14.4	13.4	1.0	....	43.2	34.0	9.3	1.5
1948	49.8	41.4	11.1	30.2	8.4	8.3	.1	....	48.3	45.9	2.4	−1.6
1949	35.6	39.0	7.5	31.5	−3.4	−2.6	−.7	....	36.2	35.3	.9	.6
1950	50.7	42.7	11.9	30.7	8.0	9.2	−1.2	....	52.0	53.8	−1.8	1.3
1951	56.9	50.8	16.1	34.8	6.1	6.5	−.4	....	60.1	59.2	.9	3.2
1952	51.0	54.8	17.4	37.4	−3.8	−3.7	−.0	....	52.7	52.1	.6	1.7
1953	49.8	56.7	18.5	38.2	−6.9	−7.1	.1	....	52.1	53.3	−1.3	2.3
1954	50.9	58.1	17.0	41.1	−7.1	−6.0	−1.1	....	52.9	52.7	.2	2.0
1955	67.5	64.4	16.4	47.9	3.1	4.4	−1.3	....	68.8	68.4	.4	1.3
1956	75.9	70.7	21.3	49.4	5.2	6.1	−.9	....	73.8	71.0	2.8	−2.1
1957	75.2	74.3	22.3	52.0	.9	2.3	−1.4	....	74.0	69.2	4.8	−1.2
1958	62.6	75.3	23.6	51.7	−12.6	−10.3	−2.4	....	62.8	61.9	.9	.2
1959	78.3	79.9	21.1	58.7	−1.6	−1.1	−.4	....	77.0	78.1	−1.2	−1.3
1960	81.1	78.0	19.7	58.3	3.1	3.0	.1	....	78.7	75.9	2.8	−2.4
1961	78.7	83.0	23.0	60.0	−4.3	−3.9	−.4	....	78.6	74.8	3.8	−.1
1962	86.7	90.5	23.3	67.2	−3.8	−4.2	.5	....	88.8	85.4	3.4	2.1
1963	93.6	92.9	21.9	71.0	.7	.3	.5	....	95.3	90.9	4.4	1.7
1964	104.0	106.3	29.6	76.7	−2.3	−3.3	1.0	....	104.2	97.4	6.8	.1
1965	120.2	119.7	33.7	86.0	.5	.5	−.0	....	119.0	113.5	5.4	−1.2
1966	127.3	128.6	36.0	92.7	−1.3	−1.8	.5	....	128.7	125.7	3.0	1.4
1967	125.7	139.9	44.3	95.6	−14.2	−13.2	−1.1	....	125.4	122.8	2.6	−.3
1968	136.0	142.0	41.9	100.0	−6.0	−6.0	.1	....	133.9	133.3	.6	−2.1
1969	153.6	143.6	40.6	103.0	9.9	8.4	1.5	....	149.7	149.3	.4	−3.9
1970	148.9	158.6	55.8	102.8	−10.6	−12.4	1.9	0.9	147.4	144.2	3.2	−1.5
1971	161.6	180.3	60.7	119.7	−19.4	−22.0	2.6	.7	165.7	166.4	−.7	4.1
1972	186.6	189.2	52.6	136.6	−3.3	−16.8	13.5	.7	189.9	195.0	−5.1	3.3
1973	235.5	227.7	79.0	148.7	7.8	−5.6	13.4	.0	236.3	229.8	6.5	.8
1974	227.8	234.5	85.1	149.4	−4.7	−11.5	6.8	[4] −2.0	231.5	228.7	2.9	3.7
1975	218.9	282.7	94.3	188.4	−63.8	−69.3	5.5	.0	224.4	206.1	18.3	5.5
1976	257.9	294.4	82.5	211.9	−36.5	−53.1	16.6	.0	263.0	257.9	5.1	5.1
1977	309.1	326.9	78.0	248.9	−17.8	−45.9	28.0	.0	310.4	324.1	−13.6	1.4
1978	374.8	374.0	89.4	284.6	.8	−29.5	30.3	.0	372.3	386.6	−14.3	−2.6
1979	422.7	407.3	96.7	310.6	14.3	−16.1	30.4	1.1	421.2	423.0	−1.8	−1.5
1980	406.2	438.3	106.2	332.1	−33.2	−61.4	28.2	1.2	410.2	402.3	7.8	3.9
1981	477.5	504.7	130.2	374.5	−28.2	−60.0	31.7	1.1	475.6	471.5	4.1	−1.9
1982 [p]	413.9	529.9	141.1	388.8	−116.1	−147.9	31.9	.0	414.0	421.9	−7.9	.1
1980:												
I	410.8	420.2	97.9	322.3	−10.6	−39.7	29.1	1.2	421.3	424.0	−2.6	10.5
II	395.8	438.8	108.6	330.2	−44.2	−67.5	23.3	1.2	399.6	391.0	8.6	3.8
III	404.4	449.2	113.1	336.1	−45.9	−73.1	27.1	1.2	406.6	384.1	22.5	2.2
IV	414.0	445.1	105.3	339.8	−32.2	−65.2	33.0	1.2	413.0	410.3	2.8	−1.0
1981:												
I	461.4	468.7	105.9	362.8	−8.3	−39.7	31.3	1.1	466.5	455.7	10.8	5.1
II	482.4	488.9	122.0	367.0	−7.6	−40.5	32.9	1.1	477.8	475.5	2.3	−4.6
III	490.0	513.4	134.4	379.0	−24.5	−58.0	33.5	1.1	489.1	486.0	3.1	−.8
IV	476.3	547.7	158.6	389.1	−72.5	−101.7	29.1	1.1	469.0	468.9	.1	−7.2
1982:												
I	428.8	519.4	139.1	380.3	−90.7	−118.4	27.7	.0	421.3	414.8	6.5	−7.5
II	441.5	529.0	144.3	384.7	−87.5	−119.6	32.1	.0	442.3	431.5	10.8	.8
III	422.4	546.1	152.0	394.1	−123.7	−156.0	32.3	.0	426.0	443.3	−17.3	3.6
IV [p]	....	....	128.9	....	....	....	....	.0	366.3	397.9	−31.7	....

[1] Undistributed corporate profits with inventory valuation and capital consumption adjustments, corporate and noncorporate capital consumption allowances with capital consumption adjustment, and private wage accruals less disbursements.

[2] Allocations of special drawing rights (SDRs), except as noted in footnote 4.

[3] Net exports of goods and services less net transfers to foreigners and interest paid by government to foreigners plus capital grants received by the United States, net.

[4] In February 1974, the U.S. Government paid to India $2,010 million in rupees under provisions of the Agricultural Trade Development and Assistance Act. This transaction is being treated as capital grants paid to foreigners, i.e., a −$2.0 billion entry in capital grants received by the United States, net.

Source: Department of Commerce, Bureau of Economic Analysis.

TABLE B–26.—*Saving by individuals, 1946–82* [1]

[Billions of dollars; quarterly data at seasonally adjusted annual rates]

Year or quarter	Total	Increase in financial assets: Total	Checkable deposits and currency	Time and savings deposits	Money market fund shares	Securities: Government securities [2]	Securities: Corporate equities [3]	Securities: Other securities [4]	Insurance and pension reserves [5]	Other financial assets [6]	Net investment [7]: Owner-occupied homes	Net investment [7]: Consumer durables	Net investment [7]: Noncorporate business assets [8]	Less: Net increase in debt: Mortgage debt on nonfarm homes	Less: Net increase in debt: Consumer credit	Less: Net increase in debt: Other debt [8] [9]
1946	24.6	18.8	5.6	6.3	...	−1.5	1.1	−0.9	5.3	2.8	3.6	6.1	2.3	3.6	3.1	−0.4
1947	20.1	13.2	.1	3.4	...	1.6	1.1	−.8	5.4	2.4	6.7	9.0	1.8	4.7	3.7	2.2
1948	24.3	9.1	−2.9	2.2	...	1.3	1.0	.0	5.3	2.2	9.1	9.8	6.9	4.6	3.2	2.8
1949	20.9	9.9	−2.0	2.6	...	1.8	.7	−.4	5.6	1.6	8.4	10.6	1.8	4.4	3.2	2.2
1950	30.6	13.7	2.6	2.4	...	−.1	.7	−.7	6.9	1.9	11.8	14.8	6.8	6.7	4.8	5.0
1951	34.7	19.1	4.6	4.7	...	−.6	1.8	.3	6.3	1.9	11.7	11.3	4.5	6.6	1.6	3.7
1952	31.3	23.2	1.6	7.8	...	2.5	1.6	.0	7.7	2.0	11.3	8.6	2.3	6.2	5.3	2.7
1953	32.5	22.8	1.0	8.1	...	2.5	1.0	.3	7.9	2.1	12.3	10.1	1.0	7.6	4.2	1.9
1954	28.2	22.2	2.2	9.1	...	1.0	.8	−.9	7.8	2.1	12.7	7.1	1.9	8.7	1.5	5.5
1955	34.1	28.0	1.2	8.6	...	5.8	1.0	.8	8.5	2.1	16.7	12.2	2.9	12.2	7.2	6.4
1956	37.2	30.2	1.8	9.4	...	3.9	2.0	1.2	9.5	2.5	15.6	8.5	1.2	11.2	3.9	3.2
1957	36.5	28.6	−.4	11.9	...	2.3	1.5	1.0	9.5	2.8	13.2	7.7	2.7	8.9	2.9	3.8
1958	34.1	31.6	3.8	13.9	...	−2.5	1.5	1.1	10.4	3.5	12.3	3.6	2.6	9.5	.5	6.0
1959	38.0	37.4	1.0	11.0	...	10.1	.5	−.3	11.9	3.3	16.3	7.3	5.0	12.8	8.0	7.2
1960	36.7	32.1	1.0	12.0	...	2.2	−.6	2.4	11.5	3.6	14.8	7.0	3.6	11.7	4.4	4.9
1961	35.9	35.4	−.9	18.3	...	1.4	.3	.1	12.1	4.3	12.7	4.3	4.7	12.2	2.5	6.5
1962	42.0	40.1	−1.2	26.1	...	1.3	−2.1	.1	12.7	3.2	13.5	8.5	7.5	14.1	6.3	7.2
1963	46.7	46.6	4.2	26.2	...	.6	−2.6	1.4	13.9	2.9	14.3	11.8	9.8	16.2	8.9	10.7
1964	56.8	55.7	5.3	26.1	...	4.8	−.2	.4	16.1	3.2	15.0	15.0	9.2	17.5	9.8	10.8
1965	65.0	58.8	7.6	27.8	...	3.7	−2.1	1.3	16.9	3.7	14.5	20.2	13.3	17.0	10.6	14.3
1966	72.8	57.9	2.4	19.0	...	11.3	−.7	2.4	19.2	4.4	13.5	23.1	10.8	13.8	6.5	12.2
1967	77.0	69.8	9.9	35.3	...	−1.2	−4.7	5.2	18.6	6.7	11.7	21.1	10.2	12.5	5.7	17.6
1968	80.5	75.6	11.1	31.1	...	5.2	−7.5	7.9	19.8	8.1	15.7	27.0	10.0	16.9	11.5	19.2
1969	71.5	65.2	−2.5	9.1	...	25.9	−2.8	10.0	21.5	4.0	16.3	26.3	12.7	18.6	10.8	19.4
1970	86.4	81.5	8.9	43.6	...	−5.4	−1.7	6.9	23.9	5.4	13.6	20.0	11.5	14.1	5.4	20.7
1971	95.6	102.1	12.2	67.7	...	−12.2	−5.5	6.5	27.4	5.8	20.7	26.6	17.5	26.2	14.7	30.3
1972	109.3	131.5	13.9	74.4	...	2.7	−5.1	4.9	29.4	11.4	28.0	34.6	20.6	41.4	19.8	44.2
1973	132.0	148.5	14.1	63.6	...	24.2	−5.8	11.1	33.0	8.3	31.0	40.4	26.6	46.5	24.3	43.8
1974	128.3	147.3	7.4	55.7	2.4	28.3	−.6	6.8	36.2	11.1	25.2	28.4	10.6	38.0	9.9	35.4
1975	153.0	174.3	6.9	83.4	1.3	25.0	−3.8	4.4	43.5	13.6	23.5	26.5	5.8	40.6	9.6	26.9
1976	165.1	210.5	15.7	107.5	−.0	11.7	−4.6	8.6	52.4	19.2	36.1	40.0	3.3	61.4	25.4	37.9
1977	167.2	233.8	20.1	107.5	.2	18.2	−3.5	4.7	67.4	19.2	52.3	49.6	15.2	91.1	40.2	52.4
1978	200.6	274.4	22.6	100.3	6.9	33.6	−5.1	12.5	73.8	29.8	63.9	56.7	25.0	111.3	48.8	59.3
1979	208.1	296.1	22.4	78.5	34.4	55.5	−15.9	18.4	68.2	34.6	67.9	52.5	26.3	121.3	45.4	68.0
1980	250.5	337.5	6.5	125.6	29.2	40.5	2.1	7.0	89.6	36.9	48.7	32.4	8.7	98.3	4.9	73.7
1981	283.1	355.2	25.8	65.6	107.5	57.3	−31.6	−6.4	98.7	38.3	43.8	38.2	27.9	81.4	25.3	75.2
1980:																
I	242.9	347.9	8.1	96.8	61.3	65.7	.6	.4	80.7	34.3	59.8	46.4	14.7	123.7	21.8	80.4
II	237.0	270.5	−11.1	81.8	62.5	−6.6	6.9	2.4	95.8	39.0	49.3	18.5	−.4	83.7	−28.4	45.7
III	263.6	361.4	41.1	120.0	5.1	40.1	−.3	13.3	100.1	42.2	40.8	27.8	6.0	94.4	14.1	63.9
IV	258.4	370.1	−11.9	203.7	−11.9	62.7	1.5	12.1	81.9	32.1	45.6	37.0	13.9	91.4	12.0	104.7
1981:																
I	256.0	328.7	55.0	25.2	148.4	5.1	−15.5	−11.3	84.6	37.2	49.0	45.7	25.3	91.6	26.5	74.7
II	257.0	365.4	−.3	92.8	59.9	103.2	−29.0	−7.4	103.5	42.6	48.4	35.2	32.9	99.5	32.2	93.2
III	320.4	387.6	5.9	84.3	137.3	83.7	−55.0	−21.9	113.3	40.1	42.4	42.8	29.6	77.8	34.2	70.1
IV	299.1	339.0	42.7	60.1	84.3	37.0	−26.8	14.9	93.6	33.2	35.7	29.0	23.4	56.8	8.3	62.8
1982:																
I	300.5	333.7	32.8	131.4	37.6	42.6	−11.0	−19.9	90.6	29.6	27.1	35.7	5.9	66.8	6.6	28.5
II	290.2	357.7	−3.9	102.4	41.2	105.2	−4.4	−30.7	112.0	36.0	29.6	37.7	7.8	51.8	25.4	65.4
III	335.9	393.3	1.7	94.7	86.5	68.9	−12.5	3.0	104.4	46.6	29.5	35.2	−.1	51.1	8.2	62.8

1 Saving by households, personal trust funds, nonprofit institutions, farms, and other noncorporate business.
2 Consists of U.S. savings bonds, other U.S. Treasury securities, U.S. Government agency securities and sponsored agency securities, mortgage pool securities, and State and local obligations.
3 Includes mutual fund shares.
4 Corporate and foreign bonds and open market paper.
5 Private life insurance reserves, private insured and noninsured pension reserves, and government insurance and pension reserves.
6 Consists of security credit, mortgages, accident and health insurance reserves, and nonlife insurance claims for households and of consumer credit, equity in sponsored agencies, and nonlife insurance claims for noncorporate business.
7 Purchases of physical assets less depreciation.
8 Includes data for corporate farms.
9 Other debt consists of security credit, policy loans, and noncorporate business debt.

Source: Board of Governors of the Federal Reserve System.

Table B–27.—*Number and median income (in 1981 dollars) of families and persons, and poverty status, by race, selected years, 1947–81*

Year	Families [1]						Persons below poverty level		Median income of persons 14 years old and over with income [2]			
	Number (millions)	Median income	Below poverty level						Males		Females	
			Total		Female householder							
			Number (millions)	Rate	Number (millions)	Rate	Number (millions)	Rate	All persons	Year-round full-time workers	All persons	Year-round full-time workers
ALL RACES												
1947	37.2	$12,341	....	....	....	....	....	....	$9,080	....	$4,141	....
1950	39.9	12,539	....	....	....	....	....	....	9,710	....	3,601	....
1955	42.9	15,006	....	....	....	....	....	....	11,405	$14,405	3,804	$9,289
1960	45.5	17,259	8.2	18.1	2.0	42.4	39.9	22.2	12,530	16,688	3,873	10,122
1961	46.4	17,435	8.4	18.1	2.0	42.1	39.6	21.9	12,735	17,217	3,888	10,157
1962	47.1	17,907	8.1	17.2	2.0	42.9	38.6	21.0	13,145	17,517	4,035	10,394
1963	47.5	18,563	7.6	15.9	2.0	40.4	36.4	19.5	13,400	18,031	4,076	10,563
1964	48.0	19,262	7.2	15.0	1.8	36.4	36.1	19.0	13,626	18,426	4,249	10,878
1965	48.5	20,054	6.7	13.9	1.9	38.4	33.2	17.3	14,479	19,019	4,384	11,000
1966 [3]	49.2	21,108	5.8	11.8	1.7	33.1	28.5	14.7	14,870	19,491	4,590	11,283
1967	50.1	21,609	5.7	11.4	1.8	33.3	27.8	14.2	15,126	19,855	4,906	11,435
1968	50.8	22,566	5.0	10.0	1.8	32.3	25.4	12.8	15,633	20,427	5,278	11,942
1969	51.6	23,402	5.0	9.7	1.8	32.7	24.1	12.1	15,950	21,504	5,289	12,595
1970	52.2	23,111	5.3	10.1	2.0	32.5	25.4	12.6	15,623	21,511	5,240	12,742
1971	53.3	23,097	5.3	10.0	2.1	33.9	25.6	12.5	15,502	21,628	5,408	12,803
1972	54.4	24,166	5.1	9.3	2.2	32.7	24.5	11.9	16,196	22,909	5,650	13,159
1973	55.1	24,663	4.8	8.8	2.2	32.2	23.0	11.1	16,487	23,470	5,722	13,278
1974 [3]	55.7	23,795	4.9	8.8	2.3	32.1	23.4	11.2	15,588	22,430	5,684	13,231
1975	56.2	23,183	5.5	9.7	2.4	32.5	25.9	12.3	14,960	21,856	5,720	13,044
1976	56.7	23,898	5.3	9.4	2.5	33.0	25.0	11.8	15,059	22,142	5,713	13,280
1977	57.2	24,027	5.3	9.3	2.6	31.7	24.7	11.6	15,193	22,617	5,915	13,228
1978	57.8	24,591	5.3	9.1	2.7	31.4	24.5	11.4	15,244	22,391	5,671	13,440
1979 [4]	59.6	24,542	5.5	9.2	2.6	30.4	26.1	11.7	14,759	21,901	5,453	13,195
1980	60.3	23,204	6.2	10.3	3.0	32.7	29.3	13.0	13,830	21,162	5,430	12,793
1981	61.0	22,388	6.9	11.2	3.3	34.6	31.8	14.0	13,473	20,692	5,458	12,457
WHITE												
1970	46.5	23,975	3.7	8.0	1.1	25.0	17.5	9.9	16,421	22,127	5,307	12,967
1971	47.6	23,966	3.8	7.9	1.2	26.5	17.8	9.9	16,252	22,237	5,497	12,951
1972	48.5	25,107	3.4	7.1	1.1	24.3	16.2	9.0	16,987	23,736	5,687	13,418
1973	48.9	25,777	3.2	6.6	1.2	24.5	15.1	8.4	17,300	24,150	5,777	13,503
1974 [3]	49.4	24,728	3.4	6.8	1.3	24.8	15.7	8.6	16,329	22,867	5,749	13,343
1975	49.9	24,110	3.8	7.7	1.4	25.9	17.8	9.7	15,715	22,361	5,779	13,074
1976	50.1	24,823	3.6	7.1	1.4	25.2	16.7	9.1	15,876	22,802	5,761	13,382
1977	50.5	25,124	3.5	7.0	1.4	24.0	16.4	8.9	15,913	23,080	6,005	13,312
1978	50.9	25,606	3.5	6.9	1.4	23.5	16.3	8.7	15,966	22,807	5,739	13,567
1979 [4]	52.2	25,610	3.6	6.9	1.4	22.3	17.2	19.0	15,418	22,534	5,504	13,311
1980	52.7	24,176	4.2	8.0	1.6	25.7	19.7	10.2	14,710	21,766	5,460	12,917
1981	53.3	23,517	4.7	8.8	1.8	27.4	21.6	11.1	14,296	21,178	5,519	12,665
BLACK												
1970	4.9	14,707	1.5	29.5	.8	54.3	7.5	33.5	9,737	15,072	4,832	10,624
1971	5.2	14,462	1.5	28.8	.9	53.5	7.4	32.5	9,692	15,205	4,817	11,435
1972	5.3	14,922	1.5	29.0	1.0	53.3	7.7	33.3	10,289	16,029	5,313	11,479
1973	5.4	14,877	1.5	28.1	1.0	52.7	7.4	31.4	10,464	16,276	5,215	11,451
1974 [3]	5.5	14,765	1.5	26.9	1.0	52.2	7.2	30.3	10,118	16,383	5,190	12,314
1975	5.6	14,835	1.5	27.1	1.0	50.1	7.5	31.3	9,395	16,641	5,250	12,491
1976	5.8	14,766	1.6	27.9	1.1	52.2	7.6	31.1	9,559	16,331	5,429	12,511
1977	5.8	14,352	1.6	28.2	1.2	51.0	7.7	31.3	9,443	15,912	5,185	12,442
1978	5.9	15,166	1.6	27.5	1.2	50.6	7.6	30.6	9,565	17,468	5,168	12,574
1979 [4]	6.2	14,502	1.7	27.8	1.2	49.4	8.1	31.0	9,544	16,240	5,009	12,197
1980	6.3	13,989	1.8	28.9	1.3	49.4	8.6	32.5	8,840	15,314	5,055	12,047
1981	6.4	13,266	2.0	30.8	1.4	52.9	9.2	34.2	8,501	14,984	4,903	11,438

[1] The term "family" refers to a group of two or more persons related by blood, marriage, or adoption and residing together; all such persons are considered members of the same family. Beginning 1979 based on householder concept and restricted to primary families.

[2] Beginning 1979, data are for persons 15 years and over.

[3] Based on revised methodology; comparable with succeeding years.

[4] Based on 1980 census population controls; comparable with succeeding years.

Note.—The poverty level is based on the poverty index adopted by a Federal interagency committee in 1969. That index reflected different consumption requirements for families based on size and composition, sex and age of family householder, and farm-nonfarm residence. Minor revisions implemented in 1981 eliminated variations in the poverty thresholds based on two of these variables, farm-nonfarm residence and sex of householder. The poverty thresholds are updated every year to reflect changes in the consumer price index. For further details see "Current Population Reports," Series P–60, No. 133.

Source: Department of Commerce, Bureau of the Census.

TABLE B–28.—*Population by age groups, 1929–82*

[Thousands of persons]

July 1	Total	Age (years)						
		Under 5	5–15	16–19	20–24	25–44	45–64	65 and over
1929	121,767	11,734	26,800	9,127	10,694	35,862	21,076	6,474
1933	125,579	10,612	26,897	9,302	11,152	37,319	22,933	7,363
1939	130,880	10,418	25,179	9,822	11,519	39,354	25,823	8,764
1940	132,122	10,579	24,811	9,895	11,690	39,868	26,249	9,031
1941	133,402	10,850	24,516	9,840	11,807	40,383	26,718	9,288
1942	134,860	11,301	24,231	9,730	11,955	40,861	27,196	9,584
1943	136,739	12,016	24,093	9,607	12,064	41,420	27,671	9,867
1944	138,397	12,524	23,949	9,561	12,062	42,016	28,138	10,147
1945	139,928	12,979	23,907	9,361	12,036	42,521	28,630	10,494
1946	141,389	13,244	24,103	9,119	12,004	43,027	29,064	10,828
1947	144,126	14,406	24,468	9,097	11,814	43,657	29,498	11,185
1948	146,631	14,919	25,209	8,952	11,794	44,288	29,931	11,538
1949	149,188	15,607	25,852	8,788	11,700	44,916	30,405	11,921
1950	152,271	16,410	26,721	8,542	11,680	45,672	30,849	12,397
1951	154,878	17,333	27,279	8,446	11,552	46,103	31,362	12,803
1952	157,553	17,312	28,894	8,414	11,350	46,495	31,884	13,203
1953	160,184	17,638	30,227	8,460	11,062	46,786	32,394	13,617
1954	163,026	18,057	31,480	8,637	10,832	47,001	32,942	14,076
1955	165,931	18,566	32,682	8,744	10,714	47,194	33,506	14,525
1956	168,903	19,003	33,994	8,916	10,616	47,379	34,057	14,938
1957	171,984	19,494	35,272	9,195	10,603	47,440	34,591	15,388
1958	174,882	19,887	36,445	9,543	10,756	47,337	35,109	15,806
1959	177,830	20,175	37,368	10,215	10,969	47,192	35,663	16,248
1960	180,671	20,341	38,494	10,683	11,134	47,140	36,203	16,675
1961	183,691	20,522	39,765	11,025	11,483	47,084	36,722	17,089
1962	186,538	20,469	41,205	11,180	11,959	47,013	37,255	17,457
1963	189,242	20,342	41,626	12,007	12,714	46,994	37,782	17,778
1964	191,889	20,165	42,297	12,736	13,269	46,958	38,338	18,127
1965	194,303	19,824	42,938	13,516	13,746	46,912	38,916	18,451
1966	196,560	19,208	43,702	14,311	14,050	47,001	39,534	18,755
1967	198,712	18,563	44,244	14,200	15,248	47,194	40,193	19,071
1968	200,706	17,913	44,622	14,452	15,786	47,721	40,846	19,365
1969	202,677	17,376	44,840	14,800	16,480	48,064	41,437	19,680
1970	205,052	17,166	44,816	15,289	17,202	48,473	41,999	20,107
1971	207,661	17,244	44,591	15,688	18,159	48,936	42,482	20,561
1972	209,896	17,101	44,203	16,039	18,153	50,482	42,898	21,020
1973	211,909	16,851	43,582	16,446	18,521	51,749	43,235	21,525
1974	213,854	16,487	42,989	16,769	18,975	53,051	43,522	22,061
1975	215,973	16,121	42,508	17,017	19,527	54,302	43,801	22,696
1976	218,035	15,617	42,099	17,194	19,986	55,852	44,008	23,278
1977	220,239	15,564	41,298	17,276	20,499	57,561	44,150	23,892
1978	222,585	15,735	40,428	17,288	20,946	59,400	44,286	24,502
1979	225,055	16,063	39,552	17,242	21,297	61,379	44,390	25,134
1980	227,658	16,448	38,814	17,131	21,605	63,465	44,487	25,708
1981	229,807	16,939	38,040	16,679	21,938	65,487	44,471	26,253
1982	231,990	......	......	......	......	......	......	......

[1] Not available.

Note.—Includes Armed Forces overseas beginning 1940. Includes Alaska and Hawaii beginning 1950.

Source: Department of Commerce, Bureau of the Census.

TABLE B–29.—*Noninstitutional population and the labor force, 1929–82*

[Monthly data seasonally adjusted, except as noted]

Year or month	Noninstitutional population [1]	Armed Forces [1]	Civilian labor force					Unemployment rate (percent of civilian labor force)	Civilian labor force participation rate [2]		
			Total	Employment			Unemployment		Total	Males	Females
				Total	Agricultural	Nonagricultural					
	Thousands of persons 14 years of age and over							Percent			
1929	...	260	49,180	47,630	10,450	37,180	1,550	3.2	...	...	...
1933	...	250	51,590	38,760	10,090	28,670	12,830	24.9	...	...	...
1939	...	370	55,230	45,750	9,610	36,140	9,480	17.2	...	...	...
1940	100,380	540	55,640	47,520	9,540	37,980	8,120	14.6	55.7	83.7	28.2
1941	101,520	1,620	55,910	50,350	9,100	41,250	5,560	9.9	56.0	84.3	28.7
1942	102,610	3,970	56,410	53,750	9,250	44,500	2,660	4.7	57.2	85.6	31.3
1943	103,660	9,020	55,540	54,470	9,080	45,390	1,070	1.9	58.7	86.4	36.0
1944	104,630	11,410	54,630	53,960	8,950	45,010	670	1.2	58.6	87.0	36.5
1945	105,530	11,440	53,860	52,820	8,580	44,240	1,040	1.9	57.2	84.8	35.9
1946	106,520	3,450	57,520	55,250	8,320	46,930	2,270	3.9	55.8	82.6	31.2
1947	107,608	1,590	60,168	57,812	8,256	49,557	2,356	3.9	56.8	84.0	31.0
	Thousands of persons 16 years of age and over										
1947	103,418	1,591	59,350	57,038	7,890	49,148	2,311	3.9	58.3	86.4	31.8
1948	104,527	1,456	60,621	58,343	7,629	50,714	2,276	3.8	58.8	86.6	32.7
1949	105,611	1,616	61,286	57,651	7,658	49,993	3,637	5.9	58.9	86.4	33.1
1950	106,645	1,649	62,208	58,918	7,160	51,758	3,288	5.3	59.2	86.4	33.9
1951	107,721	3,098	62,017	59,961	6,726	53,235	2,055	3.3	59.3	86.5	34.6
1952	108,823	3,593	62,138	60,250	6,500	53,749	1,883	3.0	59.0	86.3	34.7
1953 [3]	110,601	3,547	63,015	61,179	6,260	54,919	1,834	2.9	58.9	86.0	34.4
1954	111,671	3,350	63,643	60,109	6,205	53,904	3,532	5.5	58.8	85.5	34.6
1955	112,732	3,048	65,023	62,170	6,450	55,722	2,852	4.4	59.3	85.3	35.7
1956	113,811	2,856	66,552	63,799	6,283	57,514	2,750	4.1	60.0	85.5	36.9
1957	115,065	2,799	66,929	64,071	5,947	58,123	2,859	4.3	59.6	84.8	36.9
1958	116,363	2,636	67,639	63,036	5,586	57,450	4,602	6.8	59.5	84.2	37.1
1959	117,881	2,551	68,369	64,630	5,565	59,065	3,740	5.5	59.3	83.7	37.1
1960 [3]	119,759	2,514	69,628	65,778	5,458	60,318	3,852	5.5	59.4	83.3	37.7
1961	121,343	2,572	70,459	65,746	5,200	60,546	4,714	6.7	59.3	82.9	38.1
1962 [3]	122,981	2,827	70,614	66,702	4,944	61,759	3,911	5.5	58.8	82.0	37.9
1963	125,154	2,737	71,833	67,762	4,687	63,076	4,070	5.7	58.7	81.4	38.3
1964	127,224	2,738	73,091	69,305	4,523	64,782	3,786	5.2	58.7	81.0	38.7
1965	129,236	2,722	74,455	71,088	4,361	66,726	3,366	4.5	58.9	80.7	39.3
1966	131,180	3,122	75,770	72,895	3,979	68,915	2,875	3.8	59.2	80.4	40.3
1967	133,319	3,446	77,347	74,372	3,844	70,527	2,975	3.8	59.6	80.4	41.1
1968	135,562	3,534	78,737	75,920	3,817	72,103	2,817	3.6	59.6	80.1	41.6
1969	137,841	3,506	80,734	77,902	3,606	74,296	2,832	3.5	60.1	79.8	42.7
1970	140,272	3,188	82,771	78,678	3,463	75,215	4,093	4.9	60.4	79.7	43.3
1971	143,033	2,816	84,382	79,367	3,394	75,972	5,016	5.9	60.2	79.1	43.4
1972 [3]	146,574	2,449	87,034	82,153	3,484	78,669	4,882	5.6	60.4	78.9	43.9
1973 [3]	149,423	2,326	89,429	85,064	3,470	81,594	4,365	4.9	60.8	78.8	44.7
1974	152,349	2,229	91,949	86,794	3,515	83,279	5,156	5.6	61.3	78.7	45.7
1975	153.333	2,180	93,775	85,846	3,408	82,438	7,929	8.5	61.2	77.9	46.3
1976	158,294	2,144	96,158	88,752	3,331	85,421	7,406	7.7	61.6	77.5	47.3
1977	161,166	2,133	99,009	92,017	3,283	88,734	6,991	7.1	62.3	77.7	48.4
1978 [3]	164,027	2,117	102,251	96,048	3,387	92,661	6,202	6.1	63.2	77.9	50.0
1979	166,951	2,088	104,962	98,824	3,347	95,477	6,137	5.8	63.7	77.8	50.9
1980	169,848	2,102	106,940	99,303	3,364	95,938	7,637	7.1	63.8	77.4	51.5
1981	172,272	2,142	108,670	100,397	3,368	97,030	8,273	7.6	63.9	77.0	52.1
1982	174,451	2,179	110,204	99,526	3,401	96,125	10,678	9.7	64.0	76.6	52.6

See next page for continuation of table.

TABLE B-29.—*Noninstitutional population and the labor force, 1929–82—Continued*

[Monthly data seasonally adjusted, except as noted]

Year or month	Noninstitutional population [1]	Armed Forces [1]	Civilian labor force: Total	Civilian labor force: Employment: Total	Civilian labor force: Employment: Agricultural	Civilian labor force: Employment: Nonagricultural	Civilian labor force: Unemployment	Unemployment rate (percent of civilian labor force)	Civilian labor force participation rate [2]: Total	Civilian labor force participation rate [2]: Males	Civilian labor force participation rate [2]: Females
	Thousands of persons 16 years of age and over							Percent			
1980:											
Jan	168,625	2,081	106,546	99,872	3,313	96,559	6,674	6.3	64.0	77.7	51.6
Feb	168,846	2,086	106,637	99,963	3,387	96,576	6,674	6.3	63.9	77.8	51.5
Mar	169,073	2,090	106,394	99,677	3,412	96,265	6,717	6.3	63.7	77.5	51.3
Apr	169,289	2,092	106,552	99,204	3,318	95,886	7,348	6.9	63.7	77.4	51.4
May	169,494	2,088	106,892	98,922	3,385	95,537	7,970	7.5	63.9	77.6	51.5
June	169,735	2,092	106,832	98,769	3,309	95,460	8,063	7.5	63.7	77.5	51.4
July	170,030	2,099	107,169	98,816	3,331	95,485	8,353	7.8	63.8	77.5	51.5
Aug	170,217	2,114	107,116	98,829	3,247	95,582	8,287	7.7	63.7	77.3	51.5
Sept	170,419	2,121	107,148	99,104	3,448	95,656	8,044	7.5	63.7	77.3	51.4
Oct	170,624	2,121	107,438	99,327	3,362	95,965	8,111	7.5	63.8	77.3	51.6
Nov	170,814	2,119	107,596	99,567	3,387	96,180	8,029	7.5	63.8	77.3	51.6
Dec	171,007	2,124	107,446	99,650	3,486	96,164	7,796	7.3	63.6	77.0	51.6
1981:											
Jan	171,229	2,125	108,012	99,964	3,420	96,544	8,048	7.5	63.9	77.3	51.8
Feb	171,400	2,121	108,175	100,143	3,340	96,803	8,032	7.4	63.9	77.2	52.0
Mar	171,581	2,128	108,471	100,504	3,356	97,148	7,967	7.3	64.0	77.3	52.1
Apr	171,770	2,129	108,866	101,006	3,519	97,487	7,860	7.2	64.2	77.4	52.3
May	171,956	2,127	109,101	100,968	3,371	97,597	8,133	7.5	64.2	77.4	52.4
June	172,172	2,131	108,440	100,393	3,360	97,033	8,047	7.4	63.8	76.7	52.1
July	172,385	2,139	108,602	100,748	3,320	97,428	7,854	7.2	63.8	76.8	52.1
Aug	172,559	2,160	108,762	100,709	3,396	97,313	8,053	7.4	63.8	76.9	52.1
Sept	172,758	2,165	108,375	100,104	3,358	96,746	8,271	7.6	63.5	76.7	51.7
Oct	172,966	2,158	109,028	100,355	3,374	96,981	8,673	8.0	63.8	76.7	52.2
Nov	173,155	2,158	109,254	100,229	3,389	96,840	9,025	8.3	63.9	76.8	52.3
Dec	173,330	2,164	109,066	99,677	3,219	96,458	9,389	8.6	63.7	76.7	52.0
1982:											
Jan	173,495	2,159	109,034	99,688	3,379	96,309	9,346	8.6	63.6	76.5	52.1
Feb	173,657	2,168	109,364	99,695	3,367	96,328	9,669	8.8	63.8	76.6	52.3
Mar	173,843	2,175	109,478	99,597	3,367	96,230	9,881	9.0	63.8	76.5	52.3
Apr	174,020	2,176	109,740	99,484	3,356	96,128	10,256	9.3	63.9	76.6	52.4
May	174,201	2,175	110,378	99,994	3,446	96,548	10,384	9.4	64.2	77.0	52.7
June	174,364	2,173	110,147	99,681	3,371	96,310	10,466	9.5	64.0	76.5	52.7
July	174,544	2,180	110,416	99,588	3,445	96,143	10,828	9.8	64.1	76.5	52.9
Aug	174,707	2,196	110,614	99,683	3,429	96,254	10,931	9.9	64.1	76.6	52.9
Sept	174,889	2,198	110,858	99,543	3,363	96,180	11,315	10.2	64.2	76.8	52.8
Oct	175,069	2,188	110,752	99,176	3,413	95,763	11,576	10.5	64.1	76.7	52.7
Nov	175,238	2,180	111,042	99,136	3,466	95,670	11,906	10.7	64.2	76.8	52.8
Dec	175,380	2,182	111,129	99,093	3,411	95,682	12,036	10.8	64.2	76.6	53.0

[1] Not seasonally adjusted.

[2] Civilian labor force as percent of civilian noninstitutional population.

[3] Not strictly comparable with earlier data due to population adjustments as follows: Beginning 1953, introduction of 1950 census data added about 600,000 to population and about 350,000 to labor force, total employment, and agricultural employment. Beginning 1960, inclusion of Alaska and Hawaii added about 500,000 to population, about 300,000 to labor force, and about 240,000 to nonagricultural employment. Beginning 1962, introduction of 1960 census data reduced population by about 50,000 and labor force and employment by about 200,000. Beginning 1972, introduction of 1970 census data added about 800,000 to civilian noninstitutional population and about 333,000 to labor force and employment. A subsequent adjustment based on 1970 census in March 1973 added 60,000 to labor force and to employment. Beginning 1978, changes in sampling and estimation procedures introduced into the household survey added about 250,000 to labor force and to employment. Unemployment levels and rates were not significantly affected.

Note.—Labor force data in Tables B-29 through B-35 are based on household interviews and relate to the calendar week including the 12th of the month. For definitions of terms, area samples used, historic comparability of the data, comparability with other series, etc., see "Employment and Earnings."

Source: Department of Labor, Bureau of Labor Statistics.

TABLE B-30.—*Civilian employment and unemployment by sex and age, 1947–82*

[Thousands of persons 16 years of age and over; monthly data seasonally adjusted]

Year or month	Civilian employment							Unemployment						
	Total	Males			Females			Total	Males			Females		
		Total	16–19 years	20 years and over	Total	16–19 years	20 years and over		Total	16–19 years	20 years and over	Total	16–19 years	20 years and over
1947	57,038	40,995	2,218	38,776	16,045	1,691	14,354	2,311	1,692	270	1,422	619	144	475
1948	58,343	41,725	2,344	39,382	16,617	1,682	14,936	2,276	1,559	256	1,305	717	153	564
1949	57,651	40,925	2,124	38,803	16,723	1,588	15,137	3,637	2,572	353	2,219	1,065	223	841
1950	58,918	41,578	2,186	39,394	17,340	1,517	15,824	3,288	2,239	318	1,922	1,049	195	854
1951	59,961	41,780	2,156	39,626	18,181	1,611	16,570	2,055	1,221	191	1,029	834	145	689
1952	60,250	41,682	2,107	39,578	18,568	1,612	16,958	1,883	1,185	205	980	698	140	559
1953 [1]	61,179	42,431	2,136	40,296	18,749	1,585	17,164	1,834	1,202	184	1,019	632	123	510
1954	60,109	41,619	1,985	39,634	18,490	1,490	17,000	3,532	2,344	310	2,035	1,188	191	997
1955	62,170	42,621	2,095	40,526	19,551	1,547	18,002	2,852	1,854	274	1,580	998	176	823
1956	63,799	43,379	2,164	41,216	20,419	1,654	18,767	2,750	1,711	269	1,442	1,039	209	832
1957	64,071	43,357	2,115	41,239	20,714	1,663	19,052	2,859	1,841	300	1,541	1,018	197	821
1958	63,036	42,423	2,012	40,411	20,613	1,570	19,043	4,602	3,098	416	2,681	1,504	262	1,242
1959	64,630	43,466	2,198	41,267	21,164	1,640	19,524	3,740	2,420	398	2,022	1,320	256	1,063
1960 [1]	65,778	43,904	2,361	41,543	21,874	1,768	20,105	3,852	2,486	426	2,060	1,366	286	1,080
1961	65,746	43,656	2,315	41,342	22,090	1,793	20,296	4,714	2,997	479	2,518	1,717	349	1,368
1962 [1]	66,702	44,177	2,362	41,815	22,525	1,833	20,693	3,911	2,423	408	2,016	1,488	313	1,175
1963	67,762	44,657	2,406	42,251	23,105	1,849	21,257	4,070	2,472	501	1,971	1,598	383	1,216
1964	69,305	45,474	2,587	42,886	23,831	1,929	21,903	3,786	2,205	487	1,718	1,581	385	1,195
1965	71,088	46,340	2,918	43,422	24,748	2,118	22,630	3,366	1,914	479	1,435	1,452	395	1,056
1966	72,895	46,919	3,253	43,668	25,976	2,468	23,510	2,875	1,551	432	1,120	1,324	405	921
1967	74,372	47,479	3,186	44,294	26,893	2,496	24,397	2,975	1,508	448	1,060	1,468	391	1,078
1968	75,920	48,114	3,255	44,859	27,807	2,526	25,281	2,817	1,419	426	993	1,397	412	985
1969	77,902	48,818	3,430	45,388	29,084	2,687	26,397	2,832	1,403	440	963	1,429	413	1,015
1970	78,678	48,990	3,409	45,581	29,688	2,735	26,952	4,093	2,238	599	1,638	1,855	506	1,349
1971	79,367	49,390	3,478	45,912	29,976	2,730	27,246	5,016	2,789	693	2,097	2,227	568	1,658
1972 [1]	82,153	50,896	3,765	47,130	31,257	2,980	28,276	4,882	2,659	711	1,948	2,222	598	1,625
1973 [1]	85,064	52,349	4,039	48,310	32,715	3,231	29,484	4,365	2,275	653	1,624	2,089	583	1,507
1974	86,794	53,024	4,103	48,922	33,769	3,345	30,424	5,156	2,714	757	1,957	2,441	665	1,777
1975	85,846	51,857	3,839	48,018	33,989	3,263	30,726	7,929	4,442	966	3,476	3,486	802	2,684
1976	88,752	53,138	3,947	49,190	35,615	3,389	32,226	7,406	4,036	939	3,098	3,369	780	2,588
1977	92,017	54,728	4,174	50,555	37,289	3,514	33,775	6,991	3,667	874	2,794	3,324	789	2,535
1978 [1]	96,048	56,479	4,336	52,143	39,569	3,734	35,836	6,202	3,142	813	2,328	3,061	769	2,292
1979	98,824	57,607	4,300	53,308	41,217	3,783	37,434	6,137	3,120	811	2,308	3,018	743	2,276
1980	99,303	57,186	4,085	53,101	42,117	3,625	38,492	7,637	4,267	913	3,353	3,370	755	2,615
1981	100,397	57,397	3,815	53,582	43,000	3,411	39,590	8,273	4,577	962	3,615	3,696	800	2,895
1982	99,526	56,271	3,379	52,891	43,256	3,170	40,086	10,678	6,179	1,090	5,089	4,499	886	3,613
1981:														
Jan	99,964	57,357	3,968	53,389	42,607	3,558	39,049	8,048	4,477	998	3,479	3,571	762	2,809
Feb	100,143	57,337	3,933	53,404	42,806	3,538	39,268	8,032	4,448	988	3,500	3,544	778	2,766
Mar	100,504	57,557	3,916	53,641	42,947	3,514	39,433	7,967	4,397	958	3,439	3,570	805	2,765
Apr	101,006	57,837	3,981	53,856	43,169	3,545	39,624	7,860	4,300	947	3,353	3,560	800	2,760
May	100,968	57,739	3,892	53,847	43,229	3,504	39,725	8,133	4,495	955	3,540	3,638	792	2,846
June	100,393	57,314	3,736	53,578	43,079	3,383	39,696	8,047	4,439	947	3,492	3,608	778	2,830
July	100,748	57,614	3,786	53,828	43,134	3,413	39,721	7,854	4,226	883	3,343	3,628	761	2,867
Aug	100,709	57,540	3,796	53,744	43,169	3,443	39,726	8,053	4,444	931	3,513	3,609	760	2,849
Sept	100,104	57,404	3,758	53,646	42,700	3,344	39,356	8,271	4,499	940	3,559	3,772	819	2,953
Oct	100,355	57,257	3,750	53,507	43,098	3,263	39,835	8,673	4,764	949	3,815	3,909	866	3,043
Nov	100,229	57,062	3,683	53,379	43,167	3,247	39,920	9,025	5,052	1,026	4,026	3,973	868	3,105
Dec	99,677	56,746	3,578	53,168	42,931	3,194	39,737	9,389	5,396	1,029	4,367	3,993	819	3,174
1982:														
Jan	99,688	56,667	3,568	53,099	43,021	3,204	39,817	9,346	5,381	1,019	4,362	3,965	856	3,109
Feb	99,695	56,670	3,540	53,130	43,025	3,200	39,825	9,669	5,486	1,035	4,451	4,183	897	3,286
Mar	99,597	56,499	3,473	53,026	43,098	3,215	39,883	9,881	5,662	1,055	4,607	4,219	817	3,402
Apr	99,484	56,444	3,420	53,024	43,040	3,213	39,827	10,256	5,856	1,086	4,770	4,400	872	3,528
May	99,994	56,724	3,534	53,190	43,270	3,206	40,064	10,384	5,921	1,103	4,818	4,463	895	3,568
June	99,681	56,249	3,306	52,943	43,432	3,178	40,254	10,466	6,076	1,060	5,016	4,390	825	3,565
July	99,588	56,127	3,222	52,905	43,461	3,150	40,311	10,828	6,234	1,084	5,150	4,594	922	3,672
Aug	99,683	56,159	3,327	52,832	43,524	3,156	40,368	10,931	6,345	1,113	5,232	4,586	915	3,671
Sept	99,543	56,072	3,296	52,776	43,471	3,185	40,286	11,315	6,703	1,125	5,578	4,612	902	3,710
Oct	99,176	55,932	3,283	52,649	43,244	3,132	40,112	11,576	6,844	1,130	5,714	4,732	908	3,824
Nov	99,136	55,892	3,303	52,589	43,244	3,121	40,123	11,906	7,006	1,141	5,865	4,900	911	3,989
Dec	99,093	55,809	3,275	52,534	43,284	3,069	40,215	12,036	7,046	1,137	5,909	4,990	919	4,071

[1] See footnote 3, Table B-29.

Note.—See Note, Table B-29.

Source: Department of Labor, Bureau of Labor Statistics.

Table B-31.—*Selected employment and unemployment data, 1948–82*

[Percent; monthly data seasonally adjusted]

Year or month	Civilian employment as percent of population[1]: Total	Both sexes 16–19 years	Males 20 years and over	Females 20 years and over	White	Black and other	Unemployment rate[2]: All workers	By sex and age: Both sexes 16–19 years	Males 20 years and over	Females 20 years and over	By selected groups: Experienced wage and salary workers	Married men, spouse present[3]	Women who maintain families	Full-time workers[4]	Blue-collar workers[5]
1948	55.8	45.5	83.9	30.7	....	....	3.8	9.2	3.2	3.6	4.3	....	....	....	4.2
1949	54.6	43.0	81.6	30.6	....		5.9	13.4	5.4	5.3	6.8	3.5	....	5.4	8.0
1950	55.2	43.8	81.9	31.6	....	....	5.3	12.2	4.7	5.1	6.0	4.6	....	5.0	7.2
1951	55.7	44.9	81.6	32.6	....	....	3.3	8.2	2.5	4.0	3.7	1.5	....	2.6	3.9
1952	55.4	44.1	80.8	33.0	....	....	3.0	8.5	2.4	3.2	3.4	1.4	....	2.5	3.6
1953	55.3	43.9	80.6	32.9	....	....	2.9	7.6	2.5	2.9	3.2	1.7	....	....	3.4
1954	53.8	40.1	78.8	32.3	....	....	5.5	12.6	4.9	5.5	6.2	4.0	....	5.2	7.2
1955	55.1	41.3	80.0	33.8	....	....	4.4	11.0	3.8	4.4	4.8	2.6	....	3.8	5.8
1956	56.1	42.7	80.8	34.9	....	....	4.1	11.1	3.4	4.2	4.4	2.3	....	3.7	5.1
1957	55.7	41.1	80.2	35.0	....	....	4.3	11.6	3.6	4.1	4.6	2.8	....	4.0	6.2
1958	54.2	37.6	78.0	34.6	....	....	6.8	15.9	6.2	6.1	7.3	5.1	....	7.2	10.2
1959	54.8	38.1	79.0	35.1	....	....	5.5	14.6	4.7	5.2	5.7	3.6	....	....	7.6
1960	54.9	39.0	78.7	35.7	....	....	5.5	14.7	4.7	5.1	5.7	3.7	....	....	7.8
1961	54.2	37.5	77.6	35.5	....	....	6.7	16.8	5.7	6.3	6.8	4.6	....	6.7	9.2
1962	54.2	37.6	77.4	35.8	....	....	5.5	14.7	4.6	5.4	5.6	3.6	....	....	7.4
1963	54.1	35.8	77.3	36.2	54.0	55.2	5.7	17.2	4.5	5.4	5.6	3.4	....	5.5	7.3
1964	54.5	35.8	77.7	36.9	54.3	56.1	5.2	16.2	3.9	5.2	5.0	2.8	....	4.9	6.3
1965	55.0	37.7	77.9	37.6	54.8	56.8	4.5	14.8	3.2	4.5	4.3	2.4	....	4.2	5.3
1966	55.6	40.7	77.6	38.6	55.4	57.2	3.8	12.8	2.5	3.8	3.5	1.9	....	3.5	4.2
1967	55.8	40.4	77.4	39.3	55.7	56.9	3.8	12.9	2.3	4.2	3.6	1.8	4.9	3.4	4.4
1968	56.0	40.6	77.1	40.0	55.9	56.6	3.6	12.7	2.2	3.8	3.4	1.6	4.4	3.1	4.1
1969	56.5	42.1	76.9	41.1	56.5	56.7	3.5	12.2	2.1	3.7	3.3	1.5	4.4	3.1	3.9
1970	56.1	41.2	76.1	41.2	56.2	55.5	4.9	15.3	3.5	4.8	4.8	2.6	5.4	4.5	6.2
1971	55.5	40.4	75.3	40.8	55.7	53.8	5.9	16.9	4.4	5.7	5.7	3.2	7.3	5.5	7.4
1972	56.0	42.6	75.8	41.3	56.4	53.2	5.6	16.2	4.0	5.4	5.3	2.8	7.2	5.1	6.5
1973	56.9	44.8	76.3	42.2	57.3	54.0	4.9	14.5	3.3	4.9	4.5	2.3	7.1	4.4	5.4
1974	57.0	45.0	75.7	42.7	57.5	53.3	5.6	16.0	3.8	5.5	5.3	2.7	7.0	5.1	6.7
1975	55.3	42.3	72.9	42.3	55.9	50.4	8.5	19.9	6.8	8.0	8.2	5.1	10.0	8.1	11.7
1976	56.1	43.2	73.2	43.5	56.8	51.0	7.7	19.0	5.9	7.4	7.3	4.2	10.1	7.3	9.4
1977	57.1	45.1	73.7	44.7	57.9	51.5	7.1	17.8	5.2	7.0	6.6	3.6	9.4	6.6	8.1
1978	58.6	47.4	74.5	46.5	59.3	53.7	6.1	16.4	4.3	6.0	5.6	2.8	8.5	5.6	6.9
1979	59.2	47.7	74.7	47.6	60.0	54.0	5.8	16.1	4.2	5.7	5.5	2.8	8.3	5.3	7.0
1980	58.5	45.8	72.9	48.0	59.4	52.4	7.1	17.8	5.9	6.4	6.9	4.2	9.2	6.9	10.0
1981	58.3	43.7	72.3	48.5	59.3	51.4	7.6	19.6	6.3	6.8	7.3	4.3	10.4	7.3	10.3
1982	57.1	40.8	70.2	48.3	58.2	49.8	9.7	23.2	8.8	8.3	9.3	6.5	11.7	9.6	4.2
1981:															
Jan	58.4	45.0	72.6	48.2	59.3	52.1	7.5	19.0	6.1	6.7	7.1	4.2	10.3	7.2	10.1
Feb	58.4	44.8	72.6	48.4	59.5	51.6	7.4	19.1	6.2	6.6	7.1	4.2	9.9	7.2	10.2
Mar	58.6	44.6	72.8	48.6	59.5	52.0	7.3	19.2	6.0	6.6	7.0	4.2	9.8	7.1	10.0
Apr	58.8	45.3	73.0	48.7	59.8	52.5	7.2	18.8	5.9	6.5	6.8	3.8	9.9	6.9	9.6
May	58.7	44.6	72.8	48.8	59.7	52.0	7.5	19.1	6.2	6.7	7.2	4.0	10.4	7.1	9.9
June	58.3	43.0	72.4	48.7	59.4	51.2	7.4	19.5	6.1	6.7	7.0	4.2	10.5	7.1	9.8
July	58.4	43.6	72.6	48.6	59.5	51.3	7.2	18.6	5.8	6.7	6.9	4.0	11.2	6.9	9.6
Aug	58.4	44.0	72.4	48.6	59.5	50.9	7.4	18.9	6.1	6.7	7.0	4.0	10.2	7.0	9.7
Sept	57.9	43.2	72.1	48.0	59.0	51.1	7.6	19.9	6.2	7.0	7.3	4.3	10.6	7.3	10.2
Oct	58.0	42.8	71.8	48.5	59.1	51.0	8.0	20.6	6.7	7.1	7.6	4.7	10.7	7.7	10.9
Nov	57.9	42.4	71.5	48.6	58.9	51.0	8.3	21.5	7.0	7.2	7.9	5.0	10.8	8.0	11.6
Dec	57.5	41.5	71.2	48.3	58.6	50.6	8.6	21.4	7.6	7.4	8.4	5.6	10.3	8.5	12.6
1982:															
Jan	57.5	41.6	71.0	48.3	58.5	50.5	8.6	21.7	7.6	7.2	8.2	5.3	10.4	8.4	12.4
Feb	57.4	41.5	70.9	48.3	58.5	50.3	8.8	22.3	7.7	7.6	8.5	5.4	10.4	8.5	12.5
Mar	57.3	41.3	70.7	48.3	58.4	50.1	9.0	21.9	8.0	7.9	8.7	5.6	10.8	8.9	13.0
Apr	57.2	41.1	70.6	48.1	58.3	49.7	9.3	22.8	8.3	8.1	9.1	6.0	11.5	9.1	13.5
May	57.4	41.8	70.7	48.3	58.5	50.1	9.4	22.9	8.3	8.2	9.2	6.1	11.9	9.2	13.6
June	57.2	40.4	70.3	48.5	58.3	49.7	9.5	22.5	8.7	8.1	9.2	6.4	12.1	9.4	14.0
July	57.1	39.8	70.1	48.5	58.2	49.8	9.8	23.9	8.9	8.3	9.4	6.6	12.0	9.6	14.4
Aug	57.1	40.6	69.9	48.5	58.2	49.7	9.9	23.8	9.0	8.3	9.4	6.8	11.7	9.7	14.4
Sept	56.9	40.7	69.8	48.4	58.1	49.6	10.2	23.8	9.6	8.4	9.8	7.2	12.4	10.2	15.5
Oct	56.6	40.4	69.5	48.1	57.7	49.5	10.5	24.1	9.8	8.7	10.1	7.5	11.3	10.5	15.8
Nov	56.6	40.6	69.3	48.0	57.7	49.3	10.7	24.2	10.0	9.0	10.5	7.6	12.5	10.6	16.2
Dec	56.5	40.1	69.1	48.1	57.6	49.3	10.8	24.5	10.1	9.2	10.7	7.8	13.2	10.8	16.3

[1] Civilian employment as percent of total noninstitutional population.
[2] Unemployment as percent of civilian labor force in group specified.
[3] Data for 1949 and 1951–54 are for April; 1950, for March.
[4] Data for 1949–61 are for May.
[5] Includes craft and kindred workers, operatives, and nonfarm laborers. Data for 1948–57 are based on data for January, April, July, and October.

Note.—Data relate to persons 16 years of age and over. See footnote 3 and Note, Table B–29.

Source: Department of Labor, Bureau of Labor Statistics.

Table B-32.—*Civilian labor force participation rate by demographic characteristic, 1954–82*

[Percent;[1] monthly data seasonally adjusted]

Year or month	All civilian workers	White: Total	White: Males: Total	White: Males: 16–19 years	White: Males: 20 years and over	White: Females: Total	White: Females: 16–19 years	White: Females: 20 years and over	Black and other: Total	Black and other: Males: Total	Black and other: Males: 16–19 years	Black and other: Males: 20 years and over	Black and other: Females: Total	Black and other: Females: 16–19 years	Black and other: Females: 20 years and over
1954	58.8	58.2	85.6	57.6	87.8	33.3	40.6	32.7	64.3	85.2	61.2	87.1	46.1	31.0	47.7
1955	59.3	58.7	85.4	58.6	87.5	34.5	40.7	34.0	64.2	85.0	60.8	87.8	46.1	32.7	47.5
1956	60.0	59.4	85.6	60.4	87.6	35.7	43.1	35.1	64.9	85.1	61.5	87.8	47.3	36.3	48.4
1957	59.6	59.1	84.8	59.2	86.9	35.7	42.2	35.2	64.4	84.3	58.8	87.0	47.2	33.2	48.6
1958	59.5	58.9	84.3	56.5	86.6	35.8	40.1	35.5	64.8	84.0	57.3	87.1	48.0	31.9	49.8
1959	59.3	58.7	83.8	55.9	86.3	36.0	39.6	35.6	64.3	83.4	55.5	86.7	47.7	28.2	49.8
1960	59.4	58.8	83.4	55.9	86.0	36.5	40.3	36.2	64.5	83.0	57.6	86.2	48.2	32.9	49.9
1961	59.3	58.8	83.0	54.5	85.7	36.9	40.6	36.6	64.1	82.2	55.8	85.5	48.3	32.8	50.1
1962	58.8	58.3	82.1	53.8	84.9	36.7	39.8	36.5	63.2	80.8	53.5	84.2	48.0	33.1	49.6
1963	58.7	58.2	81.5	53.1	84.4	37.2	38.7	37.0	63.0	80.2	51.5	83.9	48.1	32.6	49.9
1964	58.7	58.2	81.1	52.7	84.2	37.5	37.8	37.5	63.1	80.0	49.9	84.1	48.5	31.7	50.7
1965	58.9	58.4	80.8	54.1	83.9	38.1	39.2	38.0	62.9	79.6	51.3	83.7	48.6	29.5	51.1
1966	59.2	58.7	80.6	55.9	83.6	39.2	42.6	38.8	63.0	79.0	51.4	83.3	49.3	33.5	51.6
1967	59.6	59.2	80.7	56.3	83.5	40.1	42.5	39.8	62.8	78.5	51.1	82.9	49.5	35.2	51.6
1968	59.6	59.3	80.4	55.9	83.2	40.7	43.0	40.4	62.2	77.6	49.7	82.2	49.3	34.8	51.4
1969	60.1	59.9	80.2	56.8	83.0	41.8	44.6	41.5	62.1	76.9	49.6	81.4	49.8	34.6	52.0
1970	60.4	60.2	80.0	57.5	82.8	42.6	45.6	42.2	61.8	76.5	47.4	81.4	49.5	34.1	51.8
1971	60.2	60.1	79.6	57.9	82.3	42.6	45.4	42.3	60.9	74.9	44.7	80.0	49.2	31.2	51.8
1972	60.4	60.4	79.6	60.1	82.0	43.2	48.1	42.7	60.2	73.9	46.0	78.6	48.8	32.3	51.2
1973	60.8	60.8	79.4	62.0	81.6	44.1	50.1	43.5	60.5	74.0	46.3	78.6	49.3	34.4	51.4
1974	61.3	61.4	79.4	62.9	81.4	45.2	51.7	44.4	60.3	73.5	47.2	78.0	49.3	34.1	51.5
1975	61.2	61.5	78.7	61.9	80.7	45.9	51.5	45.3	59.6	71.9	42.9	76.8	49.4	35.6	51.4
1976	61.6	61.8	78.4	62.3	80.3	46.9	52.8	46.2	59.8	71.2	42.3	76.1	50.4	33.6	52.8
1977	62.3	62.5	78.5	64.0	80.2	48.0	54.5	47.3	60.4	71.6	43.6	76.2	51.2	33.6	53.6
1978	63.2	63.3	78.6	65.0	80.1	49.4	56.7	48.7	62.2	72.6	45.4	77.1	53.5	38.0	55.6
1979	63.7	63.9	78.6	64.8	80.1	50.5	57.4	49.8	62.2	72.5	44.0	77.1	53.7	37.8	55.8
1980	63.8	64.1	78.2	63.7	79.8	51.2	56.2	50.6	61.7	71.5	43.5	75.9	53.6	35.9	55.9
1981	63.9	64.3	77.9	62.4	79.5	51.9	55.4	51.5	61.3	70.6	41.7	75.0	53.6	34.5	56.1
1982	64.0	64.3	77.4	60.0	79.2	52.4	55.0	52.2	61.6	71.0	40.6	75.4	53.9	34.5	56.3
1981:															
Jan	63.9	64.3	78.1	63.6	79.7	51.7	56.0	51.2	61.3	71.0	45.3	74.9	53.3	36.0	55.5
Feb	63.9	64.3	78.2	64.0	79.7	51.8	56.5	51.3	60.8	70.1	41.7	74.5	53.0	32.3	55.7
Mar	64.0	64.4	78.2	63.6	79.8	51.8	56.2	51.4	61.6	70.6	41.2	75.1	54.1	35.9	56.4
Apr	64.2	64.5	78.3	63.6	79.9	51.9	56.4	51.5	61.9	70.9	44.9	74.9	54.4	37.7	56.5
May	64.2	64.7	78.4	62.9	80.0	52.2	56.2	51.9	61.5	71.0	43.9	75.2	53.6	34.6	56.0
June	63.8	64.2	77.7	61.1	79.5	51.8	54.4	51.6	61.1	70.0	40.5	74.5	53.7	34.8	56.1
July	63.8	64.2	77.7	61.1	79.5	52.0	55.1	51.7	60.8	69.9	40.8	74.4	53.3	32.4	55.9
Aug	63.8	64.2	77.7	61.8	79.4	51.9	56.0	51.5	61.1	70.9	40.8	75.5	53.0	31.3	55.8
Sept	63.5	63.9	77.5	62.0	79.2	51.5	55.1	51.1	61.2	70.8	39.3	75.5	53.4	33.2	55.9
Oct	63.8	64.2	77.6	62.2	79.2	51.9	54.2	51.7	61.5	70.7	39.2	75.5	53.9	37.4	56.0
Nov	63.9	64.2	77.7	62.4	79.2	52.0	54.6	51.8	61.5	70.5	40.7	75.0	54.1	35.0	56.5
Dec	63.7	64.2	77.7	61.0	79.4	51.8	53.8	51.7	61.4	70.7	41.6	74.9	53.7	32.9	56.4
1982:															
Jan	63.6	64.0	77.3	61.1	79.0	51.9	54.6	51.6	61.2	70.4	39.9	74.9	53.6	33.5	56.1
Feb	63.8	64.1	77.4	60.9	79.2	52.0	54.9	51.7	61.2	70.4	41.7	74.6	53.6	34.6	56.0
Mar	63.8	64.1	77.4	60.3	79.1	52.0	54.4	51.8	61.4	70.4	40.9	74.8	54.0	33.4	56.5
Apr	63.9	64.3	77.5	60.6	79.2	52.3	55.7	51.9	61.1	70.7	38.7	75.4	53.2	31.9	55.8
May	64.2	64.6	77.9	62.4	79.5	52.5	55.4	52.2	61.7	70.8	41.1	75.2	54.2	34.1	56.7
June	64.0	64.4	77.3	58.7	79.2	52.5	54.6	52.4	61.3	70.7	37.7	75.6	53.6	31.5	56.4
July	64.1	64.4	77.2	57.9	79.2	52.8	55.0	52.6	61.6	71.2	39.3	75.9	53.8	34.9	56.1
Aug	64.1	64.4	77.4	59.7	79.1	52.7	55.0	52.5	61.8	71.1	41.4	75.5	54.2	36.9	56.2
Sept	64.2	64.6	77.7	59.4	79.5	52.7	55.3	52.4	61.9	71.4	41.7	75.8	54.1	36.4	56.2
Oct	64.1	64.4	77.6	59.4	79.4	52.4	55.2	52.1	62.0	71.4	42.0	75.8	54.2	35.6	56.4
Nov	64.2	64.5	77.6	60.0	79.4	52.6	55.1	52.4	61.8	71.5	41.3	75.9	53.7	35.3	55.9
Dec	64.2	64.6	77.5	59.6	79.3	52.8	54.6	52.6	62.1	71.5	40.7	76.0	54.3	35.8	56.5

[1] Civilian labor force as percent of civilian noninstitutional population in group specified.

Note.—Data relate to persons 16 years of age and over.
See footnote 3 and Note, Table B-29.

Source: Department of Labor, Bureau of Labor Statistics.

TABLE B-33.—*Civilian unemployment rate by demographic characteristic, 1948–82*

[Percent; [1] monthly data seasonally adjusted]

Year or month	All civilian workers	White: Total	White: Males: Total	White: Males: 16–19 years	White: Males: 20 years and over	White: Females: Total	White: Females: 16–19 years	White: Females: 20 years and over	Black and other: Total	Black and other: Males: Total	Black and other: Males: 16–19 years	Black and other: Males: 20 years and over	Black and other: Females: Total	Black and other: Females: 16–19 years	Black and other: Females: 20 years and over
1948	3.8	3.5	3.4	...	...	3.8	...	...	5.9	5.8	...	...	6.1	...	...
1949	5.9	5.6	5.6	...	...	5.7	...	...	8.9	9.6	...	...	7.9	...	...
1950	5.3	4.9	4.7	...	...	5.3	...	...	9.0	9.4	...	...	8.4	...	...
1951	3.3	3.1	2.6			4.2		...	5.3	4.9	...	...	6.1	...	...
1952	3.0	2.8	2.5	...	...	3.3	...	...	5.4	5.2	...	...	5.7	...	...
1953	2.9	2.7	2.5	...	...	3.1	...	...	4.5	4.8	...	...	4.1	...	...
1954	5.5	5.0	4.8	13.4	4.4	5.5	10.4	5.1	9.9	10.3	14.4	9.9	9.2	20.6	8.4
1955	4.4	3.9	3.7	11.3	3.3	4.3	9.1	3.9	8.7	8.8	13.4	8.4	8.5	19.2	7.7
1956	4.1	3.6	3.4	10.5	3.0	4.2	9.7	3.7	8.3	7.9	15.0	7.4	8.9	22.8	7.8
1957	4.3	3.8	3.6	11.5	3.2	4.3	9.5	3.8	7.9	8.3	18.4	7.6	7.3	20.2	6.4
1958	6.8	6.1	6.1	15.7	5.5	6.2	12.7	5.6	12.6	13.7	26.8	12.7	10.8	28.4	9.5
1959	5.5	4.8	4.6	14.0	4.1	5.3	12.0	4.7	10.7	11.5	25.2	10.5	9.4	27.7	8.3
1960	5.5	5.0	4.8	14.0	4.2	5.3	12.7	4.6	10.2	10.7	24.0	9.6	9.4	24.8	8.3
1961	6.7	6.0	5.7	15.7	5.1	6.5	14.8	5.7	12.4	12.8	26.8	11.7	11.9	29.2	10.6
1962	5.5	4.9	4.6	13.7	4.0	5.5	12.8	4.7	10.9	10.9	22.0	10.0	11.0	30.2	9.6
1963	5.7	5.0	4.7	15.9	3.9	5.8	15.1	4.8	10.8	10.5	27.3	9.2	11.2	34.7	9.4
1964	5.2	4.6	4.1	14.7	3.4	5.5	14.9	4.6	9.6	8.9	24.3	7.7	10.7	31.6	9.0
1965	4.5	4.1	3.6	12.9	2.9	5.0	14.0	4.0	8.1	7.4	23.3	6.0	9.2	31.7	7.5
1966	3.8	3.4	2.8	10.5	2.2	4.3	12.1	3.3	7.3	6.3	21.3	4.9	8.7	31.3	6.6
1967	3.8	3.4	2.7	10.7	2.1	4.6	11.5	3.8	7.4	6.0	23.9	4.3	9.1	29.6	7.1
1968	3.6	3.2	2.6	10.1	2.0	4.3	12.1	3.4	6.7	5.6	22.1	3.9	8.3	28.7	6.3
1969	3.5	3.1	2.5	10.0	1.9	4.2	11.5	3.4	6.4	5.3	21.4	3.7	7.8	27.6	5.8
1970	4.9	4.5	4.0	13.7	3.2	5.4	13.4	4.4	8.2	7.3	25.0	5.6	9.3	34.5	6.9
1971	5.9	5.4	4.9	15.1	4.0	6.3	15.1	5.3	9.9	9.1	28.8	7.3	10.9	35.4	8.7
1972	5.6	5.1	4.5	14.2	3.6	5.9	14.2	4.9	10.0	8.9	29.7	6.9	11.4	38.4	8.8
1973	4.9	4.3	3.8	12.3	3.0	5.3	13.0	4.3	9.0	7.7	26.9	5.8	10.6	34.4	8.2
1974	5.6	5.0	4.4	13.5	3.5	6.1	14.5	5.1	9.9	9.2	31.5	6.9	10.8	34.5	8.5
1975	8.5	7.8	7.2	18.3	6.2	8.6	17.4	7.5	13.8	13.6	35.2	11.6	13.9	38.3	11.5
1976	7.7	7.0	6.4	17.3	5.4	7.9	16.4	6.8	13.1	12.7	35.1	10.6	13.6	38.8	11.3
1977	7.1	6.2	5.5	15.0	4.7	7.3	15.9	6.2	13.1	12.3	36.6	10.0	13.9	39.6	11.7
1978	6.1	5.2	4.6	13.5	3.7	6.2	14.4	5.2	11.9	11.0	34.0	8.7	13.0	38.1	10.6
1979	5.8	5.1	4.5	13.9	3.6	5.9	14.0	5.0	11.3	10.4	31.3	8.5	12.3	35.6	10.2
1980	7.1	6.3	6.1	16.2	5.3	6.5	14.8	5.6	13.1	13.2	34.4	11.3	13.1	36.5	11.1
1981	7.6	6.7	6.5	17.9	5.6	6.9	16.6	5.9	14.2	14.1	37.5	12.1	14.3	38.3	12.4
1982	9.7	8.6	8.8	21.7	7.8	8.3	19.0	7.3	17.3	18.2	44.0	16.2	16.4	43.8	14.3
1981:															
Jan	7.5	6.6	6.4	17.4	5.5	6.9	15.5	6.0	13.1	13.2	39.6	10.7	13.0	33.1	11.4
Feb	7.4	6.5	6.4	18.0	5.4	6.7	16.0	5.7	13.2	13.0	36.3	11.0	13.4	34.8	11.8
Mar	7.3	6.4	6.3	17.9	5.4	6.6	15.9	5.6	13.6	12.7	32.9	11.0	14.5	42.2	12.3
Apr	7.2	6.4	6.1	17.0	5.2	6.7	16.2	5.6	13.2	12.9	36.8	10.7	13.6	35.5	11.7
May	7.5	6.6	6.5	17.6	5.5	6.9	16.6	5.9	13.6	13.6	34.1	11.7	13.5	33.3	12.0
June	7.4	6.4	6.3	17.8	5.3	6.7	16.3	5.7	14.2	14.4	38.1	12.4	14.0	37.4	12.2
July	7.2	6.3	5.9	16.7	5.1	6.8	16.3	5.8	13.7	13.8	37.0	11.9	13.6	33.2	12.2
Aug	7.4	6.3	6.2	16.7	5.3	6.5	15.7	5.6	14.8	14.9	44.5	12.4	14.7	41.2	12.8
Sept	7.6	6.6	6.4	17.8	5.4	7.0	17.2	6.0	14.6	14.2	35.7	12.5	15.1	38.8	13.3
Oct	8.0	6.9	6.8	17.9	5.9	7.1	17.5	6.1	15.2	14.8	39.1	12.9	15.6	46.1	13.0
Nov	8.3	7.3	7.2	19.7	6.2	7.4	18.3	6.3	15.2	15.5	38.4	13.6	14.8	41.4	12.8
Dec	8.6	7.6	7.8	20.2	6.8	7.4	17.7	6.4	15.7	16.2	37.7	14.4	15.1	41.4	13.1
1982:															
Jan	8.6	7.6	7.6	20.6	6.6	7.5	18.1	6.4	15.5	16.1	34.9	14.6	14.9	42.6	12.8
Feb	8.8	7.7	7.7	20.4	6.7	7.7	19.0	6.6	16.0	16.4	39.0	14.6	15.5	41.8	13.4
Mar	9.0	7.9	8.0	20.4	7.0	7.8	17.9	6.8	16.6	17.3	44.0	15.1	15.8	41.0	14.0
Apr	9.3	8.3	8.4	21.9	7.3	8.1	18.8	7.1	16.8	17.3	42.8	15.3	16.2	42.0	14.4
May	9.4	8.4	8.5	20.9	7.5	8.2	18.7	7.2	17.1	17.6	44.1	15.5	16.4	45.7	14.3
June	9.5	8.4	8.6	21.2	7.7	8.1	18.0	7.1	17.1	18.2	48.1	16.0	16.0	43.1	14.2
July	9.8	8.7	8.9	22.5	7.9	8.3	19.1	7.3	17.4	18.0	45.3	15.9	16.7	47.7	14.4
Aug	9.9	8.7	9.1	22.5	8.0	8.3	18.9	7.2	17.7	18.5	45.4	16.3	16.9	49.7	14.3
Sept	10.2	9.1	9.5	22.2	8.6	8.5	19.1	7.5	18.1	19.5	45.8	17.3	16.5	43.3	14.4
Oct	10.5	9.3	9.8	23.0	8.8	8.7	19.9	7.6	18.4	19.9	43.8	18.0	16.8	42.3	14.9
Nov	10.7	9.6	10.0	22.6	9.1	9.0	19.8	8.0	18.5	19.7	48.0	17.4	17.2	43.1	15.2
Dec	10.8	9.7	10.1	22.8	9.2	9.2	20.4	8.1	18.8	20.3	46.7	18.2	17.2	42.7	15.3

[1] Unemployment as percent of civilian labor force in group specified.

Note.—See footnote 3 and Note, Table B-29.

Source: Department of Labor, Bureau of Labor Statistics.

Table B-34.—*Unemployment by duration, 1947–82*

[Monthly data seasonally adjusted [1]]

Year or month	Total unemployment	Duration of unemployment: Less than 5 weeks	5–14 weeks	15–26 weeks	27 weeks and over	Average (mean) duration in weeks
	Thousands of persons 16 years of age and over					
1947	2,311	1,210	704	234	164	....
1948	2,276	1,300	669	193	116	8.6
1949	3,637	1,756	1,194	428	256	10.0
1950	3,288	1,450	1,055	425	357	12.1
1951	2,055	1,177	574	166	137	9.7
1952	1,883	1,135	516	148	84	8.4
1953	1,834	1,142	482	132	78	8.0
1954	3,532	1,605	1,116	495	317	11.8
1955	2,852	1,335	815	366	336	13.0
1956	2,750	1,412	805	301	232	11.3
1957	2,859	1,408	891	321	239	10.5
1958	4,602	1,753	1,396	785	667	13.9
1959	3,740	1,585	1,114	469	571	14.4
1960	3,852	1,719	1,176	503	454	12.8
1961	4,714	1,806	1,376	728	804	15.6
1962	3,911	1,663	1,134	534	585	14.7
1963	4,070	1,751	1,231	535	553	14.0
1964	3,786	1,697	1,117	491	482	13.3
1965	3,366	1,628	983	404	351	11.8
1966	2,875	1,573	779	287	239	10.4
1967	2,975	1,634	893	271	177	8.7
1968	2,817	1,594	810	256	156	8.4
1969	2,832	1,629	827	242	133	7.8
1970	4,093	2,139	1,290	428	235	8.6
1971	5,016	2,245	1,585	668	519	11.3
1972	4,882	2,242	1,472	601	566	12.0
1973	4,365	2,224	1,314	483	343	10.0
1974	5,156	2,604	1,597	574	381	9.8
1975	7,929	2,940	2,484	1,303	1,203	14.2
1976	7,406	2,844	2,196	1,018	1,348	15.8
1977	6,991	2,919	2,132	913	1,028	14.3
1978	6,202	2,865	1,923	766	648	11.9
1979	6,137	2,950	1,946	706	535	10.8
1980	7,637	3,295	2,470	1,052	820	11.9
1981	8,273	3,449	2,539	1,122	1,162	13.7
1982	10,678	3,883	3,311	1,708	1,776	15.6
1981:						
Jan	8,048	3,278	2,332	1,123	1,272	14.3
Feb	8,032	3,284	2,390	1,096	1,243	14.0
Mar	7,967	3,278	2,422	1,056	1,218	13.9
Apr	7,860	3,167	2,445	1,095	1,133	13.7
May	8,133	3,382	2,579	1,063	1,158	13.5
June	8,047	3,342	2,390	1,146	1,131	14.1
July	7,854	3,317	2,371	1,085	1,076	14.0
Aug	8,053	3,341	2,493	1,065	1,148	14.3
Sept	8,271	3,515	2,544	1,130	1,111	13.6
Oct	8,673	3,696	2,677	1,169	1,123	13.5
Nov	9,025	3,820	2,847	1,218	1,140	13.2
Dec	9,389	4,040	3,028	1,224	1,183	12.9
1982:						
Jan	9,346	3,830	3,079	1,209	1,193	13.4
Feb	9,669	3,807	3,068	1,479	1,271	14.0
Mar	9,881	3,831	3,098	1,605	1,357	13.9
Apr	10,256	3,930	3,255	1,582	1,498	14.3
May	10,384	3,871	3,281	1,633	1,634	14.9
June	10,466	3,605	3,398	1,683	1,834	16.3
July	10,828	3,959	3,249	1,780	1,789	15.6
Aug	10,931	3,933	3,346	1,808	1,829	16.1
Sept	11,315	4,004	3,549	1,830	2,026	16.6
Oct	11,576	3,930	3,511	1,951	2,216	17.1
Nov	11,906	3,963	3,549	2,191	2,333	17.3
Dec	12,036	4,019	3,460	2,125	2,607	18.0

[1] Because of independent seasonal adjustment of the various series, detail will not add to totals.

Note.—See footnote 3 and Note, Table B-29.

Source: Department of Labor, Bureau of Labor Statistics.

TABLE B–35.—*Unemployment by reason, 1967–82*

[Monthly data seasonally adjusted [1]]

Year or month	Total unemployment	Job losers	Job leavers	Reentrants	New entrants
	Thousands of persons				
1967	2,975	1,229	438	945	396
1968	2,817	1,070	431	909	407
1969	2,832	1,017	436	965	413
1970	4,093	1,811	550	1,228	504
1971	5,016	2,323	590	1,472	630
1972	4,882	2,108	641	1,456	677
1973	4,365	1,694	683	1,340	649
1974	5,156	2,242	768	1,463	681
1975	7,929	4,386	827	1,892	823
1976	7,406	3,679	903	1,928	895
1977	6,991	3,166	909	1,963	953
1978	6,202	2,585	874	1,857	885
1979	6,137	2,635	880	1,806	817
1980	7,637	3,947	891	1,927	872
1981	8,273	4,267	923	2,102	981
1982	10,678	6,268	840	2,384	1,185
1982:					
Jan	9,346	5,243	842	2,133	1,055
Feb	9,669	5,246	942	2,272	1,096
Mar	9,881	5,628	885	2,261	1,061
Apr	10,256	5,889	901	2,342	1,096
May	10,384	5,938	864	2,393	1,159
June	10,466	6,181	826	2,378	1,091
July	10,828	6,323	819	2,478	1,230
Aug	10,931	6,446	814	2,440	1,304
Sept	11,315	6,979	786	2,437	1,303
Oct	11,576	7,325	803	2,322	1,296
Nov	11,906	7,369	794	2,546	1,244
Dec	12,036	7,295	826	2,629	1,288
	Percent of civilian labor force				
1967	3.8	1.6	0.6	1.2	0.5
1968	3.6	1.3	.5	1.2	.5
1969	3.5	1.2	.5	1.2	.5
1970	4.9	2.2	.7	1.5	.6
1971	5.9	2.8	.7	1.7	.7
1972	5.6	2.4	.7	1.7	.8
1973	4.9	1.9	.8	1.5	.7
1974	5.6	2.4	.8	1.6	.7
1975	8.5	4.7	.9	2.0	.9
1976	7.7	3.8	.9	2.0	.9
1977	7.1	3.2	.9	2.0	1.0
1978	6.1	2.5	.9	1.8	.9
1979	5.8	2.5	.8	1.7	.8
1980	7.1	3.7	.8	1.8	.8
1981	7.6	3.9	.8	1.9	.9
1982	9.7	5.7	.8	2.2	1.1
1982:					
Jan	8.6	4.8	.8	2.0	1.0
Feb	8.8	4.8	.9	2.1	1.0
Mar	9.0	5.1	.8	2.1	1.0
Apr	9.3	5.4	.8	2.1	1.0
May	9.4	5.4	.8	2.2	1.1
June	9.5	5.6	.7	2.2	1.0
July	9.8	5.7	.7	2.2	1.1
Aug	9.9	5.8	.7	2.2	1.2
Sept	10.2	6.3	.7	2.2	1.2
Oct	10.5	6.6	.7	2.1	1.2
Nov	10.7	6.6	.7	2.3	1.1
Dec	10.8	6.6	.7	2.4	1.2

[1] Because of independent seasonal adjustment of the various series, detail will not add to totals.

Note.—Data relate to persons 16 years of age and over.
See footnote 3 and Note, Table B–29.

Source: Department of Labor, Bureau of Labor Statistics.

Table B–36.—*Unemployment insurance programs, selected data, 1946–82*

Year or month	All programs: Covered employment[1]	All programs: Insured unemployment (weekly average)[2 3]	All programs: Total benefits paid (millions of dollars)[2 4]	State programs: Insured unemployment	State programs: Initial claims	State programs: Exhaustions[5]	State programs: Insured unemployment as percent of covered employment	State programs: Benefits paid: Total (millions of dollars)[4]	State programs: Benefits paid: Average weekly check (dollars)[6]
	Thousands	Thousands		Weekly average; thousands	Weekly average; thousands	Weekly average; thousands			
1946	31,856	2,804	2,878.5	1,295	189	38	4.3	1,094.9	18.50
1947	33,876	1,793	1,785.5	997	187	24	3.1	775.1	17.83
1948	34,646	1,446	1,328.7	980	200	20	3.0	789.9	19.03
1949	33,098	2,474	2,269.8	1,973	340	37	6.2	1,736.0	20.48
1950	34,308	1,605	1,467.6	1,513	236	36	4.6	1,373.1	20.76
1951	36,334	1,000	862.9	969	208	16	2.8	840.4	21.09
1952	37,006	1,069	1,043.5	1,044	215	18	2.9	998.2	22.79
1953	38,072	1,067	1,050.6	990	218	15	2.8	962.2	23.58
1954	36,622	2,051	2,291.6	1,870	304	34	5.2	2,026.9	24.93
1955	40,018	1,399	1,560.2	1,265	226	25	3.5	1,350.3	25.04
1956	42,751	1,323	1,540.6	1,215	227	20	3.2	1,380.7	27.02
1957	43,436	1,571	1,913.0	1,446	270	23	3.6	1,733.9	28.17
1958	44,411	2,773	4,290.6	2,510	369	50	6.4	3,512.7	30.58
1959	45,728	1,860	2,854.3	1,684	277	33	4.4	2,279.0	30.41
1960	46,334	2,071	3,022.8	1,908	331	31	4.8	2,726.7	32.87
1961	46,266	2,994	4,358.1	2,290	350	46	5.6	3,422.7	33.80
1962	47,776	1,946	3,145.1	1,783	302	32	4.4	2,675.4	34.56
1963	48,434	[7] 1,973	3,025.9	[7] 1,806	[7] 298	30	4.3	2,774.7	35.27
1964	49,637	1,753	2,749.2	1,605	268	26	3.8	2,522.1	35.92
1965	51,580	1,450	2,360.4	1,328	232	21	3.0	2,166.0	37.19
1966	54,739	1,129	1,890.9	1,061	203	15	2.3	1,771.3	39.75
1967	56,342	1,270	2,221.5	1,205	226	17	2.5	2,092.3	41.25
1968	57,977	1,187	2,191.0	1,111	201	16	2.2	2,031.6	43.43
1969	59,999	1,177	2,298.6	1,101	200	16	2.1	2,127.9	46.17
1970	59,526	2,070	4,209.3	1,805	296	25	3.4	3,848.5	50.34
1971	59,375	2,608	6,154.0	2,150	295	39	4.1	4,957.0	54.02
1972	66,458	2,192	5,491.1	1,848	261	35	3.5	4,471.0	56.76
1973	69,897	1,793	4,517.3	1,632	247	29	2.7	4,007.6	59.00
1974	72,451	2,558	6,933.9	2,262	363	37	3.5	5,974.9	64.25
1975	71,037	4,937	16,802.4	3,986	478	81	6.0	11,754.7	70.23
1976	73,459	3,846	12,344.8	2,991	386	63	4.6	8,974.5	75.16
1977	76,419	3,308	10,998.9	2,655	375	55	3.9	8,357.2	78.79
1978	88,804	2,645	9,006.9	2,359	346	39	3.3	7,717.2	83.67
1979	92,062	2,592	9,401.3	2,434	388	39	2.9	8,612.9	89.67
1980	92,659	3,837	16,175.4	3,350	488	59	3.9	13,761.1	98.95
1981 [8]	93,300	3,410	15,283.5	3,048	460	57	3.5	13,257.8	106.54
1981:				**	**		**		
Jan	....	4,621	1,740.9	3,069	425	70	3.5	1,419.6	103.67
Feb	....	4,264	1,567.8	2,988	424	69	3.4	1,315.3	104.48
Mar	....	3,948	1,663.7	2,976	420	66	3.4	1,394.7	105.74
Apr	....	3,453	1,453.3	2,926	402	66	3.4	1,226.7	105.98
May	....	3,111	1,192.7	2,882	401	59	3.3	1,006.2	105.47
June	....	2,949	1,191.3	2,824	413	55	3.2	1,009.8	104.59
July	....	3,012	1,187.7	2,801	411	54	3.2	1,062.0	103.56
Aug	....	2,874	1,098.4	2,867	436	51	3.3	1,006.6	106.02
Sept	....	2,680	1,088.2	2,941	472	47	3.4	1,001.2	107.39
Oct	....	2,753	1,064.4	3,127	511	46	3.6	997.8	108.92
Nov	....	3,228	1,146.2	3,400	542	48	3.9	1,080.8	110.51
Dec	....	3,935	1,666.9	3,613	560	58	4.1	1,592.5	112.89
1982:									
Jan	....	4,681	1,835.1	3,577	563	61	4.1	1,764.2	114.83
Feb	....	4,723	1,904.5	3,582	529	67	4.1	1,783.4	117.05
Mar	....	4,892	2,295.2	3,775	574	74	4.3	2,072.6	117.10
Apr	....	4,760	2,141.1	3,982	573	82	4.6	1,849.9	117.61
May	....	4,387	1,871.9	3,972	579	80	4.5	1,573.4	118.08
June	....	4,328	2,003.9	4,011	560	83	4.6	1,692.2	118.64
July	....	4,495	1,929.2	3,988	539	81	4.6	1,679.4	117.28
Aug	....	4,398	2,033.0	4,136	617	83	4.7	1,746.2	118.97
Sept	....	4,282	2,003.7	4,379	654	80	5.0	1,710.6	120.78
Oct	....	4,391	1,927.3	4,615	659	83	5.3	1,646.6	122.75
Nov	....	4,635	2,044.5	4,635	618	86	5.3	1,810.3	123.22
Dec	....	....	....	4,428	546	....	5.1	....	....

**Monthly data are seasonally adjusted.

[1] Includes persons under the State, UCFE (Federal employee, effective January 1955), and RRB (Railroad Retirement Board) programs. Beginning October 1958, also includes the UCX program (unemployment compensation for ex-servicemen).

[2] Includes State, UCFE, RR, UCX, UCV (unemployment compensation for veterans, October 1952–January 1960), and SRA (Servicemen's Readjustment Act, September 1944–September 1951) programs. Also includes Federal and State extended benefit programs. Does not include FSB (Federal supplemental benefits), SUA (special unemployment assistance), and Federal supplemental compensation programs.

[3] Covered workers who have completed at least 1 week of unemployment.

[4] Annual data are net amounts and monthly data are gross amounts.

[5] Individuals receiving final payments in benefit year.

[6] For total unemployment only.

[7] Programs include Puerto Rican sugarcane workers for initial claims and insured unemployment beginning July 1963.

[8] Latest data available for all programs combined. Workers covered by State programs account for about 97 percent of wage and salary earners.

Source: Department of Labor, Employment and Training Administration.

Table B-37.—*Wage and salary workers in nonagricultural establishments, 1929–82*

[Thousands of persons; monthly data seasonally adjusted]

Year or month	Total wage and salary workers	Manufacturing			Mining	Construction	Transportation and public utilities	Wholesale and retail trade	Finance, insurance, and real estate	Services	Government	
		Total	Durable goods	Nondurable goods							Federal	State and local
1929	31,324	10,702			1,087	1,512	3,916	6,123	1,494	3,425	533	2,532
1933	23,699	7,397			744	824	2,672	4,755	1,280	2,861	565	2,601
1939	30,603	10,278	4,715	5,564	854	1,165	2,936	6,426	1,447	3,502	905	3,090
1940	32,361	10,985	5,363	5,622	925	1,311	3,038	6,750	1,485	3,665	996	3,206
1941	36,539	13,192	6,968	6,225	957	1,814	3,274	7,210	1,525	3,905	1,340	3,320
1942	40,106	15,280	8,823	6,458	992	2,198	3,460	7,118	1,509	4,066	2,213	3,270
1943	42,434	17,602	11,084	6,518	925	1,567	3,647	6,982	1,401	4,130	2,905	3,175
1944	41,864	17,328	10,856	6,472	892	1,108	3,829	7,058	1,461	4,145	2,928	3,116
1945	40,374	15,524	9,074	6,450	836	1,147	3,906	7,314	1,481	4,222	2,808	3,137
1946	41,652	14,703	7,742	6,962	862	1,683	4,061	8,376	1,675	4,697	2,254	3,341
1947	43,857	15,545	8,385	7,159	955	2,009	4,166	8,955	1,728	5,025	1,892	3,582
1948	44,866	15,582	8,326	7,256	994	2,198	4,189	9,272	1,800	5,181	1,863	3,787
1949	43,754	14,441	7,489	6,953	930	2,194	4,001	9,264	1,828	5,240	1,908	3,948
1950	45,197	15,241	8,094	7,147	901	2,364	4,034	9,386	1,888	5,357	1,928	4,098
1951	47,819	16,393	9,089	7,304	929	2,637	4,226	9,742	1,956	5,547	2,302	4,087
1952	48,793	16,632	9,349	7,284	898	2,668	4,248	10,004	2,035	5,699	2,420	4,188
1953	50,202	17,549	10,110	7,438	866	2,659	4,290	10,247	2,111	5,835	2,305	4,340
1954	48,990	16,314	9,129	7,185	791	2,646	4,084	10,235	2,200	5,969	2,188	4,563
1955	50,641	16,882	9,541	7,341	792	2,839	4,141	10,535	2,298	6,240	2,187	4,727
1956	52,369	17,243	9,833	7,411	822	3,039	4,244	10,858	2,389	6,497	2,209	5,069
1957	52,853	17,174	9,855	7,321	828	2,962	4,241	10,886	2,438	6,708	2,217	5,399
1958	51,324	15,945	8,829	7,116	751	2,817	3,976	10,750	2,481	6,765	2,191	5,648
1959	53,268	16,675	9,373	7,303	732	3,004	4,011	11,127	2,549	7,087	2,233	5,850
1960	54,189	16,796	9,459	7,337	712	2,926	4,004	11,391	2,629	7,378	2,270	6,083
1961	53,999	16,326	9,070	7,256	672	2,859	3,903	11,337	2,688	7,620	2,279	6,315
1962	55,549	16,853	9,480	7,373	650	2,948	3,906	11,566	2,754	7,982	2,340	6,550
1963	56,653	16,995	9,616	7,380	635	3,010	3,903	11,778	2,830	8,277	2,358	6,868
1964	58,283	17,274	9,816	7,458	634	3,097	3,951	12,160	2,911	8,660	2,348	7,248
1965	60,765	18,062	10,405	7,656	632	3,232	4,036	12,716	2,977	9,036	2,378	7,696
1966	63,901	19,214	11,282	7,930	627	3,317	4,158	13,245	3,058	9,498	2,564	8,220
1967	65,803	19,447	11,439	8,007	613	3,248	4,268	13,606	3,185	10,045	2,719	8,672
1968	67,897	19,781	11,626	8,155	606	3,350	4,318	14,099	3,337	10,567	2,737	9,102
1969	70,384	20,167	11,895	8,272	619	3,575	4,442	14,705	3,512	11,169	2,758	9,437
1970	70,880	19,367	11,208	8,158	623	3,588	4,515	15,040	3,645	11,548	2,731	9,823
1971	71,214	18,623	10,636	7,987	609	3,704	4,476	15,352	3,772	11,797	2,696	10,185
1972	73,675	19,151	11,049	8,102	628	3,889	4,541	15,949	3,908	12,276	2,684	10,649
1973	76,790	20,154	11,891	8,262	642	4,097	4,656	16,607	4,046	12,857	2,663	11,068
1974	78,265	20,077	11,925	8,152	697	4,020	4,725	16,987	4,148	13,441	2,724	11,446
1975	76,945	18,323	10,688	7,635	752	3,525	4,542	17,060	4,165	13,892	2,748	11,937
1976	79,382	18,997	11,077	7,920	779	3,576	4,582	17,755	4,271	14,551	2,733	12,138
1977	82,471	19,682	11,597	8,086	813	3,851	4,713	18,516	4,467	15,303	2,727	12,399
1978	86,697	20,505	12,274	8,231	851	4,229	4,923	19,542	4,724	16,252	2,753	12,919
1979	89,823	21,040	12,760	8,280	958	4,463	5,136	20,192	4,975	17,112	2,773	13,174
1980	90,406	20,285	12,187	8,098	1,027	4,346	5,146	20,310	5,160	17,890	2,866	13,375
1981	91,105	20,173	12,117	8,056	1,132	4,176	5,157	20,551	5,301	18,592	2,772	13,253
1982 p	89,619	18,849	11,114	7,735	1,122	3,912	5,057	20,547	5,350	19,000	2,733	13,051
1981:												
Jan	90,909	20,171	12,120	8,051	1,102	4,315	5,139	20,380	5,252	18,352	2,798	13,400
Feb	90,913	20,148	12,097	8,051	1,113	4,240	5,145	20,422	5,264	18,382	2,789	13,410
Mar	91,014	20,197	12,143	8,054	1,124	4,267	5,153	20,438	5,270	18,414	2,780	13,371
Apr	91,099	20,275	12,201	8,074	978	4,281	5,163	20,508	5,286	18,480	2,774	13,354
May	91,131	20,332	12,237	8,095	985	4,223	5,158	20,543	5,295	18,517	2,776	13,302
June	91,286	20,334	12,246	8,088	1,137	4,185	5,162	20,590	5,302	18,556	2,777	13,243
July	91,396	20,379	12,266	8,113	1,164	4,175	5,168	20,620	5,311	18,615	2,775	13,189
Aug	91,322	20,311	12,228	8,083	1,180	4,146	5,168	20,650	5,319	18,654	2,769	13,125
Sept	91,363	20,267	12,184	8,083	1,192	4,124	5,181	20,660	5,328	18,707	2,764	13,140
Oct	91,224	20,097	12,059	8,038	1,195	4,101	5,162	20,654	5,325	18,773	2,757	13,160
Nov	90,996	19,903	11,901	8,002	1,202	4,071	5,150	20,623	5,324	18,815	2,749	13,159
Dec	90,642	19,676	11,724	7,952	1,206	4,026	5,128	20,524	5,331	18,834	2,756	13,161
1982:												
Jan	90,460	19,517	11,622	7,895	1,201	3,966	5,125	20,630	5,326	18,831	2,741	13,123
Feb	90,459	19,454	11,575	7,879	1,203	3,974	5,115	20,670	5,326	18,867	2,737	13,113
Mar	90,304	19,319	11,490	7,829	1,197	3,934	5,100	20,655	5,336	18,904	2,736	13,123
Apr	90,083	19,169	11,375	7,794	1,182	3,938	5,094	20,584	5,335	18,929	2,730	13,122
May	90,166	19,115	11,332	7,783	1,152	3,988	5,101	20,652	5,342	18,963	2,728	13,125
June	89,839	18,930	11,203	7,727	1,124	3,940	5,078	20,595	5,352	18,988	2,739	13,093
July	89,535	18,813	11,133	7,680	1,100	3,927	5,044	20,615	5,359	19,042	2,737	12,898
Aug	89,312	18,672	10,993	7,679	1,086	3,899	5,025	20,550	5,360	19,048	2,739	12,933
Sept	89,267	18,572	10,900	7,672	1,075	3,883	5,031	20,492	5,367	19,084	2,734	13,029
Oct	88,860	18,325	10,666	7,659	1,058	3,856	5,007	20,441	5,357	19,074	2,723	13,019
Nov p	88,684	18,183	10,555	7,628	1,051	3,848	4,994	20,390	5,362	19,125	2,726	13,005
Dec p	88,518	18,134	10,533	7,601	1,036	3,818	4,979	20,297	5,376	19,143	2,728	13,007

Note.—Data in Tables B-37 through B-39 are based on reports from employing establishments and relate to full- and part-time wage and salary workers in nonagricultural establishments who worked during or received pay for any part of the pay period which includes the 12th of the month. Not comparable with labor force data (Tables B-29 through B-35), which include proprietors, self-employed persons, domestic servants, and unpaid family workers; which count persons as employed when they are not at work because of industrial disputes, bad weather, etc., even if they are not paid for the time off; and which are based on a sample of the working-age population. For description and details of the various establishment data, see "Employment and Earnings."

Source: Department of Labor, Bureau of Labor Statistics.

384-041 O - 83 - 14 : QL 3

Table B-38.—*Average weekly hours and hourly earnings in selected private nonagricultural industries, 1947–82*

[For production or nonsupervisory workers; monthly data seasonally adjusted, except as noted]

Year or month	Average weekly hours				Average gross hourly earnings, current dollars				Adjusted hourly earnings, total private nonagricultural [2]			
									Index, 1977=100		Percent change from a year earlier [4]	
	Total private nonagricultural [1]	Manufacturing	Construction	Wholesale and retail trade	Total private nonagricultural [1]	Manufacturing	Construction	Wholesale and retail trade	Current dollars	1977 dollars [3]	Current dollars	1977 dollars
1947	40.3	40.4	38.2	40.5	$1.131	$1.216	$1.540	$0.940	21.6	58.5	....	....
1948	40.0	40.0	38.1	40.4	1.225	1.327	1.712	1.010	23.4	58.9	8.3	0.7
1949	39.4	39.1	37.7	40.5	1.275	1.376	1.792	1.060	24.5	62.3	4.7	5.8
1950	39.8	40.5	37.4	40.5	1.335	1.439	1.863	1.100	25.4	64.0	3.7	2.7
1951	39.9	40.6	38.1	40.5	1.45	1.56	2.02	1.18	27.3	63.6	7.5	−.6
1952	39.9	40.7	38.9	40.0	1.52	1.64	2.13	1.23	28.7	65.5	5.1	3.0
1953	39.6	40.5	37.9	39.5	1.61	1.74	2.28	1.30	30.3	68.7	5.6	4.9
1954	39.1	39.6	37.2	39.5	1.65	1.78	2.38	1.35	31.3	70.5	3.3	2.6
1955	39.6	40.7	37.1	39.4	1.71	1.85	2.45	1.40	32.4	73.3	3.5	4.0
1956	39.3	40.4	37.5	39.1	1.80	1.95	2.57	1.47	34.0	75.9	4.9	3.5
1957	38.8	39.8	37.0	38.7	1.89	2.04	2.71	1.54	35.7	76.9	5.0	1.3
1958	38.5	39.2	36.8	38.6	1.95	2.10	2.82	1.60	37.2	78.0	4.2	1.4
1959	39.0	40.3	37.0	38.8	2.02	2.19	2.93	1.66	38.5	80.0	3.5	2.6
1960	38.6	39.7	36.7	38.6	2.09	2.26	3.07	1.71	39.8	81.4	3.4	1.8
1961	38.6	39.8	36.9	38.3	2.14	2.32	3.20	1.76	41.0	83.0	3.0	2.0
1962	38.7	40.4	37.0	38.2	2.22	2.39	3.31	1.83	42.4	85.0	3.4	2.4
1963	38.8	40.5	37.3	38.1	2.28	2.45	3.41	1.89	43.6	86.3	2.8	1.5
1964	38.7	40.7	37.2	37.9	2.36	2.53	3.55	1.97	44.8	87.5	2.8	1.4
1965	38.8	41.2	37.4	37.7	2.46	2.61	3.70	2.04	46.4	89.0	3.6	1.7
1966	38.6	41.4	37.6	37.1	2.56	2.71	3.89	2.14	48.4	90.3	4.3	1.5
1967	38.0	40.6	37.7	36.6	2.68	2.82	4.11	2.25	50.8	92.2	5.0	2.1
1968	37.8	40.7	37.3	36.1	2.85	3.01	4.41	2.41	53.9	94.0	6.1	2.0
1969	37.7	40.6	37.9	35.7	3.04	3.19	4.79	2.56	57.5	95.0	6.7	1.1
1970	37.1	39.8	37.3	35.3	3.23	3.35	5.24	2.72	61.3	95.7	6.6	.7
1971	36.9	39.9	37.2	35.1	3.45	3.57	5.69	2.88	65.7	98.3	7.2	2.7
1972	37.0	40.5	36.5	34.9	3.70	3.82	6.06	3.05	69.8	101.2	6.2	3.0
1973	36.9	40.7	36.8	34.6	3.94	4.09	6.41	3.23	74.1	101.1	6.2	−.1
1974	36.5	40.0	36.6	34.2	4.24	4.42	6.81	3.48	80.0	98.3	8.0	−2.8
1975	36.1	39.5	36.4	33.9	4.53	4.83	7.31	3.73	86.7	97.6	8.4	−.7
1976	36.1	40.1	36.8	33.7	4.86	5.22	7.71	3.97	92.9	99.0	7.2	1.4
1977	36.0	40.3	36.5	33.3	5.25	5.68	8.10	4.28	100.0	100.0	7.6	1.0
1978	35.8	40.4	36.8	32.9	5.69	6.17	8.66	4.67	108.1	100.5	8.1	.5
1979	35.7	40.2	37.0	32.6	6.16	6.70	9.27	5.06	116.8	97.4	8.0	−3.1
1980	35.3	39.7	37.0	32.2	6.66	7.27	9.94	5.48	127.3	93.5	9.0	−4.0
1981	35.2	39.8	36.9	32.2	7.25	7.99	10.80	5.93	138.9	92.6	9.1	−1.0
1982 [p]	34.8	38.9	36.7	31.9	7.67	8.50	11.55	6.22	148.4	93.3	6.8	.8
1981:												
Jan	35.6	40.4	38.6	32.3	7.00	7.69	10.40	5.72	133.7	92.8	9.9	−1.6
Feb	35.2	39.7	36.3	32.2	7.05	7.75	10.47	5.78	134.8	92.7	9.9	−1.4
Mar	35.3	39.9	37.2	32.2	7.10	7.81	10.53	5.82	135.7	92.7	9.4	−1.0
Apr	35.4	40.1	37.2	32.3	7.14	7.90	10.57	5.85	136.6	93.0	9.5	−.4
May	35.4	40.2	37.0	32.2	7.19	7.94	10.64	5.89	137.6	93.0	9.4	−.4
June	35.2	40.1	36.5	32.1	7.23	7.99	10.73	5.91	138.4	92.9	8.9	−.5
July	35.3	40.0	37.0	32.2	7.27	8.03	10.82	5.94	139.1	92.2	8.8	−1.7
Aug	35.2	39.9	36.8	32.2	7.34	8.09	10.90	5.98	140.5	92.5	9.3	−1.4
Sept	35.0	39.4	35.3	32.1	7.37	8.14	10.95	6.03	141.4	92.1	9.3	−1.4
Oct	35.1	39.5	36.8	32.0	7.40	8.16	11.06	6.03	142.0	92.1	8.6	−1.4
Nov	35.1	39.3	37.4	32.1	7.45	8.20	11.14	6.06	143.0	92.3	8.4	−.9
Dec	35.0	39.1	37.0	32.0	7.46	8.20	11.22	6.08	143.5	92.3	8.2	−.4
1982:												
Jan	34.4	37.6	35.2	31.7	7.52	8.38	11.52	6.09	144.9	92.9	8.3	.1
Feb	35.0	39.4	37.1	32.0	7.53	8.34	11.34	6.10	145.0	92.8	7.5	.1
Mar	34.9	39.0	36.9	31.9	7.54	8.37	11.39	6.12	145.4	93.3	7.2	.6
Apr	34.9	39.0	36.9	31.8	7.59	8.44	11.43	6.16	146.3	93.7	7.2	.8
May	35.0	39.1	37.5	32.0	7.65	8.48	11.54	6.20	147.7	93.7	7.3	.8
June	34.9	39.2	36.8	31.9	7.67	8.52	11.51	6.22	148.1	93.1	7.1	.2
July	34.9	39.2	37.2	31.9	7.71	8.56	11.56	6.23	148.9	93.0	7.1	.8
Aug	34.8	39.0	37.0	31.9	7.74	8.57	11.58	6.26	149.9	93.2	6.6	.8
Sept	34.8	38.8	36.4	32.1	7.72	8.56	11.56	6.25	150.1	93.2	6.1	1.2
Oct	34.7	38.8	36.3	31.9	7.77	8.56	11.71	6.32	150.8	93.2	6.2	1.2
Nov [p]	34.7	38.9	36.4	31.8	7.78	8.61	11.60	6.34	151.1	93.3	5.6	1.0
Dec [p]	34.6	38.9	36.5	31.8	7.83	8.62	11.82	6.35	151.9	94.0	5.9	1.9

[1] Also includes other private industry groups shown in Table B-37.
[2] Adjusted for overtime (in manufacturing only) and for interindustry employment shifts.
[3] Current-dollar earnings index divided by the consumer price index for urban wage earners and clerical workers on a 1977=100 base.
[4] Monthly data are computed from indexes to two decimal places and are based on data not seasonally adjusted.

Note.—See Note, Table B-37.

Source: Department of Labor, Bureau of Labor Statistics.

TABLE B–39.—*Average weekly earnings in selected private nonagricultural industries, 1947–82*

[For production or nonsupervisory workers; monthly data seasonally adjusted, except as noted]

Year or month	Average gross weekly earnings					Percent change from a year earlier, total private nonagricultural [3]	
	Total private nonagricultural [1]		Manufacturing (current dollars)	Construction (current dollars)	Wholesale and retail trade (current dollars)		
	Current dollars	1977 dollars [2]				Current dollars	1977 dollars
1947	$45.58	$123.52	$49.13	$58.83	$38.07	....	....
1948	49.00	123.43	53.08	65.23	40.80	7.5	−0.1
1949	50.24	127.84	53.80	67.56	42.93	2.5	3.6
1950	53.13	133.83	58.28	69.68	44.55	5.8	4.7
1951	57.86	134.87	63.34	76.96	47.79	8.9	.8
1952	60.65	138.47	66.75	82.86	49.20	4.8	2.7
1953	63.76	144.58	70.47	86.41	51.35	5.1	4.4
1954	64.52	145.32	70.49	88.54	53.33	1.2	.5
1955	67.72	153.21	75.30	90.90	55.16	5.0	5.4
1956	70.74	157.90	78.78	96.38	57.48	4.5	3.1
1957	73.33	158.04	81.19	100.27	59.60	3.7	.1
1958	75.08	157.40	82.32	103.78	61.76	2.4	−.4
1959	78.78	163.78	88.26	108.41	64.41	4.9	4.1
1960	80.67	164.97	89.72	112.67	66.01	2.4	.7
1961	82.60	167.21	92.34	118.08	67.41	2.4	1.4
1962	85.91	172.16	96.56	122.47	69.91	4.0	3.0
1963	88.46	175.17	99.23	127.19	72.01	3.0	1.7
1964	91.33	178.38	102.97	132.06	74.66	3.2	1.8
1965	95.45	183.21	107.53	138.38	76.91	4.5	2.7
1966	98.82	184.37	112.19	146.26	79.39	3.5	.6
1967	101.84	184.83	114.49	154.95	82.35	3.1	.2
1968	107.73	187.68	122.51	164.49	87.00	5.8	1.5
1969	114.61	189.44	129.51	181.54	91.39	6.4	.9
1970	119.83	186.94	133.33	195.45	96.02	4.6	−1.3
1971	127.31	190.58	142.44	211.67	101.09	6.2	1.9
1972	136.90	198.41	154.71	221.19	106.45	7.5	4.1
1973	145.39	198.35	166.46	235.89	111.76	6.2	−.0
1974	154.76	190.12	176.80	249.25	119.02	6.4	−4.1
1975	163.53	184.16	190.79	266.08	126.45	5.7	−3.1
1976	175.45	186.85	209.32	283.73	133.79	7.3	1.5
1977	189.00	189.00	228.90	295.65	142.52	7.7	1.2
1978	203.70	189.31	249.27	318.69	153.64	7.8	.2
1979	219.91	183.41	269.34	342.99	164.96	8.0	−3.1
1980	235.10	172.74	288.62	367.78	176.46	6.9	−5.8
1981	255.20	170.13	318.00	398.52	190.95	8.5	−1.5
1982 [p]	266.92	167.87	330.65	423.89	198.42	4.6	−1.3
1981:							
Jan	249.20	172.94	310.68	401.44	184.76	9.5	−2.0
Feb	248.16	170.56	307.68	380.06	186.12	9.1	−2.1
Mar	250.63	171.31	311.62	391.72	187.40	9.2	−1.2
Apr	252.76	172.18	316.79	393.20	188.96	9.5	−.4
May	254.53	171.98	319.19	393.68	189.66	9.9	.1
June	254.50	170.92	320.40	391.65	189.71	9.2	−.3
July	256.63	170.18	321.20	400.34	191.27	10.0	−.7
Aug	258.37	170.09	322.79	401.12	192.56	9.6	−1.1
Sept	257.95	168.05	320.72	386.54	193.56	8.4	−2.2
Oct	259.74	168.44	322.32	407.01	192.96	7.9	−2.0
Nov	261.50	168.82	322.26	416.64	194.53	7.3	−1.8
Dec	261.10	167.91	320.62	415.14	194.56	6.1	−2.4
1982:							
Jan	258.69	165.93	315.09	405.50	193.05	3.7	−4.1
Feb	263.55	168.62	328.60	420.71	195.20	6.2	−1.1
Mar	263.15	168.90	326.43	420.29	195.23	4.8	−1.6
Apr	264.89	169.69	329.16	421.77	195.89	4.5	−1.7
May	267.75	169.89	331.57	432.75	198.40	5.2	−1.2
June	267.68	168.14	333.98	423.57	198.42	4.9	−1.9
July	269.08	167.97	335.55	430.03	198.74	4.7	−1.4
Aug	269.35	167.61	334.23	428.46	199.69	4.3	−1.4
Sept	268.66	166.87	332.13	420.78	200.63	4.0	−.9
Oct	269.62	166.53	332.13	425.07	201.61	3.5	−1.4
Nov [p]	269.97	166.75	334.93	422.24	201.61	3.2	−1.2
Dec [p]	270.92	167.75	335.32	431.43	201.93	3.8	−.1

[1] Also includes other private industry groups shown in Table B–37.
[2] Earnings in current dollars divided by the consumer price index on a 1977=100 base.
[3] Based on data not seasonally adjusted.

Note.—See Note, Table B–37.

Source: Department of Labor, Bureau of Labor Statistics.

Table B–40.—*Productivity and related data, business sector, 1947–82*

[1977=100; quarterly data seasonally adjusted]

Year or quarter	Output per hour of all persons		Output [1]		Hours of all persons [2]		Compensation per hour [3]		Real compensation per hour [4]		Unit labor cost		Implicit price deflator [5]	
	Business sector	Nonfarm business sector	Business sector	Nonfarm business sector	Business sector	Nonfarm business sector	Business sector	Nonfarm business sector	Business sector	Nonfarm business sector	Business sector	Nonfarm business sector	Business sector	Nonfarm business sector
1947	43.7	49.9	35.0	34.0	80.2	68.1	17.0	18.5	46.1	50.1	38.9	37.0	38.1	36.6
1948	46.0	52.0	37.2	36.0	80.7	69.2	18.4	20.1	46.4	50.5	40.0	38.6	40.8	39.1
1949	46.7	53.1	36.5	35.3	78.1	66.6	18.7	20.6	47.6	52.5	40.1	38.9	40.3	39.4
1950	50.4	56.3	39.8	38.6	78.9	68.7	20.0	21.8	50.5	55.0	39.7	38.8	41.0	40.1
1951	51.8	57.2	42.1	41.1	81.3	71.9	22.0	23.8	51.3	55.4	42.5	41.5	44.0	42.8
1952	53.5	58.6	43.5	42.5	81.4	72.6	23.4	25.1	53.4	57.2	43.8	42.8	44.5	43.5
1953	55.2	59.5	45.4	44.3	82.2	74.5	24.9	26.5	56.4	59.9	45.1	44.4	44.9	44.4
1954	56.1	60.4	44.6	43.4	79.5	71.9	25.7	27.3	58.0	61.6	45.9	45.2	45.3	45.0
1955	58.3	62.8	48.1	47.0	82.5	74.9	26.4	28.3	59.6	64.0	45.2	45.0	46.0	46.0
1956	58.9	62.9	49.3	48.3	83.7	76.0	28.1	30.0	62.0	66.0	47.7	47.0	47.5	47.0
1957	60.4	64.0	49.8	48.9	82.5	76.4	29.9	31.7	64.4	68.2	49.5	49.5	49.2	49.3
1958	62.3	65.5	49.0	48.0	78.8	73.2	31.2	32.9	65.5	68.9	50.2	50.2	49.8	49.7
1959	64.3	67.7	52.6	51.8	81.9	76.5	32.6	34.2	67.7	71.1	50.7	50.5	50.8	50.9
1960	65.2	68.3	53.5	52.5	82.0	77.0	33.9	35.7	69.5	73.0	52.0	52.2	51.6	51.6
1961	67.3	70.3	54.4	53.5	80.8	76.1	35.2	36.8	71.3	74.6	52.3	52.4	51.8	51.9
1962	69.9	72.8	57.4	56.6	82.1	77.8	36.8	38.3	73.7	76.7	52.7	52.6	52.6	52.7
1963	72.5	75.1	59.9	59.1	82.6	78.7	38.2	39.6	75.5	78.4	52.6	52.7	53.2	53.3
1964	75.6	78.1	63.5	62.8	83.9	80.5	40.2	41.4	78.4	80.9	53.1	53.0	53.7	53.9
1965	78.3	80.5	67.8	67.2	86.6	83.5	41.7	42.8	80.1	82.2	53.3	53.2	54.7	54.8
1966	80.7	82.5	71.5	71.2	88.6	86.3	44.6	45.4	83.3	84.7	55.3	55.0	56.4	56.3
1967	82.5	84.0	73.1	72.7	88.6	86.5	47.0	47.9	85.3	86.9	56.9	57.0	57.9	58.1
1968	85.3	86.8	76.8	76.6	90.1	88.2	50.7	51.5	88.3	89.6	59.4	59.3	60.2	60.4
1969	85.5	86.5	79.0	78.8	92.5	91.1	54.2	54.8	89.6	90.6	63.4	63.4	63.2	63.3
1970	86.2	86.8	78.4	78.0	91.0	89.8	58.2	58.7	90.8	91.5	67.5	67.6	66.0	66.3
1971	89.2	89.7	80.7	80.3	90.5	89.5	62.0	62.5	92.8	93.5	69.5	69.7	69.0	69.3
1972	92.4	93.0	86.1	85.8	93.2	92.3	66.1	66.7	95.7	96.6	71.5	71.7	71.3	71.3
1973	94.7	95.3	91.8	91.7	96.8	96.2	71.3	71.7	97.3	97.8	75.3	75.3	75.3	74.0
1974	92.5	92.9	89.9	89.8	97.3	96.7	78.0	78.5	95.9	96.4	84.4	84.5	82.4	81.6
1975	94.5	94.7	88.2	87.8	93.3	92.7	85.5	86.0	96.3	96.8	90.5	90.8	90.5	90.0
1976	97.6	97.8	93.8	93.7	96.0	95.8	92.9	93.0	98.9	99.0	95.1	95.1	94.7	94.6
1977	100.0	100.0	100.0	100.0	100.0	100.0	100.0	100.0	100.0	100.0	100.0	100.0	100.0	100.0
1978	100.6	100.6	105.5	105.7	104.9	105.0	108.6	108.6	100.9	100.9	108.0	108.0	107.5	107.1
1979	99.6	99.3	107.8	108.0	108.2	108.7	119.1	118.8	99.4	99.2	119.5	119.6	117.2	116.5
1980	98.9	98.5	106.2	106.3	107.4	108.0	131.4	130.9	96.7	96.3	132.9	133.0	128.3	128.3
1981	100.7	99.9	108.9	108.6	108.2	108.7	144.1	143.6	96.0	95.7	143.1	143.8	140.4	140.8
1982 [p]	101.0	100.0	106.4	105.9	105.3	105.9	154.6	154.0	97.0	96.7	153.0	153.9	148.2	149.0
1980:														
I	99.3	98.7	107.9	107.9	108.7	109.3	126.7	126.2	97.0	96.6	127.6	127.8	123.7	123.6
II	98.2	97.6	104.7	104.6	106.6	107.2	130.0	129.3	96.4	96.0	132.3	132.5	126.9	127.2
III	98.9	98.4	105.3	105.3	106.5	107.0	133.1	132.6	96.9	96.5	134.7	134.7	129.9	129.9
IV	99.3	99.2	107.0	107.3	107.7	108.2	136.1	135.7	96.2	95.9	137.0	136.8	132.8	132.7
1981:														
I	100.7	100.4	109.1	109.2	108.3	108.8	140.0	139.5	96.2	96.0	139.0	139.0	136.5	136.5
II	100.7	100.0	109.1	109.0	108.3	109.0	142.5	142.0	96.4	96.0	141.5	141.9	138.8	138.9
III	101.0	100.0	109.6	109.1	108.5	109.1	145.6	145.1	95.7	95.4	144.2	145.1	141.9	142.3
IV	100.2	99.1	107.8	107.1	107.5	108.1	148.2	147.7	95.6	95.3	147.9	149.0	144.6	145.5
1982:														
I	100.0	99.2	106.3	106.0	106.3	106.8	150.9	150.4	96.5	96.3	150.9	151.6	146.0	146.6
II	100.3	99.4	106.4	106.1	106.1	106.7	153.4	152.7	97.1	96.6	152.9	153.5	147.5	148.1
III	101.2	100.3	106.7	106.3	105.4	106.0	155.7	155.1	96.8	96.4	153.8	154.7	149.1	149.8
IV [p]	102.2	100.9	106.0	105.3	103.7	104.3	158.0	157.4	97.5	97.2	154.5	155.9	150.4	151.7

[1] Output refers to gross domestic product originating in the sector in 1972 dollars.

[2] Hours of all persons engaged in the sector, including hours of proprietors and unpaid family workers. Estimates based primarily on establishment data.

[3] Wages and salaries of employees plus employers' contributions for social insurance and private benefit plans. Also includes an estimate of wages, salaries, and supplemental payments for the self-employed.

[4] Hourly compensation divided by the consumer price index.

[5] Current dollar gross domestic product divided by constant dollar gross domestic product.

Source: Department of Labor, Bureau of Labor Statistics.

Table B–41.—*Changes in productivity and related data, business sector, 1948–82*

[Percent change from preceding period; quarterly data at seasonally adjusted annual rates]

Year	Output per hour of all persons		Output [1]		Hours of all persons [2]		Compensation per hour [3]		Real compensation per hour [4]		Unit labor cost		Implicit price deflator [5]	
	Business sector	Nonfarm business sector	Business sector	Nonfarm business sector	Business sector	Nonfarm business sector	Business sector	Nonfarm business sector	Business sector	Nonfarm business sector	Business sector	Nonfarm business sector	Business sector	Nonfarm business sector
1948	5.3	4.3	6.1	6.0	0.7	1.6	8.5	8.6	0.7	0.8	3.0	4.1	7.0	6.8
1949	1.5	2.0	−1.9	−1.9	−3.3	−3.8	1.6	2.9	2.6	3.9	.1	.9	−1.0	.9
1950	7.9	6.0	9.1	9.4	1.1	3.1	7.1	5.8	6.0	4.8	−.8	−.2	1.6	1.7
1951	2.8	1.7	5.8	6.5	2.9	4.6	9.8	8.8	1.7	.7	6.9	6.9	7.4	6.6
1952	3.2	2.3	3.3	3.4	.1	1.0	6.4	5.5	4.1	3.2	3.0	3.1	1.1	1.8
1953	3.2	1.7	4.3	4.2	1.0	2.5	6.4	5.6	5.7	4.8	3.1	3.9	.9	2.0
1954	1.6	1.4	−1.8	−2.0	−3.3	−3.4	3.2	3.2	2.8	2.7	1.6	1.7	1.0	1.4
1955	4.0	3.9	7.9	8.2	3.8	4.1	2.5	3.6	2.8	3.9	1.4	−.3	1.6	2.2
1956	1.0	.3	2.6	2.8	1.5	2.5	6.5	6.0	4.9	4.4	5.5	5.7	3.3	3.5
1957	2.5	1.7	1.0	1.2	−1.5	−.5	6.5	5.7	2.9	2.2	3.9	3.9	3.5	3.6
1958	3.1	2.4	−1.6	−1.9	−4.5	−4.2	4.4	3.8	1.6	1.0	1.3	1.4	1.3	.9
1959	3.2	3.4	7.3	7.9	3.9	4.4	4.3	4.0	3.5	3.2	1.0	.6	2.0	2.3
1960	1.5	.8	1.6	1.5	.2	.6	4.2	4.3	2.6	2.7	2.7	3.5	1.4	1.5
1961	3.3	2.9	1.7	1.8	−1.5	−1.1	3.8	3.2	2.7	2.1	.5	.3	.6	.6
1962	3.8	3.6	5.5	5.8	1.6	2.2	4.6	4.0	3.4	2.8	.7	.4	1.5	1.5
1963	3.7	3.2	4.3	4.4	.6	1.1	3.7	3.5	2.5	2.2	.0	.2	1.1	1.2
1964	4.3	3.9	6.0	6.4	1.6	2.4	5.2	4.5	3.8	3.2	.8	.6	1.0	1.2
1965	3.5	3.1	6.8	6.9	3.2	3.7	3.9	3.4	2.2	1.7	.3	.3	1.9	1.6
1966	3.1	2.5	5.5	5.9	2.3	3.4	7.0	6.0	4.0	3.0	3.8	3.5	3.0	2.8
1967	2.2	1.9	2.2	2.1	.0	.3	5.3	5.5	2.4	2.6	3.0	3.5	2.7	3.2
1968	3.3	3.3	5.1	5.3	1.7	2.0	7.8	7.5	3.5	3.2	4.4	4.1	4.0	4.0
1969	.2	−.3	2.9	2.9	2.6	3.2	7.0	6.5	1.5	1.1	6.7	6.8	4.9	4.7
1970	.8	.3	−.8	−1.0	−1.6	−1.3	7.3	7.0	1.3	1.0	6.4	6.6	4.5	4.8
1971	3.6	3.3	3.0	2.9	−.5	−.4	6.6	6.6	2.2	2.2	2.9	3.2	4.4	4.5
1972	3.5	3.7	6.6	6.9	3.0	3.1	6.5	6.7	3.1	3.3	2.9	2.9	3.4	3.0
1973	2.6	2.4	6.6	6.8	3.9	4.3	8.0	7.6	1.6	1.3	5.3	5.0	5.5	3.8
1974	−2.4	−2.5	−2.0	−2.1	.4	.5	9.4	9.4	−1.4	−1.4	12.1	12.2	9.5	10.2
1975	2.2	2.0	−2.0	−2.2	−4.1	−4.1	9.6	9.6	.5	.4	7.3	7.5	9.8	10.3
1976	3.3	3.2	6.4	6.7	3.0	3.4	8.6	8.1	2.6	2.2	5.1	4.7	4.7	5.0
1977	2.4	2.2	6.6	6.7	4.1	4.4	7.7	7.5	1.2	1.0	5.1	5.2	5.6	5.7
1978	.6	.6	5.5	5.7	4.9	5.0	8.6	8.6	.9	.9	8.0	8.0	7.5	7.1
1979	−.9	−1.3	2.3	2.2	3.2	3.5	9.7	9.3	−1.4	−1.7	10.7	10.7	9.0	8.8
1980	−.7	−.9	−1.5	−1.5	−.7	−.7	10.4	10.2	−2.8	−2.9	11.2	11.2	9.4	10.2
1981	1.8	1.4	2.5	2.2	.7	.7	9.6	9.7	−.7	−.7	7.7	8.1	9.5	9.7
1982 p	.4	.2	−2.3	−2.5	−2.6	−2.6	7.3	7.3	1.1	1.1	6.9	7.1	5.5	5.9
1980:														
I	.6	−.4	.2	−.2	−.4	.2	12.5	11.9	−3.5	−3.9	11.8	12.4	11.2	13.2
II	−4.3	−4.6	−11.4	−11.6	−7.4	−7.4	10.7	10.2	−2.1	−2.6	15.7	15.5	10.8	12.2
III	2.6	3.4	2.1	2.7	−.5	−.7	10.1	10.4	2.2	2.5	7.3	6.8	10.0	8.6
IV	2.0	3.1	6.8	7.8	4.7	4.6	9.4	9.8	−3.1	−2.8	7.2	6.5	9.3	8.9
1981:														
I	5.6	4.9	7.9	7.2	2.1	2.2	11.7	11.8	.2	.4	5.7	6.6	11.6	12.1
II	.0	−1.3	−.1	−.8	−.1	.5	7.5	7.1	.5	.1	7.5	8.6	6.6	7.1
III	1.1	−.3	1.9	.3	.8	.6	9.0	9.0	−2.6	−2.6	7.8	9.3	9.3	10.2
IV	−2.9	−3.5	−6.4	−7.1	−3.6	−3.7	7.4	7.3	−.4	−.5	10.6	11.2	8.0	9.2
1982:														
I	−1.0	.6	−5.5	−4.2	−4.5	−4.7	7.3	7.7	3.9	4.3	8.4	7.1	3.8	3.3
II	1.4	.8	.6	.6	−.8	−.1	6.9	6.1	2.2	1.4	5.5	5.2	4.3	4.0
III	3.6	3.4	1.1	.7	−2.4	−2.7	6.1	6.6	−1.4	−.9	2.4	3.1	4.4	4.9
IV p	4.1	2.7	−2.5	−3.8	−6.4	−6.3	6.0	6.0	3.3	3.3	1.8	3.2	3.5	5.1

[1] Output refers to gross domestic product originating in the sector in 1972 dollars.

[2] Hours of all persons engaged in the sector, including hours of proprietors and unpaid family workers. Estimates based primarily on establishment data.

[3] Wages and salaries of employees plus employers' contributions for social insurance and private benefit plans. Also includes an estimate of wages, salaries, and supplemental payments for the self-employed.

[4] Hourly compensation divided by the consumer price index.

[5] Current dollar gross domestic product divided by constant dollar gross domestic product.

Note.—Data relate to all persons engaged in the sector. Percent changes are based on original data and therefore may differ slightly from percent changes based on indexes in Table B–40.

Source: Department of Labor, Bureau of Labor Statistics.

TABLE B–42.—*Industrial production indexes, major industry divisions, 1929–82*

[1967=100; monthly data seasonally adjusted]

Year or month	Total industrial production	Manufacturing: Total	Manufacturing: Durable	Manufacturing: Nondurable	Mining	Utilities
1967 proportion	100.00	87.95	51.98	35.97	6.36	5.69
1929	21.6	22.8	22.5	23.2	43.1	7.4
1933	13.7	14.0	9.1	19.9	30.6	6.7
1939	21.7	21.5	17.7	26.1	42.1	10.7
1940	25.0	25.4	23.5	27.5	46.8	11.8
1941	31.6	32.4	31.4	33.3	49.7	13.3
1942	36.3	37.8	39.9	34.6	51.3	14.9
1943	44.0	47.0	54.2	37.1	52.5	16.5
1944	47.4	50.0	60.0	38.0	56.2	17.5
1945	40.7	42.6	45.2	38.5	55.1	17.8
1946	35.0	35.3	31.6	39.7	54.2	18.6
1947	39.4	39.4	37.7	41.3	61.3	20.1
1948	41.1	40.9	39.3	42.7	64.4	22.4
1949	38.8	38.7	35.7	42.0	57.1	23.9
1950	44.9	45.0	43.5	46.7	63.8	27.2
1951	48.7	48.6	48.9	48.3	70.0	31.0
1952	50.6	50.6	51.9	49.2	69.4	33.7
1953	54.8	55.2	58.7	51.2	71.2	36.5
1954	51.9	51.5	51.8	51.6	69.9	39.3
1955	58.5	58.2	59.2	57.2	77.9	43.9
1956	61.1	60.5	61.1	60.1	82.0	48.2
1957	61.9	61.2	61.6	61.1	82.1	51.5
1958	57.9	57.0	53.9	61.6	75.3	53.9
1959	64.8	64.2	61.9	67.7	78.7	59.3
1960	66.2	65.4	62.9	69.3	80.3	63.4
1961	66.7	65.6	61.8	71.5	80.8	67.0
1962	72.2	71.5	68.6	75.8	83.1	72.0
1963	76.5	75.8	73.1	80.0	86.4	77.0
1964	81.7	81.0	78.3	85.2	89.9	83.6
1965	89.8	89.7	89.0	90.9	93.2	88.7
1966	97.8	97.9	98.9	96.7	98.2	95.5
1967	100.0	100.0	100.0	100.0	100.0	100.0
1968	106.3	106.4	106.5	106.2	104.2	108.4
1969	111.1	111.0	110.6	111.5	108.3	117.3
1970	107.8	106.4	102.3	112.3	112.2	124.5
1971	109.6	108.2	102.4	116.6	109.8	130.5
1972	119.7	118.9	113.7	126.5	113.1	139.4
1973	129.8	129.8	127.1	133.8	114.7	145.4
1974	129.3	129.4	125.7	134.6	115.3	143.7
1975	117.8	116.3	109.3	126.4	112.8	146.0
1976	130.5	130.3	122.3	141.8	114.2	151.7
1977	138.2	138.4	130.0	150.5	118.2	156.5
1978	146.1	146.8	139.7	156.9	124.0	161.4
1979	152.5	153.6	146.4	164.0	125.5	166.0
1980	147.0	146.7	136.7	161.2	132.7	168.3
1981	151.0	150.4	140.5	164.8	142.2	169.1
1982 p	138.6	137.6	124.7	156.1	126.1	169.0
1981:						
Jan	151.4	151.1	141.0	165.6	140.4	167.6
Feb	151.8	151.2	140.8	166.2	143.1	166.4
Mar	152.1	151.6	142.1	165.3	143.2	167.8
Apr	151.9	152.0	142.5	165.9	135.2	167.6
May	152.7	152.8	143.5	166.4	135.4	170.7
June	152.9	152.4	143.2	165.8	141.7	172.7
July	153.9	153.2	143.6	167.1	146.5	173.1
Aug	153.6	153.2	143.4	167.3	146.0	171.9
Sept	151.6	151.1	140.9	165.9	145.0	167.8
Oct	149.1	148.0	137.8	162.8	145.3	168.1
Nov	146.3	145.0	134.4	160.3	143.3	168.9
Dec	143.4	142.0	131.3	157.4	142.6	168.2
1982:						
Jan	140.7	138.5	127.1	155.1	144.5	171.8
Feb	142.9	140.9	129.3	157.8	142.4	170.4
Mar	141.7	140.1	128.2	157.3	138.1	170.0
Apr	140.2	138.7	126.7	156.1	134.1	171.0
May	139.2	137.9	126.1	155.0	128.9	170.9
June	138.7	137.7	125.5	155.3	123.5	169.4
July	138.8	138.1	125.9	155.7	120.1	167.7
Aug	138.4	138.0	124.9	156.9	116.9	168.5
Sept	137.3	137.1	123.5	156.7	114.7	167.5
Oct	135.8	135.0	120.5	156.0	116.4	167.8
Nov p	134.8	134.0	119.3	155.2	115.9	167.1
Dec p	134.7	133.9	119.3	155.1	118.0	165.5

Source: Board of Governors of the Federal Reserve System.

TABLE B–43.—*Industrial production indexes, market groupings, 1947–82*

[1967=100; monthly data seasonally adjusted]

Year or month	Total industrial production	Final products: Total	Consumer goods[1]: Total	Consumer goods[1]: Automotive products	Consumer goods[1]: Home goods	Equipment[2]: Total	Equipment[2]: Business	Intermediate products	Materials[3]: Total	Materials[3]: Durable goods	Materials[3]: Nondurable goods
1967 proportion	100.00	47.82	27.68	2.83	5.06	20.14	12.63	12.89	39.29	20.35	10.47
1947	39.4	38.6	42.4	45.3	37.5	30.6	38.0	41.9	39.5	38.3	....
1948	41.1	40.0	43.7	47.4	39.1	32.2	39.5	44.3	41.2	39.4	....
1949	38.8	38.8	43.4	47.0	36.2	28.7	34.5	42.0	37.6	35.3	....
1950	44.9	43.7	49.6	50.1	49.0	31.1	37.0	48.8	45.0	44.4	....
1951	48.7	47.2	49.1	52.3	43.0	43.3	45.2	51.3	49.8	50.5	....
1952	50.6	50.7	50.2	47.1	43.0	51.9	51.2	50.9	50.5	51.6	....
1953	54.8	54.1	53.2	59.5	48.6	56.3	53.3	54.5	56.1	60.3	....
1954	51.9	51.3	52.9	55.4	44.9	49.3	46.8	54.3	51.8	52.0	45.9
1955	58.5	55.4	59.0	73.6	53.0	50.4	50.8	61.7	61.3	63.7	52.5
1956	61.1	58.6	61.2	60.6	55.7	55.3	58.8	64.4	62.8	63.9	54.9
1957	61.9	60.3	62.6	63.5	54.5	57.5	61.1	64.4	62.8	63.8	54.7
1958	57.9	57.6	62.1	50.5	51.4	51.5	51.5	63.0	56.5	53.7	54.4
1959	64.8	63.2	68.1	63.3	59.0	56.5	57.9	69.5	65.2	64.0	62.1
1960	66.2	65.3	70.7	72.5	59.4	58.1	59.4	70.0	66.1	64.8	63.2
1961	66.7	65.8	72.2	66.1	61.3	57.3	57.7	71.4	66.2	63.3	65.8
1962	72.2	71.4	77.1	80.1	66.5	63.7	62.7	75.7	72.1	70.4	71.3
1963	76.5	75.5	81.3	87.7	71.8	67.5	65.8	79.9	76.7	75.1	75.6
1964	81.7	79.7	85.9	91.9	78.4	71.4	73.7	85.2	82.9	81.9	82.2
1965	89.8	87.6	92.6	113.3	88.9	80.7	84.4	90.6	92.4	93.8	90.3
1966	97.8	95.9	97.3	112.8	97.9	94.0	97.7	96.2	100.7	103.3	97.5
1967	100.0	100.0	100.0	100.0	100.0	100.0	100.0	100.0	100.0	100.0	100.0
1968	106.3	106.2	105.9	119.4	106.4	106.5	105.5	106.3	106.5	106.2	108.8
1969	111.1	109.6	109.8	118.1	113.2	109.3	112.5	112.9	112.5	112.1	115.7
1970	107.8	105.3	109.0	98.8	110.2	100.1	107.0	112.9	109.2	103.8	115.4
1971	109.6	106.3	114.7	124.4	115.6	94.7	104.1	116.7	111.3	104.9	120.2
1972	119.7	115.7	124.4	141.4	129.5	103.8	118.0	126.5	122.3	117.7	132.9
1973	129.8	124.4	131.5	153.0	142.5	114.5	134.2	137.2	133.9	134.6	142.2
1974	129.3	125.1	128.9	132.8	136.8	120.0	142.4	135.3	132.4	132.7	142.6
1975	117.8	118.2	124.0	125.8	118.8	110.2	128.2	123.1	115.5	109.1	126.6
1976	130.5	127.6	137.1	155.7	134.1	114.6	135.4	137.2	131.7	128.0	147.8
1977	138.2	135.9	145.3	175.6	141.9	123.0	147.8	145.1	138.6	136.1	155.6
1978	146.1	142.2	149.1	179.9	147.7	132.8	160.3	154.1	148.3	149.0	165.6
1979	152.5	147.2	150.8	167.7	149.2	142.2	171.3	160.5	156.4	157.8	175.9
1980	147.0	145.3	145.4	132.8	138.9	145.2	173.2	151.9	147.6	143.0	171.5
1981	151.0	149.5	147.9	137.9	142.0	151.8	181.1	154.4	151.6	149.1	174.6
1982 p	138.6	141.3	142.6	129.6	129.3	139.4	157.3	143.4	133.8	125.3	157.3
1981:											
Jan	151.4	147.8	146.9	130.4	145.6	149.1	177.7	157.5	153.8	150.0	180.2
Feb	151.8	148.2	147.8	133.9	145.2	148.7	177.5	157.7	154.3	150.6	179.9
Mar	152.1	149.0	148.3	139.2	146.1	150.0	179.3	157.1	154.4	152.2	177.5
Apr	151.9	149.9	148.9	142.9	145.0	151.4	181.0	156.3	152.9	151.8	179.3
May	152.7	151.3	150.7	151.8	144.8	152.1	182.0	156.1	153.4	152.8	179.0
June	152.9	151.4	150.3	153.1	145.0	153.0	183.6	154.9	154.0	152.4	176.9
July	153.9	152.1	150.7	147.6	145.8	154.1	184.8	156.2	155.3	153.6	176.5
Aug	153.6	151.5	149.6	137.6	145.3	154.0	184.4	156.8	155.2	154.3	175.4
Sept	151.6	150.0	147.8	139.1	141.1	152.9	182.7	154.6	152.5	150.4	175.5
Oct	149.1	148.9	146.5	132.8	138.2	152.1	180.5	151.4	148.5	145.6	170.6
Nov	146.3	147.2	144.0	121.7	134.1	151.5	179.0	148.7	144.6	141.0	164.7
Dec	143.4	146.3	142.0	119.2	125.4	152.1	179.0	145.9	139.0	134.0	158.3
1982:											
Jan	140.7	142.8	139.6	109.2	126.3	147.2	172.2	143.4	137.2	129.7	156.8
Feb	142.9	144.1	141.8	117.5	130.6	147.3	171.6	146.3	140.4	132.4	164.2
Mar	141.7	143.3	141.5	125.0	129.9	145.9	169.0	145.2	138.5	130.7	162.0
Apr	140.2	142.6	142.1	129.9	131.1	143.4	164.9	143.7	136.2	128.1	160.3
May	139.2	142.2	143.6	138.9	129.1	140.4	159.9	142.6	134.3	126.6	156.6
June	138.7	142.1	144.8	143.0	129.9	138.4	156.7	141.9	133.5	126.6	153.5
July	138.8	142.5	145.8	149.7	130.4	138.0	154.9	142.8	133.0	126.0	152.3
Aug	138.4	141.2	144.1	135.5	131.4	137.3	153.9	144.7	132.8	125.1	154.5
Sept	137.3	140.0	143.4	135.5	128.9	135.2	150.5	143.7	132.0	123.0	158.5
Oct	135.8	138.6	142.2	124.0	128.6	133.5	146.4	142.4	130.3	119.3	157.7
Nov p	134.8	137.7	141.1	121.4	126.9	133.0	144.6	141.9	128.9	118.0	155.5
Dec p	134.7	138.1	141.4	129.8	125.9	133.6	144.1	141.0	128.4	117.3	155.5

[1] Also includes clothing and consumer staples, not shown separately.
[2] Also includes defense and space equipment, not shown separately.
[3] Also includes energy materials, not shown separately.

Source: Board of Governors of the Federal Reserve System.

Table B–44.—*Industrial production indexes, selected manufactures, 1947–82*

[1967=100; monthly data seasonally adjusted]

Year or month	Durable manufactures								Nondurable manufactures			
	Primary metals		Fabricated metal products	Nonelectrical machinery	Electrical machinery	Transportation equipment		Lumber and products	Apparel products	Printing and publishing	Chemicals and products	Foods
	Total	Iron and steel				Total	Motor vehicles and parts					
1967 proportion	6.57	4.21	5.93	9.15	8.05	9.27	4.50	1.64	3.31	4.72	7.74	8.75
1947	63.3	....	49.9	39.0	22.2	31.8	....	58.9	57.8	43.3	19.7	55.8
1948	65.8	....	50.8	39.2	23.0	34.8	....	61.3	60.3	45.4	21.3	55.2
1949	55.4	....	45.8	33.4	21.6	34.9	....	54.1	59.7	46.6	21.0	55.9
1950	69.7		56.1	37.5	29.6	41.8	....	65.7	64.3	48.0	26.2	57.0
1951	75.8	....	59.9	47.7	29.8	46.6	....	65.5	63.1	49.7	29.7	59.0
1952	69.2	....	58.5	51.9	34.0	54.2	....	64.7	66.3	49.7	31.1	60.2
1953	78.5	....	66.0	54.0	39.0	68.0	....	68.4	67.2	52.0	33.6	61.4
1954	63.5	70.1	59.4	46.1	34.7	59.2	60.5	68.0	66.4	54.1	34.1	62.7
1955	82.5	93.2	67.8	50.6	39.9	68.0	81.2	75.9	73.3	59.5	39.8	66.3
1956	82.0	91.5	68.8	58.0	43.1	66.0	65.8	75.0	75.0	63.2	42.7	70.1
1957	78.5	88.2	70.6	57.9	42.8	70.7	69.0	68.8	74.9	65.4	45.2	71.1
1958	62.3	66.5	63.3	48.6	39.2	55.8	51.0	69.9	72.8	63.9	46.6	72.9
1959	72.7	76.5	71.0	56.7	47.6	63.2	66.2	79.3	80.1	68.2	54.3	76.5
1960	72.4	77.7	71.1	56.9	51.6	65.4	74.7	74.7	81.7	71.0	56.4	78.6
1961	71.1	74.2	69.4	55.4	54.8	61.5	65.5	78.2	82.2	71.3	59.2	80.9
1962	76.3	77.3	75.4	62.1	62.9	71.1	79.8	82.5	85.5	73.9	65.7	83.4
1963	82.3	84.3	77.8	66.3	64.7	78.0	88.3	86.3	89.1	77.8	71.8	86.4
1964	92.8	95.9	82.6	75.6	68.4	80.0	90.7	92.7	92.2	82.6	78.8	90.4
1965	102.1	105.2	90.8	85.0	81.7	95.1	115.9	96.3	97.4	87.9	87.8	92.4
1966	108.4	108.4	97.2	98.8	97.9	102.0	113.9	100.0	99.9	94.6	95.7	96.0
1967	100.0	100.0	100.0	100.0	100.0	100.0	100.0	100.0	100.0	100.0	100.0	100.0
1968	104.3	103.2	105.6	101.8	105.5	111.1	120.3	105.5	102.9	103.2	109.5	102.6
1969	113.8	112.6	107.9	109.3	111.9	108.4	116.5	107.9	106.7	107.4	118.4	106.1
1970	106.6	104.7	102.4	104.4	108.1	89.5	92.3	105.6	101.4	107.0	120.4	108.9
1971	100.2	96.1	103.5	100.2	107.7	97.9	118.6	113.8	104.7	107.1	125.9	112.8
1972	112.1	107.1	112.1	116.0	122.2	108.2	135.8	120.8	109.4	112.7	143.6	116.8
1973	126.7	122.3	124.7	133.7	143.1	118.3	148.8	126.0	117.3	118.2	154.5	120.9
1974	123.1	119.8	124.2	140.1	143.8	108.7	128.2	116.2	114.3	118.2	159.4	124.0
1975	96.4	95.8	109.9	125.1	116.5	97.4	111.1	107.6	107.6	113.3	147.2	123.4
1976	109.7	104.8	123.9	134.5	134.8	111.1	142.0	123.2	125.7	122.5	170.9	133.0
1977	111.1	103.8	131.0	143.6	145.4	122.2	161.1	131.2	134.2	127.6	185.7	138.8
1978	119.9	113.2	141.6	153.6	159.4	132.5	169.9	136.3	134.2	131.5	197.4	142.7
1979	121.3	113.2	148.5	163.7	175.0	135.4	159.9	136.9	134.4	136.9	211.8	147.5
1980	102.3	92.4	134.1	162.8	172.8	116.9	119.0	119.3	127.0	139.6	207.1	149.6
1981	107.9	99.8	136.4	171.2	178.4	116.1	122.3	119.1	120.4	144.2	215.6	152.1
1982 ᵖ	75.8	....	114.8	148.6	169.2	104.9	109.8	....	....	144.3	....	....
1981:												
Jan	114.1	108.7	135.8	167.3	177.6	117.4	120.0	127.4	123.8	143.9	218.9	151.9
Feb	114.5	108.4	137.6	168.3	174.9	116.1	119.9	126.2	121.6	144.8	219.8	152.5
Mar	114.9	108.0	139.2	169.2	177.4	119.5	127.1	125.6	120.2	142.7	218.5	152.4
Apr	110.6	103.4	139.5	169.7	178.8	121.3	130.7	126.3	121.6	141.6	219.8	151.9
May	111.9	105.6	138.4	172.1	179.9	123.7	136.4	126.2	122.6	141.3	220.6	152.2
June	107.4	98.5	139.3	174.1	180.1	123.4	137.5	122.5	121.1	143.1	218.4	151.3
July	109.4	99.7	140.1	176.7	180.9	119.8	130.5	122.9	122.6	144.4	221.5	151.6
Aug	113.1	105.1	140.0	176.4	182.6	115.4	123.1	119.1	122.6	146.1	219.2	151.9
Sept	108.6	99.2	136.8	173.9	180.0	114.2	120.4	113.2	122.5	145.9	216.3	150.7
Oct	102.3	92.2	133.8	169.7	179.6	110.6	113.8	109.6	117.8	145.6	208.8	151.4
Nov	96.6	87.2	130.2	167.9	175.7	106.1	105.5	104.7	113.8	143.4	204.6	153.0
Dec	89.6	79.2	126.1	167.4	170.7	103.7	100.4	104.8	114.1	145.3	199.8	152.8
1982:												
Jan	89.7	79.6	120.7	160.9	168.2	96.6	90.4	99.2	....	145.6	196.7	151.1
Feb	88.5	78.5	121.4	160.0	172.9	102.0	98.6	104.9	....	146.4	201.3	151.7
Mar	83.0	73.0	121.1	157.3	172.6	104.4	105.6	103.5	....	145.9	200.3	150.8
Apr	76.4	65.1	119.1	153.7	172.2	105.9	110.7	106.2	....	144.2	198.6	149.7
May	75.2	62.4	115.8	150.0	170.9	110.0	119.8	110.6	....	143.8	193.6	150.5
June	72.8	58.0	115.0	147.4	170.8	111.6	124.0	112.2	....	142.6	193.2	151.0
July	72.9	58.1	115.5	147.1	170.3	112.7	127.2	116.9	....	143.9	194.1	151.0
Aug	72.9	57.4	114.3	147.2	169.7	107.0	116.7	120.3	....	145.3	195.6	150.7
Sept	73.2	56.4	112.3	144.9	167.0	105.3	113.5	119.9	....	144.3	196.4	149.0
Oct	70.0	54.1	108.5	140.5	165.7	100.8	103.0	117.2	....	142.6	193.7	150.6
Nov ᵖ	67.1	51.4	107.4	138.0	164.9	100.0	101.7	119.4	....	142.6	192.8	....
Dec ᵖ	65.9	....	106.5	135.8	164.5	103.7	108.8	....	....	144.0	....	....

Source: Board of Governors of the Federal Reserve System.

TABLE B–45.—*Capacity utilization rate in manufacturing, 1948–82*

[Percent; quarterly data seasonally adjusted]

Year or quarter	FRB series[1]			Commerce series[2]				
	Total manufacturing	Primary processing	Advanced processing	Total manufacturing	Durable goods	Nondurable goods	Primary-processed goods	Advanced-processed goods
1948	82.5	87.2	80.0					
1949	74.2	76.2	73.3					
1950	82.8	88.5	79.8					
1951	85.8	90.2	83.4					
1952	85.4	84.9	85.9					
1953	89.2	89.4	89.3					
1954	80.3	80.6	80.1					
1955	87.1	92.1	84.3					
1956	86.4	89.7	84.5					
1957	83.7	84.7	83.1					
1958	75.2	75.4	75.1					
1959	81.9	83.4	81.1					
1960	80.2	79.8	80.4					
1961	77.4	77.9	77.2					
1962	81.6	81.6	81.7					
1963	83.5	83.8	83.4					
1964	85.6	87.8	84.6					
1965	89.6	91.1	88.9	86	88	85	89	85
1966	91.1	91.4	91.2	86	87	86	88	85
1967	86.9	85.7	87.6	84	83	85	87	83
1968	87.1	87.7	86.8	85	84	86	86	84
1969	86.2	88.5	85.0	85	84	86	87	84
1970	79.3	82.9	77.4	81	78	83	83	79
1971	78.4	82.3	76.3	80	78	83	82	80
1972	83.5	88.2	81.0	83	82	85	85	82
1973	87.6	92.5	85.0	86	85	86	89	84
1974	83.8	87.8	81.5	83	82	84	85	82
1975	72.9	73.7	72.5	77	76	79	76	77
1976	79.5	81.9	78.2	81	81	82	82	81
1977	81.9	84.0	80.8	83	84	82	83	83
1978	84.4	86.9	83.0	84	84	83	84	84
1979	85.7	88.1	84.3	83	83	82	84	82
1980	79.1	78.5	79.4	78	77	79	77	78
1981	78.5	78.4	78.5	76	75	78	76	76
1982 p	69.8	66.4	71.6					
1978:								
I	82.0	84.0	80.9	84	84	83	83	84
II	83.9	86.3	82.7	84	85	82	84	84
III	85.2	87.9	83.7	83	83	82	84	82
IV	86.4	89.5	84.6	84	85	83	85	84
1979:								
I	86.9	89.0	85.7	84	85	83	85	84
II	85.9	88.2	84.7	83	84	82	84	83
III	85.3	88.3	83.7	82	82	82	83	81
IV	84.4	86.9	83.0	81	80	82	83	80
1980:								
I	83.4	85.5	82.5	80	80	81	81	80
II	77.9	76.4	78.7	76	74	78	75	76
III	75.9	73.1	77.4	76	75	78	74	77
IV	79.1	79.3	78.8	78	78	78	78	78
1981:								
I	79.9	81.3	79.1	78	77	79	78	78
II	79.8	80.3	79.6	78	77	80	78	78
III	79.3	79.4	79.2	76	74	78	76	76
IV	74.8	72.7	75.9	72	70	75	71	73
1982:								
I	71.6	69.1	73.2	72	70	75	70	73
II	70.3	66.3	72.5	71	68	76	66	74
III	69.7	66.1	71.6	69	65	74	66	71
IV p	67.6	64.3	69.2					

[1] For description of the series, see "Federal Reserve Measures of Capacity and Capacity Utilization," February 1978.

[2] Quarterly data are for last month in quarter. Annual data are averages of the four indexes, except for 1965 (December index) and 1966–67 (averages of June and December indexes). For description of the series, see "Survey of Current Business," July 1974.

Sources: Board of Governors of the Federal Reserve System and Department of Commerce (Bureau of Economic Analysis).

TABLE B–46.—*New construction activity, 1929–82*

[Value put in place, billions of dollars; monthly data at seasonally adjusted annual rates]

Year or month	Total new construction	Private construction: Total	Private construction: Residential buildings[1]: Total[2]	Private construction: Residential buildings[1]: New housing units	Private construction: Nonresidential buildings and other construction[1]: Total	Private construction: Nonresidential buildings and other construction[1]: Commercial[3]	Private construction: Nonresidential buildings and other construction[1]: Industrial	Private construction: Nonresidential buildings and other construction[1]: Other[4]	Public construction: Total	Public construction: Federal	Public construction: State and local[5]
1929	10.8	8.3	3.6	3.0	4.7	1.1	0.9	2.6	2.5	0.2	2.3
1933	2.9	1.2	.5	.3	.8	.1	.2	.5	1.6	.5	1.1
1939	8.2	4.4	2.7	2.3	1.7	.3	.3	1.2	3.8	.8	3.1
1940	8.7	5.1	3.0	2.6	2.1	.3	.4	1.3	3.6	1.2	2.4
1941	12.0	6.2	3.5	3.0	2.7	.4	.8	1.5	5.8	3.8	2.0
1942	14.1	3.4	1.7	1.4	1.7	.2	.3	1.2	10.7	9.3	1.3
1943	8.3	2.0	.9	.7	1.1	.0	.2	.9	6.3	5.6	.7
1944	5.3	2.2	.8	.6	1.4	.1	.2	1.1	3.1	2.5	.6
1945	5.8	3.4	1.3	.7	2.1	.2	.6	1.3	2.4	1.7	.7
1946	14.3	12.1	6.2	4.8	5.8	1.2	1.7	3.0	2.2	.9	1.4
New series											
1947	20.0	16.7	9.9	7.8	6.9	1.0	1.7	4.2	3.3	.8	2.5
1948	26.1	21.4	13.1	10.5	8.2	1.4	1.4	5.5	4.7	1.2	3.5
1949	26.7	20.5	12.4	10.0	8.0	1.2	1.0	5.9	6.3	1.5	4.8
1950	33.6	26.7	18.1	15.6	8.6	1.4	1.1	6.1	6.9	1.6	5.2
1951	35.4	26.2	15.9	13.2	10.3	1.5	2.1	6.7	9.3	3.0	6.3
1952	36.8	26.0	15.8	12.9	10.2	1.1	2.3	6.8	10.8	4.2	6.6
1953	39.1	27.9	16.6	13.4	11.3	1.8	2.2	7.3	11.2	4.1	7.1
1954	41.4	29.7	18.2	14.9	11.5	2.2	2.0	7.2	11.7	3.4	8.3
1955	46.5	34.8	21.9	18.2	12.9	3.2	2.4	7.3	11.7	2.8	8.9
1956	47.6	34.9	20.2	16.1	14.7	3.6	3.1	8.0	12.7	2.7	10.0
1957	49.1	35.1	19.0	14.7	16.1	3.6	3.6	9.0	14.1	3.0	11.1
1958	50.0	34.6	19.8	15.4	14.8	3.6	2.4	8.8	15.5	3.4	12.1
1959	55.4	39.3	24.3	19.2	15.1	3.9	2.1	9.0	16.1	3.7	12.3
1960	54.7	38.9	23.0	17.3	15.9	4.2	2.9	8.9	15.9	3.6	12.2
1961	56.4	39.3	23.1	17.1	16.2	4.7	2.8	8.7	17.1	3.9	13.3
1962	60.2	42.3	25.2	19.4	17.2	5.1	2.8	9.2	17.9	3.9	14.0
1963	64.8	45.5	27.9	21.7	17.6	5.0	2.9	9.7	19.4	4.0	15.4
1964	68.0	47.7	28.0	21.8	19.7	5.4	3.6	10.7	20.4	3.9	16.5
1965	74.1	52.0	27.9	21.7	24.1	....	....	....	22.1	4.0	18.0
1966	76.8	52.8	25.7	19.4	27.1	....	....	....	24.0	4.0	20.0
1967	78.5	52.9	25.6	19.0	27.3	....	....	....	25.5	3.5	22.1
1968	87.5	59.9	30.6	24.0	29.3	7.8	6.0	15.5	27.6	3.4	24.2
1969	94.3	66.3	33.2	25.9	33.1	9.4	6.8	16.9	28.0	3.3	24.6
1970	95.2	67.1	31.9	24.3	35.3	9.8	6.5	19.0	28.1	3.3	24.8
1971	110.3	80.4	43.3	35.1	37.2	11.6	5.4	20.1	29.9	4.0	25.9
1972	124.4	94.2	54.3	44.9	40.0	13.5	4.7	21.8	30.2	4.4	25.8
1973	138.4	105.9	59.7	50.1	46.2	15.5	6.2	24.5	32.5	4.9	27.6
1974	139.2	100.9	50.4	40.6	50.5	15.9	7.9	26.7	38.3	5.3	33.0
1975	135.9	95.1	46.5	34.4	48.6	12.8	8.0	27.8	40.9	6.3	34.6
1976	151.1	112.0	60.5	47.3	51.4	12.8	7.2	31.5	39.1	7.0	32.1
1977	173.8	135.7	81.0	65.7	54.7	14.8	7.7	32.2	38.2	7.3	30.9
1978	205.6	159.7	93.4	75.8	66.2	18.6	11.0	36.7	45.9	8.4	37.5
1979	230.4	181.6	99.0	78.6	82.6	24.9	15.0	42.7	48.8	8.6	40.2
1980	230.7	175.7	87.3	63.1	88.4	29.9	13.8	44.7	55.1	19.7	45.4
1981	238.2	185.2	86.6	62.7	98.7	34.2	17.0	47.4	53.0	10.0	42.9

See next page for continuation of table.

TABLE B–46.—*New construction activity, 1929–82*—Continued

[Value put in place, billions of dollars; monthly data at seasonally adjusted annual rates]

Year or month	Total new construction	Private construction							Public construction		
		Total	Residential buildings [1]		Nonresidential buildings and other construction [1]				Total	Federal	State and local [5]
			Total [2]	New housing units	Total	Commercial [3]	Industrial	Other [4]			
1981:											
Jan	255.4	193.7	99.5	73.9	94.2	32.8	15.8	45.5	61.7	10.7	51.0
Feb	250.7	191.7	96.9	72.4	94.8	33.0	14.9	46.9	59.0	10.9	48.1
Mar	249.4	190.6	95.8	72.1	94.8	33.6	15.3	45.9	58.9	9.8	49.1
Apr	247.6	192.1	95.1	72.2	97.0	34.3	16.4	46.4	55.4	10.3	45.1
May	240.9	189.3	92.3	69.5	97.0	33.5	15.9	47.6	51.7	10.1	41.5
June	237.5	185.9	89.1	66.8	96.8	33.6	16.7	46.5	51.7	10.1	41.6
July	238.1	186.9	87.0	64.1	99.9	34.2	17.8	47.9	51.2	10.1	41.0
Aug	235.9	185.2	84.1	60.8	101.1	34.3	18.7	48.2	50.7	9.2	41.4
Sept	233.5	182.4	80.4	57.1	102.0	34.9	18.5	48.6	51.1	10.1	41.0
Oct	230.8	180.0	78.2	53.4	101.8	34.6	18.5	48.6	50.8	9.8	41.0
Nov	230.0	178.1	76.2	50.4	102.0	35.7	18.4	47.9	51.9	9.6	42.3
Dec	228.8	176.6	75.8	49.4	100.7	36.4	16.6	47.7	52.2	9.8	42.4
1982:											
Jan	225.1	175.5	73.7	51.0	101.8	36.2	17.1	48.5	49.6	9.2	40.4
Feb	222.6	173.0	69.2	49.2	103.9	36.8	17.2	49.8	49.6	9.6	40.0
Mar	224.6	173.6	70.0	51.0	103.6	38.4	16.6	48.6	51.0	10.0	41.0
Apr	226.1	175.1	72.3	49.6	102.8	38.4	15.9	48.5	51.0	9.8	41.1
May	228.7	179.9	75.5	51.0	104.5	36.8	17.1	50.6	48.8	9.6	39.2
June	231.6	182.7	75.3	49.8	107.4	38.0	18.4	50.9	48.9	9.5	39.4
July	227.6	178.7	73.4	51.5	105.3	37.5	16.4	51.4	48.9	9.9	39.0
Aug	228.1	176.6	72.1	52.3	104.5	36.1	16.7	51.7	51.4	10.2	41.2
Sept	228.1	177.0	71.5	53.1	105.6	37.1	16.6	51.8	51.1	10.5	40.6
Oct	229.1	177.7	74.1	52.3	103.6	35.7	17.1	50.9	51.3	10.4	40.9
Nov [p]	237.2	184.4	78.4	54.2	106.0	37.1	17.2	51.7	52.8	10.6	42.2

[1] Beginning 1960, farm residential buildings included in residential buildings; prior to 1960, included in nonresidential buildings and other construction.
[2] Total includes additions and alterations and nonhousekeeping units, not shown separately.
[3] Office buildings, warehouses, stores, restaurants, garages, etc.
[4] Religious, educational, hospital and institutional, miscellaneous nonresidential, farm (see also footnote 1), public utilities, and all other private.
[5] Includes Federal grants-in-aid for State and local projects.

Source: Department of Commerce, Bureau of the Census.

TABLE B-47.—*New housing units started and authorized, 1959–82*

[Thousands of units]

Year or month	New housing units started: Private and public[1]: Total (farm and nonfarm)	Nonfarm	Private (farm and nonfarm)[1]: Total	Type of structure: 1 unit	2 to 4 units	5 units or more	New private housing units authorized[2]: Total	Type of structure: 1 unit	2 to 4 units	5 units or more
1959	1,553.7	1,531.3	1,517.0	1,234.0	283.0		1,208.3	938.3	77.1	192.9
1960	1,296.1	1,274.0	1,252.2	994.7	257.4		998.0	746.1	64.6	187.4
1961	1,365.0	1,336.8	1,313.0	974.3	338.7		1,064.2	722.8	67.6	273.8
1962	1,492.5	1,468.7	1,462.9	991.4	471.5		1,186.6	716.2	87.1	383.3
1963	1,634.9	1,614.8	1,603.2	1,012.4	590.8		1,334.7	750.2	118.9	465.6
1964	1,561.0	1,534.0	1,528.8	970.5	108.4	450.0	1,285.8	720.1	100.8	464.9
1965	1,509.7	1,487.5	1,472.8	963.7	86.6	422.5	1,239.8	709.9	84.8	445.1
1966	1,195.8	1,172.8	1,164.9	778.6	61.1	325.1	971.9	563.2	61.0	347.7
1967	1,321.9	1,298.8	1,291.6	843.9	71.6	376.1	1,141.0	650.6	73.0	417.5
1968	1,545.4	1,521.4	1,507.6	899.4	80.9	527.3	1,353.4	694.7	84.3	574.4
1969	1,499.5	1,482.3	1,466.8	810.6	85.0	571.2	1,323.7	625.9	85.2	612.7
1970	1,469.0	(3)	1,433.6	812.9	84.8	535.9	1,351.5	646.8	88.1	616.7
1971	2,084.5	(3)	2,052.2	1,151.0	120.3	780.9	1,924.6	906.1	132.9	885.7
1972	2,378.5	(3)	2,356.6	1,309.2	141.3	906.2	2,218.9	1,033.1	148.6	1,037.2
1973	2,057.5	(3)	2,045.3	1,132.0	118.3	795.0	1,819.5	882.1	117.0	820.5
1974	1,352.5	(3)	1,337.7	888.1	68.1	381.6	1,074.4	643.8	64.3	366.2
1975	1,171.4	(3)	1,160.4	892.2	64.0	204.3	939.2	675.5	63.9	199.8
1976	1,547.6	(3)	1,537.5	1,162.4	85.9	289.2	1,296.2	893.6	93.1	309.5
1977	2,001.7	(3)	1,987.1	1,450.9	121.7	414.4	1,690.0	1,126.1	121.3	442.7
1978	2,036.1	(3)	2,020.3	1,433.3	125.0	462.0	1,800.5	1,182.6	130.6	487.3
1979	1,760.0	(3)	1,745.1	1,194.1	122.0	429.0	1,551.8	981.5	125.4	444.8
1980	1,312.6	(3)	1,292.2	852.2	109.5	330.5	1,190.6	710.4	114.5	365.7
1981	1,100.3	(3)	1,084.2	705.4	91.1	287.7	985.5	564.3	101.8	319.4
1982 p	1,070.4	(3)	1,060.6	661.0	80.7	319.0	992.5	540.0	88.6	363.9
			Seasonally adjusted annual rates							
1981:										
Jan	85.2	(3)	1,585	974	139	472	1,236	712	139	385
Feb	72.5	(3)	1,294	835	114	345	1,196	699	115	382
Mar	108.9	(3)	1,318	863	108	347	1,172	686	113	373
Apr	124.0	(3)	1,301	868	97	336	1,186	682	123	381
May	110.6	(3)	1,172	776	105	291	1,178	659	112	407
June	107.0	(3)	1,046	705	89	252	986	573	109	304
July	101.0	(3)	1,040	696	88	256	941	543	98	300
Aug	87.3	(3)	946	614	76	256	878	505	91	282
Sept	90.9	(3)	899	623	62	214	835	456	81	298
Oct	88.2	(3)	854	507	78	269	738	400	85	253
Nov	64.9	(3)	860	554	81	225	743	413	78	252
Dec	59.7	(3)	882	550	74	258	797	454	88	255
1982:										
Jan	47.6	(3)	885	592	70	223	803	450	68	285
Feb	52.0	(3)	945	568	84	293	792	436	75	281
Mar	78.7	(3)	931	621	67	243	851	460	81	310
Apr	85.1	(3)	882	566	64	252	879	450	76	353
May	99.2	(3)	1,066	631	86	349	944	488	102	354
June	91.8	(3)	908	621	83	204	929	516	91	322
July	107.2	(3)	1,193	628	102	463	1,062	500	85	477
Aug	97.2	(3)	1,033	645	88	300	888	497	83	308
Sept	108.3	(3)	1,129	677	92	360	1,003	561	96	346
Oct	111.7	(3)	1,126	701	64	361	1,172	651	86	435
Nov	111.9	(3)	1,404	883	79	442	1,192	729	96	367
Dec p	81.7	(3)	1,222	800	86	336	1,291	732	111	448

[1] Units in structures built by private developers for sale upon completion to local public housing authorities under the Department of Housing and Urban Development "Turnkey" program are classified as private housing. Military housing starts, including those financed with mortgages insured by FHA under Section 803 of the National Housing Act, are included in publicly owned starts and excluded from total private starts.

[2] Authorized by issuance of local building permit: in 16,000 permit-issuing places beginning 1978; in 14,000 places for 1972–77; in 13,000 places for 1967–71; in 12,000 places for 1963–66; and in 10,000 places prior to 1963.

[3] Not available separately beginning January 1970.

Source: Department of Commerce, Bureau of the Census.

TABLE B–48.—*Nonfarm business expenditures for new plant and equipment, 1947–83*

[Billions of dollars; quarterly data at seasonally adjusted annual rates]

Year or quarter	Total	Plant	Equipment	Plant and equipment								
				Manufacturing			Nonmanufacturing					
				Total	Durable goods	Nondurable goods	Total	Mining	Transportation	Public utilities	Trade and services[1]	Communication and other[2]
1947	21.80	8.45	13.35	8.73	3.39	5.34	13.07	0.69	2.21	1.64	6.13	2.40
1948	25.46	10.35	15.11	9.25	3.54	5.71	16.21	.93	2.66	2.67	6.92	3.04
1949	23.54	10.20	13.34	7.32	2.67	4.64	16.22	.88	2.30	3.28	7.13	2.63
1950	25.32	10.94	14.37	7.73	3.22	4.51	17.59	.84	2.38	3.42	8.37	2.58
1951	30.83	13.08	17.74	11.07	5.12	5.95	19.76	1.11	3.05	3.75	8.83	3.03
1952	31.59	13.14	18.45	12.12	5.75	6.37	19.47	1.21	2.99	3.96	8.05	3.25
1953	33.58	13.82	19.76	12.43	5.71	6.72	21.16	1.25	2.97	4.61	8.94	3.38
1954	33.13	14.09	19.03	12.00	5.49	6.51	21.13	1.29	2.42	4.23	9.59	3.60
1955	36.58	15.97	20.60	12.50	5.87	6.62	24.08	1.31	2.60	4.26	11.49	4.42
1956	44.76	19.34	25.42	16.33	8.19	8.15	28.43	1.64	3.07	4.78	13.64	5.30
1957	48.12	20.94	27.19	17.50	8.59	8.91	30.62	1.69	3.35	5.95	13.68	5.96
1958	42.17	19.41	22.76	12.98	6.21	6.77	29.19	1.43	2.34	5.74	14.11	5.58
1959	44.78	19.89	24.89	13.76	6.72	7.04	31.02	1.35	3.17	5.46	15.40	5.63
1960	48.63	20.94	27.70	16.36	8.28	8.08	32.28	1.29	3.19	5.40	16.15	6.25
1961	47.82	21.12	26.70	15.53	7.43	8.10	32.29	1.26	2.82	5.20	16.53	6.48
1962	51.28	22.12	29.16	16.03	7.81	8.22	35.25	1.41	3.26	5.12	18.27	7.19
1963	53.25	22.23	31.03	17.27	8.64	8.63	35.99	1.26	3.36	5.33	18.57	7.47
1964	61.66	24.96	36.70	21.23	10.98	10.25	40.43	1.33	4.46	5.80	20.38	8.46
1965	70.43	27.24	43.19	25.41	13.49	11.92	45.02	1.36	5.46	6.49	22.13	9.58
1966	82.22	32.21	50.01	31.37	17.23	14.15	50.84	1.42	6.43	7.82	24.69	10.49
1967	83.42	32.22	51.20	32.25	17.83	14.42	51.18	1.38	6.34	9.33	23.02	11.11
1968	88.45	35.51	52.94	32.34	17.93	14.40	56.11	1.44	6.79	10.52	25.31	12.06
1969	99.52	40.54	58.99	36.27	19.97	16.31	63.25	1.77	7.04	11.70	28.31	14.43
1970	105.61	44.24	61.36	36.99	19.80	17.19	68.62	2.02	6.95	13.03	29.77	16.85
1971	108.53	46.60	61.93	33.60	16.78	16.82	74.93	2.67	5.93	14.70	34.20	17.43
1972	120.25	49.35	70.89	35.42	18.22	17.20	84.82	2.88	6.72	16.26	40.00	18.96
1973	137.70	56.66	81.04	42.37	22.75	19.62	95.33	3.31	7.41	17.97	45.53	21.12
1974	156.98	64.29	92.69	53.21	27.44	25.76	103.78	4.62	8.23	19.83	47.79	23.30
1975	157.71	65.21	92.50	54.92	26.33	28.59	102.79	6.10	8.68	19.98	46.23	21.80
1976	171.45	71.20	100.25	59.95	28.47	31.47	111.50	7.44	8.89	22.37	49.30	23.51
1977	198.08	80.31	117.77	69.22	34.04	35.18	128.87	9.24	9.40	26.79	56.54	26.90
1978	231.24	92.70	138.54	79.72	40.43	39.29	151.52	10.21	10.68	29.95	68.66	32.02
1979	270.46	105.73	164.73	98.68	51.07	47.61	171.77	11.38	12.35	33.96	79.26	34.83
1980	295.63	117.55	178.08	115.81	58.91	56.90	179.81	13.51	12.09	35.44	81.79	36.99
1981	321.49	133.46	188.04	126.79	61.84	64.95	194.70	16.86	12.05	38.40	86.33	41.06
1982[3]	319.99			122.67	57.95	64.72	197.32	16.05	11.80	41.62	86.42	41.43
1983[3]	315.69			119.52	57.35	62.18	196.16	16.45	11.92	39.98	86.86	40.96
1981:												
I	312.24	128.57	183.67	124.50	61.24	63.27	187.74	16.20	11.74	36.05	83.43	40.32
II	316.73	131.05	185.68	125.49	63.10	62.40	191.24	16.80	11.70	37.84	85.88	39.02
III	328.25	136.40	191.85	130.11	62.58	67.53	198.13	17.55	11.61	39.55	87.55	41.89
IV	327.83	136.67	191.17	126.91	60.78	66.14	200.92	16.81	13.12	39.74	88.33	42.92
1982:												
I	327.72	139.49	188.23	128.32	60.84	67.48	199.40	17.60	11.99	40.12	87.80	41.89
II	323.22	137.95	185.28	123.77	59.03	64.74	199.46	16.56	12.32	41.40	88.85	40.33
III	315.79	135.14	180.65	119.46	57.14	62.32	196.33	14.63	11.28	43.38	87.31	39.73
IV[3]	315.21			120.50	55.80	64.70	194.71	15.56	11.82	41.66	82.01	43.65
1983:												
I[3]	316.40			121.43	57.90	63.54	194.97	16.18	10.63	40.76	85.87	41.53
II[3]	320.00			123.42	58.30	65.12	196.58	17.33	11.66	40.30	85.87	41.43

[1] Wholesale and retail trade; finance, insurance, and real estate; and personal, business, and professional services.
[2] "Other" consists of construction; social services and membership organizations; and forestry, fisheries, and agricultural services.
[3] Planned capital expenditures reported by business in late October-December 1982, corrected for biases.

Source: Department of Commerce, Bureau of Economic Analysis.

Table B–49.—*Sales and inventories in manufacturing and trade 1947–82*

[Amounts in millions of dollars; monthly data seasonally adjusted]

Year or month	Total manufacturing and trade			Manufacturing			Merchant wholesalers			Retail trade		
	Sales [1]	Inventories [2]	Ratio [3]	Sales [1]	Inventories [2]	Ratio [3]	Sales [1]	Inventories [2]	Ratio [3]	Sales [1]	Inventories [2]	Ratio [3]
1947	....	....	....	15,513	25,897	1.58	....	....	....	10,200	14,241	1.26
1948	35,260	52,507	1.42	17,316	28,543	1.57	6,808	7,957	1.13	11,135	16,007	1.39
1949	33,788	49,497	1.53	16,126	26,321	1.75	6,514	7,706	1.19	11,149	15,470	1.41
1950	38,596	59,822	1.36	18,634	31,078	1.48	7,695	9,284	1.07	12,268	19,460	1.38
1951	43,356	70,242	1.55	21,714	39,306	1.66	8,597	9,886	1.16	13,046	21,050	1.64
1952	44,840	72,377	1.58	22,529	41,136	1.78	8,782	10,210	1.12	13,529	21,031	1.52
1953	47,987	76,122	1.58	24,843	43,948	1.76	9,052	10,686	1.17	14,091	21,488	1.53
1954	46,443	73,175	1.60	23,355	41,612	1.81	8,993	10,637	1.18	14,095	20,926	1.51
1955	51,694	79,516	1.47	26,480	45,069	1.62	9,893	11,678	1.13	15,321	22,769	1.43
1956	54,063	87,304	1.55	27,740	50,642	1.73	10,513	13,260	1.19	15,811	23,402	1.47
1957	55,879	89,052	1.59	28,736	51,871	1.80	10,475	12,730	1.23	16,667	24,451	1.44
1958	54,201	87,093	1.60	27,247	50,241	1.84	10,257	12,739	1.24	16,696	24,113	1.43
1959	59,729	92,129	1.50	30,286	52,945	1.70	11,491	13,879	1.15	17,951	25,305	1.40
1960	60,827	94,713	1.56	30,879	53,780	1.75	11,656	14,120	1.22	18,294	26,813	1.45
1961	61,159	95,594	1.54	30,923	54,885	1.74	11,988	14,488	1.20	18,249	26,221	1.43
1962	65,662	101,063	1.50	33,357	58,186	1.70	12,674	14,936	1.16	19,630	27,941	1.38
1963	68,995	105,480	1.49	35,058	60,046	1.69	13,382	16,048	1.15	20,556	29,386	1.39
1964	73,682	111,503	1.47	37,331	63,409	1.64	14,529	17,000	1.14	21,823	31,094	1.40
1965	80,283	120,907	1.45	40,995	68,185	1.60	15,611	18,317	1.15	23,677	34,405	1.39
1966	87,187	136,790	1.47	44,870	77,952	1.62	16,987	20,765	1.15	25,330	38,073	1.44
1967	90,348	144,796	1.56	46,487	84,664	1.76	19,448	24,833	1.24	24,413	35,299	1.43
1968	98,104	155,697	1.54	50,228	90,618	1.74	20,846	26,134	1.23	27,030	38,945	1.38
1969	105,003	169,343	1.55	53,501	98,202	1.77	22,609	28,624	1.22	28,893	42,517	1.41
1970	107,448	177,556	1.62	52,805	101,651	1.90	23,943	32,038	1.27	30,700	43,867	1.41
1971	116,017	187,766	1.58	55,906	102,658	1.83	26,257	35,045	1.27	33,853	50,063	1.41
1972	130,030	201,950	1.49	63,023	108,238	1.67	29,584	38,633	1.24	37,422	55,079	1.40
1973	153,412	233,237	1.41	72,937	124,628	1.58	38,014	45,372	1.11	42,462	63,237	1.40
1974	177,625	285,807	1.45	84,794	157,792	1.65	47,748	56,948	1.07	45,082	71,067	1.48
1975	182,230	288,375	1.57	86,595	159,934	1.84	46,623	56,697	1.21	49,012	71,744	1.44
1976	204,277	318,544	1.48	98,802	175,193	1.69	50,694	64,078	1.19	54,781	79,273	1.38
1977	229,623	351,176	1.46	113,201	189,334	1.61	55,987	72,311	1.21	60,435	89,530	1.40
1978	259,046	397,090	1.44	126,953	210,679	1.57	65,036	83,891	1.21	67,057	102,520	1.43
1979	294,573	444,132	1.43	143,935	241,034	1.57	76,109	93,870	1.18	74,529	109,228	1.44
1980	321,504	482,570	1.45	154,249	264,016	1.66	87,931	104,441	1.13	79,325	114,114	1.41
1981	350,622	519,394	1.43	166,217	283,152	1.66	97,839	110,549	1.09	86,566	125,693	1.39
1981:												
Jan	347,858	485,396	1.40	163,902	266,798	1.63	99,852	104,233	1.04	84,104	114,365	1.36
Feb	348,653	490,291	1.41	164,676	269,146	1.63	98,776	105,027	1.06	85,201	116,118	1.36
Mar	350,281	492,399	1.41	165,936	271,062	1.63	98,217	105,189	1.07	86,128	116,148	1.35
Apr	352,855	494,177	1.40	167,649	272,060	1.62	98,944	105,149	1.06	86,263	116,968	1.36
May	353,698	497,812	1.41	168,073	274,196	1.63	99,264	105,425	1.06	86,361	118,191	1.37
June	356,524	501,531	1.41	170,951	274,616	1.61	98,274	106,904	1.09	87,299	120,010	1.37
July	355,236	504,744	1.42	170,333	276,983	1.63	97,611	105,768	1.08	87,292	121,993	1.40
Aug	354,520	510,099	1.44	169,274	279,102	1.65	97,285	107,656	1.11	87,961	123,341	1.40
Sept	353,725	515,349	1.46	168,156	282,209	1.68	97,746	108,764	1.11	87,823	124,376	1.42
Oct	346,605	518,241	1.50	163,957	284,386	1.73	96,235	108,491	1.13	86,413	125,364	1.45
Nov	344,943	521,574	1.51	161,442	285,784	1.77	96,768	110,173	1.14	86,733	125,618	1.45
Dec	341,330	519,394	1.52	159,614	283,152	1.77	95,144	110,549	1.16	86,572	125,693	1.45
1982:												
Jan	334,579	516,256	1.54	155,023	281,155	1.81	94,236	110,971	1.18	85,320	124,131	1.45
Feb	340,571	513,906	1.51	158,142	281,688	1.78	95,010	108,823	1.15	87,418	123,395	1.41
Mar	342,121	513,054	1.50	157,517	280,065	1.78	97,361	109,657	1.13	87,242	123,332	1.41
Apr	339,835	515,074	1.52	156,114	278,985	1.79	95,427	112,913	1.18	88,294	123,175	1.40
May	349,096	510,517	1.46	160,828	276,449	1.72	97,427	111,701	1.15	90,841	122,367	1.35
June	346,126	512,981	1.48	161,519	275,115	1.70	96,565	113,515	1.18	88,042	124,351	1.41
July	344,603	513,387	1.49	161,382	274,914	1.70	93,776	113,534	1.21	89,445	124,939	1.40
Aug	339,464	514,554	1.52	158,619	274,302	1.73	92,343	113,101	1.22	88,502	127,151	1.44
Sept	339,470	515,399	1.52	159,278	272,474	1.71	90,866	113,852	1.25	89,326	129,073	1.44
Oct	332,537	514,224	1.55	152,473	271,710	1.78	89,774	113,886	1.27	90,290	128,628	1.42
Nov [p]	335,938	508,553	1.51	152,343	269,297	1.77	90,982	112,669	1.24	92,613	126,587	1.37

[1] Monthly average for year and total for month.
[2] Seasonally adjusted, end of period.
[3] Inventory/sales ratio. For annual periods, ratio of weighted average inventories to average monthly sales; for monthly data, ratio of inventories at end of month to sales for month.

Note.—Earlier data are not strictly comparable with data beginning 1958 for manufacturing and beginning 1967 for wholesale and retail trade.

The inventory figures in this table do not agree with the estimates of change in business inventories included in the gross national product since these figures cover only manufacturing and trade rather than all business, and show inventories in terms of current book value without adjustment for revaluation.

Source: Department of Commerce (Bureau of Economic Analysis and Bureau of the Census).

TABLE B–50.—*Manufacturers' shipments and inventories, 1947–82*

[Millions of dollars; monthly data seasonally adjusted]

Year or month	Shipments[1]			Inventories[2]								
	Total	Durable goods industries	Nondurable goods industries	Total	Durable goods industries				Nondurable goods industries			
					Total	Materials and supplies	Work in process	Finished goods	Total	Materials and supplies	Work in process	Finished goods
1947	15,513	6,694	8,819	25,897	13,061				12,836			
1948	17,316	7,579	9,738	28,543	14,662				13,881			
1949	16,126	7,191	8,935	26,321	13,060				13,261			
1950	18,634	8,845	9,789	31,078	15,539				15,539			
1951	21,714	10,493	11,221	39,306	20,991				18,315			
1952	22,529	11,313	11,216	41,136	23,731				17,405			
1953	24,843	13,349	11,494	43,948	25,878	8,966	10,720	6,206	18,070	8,317	2,472	7,409
1954	23,355	11,828	11,527	41,612	23,710	7,894	9,721	6,040	17,902	8,167	2,440	7,415
1955	26,480	14,071	12,409	45,069	26,405	9,194	10,756	6,348	18,664	8,556	2,571	7,666
1956	27,740	14,715	13,025	50,642	30,447	10,417	12,317	7,565	20,195	8,971	2,721	8,622
1957	28,736	15,237	13,499	51,871	31,728	10,608	12,837	8,125	20,143	8,775	2,864	8,624
1958	27,247	13,563	13,684	50,241	30,258	10,032	12,387	7,839	19,983	8,662	2,828	8,491
1959	30,286	15,609	14,677	52,945	32,077	10,776	13,063	8,239	20,868	9,080	2,944	8,845
1960	30,879	15,883	14,996	53,780	32,371	10,353	12,772	9,245	21,409	9,082	2,946	9,380
1961	30,923	15,616	15,307	54,885	32,544	10,279	13,203	9,063	22,341	9,493	3,110	9,738
1962	33,357	17,262	16,095	58,186	34,632	10,810	14,159	9,662	23,554	9,813	3,296	10,444
1963	35,058	18,280	16,778	60,046	35,866	11,068	14,871	9,925	24,180	9,978	3,406	10,796
1964	37,331	19,637	17,694	63,409	38,506	11,970	16,191	10,344	24,903	10,131	3,511	11,261
1965	40,995	22,221	18,774	68,185	42,257	13,325	18,075	10,854	25,928	10,448	3,806	11,674
1966	44,870	24,649	20,220	77,952	49,920	15,489	21,939	12,491	28,032	11,155	4,204	12,673
1967	46,487	25,267	21,220	84,664	55,005	16,455	25,005	13,547	29,659	11,715	4,421	13,523
1968	50,228	27,659	22,570	90,618	58,875	17,376	27,336	14,163	31,743	12,289	4,848	14,606
1969	53,501	29,437	24,064	98,202	64,739	18,693	30,408	15,639	33,463	12,724	5,122	15,617
1970	52,805	28,188	24,617	101,651	66,780	19,182	29,848	17,751	34,871	13,150	5,274	16,448
1971	55,906	29,954	25,952	102,658	66,289	19,759	28,650	17,880	36,368	13,683	5,665	17,019
1972	63,023	34,024	29,000	108,238	70,250	20,860	30,788	18,601	37,988	14,676	5,982	17,330
1973	72,937	39,686	33,250	124,628	81,398	26,028	35,545	19,823	43,230	18,132	6,707	18,391
1974	84,794	44,228	40,567	157,792	101,739	35,151	42,603	23,985	56,053	23,699	8,175	24,179
1975	86,595	43,656	42,939	159,934	102,874	33,920	43,369	25,586	57,060	23,542	8,837	24,681
1976	98,802	50,689	48,113	175,193	112,581	37,548	46,345	28,690	62,612	25,833	9,933	26,846
1977	113,201	59,267	53,934	189,334	121,737	40,350	50,625	30,763	67,598	27,397	10,989	29,212
1978	126,953	67,848	59,104	210,679	138,045	45,334	58,694	34,018	72,634	29,354	11,913	31,367
1979	143,935	76,060	67,875	241,034	160,601	52,805	69,212	38,585	80,433	32,479	13,710	34,244
1980	154,249	77,540	76,708	264,016	174,674	55,310	76,851	42,513	89,341	36,208	15,656	37,478
1981	166,217	83,417	82,800	283,152	188,429	58,461	82,814	47,153	94,723	38,015	16,196	40,511
1981:												
Jan	163,902	81,436	82,466	266,798	176,632	56,409	78,337	41,887	90,166	36,820	15,818	37,528
Feb	164,676	82,176	82,500	269,146	177,725	56,754	78,662	42,309	91,421	37,050	16,126	38,245
Mar	165,936	83,510	82,426	271,062	178,374	56,382	79,159	42,835	92,688	36,974	16,194	39,521
Apr	167,649	84,784	82,864	272,060	179,301	56,757	79,733	42,812	92,759	37,206	16,263	39,290
May	168,073	85,439	82,634	274,196	180,010	56,394	80,435	43,180	94,186	37,305	16,509	40,372
June	170,951	86,891	84,060	274,616	181,125	57,017	80,362	43,744	93,492	37,074	16,161	40,257
July	170,333	85,739	84,594	276,983	183,229	58,016	81,041	44,172	93,754	37,531	16,174	40,048
Aug	169,274	85,223	84,051	279,102	185,022	58,121	81,635	45,266	94,080	37,447	16,251	40,382
Sept	168,156	84,671	83,485	282,209	187,686	58,908	82,621	46,158	94,523	37,606	16,213	40,705
Oct	163,957	81,265	82,692	284,386	189,461	59,117	83,588	46,756	94,925	37,720	15,912	41,293
Nov	161,442	80,279	81,163	285,784	190,222	59,216	84,058	46,946	95,561	37,834	16,174	41,555
Dec	159,614	79,133	80,481	283,152	188,429	58,461	82,814	47,153	94,723	38,015	16,196	40,511
1982:												
Jan	155,023	75,551	79,472	281,155	187,054	58,184	82,211	46,659	94,100	37,961	15,959	40,179
Feb	158,142	77,976	80,167	281,688	187,121	57,999	82,097	47,026	94,567	37,899	15,792	40,877
Mar	157,517	78,124	79,394	280,065	186,063	56,897	81,729	47,435	94,002	37,317	15,629	41,057
Apr	156,114	77,136	78,978	278,985	185,916	56,947	81,562	47,408	93,070	37,486	15,601	39,983
May	160,828	79,518	81,310	276,449	184,870	55,996	81,284	47,590	91,579	37,172	15,438	38,969
June	161,519	78,888	82,631	275,115	184,289	55,643	81,304	47,342	90,826	36,714	15,555	38,557
July	161,382	79,036	82,346	274,914	183,798	55,781	80,216	47,801	91,116	36,789	15,519	38,808
Aug	158,619	77,248	81,371	274,302	183,550	55,191	80,458	47,901	90,752	36,448	15,529	38,775
Sept	159,278	76,562	82,716	272,474	182,793	54,703	80,379	47,711	89,681	35,800	15,192	38,689
Oct	152,473	72,342	80,131	271,710	181,843	54,279	80,567	46,997	89,867	35,637	14,857	39,373
Nov [p]	152,343	72,708	79,635	269,297	179,324	53,624	79,995	45,705	89,973	35,814	14,793	39,366

[1] Monthly average for year and total for month.

[2] Book value, seasonally adjusted, end of period.

Note.—Data beginning 1958 are not strictly comparable with earlier data.

Source: Department of Commerce, Bureau of the Census.

TABLE B–51.—*Manufacturers' new and unfilled orders, 1947–82*

[Amounts in millions of dollars; monthly data seasonally adjusted]

Year or month	New orders [1]				Unfilled orders [2]			Unfilled orders—shipments ratio [3]		
	Total	Durable goods industries		Nondurable goods industries	Total	Durable goods industries	Nondurable goods industries	Total	Durable goods industries	Nondurable goods industries
		Total	Capital goods industries, nondefense							
1947	15,256	6,388	....	8,868	34,473	28,579	5,894	....	....	....
1948	17,693	8,126	....	9,566	30,736	26,619	4,117	....	....	....
1949	15,614	6,633	....	8,981	24,045	19,622	4,423	....	....	....
1950	20,110	10,165	....	9,945	41,456	35,435	6,021	....	....	....
1951	23,907	12,841	....	11,066	67,266	63,394	3,872	....	....	....
1952	23,204	12,061	....	11,143	75,857	72,680	3,177	....	....	....
1953	23,586	12,147	....	11,439	61,178	58,637	2,541	....	....	....
1954	22,335	10,768	....	11,566	48,266	45,250	3,016	3.42	4.12	0.96
1955	27,465	14,996	....	12,469	60,004	56,241	3,763	3.63	4.27	1.12
1956	28,368	15,365	....	13,003	67,375	63,880	3,495	3.87	4.55	1.04
1957	27,559	14,111	....	13,448	53,183	50,352	2,831	3.35	4.00	.85
1958	27,002	13,290	....	13,712	47,370	44,559	2,811	3.09	3.69	.86
1959	30,724	16,003	....	14,720	52,732	49,373	3,359	3.01	3.54	.94
1960	30,235	15,303	....	14,932	45,080	42,514	2,566	2.78	3.37	.72
1961	31,104	15,759	....	15,345	47,407	44,375	3,032	2.63	3.13	.79
1962	33,436	17,374	....	16,061	48,577	45,965	2,612	2.69	3.24	.68
1963	35,524	18,709	....	16,815	54,327	51,270	3,057	2.80	3.37	.73
1964	38,357	20,652	....	17,705	66,882	63,691	3,191	3.10	3.72	.72
1965	42,100	23,278	....	18,823	80,071	76,298	3,773	3.33	3.95	.80
1966	46,402	26,177	....	20,225	98,401	94,575	3,826	3.81	4.55	.76
1967	47,056	25,825	....	21,231	104,547	100,576	3,971	3.70	4.40	.73
1968	50,687	28,116	6,903	22,571	109,926	105,950	3,976	3.85	4.65	.69
1969	53,950	29,871	7,660	24,079	115,422	111,250	4,172	3.75	4.50	.69
1970	52,038	27,388	6,738	24,650	106,158	101,566	4,592	3.65	4.39	.77
1971	55,983	29,998	7,444	25,986	107,147	102,119	5,027	3.38	4.06	.77
1972	64,167	35,064	8,622	29,104	121,061	114,725	6,336	3.31	3.90	.88
1973	76,259	42,930	10,971	33,330	161,256	153,876	7,380	3.91	4.63	.93
1974	87,268	46,853	12,673	40,415	191,102	185,560	5,542	4.19	5.03	.64
1975	85,149	42,019	11,011	43,130	173,829	165,930	7,898	3.80	4.57	.84
1976	99,543	51,398	12,799	48,145	182,499	174,211	8,288	3.34	3.99	.76
1977	115,027	61,076	15,276	53,951	204,880	196,417	8,463	3.30	3.92	.70
1978	131,664	72,410	19,444	59,254	261,941	251,663	10,278	3.62	4.26	.78
1979	147,354	79,394	23,203	67,960	303,178	291,883	11,295	3.89	4.63	.76
1980	155,738	79,060	23,449	76,678	320,977	310,051	10,926	3.79	4.53	.67
1981	166,015	83,272	24,061	82,743	318,621	308,370	10,251	3.77	4.59	.59
1981:										
Jan	164,976	82,528	25,063	82,447	322,053	311,146	10,907	3.80	4.56	.66
Feb	165,375	82,699	21,857	82,677	322,749	311,666	11,084	3.77	4.53	.66
Mar	166,240	83,862	24,456	82,378	323,054	312,018	11,036	3.71	4.45	.65
Apr	169,422	86,410	25,687	83,013	324,826	313,642	11,184	3.70	4.44	.65
May	170,281	87,396	24,488	82,885	327,033	315,597	11,436	3.70	4.43	.67
June	171,022	86,911	24,039	84,111	327,105	315,618	11,487	3.66	4.37	.67
July	172,089	87,582	24,655	84,507	328,861	317,462	11,399	3.68	4.42	.65
Aug	168,797	84,819	24,867	83,979	328,384	317,057	11,327	3.68	4.42	.65
Sept	167,728	84,456	24,312	83,272	327,955	316,841	11,114	3.70	4.46	.63
Oct	159,558	77,193	22,528	82,365	323,556	312,769	10,787	3.76	4.55	.62
Nov	159,460	78,592	24,369	80,868	321,574	311,082	10,492	3.76	4.56	.60
Dec	156,660	76,421	22,130	80,239	318,621	308,370	10,251	3.77	4.59	.59
1982:										
Jan	154,519	75,061	21,717	79,458	318,114	307,877	10,237	3.90	4.76	.60
Feb	155,984	76,309	21,560	79,676	315,957	306,211	9,746	3.78	4.62	.56
Mar	157,198	77,859	22,174	79,339	315,639	305,947	9,692	3.76	4.61	.55
Apr	154,995	76,194	22,608	78,803	314,521	305,004	9,518	3.86	4.71	.57
May	156,791	75,710	20,332	81,081	310,482	301,194	9,288	3.71	4.52	.55
June	157,058	74,550	19,278	82,508	306,032	296,866	9,166	3.69	4.51	.54
July	158,588	76,446	20,322	82,142	303,235	294,272	8,963	3.67	4.49	.53
Aug	154,380	72,982	18,893	81,398	299,001	290,011	8,990	3.69	4.55	.52
Sept	156,166	73,266	20,273	82,900	295,883	286,706	9,177	3.63	4.46	.54
Oct	149,696	69,598	20,183	80,098	293,107	283,960	9,147	3.77	4.66	.54
Nov [p]	150,362	70,607	20,173	79,755	291,128	281,861	9,267	3.72	4.61	.54

[1] Monthly average for year and total for month.

[2] Seasonally adjusted, end of period.

[3] Ratio of unfilled orders at end of period to shipments for period; excludes industries with no unfilled orders. Annual figures relate to seasonally adjusted data for December.

Note.—Data beginning 1958 are not strictly comparable with earlier data.

Source: Department of Commerce, Bureau of the Census.

TABLE B–52.—*Consumer price indexes, major expenditure classes, 1929–82*

[1967=100]

Year or month	All items	Food and beverages: Total [1]	Food and beverages: Food	Housing: Total [2]	Housing: Rent, residential	Housing: Home ownership	Housing: Fuel and other utilities [3]	Apparel and upkeep	Transportation	Medical care	Entertainment	Other goods and services	Energy [4]
1929	51.3		48.3		76.0			48.5					
1933	38.8		30.6		54.1			36.9					
1939	41.6		34.6	52.2	56.0			42.4	43.0	36.7			
1940	42.0		35.2	52.4	56.2			42.8	42.7	36.8			
1941	44.1		38.4	53.7	57.2			44.8	44.2	37.0			
1942	48.8		45.1	56.2	58.5			52.3	48.1	38.0			
1943	51.8		50.3	56.8	58.5			54.0	47.9	39.9			
1944	52.7		49.6	58.1	58.6			58.5	47.9	41.1			
1945	53.9		50.7	59.1	58.8			61.5	47.8	42.1			
1946	58.5		58.1	60.6	59.2			67.5	50.3	44.4			
1947	66.9		70.6	65.2	61.1			78.2	55.5	48.1			
1948	72.1		76.6	69.8	65.1			83.3	61.8	51.1			
1949	71.4		73.5	70.9	68.0			80.1	66.4	52.7			
1950	72.1		74.5	72.8	70.4			79.0	68.2	53.7			
1951	77.8		82.8	77.2	73.2			86.1	72.5	56.3			
1952	79.5		84.3	78.7	76.2			85.3	77.3	59.3			
1953	80.1		83.0	80.8	80.3	75.0	83.0	84.6	79.5	61.4			
1954	80.5		82.8	81.7	83.2	76.3	83.5	84.5	78.3	63.4			
1955	80.2		81.6	82.3	84.3	77.0	85.1	84.1	77.4	64.8			
1956	81.4		82.2	83.6	85.9	78.3	87.3	85.8	78.8	67.2			
1957	84.3		84.9	86.2	87.5	81.7	89.9	87.3	83.3	69.9			90.1
1958	86.6		88.5	87.7	89.1	83.5	91.7	87.5	86.0	73.2			90.3
1959	87.3		87.1	88.6	90.4	84.4	93.8	88.2	89.6	76.4			91.8
1960	88.7		88.0	90.2	91.7	86.3	95.9	89.6	89.6	79.1			94.2
1961	89.6		89.1	90.9	92.9	86.9	97.1	90.4	90.6	81.4			94.4
1962	90.6		89.9	91.7	94.0	87.9	97.3	90.9	92.5	83.5			94.7
1963	91.7		91.2	92.7	95.0	89.0	98.2	91.9	93.0	85.6			95.0
1964	92.9		92.4	93.8	95.9	90.8	98.4	92.7	94.3	87.3			94.6
1965	94.5		94.4	94.9	96.9	92.7	98.3	93.7	95.9	89.5			96.3
1966	97.2		99.1	97.2	98.2	96.3	98.8	96.1	97.2	93.4			97.8
1967	100.0	100.0	100.0	100.0	100.0	100.0	100.0	100.0	100.0	100.0	100.0	100.0	100.0
1968	104.2	103.6	103.6	104.0	102.4	105.7	101.3	105.4	103.2	106.1	105.7	105.2	101.5
1969	109.8	108.8	108.9	110.4	105.7	116.0	103.6	111.5	107.2	113.4	111.0	110.4	104.2
1970	116.3	114.7	114.9	118.2	110.1	128.5	107.6	116.1	112.7	120.6	116.7	116.8	107.0
1971	121.3	118.3	118.4	123.4	115.2	133.7	115.0	119.8	118.6	128.4	122.9	122.4	111.2
1972	125.3	123.2	123.5	128.1	119.2	140.1	120.1	122.3	119.9	132.5	126.5	127.5	114.3
1973	133.1	139.5	141.4	133.7	124.3	146.7	126.9	126.8	123.8	137.7	130.0	132.5	123.5
1974	147.7	158.7	161.7	148.8	130.6	163.2	150.2	136.2	137.7	150.5	139.8	142.0	159.7
1975	161.2	172.1	175.4	164.5	137.3	181.7	167.8	142.3	150.6	168.6	152.2	153.9	176.6
1976	170.5	177.4	180.8	174.6	144.7	191.7	182.7	147.6	165.5	184.7	159.8	162.7	189.3
1977	181.5	188.0	192.2	186.5	153.5	204.9	202.2	154.2	177.2	202.4	167.7	172.2	207.3
1978	195.4	206.3	211.4	202.8	164.0	227.2	216.0	159.6	185.5	219.4	176.6	183.3	220.4
1979	217.4	228.5	234.5	227.6	176.0	262.4	239.3	166.6	212.0	239.7	188.5	196.7	275.9
1980	246.8	248.0	254.6	263.3	191.6	314.0	278.6	178.4	249.7	265.9	205.3	214.5	361.1
1981	272.4	267.3	274.6	293.5	208.2	352.7	319.2	186.9	280.0	294.5	221.4	235.7	410.0
1982	289.1	278.2	285.7	314.7	224.0	376.8	350.8	191.8	291.5	328.7	235.8	259.9	416.1
1981:													
Jan	260.5	261.4	268.6	279.1	200.9	335.8	296.7	181.1	264.7	279.5	214.4	226.2	381.7
Feb	263.2	263.7	270.8	280.9	201.9	335.8	304.5	182.0	270.9	282.6	216.7	227.4	401.1
Mar	265.1	265.0	272.2	282.6	203.0	336.8	308.4	185.1	273.5	284.7	218.2	228.7	409.3
Apr	266.8	265.7	272.9	284.8	204.2	339.3	310.5	186.4	275.3	287.0	219.2	229.9	409.8
May	269.0	265.4	272.5	288.5	205.9	345.0	314.9	186.4	277.8	289.0	220.3	232.2	411.3
June	271.3	266.5	273.6	292.2	206.8	350.4	320.2	185.8	279.9	291.5	220.8	233.4	414.0
July	274.4	268.9	276.2	297.0	207.8	358.0	325.1	184.7	282.6	295.6	221.1	234.4	415.7
Aug	276.5	270.1	277.4	299.7	210.3	361.8	327.8	187.4	283.7	299.3	222.3	235.6	416.1
Sept	279.3	270.7	278.0	303.7	211.9	367.8	331.1	190.7	285.2	301.7	224.0	243.0	417.1
Oct	279.9	270.3	277.6	303.5	213.6	366.7	330.1	191.5	287.2	304.8	225.5	245.2	414.9
Nov	280.7	269.9	277.1	304.2	215.0	367.2	329.8	191.3	289.1	308.2	226.8	245.9	414.1
Dec	281.5	270.5	277.8	305.2	216.5	367.8	331.8	190.5	289.8	310.2	227.3	246.7	414.6
1982:													
Jan	282.5	273.6	281.0	306.1	217.8	367.5	336.2	187.3	289.9	313.4	229.2	248.4	416.4
Feb	283.4	275.8	283.3	307.3	218.6	368.7	337.1	188.0	288.0	316.2	231.2	250.3	413.0
Mar	283.1	275.6	283.0	306.7	219.6	365.7	339.3	191.1	285.1	318.8	232.8	252.2	406.1
Apr	284.3	276.5	283.9	309.4	220.1	370.6	339.2	191.9	282.9	321.7	233.9	253.8	395.7
May	287.1	278.1	285.5	313.8	221.8	377.4	345.4	191.5	285.6	323.8	234.4	255.0	402.1
June	290.6	280.2	287.8	317.5	222.6	382.8	352.2	190.8	292.8	326.4	235.6	255.8	418.6
July	292.2	280.8	288.5	319.2	224.8	384.5	354.7	189.7	296.1	330.0	236.6	257.2	424.5
Aug	292.8	279.9	287.4	320.1	226.0	385.9	356.3	191.8	296.2	333.3	237.4	258.3	424.5
Sept	293.3	280.1	287.6	319.7	226.9	383.0	359.5	194.9	295.3	336.0	238.3	266.6	424.2
Oct	294.1	279.6	287.0	320.7	228.9	382.8	363.4	195.5	295.5	338.7	240.3	271.2	425.0
Nov	293.6	279.1	286.4	319.0	230.2	379.5	362.2	195.4	295.8	342.2	239.9	273.8	422.6
Dec	292.4	279.1	286.5	316.3	230.8	372.9	364.1	193.6	294.8	344.3	240.1	276.6	419.9

[1] Includes alcoholic beverages, not shown separately.
[2] Includes other items not shown separately. Series beginning 1967 not comparable with series for earlier years.
[3] Fuel oil, coal, and bottled gas; gas (piped) and electricity; and other utilities and public services.
[4] Fuel oil, coal, and bottled gas; gas (piped) and electricity; and motor fuel, motor oil, coolant, etc.

Note.—Data beginning 1978 are for all urban consumers; earlier data are for urban wage earners and clerical workers.

Source: Department of Labor, Bureau of Labor Statistics.

384-041 O - 83 - 15 : QL 3

Table B-53.—*Consumer price indexes, selected expenditure classes, 1939–82*

[1967=100]

Year or month	Food and beverages				Homeownership				Fuel and other utilities				
	Total[1]	Food			Total	Home purchase	Financing, taxes, and insurance	Maintenance and repair	Total	Household fuels			Other utilities and public services
		Total	At home	Away from home						Total	Fuel oil, coal, and bottled gas	Gas (piped) and electricity	
1939	...	34.6	...	...	...	...	...	...	...	...	37.1	82.9	...
1940	...	35.2	...	...	...	...	...	...	...	...	38.2	82.1	...
1941	...	38.4	...	...	...	...	...	...	...	...	40.5	81.4	...
1942	...	45.1	...	...	...	...	...	...	...	...	43.1	81.0	...
1943	...	50.3	...	...	...	...	...	...	...	...	45.2	80.6	...
1944	...	49.6	...	...	...	...	...	...	...	...	47.1	80.3	...
1945	...	50.7	...	...	...	...	...	...	...	...	40.0	79.0	...
1946	...	58.1	...	...	...	...	...	...	...	...	51.3	77.4	...
1947	...	70.6	73.5	...	...	...	...	...	...	...	58.4	77.1	...
1948	...	76.6	79.8	...	...	...	...	...	...	...	68.6	79.1	...
1949	...	73.5	76.7	...	...	...	...	...	...	...	70.3	81.0	...
1950	...	74.5	77.6	...	...	...	...	...	...	...	72.7	81.2	...
1951	...	82.8	86.3	...	...	...	...	...	...	...	76.5	81.5	...
1952	...	84.3	87.8	...	...	...	...	...	...	...	78.0	82.6	...
1953	...	83.0	86.2	68.9	75.0	86.5	...	71.2	83.0	...	81.5	84.2	...
1954	...	82.8	85.8	70.1	76.3	87.1	...	72.4	83.5	...	81.2	85.3	...
1955	...	81.6	84.1	70.8	77.0	87.3	...	74.1	85.1	...	82.3	87.5	...
1956	...	82.2	84.4	72.2	78.3	87.6	...	77.2	87.3	...	85.9	88.4	...
1957	...	84.9	87.2	74.9	81.7	90.0	...	80.5	89.9	...	90.3	89.3	...
1958	...	88.5	91.0	77.2	83.5	91.3	...	81.8	91.7	...	88.7	92.4	...
1959	...	87.1	88.8	79.3	84.4	91.3	...	83.2	93.8	...	89.8	94.7	...
1960	...	88.0	89.6	81.4	86.3	91.8	...	84.6	95.9	...	89.2	98.6	...
1961	...	89.1	90.4	83.2	86.9	92.3	...	85.9	97.1	...	91.0	99.4	...
1962	...	89.9	91.0	85.4	87.9	93.2	...	86.5	97.3	...	91.5	99.4	...
1963	...	91.2	92.2	87.3	89.0	94.2	...	87.7	98.2	...	93.2	99.4	...
1964	...	92.4	93.2	88.9	90.8	95.7	...	89.5	98.4	...	92.7	99.4	...
1965	...	94.4	95.5	90.9	92.7	97.0	...	91.3	98.3	...	94.6	99.4	...
1966	...	99.1	100.3	95.1	96.3	98.6	...	95.2	98.8	...	97.0	99.6	...
1967	100.0	100.0	100.0	100.0	100.0	100.0	100.0	100.0	100.0	100.0	100.0	100.0	100.0
1968	103.6	103.6	103.2	105.2	105.7	102.8	108.3	106.1	101.3	101.4	103.1	100.9	101.2
1969	108.8	108.9	108.2	111.6	116.0	109.5	123.7	115.0	103.6	103.4	105.6	102.8	104.0
1970	114.7	114.9	113.7	119.9	128.5	118.3	142.3	124.0	107.6	107.9	110.1	107.3	107.4
1971	118.3	118.4	116.4	126.1	133.7	124.8	143.5	133.7	115.0	115.3	117.5	114.7	114.7
1972	123.2	123.5	121.6	131.1	140.1	130.0	150.8	140.7	120.1	120.1	118.5	120.5	120.6
1973	139.5	141.4	141.4	141.4	146.7	132.7	160.6	151.0	126.9	128.4	136.0	126.4	124.1
1974	158.7	161.7	162.4	159.4	163.2	142.7	181.1	171.6	150.2	160.7	214.6	145.8	130.3
1975	172.1	175.4	175.8	174.3	181.7	160.3	201.9	187.6	167.8	183.8	235.3	169.6	137.1
1976	177.4	180.8	179.5	186.1	191.7	168.4	212.8	199.6	182.7	202.3	250.8	189.0	145.4
1977	188.0	192.2	190.2	200.3	204.9	179.5	227.2	214.7	202.2	228.6	283.4	213.4	152.0
1978	206.3	211.4	210.2	218.4	227.2	196.7	257.8	233.0	216.0	247.4	298.3	232.6	158.3
1979	228.5	234.5	232.9	242.9	262.4	223.1	308.9	256.4	239.3	286.4	403.1	257.8	159.5
1980	248.0	254.6	251.5	267.0	314.0	254.3	396.0	285.7	278.6	349.4	556.0	301.8	165.2
1981	267.3	274.6	269.9	291.0	352.7	267.7	472.5	314.4	319.2	407.0	675.9	345.9	181.0
1982	278.2	285.7	279.2	306.5	376.8	281.6	511.4	334.1	350.8	446.2	667.9	393.8	200.2
1981:													
Jan	261.4	268.6	265.6	280.9	335.8	266.2	435.2	296.8	296.7	375.4	625.9	318.5	171.9
Feb	263.7	270.8	267.3	284.7	335.8	263.0	437.1	302.8	304.5	387.4	675.6	322.9	173.6
Mar	265.0	272.2	268.6	286.1	336.8	261.1	441.1	306.1	308.4	393.7	693.4	326.7	174.0
Apr	265.7	272.9	268.7	288.2	339.3	260.7	447.1	309.3	310.5	396.5	690.6	330.6	175.1
May	265.4	272.5	267.7	289.3	345.0	263.0	458.3	312.9	314.9	403.3	685.8	339.6	176.2
June	266.5	273.6	268.7	290.6	350.4	266.6	467.2	315.5	320.2	411.7	682.0	350.2	177.1
July	268.9	276.2	271.6	292.4	358.0	271.4	480.0	319.3	325.1	417.2	677.9	357.6	180.8
Aug	270.1	277.4	272.8	293.7	361.8	272.6	488.3	320.5	327.8	419.5	674.6	360.8	183.7
Sept	270.7	278.0	273.2	294.8	367.8	274.5	501.8	321.6	331.1	422.4	673.4	364.5	187.4
Oct	270.3	277.6	272.1	296.2	366.7	272.5	501.8	320.8	330.1	419.0	672.7	360.6	189.4
Nov	269.9	277.1	271.0	297.2	367.2	270.2	505.6	322.8	329.8	417.6	676.1	358.3	190.7
Dec	270.5	277.8	271.7	297.7	367.8	270.5	506.3	324.1	331.8	420.0	682.5	359.9	191.9
1982:													
Jan	273.6	281.0	275.3	299.8	367.5	269.3	506.0	326.7	336.2	426.9	686.0	367.4	192.7
Feb	275.8	283.3	278.0	301.2	368.7	270.4	507.2	328.2	337.1	427.6	683.1	368.7	193.9
Mar	275.6	283.0	277.1	302.4	365.7	269.2	500.9	327.2	339.3	430.5	664.0	375.9	195.0
Apr	276.5	283.9	277.9	303.6	370.6	272.3	508.4	331.6	339.2	428.2	641.3	377.8	197.7
May	278.1	285.5	279.8	304.8	377.4	279.3	516.2	334.5	345.4	438.0	644.6	389.0	198.9
June	280.2	287.8	282.6	305.9	382.8	285.6	521.8	336.1	352.2	448.4	656.6	398.9	200.4
July	280.8	288.5	282.8	307.6	384.5	287.7	524.3	334.7	354.7	452.0	659.9	402.1	201.4
Aug	279.9	287.4	280.8	308.7	385.9	287.9	527.3	335.9	356.3	454.0	659.9	404.4	202.4
Sept	280.1	287.6	280.6	309.8	383.0	286.8	519.9	338.4	359.5	458.5	662.8	409.2	203.6
Oct	279.6	287.0	279.4	310.7	382.8	289.9	514.3	339.4	363.4	464.5	677.2	413.4	204.5
Nov	279.1	286.4	278.3	311.4	379.5	290.4	504.8	339.0	362.2	461.9	691.3	407.6	205.1
Dec	279.1	286.5	277.8	312.6	372.9	290.9	486.2	337.8	364.1	464.0	688.5	410.6	206.6

See next page for continuation of table.

TABLE B–53.—*Consumer price indexes, selected expenditure classes, 1939–82*—Continued

[1967=100]

Year or month	Transportation								Medical care		
	Total	Private transportation						Public transportation	Total	Medical care commodities	Medical care services
		Total	New cars	Used cars	Motor fuel [2]	Automobile maintenance and repair	Other				
1939	43.0	44.2	43.2	...	49.0	43.1	...	33.1	36.7	71.1	32.5
1940	42.7	43.6	43.3	...	48.1	43.0	...	33.1	36.8	70.8	32.5
1941	44.2	45.9	46.6	...	50.5	44.9	...	33.1	37.0	71.4	32.7
1942	48.1	52.3	...	...	53.4	48.8	...	33.3	38.0	73.0	33.7
1943	47.9	51.4	...	...	54.0	49.4	...	33.4	39.9	73.5	35.4
1944	47.9	51.4	...	...	54.2	50.0	...	33.5	41.1	74.3	36.9
1945	47.8	51.3	...	...	53.8	50.4	...	33.5	42.1	74.8	37.9
1946	50.3	54.3	...	...	54.9	52.0	...	34.4	44.4	76.2	40.1
1947	55.5	61.5	69.2	...	62.2	56.4	...	36.0	48.1	81.8	43.5
1948	61.8	68.2	75.6	...	70.4	59.6	...	40.7	51.1	86.1	46.4
1949	66.4	72.3	82.8	...	72.3	61.1	...	45.2	52.7	87.4	48.1
1950	68.2	72.5	83.4	...	71.8	62.3	...	48.9	53.7	88.5	49.2
1951	72.5	75.8	87.4	...	73.9	67.0	...	54.0	56.3	91.0	51.7
1952	77.3	80.8	94.9	...	75.8	68.6	...	57.5	59.3	91.8	55.0
1953	79.5	82.4	95.8	89.2	80.3	72.3	...	61.3	61.4	92.6	57.0
1954	78.3	80.3	94.3	75.9	82.5	74.8	...	65.5	63.4	93.7	58.7
1955	77.4	78.9	90.9	71.8	83.6	76.5	...	67.4	64.8	94.7	60.4
1956	78.8	80.1	93.5	69.1	86.5	79.5	...	70.0	67.2	96.7	62.8
1957	83.3	84.7	98.4	77.4	90.0	82.4	...	72.7	69.9	99.3	65.5
1958	86.0	87.4	101.5	80.2	88.8	83.7	...	76.1	73.2	102.8	68.7
1959	89.6	91.1	105.9	89.5	89.9	85.5	...	78.3	76.4	104.4	72.0
1960	89.6	90.6	104.5	83.6	92.5	87.2	...	81.0	79.1	104.5	74.9
1961	90.6	91.3	104.5	86.9	91.4	89.3	...	84.6	81.4	103.3	77.7
1962	92.5	93.0	104.1	94.8	91.9	90.4	...	87.4	83.5	101.7	80.2
1963	93.0	93.4	103.5	96.0	91.8	91.6	...	88.5	85.6	100.8	82.6
1964	94.3	94.7	103.2	100.1	91.4	92.8	...	90.1	87.3	100.5	84.6
1965	95.9	96.3	100.9	99.4	94.9	94.5	...	91.9	89.5	100.2	87.3
1966	97.2	97.5	99.1	97.0	97.0	96.2	...	95.2	93.4	100.5	92.0
1967	100.0	100.0	100.0	100.0	100.0	100.0	100.0	100.0	100.0	100.0	100.0
1968	103.2	103.0	102.8	([3])	101.4	105.5	103.4	104.6	106.1	100.2	107.3
1969	107.2	106.5	104.4	103.1	104.7	112.2	109.7	112.7	113.4	101.3	116.0
1970	112.7	111.1	107.6	104.3	105.6	120.6	119.2	128.5	120.6	103.6	124.2
1971	118.6	116.6	112.0	110.2	106.3	129.2	128.4	137.7	128.4	105.4	133.3
1972	119.9	117.5	111.0	110.5	107.6	135.1	129.1	143.4	132.5	105.6	138.2
1973	123.8	121.5	111.1	117.6	118.1	142.2	127.8	144.8	137.7	105.9	144.3
1974	137.7	136.6	117.5	122.6	159.9	156.8	132.4	148.0	150.5	109.6	159.1
1975	150.6	149.8	127.6	146.4	170.8	176.6	141.2	158.6	168.6	118.8	179.1
1976	165.5	164.6	135.7	167.9	177.9	189.7	163.1	174.2	184.7	126.0	197.1
1977	177.2	176.6	142.9	182.8	188.2	203.7	177.3	182.4	202.4	134.1	216.7
1978	185.5	185.0	153.8	186.5	196.3	220.6	184.6	187.8	219.4	143.5	235.4
1979	212.0	212.3	166.0	201.0	265.6	242.6	198.6	200.3	239.7	153.8	258.3
1980	249.7	249.2	179.3	208.1	369.1	268.3	222.6	251.6	265.9	168.1	287.4
1981	280.0	277.5	190.2	256.9	410.9	293.6	241.3	312.0	294.5	186.5	318.2
1982	291.5	287.5	197.6	296.4	389.4	315.8	257.8	346.0	328.7	205.7	356.0
1981:											
Jan	264.7	262.9	185.3	234.0	385.2	282.7	232.4	286.4	279.5	176.7	302.1
Feb	270.9	269.4	184.8	234.3	410.8	285.4	234.2	288.1	282.6	179.2	305.2
Mar	273.5	271.7	182.9	235.4	420.7	287.7	234.7	293.9	284.7	180.7	307.5
Apr	275.3	273.4	186.1	239.1	419.3	289.0	236.3	297.2	287.0	182.4	309.8
May	277.8	276.0	190.9	245.2	416.5	290.8	238.9	297.7	289.0	184.7	311.7
June	279.9	277.9	192.2	252.9	414.4	291.9	241.0	303.9	291.5	186.3	314.4
July	282.6	279.6	192.5	260.3	412.9	293.5	242.9	323.1	295.6	187.7	319.2
Aug	283.7	280.5	191.9	266.9	411.7	295.5	243.0	326.5	299.3	189.4	323.4
Sept	285.2	281.9	191.3	272.8	[2] 411.1	298.7	244.2	329.1	301.7	190.8	326.1
Oct	287.2	283.9	192.5	278.2	409.9	301.3	247.5	330.8	304.8	192.1	329.7
Nov	289.1	285.8	195.3	281.4	409.5	302.8	249.5	333.2	308.2	193.1	333.7
Dec	289.8	286.5	197.0	281.9	408.4	304.1	250.6	333.8	310.2	194.9	335.7
1982:											
Jan	289.9	286.6	197.4	280.5	406.1	305.5	253.3	334.9	313.4	195.9	339.4
Feb	288.0	284.5	195.5	279.7	399.2	307.7	253.4	336.8	316.2	197.7	342.4
Mar	285.1	281.3	194.4	280.9	384.1	310.2	254.5	336.7	318.8	200.0	345.1
Apr	282.9	278.8	196.0	285.1	366.9	311.9	255.1	339.3	321.7	202.4	348.0
May	285.6	281.5	197.5	291.4	370.6	313.6	255.7	342.1	323.8	204.1	350.2
June	292.8	288.9	198.1	298.2	392.4	316.0	258.7	345.6	326.4	205.6	353.0
July	296.1	292.3	198.6	302.4	400.2	318.0	260.8	347.2	330.0	206.5	357.3
Aug	296.2	292.4	198.7	304.4	398.4	319.2	260.8	348.1	333.3	208.2	361.0
Sept	295.3	291.1	197.7	304.6	394.2	320.6	260.0	353.3	336.0	209.9	364.0
Oct	295.5	291.1	197.7	306.7	390.7	321.9	261.4	356.3	338.7	211.6	366.9
Nov	295.8	291.4	199.0	310.5	388.3	322.3	260.7	356.0	342.2	212.9	371.0
Dec	294.8	290.4	200.1	312.6	381.7	323.1	259.6	355.6	344.3	213.7	373.4

[1] Includes alcoholic beverages, not shown separately.
[2] Includes direct pricing of diesel fuel and gasohol beginning September 1981.
[3] Not available.

Note.—Data beginning 1978 are for all urban consumers; earlier data are for urban wage earners and clerical workers.

Source: Department of Labor, Bureau of Labor Statistics.

Table B-54.—*Consumer price indexes, commodities, services, and special groups, 1939–82*

[1967=100]

Year or month	All items	Commodities: All commodities	Commodities: Food	Commodities less food: All	Commodities less food: Durable	Commodities less food: Nondurable	Services: All services	Services: Rent	Services: Services less rent	Special indexes: All items less food	Special indexes: All items less energy	Special indexes: All items less food and energy	Special indexes: Energy [1]
1939	41.6	40.2	34.6	47.7	48.5	44.3	43.5	56.0	38.1	47.2	....	....	....
1940	42.0	40.6	35.2	48.0	48.1	44.7	43.6	56.2	38.1	47.3	....	....	....
1941	44.1	43.3	38.4	50.4	51.4	46.7	44.2	57.2	38.6	48.7	....	....	....
1942	48.8	49.6	45.1	56.0	58.4	51.6	45.6	58.5	40.3	52.1	....	....	....
1943	51.8	54.0	50.3	58.4	60.3	53.8	46.4	58.5	42.1	53.6	....	....	....
1944	52.7	54.7	49.6	61.6	65.9	56.6	47.5	58.6	44.2	55.7	....	....	....
1945	53.9	56.3	50.7	64.1	70.9	58.6	48.2	58.8	45.1	56.9	....	....	....
1946	58.5	62.4	58.1	68.1	74.1	62.9	49.1	59.2	46.7	59.4	....	....	....
1947	66.9	75.0	70.6	76.8	80.3	72.2	51.1	61.1	49.0	64.5	....	....	....
1948	72.1	80.4	76.6	82.7	86.2	77.8	54.3	65.1	51.9	69.6	....	....	....
1949	71.4	78.3	73.5	81.5	87.4	76.3	56.9	68.0	54.5	70.3	....	....	....
1950	72.1	78.8	74.5	81.4	88.4	76.2	58.7	70.4	56.0	71.1	....	....	....
1951	77.8	85.9	82.8	87.5	95.1	82.0	61.8	73.2	59.3	75.7	....	....	....
1952	79.5	87.0	84.3	88.3	96.4	82.4	64.5	76.2	62.2	77.5	....	....	....
1953	80.1	86.7	83.0	88.5	95.7	83.1	67.3	80.3	64.8	79.0	....	....	....
1954	80.5	85.9	82.8	87.5	93.3	83.5	69.5	83.2	66.7	79.5	....	....	....
1955	80.2	85.1	81.6	86.9	91.5	83.5	70.9	84.3	68.2	79.7	....	....	....
1956	81.4	85.9	82.2	87.8	91.5	85.3	72.7	85.9	70.1	81.1	....	....	....
1957	84.3	88.6	84.9	90.5	94.4	87.6	75.6	87.5	73.3	83.8	83.9	83.3	90.1
1958	86.6	90.6	88.5	91.5	95.9	88.2	78.5	89.1	76.4	85.7	86.3	85.2	90.3
1959	87.3	90.7	87.1	92.7	97.3	89.3	80.8	90.4	79.0	87.3	87.0	87.0	91.8
1960	88.7	91.5	88.0	93.1	96.7	90.7	83.5	91.7	81.9	88.8	88.3	88.3	94.2
1961	89.6	92.0	89.1	93.4	96.6	91.2	85.2	92.9	83.9	89.7	89.3	89.3	94.4
1962	90.6	92.8	89.9	94.1	97.6	91.8	86.8	94.0	85.5	90.8	90.4	90.5	94.7
1963	91.7	93.6	91.2	94.8	97.9	92.7	88.5	95.0	87.3	92.0	91.6	91.6	95.0
1964	92.9	94.6	92.4	95.6	98.8	93.5	90.2	95.9	89.2	93.2	92.9	93.0	94.6
1965	94.5	95.7	94.4	96.2	98.4	94.8	92.2	96.9	91.5	94.5	94.3	94.3	96.3
1966	97.2	98.2	99.1	97.5	98.5	97.0	95.8	98.2	95.3	96.7	97.3	96.6	97.8
1967	100.0	100.0	100.0	100.0	100.0	100.0	100.0	100.0	100.0	100.0	100.0	100.0	100.0
1968	104.2	103.7	103.6	103.7	103.1	104.1	105.2	102.4	105.7	104.4	104.4	104.6	101.5
1969	109.8	108.4	108.9	108.1	107.0	108.8	112.5	105.7	113.8	110.1	110.3	110.7	104.2
1970	116.3	113.5	114.9	112.5	111.8	113.1	121.6	110.1	123.7	116.7	117.0	117.6	107.0
1971	121.3	117.4	118.4	116.8	116.5	117.0	128.4	115.2	130.8	122.1	122.0	123.1	111.2
1972	125.3	120.9	123.5	119.4	118.9	119.8	133.3	119.2	135.9	125.8	126.1	126.9	114.3
1973	133.1	129.9	141.4	123.5	121.9	124.8	139.1	124.3	141.8	130.7	133.8	131.3	123.5
1974	147.7	145.5	161.7	136.6	130.6	140.9	152.1	130.6	156.0	143.7	146.9	142.2	159.7
1975	161.2	158.4	175.4	149.1	145.5	151.7	166.6	137.3	171.9	157.1	160.2	155.3	176.6
1976	170.5	165.2	180.8	156.6	154.3	158.3	180.4	144.7	186.8	167.5	169.2	165.5	189.3
1977	181.5	174.7	192.2	165.1	163.2	166.5	194.3	153.5	201.6	178.4	179.8	175.8	207.3
1978	195.4	187.1	211.4	174.7	173.9	174.3	210.9	164.0	219.4	191.2	193.8	188.7	220.4
1979	217.4	208.4	234.5	195.1	191.1	198.7	234.2	176.0	244.9	213.0	213.1	207.0	275.9
1980	246.8	233.9	254.6	222.0	210.4	235.2	270.3	191.6	285.1	244.0	238.0	232.8	361.1
1981	272.4	253.6	274.6	241.2	227.1	257.5	305.7	208.2	324.3	270.6	261.7	257.1	410.0
1982	289.1	263.8	285.7	250.9	241.1	261.6	333.3	224.0	354.2	288.4	279.3	276.1	416.1
1981:													
Jan	260.5	245.4	268.6	232.4	221.0	245.3	287.7	200.9	304.2	257.6	251.2	245.7	381.7
Feb	263.2	248.3	270.8	235.4	220.3	253.2	290.1	201.9	306.9	260.4	252.5	246.8	401.1
Mar	265.1	249.8	272.2	237.0	219.8	257.5	292.5	203.0	309.5	262.3	253.8	248.1	409.3
Apr	266.8	250.8	272.9	238.0	221.1	258.1	295.4	204.2	312.8	264.2	255.6	250.1	409.8
May	269.0	251.9	272.5	239.6	223.9	258.2	299.6	205.9	317.4	267.0	257.9	253.0	411.3
June	271.3	253.2	273.6	241.1	226.6	258.0	303.5	206.8	321.9	269.5	260.2	255.6	414.0
July	274.4	255.0	276.2	242.6	229.6	257.5	308.8	207.8	328.1	272.7	263.5	259.0	415.7
Aug	276.5	256.2	277.4	243.8	230.9	258.4	312.2	210.3	331.7	274.9	265.6	261.3	416.1
Sept	279.3	257.7	278.0	245.5	232.6	260.3	317.3	211.9	337.5	278.2	268.6	264.8	417.1
Oct	279.9	257.9	277.6	245.9	232.9	260.7	318.6	213.6	338.7	279.0	269.4	265.9	414.9
Nov	280.7	258.0	277.1	246.2	233.2	261.1	320.6	215.0	340.8	280.1	270.4	267.2	414.1
Dec	281.5	258.4	277.8	246.5	233.7	261.1	321.8	216.5	342.0	280.8	271.1	267.9	414.6
1982:													
Jan	282.5	258.8	281.0	245.9	233.4	260.2	323.9	217.8	344.2	281.4	272.1	268.5	416.4
Feb	283.4	259.5	283.3	246.0	233.7	260.1	325.3	218.6	345.7	282.1	273.4	269.5	413.0
Mar	283.1	258.8	283.0	245.2	233.5	258.4	325.5	219.6	345.7	281.7	273.6	269.8	406.1
Apr	284.3	258.9	283.9	245.0	235.8	255.0	328.4	220.1	349.1	282.9	275.7	272.2	395.7
May	287.1	261.5	285.5	247.8	239.8	256.2	331.8	221.8	352.8	286.0	278.3	274.9	402.1
June	290.6	265.1	287.8	251.9	243.2	261.2	334.9	222.6	356.5	289.7	280.7	277.3	418.6
July	292.2	266.5	288.5	253.5	244.7	263.0	337.0	224.8	358.5	291.5	282.0	278.7	424.5
Aug	292.8	266.4	287.4	253.8	244.6	263.6	338.9	226.0	360.5	292.5	282.7	279.8	424.5
Sept	293.3	266.6	287.6	253.9	244.1	264.6	339.7	226.9	361.3	292.9	283.1	280.4	424.2
Oct	294.1	267.5	287.0	255.4	246.0	265.7	340.3	228.9	361.6	294.0	284.0	281.5	425.0
Nov	293.6	267.8	286.4	256.0	246.6	266.1	338.6	230.2	359.3	293.6	283.6	281.2	422.6
Dec	292.4	267.7	286.5	255.8	247.3	264.7	335.6	230.8	355.5	292.1	282.5	279.9	419.9

[1] Fuel oil, coal, and bottled gas; gas (piped) and electricity; and motor fuel, motor oil, coolant, etc.

Note.—Data beginning 1978 are for all urban consumers; earlier data are for urban wage earners and clerical workers.

Source: Department of Labor, Bureau of Labor Statistics.

Table B-55.—*Changes in consumer price indexes, commodities and services, 1948–82*

[Percent change]

Year or month	All items		Commodities						Services		Energy [2]	
			Total		Food		Commodities less food					
	Dec. to Dec. [1]	Year to year	Dec. to Dec. [1]	Year to year	Dec. to Dec. [1]	Year to year	Dec. to Dec. [1]	Year to year	Dec. to Dec. [1]	Year to year	Dec. to Dec. [1]	Year to year
1948	2.7	7.8	1.7	7.2	−0.8	8.5	5.3	7.7	6.1	6.3	....	....
1949	−1.8	−1.0	−4.1	−2.6	−3.7	−4.0	−4.8	−1.5	3.6	4.8	....	....
1950	5.8	1.0	7.7	.6	9.6	1.4	5.7	−.1	3.6	3.2	....	....
1951	5.9	7.9	5.9	9.0	7.4	11.1	4.6	7.5	5.2	5.3	....	....
1952	.9	2.2	−.7	1.3	−1.1	1.8	−.5	.9	4.6	4.4	....	....
1953	.6	.8	−.6	−.3	−1.3	−1.5	.2	.2	4.2	4.3	....	....
1954	−.5	.5	−1.4	−.9	−1.6	−.2	−1.4	−1.1	1.9	3.3	....	....
1955	.4	−.4	−.4	−.9	−.9	−1.4	0	−.7	2.3	2.0	....	....
1956	2.9	1.5	2.6	.9	3.1	.7	2.5	1.0	3.1	2.5	....	....
1957	3.0	3.6	2.6	3.1	2.8	3.3	2.2	3.1	4.5	4.0	....	....
1958	1.8	2.7	1.3	2.3	2.2	4.2	.8	1.1	2.7	3.8	−0.7	0.2
1959	1.5	.8	.6	.1	−.8	−1.6	1.5	1.3	3.7	2.9	4.3	1.7
1960	1.5	1.6	1.1	.9	3.1	1.0	−.3	.4	2.7	3.3	1.5	2.6
1961	.7	1.0	0	.5	−.9	1.3	.6	.3	1.9	2.0	−1.1	.2
1962	1.2	1.1	1.0	.9	1.5	.9	.7	.7	1.7	1.9	2.1	.3
1963	1.6	1.2	1.4	.9	1.9	1.4	1.2	.7	2.3	2.0	−.8	.3
1964	1.2	1.3	.8	1.1	1.4	1.3	.4	.8	1.8	1.9	−.2	−.4
1965	1.9	1.7	1.6	1.2	3.4	2.2	.7	.6	2.6	2.2	2.0	1.8
1966	3.4	2.9	2.5	2.6	3.9	5.0	1.9	1.4	4.9	3.9	1.8	1.6
1967	3.0	2.9	2.5	1.8	1.2	.9	3.1	2.6	4.0	4.4	1.4	2.2
1968	4.7	4.2	3.8	3.7	4.3	3.6	3.7	3.7	6.1	5.2	1.7	1.5
1969	6.1	5.4	5.5	4.5	7.2	5.1	4.5	4.2	7.4	6.9	3.1	2.7
1970	5.5	5.9	4.0	4.7	2.2	5.5	4.8	4.1	8.2	8.1	4.5	2.7
1971	3.4	4.3	2.9	3.4	4.3	3.0	2.3	3.8	4.1	5.6	3.1	3.9
1972	3.4	3.3	3.4	3.0	4.7	4.3	2.5	2.2	3.6	3.8	2.8	2.8
1973	8.8	6.2	10.4	7.4	20.1	14.5	5.0	3.4	6.2	4.4	16.8	8.0
1974	12.2	11.0	12.7	12.0	12.2	14.4	13.2	10.6	11.3	9.3	21.6	29.3
1975	7.0	9.1	6.3	8.9	6.5	8.5	6.2	9.2	8.1	9.5	11.6	10.6
1976	4.8	5.8	3.3	4.3	.6	3.1	5.1	5.0	7.3	8.3	6.9	7.2
1977	6.8	6.5	6.1	5.8	8.0	6.3	4.9	5.4	7.9	7.7	7.2	9.5
1978	9.0	7.7	8.9	7.1	11.8	10.0	7.7	5.8	9.3	8.5	8.0	6.3
1979	13.3	11.3	13.0	11.4	10.2	10.9	14.3	11.7	13.7	11.0	37.4	25.2
1980	12.4	13.5	11.1	12.2	10.2	8.6	11.5	13.8	14.2	15.4	18.1	30.9
1981	8.9	10.4	6.0	8.4	4.3	7.9	6.7	8.6	13.0	13.1	11.9	13.5
1982	3.9	6.1	3.6	4.0	3.1	4.0	3.8	4.0	4.3	9.0	1.3	1.5
	Change from preceding month											
	Unadjusted	Seasonally adjusted	Unadjusted	Seasonally adjusted	Unadjusted	Seasonally adjusted	Unadjusted	Seasonally adjusted	Unadjusted	Seasonally adjusted	Unadjusted	Seasonally adjusted
1981:												
Jan	0.8	0.8	0.7	0.6	0.8	0.4	0.6	0.7	1.1	1.1	3.1	....
Feb	1.0	1.0	1.2	1.1	.8	.6	1.3	1.2	.8	.8	5.1	....
Mar	.7	.6	.6	.4	.5	.3	.7	.5	.8	.8	2.0	....
Apr	.6	.4	.4	0	.3	.2	.4	−.1	1.0	1.0	.1	....
May	.8	.8	.4	.4	−.1	.1	.7	.5	1.4	1.3	.4	....
June	.9	.7	.5	.4	.4	.2	.6	.5	1.3	1.1	.7	....
July	1.1	1.1	.7	.8	1.0	.7	.6	.8	1.7	1.7	.4	....
Aug	.8	.8	.5	.6	.4	.5	.5	.6	1.1	1.2	.1	....
Sept	1.0	1.1	.6	.7	.2	.7	.7	.8	1.6	1.5	.2	....
Oct	.2	.4	.1	.4	−.1	.3	.2	.4	.4	.5	−.5	....
Nov	.3	.5	.0	.2	−.2	.1	.1	.2	.6	.9	−.2	....
Dec	.3	.4	.2	.3	.3	.1	.1	.4	.4	.5	.1	....
1982:												
Jan	.4	.3	.2	.1	1.2	.7	−.2	−.1	.7	.5	.4	....
Feb	.3	.2	.3	.2	.8	.6	.0	0	.4	.4	−.8	....
Mar	−.1	−.3	−.3	−.5	−.1	−.4	−.3	−.5	.1	.0	−1.7	....
Apr	.4	.2	.0	−.3	.3	.3	−.1	−.5	.9	.9	−2.6	....
May	1.0	1.0	1.0	.9	.6	.8	1.1	.9	1.0	.9	1.6	....
June	1.2	1.0	1.4	1.3	.8	.6	1.7	1.5	.9	.8	4.1	....
July	.6	.6	.5	.6	.2	−.1	.6	.8	.6	.6	1.4	....
Aug	.2	.3	−.0	.0	−.4	−.3	.1	.2	.6	.6	0	....
Sept	.2	.2	.1	.2	.1	.5	.0	.2	.2	.1	−.1	....
Oct	.3	.5	.3	.6	−.2	.2	.6	.8	.2	.2	.2	....
Nov	−.2	.1	.1	.3	−.2	.1	.2	.3	−.5	−.1	−.6	....
Dec	−.4	−.3	−.0	.1	.0	−.1	−.1	.2	−.9	−.8	−.6	....

[1] Changes from December to December are based on unadjusted indexes.
[2] Fuel oil, coal, and bottled gas; gas (piped) and electricity; and motor fuel, motor oil, coolant, etc.

Note.—Data beginning 1978 are for all urban consumers; earlier data are for urban wage earners and clerical workers.

Source: Department of Labor, Bureau of Labor Statistics.

Table B–56.—*Changes in special consumer price indexes, 1958–82*

[Percent change]

Year or month	All items		All items less food		All items less energy		All items less food and energy		All items less food, energy, and home purchase and finance [2]		All items X–1 [3]	
	Dec. to Dec. [1]	Year to Year	Dec. to Dec. [1]	Year to Year	Dec. to Dec. [1]	Year to Year	Dec. to Dec. [1]	Year to Year	Dec. to Dec. [1]	Year to Year	Dec. to Dec. [1]	Year to Year
1958	1.8	2.7	1.6	2.3	1.9	2.9	1.8	2.3	.....	.....	.....	.....
1959	1.5	.8	2.3	1.9	1.4	.8	2.2	2.1	.....	.....	.....	.....
1960	1.5	1.6	1.0	1.7	1.4	1.5	.8	1.5	.....	.....	.....	.....
1961	.7	1.0	1.1	1.0	.8	1.1	1.5	1.1	.....	.....	.....	.....
1962	1.2	1.1	1.2	1.2	1.2	1.2	1.1	1.3	.....	.....	.....	.....
1963	1.6	1.2	1.6	1.3	1.8	1.3	1.8	1.2	.....	.....	.....	.....
1964	1.2	1.3	1.0	1.3	1.3	1.4	1.2	1.5	.....	.....	.....	.....
1965	1.9	1.7	1.6	1.4	1.9	1.5	1.5	1.4	.....	.....	.....	.....
1966	3.4	2.9	3.3	2.3	3.5	3.2	3.3	2.4	.....	.....	.....	.....
1967	3.0	2.9	3.5	3.4	3.1	2.8	3.9	3.5	.....	.....	.....	.....
1968	4.7	4.2	4.9	4.4	4.9	4.4	5.1	4.6	4.6	4.5	3.9	3.7
1969	6.1	5.4	5.7	5.5	6.4	5.7	6.1	5.8	5.2	4.9	5.2	4.4
1970	5.5	5.9	6.5	6.0	5.6	6.1	6.6	6.2	5.7	5.2	4.5	4.9
1971	3.4	4.3	3.1	4.6	3.3	4.3	3.1	4.7	3.4	5.0	3.5	4.3
1972	3.4	3.3	3.0	3.0	3.5	3.4	3.0	3.1	2.9	2.7	3.3	3.1
1973	8.8	6.2	5.6	3.9	8.3	6.1	4.7	3.5	4.0	3.3	8.5	6.2
1974	12.2	11.0	12.2	9.9	11.5	9.8	11.3	8.3	11.1	7.8	11.1	10.1
1975	7.0	9.1	7.1	9.3	6.7	9.1	6.7	9.2	6.3	8.7	6.6	8.3
1976	4.8	5.8	6.2	6.6	4.6	5.6	6.1	6.6	6.8	6.8	5.1	5.7
1977	6.8	6.5	6.3	6.5	6.8	6.3	6.4	6.2	5.5	6.1	6.3	6.4
1978	9.0	7.7	8.5	7.2	9.2	7.8	8.5	7.3	6.9	6.0	7.9	6.8
1979	13.3	11.3	14.0	11.4	11.1	10.0	11.3	9.7	7.5	7.3	10.8	9.6
1980	12.4	13.5	12.9	14.6	11.7	11.7	12.1	12.5	9.9	9.0	10.8	11.2
1981	8.9	10.4	9.9	10.9	8.6	10.0	9.6	10.4	9.4	9.5	8.5	9.5
1982	3.9	6.1	4.0	6.6	4.2	6.7	4.5	7.4	6.0	7.6	5.0	6.1
	Change from preceding month											
	Unadjusted	Seasonally adjusted	Unadjusted	Seasonally adjusted	Unadjusted	Seasonally adjusted	Unadjusted	Seasonally adjusted	Unadjusted	Seasonally adjusted	Unadjusted	Seasonally adjusted
1981:												
Jan	0.8	0.8	0.8	0.9	0.6	.....	0.5	0.6	0.5	0.6	0.9	0.7
Feb	1.0	1.0	1.1	1.0	.5	.....	.4	.4	.8	.8	1.3	1.0
Mar	.7	.6	.7	.7	.5	.....	.5	.5	.7	.6	.8	.8
Apr	.6	.4	.7	.5	.7	.....	.8	.6	.9	.8	.6	.4
May	.8	.8	1.1	.9	.9	.....	1.2	1.0	.8	.7	.6	.5
June	.9	.7	.9	.8	.9	.....	1.0	1.1	.7	.8	.6	.5
July	1.1	1.1	1.2	1.3	1.3	.....	1.3	1.4	.9	1.0	.8	.8
Aug	.8	.8	.8	.8	.8	.....	.9	1.0	.8	.8	.7	.9
Sept	1.0	1.1	1.2	1.2	1.1	.....	1.3	1.1	1.1	.9	.8	.7
Oct	.2	.4	.3	.5	.3	.....	.4	.5	.7	.8	.4	.6
Nov	.3	.5	.4	.6	.4	.....	.5	.4	.7	.6	.4	.6
Dec	.3	.4	.2	.4	.3	.....	.3	.5	.4	.7	.4	.5
1982:												
Jan	.4	.3	.2	.2	.4	.....	.2	.3	.3	.5	.5	.4
Feb	.3	.2	.2	.2	.5	.....	.4	.4	.4	.4	.3	.1
Mar	–.1	–.3	–.1	–.2	.1	.....	.1	0	.6	.5	.2	.2
Apr	.4	.2	.4	.2	.8	.....	.9	.8	.7	.6	.2	–.2
May	1.0	1.0	1.1	1.0	.9	.....	1.0	.9	.6	.4	.7	.6
June	1.2	1.0	1.3	1.2	.9	.....	.9	.9	.6	.7	1.0	1.0
July	.6	.6	.6	.7	.5	.....	.5	.6	.4	.6	.7	.8
Aug	.2	.3	.3	.4	.2	.....	.4	.5	.4	.4	.2	.3
Sept	.2	.2	.1	.1	.1	.....	.2	.0	.8	.4	.5	.5
Oct	.3	.5	.4	.5	.3	.....	.4	.4	.6	.7	.4	.6
Nov	–.2	.1	–.1	.1	–.1	.....	–.1	–.2	.3	.2	.1	.4
Dec	–.4	–.3	–.5	–.3	–.4	.....	–.5	–.1	.2	.5	.1	.3

[1] Changes from December to December are based on unadjusted indexes.
[2] All items less food, energy, and home purchase and financing, taxes, and insurance; estimated series.
[3] An experimental measure using a rental equivalence approach for homeownership costs. Effective with data for January 1983, the consumer price index for all urban consumers will incorporate a rental equivalence measure.

Note.—Data beginning 1978 are for all urban consumers; earlier data are for urban wage earners and clerical workers.

Source: Department of Labor, Bureau of Labor Statistics.

Table B–57.—*Producer price indexes by stage of processing, 1947–82*

[1967=100]

Year or month	Finished goods: Total finished goods	Consumer foods: Total	Consumer foods: Crude	Consumer foods: Processed	Finished goods excluding consumer foods: Total	Consumer goods: Total	Consumer goods: Durable	Consumer goods: Nondurable	Capital equipment	Total finished consumer goods
1947	74.0	82.8	99.4	80.2	....	79.0	74.6	80.7	55.4	80.5
1948	79.9	90.4	107.1	87.6	....	84.0	79.7	85.8	60.4	86.5
1949	77.6	83.1	101.3	80.1	....	82.2	81.8	82.3	63.4	82.5
1950	79.0	84.7	92.2	83.4	....	83.5	82.7	83.6	64.9	83.9
1951	86.5	95.2	105.0	93.2	....	89.5	88.2	90.0	71.2	91.8
1952	86.0	94.3	112.8	91.3	....	88.3	88.9	87.8	72.4	90.7
1953	85.1	89.4	105.2	86.7	....	89.1	89.6	88.6	73.6	89.2
1954	85.3	88.7	94.7	87.6	....	89.4	90.3	88.9	74.5	89.1
1955	85.5	86.5	98.8	84.4	....	90.1	91.2	89.4	76.7	88.5
1956	87.9	86.3	98.7	84.3	....	92.3	94.3	91.1	82.4	89.8
1957	91.1	89.3	97.4	87.9	....	94.6	97.1	93.2	87.5	92.4
1958	93.2	94.5	103.5	93.1	....	94.7	98.4	92.6	89.8	94.4
1959	93.0	90.1	94.3	89.5	....	95.9	99.6	94.0	91.5	93.6
1960	93.7	92.1	100.6	90.7	....	96.3	99.2	94.7	91.7	94.5
1961	93.7	91.7	96.1	90.9	....	96.2	98.8	94.7	91.8	94.3
1962	94.0	92.5	97.0	91.7	....	96.0	98.3	94.8	92.2	94.6
1963	93.7	91.4	95.5	90.7	....	96.0	97.8	95.1	92.4	94.1
1964	94.1	91.9	98.2	90.8	....	95.9	98.2	94.8	93.3	94.3
1965	95.7	95.4	98.6	94.9	....	96.6	97.9	95.9	94.4	96.1
1966	98.8	101.6	104.8	101.0	....	98.1	98.5	97.8	96.8	99.4
1967	100.0	100.0	100.0	100.0	100.0	100.0	100.0	100.0	100.0	100.0
1968	102.8	103.6	107.5	103.0	102.6	102.1	102.2	102.2	103.5	102.7
1969	106.6	110.0	116.0	108.9	105.4	104.6	104.0	105.0	106.9	106.6
1970	110.3	113.5	116.3	113.1	109.1	107.7	106.9	108.3	112.0	109.9
1971	113.7	115.3	115.8	115.1	113.1	111.4	110.8	111.7	116.6	112.9
1972	117.2	121.7	121.2	121.7	115.4	113.5	113.3	113.6	119.5	116.6
1973	127.9	146.4	160.7	143.9	120.1	118.6	115.4	120.5	123.5	129.2
1974	147.5	166.9	180.8	164.6	139.3	138.6	125.9	146.8	141.0	149.3
1975	163.4	181.0	181.2	181.3	156.2	153.1	138.2	163.0	162.5	163.6
1976	170.6	180.4	193.9	177.8	166.1	162.6	144.5	174.8	173.4	169.7
1977	181.7	189.9	201.0	187.3	177.7	174.3	152.8	189.3	184.6	180.7
1978	195.9	207.2	216.8	204.6	190.7	186.7	166.9	200.0	199.2	194.9
1979	217.7	226.2	233.1	223.8	213.3	211.5	183.2	231.3	216.5	217.9
1980	247.0	239.5	237.2	237.8	247.8	250.8	206.2	283.9	239.8	248.9
1981	269.8	253.6	263.8	250.6	273.3	276.5	218.6	319.6	264.3	271.3
1982 [1]	280.6	259.3	252.5	257.7	285.7	287.8	226.7	333.5	279.6	280.9
1981:										
Jan	260.9	251.0	257.9	248.4	262.4	265.1	214.9	302.7	254.6	262.5
Feb	263.3	251.3	265.6	247.9	265.5	268.5	215.1	308.4	256.7	265.0
Mar	266.0	252.6	279.7	248.1	268.7	272.5	214.0	316.0	258.1	268.2
Apr	268.5	251.9	279.3	247.4	272.1	276.1	216.6	320.4	260.8	270.6
May	269.6	252.8	263.1	249.8	273.3	277.0	218.1	321.0	262.5	271.5
June	270.5	253.8	258.9	251.3	274.1	277.7	218.2	322.0	263.8	272.3
July	271.8	257.6	262.7	255.0	274.7	277.9	218.1	322.5	265.4	273.5
Aug	271.5	256.3	256.9	254.2	274.6	277.7	218.3	322.1	265.8	273.0
Sept	271.5	256.2	253.5	254.4	274.7	277.9	215.8	324.2	265.3	273.1
Oct	274.3	254.0	253.8	252.0	279.1	281.6	224.5	324.3	271.5	275.1
Nov	274.7	252.7	260.0	249.9	280.0	282.4	224.7	325.4	273.0	275.2
Dec	275.4	252.9	273.9	249.0	280.9	283.2	225.4	326.3	274.1	275.8
1982: [1]										
Jan	277.9	256.4	280.6	252.1	283.0	285.2	226.2	329.3	276.2	278.3
Feb	277.9	258.2	282.5	254.0	282.4	284.9	224.0	330.3	275.0	278.6
Mar	277.3	257.1	263.3	254.5	281.9	284.0	223.9	328.8	275.8	277.7
Apr	277.3	260.0	266.6	257.3	281.1	282.3	224.1	325.7	277.2	277.3
May	277.8	262.3	259.9	260.3	281.0	281.8	225.0	324.3	278.1	277.7
June	279.9	263.4	254.7	262.0	283.4	284.8	225.9	328.7	279.2	280.1
July	281.7	260.6	241.0	260.2	286.7	288.8	226.7	335.3	280.2	282.1
Aug	282.3	259.7	239.2	259.4	287.9	290.2	227.5	337.2	280.7	282.8
Sept	281.4	259.9	227.8	260.6	286.6	289.1	223.2	338.4	279.5	282.0
Oct	284.1	257.8	232.0	258.0	290.8	293.3	231.1	339.7	283.8	284.2
Nov	284.9	257.6	235.6	257.4	291.9	294.6	230.8	342.4	284.0	285.2
Dec	285.1	258.2	247.2	257.1	292.0	294.3	231.5	341.4	285.1	285.1

See next page for continuation of table.

TABLE B–57.—*Producer price indexes by stage of processing, 1947–82*—Continued

[1967=100]

Year or month	Intermediate materials, supplies, and components: Total	Intermediate: Foods and feeds [2]	Intermediate: Other	Materials and components: For manufacturing	Materials and components: For construction	Processed fuels and lubricants	Containers	Supplies	Crude materials for further processing: Total	Crude: Foodstuffs and feedstuffs	Crude: Other: Total	Crude: Other: Fuel	Crude: Other: Other
1947	72.4	....	70.0	72.1	66.0	85.5	66.8	77.5	101.2	111.7	....	66.6	90.6
1948	78.3	....	76.1	77.8	73.1	96.9	69.8	81.0	110.9	120.8	....	78.7	100.7
1949	75.2	....	74.2	74.5	73.2	88.2	70.1	76.3	96.0	100.3	....	78.3	91.6
1950	78.6	....	77.7	78.1	77.0	89.9	72.0	78.9	104.6	107.6	....	77.9	104.7
1951	88.1	....	87.0	88.5	84.3	93.9	84.5	88.8	120.1	124.5	....	79.4	120.7
1952	85.5	....	84.3	84.8	83.7	92.8	79.9	88.8	110.3	117.2	....	79.9	104.6
1953	86.0	....	85.3	86.2	85.1	93.4	80.0	84.3	101.9	104.9	....	82.7	100.1
1954	86.5	....	85.7	86.3	85.5	93.3	81.5	86.3	101.0	104.9	....	79.0	98.2
1955	88.1	....	88.3	88.4	88.9	93.3	82.6	84.8	97.1	95.1	....	78.8	103.8
1956	92.0	....	92.6	92.6	93.5	96.2	88.6	87.1	97.6	93.1	....	84.4	107.6
1957	94.1	....	95.0	94.8	94.0	101.9	92.5	88.0	99.8	97.2	....	89.2	106.2
1958	94.3	....	94.8	95.2	94.0	96.0	94.7	90.0	102.0	103.0	....	90.3	102.2
1959	95.6	....	96.4	96.5	96.6	95.6	94.2	91.2	99.4	96.2	....	91.9	105.8
1960	95.6	....	96.8	96.5	95.9	98.2	95.5	90.7	97.0	95.1	....	92.8	101.4
1961	95.0	....	95.5	95.3	94.6	99.4	94.7	91.8	96.5	93.8	....	92.6	102.5
1962	94.9	....	95.3	94.7	94.2	99.0	95.9	93.8	97.5	95.7	....	92.1	102.0
1963	95.2	....	95.0	94.9	94.5	98.1	94.7	95.2	95.4	92.9	....	93.2	100.7
1964	95.5	....	95.6	95.9	95.4	96.0	94.0	94.3	94.5	90.8	....	92.8	102.4
1965	96.8	....	96.9	97.4	96.2	97.4	95.8	95.2	99.3	97.1	....	93.5	104.5
1966	99.2	....	98.9	99.3	98.8	99.2	98.4	99.4	105.7	105.9	....	96.3	106.7
1967	100.0	100.0	100.0	100.0	100.0	100.0	100.0	100.0	100.0	100.0	100.0	100.0	100.0
1968	102.3	99.4	102.5	102.2	105.0	97.6	102.4	101.0	101.6	101.3	102.2	102.3	102.1
1969	105.8	102.7	106.1	105.8	110.8	98.5	106.3	102.8	108.4	109.3	106.8	106.6	106.9
1970	109.9	109.1	109.9	110.0	112.6	105.0	111.4	108.0	112.3	112.0	112.7	122.6	109.8
1971	114.1	111.7	114.3	112.8	119.7	115.2	116.6	111.0	115.1	114.2	117.0	139.0	110.7
1972	118.7	118.5	118.9	117.0	126.2	118.9	121.9	115.6	127.6	127.5	128.0	148.7	121.9
1973	131.6	168.4	128.1	127.7	136.7	131.5	129.2	140.6	174.0	180.0	162.5	164.5	161.5
1974	162.9	200.2	159.5	162.2	161.6	199.1	152.2	154.5	196.1	189.4	208.9	219.4	205.4
1975	180.0	195.3	178.6	178.7	176.4	233.0	171.4	168.1	196.9	191.8	206.9	271.5	188.3
1976	189.1	185.3	189.4	185.4	188.4	250.1	180.2	179.0	202.7	190.2	228.5	305.3	206.7
1977	201.5	190.5	202.3	195.4	203.4	282.5	188.3	188.7	209.2	192.1	245.0	372.1	212.2
1978	215.6	203.1	216.5	208.7	224.7	295.3	202.8	198.5	234.4	216.2	272.3	426.8	233.1
1979	243.2	226.1	244.4	234.4	247.4	364.8	226.8	218.2	274.3	247.9	330.0	507.6	284.5
1980	280.3	252.6	282.3	265.7	268.3	503.0	254.5	244.5	304.6	259.2	401.0	615.0	346.1
1981	306.0	250.3	310.1	286.1	287.6	595.4	276.1	263.8	329.0	257.4	482.3	751.2	413.7
1982 [1]	310.4	239.6	315.7	290.1	293.5	591.8	285.5	272.2	319.5	247.8	474.0	886.3	376.9
1981:													
Jan	296.1	270.9	298.0	279.6	279.2	551.9	264.6	257.8	328.0	270.7	450.1	677.4	391.0
Feb	298.3	261.3	301.0	280.3	280.3	569.8	268.2	257.8	336.5	267.1	484.9	697.7	427.9
Mar	302.0	255.6	305.4	281.6	282.7	598.3	270.9	258.9	334.2	262.1	488.4	703.6	430.9
Apr	305.8	254.9	309.5	284.1	288.0	608.5	274.3	262.4	336.3	263.5	492.1	716.6	432.5
May	306.7	253.1	310.7	285.1	288.5	608.7	276.4	264.0	334.4	260.6	492.4	738.4	428.3
June	307.2	253.2	311.2	285.8	289.6	605.7	277.2	264.6	335.4	264.3	487.4	759.2	418.1
July	308.5	251.1	312.7	287.9	290.4	602.0	278.8	266.0	337.3	267.2	487.2	781.2	413.1
Aug	310.1	250.2	314.5	289.8	290.7	607.8	280.3	266.1	333.0	261.8	485.3	766.7	413.9
Sept	309.7	243.5	314.6	290.2	290.0	601.4	280.6	266.1	327.4	253.4	486.0	788.7	410.2
Oct	309.4	239.3	314.6	290.2	290.1	596.9	280.9	266.6	319.9	245.7	479.2	779.0	404.1
Nov	309.0	235.2	314.5	289.5	290.2	595.1	280.6	267.2	313.9	238.3	476.3	792.5	397.8
Dec	309.4	235.2	314.9	289.3	291.1	598.1	280.2	268.3	311.5	233.7	478.6	813.0	396.2
1982: [1]													
Jan	311.0	238.8	316.4	290.4	292.0	604.4	282.5	269.8	318.4	242.6	481.5	812.9	399.5
Feb	311.1	239.4	316.4	290.9	293.0	596.8	285.5	270.4	321.6	248.3	479.3	824.5	394.8
Mar	310.6	237.7	316.0	290.4	293.3	593.0	286.3	270.6	320.0	247.9	475.2	839.7	387.1
Apr	309.9	240.9	315.1	290.6	294.0	579.9	287.0	272.1	322.6	254.4	469.9	851.2	378.8
May	309.8	245.0	314.6	291.4	293.7	570.9	287.0	273.4	328.3	262.6	470.2	864.8	376.6
June	309.9	245.1	314.7	289.8	294.5	581.1	286.5	273.4	325.6	259.9	467.7	883.9	370.0
July	311.1	243.6	316.1	289.2	294.3	600.7	286.3	273.1	323.4	255.5	469.8	901.3	369.2
Aug	310.8	240.2	316.0	288.7	293.5	603.8	285.4	272.6	319.8	249.6	471.0	906.9	369.5
Sept	310.7	238.4	316.0	290.2	293.4	593.2	285.5	272.5	316.3	242.9	474.3	926.3	369.6
Oct	310.0	234.8	315.5	289.5	293.2	590.2	285.1	272.3	312.2	236.3	475.4	919.4	372.2
Nov	310.1	234.6	315.7	288.9	293.0	594.3	284.7	273.0	313.4	236.3	479.0	955.3	369.5
Dec	310.2	235.4	315.7	288.7	294.5	593.6	284.6	273.2	312.6	237.0	475.0	949.5	366.0

[1] Data have been revised through August 1982 to reflect the availability of late reports and corrections by respondents. All data are subject to revision 4 months after original publication.

[2] Intermediate materials for food manufacturing and feeds.

Source: Department of Labor, Bureau of Labor Statistics.

Table B-58.—*Producer price indexes by stage of processing, special groups, 1974–82*

[1967=100]

Year or month	Finished goods: Total	Finished goods: Food	Finished goods: Energy	Finished goods excluding food and energy: Total	Finished goods excluding food and energy: Capital equipment	Finished goods excluding food and energy: Consumer goods excluding food and energy	Intermediate materials, supplies, and components: Total	Intermediate materials, supplies, and components: Foods and feeds[1]	Intermediate materials, supplies, and components: Energy	Intermediate materials, supplies, and components: Other	Crude materials for further processing: Total	Crude materials for further processing: Foodstuffs and feedstuffs	Crude materials for further processing: Energy	Crude materials for further processing: Other
1974	147.5	160.9	215.2	133.3	141.0	129.1	162.9	200.2	188.7	156.7	196.1	189.4	223.0	198.3
1975	163.4	181.0	252.4	148.5	162.5	141.0	180.0	195.3	220.8	174.7	196.9	191.8	266.9	165.0
1976	170.6	180.4	282.3	156.8	173.4	148.1	189.1	185.3	236.8	185.0	202.7	190.2	283.1	191.0
1977	181.7	189.9	326.7	166.3	184.6	156.6	201.5	190.5	267.3	196.1	209.2	192.1	323.5	190.1
1978	195.9	207.2	347.7	178.7	199.2	168.0	215.6	203.1	280.3	210.4	234.4	216.2	362.5	209.2
1979	217.7	226.2	469.9	194.7	216.5	183.3	243.2	226.1	348.6	234.2	274.3	247.9	439.9	253.0
1980	247.0	239.5	701.3	216.4	239.8	204.2	280.3	252.6	484.9	261.8	304.6	259.2	586.1	269.4
1981	269.8	253.6	835.4	235.1	264.3	220.1	306.0	250.3	573.6	283.4	329.0	257.4	783.4	266.0
1982 [2]	280.6	259.3	823.4	248.5	279.6	232.5	310.4	239.6	570.9	290.1	319.5	247.8	801.7	238.2
1981:														
Jan	260.9	251.0	758.1	228.2	254.6	214.4	296.1	270.9	532.0	274.3	328.0	270.7	696.0	274.1
Feb	263.3	251.3	790.2	229.5	256.7	215.4	298.3	261.3	548.8	275.9	336.5	267.1	782.6	271.1
Mar	266.0	252.6	838.7	230.2	258.1	215.8	302.0	255.6	575.4	277.8	334.2	262.1	785.1	275.5
Apr	268.5	251.9	853.9	232.8	260.8	218.3	305.8	254.9	585.3	281.3	336.3	263.5	790.5	277.9
May	269.6	252.8	854.2	234.0	262.5	219.3	306.7	253.1	586.0	282.6	334.4	260.6	798.2	272.7
June	270.5	253.8	857.3	234.7	263.8	219.7	307.2	253.2	583.4	283.4	335.4	264.3	793.5	267.5
July	271.8	257.6	852.4	235.5	265.4	220.3	308.5	251.1	580.6	285.5	337.3	267.2	793.6	267.0
Aug	271.5	256.3	842.0	236.1	265.8	220.9	310.1	250.2	585.9	287.0	333.0	261.8	786.4	269.0
Sept	271.5	256.2	847.1	235.8	265.3	220.7	309.7	243.5	579.7	287.7	327.4	253.4	795.7	263.3
Oct	274.3	254.0	841.6	240.7	271.5	225.0	309.4	239.3	575.7	288.2	319.9	245.7	786.8	257.8
Nov	274.7	252.7	842.2	241.6	273.0	225.7	309.0	235.2	574.0	288.2	313.9	238.3	791.2	249.3
Dec	275.4	252.9	846.6	242.3	274.1	226.2	309.4	235.2	576.8	288.4	311.5	233.7	800.6	246.2
1982:[2]														
Jan	277.9	256.4	842.3	244.7	276.2	228.6	311.0	238.8	582.6	289.4	318.4	242.6	801.5	250.3
Feb	277.9	258.2	832.6	244.6	275.0	229.0	311.1	239.4	575.7	290.2	321.6	248.3	796.9	249.9
Mar	277.3	257.1	814.0	245.2	275.8	229.5	310.6	237.7	572.2	290.2	320.0	247.9	788.8	248.5
Apr	277.3	260.0	775.3	246.4	277.2	230.6	309.9	240.9	560.2	290.7	322.6	254.4	778.5	246.8
May	277.8	262.3	758.2	247.3	278.1	231.5	309.8	245.0	552.0	291.1	328.3	262.6	784.0	243.7
June	279.9	263.4	789.8	248.1	279.2	232.1	309.9	245.1	561.4	290.1	325.6	259.9	792.0	234.3
July	281.7	260.6	834.7	248.8	280.2	232.6	311.1	243.6	579.3	289.6	323.4	255.5	799.4	232.9
Aug	282.3	259.7	844.3	249.5	280.7	233.3	310.8	240.2	582.2	289.2	319.8	249.6	801.7	233.3
Sept	281.4	259.9	846.6	248.0	279.5	232.0	310.7	238.4	572.4	290.3	316.3	242.9	810.0	233.2
Oct	284.1	257.8	841.7	252.7	283.8	236.7	310.0	234.8	569.2	290.1	312.2	236.3	816.7	230.6
Nov	284.9	257.6	855.3	253.0	284.0	237.0	310.1	234.6	572.4	290.0	313.4	236.3	830.2	227.5
Dec	285.1	258.2	845.9	253.7	285.1	237.4	310.2	235.4	571.2	290.2	312.6	237.0	820.1	227.6

[1] Intermediate materials for food manufacturing and feeds.

[2] Data have been revised through August 1982 to reflect the availability of late reports and corrections by respondents. All data are subject to revision 4 months after original publication.

Source: Department of Labor, Bureau of Labor Statistics.

Table B–59.—*Producer price indexes for major commodity groups, 1940–82*

[1967=100]

Year or month	Farm products and processed foods and feeds			Industrial commodities				
	Total	Farm products	Processed foods and feeds	Total	Textile products and apparel	Hides, skins, leather, and related products	Fuels and related products, and power [1]	Chemicals and allied products [1]
1940		41.4		44.0		45.2	51.4	52.4
1941		50.3		47.3		48.4	54.6	57.0
1942		64.8		50.7		52.8	56.2	63.3
1943		75.0		51.5		52.7	57.8	64.1
1944		75.5		52.3		52.2	59.5	64.8
1945		78.5		53.0		52.9	60.1	65.2
1946		90.9		58.0		61.1	64.4	70.5
1947	94.3	109.4	82.9	70.8	103.6	83.3	76.9	93.7
1948	101.6	117.5	92.7	76.9	108.1	84.2	90.5	95.9
1949	89.6	101.6	80.6	75.3	98.9	79.9	86.2	87.6
1950	93.9	106.7	83.4	78.0	102.7	86.3	87.1	88.9
1951	106.9	124.2	92.7	86.1	114.6	99.1	90.3	101.7
1952	102.7	117.2	91.6	84.1	103.4	80.1	90.1	96.5
1953	96.0	106.2	87.4	84.8	100.8	81.3	92.6	97.7
1954	95.7	104.7	88.9	85.0	98.6	77.6	91.3	98.9
1955	91.2	98.2	85.0	86.9	98.7	77.3	91.2	98.5
1956	90.6	96.9	84.9	90.8	98.7	81.9	94.0	99.1
1957	93.7	99.5	87.4	93.3	98.8	82.0	99.1	101.2
1958	98.1	103.9	91.8	93.6	97.0	82.9	95.3	102.0
1959	93.5	97.5	89.4	95.3	98.4	94.2	95.3	101.6
1960	93.7	97.2	89.5	95.3	99.5	90.8	96.1	101.8
1961	93.7	96.3	91.0	94.8	97.7	91.7	97.2	100.7
1962	94.7	98.0	91.9	94.8	98.6	92.7	96.7	99.1
1963	93.8	96.0	92.5	94.7	98.5	90.0	96.3	97.9
1964	93.2	94.6	92.3	95.2	99.2	90.3	93.7	98.3
1965	97.1	98.7	95.5	96.4	99.8	94.3	95.5	99.0
1966	103.5	105.9	101.2	98.5	100.1	103.4	97.8	99.4
1967	100.0	100.0	100.0	100.0	100.0	100.0	100.0	100.0
1968	102.4	102.5	102.2	102.5	103.7	103.2	98.9	99.8
1969	108.0	109.1	107.3	106.0	106.0	108.9	100.9	99.9
1970	111.7	111.0	112.1	110.0	107.1	110.3	106.2	102.2
1971	113.9	112.9	114.5	114.1	109.0	114.1	115.2	104.1
1972	122.4	125.0	120.8	117.9	113.6	131.3	118.6	104.2
1973	159.1	176.3	148.1	125.9	123.8	143.1	134.3	110.0
1974	177.4	187.7	170.9	153.8	139.1	145.1	208.3	146.8
1975	184.2	186.7	182.6	171.5	137.9	148.5	245.1	181.3
1976	183.1	191.0	178.0	182.4	148.2	167.8	265.6	187.2
1977	188.8	192.5	186.1	195.1	154.0	179.3	302.2	192.8
1978	206.6	212.5	202.6	209.4	159.8	200.0	322.5	198.8
1979	229.8	241.4	222.5	236.5	168.7	252.4	408.1	222.3
1980	244.7	249.4	241.2	274.8	183.5	248.9	574.0	260.3
1981	251.5	254.9	248.7	304.1	199.7	260.9	694.5	287.6
1982 [2]	248.9	242.3	251.5	312.3	204.3	263.0	693.4	292.4
1981:								
Jan	257.9	264.5	253.3	291.5	193.1	258.2	634.6	274.3
Feb	255.1	262.4	250.2	295.7	193.9	257.7	667.5	277.6
Mar	253.5	260.7	248.5	299.6	195.2	261.2	696.5	280.4
Apr	253.8	263.3	247.6	303.5	197.6	263.5	707.2	286.0
May	252.9	259.6	248.2	304.7	199.2	263.7	709.0	288.6
June	254.3	260.7	249.9	305.1	200.1	261.6	707.6	290.5
July	256.8	263.3	252.2	306.2	201.3	261.1	704.9	291.3
Aug	254.2	257.9	251.2	307.2	202.4	261.3	704.3	293.3
Sept	250.3	251.1	248.9	307.4	202.9	261.7	703.5	293.3
Oct	246.0	243.1	246.6	309.0	204.0	260.0	698.1	292.4
Nov	242.5	237.4	244.3	309.3	203.6	259.8	698.1	292.0
Dec	241.0	234.6	243.6	310.0	203.4	260.7	702.5	291.8
1982: [2]								
Jan	246.0	242.2	247.1	311.8	205.0	261.8	705.1	292.9
Feb	248.4	247.1	248.1	311.6	205.6	261.6	697.8	293.6
Mar	247.5	244.7	248.1	311.0	205.0	260.6	689.7	294.6
Apr	251.6	250.6	251.1	309.9	205.4	263.4	670.6	294.3
May	255.8	256.5	254.4	309.6	205.4	263.2	662.2	295.0
June	255.3	252.7	255.8	310.6	205.0	261.8	677.3	293.3
July	252.4	246.6	254.6	312.8	204.1	263.1	701.1	291.6
Aug	249.6	240.8	253.5	313.2	204.2	262.0	705.6	291.6
Sept	247.5	234.4	253.6	312.9	203.8	264.8	701.8	291.4
Oct	243.9	229.1	251.0	314.4	202.6	264.7	699.6	290.4
Nov	244.0	230.6	250.4	315.1	203.5	264.3	707.3	290.5
Dec	244.8	232.5	250.6	315.0	202.4	265.2	702.6	289.3

See next page for continuation of table.

TABLE B-59.—*Producer price indexes for major commodity groups, 1940–82*—Continued

[1967=100]

Year or month	Industrial commodities—Continued								
	Rubber and plastic products	Lumber and wood products	Pulp, paper, and allied products	Metals and metal products	Machinery and equipment	Furniture and household durables	Nonmetallic mineral products	Transportation equipment: Motor vehicles and equipment [3]	Miscellaneous products
1940	57.1	27.4	....	37.8	41.4	53.8	49.1	40.4	....
1941	61.5	32.7	....	38.5	42.1	57.2	50.2	43.2	....
1942	71.6	35.6	....	39.1	42.8	61.8	52.3	47.2	....
1943	73.6	37.7	....	39.0	42.4	61.4	52.4	47.2	....
1944	72.7	40.6	....	39.0	42.1	63.1	53.5	47.5	....
1945	70.5	41.2	....	39.6	42.2	63.2	55.7	48.3	....
1946	70.8	47.2	....	44.3	46.4	67.1	59.3	56.0	....
1947	70.5	73.4	72.5	54.9	53.7	77.0	66.3	64.1	73.5
1948	72.8	84.0	75.7	62.5	58.2	81.6	71.6	70.8	76.5
1949	70.5	77.7	72.4	63.0	61.0	82.9	73.5	75.7	78.0
1950	85.9	89.3	74.3	66.3	63.1	84.7	75.4	75.3	79.2
1951	105.4	97.2	88.0	73.8	70.5	91.8	80.1	79.4	83.9
1952	95.5	94.4	85.7	73.9	70.6	90.1	80.1	84.0	83.4
1953	89.1	94.3	85.5	76.3	72.2	91.9	83.3	83.6	85.6
1954	90.4	92.6	85.5	76.9	73.4	92.9	85.1	83.8	86.4
1955	102.4	97.1	87.8	82.1	75.7	93.3	87.5	86.3	86.5
1956	103.8	98.5	93.6	89.2	81.8	95.8	91.3	91.2	87.6
1957	103.4	93.5	95.4	91.0	87.6	98.3	94.8	95.1	90.2
1958	103.3	92.4	96.4	90.4	89.4	99.1	95.8	98.1	92.0
1959	102.9	98.8	97.3	92.3	91.3	99.3	97.0	100.3	92.2
1960	103.1	95.3	98.1	92.4	92.0	99.0	97.2	98.8	93.0
1961	99.2	91.0	95.2	91.9	91.9	98.4	97.6	98.6	93.3
1962	96.3	91.6	96.3	91.2	92.0	97.7	97.6	98.6	93.7
1963	96.8	93.5	95.6	91.3	92.2	97.0	97.1	97.8	94.5
1964	95.5	95.4	95.4	93.8	92.8	97.4	97.3	98.3	95.2
1965	95.9	95.9	96.2	96.4	93.9	96.9	97.5	98.5	95.9
1966	97.8	100.2	98.8	98.8	96.8	98.0	98.4	98.6	97.7
1967	100.0	100.0	100.0	100.0	100.0	100.0	100.0	100.0	100.0
1968	103.4	113.3	101.1	102.6	103.2	102.8	103.7	102.8	102.2
1969	105.3	125.3	104.0	108.5	106.5	104.9	107.7	104.8	105.2
1970	108.3	113.6	108.2	116.6	111.4	107.5	112.9	108.7	109.9
1971	109.1	127.3	110.1	118.7	115.5	110.0	122.4	114.9	112.9
1972	109.3	144.3	113.4	123.5	117.9	111.4	126.1	118.0	114.6
1973	112.4	177.2	122.1	132.8	121.7	115.2	130.2	119.2	119.7
1974	136.2	183.6	151.7	171.9	139.4	127.9	153.2	129.2	133.1
1975	150.2	176.9	170.4	185.6	161.4	139.7	174.0	144.6	147.7
1976	159.2	205.6	179.4	195.9	171.0	145.6	186.3	153.8	153.7
1977	167.6	236.3	186.4	209.0	181.7	151.5	200.5	163.7	164.3
1978	174.8	276.0	195.6	227.1	196.1	160.4	222.8	176.0	184.3
1979	194.3	300.4	219.0	259.3	213.9	171.3	248.6	190.5	208.7
1980	217.4	288.9	249.2	286.4	239.8	187.7	283.0	208.8	258.8
1981	232.6	292.8	273.8	300.4	263.3	198.5	309.5	237.6	265.7
1982 [2]	241.6	284.7	288.6	301.8	278.7	206.8	320.2	251.3	276.6
1981:									
Jan	224.8	296.5	264.4	294.0	253.3	194.0	296.6	229.0	264.3
Feb	226.4	294.7	267.2	294.0	255.3	195.2	297.9	230.9	264.9
Mar	228.4	294.4	269.0	296.4	257.5	195.8	300.9	229.5	264.0
Apr	230.8	299.4	271.4	298.8	259.6	196.4	310.8	233.9	266.0
May	231.8	298.4	272.1	299.1	260.7	197.4	312.0	236.0	266.9
June	233.4	298.1	272.9	298.4	262.1	197.3	313.6	236.7	266.3
July	232.1	296.5	274.9	302.0	264.8	199.5	314.3	237.4	263.2
Aug	234.1	294.5	275.9	304.1	266.2	199.6	314.1	238.4	262.6
Sept	235.7	289.3	277.8	304.9	268.1	201.0	313.2	232.8	267.0
Oct	237.3	284.3	279.2	305.3	269.3	201.3	313.3	247.8	268.5
Nov	238.0	282.1	280.4	304.2	270.4	202.1	313.7	248.9	267.5
Dec	238.3	285.4	281.0	303.3	272.0	202.9	313.5	249.5	267.6
1982: [2]									
Jan	237.3	285.5	285.5	304.7	274.1	203.5	315.6	250.8	268.3
Feb	239.3	285.2	286.3	304.2	275.4	204.6	319.0	246.8	273.5
Mar	240.8	285.3	287.4	302.9	276.2	205.5	319.9	246.8	272.7
Apr	241.1	286.5	288.5	303.1	277.6	206.0	320.2	247.2	273.2
May	242.1	284.6	289.6	302.8	278.2	206.5	321.2	249.2	272.2
June	242.5	289.0	289.5	299.3	278.6	207.0	320.9	251.1	271.5
July	242.0	288.6	289.1	299.5	279.6	206.8	321.1	252.0	273.4
Aug	242.6	284.2	289.3	299.2	279.9	208.1	320.5	252.8	272.0
Sept	243.3	283.0	289.2	301.8	280.3	207.7	320.2	245.0	280.3
Oct	243.0	279.6	289.2	302.1	280.9	208.4	321.2	258.1	285.9
Nov	242.6	279.9	289.6	301.0	281.3	208.3	321.5	257.5	285.7
Dec	243.0	284.8	289.5	300.9	281.8	208.6	320.9	257.9	290.3

[1] Prices for some items in this grouping are lagged and refer to 1 month earlier than the index month.
[2] Data have been revised through August 1982 to reflect the availability of late reports and corrections by respondents. All data are subject to revision 4 months after original publication.
[3] Index for total transportation equipment is not shown but is available beginning December 1968.

Source: Department of Labor, Bureau of Labor Statistics.

Table B–60.—*Changes in producer price indexes for finished goods, 1950–82*

[Percent change]

Year or month	Total finished goods		Finished consumer foods		Finished goods excluding consumer foods						Finished energy goods		Finished goods excluding food and energy	
					Total		Consumer goods		Capital equipment					
	Dec. to Dec. [1]	Year to year	Dec. to Dec. [1]	Year to year	Dec. to Dec. [1]	Year to year	Dec. to Dec. [1]	Year to year	Dec. to Dec. [1]	Year to year	Dec. to Dec. [1]	Year to year	Dec. to Dec. [1]	Year to year
1950	10.4	1.8	13.3	1.9			8.2	1.6	10.3	2.4				
1951	2.9	9.5	5.3	12.4			.9	7.2	3.4	9.7				
1952	−2.2	−.6	−5.9	−.9			−1.1	−1.3	.8	1.7				
1953	.5	−1.0	−2.2	−5.2			1.6	.9	2.3	1.7				
1954	−.1	.2	−1.9	−.8			.3	.3	1.1	1.2				
1955	1.2	.2	−2.9	−2.5			1.7	.8	5.6	3.0				
1956	4.2	2.8	3.6	−.2			2.5	2.4	8.3	7.4				
1957	3.2	3.6	5.3	3.5			1.7	2.5	4.3	6.2				
1958	.5	2.3	.4	5.8			.2	.1	1.3	2.6				
1959	−.4	−.2	−3.7	−4.7			.8	1.3	1.0	1.9				
1960	1.8	.8	5.2	2.2			.4	.4	.1	.2				
1961	−.5	0	−1.8	−.4			−.3	−.1	.2	.1				
1962	.1	.3	.5	.9			−.1	−.2	.3	.4				
1963	−.2	−.3	−1.3	−1.2			.1	0	.5	.2				
1964	.5	.4	.4	.5			.1	−.1	.9	1.0				
1965	3.3	1.7	9.1	3.8			.9	.7	1.5	1.2				
1966	2.2	3.2	1.4	6.5			1.7	1.6	3.9	2.5				
1967	1.6	1.2	−.4	−1.6			2.1	1.9	3.1	3.3				
1968	3.1	2.8	4.8	3.6	2.4	2.6	2.0	2.1	3.0	3.5				
1969	4.8	3.7	8.2	6.2	3.4	2.7	2.9	2.4	4.6	3.3				
1970	2.2	3.5	−2.5	3.2	4.3	3.5	3.9	3.0	4.9	4.8				
1971	3.2	3.1	5.9	1.6	2.1	3.7	2.0	3.4	2.4	4.1				
1972	3.8	3.1	8.0	5.6	2.1	2.0	2.0	1.9	2.0	2.5				
1973	[illegible]	[illegible]	[illegible]	[illegible]	[illegible]	[illegible]	[illegible]	[illegible]	[illegible]	[illegible]				
1974	18.3	15.3	13.0	14.0	21.2	16.0	20.5	16.9	22.6	14.2				
1975	6.6	10.8	5.5	8.4	7.2	12.1	6.7	10.5	8.2	15.2	16.4	17.3	6.1	11.4
1976	3.7	4.4	−2.5	−.3	6.2	6.3	6.0	6.2	6.4	6.7	11.5	11.8	5.6	5.6
1977	6.9	6.5	6.9	5.3	6.9	7.0	6.7	7.2	7.3	6.5	12.1	15.7	6.3	6.1
1978	9.2	7.8	11.7	9.1	8.3	7.3	8.5	7.1	7.9	7.9	8.5	6.4	8.3	7.5
1979	12.8	11.1	7.4	9.2	14.8	11.9	17.5	13.3	8.8	8.7	58.0	35.1	9.4	9.0
1980	11.8	13.5	7.5	5.9	13.3	16.2	14.2	18.6	11.4	10.8	27.8	49.2	10.7	11.1
1981	7.1	9.2	1.4	5.9	8.8	10.3	8.5	10.2	9.2	10.2	14.1	19.1	7.8	8.6
1982 [2]	3.5	4.0	2.1	2.2	4.0	4.5	3.9	4.1	4.0	5.8	−.1	−1.4	4.7	5.7
	Percent change from preceding month													
	Unadjusted	Seasonally adjusted	Unadjusted	Seasonally adjusted	Unadjusted	Seasonally adjusted	Unadjusted	Seasonally adjusted	Unadjusted	Seasonally adjusted	Unadjusted	Seasonally adjusted	Unadjusted	Seasonally adjusted
1981:														
Jan	1.4	1.2	0.7	0.6	1.6	1.4	1.6	1.4	1.5	1.2	2.2	1.9	1.5	1.2
Feb	.9	.8	.1	−.1	1.2	1.0	1.3	1.1	.8	.9	4.2	3.8	.6	.5
Mar	1.0	1.1	.5	.8	1.2	1.2	1.5	1.4	.5	.7	6.1	5.8	.3	.3
Apr	.9	.9	−.3	.2	1.3	1.2	1.3	1.2	1.0	.9	1.8	1.3	1.1	1.1
May	.4	.2	.4	.2	.4	.2	.3	.0	.7	.7	.0	−.8	.5	.4
June	.3	.6	.4	.5	.3	.6	.3	.5	.5	.8	.4	.4	.3	.6
July	.5	.4	1.5	.8	.2	.2	.1	.1	.6	.6	−.6	−.5	.3	.4
Aug	−.1	.3	−.5	.1	−.0	.3	−.1	.2	.2	.7	−1.2	−1.1	.3	.6
Sept	0	.2	−.0	−.5	.0	.4	.1	.5	−.2	.1	.6	.7	−.1	.3
Oct	1.0	.6	−.9	−.2	1.6	.8	1.3	.8	2.3	1.0	−.6	−.1	2.1	1.0
Nov	.1	.5	−.5	−.7	.3	.8	.3	.9	.6	.7	.1	1.4	.4	.7
Dec	.3	.3	.1	−.1	.3	.4	.3	.3	.4	.6	.5	.9	.3	.2
1982: [2]														
Jan	.9	.5	1.4	1.1	.7	.4	.7	.4	.8	.5	−.5	−.9	1.0	.7
Feb	0	−.2	.7	.5	−.2	−.4	−.1	−.3	−.4	−.4	−1.2	−1.6	−.0	−.1
Mar	−.2	−.1	−.4	−.1	−.2	−.1	−.3	−.4	.3	.5	−2.2	−2.6	.2	.3
Apr	0	.1	1.1	1.7	−.3	−.4	−.6	−.7	.5	.3	−4.8	−5.2	.5	.5
May	.2	−.1	.9	.6	−.0	−.2	−.2	−.5	.3	.4	−2.2	−3.0	.4	.2
June	.8	1.0	.4	.5	.9	1.1	1.1	1.3	.4	.7	4.2	4.2	.3	.6
July	.6	.5	−1.1	−1.6	1.2	1.2	1.4	1.4	.4	.4	5.7	5.7	.3	.4
Aug	.2	.6	−.3	.2	.4	.7	.5	.8	.2	.7	1.2	1.2	.3	.6
Sept	−.3	−.1	.1	−.5	−.5	−.0	−.4	.1	−.4	−.1	.3	.4	−.6	−.1
Oct	1.0	.5	−.8	−.2	1.5	.7	1.5	.8	1.5	.2	−.6	−.1	1.9	.8
Nov	.3	.6	−.1	−.2	.4	.9	.4	1.1	.1	.3	1.6	2.9	.1	.5
Dec	.1	.1	.2	.1	.0	.1	−.1	−.1	.4	.6	−1.1	−.7	.3	.2

[1] Changes from December to December are based on unadjusted indexes.

[2] Data have been revised through August 1982 to reflect the availability of late reports and corrections by respondents. All data are subject to revision 4 months after original publication.

Source: Department of Labor, Bureau of Labor Statistics.

Table B–61.—*Money stock measures and liquid assets, 1959–82*

[Averages of daily figures; billions of dollars, seasonally adjusted]

Year and month	M1	M2	M3	L	Percent change from year or 6 months earlier [3]		
	Sum of currency, demand deposits, travelers' checks, and other checkable deposits (OCD) [1]	M1 plus overnight RPs and Eurodollars, MMMF balances (general purpose and broker/dealer), and savings and small time deposits [2]	M2 plus large time deposits, term RPs, and institution-only MMMF balances	M3 plus other liquid assets	M1	M2	M3
December:							
1959	140.9	297.7	298.9	388.4			
1960	141.9	312.3	314.3	403.4	0.7	4.9	5.2
1961	146.5	335.5	339.4	430.5	3.2	7.4	8.0
1962	149.2	362.8	369.7	465.9	1.8	8.1	8.9
1963	154.7	393.4	404.1	503.7	3.7	8.4	9.3
1964	161.9	425.1	440.2	540.5	4.7	8.1	8.9
1965	169.5	459.5	480.7	584.5	4.7	8.1	9.2
1966	173.7	481.3	504.9	616.5	2.5	4.7	5.0
1967	185.1	526.6	558.6	670.1	6.6	9.4	10.6
1968	199.4	569.4	608.4	733.9	7.7	8.1	8.9
1969	205.8	591.3	614.1	765.2	3.2	3.8	.9
1970	216.5	628.8	675.2	816.5	5.2	6.3	9.9
1971	230.6	713.6	773.7	903.2	6.5	13.5	14.6
1972	251.9	806.4	882.8	1,023.6	9.2	13.0	14.1
1973	265.8	863.2	981.4	1,143.8	5.5	7.0	11.2
1974	277.4	911.2	1,064.3	1,249.8	4.4	5.6	8.4
1975	291.0	1,026.9	1,166.2	1,376.6	4.9	12.7	9.6
1976	310.4	1,171.2	1,305.0	1,531.4	6.7	14.1	11.9
1977	335.5	1,297.7	1,464.6	1,724.3	8.1	10.8	12.2
1978	363.2	1,403.9	1,629.0	1,938.9	8.3	8.2	11.2
1979	389.0	1,518.9	1,779.4	2,153.9	7.1	8.2	9.2
1980	414.5	1,656.2	1,963.1	2,370.4	6.6	9.0	10.3
1981	440.9	1,822.7	2,188.1	2,642.8	6.4	10.1	11.5
1982 p	478.5	1,999.1	2,403.7		8.5	9.7	9.9
1981:							
Jan	417.9	1,665.7	1,984.2	2,397.3	10.3	8.6	11.7
Feb	419.4	1,678.2	2,001.9	2,418.2	7.2	7.6	10.8
Mar	424.4	1,701.1	2,024.0	2,438.0	6.8	9.0	11.8
Apr	433.3	1,723.2	2,046.3	2,455.5	8.8	10.4	12.3
May	429.2	1,732.4	2,065.2	2,483.1	5.7	9.4	11.9
June	428.4	1,740.9	2,082.1	2,506.6	6.8	10.5	12.5
July	429.4	1,753.7	2,102.5	2,530.4	5.6	10.8	12.3
Aug	431.1	1,772.4	2,126.0	2,559.7	5.7	11.5	12.8
Sept	431.2	1,778.3	2,138.1	2,577.2	3.2	9.3	11.6
Oct	432.9	1,789.5	2,151.1	2,600.0	−.2	7.8	10.5
Nov	436.4	1,809.9	2,174.7	2,629.3	3.4	9.1	10.9
Dec	440.9	1,822.7	2,188.1	2,642.8	5.9	9.6	10.4
1982:							
Jan	448.6	1,841.3	2,204.3	2,667.9	9.1	10.2	9.9
Feb	447.3	1,848.1	2,215.1	2,690.5	7.7	8.7	8.6
Mar	448.3	1,865.3	2,235.9	2,717.2	8.1	10.0	9.4
Apr	452.4	1,880.9	2,258.3	2,744.2	9.2	10.5	10.2
May	451.5	1,897.7	2,279.5	2,774.4	7.0	9.9	9.9
June	451.4	1,908.2	2,296.2	2,799.5	4.8	9.6	10.1
July	451.3	1,923.8	2,320.6	2,831.9	1.2	9.2	10.8
Aug	455.2	1,946.8	2,356.4	2,858.2	3.6	11.0	13.2
Sept	460.5	1,955.0	2,364.2		5.5	9.8	11.8
Oct	468.4	1,968.2	2,382.1		7.2	9.5	11.3
Nov	475.0	1,987.2	2,401.2		10.7	9.7	11.0
Dec p	478.5	1,999.1	2,403.7		12.4	9.8	9.6

[1] Net of demand deposits due to foreign commercial banks and official institutions.

[2] M2 will differ from the sum of components shown in Table B–62 by a consolidation adjustment that represents the estimated amount of demand deposits and vault cash held by thrift institutions to service time and savings deposits.

[3] Monthly percent changes are from 6 months earlier at a compound annual rate.

Note.—See Table B–62 for components, except travelers checks not shown separately.

Source: Board of Governors of the Federal Reserve System.

Table B–62.—*Components of money stock measures and liquid assets, 1959–82*

[Averages of daily figures; billions of dollars, seasonally adjusted, except as noted]

Period	Currency	Demand deposits[1]	Other checkable deposits	Overnight repurchase agreements (RPs) (net) NSA	Overnight Eurodollars NSA	Money market mutual fund (MMMF) balances: General purpose and broker/dealer NSA	Money market mutual fund (MMMF) balances: Institution only NSA	Savings deposits	Small denomination time deposits[2]	Large denomination time deposits[2]	Term repurchase agreements (RPs) NSA	Term Eurodollars (net) NSA	Savings bonds	Short-term Treasury securities	Bankers' acceptances	Commercial paper
December:																
1959	28.9	111.6	0.0	0.0	0.0	0.0	0.0	146.0	11.8	1.2	0.0	0.7	46.1	38.6	0.5	3.6
1960	29.0	112.5	.0	.0	.0	.0	.0	158.7	12.9	2.0	.0	.8	45.7	36.7	.8	5.1
1961	29.6	116.5	.0	.0	.0	.0	.0	175.0	15.2	3.9	.0	1.4	46.5	37.0	1.0	5.2
1962	30.6	118.1	.0	.0	.0	.0	.0	194.3	20.7	6.9	.0	1.6	46.9	39.8	1.0	6.8
1963	32.5	121.7	.1	.0	.0	.0	.0	213.9	26.2	10.7	.0	1.9	48.1	40.7	1.1	7.7
1964	34.3	127.0	.1	.0	.0	.0	.0	234.8	29.9	15.2	.0	2.4	49.0	38.5	1.2	9.1
1965	36.3	132.5	.1	.0	.0	.0	.0	256.5	35.2	21.2	.0	1.7	49.6	40.7	1.5	10.2
1966	38.3	134.6	.1	.5	.0	.0	.0	252.8	55.9	23.1	.5	2.1	50.2	43.2	1.6	14.4
1967	40.4	143.9	.1	1.1	.0	.0	.0	263.3	79.0	31.0	1.0	2.1	51.2	38.7	1.7	17.8
1968	43.4	155.1	.1	1.6	.0	.0	.0	268.5	101.9	37.4	1.5	2.9	51.8	46.1	2.2	22.5
1969	46.1	158.8	.1	2.5	.0	.0	.0	263.2	121.7	20.4	2.4	2.7	51.7	59.5	3.2	34.0
1970	49.1	166.3	.1	1.4	.0	.0	.0	259.3	153.6	45.0	1.4	2.2	52.0	49.2	3.3	34.5
1971	52.5	176.8	.2	2.5	.0	.0	.0	290.8	192.0	57.6	2.5	2.7	54.3	36.3	3.5	32.7
1972	56.8	193.6	.2	3.1	.0	.0	.0	320.2	233.9	73.2	3.3	3.6	57.6	41.1	3.3	35.2
1973	61.5	202.5	.3	6.8	.0	.1	.0	325.9	267.6	111.2	7.1	5.4	60.4	50.0	4.7	41.9
1974	67.8	207.4	.4	7.2	.0	2.1	.2	337.6	290.0	144.4	8.4	8.0	63.2	53.6	10.6	50.1
1975	73.8	214.1	.9	7.5	.0	3.2	.4	387.7	340.9	129.8	9.0	9.7	67.2	77.1	8.4	48.0
1976	80.6	224.4	2.7	13.7	.0	2.8	.6	451.7	396.5	118.2	15.0	13.1	71.7	81.1	8.8	51.7
1977	88.6	239.6	4.2	17.8	1.0	2.9	.9	490.4	454.1	145.2	21.0	18.7	76.4	89.9	11.8	62.9
1978	97.4	253.9	8.4	22.1	2.0	7.1	3.1	479.9	533.9	194.6	27.5	29.9	80.3	99.3	21.4	79.2
1979	106.1	262.2	16.9	22.7	3.6	34.4	9.3	421.7	652.6	221.8	30.2	42.9	79.6	128.5	26.5	97.0
1980	116.2	267.2	26.9	30.5	4.5	61.9	13.9	398.9	751.7	257.9	37.8	48.4	72.3	156.7	31.8	98.1
1981	123.1	236.4	77.0	31.4	6.7	151.2	33.7	343.6	854.7	300.3	35.4	66.7	67.7	176.5	39.7	104.2
1982 p	132.6	240.2	101.3	39.5	6.1	177.5	43.1	400.3	904.2	332.6	33.6					
1981:																
Jan	116.3	254.1	43.2	30.6	5.2	65.8	15.0	384.5	768.1	267.5	39.2	50.2	71.7	161.1	32.4	97.7
Feb	117.2	244.8	53.3	30.4	4.9	75.2	17.3	378.5	775.7	271.7	38.1	52.2	71.0	163.6	32.5	97.0
Mar	117.8	243.0	59.5	31.9	4.6	85.4	20.2	378.5	782.0	269.8	36.1	52.1	70.6	161.9	33.3	96.1
Apr	119.1	243.5	66.5	31.8	5.0	96.0	21.3	378.8	784.1	267.6	36.7	52.6	70.3	157.6	34.5	94.2
May	119.4	240.4	65.2	34.5	6.5	98.8	19.5	373.5	795.8	278.3	37.7	57.0	70.0	158.2	35.6	97.1
June	119.7	237.7	66.7	36.5	6.4	102.9	20.1	366.8	805.5	285.6	38.8	57.9	69.7	160.3	36.4	100.3
July	120.5	236.7	68.1	35.4	6.9	112.8	21.6	361.0	814.0	293.1	37.2	58.7	69.4	161.8	37.1	100.8
Aug	120.7	236.6	69.5	35.3	7.8	122.2	23.3	350.9	830.8	299.8	33.4	61.0	68.9	164.1	37.3	102.4
Sept	121.1	234.7	71.2	32.7	6.9	130.6	26.6	343.1	839.7	302.3	33.8	61.2	68.4	168.1	37.6	103.8
Oct	121.3	235.7	71.6	30.2	5.9	137.3	29.4	339.6	849.8	302.2	33.4	63.4	67.9	176.0	37.1	104.4
Nov	121.8	235.7	74.7	30.4	6.5	144.9	32.0	340.9	856.8	300.6	35.6	65.5	67.7	179.9	38.1	103.7
Dec	123.1	236.4	77.0	31.4	6.7	151.2	33.7	343.6	854.7	300.3	35.4	66.7	67.7	176.5	39.7	104.2
1982:																
Jan	123.8	239.3	81.1	35.7	7.5	154.9	32.5	348.8	852.3	302.6	32.5	69.9	67.8	180.3	40.2	105.5
Feb	124.6	234.5	83.8	35.6	7.3	156.1	30.5	348.6	859.4	308.0	32.5	73.8	67.8	186.4	39.1	108.4
Mar	125.1	233.0	85.8	36.7	6.3	159.4	31.5	350.7	869.9	312.6	31.5	74.4	67.7	191.0	37.9	110.3
Apr	126.3	233.0	88.6	34.6	5.8	162.1	31.5	350.5	881.6	317.2	34.2	78.5	67.7	191.7	38.3	109.7
May	127.4	232.7	87.0	35.8	7.0	164.6	32.8	350.9	894.1	321.6	32.6	83.3	67.7	191.9	39.9	112.1
June	128.4	231.0	87.5	36.0	7.0	168.9	33.7	349.9	900.9	328.3	31.2	84.8	67.8	194.8	40.3	115.7
July	128.8	230.6	87.4	36.4	7.0	171.7	36.7	344.0	919.7	335.8	29.3	84.2	67.7	199.9	40.8	118.7
Aug	129.5	231.1	90.2	37.6	6.9	180.6	43.1	342.0	930.6	339.6	32.1	81.5	67.6	200.5	40.2	112.0
Sept	130.5	232.6	93.0	36.8	6.5	182.5	43.9	342.4	932.6	339.3	30.5					
Oct	131.2	236.2	96.5	39.7	6.2	184.1	44.8	352.6	923.8	342.5	31.3					
Nov	131.6	238.3	100.7	40.6	6.6	186.6	45.3	362.3	923.0	340.4	33.5					
Dec p	132.6	240.2	101.3	39.5	6.1	177.5	43.1	400.3	904.2	332.6	33.6					

[1] Demand deposits at all commercial banks other than those due to domestic banks, the U.S. Government, and foreign banks and official institutions less cash items in the process of collection and Federal Reserve float.

[2] Small denomination and large denomination deposits are those issued in amounts of less than $100,000 and more than $100,000, respectively.

Note.—NSA indicates data are not seasonally adjusted.

Travelers checks are a component of money stock but are not shown here.

See also Table B–61.

Source: Board of Governors of the Federal Reserve System.

Table B-63.—*Commercial bank loans and investments, 1939–82*

[Billions of dollars]

Year and month	Total loans and investments	Loans: Total	Loans: Commercial and industrial	Investments: U.S. Treasury securities	Investments: Other securities	Loans plus loans sold to bank affiliates
End of month [1]						
1939: Dec	40.7	17.2		16.3	7.1	
1940: Dec	43.9	18.8		17.8	7.4	
1941: Dec	50.7	21.7		21.8	7.2	
1942: Dec	67.4	19.2		41.4	6.8	
1943: Dec	85.1	19.1		59.8	6.1	
1944: Dec	105.5	21.6		77.6	6.3	
1945: Dec	124.0	26.1		90.6	7.3	
1946: Dec	114.0	31.1		74.8	8.1	
1947: Dec	116.3	38.1		69.2	9.0	
1948: Dec	114.3	42.5		62.6	9.2	
	Seasonally adjusted					
1948: Dec	113.0	41.5		62.3	9.2	
1949: Dec	118.7	42.0		66.4	10.3	
1950: Dec	124.7	51.1		61.1	12.4	
1951: Dec	130.2	56.5		60.4	13.4	
1952: Dec	139.1	62.8		62.2	14.2	
1953: Dec	143.1	66.2		62.2	14.7	
1954: Dec	153.1	69.1		67.6	16.4	
1955: Dec	157.6	80.6		60.3	16.8	
1956: Dec	161.6	88.1		57.2	16.3	
1957: Dec	166.4	91.5		56.9	17.9	
1958: Dec	181.2	95.6		65.1	20.5	
1959: Dec	188.7	110.5	39.4	57.7	20.5	
1960: Dec	197.4	116.7	42.1	59.9	20.8	
1961: Dec	212.8	123.6	43.9	65.3	23.9	
1962: Dec	231.2	137.3	47.6	64.7	29.2	
1963: Dec	250.2	153.7	52.1	61.5	35.0	
1964: Dec	272.3	172.9	58.4	60.7	38.7	
1965: Dec	300.1	198.2	69.5	57.1	44.8	
1966: Dec	316.1	213.9	78.6	53.5	48.7	
1967: Dec	352.0	231.3	86.2	59.4	61.3	
1968: Dec	390.2	258.2	95.9	60.7	71.3	
1969: Dec	401.7	279.4	105.7	51.2	71.1	283.3
1970: Dec	435.5	292.0	110.0	57.8	85.7	294.7
1971: Dec	485.7	320.9	116.2	60.6	104.2	323.7
1972: Dec	558.0	378.9	130.4	62.6	116.5	381.5
Average for month [2]						
1972: Dec	572.6	390.5	137.5	65.8	116.3	393.1
1973: Dec	647.8	460.5	165.4	58.5	128.8	464.8
1974: Dec	713.6	520.1	196.9	53.6	139.9	524.8
1975: Dec	745.2	517.4	189.6	82.2	145.6	521.8
1976: Dec	804.6	555.0	190.9	100.8	148.8	558.7
1977: Dec	891.5	632.5	210.9	99.8	159.3	637.1
1978: Dec	1,013.5	747.0	245.9	93.8	172.8	750.7
1979: Dec	1,135.9	849.9	291.2	94.5	191.5	852.9
1980: Dec	1,239.6	915.1	326.8	110.0	214.4	917.8
1981: Dec	1,316.3	973.9	358.0	111.0	231.4	976.7
1982: Dec	1,412.4	1,042.3	392.4	130.9	239.2	1,045.2
1982:						
Jan	1,320.1	974.5	360.3	114.1	231.5	977.4
Feb	1,332.4	985.2	365.5	115.1	232.0	988.0
Mar	1,342.5	995.0	370.0	114.4	233.1	997.8
Apr	1,352.5	1,002.0	373.1	116.6	234.0	1,004.8
May	1,362.0	1,010.8	378.9	116.3	234.9	1,013.5
June	1,368.8	1,017.1	383.4	115.8	235.9	1,020.1
July	1,376.1	1,023.7	386.7	116.5	235.9	1,026.5
Aug	1,383.1	1,028.3	387.9	117.8	237.1	1,031.1
Sept	1,389.4	1,033.5	392.5	118.2	237.6	1,036.4
Oct	1,397.5	1,038.1	394.8	122.3	237.2	1,040.9
Nov	1,398.5	1,036.4	392.0	126.4	235.8	1,039.3
Dec	1,412.4	1,042.3	392.4	130.9	239.2	1,045.2

[1] Data are for December 31 call dates.

[2] Data are prorated averages of Wednesday figures for domestically chartered banks and averages of current and previous month-end data for foreign-related institutions. Lease financing receivables are included in total loans and investments and in total loans.

Note.—Beginning December 1981, levels have been reduced because of shifts from U.S. banking offices to International Banking Facilities (IBFs).

Source: Board of Governors of the Federal Reserve System.

TABLE B–64.—*Total funds raised in credit markets by nonfinancial sectors, 1974–82*

[Billions of dollars; quarterly data at seasonally adjusted annual rates]

Item	1974	1975	1976	1977	1978	1979	1980	1981
Total funds raised by nonfinancial sectors	193.9	214.4	273.5	334.3	401.7	402.0	397.1	406.9
U.S. Government	11.8	85.4	69.0	56.8	53.7	37.4	79.2	87.4
Foreign	14.8	11.5	19.6	13.9	33.2	21.0	29.3	27.3
Private domestic nonfinancial sectors	167.4	117.5	184.9	263.6	314.8	343.6	288.7	292.3
Corporate equities	4.1	9.9	10.5	2.7	–.1	–7.8	12.9	–11.5
Debt instruments	163.3	107.5	174.3	260.9	314.9	351.5	275.8	303.7
Debt capital instruments	100.6	100.9	123.6	169.8	198.7	216.0	204.1	175.0
State and local government obligations	16.5	16.1	15.7	21.9	28.4	29.8	35.9	32.9
Corporate bonds	19.7	27.2	22.8	21.0	20.1	22.5	33.2	23.9
Mortgages	64.4	57.6	85.1	126.9	150.2	163.7	135.1	118.3
Home	37.3	42.0	63.9	94.3	112.1	120.1	96.7	78.6
Multi-family residential	6.9	–.0	3.9	7.1	9.2	7.8	8.8	4.6
Commercial	15.1	11.0	11.6	18.4	21.7	23.9	20.2	25.3
Farm	5.0	4.6	5.7	7.1	7.2	11.8	9.3	9.8
Other debt instruments	62.7	6.6	50.7	91.1	116.2	135.5	71.7	128.8
Consumer credit	9.9	9.6	25.4	40.2	48.8	45.4	4.9	25.3
Bank loans n.e.c.	32.6	–10.5	4.4	26.7	37.1	49.2	35.4	51.1
Open-market paper	6.6	–2.6	4.0	2.9	5.2	11.1	6.6	19.2
Other	13.5	10.1	16.9	21.3	25.1	29.7	24.9	33.1
By borrowing sector: Total	167.4	117.5	184.9	263.6	314.8	343.6	288.7	292.3
State and local governments	15.5	13.7	15.2	15.4	19.1	20.2	27.3	22.3
Households	53.9	52.1	89.5	137.3	169.3	176.5	117.5	120.4
Nonfinancial business	98.0	51.6	80.2	110.9	126.3	146.9	143.9	149.5
Farm	7.8	8.5	10.2	12.3	14.6	21.4	14.4	16.4
Nonfarm noncorporate	20.2	12.5	15.4	28.3	32.4	34.4	33.8	40.5
Corporate	69.9	30.7	54.5	70.4	79.3	91.2	95.7	92.6
Debt instruments	65.9	20.8	44.0	67.6	79.4	99.0	82.8	104.1
Equities	4.1	9.9	10.5	2.7	–.1	–7.8	12.9	–11.5
Total funds supplied to nonfinancial sectors	193.9	214.4	273.5	334.3	401.7	402.0	397.1	406.9
Financed directly or indirectly by:								
Private domestic nonfinancial sectors	123.5	148.1	173.5	184.0	219.7	258.9	271.1	291.3
Deposits and currency	73.7	101.2	133.4	148.5	152.3	151.9	179.2	221.0
Checkable deposits and currency	8.5	15.6	17.8	25.5	25.6	27.2	14.5	27.8
Time and savings deposits	65.3	83.3	111.7	119.3	110.3	82.2	127.8	82.9
Money market fund shares	2.4	1.3	–.0	.2	6.9	34.4	29.2	107.5
Security repurchase agreements	–2.2	.2	2.3	2.2	7.5	6.6	6.5	2.5
Foreign deposits	–.2	.8	1.7	1.3	2.0	1.5	1.1	.3
Credit market instruments	50.4	50.7	44.7	39.0	72.5	122.9	89.7	101.9
Corporate equities	–.6	–3.8	–4.6	–3.5	–5.1	–15.9	2.1	–31.6
Foreign funds	21.8	2.1	13.2	43.5	46.7	22.7	5.6	13.6
At banks	10.1	–8.7	–4.7	1.2	6.3	25.6	–23.0	–8.8
Credit and equity instruments	11.7	10.8	17.9	42.3	40.5	–2.9	28.6	22.3
U.S. Government-related loans, net	19.1	23.2	20.4	17.6	27.2	31.8	29.0	34.2
U.S. Government cash balances	–4.6	2.8	3.0	.9	3.7	.5	–3.6	.1
Private insurance and pension reserves	33.4	39.7	47.7	60.7	66.6	60.0	80.8	88.5
Other sources	.8	–1.6	15.7	27.5	37.8	28.1	14.2	–20.8

See next page for continuation of table.

TABLE B-64.—*Total funds raised in credit markets by nonfinancial sectors, 1974–82*—Continued

[Billions of dollars; quarterly data at seasonally adjusted annual rates]

Item	1981				1982		
	I	II	III	IV	I	II	III
Total funds raised by nonfinancial sectors	431.9	444.5	380.8	370.6	361.8	399.5	479.7
U.S. Government	111.3	52.5	62.7	123.0	94.8	101.4	221.2
Foreign	33.6	35.7	18.9	20.9	15.5	16.5	1.3
Private domestic nonfinancial sectors	287.0	356.3	299.2	226.7	251.5	281.6	257.2
Corporate equities	5.2	−3.4	−24.6	−23.0	−5.3	5.0	.0
Debt instruments	281.8	359.7	323.8	249.7	256.8	276.6	257.2
Debt capital instruments	192.7	200.3	156.9	150.0	159.7	153.6	172.9
State and local government obligations	36.0	34.2	26.3	35.0	38.3	57.5	54.3
Corporate bonds	25.0	24.5	19.5	26.4	20.3	16.7	42.5
Mortgages	131.8	141.6	111.1	88.6	101.2	79.4	76.2
Home	93.4	96.9	72.5	51.6	67.2	51.8	51.4
Multi-family residential	4.4	5.7	4.1	4.2	6.2	3.9	7.1
Commercial	25.3	29.4	23.7	22.6	20.5	20.1	11.0
Farm	8.5	9.5	10.8	10.2	7.3	3.6	6.6
Other debt instruments	89.1	159.4	166.8	99.6	97.1	123.0	84.3
Consumer credit	26.5	32.2	34.2	8.3	6.6	25.4	8.2
Bank loans n.e.c.	22.8	72.6	66.0	43.2	69.9	86.6	46.6
Open-market paper	11.3	10.1	32.9	22.3	12.2	−5.3	−.9
Other	28.5	44.5	33.8	25.9	8.4	16.4	30.4
By borrowing sector: Total	287.0	356.3	299.2	226.7	251.5	281.6	257.2
State and local governments	27.1	23.1	14.8	24.3	25.6	46.9	39.2
Households	135.0	147.1	128.1	71.7	82.1	97.2	81.6
Nonfinancial business	125.0	186.1	156.4	130.7	143.8	137.4	136.5
Farm	19.2	20.5	16.1	9.6	5.6	11.3	12.5
Nonfarm noncorporate	37.1	46.5	40.1	38.5	28.0	32.8	25.9
Corporate	68.7	119.1	100.2	82.5	110.2	93.3	98.0
Debt instruments	63.5	122.5	124.8	105.5	115.5	88.3	98.0
Equities	5.2	−3.4	−24.6	−23.0	−5.3	5.0	.0
Total funds supplied to nonfinancial sectors	431.9	444.5	380.8	370.6	361.8	399.5	479.7
Financed directly or indirectly by:							
Private domestic nonfinancial sectors	309.3	278.3	285.5	291.9	242.6	296.5	329.9
Deposits and currency	284.0	153.2	217.5	229.2	205.3	149.7	204.6
Checkable deposits and currency	69.7	−5.2	−6.6	53.2	27.3	−9.5	−5.8
Time and savings deposits	39.2	108.3	103.8	80.2	148.2	112.1	123.5
Money market fund shares	148.4	59.9	137.3	84.3	37.6	41.2	86.5
Security repurchase agreements	16.9	−1.6	−13.8	8.6	.3	1.7	7.6
Foreign deposits	9.7	−8.2	−3.2	2.8	−8.1	4.1	−7.2
Credit market instruments	40.9	154.2	123.0	89.5	48.3	151.2	137.8
Corporate equities	−15.5	−29.0	−55.0	−26.8	−11.0	−4.4	−12.5
Foreign funds	21.8	55.0	3.2	−25.7	−32.9	23.7	−40.8
At banks	−25.4	24.0	11.9	−45.6	−46.0	−16.3	−61.7
Credit and equity instruments	47.2	31.0	8.7	19.9	13.0	40.0	20.9
U.S. Government-related loans, net	27.2	23.3	37.4	49.0	10.0	10.1	53.2
U.S. Government cash balances	14.1	−2.5	−7.2	−3.8	23.2	−29.6	42.3
Private insurance and pension reserves	79.3	94.7	95.0	85.3	84.2	99.1	85.4
Other sources	−19.7	−4.3	−33.0	−26.1	34.7	−.4	9.7

Source: Board of Governors of the Federal Reserve System.

TABLE B–65.—*Federal Reserve Bank credit and member bank reserves, 1929–82*

[Averages of daily figures; millions of dollars]

Year and month	Reserve Bank credit outstanding					Member bank reserves [1]		
	Total	U.S. Government and Federal agency securities	Member bank borrowings		Other	Total	Required	Excess
			Total	Seasonal				
1929: Dec	1,643	446	801		396	2,395	2,347	48
1933: Dec	2,669	2,432	95		142	2,588	[2] 1,822	[2] 766
1939: Dec	2,612	2,510	3		99	11,473	6,462	5,011
1940: Dec	2,305	2,188	3		114	14,049	7,403	6,646
1941: Dec	2,404	2,219	5		180	12,812	9,422	3,390
1942: Dec	6,035	5,549	4		482	13,152	10,776	2,376
1943: Dec	11,914	11,166	90		658	12,749	11,701	1,048
1944: Dec	19,612	18,693	265		654	14,168	12,884	1,284
1945: Dec	24,744	23,708	334		702	16,027	14,536	1,491
1946: Dec	24,746	23,767	157		822	16,517	15,617	900
1947: Dec	22,858	21,905	224		729	17,261	16,275	986
1948: Dec	23,978	23,002	134		842	19,990	19,193	797
1949: Dec	19,012	18,287	118		607	16,291	15,488	803
1950: Dec	21,606	20,345	142		1,119	17,391	16,364	1,027
1951: Dec	25,446	23,409	657		1,380	20,310	19,484	826
1952: Dec	27,299	24,400	1,593		1,306	21,180	20,457	723
1953: Dec	27,107	25,639	441		1,027	19,920	19,227	693
1954: Dec	26,317	24,917	246		1,154	19,279	18,576	703
1955: Dec	26,853	24,602	839		1,412	19,240	18,646	594
1956: Dec	27,156	24,765	688		1,703	19,535	18,883	652
1957: Dec	26,186	23,982	710		1,494	19,420	18,843	577
1958: Dec	28,412	26,312	557		1,543	18,899	18,383	516
1959: Dec	29,435	27,036	906		1,493	18,932	18,450	482
1960: Dec	29,060	27,248	87		1,725	19,283	18,514	769
1961: Dec	31,217	29,098	149		1,970	20,118	19,550	568
1962: Dec	33,218	30,546	304		2,368	20,040	19,468	572
1963: Dec	36,610	33,729	327		2,554	20,746	20,210	536
1964: Dec	39,873	37,126	243		2,504	21,609	21,198	411
1965: Dec	43,853	40,885	454		2,514	22,719	22,267	452
1966: Dec	46,864	43,760	557		2,547	23,830	23,438	392
1967: Dec	51,268	48,891	238		2,139	25,260	24,915	345
1968: Dec	56,610	52,529	765		3,316	27,221	26,766	455
1969: Dec	64,100	57,500	1,086		5,514	28,031	27,774	257
1970: Dec	66,708	61,688	321		4,699	29,265	28,993	272
1971: Dec	74,255	69,158	107		4,990	31,329	31,164	165
1972: Dec	76,851	71,094	1,049		4,708	31,353	31,134	219
1973: Dec	85,642	79,701	1,298	41	4,643	35,068	34,806	262
1974: Dec	93,967	86,679	703	32	6,585	36,941	36,602	339
1975: Dec	99,651	92,108	127	13	7,416	34,989	34,727	262
1976: Dec	107,632	100,328	62	12	7,242	35,136	34,964	172
1977: Dec	116,382	107,948	558	54	7,876	36,471	36,297	174
1978: Dec	129,330	117,344	874	134	11,112	41,572	41,447	125
1979: Dec	139,896	126,276	1,473	82	12,147	43,972	43,578	394
1980: Dec	143,250	127,895	1,617	116	13,738	[3] 40,097	40,067	[4] 30
1981: Dec	151,920	137,796	642	53	13,482	41,918	41,606	312
1982: Dec *p*	159,968	146,358	699	33	12,911	42,172	41,354	818
1982:								
Jan	152,297	136,657	1,526	75	14,114	43,210	42,785	425
Feb	150,554	136,050	1,713	132	12,791	41,280	40,981	299
Mar	146,815	133,635	1,611	174	11,569	39,230	38,873	357
Apr	150,361	136,649	1,581	167	12,131	39,558	39,284	274
May	151,333	138,809	1,105	237	11,419	39,552	39,192	360
June	152,140	139,814	1,205	239	11,121	39,567	39,257	310
July	153,468	141,623	669	225	11,176	39,864	39,573	291
Aug	153,903	141,791	510	119	11,602	40,177	39,866	311
Sept	153,324	140,962	976	102	11,386	39,963	39,579	384
Oct	153,666	141,443	455	86	11,768	40,587	40,183	404
Nov	156,151	143,442	579	47	12,130	41,199	40,797	402
Dec *p*	159,968	146,358	699	33	12,911	42,172	41,354	818

[1] Beginning December 1959, part of currency and cash held by member banks allowed as reserves; beginning November 1960 all such currency and cash allowed.

Beginning November 1972, includes reserve deficiencies on which Federal Reserve Banks were allowed to waive penalties for a transition period in connection with bank adaptation to Regulation J as amended effective November 9, 1972. Transition period ended after second quarter 1974.

Effective November 1975, includes reserve deficiencies on which penalties are waived over a 24-month period when a nonmember bank merges into an existing member bank, or when a nonmember bank joins the Federal Reserve System.

[2] Data are for licensed banks only.

[3] Includes all reserve balances of depository institutions plus vault cash at institutions with required reserve balances plus vault cash equal to required reserves at other institutions.

[4] Reserve balances with Federal Reserve Banks plus vault cash used to satisfy reserve requirements less required reserves. (This measure of excess reserves is comparable to the old excess reserves concept published historically.)

Source: Board of Governors of the Federal Reserve System.

TABLE B–66.—*Aggregate reserves of depository institutions and monetary base, 1959–82*

[Averages of daily figures; billions of dollars]

Year and month	Adjusted for changes in reserve requirements [1]							
	Seasonally adjusted				Not seasonally adjusted			
	Reserves of depository institutions			Monetary base [3]	Reserves of depository institutions			Monetary base [3]
	Total [2]	Nonborrowed	Required		Total [2]	Nonborrowed	Required	
1959: Dec	14.94	13.99	14.43	44.3	15.22	14.28	14.72	45.2
1960: Dec	15.13	15.06	14.39	44.5	15.42	15.34	14.67	45.5
1961: Dec	15.67	15.54	15.09	45.7	15.96	15.82	15.37	46.7
1962: Dec	16.04	15.78	15.47	47.1	16.31	16.05	15.74	48.1
1963: Dec	16.46	16.13	15.97	49.4	16.71	16.38	16.22	50.4
1964: Dec	17.07	16.80	16.66	51.9	17.32	17.06	16.92	52.9
1965: Dec	17.77	17.33	17.35	54.7	18.06	17.62	17.64	55.8
1966: Dec	17.83	17.30	17.49	56.8	18.16	17.63	17.82	57.9
1967: Dec	19.51	19.28	19.14	60.5	19.82	19.59	19.45	61.8
1968: Dec	20.70	19.96	20.28	64.8	20.72	19.97	20.29	65.8
1969: Dec	21.01	19.89	20.72	67.9	21.00	19.88	20.72	68.8
1970: Dec	22.13	21.80	21.88	72.0	22.14	21.81	21.89	73.0
1971: Dec	23.58	23.45	23.39	77.1	23.63	23.51	23.45	78.2
1972: Dec	26.32	25.27	26.03	84.2	26.35	25.30	26.06	85.4
1973: Dec	27.63	26.33	27.33	90.3	27.85	26.55	27.55	91.7
1974: Dec	29.25	28.52	28.99	98.3	29.59	28.86	29.33	100.0
1975: Dec	29.29	29.16	29.02	104.5	29.70	29.57	29.43	106.3
1976: Dec	29.86	29.81	29.59	112.0	30.27	30.22	30.00	114.1
1977: Dec	31.17	30.60	30.98	121.4	31.67	31.11	31.48	123.7
1978: Dec	32.82	31.95	32.59	132.2	33.37	32.50	33.13	134.8
1979: Dec	34.26	32.79	33.93	142.5	34.83	33.35	34.50	145.4
1980: Dec	36.46	34.77	35.95	155.0	37.11	35.42	36.59	158.0
1981: Dec	37.99	37.35	37.67	162.7	38.66	38.03	38.34	165.8
1982: Dec [p]	40.91	40.28	40.39	175.1	41.59	40.96	41.07	178.4
1981:								
Jan	36.52	35.12	36.14	155.4	38.01	36.62	37.64	156.5
Feb	36.52	35.22	36.17	156.0	36.28	34.97	35.93	154.3
Mar	36.85	35.85	36.57	156.7	36.24	35.24	35.96	154.9
Apr	37.02	35.68	36.85	158.0	36.88	35.54	36.71	157.0
May	37.18	34.95	36.92	158.5	36.89	34.66	36.63	157.9
June	37.20	35.17	36.86	158.9	36.68	34.65	36.35	158.4
July	37.28	35.60	36.94	159.6	37.24	35.56	36.90	160.5
Aug	37.34	35.92	37.05	160.0	37.06	35.64	36.77	160.3
Sept	37.72	36.27	37.31	160.6	37.52	36.06	37.11	160.2
Oct	37.60	36.42	37.33	160.8	37.70	36.52	37.42	160.8
Nov	37.62	36.95	37.27	161.2	37.78	37.12	37.44	162.6
Dec	37.99	37.35	37.67	162.7	38.66	38.03	38.34	165.8
1982:								
Jan	38.71	37.20	38.30	164.3	40.04	38.52	39.62	165.3
Feb	38.26	36.47	37.96	164.7	38.05	36.26	37.75	162.9
Mar	38.36	36.80	37.99	165.2	37.80	36.24	37.44	163.3
Apr	38.43	36.87	38.16	166.5	38.33	36.76	38.06	165.6
May	38.50	37.39	38.15	167.7	38.19	37.07	37.83	167.1
June	38.58	37.37	38.27	168.8	38.07	36.86	37.76	168.2
July	38.52	37.83	38.21	169.2	38.43	37.74	38.12	170.0
Aug	38.80	38.29	38.49	170.1	38.51	38.00	38.20	170.4
Sept	39.57	38.63	39.18	171.9	39.35	38.42	38.97	171.4
Oct	39.88	39.40	39.47	172.8	40.00	39.52	39.59	172.9
Nov	40.46	39.84	40.06	173.7	40.68	40.06	40.28	175.1
Dec [p]	40.91	40.28	40.39	175.1	41.59	40.96	41.07	178.4

[1] Reserve aggregates include required reserves of member banks and Edge Act corporations and other depository institutions. Discontinuities associated with the implementation of the Monetary Control Act, the inclusion of Edge Act corporation reserves, and other changes in Regulation D have been removed. Beginning with the week ended December 23, 1981, reserves aggregates have been reduced by shifts of reservable liabilities to international banking facilities (IBFS). On the basis of reports of liabilities transferred to IBFS by U.S. commercial banks and U.S. agencies and branches of foreign banks, it is estimated that required reserves were lowered on average by $10 to $20 million in December 1981 and $40 to $70 million in January 1982.

[2] Reserve balances with Federal Reserve Banks (which exclude required clearing balances) plus vault cash at institutions with required reserve balances plus vault cash equal to required reserves at other institutions.

[3] Includes reserve balances and required clearing balances at Federal Reserve Banks in the current week plus vault cash held two weeks earlier used to satisfy reserve requirements at all depository institutions plus currency outside the U.S. Treasury, Federal Reserve Banks, the vaults of depository institutions, and surplus vault cash at depository institutions.

Source: Board of Governors of the Federal Reserve System.

TABLE B-67.—*Bond yields and interest rates, 1929–82*

[Percent per annum]

Year or month	U.S. Treasury securities				Corporate bonds (Moody's)		High-grade municipal bonds (Standard & Poor's)	New-home mortgage yields (FHLBB) [3]	Prime commercial paper, 4–6 months	Prime rate charged by banks [4]	Discount rate, Federal Reserve Bank of New York [4]	Federal funds rate [5]
	Bills (new issues) [1]		Constant maturities [2]		Aaa	Baa						
	3-month	6-month	3 years	10 years								
1929	......	......	......	......	4.73	5.90	4.27	......	5.85	5.50–6.00	5.16	......
1933	0.515	......	......	......	4.49	7.76	4.71	......	1.73	1.50–4.00	2.56	......
1939	.023	......	......	......	3.01	4.96	2.76	......	.59	1.50	1.00	......
1940	.014	......	......	......	2.84	4.75	2.50	......	.56	1.50	1.00	......
1941	.103	......	......	......	2.77	4.33	2.10	......	.53	1.50	1.00	......
1942	.326	......	......	......	2.83	4.28	2.36	......	.66	1.50	[6] 1.00	......
1943	.373	......	......	......	2.73	3.91	2.06	......	.69	1.50	[6] 1.00	......
1944	.375	......	......	......	2.72	3.61	1.86	......	.73	1.50	[6] 1.00	......
1945	.375	......	......	......	2.62	3.29	1.67	......	.75	1.50	[6] 1.00	......
1946	.375	......	......	......	2.53	3.05	1.64	......	.81	1.50	[6] 1.00	......
1947	.594	......	......	......	2.61	3.24	2.01	......	1.03	1.50–1.75	1.00	......
1948	1.040	......	......	......	2.82	3.47	2.40	......	1.44	1.75–2.00	1.34	......
1949	1.102	......	......	......	2.66	3.42	2.21	......	1.49	2.00	1.50	......
1950	1.218	......	......	......	2.62	3.24	1.98	......	1.45	2.07	1.59	......
1951	1.552	......	......	......	2.86	3.41	2.00	......	2.16	2.56	1.75	......
1952	1.766	......	......	......	2.96	3.52	2.19	......	2.33	3.00	1.75	......
1953	1.931	......	2.47	2.85	3.20	3.74	2.72	......	2.52	3.17	1.99	......
1954	.953	......	1.63	2.40	2.90	3.51	2.37	......	1.58	3.05	1.60	......
1955	1.753	......	2.47	2.82	3.06	3.53	2.53	......	2.18	3.16	1.89	1.78
1956	2.658	......	3.19	3.18	3.36	3.88	2.93	......	3.31	3.77	2.77	2.73
1957	3.267	......	3.98	3.65	3.89	4.71	3.60	......	3.81	4.20	3.12	3.11
1958	1.839	......	2.84	3.32	3.79	4.73	3.56	......	2.46	3.83	2.15	1.57
1959	3.405	3.832	4.46	4.33	4.38	5.05	3.95	......	3.97	4.48	3.36	3.30
1960	2.928	3.247	3.98	4.12	4.41	5.19	3.73	......	3.85	4.82	3.53	3.22
1961	2.378	2.605	3.54	3.88	4.35	5.08	3.46	......	2.97	4.50	3.00	1.96
1962	2.778	2.908	3.47	3.95	4.33	5.02	3.18	......	3.26	4.50	3.00	2.68
1963	3.157	3.253	3.67	4.00	4.26	4.86	3.23	5.89	3.55	4.50	3.23	3.18
1964	3.549	3.686	4.03	4.19	4.40	4.83	3.22	5.82	3.97	4.50	3.55	3.50
1965	3.954	4.055	4.22	4.28	4.49	4.87	3.27	5.81	4.38	4.54	4.04	4.07
1966	4.881	5.082	5.23	4.92	5.13	5.67	3.82	6.25	5.55	5.63	4.50	5.11
1967	4.321	4.630	5.03	5.07	5.51	6.23	3.98	6.46	5.10	5.61	4.19	4.22
1968	5.339	5.470	5.68	5.65	6.18	6.94	4.51	6.97	5.90	6.30	5.16	5.66
1969	6.677	6.853	7.02	6.67	7.03	7.81	5.81	7.80	7.83	7.96	5.87	8.20
1970	6.458	6.562	7.29	7.35	8.04	9.11	6.51	8.45	7.71	7.91	5.95	7.18
1971	4.348	4.511	5.65	6.16	7.39	8.56	5.70	7.74	5.11	5.72	4.88	4.66
1972	4.071	4.466	5.72	6.21	7.21	8.16	5.27	7.60	4.73	5.25	4.50	4.43
1973	7.041	7.178	6.95	6.84	7.44	8.24	5.18	7.96	8.15	8.03	6.44	8.73
1974	7.886	7.926	7.82	7.56	8.57	9.50	6.09	8.92	9.84	10.81	7.83	10.50
1975	5.838	6.122	7.49	7.99	8.83	10.61	6.89	9.00	6.32	7.86	6.25	5.82
1976	4.989	5.266	6.77	7.61	8.43	9.75	6.49	9.00	5.34	6.84	5.50	5.04
1977	5.265	5.510	6.69	7.42	8.02	8.97	5.56	9.02	5.61	6.83	5.46	5.54
1978	7.221	7.572	8.29	8.41	8.73	9.49	5.90	9.56	7.99	9.06	7.46	7.93
1979	10.041	10.017	9.72	9.44	9.63	10.69	6.39	10.78	[7] 10.91	12.67	10.28	11.19
1980	11.506	11.374	11.55	11.46	11.94	13.67	8.51	12.66	12.29	15.27	11.77	13.36
1981	14.077	13.811	14.44	13.91	14.17	16.04	11.23	14.70	14.76	18.87	13.42	16.38
1982	10.686	11.084	12.92	13.00	13.79	16.11	11.57	15.14	11.89	14.86	11.02	12.26

See next page for continuation of table.

TABLE B–67.—*Bond yields and interest rates, 1929–82*—Continued

[Percent per annum]

Year or month	U.S. Treasury securities: Bills (new issues)[1]: 3-month	U.S. Treasury securities: Bills (new issues)[1]: 6-month	U.S. Treasury securities: Constant maturities[2]: 3 years	U.S. Treasury securities: Constant maturities[2]: 10 years	Corporate bonds (Moody's): Aaa	Corporate bonds (Moody's): Baa	High-grade municipal bonds (Standard & Poor's)	New-home mortgage yields (FHLBB)[3]	Prime commercial paper, 4–6 months	Prime rate charged by banks (high low)[4]	Discount rate, Federal Reserve Bank of New York (high-low)*	Federal funds rate[5]
1980:												
Jan	12.036	11.851	10.88	10.80	11.09	12.42	7.21	11.87	12.66	15.25–15.25	12.00–12.00	13.82
Feb	12.814	12.721	12.84	12.41	12.38	13.57	8.04	11.93	13.60	16.75–15.25	13.00–12.00	14.13
Mar	15.526	15.100	14.05	12.75	12.96	14.45	9.09	12.62	16.50	19.50–16.75	13.00–13.00	17.19
Apr	14.003	13.618	12.02	11.47	12.04	14.19	8.40	13.03	14.93	20.00–19.50	13.00–13.00	17.61
May	9.150	9.149	9.44	10.18	10.99	13.17	7.37	13.68	9.29	19.00–14.00	13.00–12.00	10.98
June	6.995	7.218	8.91	9.78	10.58	12.71	7.60	12.66	8.03	14.00–12.00	12.00–11.00	9.47
July	8.126	8.101	9.27	10.25	11.07	12.65	8.08	12.48	8.29	12.00–11.00	11.00–10.00	9.03
Aug	9.259	9.443	10.63	11.10	11.64	13.15	8.62	12.25	9.61	11.50–11.00	10.00–10.00	9.61
Sept	10.321	10.546	11.57	11.51	12.02	13.70	8.95	12.35	11.04	13.00–11.50	11.00–10.00	10.87
Oct	11.580	11.566	12.01	11.75	12.31	14.23	9.11	12.61	12.32	14.50–13.50	11.00–11.00	12.81
Nov	13.888	13.612	13.31	12.68	12.97	14.64	9.55	13.04	14.73	17.75–14.50	12.00–11.00	15.85
Dec	15.661	14.770	13.65	12.84	13.21	15.14	10.09	13.28	16.49	21.50–17.75	13.00–12.00	18.90
1981:												
Jan	14.724	13.883	13.01	12.57	12.81	15.03	9.65	13.26	15.10	21.50–20.00	13.00–13.00	19.08
Feb	14.905	14.134	13.65	13.19	13.35	15.37	10.03	13.54	14.87	20.00–19.00	13.00–13.00	15.93
Mar	13.478	12.983	13.51	13.12	13.33	15.34	10.12	14.02	13.59	19.00–17.50	13.00–13.00	14.70
Apr	13.635	13.434	14.09	13.68	13.88	15.56	10.55	14.15	14.17	18.00–17.00	13.00–13.00	15.72
May	16.295	15.334	15.08	14.10	14.32	15.95	10.73	14.10	16.66	20.50–18.00	14.00–13.00	18.52
June	14.557	13.947	14.29	13.47	13.75	15.80	10.56	14.67	15.22	20.50–20.00	14.00–14.00	19.10
July	14.699	14.402	15.15	14.28	14.38	16.17	11.03	14.72	16.09	20.50–20.00	14.00–14.00	19.04
Aug	15.612	15.548	16.00	14.94	14.89	16.34	12.13	15.27	16.62	20.50–20.50	14.00–14.00	17.82
Sept	14.951	15.057	16.22	15.32	15.49	16.92	12.86	15.29	15.93	20.50–19.50	14.00–14.00	15.87
Oct	13.873	14.013	15.50	15.15	15.40	17.11	12.67	15.65	14.72	19.50–18.00	14.00–14.00	15.08
Nov	11.269	11.530	13.11	13.39	14.22	16.39	11.71	16.38	11.96	18.00–16.00	14.00–13.00	13.31
Dec	10.926	11.471	13.66	13.72	14.23	16.55	12.77	15.87	12.14	15.75–15.75	13.00–12.00	12.37
1982:												
Jan	12.412	12.930	14.64	14.59	15.18	17.10	13.16	15.25	13.35	15.75–15.75	12.00–12.00	13.22
Feb	13.780	13.709	14.73	14.43	15.27	17.18	12.81	15.12	14.27	17.00–15.75	12.00–12.00	14.78
Mar	12.493	12.621	14.13	13.86	14.58	16.82	12.72	15.67	13.47	16.50–16.50	12.00–12.00	14.68
Apr	12.821	12.861	14.18	13.87	14.46	16.78	12.45	15.84	13.64	16.50–16.50	12.00–12.00	14.94
May	12.148	12.220	13.77	13.62	14.26	16.64	11.99	15.89	13.02	16.50–16.50	12.00–12.00	14.45
June	12.108	12.310	14.48	14.30	14.81	16.92	12.42	15.40	13.79	16.50–16.50	12.00–12.00	14.15
July	11.914	12.236	14.00	13.95	14.61	16.80	12.11	15.70	13.00	16.50–15.50	12.00–11.50	12.59
Aug	9.006	10.105	12.62	13.06	13.71	16.32	11.12	15.68	10.80	15.50–13.50	11.50–10.00	10.12
Sept	8.196	9.539	12.03	12.34	12.94	15.63	10.61	14.98	10.86	13.50–13.50	10.00–10.00	10.31
Oct	7.750	8.299	10.62	10.91	12.12	14.73	9.59	14.41	9.21	13.50–12.00	10.00–9.50	9.71
Nov	8.042	8.319	9.98	10.55	11.68	14.30	9.97	13.81	8.72	12.00–11.50	9.50–9.00	9.20
Dec	8.013	8.225	9.88	10.54	11.83	14.14	9.91	13.70	8.50	11.50–11.50	9.00–8.50	8.95

[1] Rate on new issues within period; bank-discount basis.
[2] Yields on the more actively traded issues adjusted to constant maturities by the Treasury Department.
[3] Effective rate (in the primary market) on conventional mortgages, reflecting fees and charges as well as contract rate and assuming on the average, repayment at end of 10 years. Rates beginning January 1973 not strictly comparable with prior rates.
[4] For monthly data, high and low for the period. Prime rate for 1929–33 and 1947–48 are ranges of the rate in effect during the period.
[5] Since July 19, 1975, the daily effective rate is an average of the rates on a given day weighted by the volume of transactions at these rates. Prior to that date, the daily effective rate was the rate considered most representative of the day's transactions, usually the one at which most transactions occurred.
[6] From October 30, 1942, to April 24, 1946, a preferential rate of 0.50 percent was in effect for advances secured by Government securities maturing in 1 year or less.
[7] Beginning November 1979, data are for 6-months paper.

Sources: Department of the Treasury, Board of Governors of the Federal Reserve System, Federal Home Loan Bank Board (FHLBB), Moody's Investors Service, and Standard & Poor's Corporation.

Table B-68.—*Consumer credit outstanding and net change, 1950–82*

[Millions of dollars]

Year and month	Amount outstanding (end of month)							Net change from preceding period			
	Total	Installment credit [1]					Noninstallment credit [4]	Total	Installment credit [1]		Noninstallment credit [4]
		Total	Automobile	Revolving [2]	Mobile home [3]	Other			Total	Automobile	
1950: Dec	25,641	15,503	6,015			9,488	10,138	4,789	3,271	1,537	1,518
1951: Dec	27,268	16,220	5,958			10,262	11,048	1,627	717	−57	910
1952: Dec	32,551	20,470	7,635			12,835	12,081	5,283	4,250	1,677	1,033
1953: Dec	36,736	24,254	9,685			14,569	12,482	4,185	3,784	2,050	401
1954: Dec	38,192	24,891	9,747			15,144	13,301	1,456	637	62	819
1955: Dec	45,348	30,269	13,471			16,798	15,079	7,156	5,378	3,724	1,778
1956: Dec	49,268	33,171	14,484			18,687	16,097	3,920	2,902	1,013	1,018
1957: Dec	52,191	35,443	15,472			19,971	16,748	2,923	2,272	988	651
1958: Dec	52,702	35,339	14,258			21,081	17,363	511	−104	−1,214	615
1959: Dec	60,741	41,123	16,632			24,491	19,618	8,039	5,784	2,374	2,255
1960: Dec	65,104	45,051	18,083			26,968	20,053	4,363	3,928	1,451	435
1961: Dec	67,635	46,027	17,599			28,428	21,608	2,531	976	−484	1,555
1962: Dec	73,917	50,994	19,924			31,070	22,923	6,282	4,967	2,325	1,315
1963: Dec	82,805	57,829	22,842			34,987	24,976	8,888	6,835	2,918	2,053
1964: Dec	92,591	65,572	25,817			39,755	27,019	9,786	7,743	2,975	2,043
1965: Dec	103,207	73,881	29,355			44,526	29,326	10,616	8,309	3,538	2,307
1966: Dec	109,749	79,339	30,992			48,347	30,410	6,542	5,458	1,637	1,084
1967: Dec	115,430	83,148	31,131			52,017	32,282	5,681	3,809	139	1,872
1968: Dec	126,949	91,681	34,348	2,105		55,228	35,268	11,519	8,533	3,217	2,986
1969: Dec	137,742	101,161	36,946	3,720		60,495	36,581	10,793	9,480	2,598	1,313
1970: Dec	143,113	105,528	36,325	5,128	2,461	61,614	37,585	5,371	4,367	−621	1,004
1971: Dec	157,795	118,255	40,519	8,528	7,226	61,982	39,540	14,682	12,727	4,194	1,955
1972: Dec	177,639	133,173	47,862	9,700	9,526	66,085	44,466	19,844	14,918	7,343	4,926
1973: Dec	203,077	155,108	53,772	11,709	13,580	76,047	47,969	25,438	21,935	5,910	3,503
1974: Dec	213,427	164,594	54,266	13,681	14,642	82,005	48,833	10,350	9,486	494	864
1975: Dec	223,140	171,996	57,242	15,019	14,434	85,301	51,144	9,713	7,402	2,976	2,311
1976: Dec	248,916	193,525	67,707	17,189	14,573	94,056	55,391	25,776	21,529	10,465	4,247
1977: Dec	289,133	230,564	82,911	39,274	14,945	93,434	58,569	40,217	37,039	15,204	3,178
1978: Dec	337,917	273,645	101,647	48,309	15,235	108,454	64,271	48,784	43,081	18,736	5,703
1979: Dec	383,363	312,024	116,362	56,937	16,838	121,887	71,339	45,446	38,379	14,715	7,067
1980: Dec	388,239	313,472	116,838	58,352	17,322	120,960	74,767	4,876	1,448	476	3,428
1981: Dec	413,544	333,375	126,431	63,049	18,486	125,409	80,169	25,305	19,903	9,593	5,402
								Seasonally adjusted [5]			
1981:											
Jan	384,847	310,760	115,778	57,556	17,202	120,224	74,087	1,704	1,206	31	498
Feb	383,232	309,385	116,195	56,047	17,113	120,030	73,847	1,962	1,845	831	117
Mar	385,685	311,071	118,049	55,356	17,162	120,504	74,614	3,208	2,971	1,526	237
Apr	388,857	313,669	119,076	55,716	17,342	121,535	75,188	3,518	2,722	648	796
May	391,077	315,679	119,582	55,820	17,576	122,701	75,398	2,078	1,571	−114	507
June	394,531	318,792	120,400	56,798	17,704	123,890	75,739	2,708	2,031	149	677
July	397,210	320,656	121,476	56,764	17,760	124,656	76,554	2,791	1,551	1,056	1,240
Aug	401,449	324,161	123,481	57,280	17,959	125,441	77,288	2,557	2,428	1,859	129
Sept	406,234	328,187	125,703	58,318	18,124	126,042	78,047	3,430	2,975	2,079	455
Oct	406,670	328,652	126,344	58,451	18,300	125,557	78,018	584	1,002	1,024	−418
Nov	407,970	329,053	126,385	58,923	18,380	125,365	78,917	1,212	600	564	612
Dec	413,544	333,375	126,431	63,049	18,486	125,409	80,169	432	−33	68	465
1982:											
Jan	409,444	330,135	125,525	61,433	18,397	124,780	79,309	1,620	443	−121	1,177
Feb	406,682	327,435	125,294	59,514	18,343	124,284	79,247	−516	75	−56	−591
Mar	406,520	327,131	125,559	58,491	18,363	124,718	79,389	554	990	−28	−436
Apr	408,109	328,363	126,201	58,641	18,402	125,119	79,746	2,058	1,175	233	883
May	409,500	329,338	127,220	58,647	18,479	124,992	80,162	2,001	1,399	959	602
June	412,599	331,851	128,415	59,302	18,543	125,591	80,748	2,279	1,349	655	930
July	413,366	332,471	128,359	59,824	18,601	125,687	80,895	992	570	61	422
Aug	415,140	333,808	128,281	60,475	18,741	126,311	81,332	−149	66	−402	−215
Sept	417,624	335,948	129,085	60,932	18,778	127,153	81,676	1,138	1,092	505	46
Oct	417,422	334,977	128,619	60,917	18,814	126,627	82,445	54	−324	−78	378
Nov	419,768	336,991	129,594	61,500	18,821	127,076	82,777	2,656	2,523	1,816	133

[1] Installment credit covers most short- and intermediate-term credit extended to individuals through regular business channels, usually to finance the purchase of consumer goods and services or to refinance debts incurred for such purposes, and scheduled to be repaid (or with the option of repayment) in two or more installments. Credit secured by real estate is generally excluded.

[2] Consists of credit cards at retailers, gasoline companies, and commercial banks, and check credit at commercial banks. Prior to 1968, included in "other," except gasoline companies, included in noninstallment credit prior to 1971. Beginning 1977, includes open-end credit at retailers, previously included in "other." Also beginning 1977, some retail credit was reclassified from commercial into consumer credit.

[3] Not reported separately prior to July 1970.

[4] Because of inconsistencies in the data and infrequent benchmarking, series on noninstallment credit is no longer published by the Federal Reserve Board on a regular basis. Data are shown here as a general indication of trends.

[5] For installment credit, computed as the difference between extensions and liquidations (both seasonally adjusted); see also Table B-69. For noninstallment credit, computed as the change from one month to another in the seasonally adjusted amount outstanding.

Source: Board of Governors of the Federal Reserve System.

TABLE B-69.—*Consumer installment credit extended and liquidated, 1950–82*

[Millions of dollars; monthly data seasonally adjusted]

Year or month	Total		Automobile		Revolving [1]		Mobile home [2]		Other	
	Ex-tended	Liqui-dated	Ex-tended	Liqui-dated	Ex-tended	Liqui-dated	Ex-tended	Liqui-dated	Ex-tended	Liqui-dated
1950	22,130	18,861	8,445	6,906	...	...	...	...	13,685	11,955
1951	24,583	23,867	8,951	9,008	...	...	...	...	15,632	14,859
1952	30,616	26,355	11,610	9,932	...	...	...	...	19,006	16,423
1953	32,579	28,794	12,740	10,689	...	...	...	...	19,839	18,105
1954	32,265	31,625	11,741	11,679	...	...	...	...	20,524	19,946
1955	40,263	34,882	16,732	13,008	...	...	...	...	23,531	21,874
1956	40,886	37,899	15,572	14,559	...	...	...	...	25,314	23,340
1957	43,101	40,759	16,554	15,567	...	...	...	...	26,547	25,192
1958	40,956	41,290	14,287	15,501	...	...	...	...	26,669	25,789
1959	49,134	43,395	18,008	15,638	...	...	...	...	31,126	27,757
1960	50,827	47,022	18,112	16,661	...	...	...	...	32,715	30,361
1961	50,598	49,735	16,477	16,960	...	...	...	...	34,121	32,775
1962	57,562	52,601	20,164	17,840	...	...	...	...	37,398	34,761
1963	64,660	57,822	22,617	19,699	...	...	...	...	42,043	38,123
1964	72,445	64,616	24,792	21,815	...	...	...	...	47,653	42,801
1965	79,918	71,616	27,913	24,386	...	...	...	...	52,005	47,230
1966	83,821	78,365	27,844	26,206	...	...	...	...	55,977	52,159
1967	89,058	85,194	27,623	27,482	...	...	...	...	61,435	57,712
1968	101,426	92,075	32,228	29,013	3,481	2,726	...	...	65,717	60,336
1969	109,422	99,945	33,686	31.090	6,182	4,567	...	...	69,554	64,288
1970	115,007	110,352	30,857	31,414	8,689	7,278	612	478	74,849	71,188
1971	138,046	127,789	36,706	32,512	21,862	20,818	2,521	1,754	76,957	72,705
1972	152,275	136,787	43,702	38,081	24,659	23,485	5,121	2,975	78,793	72,246
1973	173,035	152,817	49,606	43,696	28,702	26,699	7,061	4,184	87,666	78,238
1974	172,765	163,276	46,514	46,019	33,213	31,243	5,788	4,720	87,250	81,294
1975	180,083	172,675	52,420	49,444	36,956	35,616	4,326	4,536	86,381	83,079
1976	210,740	189,179	63,743	53,278	43,934	41,764	4,859	4,720	98,204	89,417
1977	257,600	222,138	75,641	60,437	87,596	81,348	5,712	5,341	88,651	75,012
1978	297,668	254,589	87,981	69,245	105,125	96,090	5,412	5,126	99,150	84,128
1979	324,777	286,396	93,901	79,186	120,174	111,546	6,471	4,868	104,231	90,796
1980	306,076	304,628	83,454	82,977	128,068	126,653	5,093	4,610	89,461	90,388
1981	336,341	316,447	94,404	84,809	140,135	135,438	6,028	4,867	95,774	91,333
1981:										
Jan	27,466	26,260	7,343	7,312	11,535	10.944	392	451	8,196	7,553
Feb	28,682	26,837	8,229	7,398	11,738	11,419	405	492	8,310	7,528
Mar	29,370	26,399	8,499	6,973	11,620	11,110	616	552	8,635	7,764
Apr	29,271	26,549	7,459	6,811	12,383	11,443	593	410	8,836	7,885
May	28,377	26,806	7,384	7,498	11,876	11,520	620	372	8,497	7,416
June	29,223	27,192	7,515	7,366	12,658	11,651	509	399	8,541	7,776
July	28,290	26,739	8,059	7,003	11,706	11,590	445	386	8,080	7,760
Aug	28,323	25,895	8,396	6,537	11,663	11,486	520	364	7,744	7,508
Sept	29,406	26,431	9,000	6,921	12,263	11,692	532	375	7,611	7,443
Oct	26,836	25,834	7,490	6,466	11,753	11,429	475	353	7,118	7,586
Nov	27,370	26,770	8,073	7,509	11,379	11,358	479	404	7,439	7,499
Dec	26,656	26,689	7,352	7,284	11,592	11,533	508	365	7,204	7,507
1982:										
Jan	26,888	26,445	7,474	7,595	11,070	11,266	434	460	7,910	7,124
Feb	27,150	27,075	7,283	7,339	11,730	11,885	364	408	7,773	7,443
Mar	27,462	26,472	7,183	7,211	12,143	11,836	411	396	7,725	7,029
Apr	28,684	27,509	7,871	7,638	12,416	11,917	544	493	7,853	7,461
May	29,197	27,798	8,429	7,470	12,528	11,991	478	408	7,762	7,929
June	29,737	28,388	8,182	7.527	13,361	12,854	459	392	7,735	7,615
July	27,514	26,944	7,332	7,271	12,551	11,939	441	378	7,190	7,356
Aug	27,579	27,513	7,112	7,514	12,497	12,354	581	440	7,389	7,205
Sept	28,268	27,176	7,546	7,041	12,464	12,254	452	442	7,806	7,439
Oct	28,062	28,386	7,970	8,048	12,340	12,232	476	480	7,270	7,626
Nov	31,610	29,087	10,329	8,513	12,489	12,382	484	444	8,308	7,748

[1] Consists of credit cards at retailers, gasoline companies, and commercial banks, and check credit at commercial banks. Prior to 1968, included in "other," except gasoline companies, included in noninstallment credit prior to 1971. Beginning 1977, includes open-end credit at retailers, previously included in "other." Also beginning 1977, some retail credit was reclassified from commercial into consumer credit.

[2] Not reported separately prior to July 1970.

Note.—Installment credit covers most short- and intermediate-term credit extended to individuals through regular business channels, usually to finance the purchase of consumer goods and services or to refinance debts incurred for such purposes, and scheduled to be repaid (or with the option of repayment) in two or more installments. Credit secured by real estate is generally excluded.

Liquidated credit includes repayments, chargeoffs, and other credit.

See also Table B–68.

Source: Board of Governors of the Federal Reserve System.

Table B–70.—*Mortgage debt outstanding by type of property and of financing, 1939–82*

[Billions of dollars]

End of year or quarter	All properties	Farm properties	Nonfarm properties				Nonfarm properties by type of mortgage					
							Government underwritten				Conventional [3]	
			Total	1- to 4-family houses	Multifamily properties	Commercial properties [1]	Total [2]	1- to 4-family houses			Total	1- to 4-family houses
								Total	FHA insured	VA guaranteed		
1939	35.5	6.6	28.9	16.3	5.6	7.0	1.8	1.8	1.8	...	27.1	14.5
1940	36.5	6.5	30.0	17.4	5.7	6.9	2.3	2.3	2.3	...	27.7	15.1
1941	37.6	6.4	31.2	18.4	5.9	7.0	3.0	3.0	3.0	...	28.2	15.4
1942	36.7	6.0	30.8	18.2	5.8	6.7	3.7	3.7	3.7	...	27.1	14.5
1943	35.3	5.4	29.9	17.8	5.8	6.3	4.1	4.1	4.1	...	25.8	13.7
1944	34.7	4.9	29.7	17.9	5.6	6.2	4.2	4.2	4.2	...	25.5	13.7
1945	35.5	4.8	30.8	18.6	5.7	6.4	4.3	4.3	4.1	0.2	26.5	14.3
1946	41.8	4.9	36.9	23.0	6.1	7.7	6.3	6.1	3.7	2.4	30.6	16.9
1947	48.9	5.1	43.9	28.2	6.6	9.1	9.8	9.3	3.8	5.5	34.1	18.9
1948	56.2	5.3	50.9	33.3	7.5	10.2	13.6	12.5	5.3	7.2	37.3	20.8
1949	62.7	5.6	57.1	37.6	8.6	10.8	17.1	15.0	6.9	8.1	40.0	22.6
1950	72.8	6.1	66.7	45.2	10.1	11.5	22.1	18.8	8.5	10.3	44.7	26.3
1951	82.3	6.7	75.6	51.7	11.5	12.5	26.6	22.9	9.7	13.2	49.1	28.9
1952	91.4	7.2	84.2	58.5	12.3	13.4	29.3	25.4	10.8	14.6	54.9	33.2
1953	101.3	7.7	93.6	66.1	12.9	14.5	32.1	28.1	12.0	16.1	61.5	38.0
1954	113.7	8.2	105.4	75.7	13.5	16.3	36.2	32.1	12.8	19.3	69.3	43.6
1955	129.9	9.0	120.9	88.2	14.3	18.3	42.9	38.9	14.3	24.6	78.0	49.3
1956	144.5	9.8	134.6	99.0	14.9	20.7	47.8	43.9	15.5	28.4	86.8	55.1
1957	156.5	10.4	146.1	107.6	15.3	23.2	51.6	47.2	16.5	30.7	94.6	60.4
1958	171.8	11.1	160.7	117.7	16.8	26.1	55.2	50.1	19.7	30.4	105.5	67.6
1959	190.8	12.1	178.7	130.9	18.7	29.2	59.3	53.8	23.8	30.0	119.4	77.0
1960	207.5	12.8	194.7	141.9	20.3	32.4	62.3	56.4	26.7	29.7	132.3	85.5
1961	228.0	13.9	214.1	154.6	23.0	36.5	65.6	59.1	29.5	29.6	148.5	95.5
1962	251.4	15.2	236.2	169.3	25.8	41.1	69.4	62.2	32.3	29.9	166.9	107.1
1963	278.5	16.8	261.7	186.4	29.0	46.2	73.4	65.9	35.0	30.9	188.2	120.5
1964	305.9	18.9	287.0	203.4	33.6	50.0	77.2	69.2	38.3	30.9	209.8	134.1
1965	333.3	21.2	312.1	220.5	37.2	54.5	81.2	73.1	42.0	31.1	231.0	147.4
1966	356.5	23.1	333.4	232.9	40.3	60.1	84.1	76.1	44.8	31.3	249.3	156.9
1967	381.2	25.1	356.1	247.3	43.9	64.8	88.2	79.9	47.4	32.5	267.9	167.4
1968	410.9	27.4	383.5	264.8	47.3	71.4	93.4	84.4	50.6	33.8	290.1	180.4
1969	441.4	29.2	412.2	283.2	52.2	76.9	100.2	90.2	54.5	35.7	312.0	193.0
1970	474.2	30.3	443.8	298.1	60.1	85.6	109.2	97.3	59.9	37.3	334.6	200.8
1971	526.5	32.2	494.3	328.3	70.1	95.9	120.7	105.2	65.7	39.5	373.5	223.1
1972	603.4	35.8	567.7	372.2	82.8	112.7	131.1	113.0	68.2	44.7	436.5	259.2
1973	681.6	41.3	640.3	415.5	93.1	131.7	135.0	116.2	66.2	50.0	505.3	299.2
1974	744.3	46.3	698.0	451.2	100.0	146.9	140.2	121.3	65.1	56.2	557.8	329.9
1975	806.1	51.1	755.0	495.0	100.6	159.3	147.0	127.7	66.1	61.6	608.0	367.3
1976	893.0	56.6	836.4	560.7	104.5	171.2	154.1	133.5	66.5	67.0	682.3	427.1
1977	1,022.6	63.6	958.9	657.8	111.5	189.6	161.7	141.6	68.0	73.6	797.2	516.2
1978	1,173.6	70.8	1,102.8	770.6	120.7	211.4	176.4	153.4	71.4	82.0	926.4	617.3
1979	1,337.7	82.7	1,255.1	891.1	128.4	235.6	199.0	172.9	81.0	92.0	1,056.1	718.1
1980	1,471.8	92.0	1,379.8	987.0	137.1	255.7	225.1	195.2	93.6	101.6	1,154.7	791.8
1981	1,583.5	101.7	1,481.8	1,060.5	141.4	279.9	239.0	207.6	101.3	106.2	1,242.8	852.9
1980:												
I	1,371.1	86.0	1,285.1	914.3	130.0	240.9	207.5	180.8	86.0	94.8	1,077.6	733.4
II	1,398.1	89.0	1,309.0	931.6	132.4	245.1	211.6	184.1	87.4	96.7	1,097.4	747.5
III	1,435.5	90.6	1,344.9	960.7	134.6	249.6	218.9	190.0	90.6	99.4	1,126.0	770.7
IV	1,471.8	92.0	1,379.8	987.0	137.1	255.7	225.1	195.2	93.6	101.6	1,154.7	791.8
1981:												
I	1,497.6	94.5	1,403.1	1,004.0	138.1	261.0	229.1	198.8	95.7	103.1	1,174.0	805.2
II	1,533.2	97.5	1,435.7	1,028.3	139.3	268.1	233.6	202.7	98.1	104.6	1,202.0	825.6
III	1,561.6	100.0	1,461.6	1,047.6	140.2	273.7	237.0	205.9	100.0	105.9	1,224.6	841.7
IV	1,583.5	101.7	1,481.8	1,060.5	141.4	279.9	239.0	207.6	101.3	106.2	1,242.8	852.9
1982:												
I	1,602.8	103.6	1,499.2	1,071.9	142.9	284.4	240.6	209.0	102.0	107.0	1,258.6	862.9
II	1,624.2	105.5	1,518.7	1,085.2	143.8	289.7	...	...	...	...	...	...
III	1,635.8	106.7	1,529.1	1,092.3	144.7	292.2	...	...	...	...	...	...

[1] Includes negligible amount of farm loans held by savings and loan associations.
[2] Includes FHA insured multifamily properties, not shown separately.
[3] Derived figures. Total includes multifamily and commercial properties, not shown separately.

Source: Board of Governors of the Federal Reserve System, based on data from various Government and private organizations.

TABLE B–71.—*Mortgage debt outstanding by holder, 1939–82*

[Billions of dollars]

End of year or quarter	Total	Major financial institutions: Total	Savings and loan associations	Mutual savings banks	Commercial banks [1]	Life insurance companies	Other holders: Federal and related agencies [2]	Individuals and others
1939	35.5	18.6	3.8	4.8	4.3	5.7	5.0	11.9
1940	36.5	19.5	4.1	4.9	4.6	6.0	4.9	12.0
1941	37.6	20.7	4.6	4.8	4.9	6.4	4.7	12.2
1942	36.7	20.7	4.6	4.6	4.7	6.7	4.3	11.7
1943	35.3	20.2	4.6	4.4	4.5	6.7	3.6	11.5
1944	34.7	20.2	4.8	4.3	4.4	6.7	3.0	11.5
1945	35.5	21.0	5.4	4.2	4.8	6.6	2.4	12.1
1946	41.8	26.0	7.1	4.4	7.2	7.2	2.0	13.8
1947	48.9	31.8	8.9	4.9	9.4	8.7	1.8	15.3
1948	56.2	37.8	10.3	5.8	10.9	10.8	1.8	16.6
1949	62.7	42.9	11.6	6.7	11.6	12.9	2.3	17.5
1950	72.8	51.7	13.7	8.3	13.7	16.1	2.8	18.4
1951	82.3	59.5	15.6	9.9	14.7	19.3	3.5	19.3
1952	91.4	66.9	18.4	11.4	15.9	21.3	4.1	20.4
1953	101.3	75.1	22.0	12.9	16.9	23.3	4.6	21.7
1954	113.7	85.7	26.1	15.0	18.6	26.0	4.8	23.2
1955	129.9	99.3	31.4	17.5	21.0	29.4	5.3	25.3
1956	144.5	111.2	35.7	19.7	22.7	33.0	6.2	27.1
1957	156.5	119.7	40.0	21.2	23.3	35.2	7.7	29.1
1958	171.8	131.5	45.6	23.3	25.5	37.1	8.0	32.3
1959	190.8	145.5	53.1	25.0	28.1	39.2	10.2	35.1
1960	207.5	157.6	60.1	26.9	28.8	41.8	11.5	38.4
1961	228.0	172.6	68.8	29.1	30.4	44.2	12.2	43.1
1962	251.4	192.5	78.8	32.3	34.5	46.9	12.6	46.3
1963	278.5	217.1	90.9	36.2	39.4	50.5	11.8	49.5
1964	305.9	241.0	101.3	40.6	44.0	55.2	12.2	52.7
1965	333.3	264.6	110.3	44.6	49.7	60.0	13.5	55.2
1966	356.5	280.8	114.4	47.3	54.4	64.6	17.5	58.2
1967	381.2	298.8	121.8	50.5	59.0	67.5	20.9	61.4
1968	410.9	319.9	130.8	53.5	65.7	70.0	25.1	65.9
1969	441.4	339.1	140.2	56.1	70.7	72.0	31.1	71.2
1970	474.2	355.9	150.3	57.9	73.3	74.4	38.3	79.9
1971	526.5	394.2	174.3	62.0	82.5	75.5	46.4	85.9
1972	603.4	450.0	206.2	67.6	99.3	76.9	54.6	98.9
1973	681.6	505.4	231.7	73.2	119.1	81.4	64.8	111.4
1974	744.3	542.6	249.3	74.9	132.1	86.2	82.1	119.7
1975	806.1	581.2	278.6	77.2	136.2	89.2	101.0	123.8
1976	893.0	647.5	323.0	81.6	151.3	91.6	116.6	128.9
1977	1,022.6	745.0	381.2	88.1	179.0	96.8	140.3	137.2
1978	1,173.6	848.2	432.8	95.2	214.0	106.2	170.4	155.0
1979	1,337.7	938.6	475.7	98.9	245.2	118.8	215.7	183.4
1980	1,471.8	997.2	503.2	99.9	263.0	131.1	256.6	218.1
1981	1,583.5	1,040.6	518.4	100.0	284.5	137.7	289.1	253.8
1980:								
I	1,371.1	951.2	479.0	99.2	250.7	122.4	228.6	191.4
II	1,398.1	958.8	481.1	99.2	253.0	125.6	238.2	201.1
III	1,435.5	977.5	492.1	99.3	258.0	128.1	247.1	210.9
IV	1,471.8	997.2	503.2	99.9	263.0	131.1	256.6	218.1
1981:								
I	1,497.6	1,006.9	507.6	99.7	266.7	132.9	263.5	227.2
II	1,533.2	1,023.1	515.3	100.0	273.2	134.7	271.4	238.6
III	1,561.6	1,033.8	518.8	100.0	279.0	136.0	279.9	247.9
IV	1,583.5	1,040.6	518.4	100.0	284.5	137.7	289.1	253.8
1982:								
I	1,602.8	1,041.5	515.9	97.5	289.4	138.8	301.0	260.3
II	1,624.2	1,042.7	512.7	96.3	294.0	139.5	315.1	266.4
III	1,635.8	1,028.8	495.4	94.2	298.3	140.8	333.2	273.8

[1] Includes loans held by nondeposit trust companies, but not by bank trust departments.

[2] Includes former Federal National Mortgage Association (FNMA) and new Government National Mortgage Association (GNMA), as well as Federal Housing Administration, Veterans Administration, Public Housing Administration, Farmers Home Administration, and in earlier years Reconstruction Finance Corporation, Homeowners Loan Corporation, and Federal Farm Mortgage Corporation. Also includes GNMA Pools and U.S.-sponsored agencies such as new FNMA, Federal Land Banks, and Federal Home Loan Mortgage Corporation. Other U.S. agencies (amounts small or current separate data not readily available) included with "individuals and others."

Source: Board of Governors of the Federal Reserve System, based on data from various Government and private organizations.

384-041 O - 83 - 16 : QL 3

TABLE B–72.—*Federal budget receipts, outlays, and debt, fiscal years 1973–84*

[Millions of dollars; fiscal years]

Description	Actual						
	1973	1974	1975	1976	Transition quarter	1977	1978
BUDGET RECEIPTS AND OUTLAYS:							
Total receipts	230,799	263,224	279,090	298,060	81,232	355,559	399,561
Federal funds	161,357	181,219	187,505	201,099	54,085	241,312	270,490
Trust funds	90,766	103,138	116,683	131,750	31,530	150,560	165,568
Interfund transactions	–21,325	–21,133	–25,098	–34,789	–4,383	–36,313	–36,498
Total outlays	245,647	267,912	324,245	364,473	94,188	400,506	448,368
Federal funds	186,951	199,918	240,081	269,921	65,088	295,756	331,991
Trust funds	80,021	89,126	109,261	129,341	33,482	141,063	152,874
Interfund transactions	–21,325	–21,133	–25,098	–34,789	–4,383	–36,313	–36,498
Total surplus or deficit (–)	–14,849	–4,688	–45,154	–66,413	–12,956	–44,948	–48,807
Federal funds	–25,593	–18,699	–52,576	–68,822	–11,004	–54,444	–61,501
Trust funds	10,745	14,011	7,422	2,409	–1,952	9,496	12,694
OUTSTANDING DEBT, END OF PERIOD:							
Gross Federal debt	468,426	486,247	544,131	631,866	646,379	709,138	780,425
Held by Government agencies	125,381	140,194	147,225	151,566	148,052	157,295	169,477
Held by the public	343,045	346,053	396,906	480,300	498,327	551,843	610,948
Federal Reserve System	75,181	80,648	84,993	94,714	96,702	105,004	115,480
Other	267,863	265,405	311,913	385,586	401,625	446,839	495,468
BUDGET RECEIPTS	230,799	263,224	279,090	298,060	81,232	355,559	399,561
Individual income taxes	103,246	118,952	122,386	131,603	38,801	157,626	180,988
Corporation income taxes	36,153	38,620	40,621	41,409	8,460	54,892	59,952
Social insurance taxes and contributions	63,115	75,071	84,534	90,769	25,219	106,485	120,967
Excise taxes	16,260	16,844	16,551	16,963	4,473	17,548	18,376
Estate and gift taxes	4,917	5,035	4,611	5,216	1,455	7,327	5,285
Customs duties	3,188	3,334	3,676	4,074	1,212	5,150	6,573
Miscellaneous receipts:							
Deposits of earnings by Federal Reserve System	3,495	4,845	5,777	5,451	1,500	5,908	6,641
All other	425	523	935	2,576	111	623	778
BUDGET OUTLAYS	245,647	267,912	324,245	364,473	94,188	400,506	448,368
National defense	74,541	77,781	85,552	89,430	22,307	97,501	105,186
International affairs	4,066	5,681	6,922	5,554	2,191	4,819	5,922
General science, space, and technology	4,030	3,977	3,989	4,370	1,161	4,677	4,742
Energy	1,179	837	2,169	3,127	794	4,172	5,861
Natural resources and environment	4,763	5,670	7,336	8,124	2,532	10,000	10,925
Agriculture	4,852	2,227	1,659	2,502	584	5,526	7,731
Commerce and housing credit	924	3,925	5,607	3,792	1,392	98	3,331
Transportation	9,065	9,172	10,388	13,435	3,304	14,636	15,445
Community and regional development	4,595	4,134	3,738	4,767	1,340	6,348	11,070
Education, training, employment, and social services	12,735	12,344	15,870	18,737	5,162	20,985	26,463
Health	17,405	20,364	25,742	31,503	8,181	36,582	41,232
Income security	72,965	84,437	108,576	127,390	32,797	137,900	146,180
Veterans benefits and services	12,013	13,386	16,597	18,432	3,962	18,038	18,974
Administration of justice	2,131	2,462	2,942	3,320	859	3,600	3,802
General government	2,568	3,243	3,133	2,948	883	3,169	3,706
General purpose fiscal assistance	7,351	6,890	7,187	7,235	2,092	9,499	9,601
Net interest	17,346	21,449	23,244	26,711	6,946	29,877	35,435
Allowances							
Undistributed offsetting receipts	–6,882	–10,068	–6,408	–6,904	–2,296	–6,922	–7,242
Composition of undistributed offsetting receipts:							
Employer share, employee retirement	–2,927	–3,319	–3,980	–4,242	–985	–4,548	–4,983
Rents and royalties on the Outer Continental Shelf	–3,956	–6,748	–2,428	–2,662	–1,311	–2,374	–2,259

See next page for continuation of table.

Table B–72.—*Federal budget receipts, outlays, and debt, fiscal years 1973–84*—Continued

[Millions of dollars; fiscal years]

Description	Actual				Estimates	
	1979	1980	1981	1982	1983	1984
BUDGET RECEIPTS AND OUTLAYS:						
Total receipts	463,302	517,112	599,272	617,766	597,494	659,702
Federal funds	316,366	350,856	410,422	409,253	376,945	404,745
Trust funds	186,988	210,930	239,413	268,407	314,755	330,210
Interfund transactions	−40,052	−44,674	−50,563	−59,894	−94,206	−75,253
Total outlays	490,997	576,675	657,204	728,375	805,202	848,483
Federal funds	362,396	419,220	475,171	526,113	603,047	610,467
Trust funds	168,653	202,129	232,596	262,155	296,361	313,269
Interfund transactions	−40,052	−44,674	−50,563	−59,894	−94,206	−75,253
Total surplus or deficit (−)	−27,694	−59,563	−57,932	−110,609	−207,708	−188,781
Federal funds	−46,030	−68,364	−64,749	−116,860	−226,102	−205,721
Trust funds	18,335	8,801	6,817	6,252	18,393	16,941
OUTSTANDING DEBT, END OF PERIOD:						
Gross Federal debt	833,751	914,317	1,003,941	1,146,987	1,383,744	1,606,339
Held by Government agencies	189,162	199,212	209,507	217,560	239,317	258,912
Held by the public	644,589	715,105	794,434	929,427	1,144,427	1,347,427
Federal Reserve System	115,594	120,846	124,466	134,497		
Other	528,996	594,259	669,968	794,929		
BUDGET RECEIPTS	463,302	517,112	599,272	617,766	597,494	659,702
Individual income taxes	217,841	244,069	285,917	297,744	285,194	295,589
Corporation income taxes	65,677	64,600	61,137	49,207	35,286	51,770
Social insurance taxes and contributions	138,939	157,803	182,720	201,498	210,313	242,937
Excise taxes	18,745	24,329	40,839	36,311	37,257	40,353
Estate and gift taxes	5,411	6,389	6,787	7,991	6,114	5,902
Customs duties	7,439	7,174	8,083	8,854	8,819	9,137
Miscellaneous receipts:						
Deposits of earnings by Federal Reserve System	8,327	11,767	12,834	15,186	13,406	12,819
All other	925	981	956	975	1,105	1,195
BUDGET OUTLAYS	490,997	576,675	657,204	728,375	805,202	848,483
National defense	117,681	135,856	159,765	187,418	214,769	245,305
International affairs	6,091	10,733	11,130	9,982	11,939	13,250
General science, space, and technology	5,041	5,722	6,359	7,070	7,759	8,250
Energy	6,856	6,313	10,277	4,674	4,506	3,306
Natural resources and environment	12,091	13,812	13,525	12,934	12,087	9,832
Agriculture	6,238	4,762	5,572	14,875	21,075	12,150
Commerce and housing credit	2,579	7,788	3,946	3,865	1,928	413
Transportation	17,459	21,120	23,381	20,560	21,876	25,145
Community and regional development	9,542	10,068	9,394	7,165	7,373	6,951
Education, training, employment, and social services	29,685	30,767	31,402	26,300	26,676	25,256
Health	46,962	55,220	65,982	74,017	82,362	90,647
Income security	160,159	193,100	225,101	248,343	282,472	282,422
Veterans benefits and services	19,928	21,183	22,988	23,955	24,411	25,724
Administration of justice	4,153	4,570	4,696	4,671	5,273	5,491
General government	4,093	4,505	4,614	4,726	5,794	5,993
General purpose fiscal assistance	8,372	8,584	6,856	6,393	6,382	6,968
Net interest	42,606	52,458	68,726	84,697	88,936	103,180
Allowances						949
Undistributed offsetting receipts	−8,538	−9,887	−16,509	−13,270	−20,414	−22,750
Composition of undistributed offsetting receipts:						
Employer share, employee retirement	−5,271	−5,787	−6,371	−7,020	−8,214	−9,853
Rents and royalties on the Outer Continental Shelf	−3,267	−4,101	−10,138	−6,250	−11,793	−11,895

Note.—Under provisions of the Congressional Budget Act of 1974, the fiscal year for the Federal Government shifted beginning with fiscal year 1977. Through fiscal year 1976, the fiscal year was on a July 1–June 30 basis. Beginning October 1976 (fiscal year 1977), the fiscal year is on an October 1–September 30 basis. The period July 1, 1976 through September 30, 1976 is a separate fiscal period known as the transition quarter.

Refunds of receipts are excluded from receipts and outlays.

See "Budget of the United States Government, Fiscal Year 1984" for additional information.

Sources: Department of the Treasury and Office of Management and Budget.

Table B–73.—*Federal budget receipts and outlays, off-budget outlays, and debt, fiscal years 1929–84*

[Billions of dollars]

Fiscal year	Budget			Off-budget outlays	Budget and off-budget surplus or deficit (−)	Gross Federal debt (end of period)	
	Receipts	Outlays	Surplus or deficit (−)			Total	Held by the public
1929	3.9	3.1	.7			[1] 16.9	
1933	2.0	4.6	−2.6			[1] 22.5	
1939	5.0	8.8	−3.9			48.2	41.4
1940	6.4	9.5	−3.1			50.7	42.8
1941	8.6	13.6	−5.0			57.5	48.2
1942	14.4	35.1	−20.8			79.2	67.8
1943	23.6	78.5	−54.9			142.6	127.0
1944	44.3	91.3	−47.0			204.1	184.8
1945	45.2	92.7	−47.5			260.1	235.2
1946	39.3	55.2	−15.9			271.0	241.9
1947	38.4	34.5	3.9			257.1	224.3
1948	41.8	29.8	12.0			252.0	216.3
1949	39.4	38.8	.6			252.6	214.3
1950	39.5	42.6	−3.1			256.9	219.0
1951	51.6	45.5	6.1			255.3	214.3
1952	66.2	67.7	−1.5			259.1	214.8
1953	69.6	76.1	−6.5			266.0	218.4
1954	69.7	70.9	−1.2			270.8	224.5
1955	65.5	68.5	−3.0			274.4	226.6
1956	74.5	70.5	4.1			272.8	222.2
1957	80.0	76.7	3.2			272.4	219.4
1958	79.6	82.6	−2.9			279.7	226.4
1959	79.2	92.1	−12.9			287.8	235.0
1960	92.5	92.2	.3			290.9	237.2
1961	94.4	97.8	−3.4			292.9	238.6
1962	99.7	106.8	−7.1			303.3	248.4
1963	106.6	111.3	−4.8			310.8	254.5
1964	112.7	118.6	−5.9			316.8	257.6
1965	116.8	118.4	−1.6			323.2	261.6
1966	130.9	134.7	−3.8			329.5	264.7
1967	148.9	157.6	−8.7			341.3	267.5
1968	153.0	178.1	−25.2			369.8	290.6
1969	186.9	183.6	3.2			367.1	279.5
1970	192.8	195.7	−2.8			382.6	284.9
1971	187.1	210.2	−23.0			409.5	304.3
1972	207.3	230.7	−23.4			437.3	323.8
1973	230.8	245.6	−14.8	0.1	−14.9	468.4	343.0
1974	263.2	267.9	−4.7	1.4	−6.1	486.2	346.1
1975	279.1	324.2	−45.2	8.1	−53.2	544.1	396.9
1976	298.1	364.5	−66.4	7.3	−73.7	631.9	480.3
Transition quarter	81.2	94.2	−13.0	1.8	−14.7	646.4	498.3
1977	355.6	400.5	−44.9	8.7	−53.6	709.1	551.8
1978	399.6	448.4	−48.8	10.4	−59.2	780.4	610.9
1979	463.3	491.0	−27.7	12.5	−40.2	833.8	644.6
1980	517.1	576.7	−59.6	14.2	−73.8	914.3	715.1
1981	599.3	657.2	−57.9	21.0	−78.9	1,003.9	794.4
1982	617.8	728.4	−110.6	17.3	−127.9	1,147.0	929.4
1983 [2]	597.5	805.2	−207.7	17.0	−224.8	1,383.7	1,144.4
1984 [2]	659.7	848.5	−188.8	14.0	−202.8	1,606.3	1,347.4

[1] Not strictly comparable with later data.
[2] Estimates.

Note.—Under provisions of the Congressional Budget Act of 1974, the fiscal year for the Federal Government shifted beginning with fiscal year 1977. Through fiscal year 1976, the fiscal year was on a July 1–June 30 basis; beginning October 1976 (fiscal year 1977), the fiscal year is on an October 1–September 30 basis. The 3-month period from July 1, 1976 through September 30, 1976 is a separate fiscal period known as the transition quarter.

Data for 1929–39 are according to the administrative budget and those beginning 1940 according to the unified budget.

Refunds of receipts are excluded from receipts and outlays.

See "Budget of the United States Government, Fiscal Year 1984" for additional information.

Sources: Department of the Treasury and Office of Management and Budget.

TABLE B-74.—*Relation of Federal Government receipts and expenditures in the national income and product accounts to the unified budget, fiscal years 1982–84*

[Billions of dollars; fiscal years]

Receipts and expenditures	1982	Estimate	
		1983	1984
RECEIPTS			
Total budget receipts	617.8	597.5	659.7
Government contribution for employee retirement (grossing)	10.7	12.2	14.0
Other netting and grossing	9.3	11.7	13.9
Adjustment to accruals	−18.2	8.2	−.3
Geographic exclusions	−1.6	−1.7	−1.9
Other	.2	.0	.2
Federal sector, national income and product accounts, receipts	618.2	627.9	685.6
EXPENDITURES			
Total budget outlays	728.4	805.2	848.5
Lending and financial transactions	−5.3	−3.8	−3.8
Government contribution for employee retirement (grossing)	10.7	12.2	14.0
Other netting and grossing	9.3	11.7	13.9
Defense timing adjustment	−1.2	−1.7	−2.5
Bonuses on Outer Continental Shelf land leases	2.7	8.3	7.9
Geographic exclusions	−4.6	−4.8	−4.9
Other	−.3	1.9	4.2
Federal sector, national income and product accounts, expenditures	739.7	829.0	877.3

Note.—See Note, Table B–73.

See Special Analysis B, "Special Analyses, Budget of the United States Government, Fiscal Year 1984" for description of these categories.

Sources: Department of Commerce (Bureau of Economic Analysis), Department of the Treasury, and Office of Management and Budget.

Table B–75.—*Government receipts and expenditures, national income and product accounts, 1929–82*

[Billions of dollars; quarterly data at seasonally adjusted annual rates]

Calendar year or quarter	Total government			Federal Government			State and local government		
	Receipts	Expenditures	Surplus or deficit (−), national income and product accounts	Receipts	Expenditures	Surplus or deficit (−), national income and product accounts	Receipts	Expenditures	Surplus or deficit (−), national income and product accounts
1929	11.3	10.3	1.0	3.8	2.6	1.2	7.6	7.8	−0.2
1933	9.3	10.7	−1.4	2.7	4.0	−1.3	7.2	7.2	−.1
1939	15.4	17.6	−2.2	6.7	8.9	−2.2	9.6	9.6	.0
1940	17.7	18.4	−.7	8.6	10.0	−1.3	10.0	9.3	.6
1941	25.0	28.8	−3.8	15.4	20.5	−5.1	10.4	9.1	1.3
1942	32.6	64.0	−31.4	22.9	56.1	−33.1	10.6	8.8	1.8
1943	49.2	93.3	−44.1	39.3	85.8	−46.6	10.9	8.4	2.5
1944	51.2	103.0	−51.8	41.0	95.5	−54.5	11.1	8.5	2.7
1945	53.2	92.7	−39.5	42.5	84.6	−42.1	11.6	9.0	2.6
1946	51.0	45.6	5.4	39.1	35.6	3.5	13.0	11.1	1.9
1947	56.9	42.5	14.4	43.2	29.8	13.4	15.4	14.4	1.0
1948	58.9	50.5	8.4	43.2	34.9	8.3	17.7	17.6	.1
1949	55.9	59.3	−3.4	38.7	41.3	−2.6	19.5	20.2	−.7
1950	69.0	61.0	8.0	50.0	40.8	9.2	21.3	22.5	−1.2
1951	85.2	79.2	6.1	64.3	57.8	6.5	23.4	23.9	−.4
1952	90.1	93.9	−3.8	67.3	71.1	−3.7	25.4	25.5	−.0
1953	94.6	101.6	−6.9	70.0	77.1	−7.1	27.4	27.3	.1
1954	89.9	97.0	−7.1	63.7	69.8	−6.0	29.0	30.2	−1.1
1955	101.1	98.0	3.1	72.6	68.1	4.4	31.7	32.9	−1.3
1956	109.7	104.5	5.2	78.0	71.9	6.1	35.0	35.9	−.9
1957	116.2	115.2	.9	81.9	79.6	2.3	38.5	39.8	−1.4
1958	115.0	127.6	−12.6	78.7	88.9	−10.3	42.0	44.3	−2.4
1959	129.4	131.0	−1.6	89.8	91.0	−1.1	46.4	46.9	−.4
1960	139.5	136.4	3.1	96.1	93.1	3.0	49.9	49.8	.1
1961	144.8	149.1	−4.3	98.1	101.9	−3.9	54.0	54.4	−.4
1962	156.7	160.5	−3.8	106.2	110.4	−4.2	58.5	58.0	.5
1963	168.5	167.8	.7	114.4	114.2	.3	63.2	62.8	.5
1964	174.0	176.3	−2.3	114.9	118.2	−3.3	69.5	68.5	1.0
1965	188.3	187.8	.5	124.3	123.8	.5	75.1	75.1	−.0
1966	212.3	213.6	−1.3	141.8	143.6	−1.8	84.8	84.3	.5
1967	228.2	242.4	−14.2	150.5	163.7	−13.2	93.6	94.7	−1.1
1968	263.1	269.1	−6.0	174.4	180.5	−6.0	107.3	107.2	.1
1969	296.7	286.8	9.9	196.9	188.4	8.4	120.2	118.7	1.5
1970	302.8	313.4	−10.6	191.9	204.3	−12.4	135.4	133.5	1.9
1971	322.6	342.0	−19.4	198.6	220.6	−22.0	153.0	150.4	2.6
1972	368.3	371.6	−3.3	227.5	244.3	−16.8	178.3	164.8	13.5
1973	413.1	405.3	7.8	258.6	264.2	−5.6	195.0	181.6	13.4
1974	455.2	460.0	−4.7	287.8	299.3	−11.5	211.4	204.6	6.8
1975	470.5	534.3	−63.8	287.3	356.6	−69.3	237.7	232.2	5.5
1976	538.4	574.9	−36.5	331.8	384.8	−53.1	267.8	251.2	16.6
1977	605.4	623.3	−17.8	375.2	421.1	−45.9	297.7	269.7	28.0
1978	681.9	681.1	.8	431.6	461.0	−29.5	327.6	297.3	30.3
1979	765.1	750.8	14.3	493.6	509.7	−16.1	352.0	321.5	30.4
1980	838.0	871.2	−33.2	540.7	602.1	−61.4	385.9	357.8	28.2
1981	957.3	985.5	−28.2	628.2	688.2	−60.0	416.8	385.0	31.7
1982 *p*	968.4	1,084.5	−116.1	614.7	762.6	−147.9	437.3	405.4	31.9
1980:									
I	814.6	825.2	−10.6	525.7	565.4	−39.7	374.5	345.3	29.1
II	809.2	853.4	−44.2	520.2	587.7	−67.5	376.6	353.3	23.3
III	842.8	888.8	−45.9	542.4	615.4	−73.1	389.3	362.2	27.1
IV	885.2	917.4	−32.2	574.6	639.9	−65.2	403.3	370.3	33.0
1981:									
I	939.8	948.1	−8.3	620.0	659.7	−39.7	410.0	378.6	31.3
II	951.5	959.1	−7.6	627.0	667.5	−40.5	415.2	382.2	32.9
III	974.3	998.7	−24.5	640.2	698.2	−58.0	420.3	386.9	33.5
IV	963.6	1,036.1	−72.5	625.7	727.4	−101.7	421.5	392.4	29.1
1982:									
I	951.1	1,041.8	−90.7	609.9	728.3	−118.4	424.2	396.5	27.7
II	966.2	1,053.7	−87.5	617.0	736.6	−119.6	434.3	402.2	32.1
III	972.2	1,095.9	−123.7	613.7	769.7	−156.0	440.5	408.2	32.3
IV *p*	....	1,146.7	....	....	815.9	....	....	414.9	....

Note.—Federal grants-in-aid to State and local governments are reflected in Federal expenditures and State and local receipts. Total government receipts and expenditures have been adjusted to eliminate this duplication.

Source: Department of Commerce, Bureau of Economic Analysis.

TABLE B-76.—*Federal Government receipts and expenditures, national income and product accounts, 1958–84*

[Billions of dollars; quarterly data at seasonally adjusted annual rates]

Year or quarter	Receipts					Expenditures							Surplus or deficit (−), national income and product accounts
	Total	Personal tax and nontax receipts	Corporate profits tax accruals	Indirect business tax and nontax accruals	Contributions for social insurance	Total [1]	Purchases of goods and services	Transfer payments: To persons	Transfer payments: To foreigners	Grants-in-aid to State and local governments	Net interest paid	Subsidies less current surplus of government enterprises	
Fiscal year: [2]													
1958	78.1	36.3	17.9	11.6	12.3	82.8	51.1	17.8	1.7	4.7	5.4	2.4	−4.7
1959	85.4	38.2	21.4	12.0	13.9	91.2	54.8	19.9	1.8	6.2	5.6	2.5	−5.8
1960	94.8	42.5	22.3	13.2	16.7	91.3	52.9	20.6	1.8	6.9	6.8	2.4	3.4
1961	95.0	43.6	20.0	13.3	18.1	98.1	55.8	23.6	2.1	6.9	6.4	3.3	−3.1
1962	104.0	47.3	22.7	14.2	19.9	106.2	61.0	25.1	2.1	7.6	6.4	4.1	−2.2
1963	110.0	49.6	23.3	15.0	22.1	111.7	63.7	26.5	2.1	8.3	7.1	4.0	−1.7
1964	115.6	50.7	25.7	15.6	23.6	117.2	65.9	27.4	2.2	9.8	7.7	4.1	−1.5
1965	120.0	51.4	27.1	16.9	24.5	118.5	64.6	28.4	2.2	10.9	8.2	4.3	1.4
1966	132.7	57.5	30.8	15.5	28.9	132.7	72.4	31.8	2.3	12.7	8.7	4.8	.0
1967	146.0	64.4	30.3	15.8	35.5	154.9	86.0	37.2	2.2	14.8	9.6	5.2	−8.9
1968	159.9	71.4	33.1	17.1	38.3	172.2	95.0	42.7	2.1	17.8	10.4	4.1	−12.3
1969	189.8	90.2	36.8	18.6	44.2	184.6	98.0	48.7	2.2	19.2	11.9	4.7	5.2
1970	194.8	94.0	32.9	19.2	48.8	195.5	97.1	55.0	2.0	22.6	13.5	5.5	−.7
1971	192.4	87.9	31.9	20.0	52.6	212.9	94.9	67.7	2.3	26.8	14.0	7.0	−20.5
1972	213.4	100.5	34.2	19.9	58.9	232.7	100.6	76.1	2.8	32.6	14.0	6.5	−19.2
1973	240.7	107.4	41.2	20.7	71.5	255.7	101.1	87.2	2.7	40.4	15.7	9.2	−14.9
1974	271.6	122.7	43.4	21.4	84.2	278.2	104.5	101.8	3.0	41.6	19.6	7.6	−6.6
1975	283.4	127.5	41.8	22.2	91.9	328.8	117.9	131.4	3.1	48.4	21.7	6.0	−45.4
1976	314.9	137.2	52.5	24.3	101.0	370.7	125.1	153.8	3.0	57.5	25.2	6.2	−55.8
1977	365.9	166.3	58.9	24.5	116.2	411.2	139.8	166.6	3.2	66.3	28.4	6.9	−45.3
1978	414.3	186.5	67.3	27.2	133.3	450.4	150.4	178.7	3.5	74.7	33.5	9.7	−36.1
1979	480.8	222.6	76.1	29.1	153.1	495.6	164.1	197.8	4.1	79.1	40.6	9.9	−14.8
1980	525.1	250.1	70.0	34.7	170.3	577.0	189.8	234.6	4.8	86.7	50.6	10.5	−51.9
1981	614.7	291.7	70.9	55.7	196.3	666.5	218.1	273.4	5.7	90.1	66.2	13.1	−51.9
1982	618.2	303.0	50.1	50.7	214.4	739.7	250.1	304.8	6.0	83.4	82.5	12.8	−121.5
1983 [3]	627.9	293.1	50.5	55.2	229.1	829.0	279.0	342.2	6.4	86.9	92.4	22.1	−201.1
1984 [3]	685.6	304.1	59.4	59.3	262.8	877.3	302.5	350.9	6.5	90.1	106.6	20.7	−191.7
Calendar year:													
1958	78.7	36.8	18.0	11.5	12.4	88.9	53.9	19.6	1.8	5.6	5.2	2.8	−10.3
1959	89.8	39.9	22.5	12.5	14.9	91.0	53.9	20.1	1.8	6.8	6.2	2.1	−1.1
1960	96.1	43.6	21.4	13.4	17.6	93.1	53.7	21.6	1.9	6.5	6.8	2.6	3.0
1961	98.1	44.7	21.5	13.6	18.3	101.9	57.4	25.0	2.1	7.2	6.2	4.0	−3.9
1962	106.2	48.6	22.5	14.6	20.5	110.4	63.7	25.6	2.2	8.0	6.8	4.2	−4.2
1963	114.4	51.5	24.6	15.3	23.1	114.2	64.6	27.0	2.2	9.1	7.3	3.9	.3
1964	114.9	48.6	26.1	16.2	24.0	118.2	65.2	27.9	2.2	10.4	8.0	4.5	−3.3
1965	124.3	53.9	28.9	16.5	25.0	123.8	67.3	30.3	2.2	11.1	8.4	4.6	.5
1966	141.8	61.7	31.4	15.6	33.1	143.6	78.8	33.5	2.3	14.4	9.2	5.5	−1.8
1967	150.5	67.5	30.0	16.3	36.7	163.7	90.9	40.1	2.2	15.9	9.8	4.7	−13.2
1968	174.4	79.7	36.1	18.0	40.7	180.5	98.0	46.0	2.1	18.6	11.3	4.5	−6.0
1969	196.9	95.1	36.1	19.0	46.7	188.4	97.6	50.6	2.1	20.3	12.7	5.2	8.4
1970	191.9	92.6	30.6	19.3	49.3	204.3	95.7	61.3	2.2	24.4	14.1	6.5	−12.4
1971	198.6	90.3	33.5	20.4	54.4	220.6	96.2	72.7	2.6	29.0	13.8	6.3	−22.0
1972	227.5	108.2	36.6	20.0	62.7	244.3	101.7	80.5	2.7	37.5	14.4	7.9	−16.8
1973	258.6	114.7	43.3	21.2	79.5	264.2	102.0	93.3	2.6	40.6	18.0	7.8	−5.6
1974	287.8	131.3	45.1	21.7	89.8	299.3	111.0	114.5	3.2	43.9	20.7	5.5	−11.5
1975	287.3	125.8	43.6	23.9	94.1	356.6	122.7	146.3	3.1	54.6	23.1	6.9	−69.3
1976	331.8	147.3	54.6	23.4	106.5	384.8	129.2	158.8	3.2	61.1	26.8	5.8	−53.1
1977	375.2	170.1	61.6	25.0	118.5	421.1	143.4	169.6	3.3	67.5	29.1	8.2	−45.9
1978	431.6	194.9	71.3	28.1	137.2	461.0	153.6	181.8	3.8	77.3	35.2	9.5	−29.5
1979	493.6	230.6	74.2	29.4	159.5	509.7	168.3	205.0	4.2	80.5	42.4	9.2	−16.1
1980	540.7	257.5	70.3	38.9	174.1	602.1	197.2	246.2	5.2	88.7	53.1	11.7	−61.4
1981	628.2	298.1	67.3	58.5	204.3	688.2	228.9	280.9	5.7	87.7	71.9	13.1	−60.0
1982 P	614.7	300.1	48.1	50.0	216.5	762.6	257.3	315.7	6.1	83.6	84.8	15.1	−147.9
1981:													
I	620.0	286.4	76.1	57.5	199.9	659.7	217.0	268.8	5.2	90.2	66.3	12.2	−39.7
II	627.0	297.0	65.6	61.5	202.8	667.5	218.2	271.9	4.8	90.6	68.3	13.7	−40.5
III	640.2	307.9	68.4	57.8	206.1	698.2	230.0	289.0	6.1	86.3	74.0	13.0	−58.0
IV	625.7	300.9	59.1	57.2	208.4	727.4	250.5	294.0	6.6	83.6	79.0	13.6	−101.7
1982:													
I	609.9	299.9	46.5	48.7	214.9	728.3	249.7	297.2	6.0	83.0	79.6	12.7	−118.4
II	617.0	305.8	45.2	49.8	216.2	736.6	244.3	307.0	5.8	85.0	82.8	11.6	−119.6
III	613.7	295.6	49.8	50.8	217.5	769.7	259.0	321.8	5.6	82.0	88.7	12.6	−156.0
IV P	....	299.3	....	50.7	217.4	815.9	276.1	337.0	7.0	84.2	88.2	23.4	....

[1] Includes an item for the difference between wage accruals and disbursements, not shown separately.

[2] Under provisions of the Congressional Budget Act of 1974, the fiscal year for the Federal Government shifted beginning with fiscal year 1977. Through fiscal year 1976, the fiscal year was on a July 1–June 30 basis; beginning October 1976 (fiscal year 1977), the fiscal year is on an October 1–September 30 basis. The 3-month period from July 1, 1976 through September 30, 1976 is a separate fiscal period known as the transition quarter.

[3] Estimates.

Sources: Department of Commerce (Bureau of Economic Analysis) and Office of Management and Budget.

Table B–77.—*State and local government receipts and expenditures, national income and product accounts, 1946–82*

[Billions of dollars; quarterly data at seasonally adjusted annual rates]

Calendar year or quarter	Receipts: Total	Receipts: Personal tax and nontax receipts	Receipts: Corporate profits tax accruals	Receipts: Indirect business tax and nontax accruals	Receipts: Contributions for social insurance	Receipts: Federal grants-in-aid	Expenditures: Total [1]	Expenditures: Purchases of goods and services	Expenditures: Transfer payments to persons	Expenditures: Net interest paid less dividends received	Expenditures: Subsidies less current surplus of government enterprises	Surplus or deficit (−), national income and product accounts
1946	13.0	1.5	0.5	9.3	0.6	1.1	11.1	9.9	1.7	0.2	−0.7	1.9
1947	15.4	1.7	.6	10.7	.7	1.7	14.4	12.8	2.3	.1	−.8	1.0
1948	17.7	2.1	.7	12.2	.8	2.0	17.6	15.3	3.0	.1	−.8	.1
1949	19.5	2.4	.6	13.3	.9	2.2	20.2	18.0	3.0	.1	−.9	−.7
1950	21.3	2.5	.8	14.6	1.1	2.3	22.5	19.8	3.6	.1	−.9	−1.2
1951	23.4	2.8	.9	15.9	1.4	2.5	23.9	21.8	3.1	.0	−1.0	−.4
1952	25.4	3.0	.8	17.4	1.6	2.6	25.5	23.2	3.3	.0	−1.1	−.0
1953	27.4	3.2	.8	18.8	1.7	2.8	27.3	25.0	3.5	.0	−1.2	.1
1954	29.0	3.5	.8	19.9	2.0	2.9	30.2	27.8	3.6	.1	−1.3	−1.1
1955	31.7	3.9	1.0	21.6	2.1	3.1	32.9	30.6	3.8	.1	−1.5	−1.3
1956	35.0	4.5	1.0	23.8	2.3	3.3	35.9	33.5	3.9	.1	−1.6	−.9
1957	38.5	5.0	1.0	25.7	2.6	4.2	39.8	37.1	4.3	.1	−1.7	−1.4
1958	42.0	5.4	1.0	27.2	2.8	5.6	44.3	41.1	4.8	.1	−1.7	−2.4
1959	46.4	6.1	1.2	29.3	3.1	6.8	46.9	43.7	5.1	.1	−2.0	−.4
1960	49.9	6.7	1.2	32.0	3.4	6.5	49.8	46.5	5.4	.1	−2.2	.1
1961	54.0	7.4	1.3	34.4	3.7	7.2	54.4	50.8	5.8	.1	−2.3	−.4
1962	58.5	8.2	1.5	37.0	3.9	8.0	58.0	54.3	6.0	.1	−2.5	.5
1963	63.2	8.8	1.7	39.4	4.2	9.1	62.8	59.0	6.4	.1	−2.8	.5
1964	69.5	10.0	1.8	42.6	4.7	10.4	68.5	64.6	6.9	−.1	−2.8	1.0
1965	75.1	10.9	2.0	46.1	5.0	11.1	75.1	71.1	7.3	−.3	−3.0	−.0
1966	84.8	12.8	2.2	49.7	5.7	14.4	84.3	79.8	8.1	−.7	−3.0	.5
1967	93.6	14.6	2.5	54.0	6.7	15.9	94.7	89.3	9.4	−.9	−3.1	−1.1
1968	107.3	17.5	3.1	60.9	7.2	18.6	107.2	101.0	10.5	−1.1	−3.2	.1
1969	120.2	20.6	3.4	67.6	8.3	20.3	118.7	111.2	12.2	−1.4	−3.3	1.5
1970	135.4	23.2	3.5	75.0	9.2	24.4	133.5	124.4	14.7	−2.0	−3.6	1.9
1971	153.0	26.4	4.1	83.3	10.2	29.0	150.4	138.7	17.3	−1.7	−3.7	2.6
1972	178.3	32.8	5.0	91.5	11.5	37.5	164.8	151.4	19.3	−1.9	−4.2	13.5
1973	195.0	36.0	5.8	99.7	13.0	40.6	181.6	168.5	20.7	−3.3	−4.3	13.4
1974	211.4	39.0	6.5	107.4	14.6	43.9	204.6	193.1	20.9	−5.0	−4.4	6.8
1975	237.7	43.1	7.1	116.2	16.8	54.6	232.2	217.2	24.6	−5.1	−4.5	5.5
1976	267.8	49.6	9.3	128.3	19.5	61.1	251.2	232.9	27.6	−4.5	−4.8	16.6
1977	297.7	56.3	11.1	140.7	22.1	67.5	269.7	250.4	29.7	−5.3	−5.1	28.0
1978	327.6	63.8	11.9	150.0	24.7	77.3	297.3	278.3	32.8	−7.9	−5.7	30.3
1979	352.0	70.4	13.4	160.2	27.4	80.5	321.5	306.0	35.0	−13.8	−5.9	30.4
1980	385.9	78.8	14.4	174.1	29.9	88.7	357.8	341.2	39.6	−16.9	−6.2	28.2
1981	416.8	88.6	13.9	192.8	33.8	87.7	385.0	368.0	43.0	−19.5	−6.5	31.7
1982 [p]	437.3	97.1	10.7	208.8	37.2	83.6	405.4	389.8	45.1	−22.7	−6.8	31.9
1980:												
I	374.5	75.5	15.9	168.8	28.7	85.5	345.3	329.6	37.7	−16.1	−6.0	29.1
II	376.6	77.3	12.5	170.5	28.8	87.6	353.3	337.2	38.9	−16.7	−6.1	23.3
III	389.3	79.6	14.2	176.1	30.6	88.9	362.2	345.2	40.5	−17.3	−6.2	27.1
IV	403.3	82.7	15.0	181.2	31.6	92.7	370.3	352.8	41.4	−17.7	−6.3	33.0
1981:												
I	410.0	84.8	15.4	187.1	32.5	90.2	378.6	361.1	42.0	−18.1	−6.4	31.3
II	415.2	87.2	13.6	190.4	33.4	90.6	382.2	365.0	42.8	−19.1	−6.4	32.9
III	420.3	90.3	14.0	195.5	34.2	86.3	386.9	370.1	43.3	−20.1	6.5	33.5
IV	421.5	92.3	12.5	198.0	35.1	83.6	392.4	375.7	43.9	−20.7	−6.6	29.1
1982:												
I	424.2	93.6	10.1	201.5	36.0	83.0	396.5	380.4	44.3	−21.5	−6.6	27.7
II	434.3	95.4	10.2	206.9	36.9	85.0	402.2	386.6	44.7	−22.4	−6.7	32.1
III	440.5	98.8	11.2	210.9	37.7	82.0	408.2	392.7	45.4	−23.2	−6.8	32.3
IV [p]	....	100.5	....	215.8	38.4	84.2	414.9	399.6	46.0	−23.8	−6.9	....

[1] Includes an item for the difference between wage accruals and disbursements, not shown separately.

Source: Department of Commerce, Bureau of Economic Analysis.

TABLE B–78.—*State and local government revenues and expenditures, selected fiscal years, 1927–81*

[Millions of dollars]

Fiscal year [1]	General revenues by source [2]							General expenditures by function [2]				
	Total	Property taxes	Sales and gross receipts taxes	Individual income taxes	Corporation net income taxes	Revenue from Federal Government	All other [3]	Total	Education	Highways	Public welfare	All other [4]
1927	7,271	4,730	470	70	92	116	1,793	7,210	2,235	1,809	151	3,015
1932	7,267	4,487	752	74	79	232	1,643	7,765	2,311	1,741	444	3,269
1934	7,678	4,076	1,008	80	49	1,016	1,449	7,181	1,831	1,509	889	2,952
1936	8,395	4,093	1,484	153	113	948	1,604	7,644	2,177	1,425	827	3,215
1938	9,228	4,440	1,794	218	165	800	1,811	8,757	2,491	1,650	1,069	3,547
1940	9,609	4,430	1,982	224	156	945	1,872	9,229	2,638	1,573	1,156	3,862
1942	10,418	4,537	2,351	276	272	858	2,123	9,190	2,586	1,490	1,225	3,889
1944	10,908	4,604	2,289	342	451	954	2,269	8,863	2,793	1,200	1,133	3,737
1946	12,356	4,986	2,986	422	447	855	2,661	11,028	3,356	1,672	1,409	4,591
1948	17,250	6,126	4,442	543	592	1,861	3,685	17,684	5,379	3,036	2,099	7,170
1950	20,911	7,349	5,154	788	593	2,486	4,541	22,787	7,177	3,803	2,940	8,867
1952	25,181	8,652	6,357	998	846	2,566	5,763	26,098	8,318	4,650	2,788	10,342
1953	27,307	9,375	6,927	1,065	817	2,870	6,252	27,910	9,390	4,987	2,914	10,619
1954	29,012	9,967	7,276	1,127	778	2,966	6,897	30,701	10,557	5,527	3,060	11,557
1955	31,073	10,735	7,643	1,237	744	3,131	7,584	33,724	11,907	6,452	3,168	12,197
1956	34,667	11,749	8,691	1,538	890	3,335	8,465	36,711	13,220	6,953	3,139	13,399
1957	38,164	12,864	9,467	1,754	984	3,843	9,250	40,375	14,134	7,816	3,485	14,940
1958	41,219	14,047	9,829	1,759	1,018	4,865	9,699	44,851	15,919	8,567	3,818	16,547
1959	45,306	14,983	10,437	1,994	1,001	6,377	10,516	48,887	17,283	9,592	4,136	17,876
1960	50,505	16,405	11,849	2,463	1,180	6,974	11,634	51,876	18,719	9,428	4,404	19,325
1961	54,037	18,002	12,463	2,613	1,266	7,131	12,563	56,201	20,574	9,844	4,720	21,063
1962	58,252	19,054	13,494	3,037	1,308	7,871	13,489	60,206	22,216	10,357	5,084	22,549
1963	62,890	20,089	14,456	3,269	1,505	8,722	14,850	64,816	23,776	11,136	5,481	24,423
1962–63 [5]	62,269	19,833	14,446	3,267	1,505	8,663	14,556	63,977	23,729	11,150	5,420	23,678
1963–64 [5]	68,443	21,241	15,762	3,791	1,695	10,002	15,951	69,302	26,286	11,664	5,766	25,586
1964–65 [5]	74,000	22,583	17,118	4,090	1,929	11,029	17,250	74,546	28,563	12,221	6,315	27,447
1965–66 [5]	83,036	24,670	19,085	4,760	2,038	13,214	19,269	82,843	33,287	12,770	6,757	30,029
1966–67 [5]	91,197	26,047	20,530	5,826	2,227	15,370	21,197	93,350	37,919	13,932	8,218	33,281
1967–68 [5]	101,264	27,747	22,911	7,308	2,518	17,181	23,598	102,411	41,158	14,481	9,857	36,915
1968–69 [5]	114,550	30,673	26,519	8,908	3,180	19,153	26,118	116,728	47,238	15,417	12,110	41,963
1969–70 [5]	130,756	34,054	30,322	10,812	3,738	21,857	29,971	131,332	52,718	16,427	14,679	47,508
1970–71 [5]	144,927	37,852	33,233	11,900	3,424	26,146	32,374	150,674	59,413	18,095	18,226	54,940
1971–72 [5]	166,352	42,133	37,488	15,237	4,416	31,253	35,826	166,873	64,886	19,010	21,070	61,907
1972–73 [5]	190,214	45,283	42,047	17,994	5,425	39,256	40,210	181,227	69,714	18,615	23,582	69,316
1973–74 [5]	207,670	47,705	46,098	19,491	6,015	41,820	46,541	198,959	75,833	19,946	25,085	78,096
1974–75 [5]	228,171	51,491	49,815	21,454	6,642	47,034	51,735	230,721	87,858	22,528	28,155	92,180
1975–76 [5]	256,176	57,001	54,547	24,575	7,273	55,589	57,191	256,731	97,216	23,907	32,604	103,004
1976–77 [5]	285,796	62,535	60,595	29,245	9,174	62,575	61,673	274,388	102,805	23,105	35,941	112,537
1977–78 [5]	315,960	66,422	67,596	33,176	10,738	69,592	68,436	296,983	110,758	24,609	39,140	122,476
1978–79 [5]	343,278	64,944	74,247	36,932	12,128	75,164	79,864	327,517	119,448	28,440	41,898	137,731
1979–80 [5]	382,322	68,499	79,927	42,080	13,321	83,029	95,466	369,086	133,211	33,311	47,288	155,277
1980–81 [5]	423,404	74,969	85,971	46,426	14,143	90,294	111,599	407,449	145,784	34,603	54,121	172,941

[1] Fiscal years not the same for all governments. See footnote 5.
[2] Excludes revenues or expenditures of publicly owned utilities and liquor stores, and of insurance-trust activities. Intergovernmental receipts and payments between State and local governments are also excluded.
[3] Includes licenses and other taxes and charges and miscellaneous revenues.
[4] Includes expenditures for health, hospitals, police, local fire protection, natural resources, sanitation, housing and urban renewal, local parks and recreation, general control, financial administration, interest on general debt, and unallocable expenditures.
[5] Data for fiscal year ending in the 12-month period through June 30. Data for 1963 and earlier years include local government amounts grouped in terms of fiscal years ended during the particular calendar year.

Note.—Data are not available for intervening years.

Source: Department of Commerce, Bureau of the Census.

TABLE B–79.—*Interest-bearing public debt securities by kind of obligation, 1967–82*

[Millions of dollars]

End of year or month	Total interest-bearing public debt securities	Marketable: Total	Marketable: Treasury bills	Marketable: Treasury notes	Marketable: Treasury bonds [1]	Nonmarketable: Total	Nonmarketable: U.S. savings bonds	Nonmarketable: Foreign government and public series [2]	Nonmarketable: Government account series	Nonmarketable: Other [3]
Fiscal year:										
1967	322,286	[4] 210,672	58,535	49,108	97,418	111,614	51,213	1,514	56,155	2,731
1968	344,401	226,592	64,440	71,073	91,079	117,808	51,712	3,741	59,526	2,828
1969	351,729	226,107	68,356	78,946	78,805	125,623	51,711	4,070	66,790	3,051
1970	369,026	232,599	76,154	93,489	62,956	136,426	51,281	4,755	76,323	4,068
1971	396,289	245,473	86,677	104,807	53,989	150,816	53,003	9,270	82,784	5,759
1972	425,360	257,202	94,648	113,419	49,135	168,158	55,921	18,985	89,598	3,654
1973	456,353	262,971	100,061	117,840	45,071	193,382	59,418	28,521	101,700	3,701
1974	473,238	266,575	105,019	128,419	33,137	206,663	61,921	25,011	115,442	4,289
1975	532,122	315,606	128,569	150,257	36,779	216,516	65,482	23,216	124,173	3,644
1976	619,254	392,581	161,198	191,758	39,626	226,673	69,733	21,500	130,557	4,883
1977	697,629	443,508	156,091	241,692	45,724	254,121	75,411	21,799	140,113	16,797
1978	766,971	485,155	160,936	267,865	56,355	281,816	79,798	21,680	153,271	27,067
1979	819,007	506,693	161,378	274,242	71,073	312,314	80,440	28,115	176,360	27,400
1980	906,402	594,506	199,832	310,903	83,772	311,896	72,727	25,158	189,848	24,164
1981	996,495	683,209	223,388	363,643	96,178	313,286	68,017	20,499	201,052	23,718
1982	1,140,883	824,422	277,900	442,890	103,631	316,461	67,274	14,641	210,462	24,085
1981:										
Jan	929,825	628,482	220,423	321,176	86,883	301,343	71,057	23,804	182,197	24,287
Feb	946,455	642,905	228,972	324,540	89,393	303,550	70,443	23,986	185,020	24,102
Mar	963,207	661,142	235,315	336,505	89,323	302,065	70,057	24,162	183,833	24,015
Apr	962,779	657,906	225,849	341,052	91,006	304,873	69,518	24,411	186,979	23,965
May	[illegible]	[illegible]	[illegible]	[illegible]	[illegible]	[illegible]	[illegible]	24,789	190,839	23,750
June	969,921	660,769	218,786	348,788	93,196	309,152	68,934	23,514	192,962	23,741
July	972,053	666,405	217,532	354,005	94,868	305,647	68,719	21,943	191,647	23,339
Aug	978,920	673,765	219,854	357,603	96,308	305,155	68,355	21,431	192,060	23,310
Sept	996,495	683,209	223,388	363,643	96,178	313,286	68,017	20,499	201,052	23,718
Oct	999,451	689,578	229,061	362,649	97,867	309,874	67,718	20,471	198,053	23,632
Nov	1,011,936	704,819	233,905	370,794	100,119	307,117	67,739	20,309	195,541	23,529
Dec	1,027,300	720,293	245,015	375,332	99,946	307,007	67,837	19,025	196,665	23,480
1982:										
Jan	1,032,678	726,542	250,562	374,357	101,623	306,136	67,581	18,920	196,393	23,243
Feb	1,042,198	737,532	254,037	382,070	101,426	304,666	67,378	18,384	195,722	23,182
Mar	1,059,815	752,620	256,212	395,042	101,366	307,195	67,163	19,641	196,707	23,684
Apr	1,064,538	755,833	254,880	399,700	101,253	308,705	67,034	19,446	198,538	23,687
May	1,066,410	755,688	256,114	398,408	101,166	310,722	67,082	18,395	201,290	23,955
June	1,078,431	763,995	256,007	406,925	101,063	314,436	67,122	17,457	205,954	23,902
July	1,083,296	774,077	262,009	411,070	100,998	309,218	67,132	16,643	201,502	23,941
Aug	1,108,131	801,427	273,066	427,426	100,935	306,704	67,148	15,606	199,896	24,054
Sept	1,140,883	824,422	277,900	442,890	103,631	316,461	67,274	14,641	210,462	24,085
Oct	1,136,826	824,662	283,923	438,068	102,672	312,164	67,514	14,627	205,717	24,305
Nov	1,160,489	852,463	293,531	454,229	104,702	308,026	67,801	14,863	199,903	25,459
Dec.	1,195,496	881,476	311,820	465,030	104,627	314,020	67,719	14,691	205,427	26,183

[1] Includes Treasury bonds and minor amounts of Panama Canal and postal savings bonds.
[2] Nonmarketable certificates of indebtedness, notes, bonds, and bills in the Treasury foreign series of dollar-denominated and foreign-currency denominated issues.
[3] Includes depository bonds, retirement plan bonds, Rural Electrification Administration bonds, State and local bonds, and special issues held only by U.S. Government agencies and trust funds and the Federal home loan banks.
[4] Includes $5,610 million in certificates not shown separately.

Note.—Through fiscal year 1976, the fiscal year was on a July 1–June 30 basis; beginning October 1976 (fiscal year 1977) the fiscal year is on an October 1–September 30 basis.

Source: Department of the Treasury.

TABLE B–80.—*Estimated ownership of public debt securities, 1967–82*

[Par values; [1] billions of dollars]

End of year or month	Public debt securities: Total [2]	Held by Government accounts	Held by Federal Reserve Banks	Held by private investors: Total [3]	Commercial banks [4]	Mutual savings banks and insurance companies	Corporations [5]	State and local governments [6]	Individuals [7]	Miscellaneous investors [3] [8]
Fiscal year:										
1967	322.9	71.8	46.7	204.4	55.5	13.2	11.0	23.6	70.4	30.7
1968	345.4	76.1	52.2	217.0	59.7	12.5	12.0	25.1	74.2	33.4
1969	352.9	84.8	54.1	214.0	55.3	11.6	11.1	26.4	77.3	32.3
1970	370.1	95.2	57.7	217.2	52.6	10.4	8.5	29.0	81.8	35.0
1971	397.3	102.9	65.5	228.9	61.0	10.3	7.4	25.9	75.4	49.1
1972	426.4	111.5	71.4	243.6	60.9	10.2	9.3	26.9	73.2	63.2
1973	457.3	123.4	75.0	258.9	58.8	9.6	9.8	28.8	75.9	76.0
1974	474.2	138.2	80.5	255.6	53.2	8.5	10.8	28.3	80.7	74.2
1975	533.2	145.3	84.7	303.2	69.0	10.6	13.8	31.7	86.8	91.3
1976	620.4	149.6	94.4	376.4	92.5	16.0	24.7	39.3	96.2	107.7
1977	698.8	155.5	104.7	438.6	99.8	20.5	21.2	48.2	106.5	142.4
1978	771.5	167.9	115.3	488.3	94.4	21.2	18.1	63.8	113.9	176.9
1979	826.5	187.7	115.5	523.4	92.5	21.5	22.1	66.5	115.5	205.3
1980	907.7	197.7	120.7	589.2	109.7	24.3	25.9	77.0	123.0	229.3
1981	997.9	208.1	124.3	665.4	112.2	26.2	37.8	86.2	140.3	262.7
1982	1,142.0	216.4	134.4	791.2						
1981:										
Jan	934.1	189.5	117.2	627.4	117.2	25.5	30.4	77.3	134.2	242.8
Feb	950.5	192.0	118.9	639.6	116.4	25.3	35.2	80.4	136.2	246.1
Mar	964.5	190.9	119.0	654.6	117.5	23.7	40.0	82.3	138.6	252.5
Apr	964.0	193.9	119.7	650.4	113.5	23.7	40.4	83.6	138.2	251.0
May	968.5	197.8	118.3	652.3	113.2	25.3	38.8	85.1	139.9	250.0
June	971.2	199.9	120.0	651.2	113.3	24.0	38.7	83.0	139.6	252.6
July	973.3	198.6	123.4	651.3	114.2	25.4	37.8	86.0	139.5	248.4
Aug	980.2	199.0	124.5	656.7	115.0	26.1	38.0	86.2	140.2	251.2
Sept	997.9	208.1	124.3	665.4	112.2	26.2	37.8	86.2	140.3	262.7
Oct	1,005.0	204.9	123.0	677.2	111.3	24.7	38.6	88.3	141.0	273.3
Nov	1,013.3	202.1	126.5	684.6	110.0	24.6	38.3	87.5	141.6	282.6
Dec	1,028.7	203.3	129.9	694.5	109.4	24.3	37.8	85.6	143.7	293.7
1982:										
Jan	1,038.4	202.8	128.3	707.3	111.4	24.9	37.9	86.2	144.1	302.8
Feb	1,048.2	201.1	126.2	720.8	111.8	24.1	37.5	88.2	144.7	314.5
Mar	1,061.3	202.5	125.6	733.3	114.3	25.6	37.5	88.3	146.5	321.1
Apr	1,065.7	204.3	134.3	727.1	110.1	26.8	36.5	88.5	145.7	319.5
May	1,071.7	206.7	129.8	735.2	109.4	27.2	38.8	91.8	146.2	321.8
June	1,079.6	211.7	127.0	740.9	117.0	27.9	38.9	91.2	146.2	319.7
July	1,089.6	206.3	133.8	749.6	110.0	28.2	39.9	88.7	146.4	336.4
Aug	1,109.2	206.5	132.9	769.8						
Sept	1,142.0	216.4	134.4	791.2						
Oct	1,142.8	211.0	132.1	799.7						
Nov	1,161.7	203.9	137.7	820.1						
Dec	1,197.1	209.4	139.9	849.4						

[1] U.S. savings bonds, series A–F and J, and U.S. savings notes are included at current redemption value.

[2] As of July 31, 1974, public debt outstanding has been adjusted to exclude the notes of the International Monetary Fund to conform with the Budget presentation. This adjustment applies to the 1967–82 data in this table.

[3] For comparability with 1975–82 published data, published data for 1967–74 have been adjusted to exclude notes of the International Monetary Fund. These adjustments amounted to $3.3 billion in 1967, $2.2 billion in 1968, and $0.8 billion in each year 1969 through 1974. These adjustments were necessary in order to add to the total public debt figures as published by the Department of the Treasury. The Treasury Survey of Ownership on which private investor group estimates were based was discontinued in July 1982.

[4] Includes commercial banks, trust companies, and stock savings banks in the United States and Territories and island possessions; figures exclude securities held in trust departments.

[5] Exclusive of banks and insurance companies.

[6] Includes trust, sinking, and investment funds of State and local governments and their agencies, and of Territories and possessions.

[7] Includes partnerships and personal trust accounts.

[8] Includes savings and loan associations, nonprofit institutions, corporate pension trust funds, dealers and brokers, certain government deposit accounts and government-sponsored agencies, and investments of foreign balances and international accounts in the United States.

Note.—Through fiscal year 1976, the fiscal year was on a July 1—June 30 basis; beginning October 1976 (fiscal year 1977), the fiscal year is on an October 1—September 30 basis.

Source: Department of the Treasury.

Table B–81.—*Maturity distribution and average length of marketable interest-bearing public debt securities held by private investors, 1967–82*

End of year or month	Amount outstanding, privately held	Maturity class					Average length	
		Within 1 year	1 to 5 years	5 to 10 years	10 to 20 years	20 years and over		
	Millions of dollars						Years	Months
Fiscal year:								
1967	150,321	56,561	53,584	21,057	6,153	12,968	5	1
1968	159,671	66,746	52,295	21,850	6,110	12,670	4	5
1969	156,008	69,311	50,182	18,078	6,097	12,337	4	2
1970	157,910	76,443	57,035	8,286	7,876	8,272	3	0
1971	161,863	74,803	58,557	14,503	6,357	7,645	3	6
1972	165,978	79,509	57,157	16,033	6,358	6,922	3	3
1973	167,869	84,041	54,139	16,385	8,741	4,564	3	1
1974	164,862	87,150	50,103	14,197	9,930	3,481	2	11
1975	210,382	115,677	65,852	15,385	8,857	4,611	2	8
1976	279,782	151,723	89,151	24,169	8,087	6,652	2	7
1977	326,674	161,329	113,319	33,067	8,428	10,531	2	11
1978	356,501	163,819	132,993	33,500	11,383	14,805	3	3
1979	380,530	181,883	127,574	32,279	18,489	20,304	3	7
1980	463,717	220,084	156,244	38,809	25,901	22,679	3	9
1981	549,863	256,187	182,237	48,743	32,569	30,127	4	0
1982	682,043	314,436	221,783	75,749	33,017	37,058	3	11
1981:								
Jan	502,248	247,958	156,845	42,060	27,011	[illegible]	3	9
Feb	515,178	256,007	160,163	43,382	28,690	26,936	3	10
Mar	532,800	263,208	167,226	46,786	28,662	26,918	3	9
Apr	528,992	254,533	167,570	49,616	28,587	28,685	3	10
May	529,057	258,101	167,865	43,842	30,296	28,953	3	11
June	531,525	252,489	172,784	47,032	30,268	28,952	3	11
July	533,778	251,307	171,504	50,242	30,172	30,553	4	0
Aug	540,228	251,533	180,669	45,297	32,602	30,127	4	1
Sept	549,863	256,187	182,237	48,743	32,569	30,127	4	0
Oct	558,169	263,717	177,834	52,201	32,536	31,881	4	0
Nov	569,534	266,163	189,570	47,615	34,164	32,022	4	1
Dec	580,670	275,322	188,422	50,851	34,055	32,020	4	0
1982:								
Jan	590,139	284,171	183,843	54,370	34,069	33,686	4	0
Feb	604,671	290,697	194,457	49,120	35,819	34,578	4	1
Mar	619,030	295,476	200,544	52,612	35,822	34,576	4	0
Apr	613,576	289,000	199,278	55,329	35,565	34,404	4	0
May	618,699	290,476	203,612	54,361	35,701	34,549	4	1
June	628,997	293,266	207,106	58,425	35,651	34,549	4	0
July	634,556	295,118	206,380	63,022	35,583	34,453	4	0
Aug	660,583	309,446	217,258	66,347	33,097	34,435	3	11
Sept	682,043	314,436	221,783	75,749	33,017	37,058	3	11
Oct	685,969	321,081	218,673	75,944	33,065	37,206	3	10
Nov	708,769	327,565	235,443	72,644	35,750	37,367	3	11
Dec	736,148	346,321	239,262	77,570	35,677	37,318	3	10

Note.—All issues classified to final maturity.

Through fiscal year 1976, the fiscal year was on a July 1—June 30 basis; beginning October 1976 (fiscal year 1977), the fiscal year is on an October 1—September 30 basis.

Source: Department of the Treasury.

TABLE B–82.—*Corporate profits with inventory valuation and capital consumption adjustments, 1929–82*

[Billions of dollars; quarterly data at seasonally adjusted annual rates]

Year or quarter	Corporate profits with inventory valuation and capital consumption adjustments	Corporate profits tax liability	Profits after tax with inventory valuation and capital consumption adjustments		
			Total	Dividends	Undistributed profits with inventory valuation and capital consumption adjustments
1929	9.0	1.4	7.7	5.8	1.9
1933	−1.7	.5	−2.3	2.0	−4.3
1939	5.3	1.4	3.9	3.8	.1
1940	8.6	2.8	5.8	4.0	1.8
1941	14.1	7.6	6.5	4.4	2.1
1942	19.3	11.4	7.9	4.3	3.6
1943	23.5	14.1	9.5	4.4	5.0
1944	23.6	12.9	10.7	4.6	6.1
1945	19.0	10.7	8.4	4.6	3.8
1946	16.6	9.1	7.5	5.6	1.9
1947	22.3	11.3	11.0	6.3	4.7
1948	29.4	12.4	17.0	7.0	10.0
1949	27.1	10.2	16.9	7.2	9.7
1950	33.9	17.9	16.0	8.8	7.2
1951	38.7	22.6	16.1	8.5	7.6
1952	36.1	19.4	16.7	8.5	8.2
1953	36.3	20.3	16.0	8.8	7.2
1954	35.2	17.6	17.5	9.1	8.4
1955	45.5	22.0	23.4	10.3	13.1
1956	43.7	22.0	21.8	11.1	10.7
1957	43.3	21.4	21.8	11.5	10.3
1958	38.5	19.0	19.5	11.3	8.2
1959	49.6	23.6	26.0	12.2	13.8
1960	47.6	22.7	24.9	12.9	12.1
1961	48.6	22.8	25.8	13.3	12.5
1962	56.6	24.0	32.6	14.4	18.2
1963	62.1	26.2	35.9	15.5	20.4
1964	69.2	28.0	41.2	17.3	23.9
1965	80.0	30.9	49.1	19.1	30.0
1966	85.1	33.7	51.4	19.4	32.0
1967	82.4	32.5	49.9	20.2	29.7
1968	89.1	39.2	50.0	22.0	27.9
1969	85.1	39.5	45.6	22.5	23.1
1970	71.4	34.2	37.2	22.5	14.8
1971	83.2	37.5	45.7	22.9	22.8
1972	96.6	41.6	55.0	24.4	30.5
1973	108.3	49.0	59.3	27.0	32.3
1974	94.9	51.6	43.3	29.9	13.4
1975	110.5	50.6	59.9	30.8	29.1
1976	138.1	63.8	74.3	37.4	36.9
1977	167.3	72.7	94.6	40.8	53.7
1978	192.4	83.2	109.1	47.0	62.2
1979	194.8	87.6	107.2	52.7	54.5
1980	181.6	84.7	97.0	58.1	38.9
1981	190.6	81.2	109.5	65.1	44.4
1982 p	161.1	58.8	102.3	70.3	32.1
1980:					
I	195.3	95.3	100.0	56.2	43.9
II	172.2	73.3	98.9	57.8	41.0
III	177.8	82.2	95.6	58.7	36.9
IV	181.2	87.8	93.3	59.6	33.7
1981:					
I	200.3	91.5	108.9	61.5	47.3
II	185.1	79.2	105.9	64.0	42.0
III	193.1	82.4	110.7	66.8	43.9
IV	183.9	71.6	112.3	68.1	44.3
1982:					
I	157.1	56.7	100.4	68.8	31.6
II	155.4	55.3	100.0	69.3	30.7
III	166.2	60.9	105.3	70.5	34.8

Source: Department of Commerce, Bureau of Economic Analysis.

384-041 O - 83 - 17 : QL 3

TABLE B–83.—*Corporate profits by industry, 1929–82*

[Billions of dollars; quarterly data at seasonally adjusted annual rates]

Year or quarter	Corporate profits with inventory valuation adjustment and without capital consumption adjustment										
	Total	Domestic industries									Rest of the world
		Total	Financial[1]			Nonfinancial					
			Total	Federal Reserve banks	Other	Total	Manufacturing[2]	Transportation and public utilities	Wholesale and retail trade	Other	
1929	10.5	10.2	1.3	0.0	1.3	8.9	5.2	1.8	1.0	0.9	0.2
1933	−1.2	−1.2	.3	.0	.3	−1.5	−.4	.0	−.5	−.7	.0
1939	6.5	6.1	.8	.0	.8	5.3	3.3	1.0	.7	[illegible]	[illegible]
1940	9.8	9.6	1.0	.0	.9	8.6	5.5	1.3	1.2	.6	.3
1941	15.4	15.0	1.1	.0	1.0	14.0	9.5	2.0	1.4	1.1	.4
1942	20.5	20.1	1.2	.0	1.2	18.9	11.8	3.4	2.2	1.5	.4
1943	24.5	24.1	1.3	.0	1.3	22.8	13.8	4.4	3.0	1.6	.4
1944	24.0	23.5	1.6	.1	1.6	21.9	13.2	3.9	3.2	1.6	.4
1945	19.3	18.9	1.7	.1	1.6	17.3	9.7	2.7	3.3	1.5	.3
1946	19.6	18.9	2.1	.1	2.0	16.8	9.0	1.8	3.8	2.1	.7
1947	25.9	24.9	1.7	.1	1.6	23.2	13.6	2.2	4.6	2.9	1.0
1948	33.4	32.2	2.6	.2	2.3	29.6	17.6	3.0	5.5	3.6	1.3
1949	31.1	29.9	3.1	.2	2.9	26.8	16.2	3.0	4.5	3.1	1.1
1950	37.9	36.7	3.1	.2	3.0	33.5	20.9	4.0	5.0	3.6	1.3
1951	43.3	41.5	3.6	.3	3.3	37.9	24.6	4.6	5.0	3.7	1.7
1952	40.6	38.7	4.0	.4	3.7	34.7	21.7	4.9	4.8	3.3	1.9
1953	40.2	38.4	4.5	.4	4.1	33.9	22.0	5.0	3.8	3.1	1.8
1954	38.4	36.4	4.6	.3	4.3	31.8	19.9	4.7	3.8	3.4	2.0
1955	[illegible]	[illegible]	[illegible]	[illegible]	[illegible]	[illegible]	20.0	5.8	5.0	3.6	2.4
1956	46.9	44.1	5.0	.5	4.5	39.1	24.7	5.9	4.5	4.1	2.8
1957	46.6	43.5	5.2	.6	4.6	38.3	24.0	5.8	4.4	4.0	3.1
1958	41.6	39.1	5.7	.6	5.1	33.5	19.4	5.9	4.6	3.6	2.5
1959	52.3	49.6	6.8	.7	6.0	42.9	26.4	7.0	5.9	3.6	2.7
1960	49.7	46.7	7.2	1.0	6.2	39.5	23.6	7.4	4.9	3.6	3.0
1961	50.0	46.8	7.0	.8	6.3	39.8	23.3	7.8	5.0	3.7	3.2
1962	55.1	51.5	7.3	.9	6.4	44.2	26.0	8.4	5.8	3.9	3.6
1963	59.7	55.8	6.8	1.0	5.8	49.0	29.3	9.3	5.9	4.4	3.9
1964	66.0	61.8	6.9	1.1	5.8	54.9	32.3	10.0	7.5	5.1	4.2
1965	76.0	71.5	7.5	1.4	6.2	64.0	39.3	11.0	8.1	5.6	4.5
1966	80.9	76.7	8.5	1.7	6.8	68.2	41.9	11.8	8.2	6.3	4.2
1967	78.1	73.7	9.0	2.0	7.0	64.8	38.5	10.7	9.1	6.5	4.4
1968	84.9	79.7	10.4	2.5	7.9	69.3	41.2	10.8	10.4	6.9	5.2
1969	80.8	74.6	11.1	3.1	8.0	63.5	36.6	10.3	10.5	6.1	6.1
1970	68.9	62.4	12.1	3.6	8.6	50.2	26.6	8.2	9.5	5.9	6.5
1971	82.0	74.9	14.1	3.3	10.7	60.8	34.1	8.5	11.7	6.5	7.1
1972	94.0	85.3	15.3	3.4	11.9	70.0	40.7	9.0	13.4	6.9	8.6
1973	105.6	92.0	15.9	4.5	11.4	76.0	45.5	8.7	13.9	8.0	13.7
1974	96.7	80.4	15.0	5.7	9.3	65.4	39.0	6.1	12.5	7.9	16.3
1975	120.6	107.6	11.8	5.7	6.2	95.8	52.6	10.0	21.3	11.9	13.0
1976	151.6	137.4	17.1	6.0	11.1	120.3	69.2	14.5	22.4	14.2	14.3
1977	178.5	163.4	23.1	6.2	16.9	140.3	78.3	17.8	26.6	17.6	15.1
1978	205.1	185.4	31.0	7.7	23.3	154.4	86.9	20.6	26.9	20.0	19.7
1979	209.6	179.0	30.3	9.6	20.7	148.6	85.6	15.9	27.1	20.1	30.6
1980	199.4	169.1	29.2	11.9	17.2	140.0	74.5	17.4	24.6	23.4	30.3
1981	207.5	184.6	22.7	14.5	8.1	162.0	86.3	19.1	33.4	23.1	22.8
1982 [p]	166.0	149.6	22.5	15.7	6.8	127.1	59.8	18.7	28.1	20.6	16.4
1980:											
I	211.0	175.9	31.5	11.6	19.9	144.4	85.2	16.8	19.7	22.7	35.1
II	189.4	157.8	28.6	12.5	16.1	129.2	64.7	13.9	27.1	23.5	31.7
III	197.0	167.5	27.2	11.4	15.8	140.3	70.0	21.5	24.4	24.3	29.6
IV	200.4	175.5	29.4	12.2	17.1	146.1	78.1	17.5	27.3	23.3	24.9
1981:											
I	217.6	193.8	26.8	13.2	13.6	167.0	90.3	20.1	33.0	23.6	23.8
II	202.6	181.7	22.7	14.2	8.6	159.0	88.9	15.6	32.1	22.5	20.8
III	210.3	189.3	20.8	15.2	5.5	168.5	92.2	19.6	33.0	23.7	21.0
IV	199.4	173.7	20.4	15.6	4.8	153.3	73.7	21.2	35.7	22.7	25.7
1982:											
I	167.2	150.3	20.0	16.1	3.9	130.4	57.7	18.8	31.9	21.9	16.9
II	162.2	144.1	22.2	16.0	6.2	121.9	56.6	18.5	26.8	20.0	18.2
III	170.0	153.7	24.2	15.8	8.4	129.5	62.7	19.2	27.4	20.3	16.3

[1] Consists of the following industries: Banking; credit agencies other than banks; security and commodity brokers, dealers, and services; insurance carriers; regulated investment companies; small business investment companies; and real estate investment trusts.
[2] See Table B–84 for industry detail.

Note.—The industry classification is on a company basis and is based on the 1972 Standard Industrial Classification (SIC) beginning 1948, and on the 1942 SIC prior to 1948.

Source: Department of Commerce, Bureau of Economic Analysis.

Table B–84.—*Corporate profits of manufacturing industries, 1929–82*

[Billions of dollars; quarterly data at seasonally adjusted annual rates]

Year or quarter	Corporate profits with inventory valuation adjustment and without capital consumption adjustment												
	Total manufacturing	Durable goods							Nondurable goods				
		Total	Primary metal industries	Fabricated metal products	Machinery, except electrical	Electric and electronic equipment	Motor vehicles and equipment	Other	Total	Food and kindred products	Chemicals and allied products	Petroleum and coal products	Other
1929	5.2	2.6							2.6				
1933	−.4	−.4							.0				
1939	3.3	1.7							1.7				
1940	5.5	3.1							2.4				
1941	9.5	6.4							3.1				
1942	11.8	7.2							4.6				
1943	13.8	8.1							5.7				
1944	13.2	7.4							5.9				
1945	9.7	4.5							5.2				
1946	9.0	2.4							6.6				
1947	13.6	5.8							7.8				
1948	17.6	7.5	1.6	.8	1.2	.7	1.4	1.8	10.0	1.9	1.7	2.8	3.7
1949	16.2	8.1	1.5	.7	1.3	.8	2.1	1.7	8.1	1.6	1.8	1.9	2.8
1950	20.9	12.0	2.3	1.1	1.6	1.2	3.1	2.6	8.9	1.6	2.3	2.3	2.7
1951	24.6	13.2	3.1	1.3	2.3	1.3	2.4	2.8	11.4	1.4	2.8	2.7	4.4
1952	21.7	11.7	1.9	1.0	2.3	1.5	2.4	2.6	9.9	1.7	2.3	2.3	3.6
1953	22.0	11.9	2.5	1.0	1.9	1.4	2.6	2.6	10.1	1.8	2.2	2.8	3.3
1954	19.9	10.5	1.7	.9	1.7	1.2	2.1	2.9	9.4	1.6	2.2	2.7	2.9
1955	26.0	14.3	2.9	1.0	1.7	1.1	4.1	3.5	11.8	2.2	3.0	3.0	3.6
1956	24.7	12.8	3.0	1.1	2.1	1.2	2.2	3.2	11.9	1.8	2.8	3.3	4.1
1957	24.0	13.3	3.0	1.1	2.0	1.5	2.6	3.1	10.7	1.8	2.8	2.6	3.6
1958	19.4	9.3	1.9	.9	1.4	1.3	.9	2.9	10.0	2.1	2.5	2.1	3.3
1959	26.4	13.7	2.3	1.1	2.1	1.7	3.0	3.5	12.7	2.4	3.5	2.5	4.3
1960	23.6	11.6	2.0	.8	1.8	1.3	3.0	2.7	12.0	2.2	3.1	2.5	4.2
1961	23.3	11.4	1.6	1.0	1.9	1.3	2.5	3.1	11.9	2.3	3.2	2.2	4.1
1962	26.0	14.0	1.6	1.1	2.3	1.5	4.0	3.5	12.0	2.3	3.2	2.2	4.3
1963	29.3	16.3	2.0	1.3	2.5	1.6	4.9	4.0	13.1	2.7	3.6	2.1	4.6
1964	32.3	17.9	2.5	1.4	3.3	1.7	4.7	4.4	14.4	2.7	4.0	2.4	5.3
1965	39.3	23.0	3.1	2.0	3.9	2.7	6.2	5.1	16.3	2.8	4.6	2.9	6.0
1966	41.9	23.8	3.6	2.4	4.5	3.0	5.1	5.2	18.1	3.2	4.9	3.2	6.8
1967	38.5	20.9	2.7	2.4	4.1	2.9	3.9	4.9	17.6	3.2	4.3	3.9	6.3
1968	41.2	22.2	1.9	2.3	4.1	2.8	5.5	5.7	19.1	3.2	5.2	3.7	7.0
1969	36.6	18.9	1.4	2.0	3.7	2.3	4.7	4.9	17.7	3.0	4.5	3.2	6.9
1970	26.6	10.2	.8	1.1	2.9	1.2	1.2	2.9	16.5	3.2	3.9	3.5	5.9
1971	34.1	16.3	.7	1.5	2.9	1.9	5.0	4.3	17.8	3.5	4.4	3.5	6.4
1972	40.7	22.4	1.6	2.1	4.3	2.8	5.9	5.7	18.3	2.9	5.2	3.0	7.2
1973	45.5	24.3	2.2	2.5	4.6	3.0	5.7	6.2	21.2	2.4	6.0	5.0	7.8
1974	39.0	13.2	5.4	1.6	2.9	.4	.1	2.9	25.8	2.8	5.6	10.5	6.8
1975	52.6	18.9	2.9	3.0	4.7	2.1	1.9	4.3	33.6	8.6	6.5	9.6	8.9
1976	69.2	30.4	2.1	3.8	6.3	3.4	7.2	7.6	38.8	6.9	8.3	12.6	11.0
1977	78.3	38.1	1.1	4.4	8.8	5.6	9.4	8.8	40.2	6.8	7.9	11.6	13.8
1978	86.9	44.3	3.5	4.9	9.4	6.5	8.9	11.0	42.6	6.0	8.3	13.8	14.5
1979	85.6	37.1	3.5	5.2	8.9	5.1	4.7	9.8	48.4	5.7	7.1	20.7	14.8
1980	74.5	20.7	2.9	4.4	7.2	4.4	−5.0	6.8	53.8	6.2	6.7	28.0	13.0
1981	86.3	28.4	4.1	4.9	9.3	5.1	−1.1	6.2	57.9	8.7	8.2	26.6	14.4
1982 [p]	59.8	11.4	−5.1	4.4	5.1	3.5	1.1	2.3	48.4	6.5	5.7	24.4	11.7
1980:													
I	85.2	25.5	4.7	5.4	7.2	5.2	−3.7	6.7	59.6	6.6	7.4	31.5	14.1
II	64.7	12.4	2.6	2.8	7.0	3.5	−10.6	7.1	52.3	5.5	5.5	29.1	12.2
III	70.0	18.2	.1	4.3	7.4	4.3	−4.1	6.3	51.8	4.9	6.6	27.7	12.7
IV	78.1	26.5	4.2	5.0	7.2	4.5	−1.4	7.1	51.6	7.0	7.4	23.5	12.9
1981:													
I	90.3	32.1	7.0	4.7	8.4	6.2	−2.6	8.4	58.2	10.4	9.4	23.5	14.9
II	88.9	35.2	4.7	6.0	9.2	4.9	2.6	7.8	53.7	8.5	7.5	23.3	14.4
III	92.2	27.4	4.1	5.4	9.6	4.8	−2.8	6.3	64.8	7.7	8.0	35.1	14.1
IV	73.7	18.9	.7	3.4	9.9	4.3	−1.8	2.4	54.7	8.1	7.8	24.7	14.1
1982:													
I	57.7	9.1	−3.1	4.4	8.3	3.6	−4.1	.0	48.6	6.7	6.5	25.4	10.0
II	56.6	12.7	−6.5	3.8	4.8	3.7	3.3	3.5	43.9	6.3	5.8	20.4	11.4
III	62.7	12.2	−5.4	4.7	3.7	3.2	3.2	2.7	50.5	7.0	5.1	25.9	12.5

Note.—The industry classification is on a company basis and is based on the 1972 Standard Industrial Classification (SIC) beginning 1948, and on the 1942 SIC prior to 1948.

Source: Department of Commerce, Bureau of Economic Analysis.

Table B–85.—*Sales, profits, and stockholders' equity, all manufacturing corporations, 1950–82*

[Billions of dollars]

Year or quarter	All manufacturing corporations				Durable goods industries				Nondurable goods industries			
	Sales (net)	Profits		Stock-holders' equity[2]	Sales (net)	Profits		Stock-holders' equity[2]	Sales (net)	Profits		Stock-holders' equity[2]
		Before income taxes[1]	After income taxes			Before income taxes[1]	After income taxes			Before income taxes[1]	After income taxes	
1950	181.9	23.2	12.9	83.3	86.8	12.9	6.7	39.9	95.1	10.3	6.1	43.5
1951	245.0	27.4	11.9	98.3	116.8	15.4	6.1	47.2	128.1	12.1	5.7	51.1
1952	250.2	22.9	10.7	103.7	122.0	12.9	5.5	49.8	128.0	10.0	5.2	53.9
1953	265.9	24.4	11.3	108.2	137.9	14.0	5.8	52.4	128.0	10.4	5.5	55.7
1954	248.5	20.9	11.2	113.1	122.8	11.4	5.6	54.9	125.7	9.6	5.6	58.2
1955	278.4	28.6	15.1	120.1	142.1	16.5	8.1	58.8	136.3	12.1	7.0	61.3
1956	307.3	29.8	16.2	131.6	159.5	16.5	8.3	65.2	147.8	13.2	7.8	66.4
1957	320.0	28.2	15.4	141.1	166.0	15.8	7.9	70.5	154.1	12.4	7.5	70.6
1958	305.3	22.7	12.7	147.4	148.6	11.4	5.0	72.8	156.7	11.3	6.9	74.6
1959	338.0	29.7	16.3	157.1	169.4	15.8	8.1	77.9	168.5	13.9	8.3	79.2
1960	345.7	27.5	15.2	165.4	173.9	14.0	7.0	82.3	171.8	13.5	8.2	83.1
1961	356.4	27.5	15.3	172.6	175.2	13.6	6.9	84.9	181.2	13.9	8.5	87.7
1962	389.4	31.9	17.7	181.4	195.3	16.8	8.6	89.1	194.1	15.1	9.2	92.3
1963	412.7	34.9	19.5	189.7	209.0	18.5	9.5	93.3	203.6	16.4	10.0	96.3
1964	443.1	39.6	23.2	199.8	226.3	21.2	11.6	98.5	216.8	18.3	11.6	101.3
1965	492.2	46.5	27.5	211.7	257.0	26.2	14.5	105.4	235.2	20.3	13.0	106.3
1966	554.2	51.8	30.9	230.3	291.7	29.2	16.4	115.2	262.4	22.6	14.6	115.1
1967	575.4	47.8	29.0	247.6	300.6	25.7	14.6	125.0	274.8	22.0	14.4	122.6
1968	631.9	55.4	32.1	265.9	335.5	30.6	16.5	135.6	296.4	24.8	15.5	130.3
1969	694.6	58.1	33.2	289.9	366.5	31.5	16.9	147.6	328.1	26.6	16.4	142.3
1970	708.8	48.1	28.6	306.8	363.1	23.0	12.9	155.1	345.7	25.2	15.7	151.7
1971	751.1	52.9	31.0	320.8	381.8	26.5	14.5	160.4	369.3	26.5	16.5	160.5
1972	849.5	63.2	36.5	343.4	435.8	33.6	18.4	171.4	413.7	29.6	18.0	172.0
1973	1,017.2	81.4	48.1	374.1	527.3	43.6	24.8	188.7	489.9	37.8	23.3	185.4
1973: IV	275.1	21.4	13.0	386.4	140.1	10.8	6.3	194.7	135.0	10.6	6.7	191.7
New series:												
1973: IV	236.6	20.6	13.2	368.0	122.7	10.1	6.2	185.8	113.9	10.5	7.0	182.1
1974	1,060.6	92.1	58.7	395.0	529.0	41.1	24.7	196.0	531.6	51.0	34.1	199.0
1975	1,065.2	79.9	49.1	423.4	521.1	35.3	21.4	208.1	544.1	44.6	27.7	215.3
1976	1,203.2	104.9	64.5	462.7	589.6	50.7	30.8	224.3	613.7	54.3	33.7	238.4
1977	1,328.1	115.1	70.4	496.7	657.3	57.9	34.8	239.9	670.8	57.2	35.5	256.8
1978	1,496.4	132.5	81.1	540.5	760.7	69.6	41.8	262.6	735.7	62.9	39.3	277.9
1979	1,741.8	154.2	98.7	600.5	865.7	72.4	45.2	292.5	876.1	81.8	53.5	308.0
1980	1,912.8	145.8	92.6	668.1	889.1	57.4	35.6	317.7	1,023.7	88.4	56.9	350.4
1981	2,144.7	158.5	101.3	743.4	979.5	67.2	41.7	350.4	1,165.2	91.3	59.6	393.0
1979:												
I	406.6	36.5	22.7	576.2	207.5	18.8	11.4	281.9	199.1	17.7	11.2	294.3
II	436.4	42.6	26.8	592.5	222.6	21.6	13.3	289.3	213.8	21.1	13.5	303.2
III	437.5	38.2	24.7	609.2	213.6	16.4	10.3	296.5	223.9	21.9	14.4	312.6
IV	461.2	36.8	24.5	624.0	221.9	15.7	10.1	302.1	239.3	21.2	14.4	321.9
1980:												
I	465.7	39.5	24.8	643.9	219.8	15.8	9.7	308.0	245.9	23.7	15.1	335.9
II	466.3	35.9	22.4	658.1	218.7	13.5	8.2	312.6	247.6	22.4	14.2	345.5
III	464.2	33.2	21.0	670.5	212.6	11.9	7.2	317.2	251.6	21.3	13.7	353.3
IV	516.6	37.2	24.4	699.7	238.0	16.2	10.4	332.8	278.6	21.0	14.0	366.9
1981:												
I	520.8	39.0	24.4	718.4	234.1	16.7	10.1	339.4	286.7	22.3	14.2	379.1
II	549.6	45.6	28.9	739.4	257.2	20.7	12.7	349.7	292.4	24.9	16.2	389.7
III	539.9	40.0	25.2	753.5	245.1	16.4	10.3	354.2	294.8	23.5	14.9	399.4
IV	534.4	34.0	22.9	762.3	243.0	13.4	8.5	358.3	291.3	20.6	14.3	404.0
1982:												
I	501.0	28.9	19.0	756.5	226.4	10.8	6.8	353.0	274.6	18.1	12.2	403.5
II	520.1	30.9	20.0	764.1	240.3	12.7	8.2	356.5	279.8	18.2	11.8	407.6
III	507.1	27.8	17.8	774.3	225.3	8.5	5.3	360.1	281.8	19.3	12.5	414.2

[1] In the old series, "income taxes" refers to Federal income taxes only, as State and local income taxes had already been deducted. In the new series, no income taxes have been deducted.

[2] Annual data are average equity for the year (using four end-of-quarter figures).

Note.—Data are not necessarily comparable from one period to another due to changes in accounting procedures, industry classifications, sampling procedures, etc. For explanatory notes concerning compilation of the series, see "Quarterly Financial Report for Manufacturing, Mining, and Trade Corporations," Federal Trade Commission.

Source: Federal Trade Commission.

TABLE B–86.—*Relation of profits after taxes to stockholders' equity and to sales, all manufacturing corporations, 1947–82*

Year or quarter	Ratio of profits after income taxes (annual rate) to stockholders' equity—percent[1]			Profits after income taxes per dollar of sales—cents		
	All manufacturing corporations	Durable goods industries	Nondurable goods industries	All manufacturing corporations	Durable goods industries	Nondurable goods industries
1947	15.6	14.4	16.6	6.7	6.7	6.7
1948	16.0	15.7	16.2	7.0	7.1	6.8
1949	11.6	12.1	11.2	5.8	6.4	5.4
1950	15.4	16.9	14.1	7.1	7.7	6.5
1951	12.1	13.0	11.2	4.9	5.3	4.5
1952	10.3	11.1	9.7	4.3	4.5	4.1
1953	10.5	11.1	9.9	4.3	4.2	4.3
1954	9.9	10.3	9.6	4.5	4.6	4.4
1955	12.6	13.8	11.4	5.4	5.7	5.1
1956	12.3	12.8	11.8	5.3	5.2	5.3
1957	10.9	11.3	10.6	4.8	4.8	4.9
1958	8.6	8.0	9.2	4.2	3.9	4.4
1959	10.4	10.4	10.4	4.8	4.8	4.9
1960	9.2	8.5	9.8	4.4	4.0	4.8
1961	8.9	8.1	9.6	4.3	3.9	4.7
1962	9.8	9.6	9.9	4.5	4.4	4.7
1963	10.3	10.1	10.4	4.7	4.5	4.9
1964	11.6	11.7	11.5	5.2	5.1	5.4
1965	13.0	13.8	12.2	5.6	5.7	5.5
1966	13.4	14.2	12.7	5.6	5.6	5.6
1967	11.7	11.7	11.8	5.0	4.8	5.3
1968	12.1	12.2	11.9	5.1	4.9	5.2
1969	11.5	11.4	11.5	4.8	4.6	5.0
1970	9.3	8.3	10.3	4.0	3.5	4.5
1971	9.7	9.0	10.3	4.1	3.8	4.5
1972	10.6	10.8	10.5	4.3	4.2	4.4
1973	12.8	13.1	12.6	4.7	4.7	4.8
1973: IV	13.4	12.9	14.0	4.7	4.5	5.0
New series:						
1973: IV	14.3	13.3	15.3	5.6	5.0	6.1
1974	14.9	12.6	17.1	5.5	4.7	6.4
1975	11.6	10.3	12.9	4.6	4.1	5.1
1976	13.9	13.7	14.2	5.4	5.2	5.5
1977	14.2	14.5	13.8	5.3	5.3	5.3
1978	15.0	16.0	14.2	5.4	5.5	5.3
1979	16.4	15.4	17.4	5.7	5.2	6.1
1980	13.9	11.2	16.3	4.8	4.0	5.6
1981	13.6	11.9	15.2	4.7	4.3	5.1
1979:						
I	15.7	16.2	15.3	5.6	5.5	5.6
II	18.1	18.4	17.8	6.1	6.0	6.3
III	16.3	14.0	18.4	5.7	4.8	6.4
IV	15.7	13.4	17.9	5.3	4.6	6.0
1980:						
I	15.4	12.6	18.0	5.3	4.4	6.1
II	13.6	10.6	16.4	4.8	3.8	5.7
III	12.5	9.1	15.6	4.5	3.4	5.5
IV	14.0	12.6	15.2	4.7	4.4	5.0
1981:						
I	13.6	12.0	15.0	4.7	4.3	5.0
II	15.6	14.6	16.6	5.3	4.9	5.5
III	13.4	11.6	14.9	4.7	4.2	5.1
IV	12.0	9.5	14.2	4.3	3.5	4.9
1982:						
I	10.1	7.7	12.1	3.8	3.0	4.4
II	10.5	9.2	11.6	3.9	3.4	4.2
III	9.2	5.9	12.1	3.5	2.4	4.4

[1] Annual ratios based on average equity for the year (using four end-of-quarter figures). Quarterly ratios based on equity at end of quarter only.

Note.—Based on data in millions of dollars.
See Note, Table B–85.
Source: Federal Trade Commission.

TABLE B–87.—*Relation of profits after taxes to stockholders' equity and to sales, all manufacturing corporations, by industry group, 1981–82*

Industry	Ratio of profits after income taxes (annual rate) to stockholders' equity—percent [1]					Profits after income taxes per dollar of sales—cents				
	1981		1982			1981		1982		
	III	IV	I	II	III	III	IV	I	II	III
All manufacturing corporations	13.4	12.0	10.1	10.5	9.2	4.7	4.3	3.8	3.9	3.5
Durable goods industries	11.6	9.5	7.7	9.2	5.9	4.2	3.5	3.0	3.4	2.4
Stone, clay, and glass products	11.9	5.8	−3.7	4.6	7.3	4.6	2.5	−1.8	1.9	2.9
Primary metal industries	13.9	3.0	.9	−3.4	−8.3	4.9	1.2	.4	−1.3	−3.7
Iron and steel	18.4	.1	.4	−6.2	−13.2	5.9	.0	.1	−2.3	−5.5
Nonferrous metals	6.3	8.0	1.8	1.0	−.9	2.6	3.6	.8	.4	−.5
Fabricated metal products	14.1	9.4	9.8	9.0	6.1	4.2	2.9	3.2	3.1	1.7
Machinery, except electrical	14.1	15.5	11.8	10.8	7.3	6.3	6.8	5.7	5.2	3.8
Electrical and electronic equipment	12.9	12.3	12.6	12.6	11.4	4.5	4.3	4.7	4.6	4.4
Transportation equipment [2]	1.9	3.8	4.3	11.6	4.6	.6	1.1	1.3	3.2	1.4
Motor vehicles and equipment	−6.9	−1.6	.0	11.8	−.2	−2.2	−.5	.0	3.2	−.1
Aircraft, guided missiles, and parts	13.9	11.7	10.8	11.6	12.6	4.1	3.1	3.2	3.2	3.7
Instruments and related products	17.7	14.9	13.3	15.3	14.7	9.4	7.9	7.6	8.3	7.9
Other durable manufacturing products	9.8	5.9	2.4	8.3	6.9	2.8	1.8	.8	2.5	2.1
Nondurable goods industries	14.9	14.2	12.1	11.6	12.1	5.1	4.9	4.4	4.2	4.4
Food and kindred products	13.8	14.6	12.6	12.3	11.9	3.2	3.3	3.1	2.9	2.8
Tobacco manufactures	19.4	18.6	18.4	21.3	20.8	11.3	10.9	11.4	12.5	12.2
Textile mill products	[illegible]	[illegible]	2.6	4.9	8.4	2.6	1.7	.8	1.4	2.5
Paper and allied products	9.7	12.5	6.2	6.5	6.1	3.9	5.4	2.8	2.8	2.7
Printing and publishing	15.6	15.5	9.7	13.8	13.5	5.2	5.1	3.4	4.7	4.5
Chemicals and allied products [2]	13.9	13.3	13.0	12.2	10.7	6.5	6.7	6.4	6.0	5.3
Industrial chemicals and synthetics	11.9	11.4	8.9	7.7	5.6	5.3	5.6	4.3	4.0	2.8
Drugs	16.1	18.6	20.8	17.6	18.9	10.2	12.4	13.6	11.8	12.3
Petroleum and coal products	17.4	15.4	13.9	11.6	13.8	6.4	5.8	5.7	4.9	6.0
Rubber and miscellaneous plastics products	11.4	9.1	8.7	10.4	9.0	3.3	2.8	2.7	3.1	2.9
Other nondurable manufacturing products	14.4	15.0	7.0	9.6	12.0	3.3	3.3	1.7	2.4	2.7

[1] Ratios based on equity at end of quarter.
[2] Includes other industries not shown separately.

Source: Federal Trade Commission.

Table B-88.—*Determinants of business fixed investment 1955–82*

[Percent, except as noted]

Year	Real investment as percent of real GNP	Capacity utilization rate in manufacturing [1]	Nonfinancial corporations: Cash flow as percent of GNP [2]	Rate of return on depreciable assets [3]: Before tax	Rate of return on depreciable assets [3]: After tax	Rate of return on stockholders' equity [4]: Before tax	Rate of return on stockholders' equity [4]: After tax	Ratio of market value to replacement cost of net assets [5]
1955	9.3	87.1	9.3	19.8	9.8	13.1	6.2	1.112
1956	9.7	86.4	8.9	16.8	7.9	11.6	5.4	1.104
1957	9.7	83.7	8.9	15.2	7.4	10.6	5.0	1.018
1958	8.7	75.2	8.6	12.8	6.5	8.4	3.9	1.041
1959	8.8	81.9	9.3	16.4	8.5	10.5	5.1	1.252
1960	9.1	80.2	8.9	15.0	8.0	9.9	5.0	1.222
1961	8.8	77.4	8.8	15.1	8.2	9.5	4.6	1.350
1962	9.0	81.6	9.4	17.4	10.3	11.2	6.1	1.282
1963	9.0	83.5	9.7	18.8	11.2	12.1	6.7	1.419
1964	9.4	85.6	10.1	20.2	12.5	13.3	7.8	1.521
1965	10.5	89.6	10.6	22.1	14.0	15.5	9.6	1.621
1966	11.0	91.1	10.3	21.8	13.7	15.2	9.2	1.466
1967	10.4	86.9	10.0	19.3	12.4	13.4	8.2	1.480
1968	10.3	87.1	9.4	18.9	11.3	13.8	8.0	1.523
1969	10.7	86.2	8.6	16.5	9.7	12.5	7.1	1.353
1970	10.5	79.3	7.8	12.8	7.9	8.8	4.7	1.091
1971	10.0	78.4	8.3	13.5	8.5	9.9	5.7	1.176
1972	10.2	83.5	8.6	14.3	9.1	10.5	6.2	1.258
1973	11.0	87.6	8.0	14.3	8.7	12.8	8.3	1.157
1974	10.9	83.8	7.0	11.0	6.1	11.2	7.3	.827
1975	9.7	72.9	9.0	11.9	7.7	8.5	5.2	.811
1976	9.7	79.5	9.3	12.9	7.9	8.6	4.8	.911
1977	10.2	81.9	9.7	13.9	8.7	10.2	6.3	.797
1978	11.0	84.4	9.5	13.7	8.6	10.7	6.8	.761
1979	11.5	85.7	8.9	12.1	7.4	10.2	6.6	.709
1980	11.3	79.1	8.7	10.5	6.6	8.4	5.5	.666
1981	11.4	78.5	9.5	11.0	7.7	7.7	5.1	.694
1982 *p*	11.2	69.8	9.6	9.5	7.5	(6)	(6)	.690

[1] Federal Reserve Board index.
[2] Cash flow calculated as after-tax profits plus capital consumption allowance plus inventory valuation adjustment.
[3] Profits plus capital consumption adjustment and inventory valuation adjustment plus net interest paid divided by the stock of depreciable assets valued at current replacement cost.
[4] Profits corrected for inflation effects divided by net worth (physical capital component valued at current replacement cost).
[5] Equity plus interest-bearing debt divided by current replacement cost of net assets.
[6] Not available.

Sources: Department of Commerce (Bureau of Economic Analysis), Board of Governors of the Federal Reserve System, and Council of Economic Advisers.

TABLE B-89.—*Sources and uses of funds, nonfarm nonfinancial corporate business, 1946–82*

[Billions of dollars; quarterly data at seasonally adjusted annual rates]

Year or quarter	Sources							Uses			Discrepancy (sources less uses)
	Total	Internal [1]	External					Total	Capital expenditures [3]	Increase in financial assets	
			Total	Credit market funds			Other [2]				
				Total	Securities and mortgages	Loans and short-term paper					
1946	18.7	8.1	10.6	6.9	3.6	3.3	3.7	16.8	18.1	−1.4	1.9
1947	27.0	12.9	14.1	8.4	5.4	3.0	5.8	25.6	17.3	8.4	1.4
1948	28.9	19.1	9.7	6.5	6.7	−.2	3.3	25.3	20.3	5.0	3.6
1949	19.9	19.5	.4	3.1	4.9	−1.8	−2.7	18.3	14.8	3.5	1.6
1950	42.1	18.0	24.0	8.1	4.2	3.9	15.9	40.4	24.0	16.4	1.7
1951	36.4	20.2	16.2	10.5	6.4	4.1	5.7	37.6	30.2	7.4	−1.2
1952	29.9	21.9	8.0	9.5	8.0	1.4	−1.5	29.2	24.6	4.6	.6
1953	27.8	21.7	6.1	5.7	6.0	−.4	.5	28.0	25.7	2.3	−.1
1954	29.6	23.9	5.7	6.5	6.7	−.2	−.8	27.8	22.9	4.9	1.8
1955	52.7	29.5	23.2	10.2	6.4	3.7	13.1	49.1	32.6	16.5	3.5
1956	44.9	29.5	15.4	12.8	7.5	5.3	2.5	40.8	36.8	4.0	4.1
1957	43.4	31.5	11.9	12.3	10.4	1.9	−.4	39.1	34.9	4.2	4.3
1958	41.9	30.3	11.7	10.5	10.5	−.0	1.2	38.5	27.7	10.8	3.4
1959	56.3	36.0	20.2	12.3	8.1	4.2	7.9	51.2	37.0	14.2	5.0
1960	48.6	35.4	13.2	12.1	7.5	4.6	1.2	41.4	37.5	3.9	7.2
1961	56.3	36.5	19.8	12.9	10.7	2.2	6.9	51.0	36.7	14.2	5.3
1962	60.1	42.8	17.3	12.8	9.4	3.4	4.6	55.5	43.2	12.3	4.6
1963	68.4	46.5	22.0	12.5	8.4	4.0	9.5	60.4	44.7	15.7	8.0
1964	73.9	51.8	22.1	14.1	7.8	6.2	8.0	64.9	50.1	14.8	9.0
1965	91.8	58.5	33.3	18.5	7.6	11.0	14.8	82.7	61.0	21.8	9.1
1966	97.6	62.6	35.0	23.8	14.3	9.5	11.2	91.3	74.7	16.6	6.4
1967	94.7	63.6	31.1	27.8	19.1	8.7	3.3	88.5	72.2	16.3	6.2
1968	113.5	65.0	48.5	27.7	15.0	12.6	20.9	106.0	75.4	30.6	7.5
1969	115.5	64.4	51.1	32.3	14.6	17.7	18.8	115.3	83.7	31.6	.2
1970	102.3	61.8	40.5	35.3	26.3	9.0	5.3	98.7	80.0	18.7	3.6
1971	125.3	73.5	51.8	37.2	32.8	4.4	14.6	122.7	86.0	36.7	2.6
1972	151.6	85.0	66.6	43.4	26.4	16.9	23.2	149.1	99.0	50.1	2.4
1973	192.4	91.7	100.7	56.7	20.7	36.0	44.0	191.9	121.5	70.5	.5
1974	190.1	85.6	104.4	69.9	26.3	43.6	34.5	190.1	137.9	52.2	.0
1975	156.9	119.7	37.2	30.7	38.7	−8.0	6.5	150.9	109.7	41.2	6.0
1976	210.8	134.2	76.6	54.5	38.2	16.3	22.1	201.8	148.3	53.5	9.0
1977	252.2	157.4	94.9	70.4	33.9	36.5	24.5	237.6	175.1	62.5	14.7
1978	315.4	175.7	139.7	79.3	31.9	47.4	60.4	294.2	202.2	92.0	21.2
1979	346.3	188.8	157.5	91.2	25.9	65.3	66.3	347.1	219.8	127.3	−.8
1980	333.7	197.5	136.2	95.7	57.5	38.2	40.6	317.9	220.5	97.4	15.8
1981	352.2	231.1	121.1	92.6	23.1	69.6	28.5	314.8	260.9	53.9	37.4
1980:											
I	363.2	192.6	170.6	114.7	46.1	68.6	55.9	341.2	231.3	109.9	22.0
II	263.4	197.4	66.0	62.6	58.6	4.0	3.4	248.7	215.6	33.1	14.7
III	326.4	199.3	127.2	86.6	63.7	22.9	40.5	314.2	209.9	104.3	12.2
IV	381.9	200.8	181.1	118.7	61.7	57.1	62.4	367.5	225.2	142.3	14.4
1981:											
I	333.6	222.4	111.3	68.7	41.6	27.1	42.6	318.2	233.5	84.7	15.4
II	381.2	225.4	155.8	119.1	34.8	84.3	36.7	352.2	260.0	92.2	29.0
III	348.9	235.2	113.7	100.2	3.2	97.0	13.5	304.6	284.6	20.0	44.2
IV	345.0	241.4	103.6	82.5	12.7	69.9	21.1	284.0	265.5	18.5	61.0
1982:											
I	297.7	232.6	65.0	110.2	30.6	79.7	−45.2	225.3	241.9	−16.6	72.3
II	348.2	234.3	113.9	93.3	33.1	60.3	20.5	304.9	248.5	56.4	43.3
III [p]	371.7	240.3	131.3	98.0	59.3	38.7	33.3	328.5	264.2	64.3	43.1

[1] Undistributed profits (after inventory valuation and capital consumption adjustments), capital consumption allowances, and foreign branch profits, dividends, and subsidiaries' earnings retained abroad.

[2] Consists of tax liabilities, trade debt, and direct foreign investment in the United States.

[3] Plant and equipment, residential structures, inventory investment, and mineral rights from U.S. Government.

Source: Board of Governors of the Federal Reserve System.

TABLE B–90.—*Current assets and liabilities of U.S. corporations, 1939–82*

[Billions of dollars]

End of year or quarter	Current assets						Current liabilities			Net working capital	Current ratio[3]
	Total	Cash[1]	U.S. Government securities[2]	Notes and accounts receivable	Inventories	Other current assets	Total	Notes and accounts payable	Other current liabilities		
	All corporations[4]										
SEC series:[5]											
1939	54.5	10.8	2.2	22.1	18.0	1.4	30.0	21.9	8.1	24.5	1.817
1940	60.3	13.1	2.0	24.0	19.8	1.5	32.8	23.2	9.6	27.5	1.838
1941	72.9	13.9	4.0	28.0	25.6	1.4	40.7	26.4	14.3	32.3	1.791
1942	83.6	17.6	10.1	27.3	27.3	1.3	47.3	26.0	21.3	36.3	1.767
1943	93.8	21.6	16.4	26.9	27.6	1.3	51.6	26.3	25.3	42.1	1.818
1944	97.2	21.6	20.9	26.5	26.8	1.4	51.7	26.8	24.9	45.6	1.880
1945	97.4	21.7	21.1	25.9	26.3	2.4	45.8	25.7	20.1	51.6	2.127
1946	108.1	22.8	15.3	30.7	37.6	1.7	51.9	31.6	20.3	56.2	2.083
1947	123.6	25.0	14.1	38.3	44.6	1.6	61.5	37.6	23.9	62.1	2.010
1948	133.0	25.3	14.8	42.4	48.9	1.6	64.4	39.3	25.0	68.6	2.065
1949	133.1	26.5	16.8	43.0	45.3	1.4	60.7	37.5	23.3	72.4	2.193
1950	161.5	28.1	19.7	56.8	55.1	1.7	79.8	48.3	31.6	81.6	2.024
1951	179.1	30.0	20.7	61.5	64.9	2.1	92.6	54.9	37.8	86.5	1.934
1952	186.2	30.8	19.9	67.4	65.8	2.4	96.1	59.3	36.8	90.1	1.938
1953	190.6	31.1	21.5	68.5	67.2	2.4	98.9	59.5	39.4	91.8	1.927
1954	194.6	33.4	19.2	73.6	65.3	3.1	99.7	61.7	38.0	94.9	1.952
1955	224.0	34.6	23.5	88.9	72.8	4.2	121.0	76.1	45.0	103.0	1.851
1956	237.9	34.8	19.1	97.7	80.4	5.9	130.5	83.9	46.6	107.4	1.823
1957	244.7	34.9	18.6	102.2	82.2	6.7	133.1	86.6	46.5	111.6	1.838
1958	255.3	37.4	18.8	109.7	81.9	7.5	136.6	90.4	46.2	118.7	1.869
1959	277.3	36.3	22.8	120.6	88.4	9.1	153.1	101.0	52.0	124.2	1.811
1960	289.0	37.2	20.1	129.2	91.8	10.6	160.4	106.8	53.6	128.6	1.802
1961	306.8	41.1	20.0	139.2	95.2	11.4	171.2	114.6	56.6	135.6	1.792
	Nonfinancial corporations[6]										
SEC series:[5]											
1961	254.7	34.8	16.5	97.9	95.0	10.5	123.7	84.4	39.3	131.0	2.059
1962	269.7	37.1	16.8	103.2	100.5	12.1	132.4	88.7	43.7	137.3	2.037
1963	288.2	39.8	16.7	110.5	106.8	14.4	145.5	97.0	48.5	142.7	1.981
1964	305.6	40.5	15.8	119.9	113.1	16.3	156.6	104.9	51.7	149.0	1.951
1965	336.0	42.8	14.4	134.1	126.6	18.1	178.8	121.5	57.3	157.2	1.879
1966	364.0	41.9	13.0	146.6	142.8	19.7	199.4	137.5	61.9	164.6	1.825
1967	386.2	45.5	10.3	155.3	153.1	22.0	211.3	147.1	64.2	174.9	1.828
1968	426.5	48.2	11.5	173.9	166.0	26.9	244.1	168.8	75.3	182.4	1.747
1969	473.6	47.9	10.6	197.0	186.4	31.6	287.8	199.2	88.6	185.7	1.646
1970	492.3	50.2	7.7	206.1	193.3	35.0	304.9	211.3	93.6	187.4	1.615
1971	529.6	53.3	11.0	221.1	200.4	43.8	326.0	220.5	105.5	203.6	1.625
1972	599.3	59.0	10.6	248.2	225.7	55.8	375.6	282.9	92.7	223.7	1.595
1973	697.8	66.3	12.8	288.5	263.9	66.4	450.9	340.3	110.7	246.9	1.548
1974	790.7	71.1	12.3	322.1	313.6	71.7	530.4	402.3	128.1	260.3	1.491
FTC–FRB series:[7]											
1974	735.4	73.2	11.1	265.8	319.5	65.9	453.4	269.8	183.6	282.0	1.622
1975	759.0	82.1	19.0	272.1	315.9	69.9	451.6	264.2	187.4	307.4	1.681
1976	827.4	88.2	23.5	292.9	342.5	80.3	495.1	282.1	213.0	332.4	1.671
1977	912.7	97.2	18.2	330.3	376.9	90.1	557.1	317.6	239.6	355.5	1.638
1978	1,043.7	105.5	17.3	388.0	431.6	101.3	669.3	382.9	286.4	374.4	1.559
1979	1,218.2	118.0	17.0	461.1	505.5	116.7	807.8	461.2	346.6	410.5	1.508
1980	1,333.5	127.1	19.3	510.6	543.7	132.7	890.9	515.2	375.7	442.6	1.497
1981	1,427.1	131.7	17.9	536.7	587.1	153.6	980.0	562.9	417.1	447.1	1.456
1981:											
I	1,374.5	126.6	19.2	528.0	560.2	140.5	923.2	520.3	402.9	451.3	1.489
II	1,388.3	126.2	19.9	533.1	565.3	143.8	931.5	525.9	405.5	456.8	1.490
III	1,410.9	125.1	18.0	542.4	577.0	148.3	967.2	549.5	417.7	443.7	1.459
IV	1,427.1	131.7	17.9	536.7	587.1	153.6	980.0	562.9	417.1	447.1	1.456
1982:											
I	1,423.6	121.3	17.1	537.8	593.8	153.6	985.7	555.0	430.8	437.9	1.444
II	1,419.4	123.4	17.4	534.4	589.2	155.0	982.6	554.9	427.8	436.8	1.445

[1] Includes time certificates of deposit.
[2] Includes Federal agency issues.
[3] Total current assets divided by total current liabilities.
[4] Excludes banks, savings and loan associations, and insurance companies.
[5] Based on data from "Statistics of Income," Department of the Treasury.
[6] Excludes banks, savings and loan associations, insurance companies, investment companies, finance companies (personal and commercial), real estate companies, and security and commodity brokers, dealers, and exchanges.
[7] Based on data from "Quarterly Financial Report for Manufacturing, Mining, and Trade Corporations," Federal Trade Commission. See "Federal Reserve Bulletin," July 1978, for details regarding the series.

Note.—SEC series not available after 1974.

Sources: Board of Governors of the Federal Reserve System, Federal Trade Commission, and Securities and Exchange Commission.

TABLE B-91.—*State and municipal and corporate securities offered, 1934–82*

[Millions of dollars]

Year or quarter	State and municipal securities offered for cash (principal amounts)	Corporate securities offered for cash								
		Total corporate offerings	Type of corporate security			Industry of corporate issuer				
			Common stock	Preferred stock	Bonds and notes	Manufacturing [1]	Electric, gas, and water [2]	Transportation [3]	Communication	Other
1934	939	397	19	6	372	67	133	176		21
1939	1,128	2,164	87	98	1,979	604	1,271	186		103
1940	1,238	2,677	108	183	2,386	992	1,203	324		159
1941	956	2,667	110	167	2,389	848	1,357	366		96
1942	524	1,062	34	112	917	539	472	48		4
1943	435	1,170	56	124	990	510	477	161		21
1944	661	3,202	163	369	2,670	1,061	1,422	609		109
1945	795	6,011	397	758	4,855	2,026	2,319	1,454		211
1946	1,157	6,900	891	1,127	4,882	3,701	2,158	711		329
1947	2,324	6,577	779	762	5,036	2,742	3,257	286		293
1948	2,690	7,078	614	492	5,973	2,226	2,187	755	902	1,008
1949	2,907	6,052	736	425	4,890	1,414	2,320	800	571	946
1950	3,532	6,362	811	631	4,920	1,200	2,649	813	399	1,300
1951	3,189	7,741	1,212	838	5,691	3,122	2,455	494	612	1,058
1952	4,401	9,534	1,369	564	7,601	4,039	2,675	992	760	1,068
1953	5,558	8,898	1,326	489	7,083	2,254	3,029	595	882	2,138
1954	6,969	9,516	1,213	816	7,488	2,268	3,713	778	720	2,037
1955	5,977	10,240	2,185	635	7,420	2,994	2,464	893	1,132	2,757
1956	5,446	10,939	2,301	636	8,002	3,647	2,529	724	1,419	2,619
1957	6,958	12,884	2,516	411	9,957	4,234	3,938	824	1,462	2,426
1958	7,449	11,558	1,334	571	9,653	3,515	3,804	824	1,424	1,991
1959	7,681	9,748	2,027	531	7,190	2,073	3,258	967	717	2,733
1960	7,230	10,154	1,664	409	8,081	2,152	2,851	718	1,050	3,383
1961	8,360	13,165	3,294	450	9,420	4,077	3,032	694	1,834	3,527
1962	8,558	10,705	1,314	422	8,969	3,249	2,825	567	1,303	2,761
1963	10,107	12,211	1,011	343	10,856	3,514	2,677	957	1,105	3,957
1964	10,544	13,957	2,679	412	10,865	3,046	2,760	982	2,189	4,980
1965	11,148	14,782	1,473	724	12,585	5,414	2,934	702	945	4,787
1966	11,089	17,385	1,901	580	14,904	7,056	3,666	1,494	2,003	3,167
1967	14,288	24,014	1,927	881	21,206	11,069	4,935	1,639	1,975	4,396
1968	16,374	21,261	3,885	636	16,740	6,958	5,293	1,564	1,775	5,671
1969	11,460	25,997	7,640	691	17,666	6,346	6,715	1,779	2,172	8,985
1970	17,762	37,451	7,037	1,390	29,023	10,647	11,009	1,253	5,291	9,252
1971	24,370	43,229	9,485	3,683	30,061	11,651	11,721	1,148	5,840	12,867
1972	22,941	39,705	10,707	3,371	25,628	6,398	11,314	860	4,836	16,298
1973	22,953	31,680	7,642	3,341	20,700	4,832	10,269	811	4,872	10,897
1974	22,824	37,820	4,050	2,273	31,497	10,511	12,836	1,005	3,932	9,632
1975	29,326	53,632	7,414	3,459	42,759	18,652	15,893	3,637	4,466	10,983
1976	33,845	53,314	8,305	2,803	42,206	15,496	14,418	4,649	3,562	15,194
1977	45,060	54,229	8,047	3,916	42,266	13,757	13,704	3,218	4,443	19,113
1978	46,215	48,212	7,937	2,832	37,443	11,062	12,253	2,696	3,640	18,565
1979	42,261	53,093	8,706	3,530	40,857	11,563	13,736	3,297	4,694	19,803
1980	47,133	78,896	18,996	3,635	56,265	24,398	15,940	3,727	7,401	27,429
1981	46,134	72,503	25,107	1,788	45,606	17,395	14,495	2,779	6,158	31,676
1982: First 3 quarters	49,231	54,587	14,993	3,497	36,097	9,847	13,127	1,310	1,765	28,535
1981:										
I	9,159	16,681	5,011	804	10,865	5,577	3,269	858	1,354	5,623
II	13,361	23,758	9,647	437	13,674	6,044	4,516	1,211	2,294	9,693
III	9,882	11,529	5,093	267	6,168	1,862	2,986	410	1,807	4,464
IV	13,732	20,535	5,356	280	14,899	3,912	3,724	300	703	11,896
1982:										
I	12,770	15,572	4,657	582	10,333	2,348	4,269	399	519	8,037
II	17,627	15,960	5,800	1,126	9,034	1,771	4,372	280	556	8,978
III	18,834	23,055	4,536	1,789	16,730	5,728	4,486	631	690	11,520

[1] Prior to 1948, also includes extractive, radio broadcasting, airline companies, commercial, and miscellaneous company issues.
[2] Prior to 1948, also includes telephone, street railway, and bus company issues.
[3] Prior to 1948, includes railroad issues only.

Note.—Covers substantially all new issues of State, municipal, and corporate securities offered for cash sale in the United States in amounts over $100,000 and with terms to maturity of more than 1 year; excludes notes issued exclusively to commercial banks, intercorporate transactions, and issues to be sold over an extended period, such as employee-purchase plans. Closed-end investment company issues are included beginning 1973.

Sources: Securities and Exchange Commission, "The Commercial and Financial Chronicle," and "The Bond Buyer."

TABLE B–92.—*Common stock prices and yields, 1949–82*

Year or month	Common stock prices [1]							Common stock yields (percent) [5]	
	New York Stock Exchange indexes (Dec. 31, 1965=50) [2]					Dow Jones industrial average [3]	Standard & Poor's composite index (1941–43=10) [4]	Dividend-price ratio [6]	Earnings-price ratio [7]
	Composite	Industrial	Transportation	Utility	Finance				
1949	9.02	...	...	...	...	179.48	15.23	6.59	15.48
1950	10.87	...	...	...	...	216.31	18.40	6.57	13.99
1951	13.08	...	...	...	...	257.64	22.34	6.13	11.82
1952	13.81	...	...	...	...	270.76	24.50	5.80	9.47
1953	13.67	...	...	...	...	275.97	24.73	5.80	10.26
1954	16.19	...	...	...	...	333.94	29.69	4.95	8.57
1955	21.54	...	...	...	...	442.72	40.49	4.08	7.95
1956	24.40	...	...	...	...	493.01	46.62	4.09	7.55
1957	23.67	...	...	...	...	475.71	44.38	4.35	7.89
1958	24.56	...	...	...	...	491.66	46.24	3.97	6.23
1959	30.73	...	...	...	...	632.12	57.38	3.23	5.78
1960	30.01	...	...	...	...	618.04	55.85	3.47	5.90
1961	35.37	...	...	...	...	691.55	66.27	2.98	4.62
1962	33.49	...	...	...	...	639.76	62.38	3.37	5.82
1963	37.51	...	...	...	...	714.81	69.87	3.17	5.50
1964	43.76	...	...	...	...	834.05	81.37	3.01	5.32
1965	47.39	...	...	...	...	910.88	88.17	3.00	5.59
1966	46.15	46.18	50.26	45.41	44.45	873.60	85.26	3.40	6.63
1967	50.77	51.97	53.51	45.43	49.82	879.12	91.93	3.20	5.73
1968	55.37	58.00	50.58	44.19	65.85	906.00	98.70	3.07	5.67
1969	54.67	57.44	46.96	42.80	70.49	876.72	97.84	3.24	6.08
1970	45.72	48.03	32.14	37.24	60.00	753.19	83.22	3.83	6.45
1971	54.22	57.92	44.35	39.53	70.38	884.76	98.29	3.14	5.41
1972	60.29	65.73	50.17	38.48	78.35	950.71	109.20	2.84	5.50
1973	57.42	63.08	37.74	37.69	70.12	923.88	107.43	3.06	7.12
1974	43.84	48.08	31.89	29.79	49.67	759.37	82.85	4.47	11.59
1975	45.73	50.52	31.10	31.50	47.14	802.49	86.16	4.31	9.15
1976	54.46	60.44	39.57	36.97	52.94	974.92	102.01	3.77	8.90
1977	53.69	57.86	41.09	40.92	55.25	894.63	98.20	4.62	10.79
1978	53.70	58.23	43.50	39.22	56.65	820.23	96.02	5.28	12.03
1979	58.32	64.76	47.34	38.20	61.42	844.40	103.01	5.47	13.46
1980	68.10	78.70	60.61	37.35	64.25	891.41	118.78	5.26	12.66
1981	74.02	85.44	72.61	38.91	73.52	932.92	128.05	5.20	11.96
1982	68.93	78.18	60.41	39.75	71.99	884.36	119.71	5.81	...
1981:									
Jan	76.24	89.23	74.43	38.53	70.04	962.13	132.97	4.80	...
Feb	73.52	85.74	72.76	37.59	68.48	945.50	128.40	5.00	...
Mar	76.46	89.39	77.09	37.82	72.82	987.18	133.19	4.88	10.72
Apr	77.60	90.57	80.63	38.34	74.59	1,004.86	134.43	4.86	...
May	76.28	88.78	76.78	38.27	74.65	979.52	131.73	4.98	...
June	76.80	88.63	76.71	39.23	79.79	996.27	132.28	5.03	11.44
July	74.98	86.64	74.42	38.90	74.97	947.94	129.13	5.18	...
Aug	75.24	86.72	73.27	40.22	73.76	926.25	129.63	5.16	...
Sept	68.37	78.07	63.67	38.17	69.38	853.38	118.27	5.69	13.13
Oct	69.40	78.93	65.65	38.87	72.56	853.25	119.80	5.65	...
Nov	71.49	80.86	67.68	40.73	76.47	860.44	122.92	5.54	...
Dec	71.81	81.70	68.27	40.22	74.74	878.28	123.79	5.57	12.53
1982:									
Jan	67.91	76.85	62.04	39.30	70.99	853.41	117.28	5.95	...
Feb	66.16	74.78	59.09	38.32	70.50	833.15	114.50	6.06	...
Mar	63.86	71.51	55.19	38.57	69.08	812.33	110.84	6.28	13.23
Apr	66.97	75.59	57.91	39.20	71.44	844.96	116.31	5.99	...
May	67.07	75.97	56.84	39.40	69.16	846.72	116.35	5.97	...
June	63.10	71.59	53.07	37.34	63.19	804.37	109.70	6.28	12.93
July	62.82	71.37	53.40	37.20	61.59	818.41	109.38	6.31	...
Aug	62.91	70.98	53.98	38.19	62.84	832.11	109.65	6.32	...
Sept	70.21	80.08	61.39	40.36	69.66	917.27	122.43	5.63	...
Oct	76.10	86.67	66.64	42.67	80.59	988.71	132.66	5.12	...
Nov	79.75	90.76	71.92	43.46	88.66	1,027.76	138.10	4.92	...
Dec	80.30	92.00	73.40	42.93	86.22	1,033.08	139.37	4.93	...

[1] Averages of daily closing prices, except New York Stock Exchange data through May 1964 are averages of weekly closing prices.
[2] Includes all the stocks (more than 1,500) listed on the New York Stock Exchange.
[3] Includes 30 stocks.
[4] Includes 500 stocks.
[5] Standard & Poor's series, based on 500 stocks in the composite index.
[6] Aggregate cash dividends (based on latest known annual rate) divided by aggregate market value based on Wednesday closing prices. Monthly data are averages of weekly figures; annual data are averages of monthly figures.
[7] Quarterly data are ratio of earnings (after taxes) for 4 quarters ending with particular quarter to price index for last day of that quarter. Annual ratios are averages of quarterly ratios.

Note.—All data relate to stocks listed on the New York Stock Exchange.

Sources: New York Stock Exchange, Dow Jones & Co., Inc., and Standard & Poor's Corporation.

TABLE B-93.—*Business formation and business failures, 1929–82*

Year or month	Index of net business formation (1967=100)	New business incorporations (number)	Business failures [1]						
			Business failure rate [2]	Number of failures			Amount of current liabilities (millions of dollars)		
				Total	Liability size class		Total	Liability size class	
					Under $100,000	$100,000 and over		Under $100,000	$100,000 and over
1929			103.9	22,909	22,165	744	483.3	261.5	221.8
1933 [3]			100.3	19,859	18,880	979	457.5	215.5	242.0
1939 [3]			69.6	14,768	14,541	227	182.5	132.9	49.7
1940			63.0	13,619	13,400	219	166.7	119.9	46.8
1941			54.4	11,848	11,685	163	136.1	100.7	35.4
1942			44.6	9,405	9,282	123	100.8	80.3	20.5
1943			16.4	3,221	3,155	66	45.3	30.2	15.1
1944			6.5	1,222	1,176	46	31.7	14.5	17.1
1945			4.2	809	759	50	30.2	11.4	18.8
1946		132,916	5.2	1,129	1,003	126	67.3	15.7	51.6
1947		112,897	14.3	3,474	3,103	371	204.6	63.7	140.9
1948	104.8	96,346	20.4	5,250	4,853	397	234.6	93.9	140.7
1949	86.4	85,640	34.4	9,246	8,708	538	308.1	161.4	146.7
1950	90.8	93,092	34.3	9,162	8,746	416	248.3	151.2	97.1
1951	90.1	83,778	30.7	8,058	7,626	432	259.5	131.6	128.0
1952	94.5	92,946	28.7	7,611	7,081	530	283.3	131.9	151.4
1953	92.4	102,706	33.2	8,862	8,075	787	394.2	167.5	226.6
1954	90.8	117,411	42.0	11,086	10,226	860	462.6	211.4	251.2
1955	98.2	139,915	41.6	10,969	10,113	856	449.4	206.4	243.0
1956	95.4	141,163	48.0	12,686	11,615	1,071	562.7	239.8	322.9
1957	91.4	137,112	51.7	13,739	12,547	1,192	615.3	267.1	348.2
1958	91.1	150,781	55.9	14,964	13,499	1,465	728.3	297.6	430.7
1959	98.1	193,067	51.8	14,053	12,707	1,346	692.8	278.9	413.9
1960	94.5	182,713	57.0	15,445	13,650	1,795	938.6	327.2	611.4
1961	91.1	181,535	64.4	17,075	15,006	2,069	1,090.1	370.1	720.0
1962	92.8	182,057	60.8	15,782	13,772	2,010	1,213.6	346.5	867.1
1963	94.7	186,404	56.3	14,374	12,192	2,182	1,352.6	321.0	1,031.6
1964	98.0	197,724	53.2	13,501	11,346	2,155	1,329.2	313.6	1,015.6
1965	99.5	203,897	53.3	13,514	11,340	2,174	1,321.7	321.7	1,000.0
1966	98.9	200,010	51.6	13,061	10,833	2,228	1,385.7	321.5	1,064.1
1967	100.0	206,569	49.0	12,364	10,144	2,220	1,265.2	297.9	967.3
1968	107.6	233,635	38.6	9,636	7,829	1,807	941.0	241.1	699.9
1969	113.5	274,267	37.3	9,154	7,192	1,962	1,142.1	231.3	910.8
1970	107.1	264,209	43.8	10,748	8,019	2,729	1,887.8	269.3	1,618.4
1971	109.5	287,577	41.7	10,326	7,611	2,715	1,916.9	271.3	1,645.6
1972	115.5	316,601	38.3	9,566	7,040	2,526	2,000.2	258.8	1,741.5
1973	115.5	329,358	36.4	9,345	6,627	2,718	2,298.6	235.6	2,063.0
1974	111.2	319,149	38.4	9,915	6,733	3,182	3,053.1	256.9	2,796.3
1975	108.8	326,345	42.6	11,432	7,504	3,928	4,380.2	298.6	4,081.6
1976	117.2	375,766	34.8	9,628	6,176	3,452	3,011.3	257.8	2,753.4
1977	126.5	436,170	28.4	7,919	4,861	3,058	3,095.3	208.3	2,887.0
1978	132.9	478,019	23.9	6,619	3,712	2,907	2,656.0	164.7	2,491.3
1979	131.7	524,565	27.8	7,564	3,930	3,634	2,667.4	179.9	2,487.5
1980	121.1	533,520	42.1	11,742	5,682	6,060	4,635.1	272.5	4,362.6
1981	113.5	581,242	61.3	16,794	8,233	8,561	6,955.2	405.8	6,549.3
	Seasonally adjusted								
1981:									
Jan	118.1	46,039	48.6	1,109	559	550	341.4	27.6	313.8
Feb	117.1	48,588	47.8	1,133	546	587	789.2	25.7	763.5
Mar	117.7	47,972	47.6	1,212	572	640	485.3	28.0	457.3
Apr	118.0	49,413	61.8	1,557	736	821	536.9	44.8	492.1
May	115.4	48,997	62.0	1,464	730	734	428.2	35.1	393.1
June	114.6	49,172	60.8	1,408	711	697	408.5	32.3	376.3
July	113.1	49,038	65.9	1,432	739	693	619.5	37.7	581.8
Aug	113.6	48,631	53.3	1,172	576	596	450.4	27.5	422.9
Sept	111.5	48,450	87.0	1,777	879	898	752.3	42.6	709.7
Oct	107.6	47,947	69.4	1,604	768	836	897.9	36.7	861.2
Nov	108.8	49,413	65.7	1,368	655	713	618.8	30.7	588.1
Dec	106.2	47,556	72.2	1,558	762	796	626.7	37.2	589.5
1982: [4]									
Jan	(4)	43,330	(4)	(4)	(4)	(4)	(4)	(4)	(4)
Feb	(4)	47,234	(4)	(4)	(4)	(4)	(4)	(4)	(4)
Mar	(4)	46,899	(4)	(4)	(4)	(4)	(4)	(4)	(4)
Apr	(4)	46,876	(4)	(4)	(4)	(4)	(4)	(4)	(4)
May	(4)	46,995	(4)	(4)	(4)	(4)	(4)	(4)	(4)
June	(4)	45,936	(4)	(4)	(4)	(4)	(4)	(4)	(4)
July	(4)	44,525	(4)	(4)	(4)	(4)	(4)	(4)	(4)
Aug	(4)	46,981	(4)	(4)	(4)	(4)	(4)	(4)	(4)
Sept	(4)	45,552	(4)	(4)	(4)	(4)	(4)	(4)	(4)

[1] Commercial and industrial failures only. Excludes failures of banks and railroads and, beginning 1933, of real estate, insurance, holding, and financial companies, steamship lines, travel agencies, etc.
[2] Failure rate per 10,000 listed enterprises.
[3] Series revised; not strictly comparable with earlier data.
[4] Not available.
Sources: Department of Commerce (Bureau of Economic Analysis) and Dun & Bradstreet, Inc.

TABLE B–94.—*Farm income, 1929–82*

[Billions of dollars; quarterly data at seasonally adjusted annual rates]

Year or quarter	Income of farm operators from farming: Gross farm income: Total[1]	Gross farm income: Cash marketing receipts: Total	Cash marketing receipts: Livestock and products	Cash marketing receipts: Crops	Gross farm income: Value of inventory changes[2]	Production expenses	Net farm income: Current dollars	Net farm income: 1967 dollars[3]
1929	13.8	11.3	6.2	5.1	−0.1	7.7	6.2	12.0
1933	6.9	5.3	2.8	2.5	−.2	4.4	2.6	6.6
1939	10.7	7.9	4.5	3.3	.1	6.3	4.4	10.6
1940	11.3	8.4	4.9	3.5	.3	6.9	4.5	10.7
1941	14.3	11.1	6.5	4.6	.4	7.8	6.5	14.7
1942	19.9	15.6	9.0	6.5	1.1	10.0	9.9	20.2
1943	23.3	19.6	11.5	8.1	−.1	11.6	11.7	22.7
1944	24.0	20.5	11.4	9.2	−.4	12.3	11.7	22.2
1945	25.4	21.7	12.0	9.7	−.4	13.1	12.3	22.8
1946	29.6	24.8	13.8	11.0	.0	14.5	15.1	25.8
1947	32.4	29.6	16.5	13.1	−1.8	17.0	15.4	23.0
1948	36.5	30.2	17.1	13.1	1.7	18.8	17.7	24.5
1949	30.8	27.8	15.4	12.4	−.9	18.0	12.8	17.9
1950	33.1	28.5	16.1	12.4	.8	19.5	13.6	18.9
1951	38.3	32.9	19.6	13.2	1.2	22.3	15.9	20.5
1952	37.8	32.5	18.2	14.3	.9	22.8	15.0	18.8
1953	34.4	31.0	16.9	14.1	−.6	21.5	13.0	16.2
1954	34.2	29.8	16.3	13.6	.5	21.8	12.4	15.4
1955	33.5	29.5	16.0	13.5	.2	22.2	11.3	14.1
1956	34.0	30.4	16.4	14.0	−.5	22.7	11.3	13.8
1957	34.8	29.7	17.4	12.3	.6	23.7	11.1	13.1
1958	39.0	33.5	19.2	14.2	.8	25.8	13.2	15.2
1959	37.9	33.6	18.9	14.7	.0	27.2	10.7	12.3
1960	38.9	34.2	19.0	15.3	.4	27.4	11.5	13.0
1961	40.5	35.2	19.5	15.7	.3	28.6	12.0	13.3
1962	42.3	36.5	20.2	16.3	.6	30.3	12.1	13.3
1963	43.4	37.5	20.0	17.4	.6	31.6	11.8	12.8
1964	42.3	37.3	19.9	17.4	−.8	31.8	10.5	11.3
1965	46.5	39.4	21.9	17.5	1.0	33.7	12.9	13.7
1966	50.5	43.4	25.0	18.4	−.1	36.5	14.0	14.4
1967	50.5	42.8	24.4	18.4	.7	38.2	12.3	12.3
1968	51.8	44.2	25.5	18.7	.1	39.5	12.3	11.8
1969	56.4	48.2	28.6	19.6	.1	42.1	14.3	13.0
1970	58.7	50.5	29.5	21.0	.0	44.4	14.2	12.2
1971	62.0	52.7	30.5	22.3	1.4	47.2	14.8	12.2
1972	71.0	61.1	35.6	25.5	.9	52.1	18.9	15.1
1973	98.8	86.9	45.8	41.1	3.4	65.4	33.4	25.1
1974	98.0	92.4	41.3	51.1	−1.6	72.0	26.0	17.6
1975	101.0	88.9	43.1	45.8	3.4	75.8	25.2	15.6
1976	101.9	95.4	46.3	49.0	−2.4	83.3	18.7	11.0
1977	108.6	96.2	47.6	48.6	1.0	90.2	18.4	10.2
1978	127.3	112.5	58.8	53.7	1.1	100.6	26.7	13.6
1979	151.3	131.7	68.6	63.1	5.6	119.0	32.4	14.9
1980	150.6	139.5	67.8	71.7	−4.3	130.5	20.1	8.2
1981	166.8	143.5	68.5	75.0	5.5	141.6	25.1	9.2
1982 p	163.7	142.9	69.0	73.9	−.2	144.2	19.5	6.7
1980:								
I	148.6	135.3	66.7	68.6	−1.4	125.7	22.9	9.5
II	145.2	134.3	64.4	69.9	4.2	128.7	16.5	6.8
III	153.2	143.6	69.3	74.3	−6.0	132.0	21.2	8.5
IV	155.4	144.8	70.8	74.0	−5.6	135.4	20.0	7.8
1981:								
I	161.8	142.5	67.9	74.6	2.5	139.0	22.8	8.6
II	164.7	142.3	69.4	72.9	5.3	141.0	23.7	8.8
III	171.5	146.7	71.0	75.7	7.2	143.2	28.3	10.2
IV	168.8	142.5	65.7	76.8	7.0	143.2	25.6	9.1
1982:								
I	162.0	143.4	67.4	76.0	−1.0	143.7	18.3	6.5
II	163.0	144.4	70.1	74.3	−.5	144.2	18.8	6.6
III	161.6	143.2	70.4	72.8	.0	144.3	17.3	5.9
IV p	168.1	140.6	68.1	72.5	.5	144.6	23.5	8.0

[1] Cash marketing receipts and inventory changes plus Government payments, other farm cash income, and nonmoney income furnished by farms.
[2] Physical changes in end-of-period inventory of crop and livestock commodities valued at average prices during the period.
[3] Income in current dollars divided by the consumer price index (Department of Labor).

Source: Department of Agriculture, except as noted.

TABLE B-95.—*Farm output and productivity indexes, 1929–82*

[1977=100]

Year	Farm output						Productivity indicators				
	Total [1]	Crops [2]				Live-stock and prod-ucts [2]	Farm output per unit of total input	Crop produc-tion per acre [4]	Farm output per hour of farm work		
		Total [3]	Feed grains	Food grains	Oil crops				Total	Crops	Live-stock and prod-ucts
1929	44	48	38	39	6	50	45	48	9	10	14
1933	42	43	35	27	5	54	45	43	9	10	13
1939	48	49	40	36	14	56	50	51	11	12	14
1940	50	51	41	40	16	57	53	53	12	10	14
1941	52	52	44	45	16	60	53	54	13	14	15
1942	58	58	51	48	23	67	58	59	14	15	16
1943	57	55	47	41	23	72	56	55	14	15	16
1944	59	58	49	51	20	69	57	58	14	16	16
1945	58	56	47	53	20	68	58	57	15	16	16
1946	60	59	51	55	19	66	60	60	16	18	17
1947	58	56	39	64	22	65	58	57	16	18	17
1948	63	64	57	62	27	64	63	64	18	20	18
1949	62	61	50	53	26	67	60	60	19	20	18
1950	61	59	51	49	26	70	60	59	19	22	19
1951	63	60	47	49	26	73	61	59	20	22	20
1952	66	62	50	63	26	74	63	62	22	24	21
1953	66	62	49	57	26	74	64	62	23	25	22
1954	66	61	51	51	28	77	64	61	24	26	23
1955	69	63	54	48	30	79	67	63	26	28	24
1956	69	63	54	50	34	79	68	64	28	30	25
1957	67	62	58	47	33	78	68	65	29	33	26
1958	73	69	64	69	39	79	74	73	33	38	28
1959	74	68	66	55	36	83	74	72	35	37	31
1960	76	72	69	66	38	82	77	77	37	41	32
1961	76	70	62	60	43	86	78	78	39	42	35
1962	77	71	62	56	44	86	79	81	41	45	37
1963	80	74	68	59	46	89	82	83	45	47	40
1964	79	72	59	65	46	91	81	81	47	49	43
1965	82	76	70	67	53	89	85	85	52	56	45
1966	79	73	70	67	55	91	83	83	53	59	49
1967	83	77	79	76	56	94	85	86	58	63	53
1968	85	79	75	80	64	94	87	89	62	66	55
1969	85	80	78	74	65	95	88	91	63	68	59
1970	84	77	71	69	66	99	87	88	66	70	64
1971	92	86	92	81	68	100	94	96	74	79	68
1972	91	87	88	77	74	101	94	99	78	84	73
1973	93	92	91	86	87	99	95	99	81	87	76
1974	88	84	74	91	71	100	90	88	79	80	82
1975	95	93	91	108	86	95	99	96	89	89	85
1976	97	92	96	107	74	99	97	94	94	91	93
1977	100	100	100	100	100	100	100	100	100	100	100
1978	104	102	108	93	105	101	102	105	109	105	109
1979	111	113	116	108	129	104	106	113	119	118	118
1980	103	101	97	121	99	108	100	99	112	104	129
1981	115	116	121	143	114	108	112	113	129	121	138
1982 p	117	120	124	140	103	107	114	118	131	126	137

[1] Farm output measures the annual volume of net farm production available for eventual human use through sales from farms or consumption in farm households.
[2] Gross production.
[3] Includes items not included in groups shown.
[4] Computed from variable weights for individual crops produced each year.

Source: Department of Agriculture.

TABLE B–96.—*Farm input use, selected inputs, 1929–82*

Year	Farm population April [1]: Number (thousands)	Farm population April [1]: As percent of total population [2]	Farm employment (thousands) [3]: Total	Farm employment (thousands) [3]: Family workers	Farm employment (thousands) [3]: Hired workers	Crops harvested (millions of acres) [4]	Selected indexes of input use (1977=100): Total	Farm labor	Farm real estate	Mechanical power and machinery	Agricultural chemicals [5]	Feed, seed, and livestock purchases [6]
1929	30,580	25.1	12,763	9,360	3,403	365	100	469	106	33	6	28
1933	32,393	25.8	12,739	9,874	2,865	340	94	457	99	27	4	26
1939	30,840	23.5	11,338	8,611	2,727	331	96	419	104	34	7	37
1940	30,547	23.1	10,979	8,300	2,679	341	97	417	106	36	9	39
1941	30,118	22.6	10,669	8,017	2,652	344	98	411	104	38	9	42
1942	28,914	21.4	10,504	7,949	2,555	348	101	421	102	44	10	44
1943	26,186	19.2	10,446	8,010	2,436	357	102	416	101	47	11	48
1944	24,815	17.9	10,219	7,988	2,231	362	103	412	100	49	13	48
1945	24,420	17.5	10,000	7,881	2,119	354	101	386	101	50	13	50
1946	25,403	18.0	10,295	8,106	2,189	352	99	371	105	49	14	49
1947	25,829	17.9	10,382	8,115	2,267	355	99	351	105	55	15	51
1948	24,383	16.6	10,363	8,026	2,337	356	100	342	106	62	16	52
1949	24,194	16.2	9,964	7,712	2,252	360	103	329	107	68	18	56
1950	23,048	15.2	9,926	7,597	2,329	345	102	310	108	72	19	58
1951	21,890	14.2	9,546	7,310	2,236	344	105	310	108	77	21	62
1952	21,748	13.9	9,149	7,005	2,144	349	105	296	107	81	23	63
1953	19,874	12.5	8,864	6,775	2,089	348	104	285	107	82	24	63
1954	19,019	11.7	8,651	6,570	2,081	346	103	274	107	82	24	65
1955	19,078	11.5	8,381	6,345	2,036	340	103	264	107	83	26	66
1956	18,712	11.1	7,852	5,900	1,952	324	101	249	105	84	27	69
1957	17,656	10.3	7,600	5,660	1,940	324	99	231	104	83	27	68
1958	17,128	9.8	7,503	5,521	1,982	324	98	222	103	83	28	73
1959	16,592	9.3	7,342	5,390	1,952	324	100	216	104	84	32	77
1960	15,635	8.7	7,057	5,172	1,885	324	98	207	102	83	32	77
1961	14,803	8.1	6,919	5,029	1,890	302	98	198	102	81	35	81
1962	14,313	7.7	6,700	4,873	1,827	295	98	189	103	80	38	83
1963	13,367	7.1	6,518	4,738	1,780	298	98	183	103	80	43	83
1964	12,954	6.7	6,110	4,506	1,604	298	98	174	103	80	46	85
1965	12,363	6.4	5,610	4,128	1,482	298	96	156	102	80	49	86
1966	11,595	5.9	5,214	3,854	1,360	294	96	147	101	82	56	89
1967	10,875	5.5	4,903	3,650	1,253	306	98	143	103	86	66	92
1968	10,454	5.2	4,749	3,535	1,213	300	98	138	102	87	69	89
1969	10,307	5.1	4,596	3,419	1,176	290	97	133	101	86	73	93
1970	9,712	4.7	4,523	3,348	1,175	293	97	126	104	86	75	96
1971	9,425	4.5	4,436	3,275	1,161	305	98	123	102	87	81	102
1972	9,610	4.6	4,373	3,228	1,146	294	98	117	101	87	86	104
1973	9,472	4.5	4,337	3,169	1,168	321	98	115	100	90	90	107
1974	9,264	4.3	4,389	3,075	1,314	328	98	112	98	93	92	99
1975	8,864	4.1	4,342	3,026	1,317	336	97	107	97	96	83	93
1976	8,253	3.8	4,374	2,997	1,377	337	99	103	98	98	96	101
1977	[7] 6,194	[7] 2.8	4,155	2,859	1,296	345	100	100	100	100	100	100
1978	[7] 6,501	[7] 2.9	3,957	2,689	1,268	338	101	95	100	104	107	104
1979	[7] 6,241	[7] 2.8	3,774	2,501	1,273	349	104	93	100	107	118	111
1980	[7] 6,051	[7] 2.7	3,705	2,402	1,303	352	103	92	101	105	120	108
1981	[7] 5,790	[7] 2.5	[8] 3,816	[8] 2,456	[8] 1,360	366	103	90	101	105	123	106
1982 [p]	....	....	3,700	2,405	1,295	365	....	....	....	....	....	....

[1] Farm population as defined by Department of Agriculture and Department of Commerce, i.e., civilian population living on farms in rural areas, regardless of occupation. See also footnote 7.

[2] Total population of United States including Armed Forces overseas, as of July 1.

[3] Includes persons doing farmwork on all farms. These data, published by the Department of Agriculture, differ from those on agricultural employment by the Department of Labor (see Table B–31) because of differences in the method of approach, in concepts of employment, and in time of month for which the data are collected.

[4] Acreage harvested plus acreages in fruits, tree nuts, and farm gardens.

[5] Fertilizer, lime, and pesticides.

[6] Nonfarm constant dollar value of feed, seed, and livestock purchases.

[7] Based on new definition of a farm. Under old definition of a farm, farm population (in thousands and as percent of total population) for 1977, 1978, 1979, 1980 and 1981 is 7,806 and 3.5; 8,005 and 3.6; 7,553 and 3.4; 7,241 and 3.2; and 6,942 and 3.0, respectively.

[8] Previous basis for farm employment series has been discontinued. Employment after 1980 is estimated.

Note.—Population includes Alaska and Hawaii beginning 1960.

Sources: Department of Agriculture and Department of Commerce (Bureau of the Census).

Table B–97.—*Indexes of prices received and prices paid by farmers, 1940–82*

[1977=100]

Year or month	Prices received by farmers: All farm products	Prices received by farmers: Crops	Prices received by farmers: Livestock and products	Prices paid by farmers: All commodities, services, interest, taxes, and wage rates [1]	Production items: Total [2]	Production items: Tractors and self-propelled machinery	Production items: Fertilizer	Production items: Fuels and energy	Wage rates	Addendum: Average farm real estate value per acre [3]
1940	22	21	23	18	21	...	37	...	7	7
1941	27	25	29	19	22	...	37	...	8	7
1942	35	34	36	22	26	...	41	...	10	7
1943	42	43	41	25	28	...	44	...	14	8
1944	43	46	41	26	30	...	44	...	17	9
1945	45	47	44	28	30	...	45	...	19	10
1946	52	53	50	30	33	...	45	...	20	11
1947	60	61	60	35	39	...	50	...	22	13
1948	63	59	65	38	43	...	55	...	23	14
1949	55	52	56	36	41	...	56	...	22	14
1950	56	54	58	37	42	...	54	...	22	14
1951	66	61	70	41	47	...	57	...	25	16
1952	63	62	64	42	47	...	59	...	26	18
1953	56	55	56	40	44	...	59	...	27	18
1954	54	56	52	40	44	...	59	...	27	18
1955	51	53	49	40	43	...	58	...	27	19
1956	50	54	47	40	43	...	57	...	28	19
1957	51	52	51	42	44	...	58	...	29	21
1958	55	52	57	43	46	...	58	...	30	22
1959	53	51	53	43	46	...	57	...	32	23
1960	52	51	53	44	46	...	57	...	33	24
1961	53	52	52	44	46	...	58	...	33	25
1962	53	54	53	45	47	...	58	...	34	26
1963	53	55	51	45	47	...	57	...	35	27
1964	52	55	49	45	47	...	57	...	36	29
1965	54	53	54	47	48	39	57	49	38	31
1966	58	55	60	49	50	40	56	49	41	33
1967	55	52	57	49	50	42	55	50	44	35
1968	56	52	60	51	50	44	52	50	48	38
1969	59	50	67	53	52	47	48	51	53	40
1970	60	52	67	55	54	49	48	52	57	42
1971	62	56	67	58	57	51	50	53	59	43
1972	69	60	77	62	61	54	52	54	63	47
1973	98	91	104	71	73	58	56	57	69	53
1974	105	117	94	81	83	68	92	79	79	66
1975	101	105	98	89	91	82	120	88	85	75
1976	102	102	101	95	97	91	102	93	93	86
1977	100	100	100	100	100	100	100	100	100	100
1978	115	105	124	108	108	109	100	105	107	109
1979	132	116	147	123	125	122	108	137	117	125
1980	134	125	144	138	138	136	134	188	127	145
1981	138	134	143	150	148	152	144	213	136	158
1982 [p]	133	122	144	155	150	165	144	211	136	157
1981:										
Jan	145	144	146	147	146	142	136	201	140	...
Feb	144	144	145	148	146	142	136	212	140	158
Mar	143	145	141	149	147	146	145	216	140	...
Apr	143	143	144	150	149	146	145	217	135	...
May	142	142	143	150	149	146	147	216	135	...
June	142	138	147	150	150	155	147	215	135	...
July	142	138	147	150	148	155	147	214	135	...
Aug	138	130	146	151	148	155	147	214	135	...
Sept	133	120	145	151	148	159	147	214	135	...
Oct	130	120	140	150	147	159	144	214	135	...
Nov	130	121	138	150	147	159	144	214	135	...
Dec	128	122	133	150	145	159	143	214	135	...
1982:										
Jan	132	126	137	153	148	159	143	217	136	...
Feb	133	123	142	153	148	159	143	215	136	...
Mar	133	120	145	154	150	161	147	207	136	...
Apr	135	123	147	154	150	161	147	200	136	157
May	139	125	151	155	150	161	146	202	136	...
June	137	125	149	156	151	167	146	212	136	...
July	136	124	148	156	151	167	146	214	136	...
Aug	133	119	147	156	151	167	146	213	136	...
Sept	136	125	146	156	150	168	146	213	136	...
Oct	128	114	142	155	149	168	141	212	136	...
Nov	129	118	140	156	149	168	141	213	136	...
Dec [p]	127	116	138	155	149	168	139	209	136	...

[1] Includes items used for family living, not shown separately.
[2] Includes other items not shown separately.
[3] Average for 48 States. Annual data are for March 1 of each year through 1975, for February 1 for 1976 through 1981, and for April 1, for 1982. Monthly data are for first of month.

Source: Department of Agriculture.

TABLE B–98.—*U.S. exports and imports of agricultural commodities, 1940–82*

[Billions of dollars]

Year	Exports							Imports					Agricultural trade balance
	Total [1]	Feed grains	Food grains [2]	Oilseeds and products	Cotton	Tobacco	Animals and products	Total [1]	Crops, fruits, and vegetables [3]	Animals and products	Coffee	Cocoa beans and products	
1940	0.5	(4)	(4)	(4)	0.2	(4)	0.1	1.3	(4)	0.2	0.1	(4)	−0.8
1941	.7	(4)	0.1	(4)	.1	0.1	.3	1.7	0.1	.3	.2	(4)	−1.0
1942	1.2	(4)	(4)	(4)	.1	.1	.8	1.3	(4)	.5	.2	(4)	−.1
1943	2.1	(4)	.1	0.1	.2	.2	1.2	1.5	.1	.4	.3	(4)	.6
1944	2.1	(4)	.1	.1	.1	.1	1.3	1.8	.1	.3	.3	(4)	.3
1945	2.3	(4)	.4	(4)	.3	.2	.9	1.7	.1	.4	.3	(4)	.5
1946	3.1	0.1	.7	(4)	.5	.4	.9	2.3	.2	.4	.5	0.1	.8
1947	4.0	.4	1.4	.1	.4	.3	.7	2.8	.1	.4	.6	.2	1.2
1948	3.5	.1	1.5	.2	.5	.2	.5	3.1	.2	.6	.7	.2	.3
1949	3.6	.3	1.1	.3	.9	.3	.4	2.9	.2	.4	.8	.1	.7
1950	2.9	.2	.6	.2	1.0	.3	.3	4.0	.2	.7	1.1	.2	−1.1
1951	4.0	.3	1.1	.3	1.1	.3	.5	5.2	.2	1.1	1.4	.2	−1.1
1952	3.4	.3	1.1	.2	.9	.2	.3	4.5	.2	.7	1.4	.2	−1.1
1953	2.8	.3	.7	.2	.5	.3	.4	4.2	.2	.6	1.5	.2	−1.3
1954	3.1	.2	.5	.3	.8	.3	.5	4.0	.2	.5	1.5	.3	−.9
1955	3.2	.3	.6	.4	.5	.4	.6	4.0	.2	.5	1.4	.2	−.8
1956	4.2	.4	1.0	.5	.7	.3	.7	4.0	.2	.4	1.4	.2	.2
1957	4.5	.3	1.0	.5	1.0	.4	.7	4.0	.2	.5	1.4	.2	.6
1958	3.9	.5	.8	.4	.7	.4	.5	3.9	.2	.7	1.2	.2	(4)
1959	4.0	.6	.9	.6	.4	.3	.6	4.1	.2	.8	1.1	.2	−.1
1960	4.8	.5	1.2	.6	1.0	.4	.6	3.8	.2	.6	1.0	.2	1.0
1961	5.0	.5	1.4	.6	.9	.4	.6	3.7	.2	.7	1.0	.2	1.3
1962	5.0	.8	1.3	.7	.5	.4	.6	3.9	.2	.9	1.0	.2	1.2
1963	5.6	.8	1.5	.8	.6	.4	.7	4.0	.3	.9	1.0	.2	1.6
1964	6.3	.9	1.7	1.0	.7	.4	.8	4.1	.3	.8	1.2	.2	2.3
1965	6.2	1.1	1.4	1.2	.5	.4	.8	4.1	.3	.9	1.1	.1	2.1
1966	6.9	1.3	1.8	1.2	.4	.5	.7	4.5	.4	1.2	1.1	.1	2.4
1967	6.4	1.1	1.5	1.3	.5	.5	.7	4.5	.4	1.1	1.0	.2	1.9
1968	6.3	.9	1.4	1.3	.5	.5	.7	5.0	.5	1.3	1.2	.2	1.3
1969	6.0	.9	1.2	1.3	.3	.6	.8	5.0	.5	1.4	.9	.2	1.1
1970	7.3	1.1	1.4	1.9	.4	.5	.9	5.8	.5	1.6	1.2	.3	1.5
1971	7.7	1.0	1.3	2.2	.6	.5	1.0	5.8	.6	1.5	1.2	.2	1.9
1972	9.4	1.5	1.8	2.4	.5	.7	1.1	6.5	.7	1.8	1.3	.2	2.9
1973	17.7	3.5	4.7	4.3	.9	.7	1.6	8.4	.8	2.6	1.7	.3	9.3
1974	21.9	4.6	5.4	5.7	1.3	.8	1.8	10.2	.8	2.2	1.6	.5	11.7
1975	21.9	5.2	6.2	4.5	1.0	.9	1.7	9.3	.8	1.8	1.7	.5	12.6
1976	23.0	6.0	4.7	5.1	1.0	.9	2.4	11.0	.9	2.3	2.9	.6	12.0
1977	23.6	4.9	3.6	6.6	1.5	1.1	2.7	13.4	1.2	2.3	4.2	1.0	10.2
1978	29.4	5.9	5.5	8.2	1.7	1.4	3.0	14.8	1.5	3.1	4.0	1.4	14.6
1979	34.7	7.7	6.3	8.9	2.2	1.2	3.8	16.7	1.7	3.9	4.2	1.2	18.0
1980	41.2	9.8	7.9	9.4	2.9	1.3	3.8	17.4	1.7	3.8	4.2	.9	23.9
1981	43.3	9.4	9.6	9.6	2.3	1.5	4.2	16.8	2.0	3.5	2.9	.9	26.6
Jan–Nov:													
1981	39.7	8.7	8.9	8.7	2.0	1.3	3.9	15.4	1.9	3.2	2.6	.9	24.3
1982	33.7	5.9	7.4	8.3	1.8	1.4	3.6	14.0	2.2	3.3	2.6	.7	19.7

[1] Total includes items not shown separately.
[2] Rice, wheat, and wheat flour.
[3] Includes nuts, fruits, and vegetable preparations.
[4] Less than $50 million.

Note.—Data derived from official estimates released by the Bureau of the Census, Department of Commerce. Agricultural commodities are defined as (1) nonmarine food products and (2) other products of agriculture which have not passed through complex processes of manufacture. Export value, at U.S. port of exportation, is based on the selling price and includes inland freight, insurance, and other charges to the port. Import value, defined generally as the market value in the foreign country, excludes import duties, ocean freight, and marine insurance.

Source: Department of Agriculture.

384-041 O - 83 - 18 : QL 3

Table B-99.—*Balance sheet of the farming sector, 1929–83*

[Billions of dollars]

Beginning of year	Assets									Claims			
				Other physical assets			Financial assets						
	Total	Real estate	Livestock [1]	Machinery and motor vehicles	Crops [2]	Household equipment and furnishings	Deposits and currency	U.S. savings bonds	Investments in cooperatives	Total	Real estate debt	Other debt	Proprietors' equities
1929	....	48.0	6.6	3.2	....	....	....	....	....	....	9.8	....	....
1933	....	30.8	3.0	2.5	....	....	....	....	....	....	8.5	....	....
1939	....	34.1	5.1	3.2	....	....	....	....	....	....	6.8	....	....
1940	53.0	33.6	5.1	3.1	2.7	4.2	3.2	0.2	0.8	53.0	6.6	3.4	43.0
1941	54.8	34.4	5.3	3.3	3.0	4.1	3.5	.4	.9	54.8	6.5	4.0	44.3
1942	62.9	37.5	7.1	4.0	3.8	4.8	4.2	.5	.9	62.9	6.4	4.1	52.5
1943	73.6	41.6	9.6	4.9	5.1	4.8	5.4	1.1	1.0	73.6	6.0	3.9	63.8
1944	84.0	48.2	9.7	5.4	6.1	4.7	6.6	2.2	1.1	84.0	5.4	3.5	75.1
1945	93.8	53.9	9.0	6.5	6.7	5.2	7.9	3.4	1.2	93.8	4.9	3.4	85.4
1946	102.9	61.0	9.7	5.4	6.3	5.6	9.4	4.2	1.4	102.9	4.8	3.1	95.0
1947	115.9	68.5	11.9	5.3	7.1	7.2	10.2	4.2	1.5	115.9	4.9	3.5	107.5
1948	127.4	73.7	13.3	7.4	9.0	8.1	9.9	4.4	1.7	127.4	5.1	4.1	118.1
1949	134.6	76.6	14.4	10.1	8.6	8.9	9.6	4.6	1.9	134.6	5.3	6.1	123.3
1950	134.5	77.6	12.9	12.2	7.6	8.4	9.1	4.7	2.1	134.5	5.6	6.9	122.1
1951	154.3	89.5	17.1	14.1	7.9	9.6	9.1	4.7	2.3	154.3	6.1	7.0	141.3
1952	170.1	98.5	19.5	16.7	8.8	10.1	9.4	4.7	2.5	170.1	6.7	7.9	155.5
1953	167.6	100.1	14.8	17.4	9.0	9.6	9.4	4.6	2.7	167.6	7.2	8.9	151.5
1954	164.5	98.7	11.7	18.4	9.1	9.5	9.4	4.7	2.9	164.5	7.7	9.2	147.6
1955	168.9	102.2	11.2	18.7	9.6	9.7	9.4	5.0	3.0	168.9	8.2	9.5	151.2
1956	173.6	107.5	10.6	19.3	8.3	10.0	9.5	5.2	3.2	173.6	9.0	9.8	154.9
1957	182.8	115.7	11.0	20.2	8.3	9.6	9.4	5.1	3.5	182.8	9.8	9.5	163.4
1958	191.3	121.8	13.9	20.1	7.6	9.6	9.5	5.1	3.7	191.3	10.4	10.0	170.8
1959	207.6	131.1	17.7	21.8	9.3	9.4	10.0	5.2	3.9	207.6	11.1	12.6	183.9
1960	210.2	137.2	15.2	22.7	7.7	9.2	9.2	4.7	4.2	210.2	12.0	12.7	185.4
1961	210.9	138.5	15.6	22.2	8.0	8.7	8.7	4.6	4.5	210.9	12.8	13.4	184.7
1962	219.3	144.5	16.4	22.5	8.8	8.9	8.8	4.5	4.8	219.3	13.9	14.6	190.9
1963	227.6	150.2	17.3	23.5	9.3	8.8	9.2	4.4	5.0	227.6	15.2	16.2	196.2
1964	235.8	158.6	15.9	23.9	9.8	8.8	9.2	4.2	5.4	235.8	16.8	17.6	201.4
1965	243.8	167.5	14.5	24.8	9.2	8.4	9.6	4.2	5.6	243.8	18.9	17.9	207.0
1966	260.8	179.2	17.6	26.0	9.7	8.4	10.0	4.1	5.9	260.8	21.2	19.5	220.1
1967	274.3	189.1	19.0	27.4	10.0	8.3	10.3	3.9	6.2	274.3	23.1	20.9	230.2
1968	288.0	199.7	18.8	29.8	9.6	8.8	10.9	3.8	6.5	288.0	25.1	22.3	240.6
1969	302.8	209.2	20.2	31.3	10.6	9.4	11.5	3.8	6.8	302.8	27.4	23.1	252.3
1970	314.9	215.8	23.5	32.3	10.9	9.6	11.9	3.7	7.2	314.9	29.2	23.8	261.9
1971	326.0	223.2	23.7	34.4	10.7	10.0	12.4	3.6	8.0	326.0	30.3	24.1	271.5
1972	351.8	239.6	27.3	36.6	11.8	10.8	13.2	3.7	8.8	351.8	32.2	27.4	292.2
1973	394.8	267.3	34.1	39.3	14.5	11.9	14.0	4.0	9.8	394.8	35.1	29.8	329.9
1974	478.6	327.8	42.4	44.2	22.0	12.3	14.9	4.1	10.9	478.6	39.5	33.8	405.3
1975 [3]	502.6	359.7	24.5	54.7	23.3	11.2	14.0	3.8	11.4	502.6	44.6	37.0	421.0
1976	576.3	418.1	29.4	64.0	21.3	11.7	14.5	3.9	13.4	576.3	49.6	41.9	484.8
1977	664.2	496.4	29.0	71.0	22.1	12.1	14.8	3.8	14.9	664.2	55.2	48.7	560.3
1978	736.3	554.7	31.9	77.0	24.8	13.8	15.2	3.9	15.2	736.3	63.3	59.4	613.6
1979	873.4	655.0	51.3	85.1	28.0	16.0	15.5	4.2	18.3	873.4	71.4	69.4	732.6
1980	1,004.8	755.9	61.4	96.7	33.5	17.2	15.9	4.0	20.2	1,004.8	85.4	80.4	839.0
1981	1,091.0	830.0	60.8	102.8	35.9	19.4	16.2	3.8	22.2	1,091.0	95.5	86.4	909.0
1982	1,091.8	823.8	53.6	111.4	36.5	21.7	16.8	3.6	24.4	1,091.8	105.6	96.1	890.1
1983 [4]	1,070.0	789.1	58.3	115.3	37.5	22.4	17.3	3.5	26.6	1,070.0	110.0	105.0	855.0

[1] Beginning with 1961, horses and mules are excluded.
[2] Includes all crops held on farms and crops held off farms by farmers as security for Commodity Credit Corporation loans.
[3] Beginning 1975, data are for farms included in the new farm definition, that is, places with sales of $1,000 or more annually.
[4] Forecast.

Note.—Beginning 1960, data include Alaska and Hawaii.

Source: Department of Agriculture.

Table B–100.—*Exchange rates, 1967–82*

[Cents per unit of foreign currency, except as noted]

Year and month	Belgian franc	Canadian dollar	French franc	German mark	Italian lira	Japanese yen
March 1973	2.5378	100.333	22.191	35.548	0.17604	0.38190
1967	2.0125	92.689	20.323	25.084	.16022	.27613
1968	2.0026	92.801	20.191	25.048	.16042	.27735
1969	1.9942	92.855	19.302	25.491	.15940	.27903
1970	2.0130	95.802	18.087	27.424	.15945	.27921
1971	2.0598	99.021	18.148	28.768	.16174	.28779
1972	2.2716	100.937	19.825	31.364	.17132	.32995
1973	2.5761	99.977	22.536	37.758	.17192	.36915
1974	2.5713	102.257	20.805	38.723	.15372	.34302
1975	2.7253	98.297	23.354	40.729	.15338	.33705
1976	2.5921	101.410	20.942	39.737	.12044	.33741
1977	2.7911	94.112	20.344	43.079	.11328	.37342
1978	3.1809	87.729	22.218	49.867	.11782	.47981
1979	3.4098	85.386	23.504	54.561	.12035	.45834
1980	3.4247	85.530	23.694	55.089	.11694	.44311
1981	2.7007	83.408	18.489	44.362	.08842	.45432
1982	2.1844	81.011	15.199	41.186	.07386	.40151
1981:						
I	2.9633	83.784	20.609	48.008	.09995	.48644
II	2.6899	83.427	18.484	43.958	.08827	.45491
III	2.5157	82.547	17.247	41.170	.08232	.43172
IV	2.6465	83.918	17.682	44.508	.08352	.44572
1982:						
I	2.4166	87.721	16.686	42.630	.07932	.42821
II	2.2216	80.366	15.949	42.048	.07575	.41003
III	2.1017	80.022	14.396	40.268	.07169	.38614
IV	2.0529	81.199	14.143	39.998	.06968	.38697

	Netherlands guilder	Swedish krona	Swiss franc	United Kingdom pound	Multilateral trade-weighted value of the U.S. dollar (March 1973=100)	
					Nominal	Real [1]
March 1973	34.834	22.582	31.084	247.24	100.0	100.0
1967	27.759	19.373	23.104	275.04	120.0	
1968	27.626	19.349	23.169	239.35	122.1	
1969	27.592	19.342	23.186	239.01	122.4	
1970	27.651	19.282	23.199	239.59	121.1	
1971	28.650	19.592	24.325	244.42	117.8	
1972	31.153	21.022	21.193	250.08	109.1	
1973	35.977	22.970	31.700	245.10	99.1	98.8
1974	37.267	22.563	33.688	234.03	101.4	99.2
1975	39.632	24.141	38.743	222.16	98.5	93.9
1976	37.846	22.957	40.013	180.48	105.6	97.3
1977	40.752	22.383	41.714	174.49	103.3	93.1
1978	46.284	22.139	56.283	191.84	92.4	84.2
1979	49.843	23.323	60.121	212.24	88.1	83.2
1980	50.369	23.647	59.697	232.58	87.4	84.8
1981	40.191	19.860	51.025	202.43	102.9	100.8
1982	37.427	15.914	49.190	174.80	116.6	111.7
1981:						
I	43.864	21.976	52.818	230.96	94.5	92.3
II	39.567	20.520	49.098	207.91	103.1	100.3
III	37.057	18.866	47.757	183.62	110.0	108.0
IV	40.500	18.096	54.726	188.22	105.4	102.7
1982:						
I	38.836	17.432	53.358	184.61	109.9	106.0
II	37.920	16.929	50.124	177.95	114.0	109.2
III	36.609	16.229	47.272	172.41	119.8	115.3
IV	36.526	13.660	46.739	164.81	122.2	116.2

[1] Adjusted by the consumer price index for all urban consumers.

Source: Board of Governors of the Federal Reserve System.

TABLE B–101.—*U.S. international transactions, 1946–82*

[Millions of dollars; quarterly data seasonally adjusted, except as noted. Credits (+), debits (–)]

Year or quarter	Merchandise [1] [2]			Investment income [3]			Net military transactions	Net travel and transportation receipts	Other services, net [3]	Balance on goods and services [1] [4]	Remittances, pensions, and other unilateral transfers [1]	Balance on current account [1] [4]
	Exports	Imports	Net	Receipts	Payments	Net						
1946	11,764	–5,067	6,697	772	–212	560	–493	733	310	7,807	–2,922	4,885
1947	16,097	–5,973	10,124	1,102	–245	857	–455	946	145	11,617	–2,625	8,992
1948	13,265	–7,557	5,708	1,921	–437	1,484	–799	374	175	6,942	–4,525	2,417
1949	12,213	–6,874	5,339	1,831	–476	1,355	–621	230	208	6,511	–5,638	873
1950	10,203	–9,081	1,122	2,068	–559	1,509	–576	–120	242	2,177	–4,017	–1,840
1951	14,243	–11,176	3,067	2,633	–583	2,050	–1,270	298	254	4,399	–3,515	884
1952	13,449	–10,838	2,611	2,751	–555	2,196	–2,054	83	309	3,145	–2,531	614
1953	12,412	–10,975	1,437	2,736	–624	2,112	–2,423	–238	307	1,195	–2,481	–1,286
1954	12,929	–10,353	2,576	2,929	–582	2,347	–2,460	–269	305	2,499	–2,280	219
1955	14,424	–11,527	2,897	3,406	–676	2,730	–2,701	–297	299	2,928	–2,498	430
1956	17,556	–12,803	4,753	3,837	–735	3,102	–2,788	–361	447	5,153	–2,423	2,730
1957	19,562	–13,291	6,271	4,180	–796	3,384	–2,841	–189	482	7,107	–2,345	4,762
1958	16,414	–12,952	3,462	3,790	–825	2,965	–3,135	–633	486	3,145	–2,361	784
1959	16,458	–15,310	1,148	4,132	–1,061	3,071	–2,805	–821	573	1,166	–2,448	–1,282
1960	19,650	–14,758	4,892	4,616	–1,237	3,379	–2,752	–964	579	5,132	–2,308	2,824
1961	20,108	–14,537	5,571	4,999	–1,245	3,754	–2,596	–978	594	6,346	–2,524	3,822
1962	20,781	–16,260	4,521	5,618	–1,324	4,294	–2,449	–1,152	809	6,025	–2,638	3,387
1963	22,272	–17,048	5,224	6,157	–1,561	4,596	–2,304	–1,309	960	7,167	–2,754	4,414
1964	25,501	–18,700	6,801	6,824	–1,784	5,040	–2,133	–1,146	1,041	9,604	–2,781	6,823
1965	26,461	–21,510	4,951	7,437	–2,088	5,349	–2,122	–1,280	1,387	8,285	–2,854	5,432
1966	29,310	–25,493	3,817	7,528	–2,481	5,047	–2,935	–1,331	1,365	5,963	–2,932	3,031
1967	30,666	–26,866	3,800	8,020	–2,747	5,273	–3,226	–1,750	1,612	5,708	–3,125	2,583
1968	33,626	–32,991	635	9,368	–3,378	5,990	–3,143	–1,548	1,630	3,563	–2,952	611
1969	36,414	–35,807	607	10,912	–4,869	6,043	–3,328	–1,763	1,833	3,393	–2,994	399
1970	42,469	–39,866	2,603	11,747	–5,516	6,231	–3,354	–2,038	2,180	5,625	–3,294	2,331
1971	43,319	–45,579	–2,260	12,707	–5,436	7,271	–2,893	–2,345	2,495	2,269	–3,701	–1,433
1972	49,381	–55,797	–6,416	14,764	–6,572	8,192	–3,420	–3,063	2,766	–1,941	–3,854	–5,795
1973	71,410	–70,499	911	21,808	–9,655	12,153	–2,070	–3,158	3,184	11,021	–3,881	7,140
1974	98,306	–103,649	–5,343	27,587	–12,084	15,503	–1,653	–3,184	3,986	9,309	[5] –7,186	2,124
1975	107,088	–98,041	9,047	25,351	–12,564	12,787	–746	–2,792	4,598	22,893	–4,613	18,280
1976	114,745	–124,051	–9,306	29,286	–13,311	15,975	559	–2,558	4,711	9,382	–4,998	4,384
1977	120,816	–151,689	–30,873	32,179	–14,217	17,962	1,528	–3,293	5,224	–9,451	–4,617	–14,068
1978	142,054	–175,813	–33,759	42,245	–21,680	20,565	621	–3,125	5,955	–9,743	–5,030	–14,773
1979	184,473	–211,819	–27,346	64,129	–32,914	31,215	–2,035	–2,429	5,690	5,095	–5,561	–466
1980	224,237	–249,575	–25,338	72,686	–42,776	29,910	–2,471	–940	7,144	8,303	–6,783	1,520
1981	236,254	–264,143	–27,889	85,945	–52,908	33,037	–1,541	–231	7,702	11,079	–6,608	4,471
1980:												
I	54,752	–64,431	–9,679	19,944	–10,505	9,439	–931	–436	1,644	37	–1,837	–1,800
II	55,843	–62,363	–6,520	16,016	–10,268	5,748	–514	–216	1,808	306	–1,306	–1,000
III	55,786	–59,735	–3,949	17,848	–10,485	7,363	–286	–114	1,810	4,824	–1,444	3,380
IV	57,856	–63,046	–5,190	18,877	–11,519	7,358	–742	–174	1,879	3,131	–2,195	936
1981:												
I	60,683	–64,995	–4,312	20,528	–12,405	8,123	–487	–495	1,838	4,667	–1,422	3,245
II	60,284	–66,831	–6,547	21,642	–13,441	8,201	–587	–139	1,981	2,909	–1,510	1,399
III	57,694	–65,539	–7,845	22,048	–13,865	8,183	61	200	1,960	2,559	–1,808	751
IV	57,593	–66,778	–9,185	21,727	–13,198	8,529	–528	203	1,924	943	–1,870	–927
1982:												
I	55,780	–61,653	–5,873	20,890	–14,029	6,861	167	–66	2,034	3,123	–2,048	1,075
II	55,174	–60,869	–5,695	22,562	–14,874	7,688	247	–319	2,050	3,971	–1,740	2,231
III *p*	52,480	–64,938	–12,458	21,880	–14,462	7,418	527	–201	2,140	2,574	–1,653	–4,227

[1] Excludes military.
[2] Adjusted from Census data for differences in valuation, coverage, and timing.
[3] Fees and royalties from U.S. direct investments abroad or from foreign direct investments in the United States are excluded from investment income and included in other services, net.
[4] In concept, balance on goods and services is equal to net exports and imports in the national income and product accounts (and the sum of balance on current account and allocations of special drawing rights is equal to net foreign investment in the accounts), although the series differ because of different handling of certain items (gold, extraordinary military shipments, etc.), revisions, etc.
[5] Includes extraordinary U.S. Government transactions with India.

See next page for continuation of table.

TABLE B–101.—*U.S. international transactions, 1946–82*—Continued

[Millions of dollars; quarterly data seasonally adjusted, except as noted]

Year or quarter	U.S. assets abroad, net [increase/capital outflow (−)]				Foreign assets in the U.S., net [increase/capital inflow (+)]			Allocations of special drawing rights (SDRs)	Statistical discrepancy	
	Total	U.S. official reserve assets [6]	Other U.S. Government assets	U.S. private assets	Total	Foreign official assets	Other foreign assets		Total (sum of the items with sign reversed)	Of which: Seasonal adjustment discrepancy
1946	...	−623	...	...	...	...	...	...	...	...
1947	...	−3,315	...	...	...	...	...	...	...	...
1948	...	−1,736	...	...	...	...	...	...	...	...
1949	...	−266	...	...	...	...	...	...	...	...
1950	...	1,758	...	...	...	...	...	...	...	...
1951	...	−33	...	...	...	...	...	...	...	...
1952	...	−415	...	...	...	...	...	...	...	...
1953	...	1,256	...	...	...	...	...	...	...	...
1954	...	480	...	...	...	...	...	...	...	...
1955	...	182	...	...	...	...	...	...	...	...
1956	...	−869	...	...	...	...	...	...	...	...
1957	...	−1,165	...	...	...	...	...	...	...	...
1958	...	2,292	...	...	...	...	...	...	...	...
1959	...	1,035	...	...	...	...	...	...	...	...
1960	−4,099	2,145	−1,100	−5,144	2,294	1,473	821	...	−1,019	...
1961	−5,538	607	−910	−5,235	2,705	765	1,939	...	−989	...
1962	−4,174	1,535	−1,085	−4,623	1,911	1,270	641	...	−1,124	...
1963	−7,270	378	−1,662	−5,986	3,217	1,986	1,231	...	−360	...
1964	−9,560	171	−1,680	−8,050	3,643	1,660	1,983	...	−907	...
1965	−5,716	1,225	−1,605	−5,336	742	134	607	...	−458	...
1966	−7,321	570	−1,543	−6,347	3,661	−672	4,333	...	629	...
1967	−9,757	53	−2,423	−7,386	7,379	3,451	3,928	...	−205	...
1968	−10,977	−870	−2,274	−7,833	9,928	−774	10,703	...	438	...
1969	−11,585	−1,179	2,200	8,206	12,702	−1,301	14,002	...	−1,516	...
1970	−9,337	2,481	−1,589	−10,229	6,359	6,908	−550	867	−219	...
1971	−12,475	2,349	−1,884	−12,940	22,970	26,879	−3,909	717	−9,779	...
1972	−14,497	−4	−1,568	−12,925	21,461	10,475	10,986	710	−1,879	...
1973	−22,874	158	−2,644	−20,388	18,388	6,026	12,362	...	−2,654	...
1974	−34,745	−1,467	[5] 366	−33,643	34,241	10,546	23,696	...	−1,620	...
1975	−39,703	−849	−3,474	−35,380	15,670	7,027	8,643	...	5,753	...
1976	−51,269	−2,558	−4,214	−44,498	36,518	17,693	18,826	...	10,367	...
1977	−34,785	−375	−3,693	−30,717	51,319	36,816	14,503	...	−2,465	...
1978	−61,130	732	−4,660	−57,202	64,036	33,678	30,358	...	11,866	...
1979	−64,344	−1,133	−3,743	−59,469	38,460	−13,697	52,157	1,139	25,212	...
1980	−86,026	−8,155	−5,126	−72,746	54,484	15,442	39,042	1,152	28,870	...
1981	−109,294	−5,175	−5,137	−98,982	77,921	4,785	73,136	1,093	25,809	...
1980:										
I	−12,916	−3,268	−1,438	−8,210	7,865	−7,421	15,286	1,152	5,700	−643
II	−24,962	502	−1,143	−24,321	8,616	7,644	972	...	17,346	795
III	−19,635	−1,109	−1,390	−17,136	12,647	7,541	5,106	...	3,608	−2,754
IV	−28,512	−4,279	−1,154	−23,079	25,356	7,678	17,677	...	2,219	2,605
1981:										
I	−22,796	−4,529	−1,375	−16,892	8,470	5,361	3,109	1,093	9,988	−829
II	−21,566	−905	−1,518	−19,143	13,464	−2,861	16,324	...	6,703	503
III	−17,257	−4	−1,257	−15,996	16,880	−5,835	22,715	...	−374	−2,144
IV	−47,677	262	−987	−46,952	39,107	8,119	30,988	...	9,497	2,474
1982:										
I	−31,201	−1,089	−904	−29,208	25,080	−3,122	28,202	...	5,045	−899
II	−37,790	−1,132	−1,547	−35,111	29,619	1,998	27,621	...	5,940	574
III p	−26,364	−794	−2,418	−23,152	16,054	2,102	13,952	...	14,537	−1,973

[6] Consists of gold, special drawing rights, convertible currencies, and the U.S. reserve position in the International Monetary Fund (IMF).

Note.—Quarterly data for U.S. official reserve assets and foreign assets in the United States are not seasonally adjusted.

Source: Department of Commerce, Bureau of Economic Analysis.

Table B–102.—*U.S. merchandise exports and imports by principal end-use category, 1965–82*

[Millions of dollars; quarterly data seasonally adjusted]

Year or quarter	Exports					Imports				
	Total	Agricultural	Nonagricultural			Total	Petroleum and products	Nonpetroleum		
			Total	Capital goods except automotive	Other goods			Total	Industrial supplies and materials	Other goods
1965	26,461	6,305	20,156	8,052	12,104	21,510	2,034	19,476	9,123	10,353
1966	29,310	6,949	22,361	8,907	13,454	25,493	2,078	23,415	10,235	13,180
1967	30,666	6,453	24,213	9,934	14,279	26,866	2,091	24,775	9,956	14,819
1968	33,626	6,297	27,329	11,111	16,218	32,991	2,384	30,607	12,027	18,580
1969	36,414	6,096	30,318	12,369	17,949	35,807	2,649	33,158	11,798	21,360
1970	42,469	7,374	35,095	14,659	20,436	39,866	2,927	36,939	12,416	24,523
1971	43,319	7,831	35,488	15,372	20,116	45,579	3,650	41,929	13,794	28,135
1972	49,381	9,513	39,868	16,914	22,954	55,797	4,650	51,147	16,308	34,839
1973	71,410	17,978	53,432	21,999	31,433	70,499	8,415	62,084	19,636	42,448
1974	98,306	22,412	75,894	30,878	45,016	103,649	26,609	77,040	27,819	49,221
1975	107,088	22,242	84,846	36,639	48,207	98,041	27,017	71,024	24,013	47,011
1976	114,745	23,381	91,364	39,112	52,252	124,051	34,573	89,478	29,759	59,719
1977	120,816	24,331	96,485	39,767	56,718	151,689	44,983	106,706	35,670	71,036
1978	142,054	29,902	112,152	46,470	65,682	175,813	42,312	133,501	42,542	90,959
1979	184,473	35,594	148,879	58,842	90,037	211,819	60,482	151,337	49,880	101,457
1980	224,237	42,156	182,081	74,178	107,903	249,575	79,414	170,161	55,632	114,529
1981	236,254	44,264	191,990	81,666	110,324	264,143	77,579	186,564	60,281	126,283
1980:										
I	54,752	10,159	44,593	17,070	27,523	64,431	21,049	43,382	15,331	28,051
II	55,843	10,159	45,684	18,458	27,226	62,363	20,834	41,529	13,624	27,905
III	55,786	10,706	45,080	18,965	26,115	59,735	17,735	42,000	13,167	28,833
IV	57,856	11,132	46,724	19,685	27,039	63,046	19,796	43,250	13,510	29,740
1981:										
I	60,683	12,575	48,108	20,122	27,986	64,995	20,533	44,462	14,474	29,988
II	60,284	11,151	49,133	21,107	28,026	66,831	20,798	46,034	15,205	30,829
III	57,694	9,947	47,747	20,236	27,511	65,539	18,158	47,382	15,498	31,884
IV	57,593	10,591	47,002	20,201	26,801	66,778	18,091	48,687	15,102	33,585
1982:										
I	55,780	10,510	45,270	19,354	25,916	61,653	15,652	46,001	14,230	31,771
II	55,174	10,673	44,501	19,310	25,191	60,869	13,416	47,453	13,422	34,031
III [p]	52,480	8,496	43,984	18,571	25,413	64,938	16,453	48,485	13,485	35,000

Note.—Data are on an international transactions basis and exclude military shipments.

Source: Department of Commerce, Bureau of Economic Analysis.

TABLE B–103.—*U.S. merchandise exports and imports by area, 1973–82*

[Millions of dollars]

Item	1973	1974	1975	1976	1977	1978	1979	1980	1981	1982 first 3 quarters at annual rate [1]
Exports	71,410	98,306	107,088	114,745	120,816	142,054	184,473	224,237	236,254	217,912
Industrial countries	48,529	64,487	66,496	72,335	76,970	87,948	115,930	137,152	141,134	130,069
Canada	16,710	21,842	23,537	26,336	28,533	31,229	38,690	41,626	45,250	40,099
Japan	8,356	10,724	9,567	10,196	10,566	12,960	17,629	20,806	21,796	20,839
Western Europe	21,216	28,164	29,884	31,883	34,094	39,546	54,177	67,603	65,090	60,952
Australia, New Zealand, and South Africa	2,247	3,757	3,508	3,920	3,777	4,213	5,434	7,117	8,998	8,180
Other countries, except Eastern Europe	20,834	32,082	37,343	38,287	40,951	50,213	62,630	82,942	90,636	83,820
OPEC [2]	3,414	6,219	9,956	11,561	12,877	14,846	14,537	17,364	21,093	21,103
Other [3]	17,420	25,863	27,387	26,726	28,074	35,367	48,093	65,578	69,543	62,717
Eastern Europe	2,047	1,737	3,249	4,123	2,895	3,893	5,913	4,143	4,461	4,023
Imports	70,499	103,649	98,041	[4] 124,051	[4] 151,689	[4] 175,813	[4] 211,819	[4] 249,575	[4] 264,143	[4] 249,947
Industrial countries	48,985	61,092	55,973	67,488	79,228	99,151	112,600	127,702	143,395	145,681
Canada	17,694	22,392	21,710	26,475	29,645	33,552	39,020	42,697	47,316	48,863
Japan	9,665	12,414	11,257	15,531	18,565	24,541	26,261	31,217	37,598	38,775
Western Europe	19,774	24,267	20,764	23,003	28,226	36,618	41,826	47,255	52,873	52,955
Australia, New Zealand, and South Africa	1,852	2,019	2,242	2,479	2,792	4,440	5,493	6,533	5,608	5,089
Other countries, except Eastern Europe	20,913	41,580	41,334	55,379	70,680	74,402	96,137	119,142	119,196	103,102
OPEC [2]	5,097	17,234	18,897	27,409	35,778	33,286	45,039	55,602	49,934	32,433
Other [3]	15,816	24,346	22,437	27,970	34,902	41,116	51,098	63,540	69,262	70,669
Eastern Europe	601	977	734	875	1,127	1,508	1,896	1,444	1,552	1,132

[1] Preliminary; seasonally adjusted.
[2] Algeria, Ecuador, Gabon, Indonesia, Iran, Iraq, Kuwait, Libya, Nigeria, Qatar, Saudi Arabia, United Arab Emirates, and Venezuela.
[3] Latin American Republics, other Western Hemisphere, and other countries in Asia and Africa, less members of OPEC.
[4] Trade with international organizations is included in totals for 1976–82, but not in area detail. This includes imports of nonmonetary gold from International Monetary Fund in 1976–80; an export of tin to International Tin Council (ITC) in 1981; and an import of tin from ITC in 1982.

Note.—Data are on an international transactions basis and exclude military.

Source: Department of Commerce, Bureau of Economic Analysis.

TABLE B–104.—*U.S. merchandise exports and imports by commodity groups, 1960–82*

[Millions of dollars; monthly data seasonally adjusted]

Year or month	Merchandise exports[1]					Merchandise imports					Merchandise trade balance		
	Total domestic and foreign exports[2]	Domestic exports				General imports[6]				Total, c.i.f. value[7]	Exports less imports, customs value	Exports less imports, f.a.s.	Exports less imports, c.i.f.
		Total[2 3]	Food, beverages, and tobacco	Crude materials and fuels[4]	Manufactured goods[5]	Total[3]	Food, beverages, and tobacco	Crude materials and fuels[4]	Manufactured goods[5]				
	F.a.s. value[8]					Customs value							
1960	19,659	19,459	3,167	3,942	12,583	15,073	3,392	4,418	6,863		4,586		
1961	20,226	19,982	3,466	3,864	12,784	14,761	3,455	4,334	6,537		5,465		
1962	20,986	20,717	3,743	3,356	13,668	16,464	3,674	4,691	7,649		4,522		
1963	22,467	22,182	4,188	3,775	14.297	17,207	3,863	4,755	8,070		5,260		
1964	25,832	25,479	4,637	4,337	16,529	18,749	4,022	5,029	9,106		7,083		
1965	26,742	26,399	4,519	4,273	17,433	21,427	4,013	5,440	11,244		5,315		
1966	29,490	29,054	5,186	4,404	19,218	25,618	4,590	5,718	14,446		3,872		
1967	31,030	30,646	4,710	4,726	20,844	26,889	4,701	5,367	15,756	28,745	4,141		2,283
1968	34,063	33,626	4,592	4,865	23,818	33,226	5,365	6,031	20,624	35,320	837		–1,257
1969	37,332	36,788	4,446	5,006	26,785	36,043	5,308	6,391	23,011	38,241	1,289		–909
1970	42,659	42,025	5,058	6,692	29,344	39,951	6,230	6,542	25,907	42,429	2,708		230
1971	43,549	42,911	5,076	6,441	30,443	45,563	6,404	7,268	30,414	48,342	–2,014		–4,793
1972	49,199	48,399	6,569	7,091	33,740	55,583	7,379	8,838	37,767	58,862	–6,384		–9,663
1973	70,823	69,730	12,938	10,735	44,731	69,476	9,235	13,446	45,001	73,573	1,348		2,752
1974	97,998	96,634	15,233	15,802	63,523	101,394	10,701	31,842	56,202	108,392	–3,396		–10,395
						F.a.s. value[8]							
1974*	98,092	96,679	15,233	15,802	63,523	102,559	10,709	32,064	55,223	110,875		–4,467	–12,783
1975*	107,652	106,161	16,793	15,197	70,951	98,503	9,923	32,596	51,080	105,880		9,149	1,772
1976*	115,223	113,549	17,234	16,095	77,241	123,477	11,891	41,474	64,775	132,498		–8,254	–17,274
1977*	121,232	119,024	15,963	18,579	80,151	150,390	14,227	53,554	76,554	160,411		–29,158	–39,179
1978*	143,681	141,142	20,604	20,957	94,473	174,757	15,743	51,901	100,317	186,045		–31,076	–42,364
1979*	181,860	178,633	24,587	28,222	116,587	209,458	17,735	71,390	112,226	222,228		–27,599	–40,368
1980	220,630	216,515	30,407	33,719	143,891	244,871	18,551	93,973	125,122	256,984		–24,241	–36,354
						Customs value							
1981	233,677	228,899	33,206	33,022	154,283	260,982	18,350	92,873	142,475	273,352	–27,305		–39,675
1982	212,193	207,076	26,977	33,518	139,716	243,952	17,817	74,404	144,022	254,885	–31,759		–42,691
1981:													
Jan	18,902	18,536	2,934	2,815	12,065	22,616	1,736	8,976	11,278	23,679	–3,714		–4,777
Feb	19,788	19,465	2,943	2,958	12,813	21,916	1,589	9,099	10,750	22,917	–2,127		–3,129
Mar	21,278	20,843	3,304	3,219	13,558	21,029	1,612	7,471	11,379	21,983	249		–705
Apr	19,786	19,377	2,891	2,530	13,276	22,249	1,471	8,878	11,325	23,266	–2,463		–3,480
May	18,899	18,528	2,667	2,526	12,619	21,232	1,665	7,146	11,816	22,248	–2,333		–3,349
June	19,750	19,340	2,573	2,342	13,456	22,005	1,472	8,249	11,645	23,033	–2,255		–3,283
July	19,289	18,919	2,549	2,430	13,060	20,114	1,390	6,576	11,622	21,074	–825		–1,784
Aug	19,031	18,720	2,470	2,662	12,991	23,242	1,479	7,779	13,361	24,398	–4,212		–5,367
Sept	19,551	19,108	2,772	2,795	12,947	21,274	1,393	7,411	11,971	22,317	–1,724		–2,766
Oct	19,163	18,733	2,920	2,863	12,458	23,077	1,583	7,642	13,127	24,194	–3,914		–5,031
Nov	19,153	18,751	2,675	2,872	12,590	22,508	1,413	7,468	12,826	23,568	–3,356		–4,415
Dec	18,885	18,377	2,515	2,934	12,318	19,746	1,542	6,174	11,414	20,699	–861		–1,814
1982:													
Jan	18,737	18,350	2,279	3,076	12,463	22,829	1,340	8,269	12,584	23,870	–4,092		–5,134
Feb	18,704	18,341	2,482	3,434	11,876	19,090	1,154	5,845	11,527	19,900	–387		–1,197
Mar	18,602	18,127	2,673	3,151	11,822	20,349	1,529	5,717	12,402	21,237	–1,747		–2,635
Apr	17,843	17,441	2,506	2,898	11,428	17,387	1,435	5,033	10,337	18,165	456		–322
May	18,218	17,807	2,478	2,912	11,837	20,558	1,569	4,906	13,219	21,509	–2,340		–3,291
June	18,822	18,386	2,421	2,797	12,563	21,310	1,567	6,198	12,899	22,259	–2,488		–3,437
July	18,027	17,638	1,896	2,617	12,590	19,559	1,389	6,645	10,982	20,449	–1,532		–2,422
Aug	17,498	17,177	2,162	2,642	11,882	23,494	1,617	7,168	14,111	24,578	–5,996		–7,080
Sept	17,387	16,651	1,909	2,832	11,334	20,644	1,581	5,968	12,434	21,580	–3,257		–4,192
Oct	16,698	16,310	2,132	2,665	10,987	21,096	1,667	6,711	12,028	22,024	–4,398		–5,326
Nov	15,693	15,317	2,086	2,361	10,369	18,937	1,498	5,770	11,038	19,783	–3,244		–4,090
Dec	16,335	15,902	1,943	2,420	10,660	18,865	1,469	6,181	10,621	19,701	–2,529		–3,366

[1] Beginning 1960, data have been adjusted for comparability with the revised commodity classifications effective in 1965.

[2] Department of Defense shipments of grant-aid military supplies and equipment under the Military Assistance Program are excluded from total exports.

[3] Total includes commodities and transactions not classified according to kind.

[4] Includes fats and oils.

[5] Includes machinery, transportation equipment, chemicals, metals, and other manufactures. Export data for these items include military grant-aid shipments through 1977 and exclude them thereafter.

[6] Total arrivals of imported goods other than intransit shipments.

[7] C.i.f. (cost, insurance, and freight) import value at first port of entry into United States. Data for 1967–73 are estimates.

[8] F.a.s. (free alongside ship) value basis at U.S. port of exportation for exports and at foreign port of exportation for imports.

Note.—Data are as reported by the Bureau of the Census adjusted to include silver ore and bullion reported separately prior to 1969. Trade in gold is included beginning 1974. Export statistics cover all merchandise shipped from the U.S. customs area, except supplies for the U.S. Armed Forces. Exports include shipments under Agency for International Development and Food for Peace programs as well as other private relief shipments.

Data for 1980 and 1981 include trade of the U.S. Virgin Islands, except that for 1980 Virgin Islands exports are reflected only in the figures for domestic and foreign exports combined, total domestic exports, and trade balance.

*Data for 1974–79 for domestic and foreign exports combined, total domestic exports, total general imports, and trade balance include trade of the Virgin Islands.

Source: Department of Commerce (Bureau of the Census and International Trade Administration, Office of Trade Investment and Analysis, Trade Performance Division).

TABLE B–105.—*International investment position of the United States at year-end, selected years, 1970–81*

[Billions of dollars]

Type of investment	1970	1972	1974	1976	1978	1979	1980	1981
Net international investment position of the United States	58.6	37.1	58.8	83.8	76.2	94.9	121.6	160.3
U.S. assets abroad	165.5	199.0	255.7	347.2	447.9	510.6	606.9	717.4
U.S. official reserve assets	14.5	13.2	15.9	18.7	18.7	19.0	26.8	30.1
Gold	11.1	10.5	11.7	11.6	11.7	11.2	11.2	11.2
Special drawing rights (SDRs)	.9	2.0	2.4	2.4	1.6	2.7	2.6	4.1
Reserve position in the International Monetary Fund (IMF)	1.9	.5	1.9	4.4	1.0	1.3	2.9	5.1
Foreign currency reserves	.6	.2	.0	.3	4.4	3.8	10.1	9.8
Other U.S. Government assets	32.1	36.1	38.4	46.0	54.2	58.4	63.5	68.5
U.S. loans and other long-term assets	29.7	34.1	36.3	44.1	52.3	56.5	61.9	67.2
U.S. short-term assets other than reserves	2.5	2.0	2.1	1.9	1.9	1.9	1.7	1.3
U.S. private assets	118.8	149.7	201.5	282.4	375.0	433.2	516.6	618.8
Direct investments abroad (book value)	75.5	89.9	110.1	136.8	162.7	187.9	215.6	227.3
Foreign securities	21.0	27.6	28.2	44.2	53.4	56.8	62.5	62.9
Claims on foreigners reported by U.S. banks, not included elsewhere	13.8	20.7	46.2	81.1	130.8	157.0	203.9	293.5
Claims on unaffiliated foreigners reported by U.S. nonbanks	8.5	11.4	17.0	20.3	28.1	31.5	34.7	35.0
Foreign assets in the United States	106.8	161.8	196.9	263.4	371.6	415.7	485.3	557.1
Foreign official assets	26.1	63.2	79.8	104.2	173.0	159.7	175.8	180.1
U.S. Government securities[1]	17.7	52.9	58.1	72.6	128.5	106.6	118.2	125.1
Other U.S. Government liabilities	1.7	1.6	2.6	8.8	12.7	12.6	13.1	13.1
Liabilities reported by U.S. banks, not included elsewhere	6.7	8.5	18.4	17.2	23.3	30.5	30.4	26.3
Other official assets	.0	.2	.6	5.6	8.5	9.9	14.1	15.6
Other foreign assets	80.7	98.7	117.1	159.1	198.7	256.0	309.4	377.1
Direct investments in the United States (book value)	13.3	14.9	25.1	30.8	42.5	54.5	68.4	89.8
Liabilities reported by U.S. banks, not included elsewhere	22.7	21.2	41.8	53.5	77.7	110.3	121.1	164.7
U.S. Treasury securities	1.2	1.2	1.7	7.0	8.9	14.2	16.1	18.5
Other U.S. securities[2]	34.7	50.7	34.9	54.9	53.6	58.6	74.1	75.3
Liabilities to unaffiliated foreigners reported by U.S. nonbanks	8.8	10.7	13.6	13.0	16.0	18.4	29.8	28.9

[1] Includes Treasury and agency issues of securities.
[2] Corporate and other bonds and corporate stocks.

Source: Department of Commerce, Bureau of Economic Analysis.

TABLE B–106.—*World trade: Exports and imports, 1965, 1970, 1975, and 1979–82*

[Billions of U.S. dollars]

Area and country	1965	1970	1975	1979	1980	1981	1982 [1]
	Exports, f.o.b. [2]						
Developed countries [3]	130.1	226.7	585.7	1,085.7	1.283.9	1.258.9	1,199.7
United States	27.5	43.2	108.1	182.0	220.8	233.7	212.9
Canada	8.4	16.7	34.1	58.3	67.7	72.6	71.1
Japan	8.5	19.3	55.7	102.3	130.4	151.5	140.3
European Community [4]	65.2	113.6	300.6	577.2	665.8	612.8	599.3
France	10.2	18.1	53.1	100.7	116.0	106.4	96.4
West Germany	17.9	34.2	90.2	171.8	192.9	176.1	175.7
Italy	7.2	13.2	34.8	72.2	77.7	75.3	77.3
United Kingdom	13.8	19.6	44.5	86.4	110.1	102.7	95.5
Other developed countries	20.5	33.7	87.1	165.8	199.1	188.2	176.1
Developing countries	40.2	61.7	226.5	452.8	608.8	606.1	525.9
Oil exporting countries [5]	10.5	17.5	113.6	214.3	301.2	276.4	212.8
Other	29.6	44.2	113.0	238.5	307.6	329.6	313.1
Communist countries [6]	23.2	34.9	90.5	170.4	203.1	213.2	215.6
U.S.S.R.	8.2	12.8	33.4	64.9	76.4	79.4	80.9
Eastern Europe	11.8	18.2	45.3	77.9	87.5	91.1	90.1
China	2.0	2.2	7.3	13.5	18.9	21.4	23.0
TOTAL	193.5	323.3	902.7	1,708.9	2,095.8	2,078.2	1,941.2
	Imports, c.i.f. [7]						
Developed countries [3]	137.5	237.8	618.1	1,182.7	1,427.1	1,358.3	1,290.4
United States	23.2	42.7	105.9	222.2	257.0	273.4	261.4
Canada	8.7	14.3	36.2	57.0	62.8	70.0	60.8
Japan	8.2	18.9	57.8	109.8	141.3	142.9	132.0
European Community [4]	70.5	118.9	306.4	611.1	729.2	644.2	628.1
France	10.4	19.1	54.0	107.0	134.9	121.0	116.6
West Germany	17.6	29.9	74.9	159.6	188.0	163.9	154.9
Italy	7.4	15.0	38.4	77.9	99.5	91.1	90.5
United Kingdom	16.1	22.0	53.3	99.6	115.8	102.0	100.1
Other developed countries	27.0	43.1	111.8	182.6	236.8	227.9	208.1
Developing countries	43.5	67.8	221.6	408.0	540.1	595.2	562.4
Oil exporting countries [5]	6.4	9.9	52.8	100.1	137.2	162.0	163.9
Other	37.2	57.9	168.9	307.8	402.9	433.2	398.5
Communist countries [6]	22.5	34.1	100.8	170.9	202.8	211.2	209.3
U.S.S.R.	8.0	11.7	37.1	58.0	68.5	73.2	80.1
Eastern Europe	11.6	18.5	51.3	83.0	93.1	97.3	89.2
China	1.8	2.2	7.4	15.7	20.9	19.6	19.1
TOTAL	203.5	339.7	940.5	1,761.6	2,170.0	2,164.7	2,062.1

[1] Preliminary estimates.
[2] Free-on-board ship value.
[3] Includes the OECD countries, South Africa, and non-OECD Europe.
[4] Includes Belgium-Luxembourg, Denmark, Greece, Ireland, and the Netherlands, not shown separately.
[5] Includes Algeria, Ecuador, Gabon, Indonesia, Iran, Iraq, Kuwait, Libya, Nigeria, Oman, Qatar, Saudi Arabia, United Arab Emirates, and Venezuela.
[6] Includes North Korea, Vietnam, Albania, Cuba, Mongolia, and Yugoslavia, not shown separately.
[7] Cost, insurance, and freight value, except Eastern Europe (except Hungary) and U.S.S.R., which are f.o.b (free on board).

Sources: International Monetary Fund, Organization for Economic Cooperation and Development, and Council of Economic Advisers.

TABLE B–107.—*World trade balance and current account balances, 1965, 1970, 1975, and 1979–82*

[Billions of U.S. dollars]

Area and country	1965	1970	1975	1979	1980	1981	1982 [1]
	World trade balance [2]						
Developed countries [3]	−7.4	−11.2	−32.5	−97.1	−143.2	−99.4	−90.7
United States	4.3	.5	2.2	−40.2	−36.2	−39.6	−48.5
Canada	−.2	2.5	−2.1	1.3	4.9	2.6	10.3
Japan	.3	.4	−2.1	−7.5	−10.9	8.6	8.3
European Community [4]	5.3	−5.2	−5.7	−33.9	−63.3	−31.4	−28.8
France	−.2	−1.0	−.8	−6.3	−18.9	−14.5	−20.2
West Germany	.3	4.3	15.2	12.2	4.9	12.2	20.8
Italy	−.2	−1.8	−3.6	−5.7	−21.8	−15.8	−13.2
United Kingdom	−2.3	−2.4	−8.8	−13.2	−5.7	.7	−4.6
Other developed countries	−6.4	−9.4	−24.7	−16.8	−37.7	−39.7	−32.0
Developing countries	−3.3	−6.1	4.9	44.8	68.6	10.8	−36.5
Oil-exporting countries [5]	4.2	7.6	60.8	114.2	164.0	114.4	48.9
Other	−7.5	−13.6	−55.9	−69.4	−95.4	−103.6	−85.4
Communist countries [6]	.7	.8	−10.3	−.5	.3	2.0	6.3
U.S.S.R.	.2	1.1	−3.7	6.9	7.9	6.2	.8
Eastern Europe	.2	−.3	−6.0	−5.1	−5.6	−6.1	.8
China	.2	.0	−.1	−2.2	−2.0	1.8	3.9
TOTAL [7]	−10.0	−16.4	−37.8	−52.7	−74.2	−86.5	−120.9
	Current account balances [8]						
Developed countries [3]	3.2	4.7	−2.7	29.8	70.6	−40.1	−43.8
United States	5.4	2.3	18.3	−.5	1.5	4.2	−8.8
Canada	−1.1	.8	−4.7	−4.2	−.9	−4.4	1.0
Japan	.9	2.0	−.6	−8.7	−10.7	5.1	6.5
European Community [4]	.8	2.8	2.5	−8.7	−37.3	−14.2	−17.0
France	.4	−.1	1.6	5.2	−3.6	−3.0	−11.5
West Germany	−1.6	.9	4.0	−6.1	−16.4	−7.1	−.3
Italy	2.2	.9	−.6	5.4	−9.8	−8.5	−5.5
United Kingdom	−.1	2.0	−3.4	−1.7	6.9	12.4	4.5
Other developed countries	−2.9	−3.1	−18.2	−7.7	−23.2	−30.7	−25.5
Developing countries			−16.5	−18.3	−1.3	−25.0	−61.0
Oil exporting countries [5]			19.4	27.9	72.1	56.5	2.0
Other			−35.9	−46.2	−73.4	−81.5	−63.0
Communist countries [6]	.3	−1.8	−11.2	−4.9	−3.0	2.7	6.7
U.S.S.R.			−4.7	3.8	3.5	2.7	3.1
Eastern Europe		−.8	−6.4	−7.6	−5.5	−3.5	−2.0
China		−.1	−.1	−1.1	−1.0	3.5	5.6
TOTAL			−30.4	−53.0	−74.9	−62.4	−98.1

[1] Preliminary estimates.
[2] Exports f.o.b. (free-on-board ship value) less imports c.i.f. (cost, insurance, and freight).
[3] Includes the OECD countries, South Africa, and non-OECD Europe.
[4] Includes Belgium-Luxembourg, Denmark, Greece, Ireland, and the Netherlands, not shown separately.
[5] Includes Algeria, Ecuador, Gabon, Indonesia, Iran, Iraq, Kuwait, Libya, Nigeria, Oman, Qatar, Saudi Arabia, United Arab Emirates, and Venezuela.
[6] Includes North Korea, Vietnam, Albania, Cuba, Mongolia, and Yugoslavia, not shown separately.
[7] Asymmetries arise in global payments aggregations because of discrepancies in coverage, classification, timing, and valuation in the recording of transactions by the countries involved.
[8] OECD basis.

Sources: International Monetary Fund, Organization for Economic Cooperation and Development, and Council of Economic Advisers.

TABLE B–108.—*International reserves, selected years, 1952–82*

[Millions of SDRs; end of period]

Area and country	1952	1962	1972	1979	1980	1981	1982 November
All countries [1]	[2] 49,391	62,851	147,443	306,995	358,706	375,793	364,589
Industrial countries [3]	38,582	52,535	110,282	180,775	211,490	212,732	207,396
United States	24,714	17,220	12,112	15,170	21,479	25,502	30,415
Canada	1,944	2,561	5,572	2,951	3,159	3,755	3,396
Australia	920	1,168	5,656	1,359	1,603	1,713	5,539
Japan	1,101	2,021	16,916	15,667	20,164	25,083	22,150
New Zealand	183	251	767	344	277	580	523
Austria	116	1,081	2,505	3,832	4,879	5,279	5,157
Belgium	1,133	1,753	3,564	5,307	7,330	5,451	5,086
Denmark	150	256	787	2,514	2,712	2,246	2,004
Finland	132	237	664	1,204	1,501	1.319	1,254
France	686	4,049	9,224	16,212	24,301	21,991	15,230
Germany	960	6,958	21,908	43,225	40,976	40,892	43,580
Iceland	8	32	78	125	138	199	132
Ireland	318	359	1,038	1,693	2,255	2,290	2,151
Italy	722	4,068	5,605	16,149	20,477	19,631	14,605
Netherlands	953	1,943	4,407	7,301	10,669	9,562	10,056
Norway	164	304	1,220	3,241	4,783	5,414	6,808
Spain	134	1,045	4,618	10,550	9,813	9,794	[4] 7,675
Sweden	504	802	1,453	2,880	2,893	3,306	3,499
Switzerland	1,667	2,919	6,961	15,391	15,190	14,925	15,448
United Kingdom	1,956	3,308	5,201	15,626	16,851	13,757	12,770
Oil-exporting countries	1,699	2,030	10,071	56,318	73,601	81,428	76,989
Algeria	84	186	454	2,214	3,153	3,370	2,511
Indonesia	314	108	531	3,093	4,311	4,416	3,041
Iran	177	211	885	11,682	...	...	...
Iraq	131	193	720	...	...	...	...
Kuwait	50	97	335	2,268	3,169	3,583	5,263
Libya	...	96	2,694	4,902	10,372	7,860	6,239
Nigeria	500	289	346	4,235	8,049	3,371	1,128
Oman	...	...	149	445	692	988	[4] 1,049
Qatar	...	...	56	228	286	339	...
Saudi Arabia	...	268	2,303	14,790	18,536	27,855	26,929
United Arab Emirates	...	...	...	1,107	1,600	2,775	[4] 2,957
Venezuela	443	583	1,595	5,958	5,579	7,415	6,721
Non-oil developing countries	8,576	8,171	26,132	68,703	71,776	75,303	73,035
Africa	1,202	1,635	3,168	4,286	4,444	4,175	4,218
Asia	3,407	2,550	6,640	23,205	24,947	27,441	32,628
Europe	966	1,346	6,428	7,400	8,060	8,159	6,972
Middle East	825	940	2,402	7,442	8,311	9,001	8,753
Western Hemisphere	2,175	1,700	7,494	26,370	26,014	26,527	20,464

[1] Includes Taiwan, not shown in area detail.
[2] Includes Cuba.
[3] Includes Luxembourg.
[4] Data are for October 1982.

Note.—International reserves is comprised of monetary authorities' holdings of gold, special drawing rights (SDRs), reserve positions in the International Monetary Fund, and foreign exchange. Data exclude U.S.S.R., other Eastern European countries, and Cuba (after 1960).

U.S. dollars per SDR (end of period) are: 1952 and 1962—1.00000; 1972—1.08571; 1977—1.21471; 1978—1.30279; 1979—1.31733; 1980—1.27541; 1981—1.6396; and November 1982—1.07953.

Source: International Monetary Fund, *"International Financial Statistics."*

TABLE B–109.—*Growth rates in real gross national product, 1960–82*

[Percent change]

Area and country	1960–73 annual average	1974–81 annual average	1978	1979	1980	1981	1982 [1]	U.S. dollar value in 1981 (billions) [2]
Developed countries [3]	5.1	2.7	4.1	3.5	1.2	1.4	–.5	7,020
United States	4.1	2.7	4.8	3.2	–.2	2.0	–1.8	2,926
Canada	5.6	2.6	3.7	3.0	.0	3.0	–5.0	280
Japan	10.4	4.4	5.1	5.6	4.2	2.9	2.5	1,150
European Community [4]	4.7	1.9	3.1	3.4	1.3	–.4	.3	2,420
France	5.8	2.5	3.7	3.5	1.6	.3	1.5	577
West Germany	4.7	2.2	3.6	4.3	1.8	–.3	–1.3	687
Italy	5.2	2.1	2.7	4.9	4.0	–.2	.8	299
United Kingdom	3.1	.9	3.3	1.4	–1.7	–.8	.5	502
Other developed countries	5.1	1.9	2.1	–1.7	4.0	5.2	([5])	245
Developing countries	5.8	4.4	4.3	4.1	4.5	2.7	.8	1,965
Oil exporting countries [6]	....	3.7	6.7	3.2	2.0	–.5	1.2	540
Other	....	4.6	3.3	4.5	5.6	3.1	.7	1,425
Communist countries [7]	5.2	2.7	4.2	1.6	1.9	1.2	1.4	2,740
U.S.S.R.	5.2	2.3	3.4	.8	1.5	1.8	1.6	1,587
Eastern Europe	4.1	1.8	3.0	1.3	.4	–1.0	–.7	671
China	6.5	5.9	12.3	6.9	6.9	3.0	5.0	328
TOTAL	5.2	2.9	3.8	2.8	1.8	1.8	.2	11,725

[1] Preliminary estimates.
[2] Estimates based on conversion at average rates of exchange for 1980, except for those of the Communist countries, which were converted at U.S. purchasing power equivalents.
[3] Includes the OECD countries, South Africa, and non-OECD Europe.
[4] Includes Belgium-Luxembourg, Denmark, Greece, Ireland, and the Netherlands, not shown separately.
[5] Not available.
[6] Includes Algeria, Ecuador, Gabon, Indonesia, Iran, Iraq, Kuwait, Libya, Nigeria, Oman, Qatar, Saudi Arabia, United Arab Emirates, and Venezuela.
[7] Includes North Korea, Vietnam, Albania, Cuba, Mongolia, and Yugoslavia, not shown separately.

Sources: Department of Commerce, International Monetary Fund, Organization for Economic Cooperation and Development (OECD), and Council of Economic Advisers.

TABLE B–110.—*Industrial production and consumer prices, major industrial countries, 1960–82*

[1967=100]

Year or quarter	United States	Canada	Japan	European Community[1]	France	West Germany	Italy	United Kingdom
	Industrial production[2]							
1960	66.2	63.1	43.0	74.7	70	78.4	59.2	84.4
1961	66.7	65.6	51.2	78.1	73	82.8	65.5	84.3
1962	72.2	71.2	55.4	81.3	78	86.1	71.9	85.1
1963	76.5	75.7	61.7	84.8	86	88.9	78.4	88.4
1964	81.7	82.6	71.4	91.0	90	96.6	79.2	95.0
1965	89.8	89.7	74.2	94.7	93	102.1	82.8	97.7
1966	97.8	96.2	83.8	98.4	98	103.0	93.3	99.2
1967	100.0	100.0	100.0	100.0	100	100.0	100.0	100.0
1968	106.3	106.4	115.2	107.4	104	109.2	106.4	106.7
1969	111.1	113.7	133.4	117.6	114	123.2	110.5	110.3
1970	107.8	115.3	151.8	123.3	120	131.1	117.6	110.9
1971	109.6	121.5	155.7	126.1	128	133.6	117.5	110.6
1972	119.7	130.7	167.0	131.7	135	138.7	122.7	113.2
1973	129.8	144.6	190.5	141.4	145	147.7	134.6	123.0
1974	129.3	149.2	183.1	142.3	148	145.1	140.6	120.0
1975	117.8	140.3	163.9	132.8	139	137.1	127.6	114.3
1976	130.5	148.5	182.0	142.6	149	149.1	143.5	117.4
1977	138.2	152.2	189.7	145.9	152	152.0	145.1	122.9
1978	146.1	157.8	201.1	149.7	155	154.1	147.9	126.9
1979	152.5	167.4	217.7	156.8	163	161.8	157.6	132.2
1980	147.0	164.6	232.5	155.6	160	162.3	166.5	123.6
1981	151.0	167.3	239.5	152.3	157	159.9	162.7	118.8
1982 p	138.6	....	....	....	....	....	....	....
1981:								
I	151.8	167.8	235.4	151.5	158	162	157.7	117.8
II	152.5	172.8	236.1	152.1	160	160	160.1	118.5
III	153.0	168.1	241.1	152.1	161	161	152.3	118.6
IV	146.3	160.7	245.9	151.8	161	160	159.8	120.0
1982:								
I	141.8	156.1	243.6	151.9	158	162	161.0	119.2
II	139.4	151.9	239.7	151.5	159	159	158.6	119.8
III	138.2	147.7	243.5	148.6	151	154	146.6	119.8
IV p	135.1	....	....	....	....	....	....	....
	Consumer prices							
1960	88.7	85.9	68.3	77.0	[3] 78.0	82.9	74.1	79.0
1961	89.6	86.7	71.8	81.1	[3] 80.6	84.8	75.7	81.6
1962	90.6	87.7	76.7	84.5	85.4	87.4	79.2	85.1
1963	91.7	89.2	82.5	87.6	89.5	89.9	85.1	86.8
1964	92.9	90.9	85.8	90.8	92.5	92.0	90.1	89.6
1965	94.5	93.1	91.6	94.2	94.8	95.0	94.2	93.9
1966	97.2	96.5	96.3	97.5	97.4	98.4	96.4	97.6
1967	100.0	100.0	100.0	100.0	100.0	100.0	100.0	100.0
1968	104.2	104.0	105.3	103.7	104.5	101.6	101.4	104.8
1969	109.8	108.8	110.9	108.0	111.3	103.5	104.1	110.3
1970	116.3	112.4	119.3	113.3	117.1	107.1	109.2	117.4
1971	121.3	115.6	126.5	120.3	123.5	112.7	114.4	128.5
1972	125.3	121.2	132.3	127.6	131.1	119.0	121.0	137.7
1973	133.1	130.3	147.9	138.3	140.7	127.2	134.0	150.2
1974	147.7	144.5	184.0	156.4	160.0	136.1	159.7	174.3
1975	161.2	160.1	205.8	176.7	178.9	144.2	186.8	216.5
1976	170.5	172.1	224.9	195.2	196.1	150.4	218.1	252.4
1977	181.5	185.9	243.0	214.7	214.5	155.9	255.2	292.4
1978	195.4	202.5	252.3	229.9	233.9	160.2	286.2	316.6
1979	217.4	221.0	261.3	250.7	259.1	166.8	328.5	359.0
1980	246.8	243.5	282.2	281.6	294.2	175.9	398.0	423.6
1981	272.4	273.9	296.2	314.1	332.7	186.3	472.4	473.9
1982	289.1	303.4	....	....	....	....	....	514.7
1981:								
I	262.9	262.0	291.4	300.7	315.7	182.2	448.4	450.4
II	269.0	270.2	296.3	310.4	326.1	185.5	468.0	472.3
III	276.7	278.2	296.9	317.8	338.9	187.8	482.1	480.5
IV	280.7	285.0	300.1	326.3	349.9	190.0	504.9	492.3
1982:								
I	283.0	292.2	300.3	333.9	359.8	192.7	523.7	500.5
II	287.3	301.2	303.5	344.3	371.0	195.4	539.6	516.6
III	292.8	307.6	304.8	348.2	376.0	197.6	562.7	518.9
IV	293.4	312.6	....	....	....	....	....	522.7

[1] Consists of Belgium-Luxembourg, Denmark, France, Greece, Ireland, Italy, Netherlands, United Kingdom, and West Germany. Industrial production prior to July 1981 excludes data for Greece, which joined the EC in 1981.
[2] All data exclude construction. Quarterly data are seasonally adjusted.
[3] Data for 1960 and 1961 are for Paris only.

Sources: Department of Commerce (International Trade Administration, Office of Trade Investment and Analysis, Trade Performance Division) and Department of Labor (Bureau of Labor Statistics).

TABLE B–111.—*Unemployment rate, and hourly compensation, major industrial countries, 1960–82*

[Quarterly data seasonally adjusted]

Year or quarter	United States	Canada	Japan	France	West Germany	Italy	United Kingdom
	Unemployment rate (percent)[1]						
1960	5.5	7.0	1.7	1.6	1.1	3.8	2.1
1961	6.7	7.1	1.5	1.4	.6	3.2	1.9
1962	5.5	5.9	1.3	1.3	.6	2.8	2.7
1963	5.7	5.5	1.3	1.2	.5	2.4	3.3
1964	5.2	4.7	1.2	1.3	.4	2.6	2.4
1965	4.5	3.9	1.2	1.4	.3	3.5	2.1
1966	3.8	3.4	1.4	1.8	.3	3.8	2.2
1967	3.8	3.8	1.3	1.8	1.3	3.4	3.2
1968	3.6	4.5	1.2	2.4	1.1	3.4	3.2
1969	3.5	4.4	1.1	2.2	.6	3.3	3.0
1970	4.9	5.7	1.2	2.4	.5	3.1	3.1
1971	5.9	6.2	1.3	2.7	.6	3.1	3.9
1972	5.6	6.2	1.4	2.8	.7	3.6	4.2
1973	4.9	5.5	1.3	2.7	.7	3.4	3.2
1974	5.6	5.3	1.4	2.9	1.6	2.8	3.1
1975	8.5	6.9	1.9	4.2	3.5	3.2	4.6
1976	7.7	7.1	2.0	4.6	3.5	3.6	6.0
1977	7.1	8.1	2.0	5.0	3.5	3.6	6.4
1978	6.1	8.4	2.3	5.4	3.4	3.7	6.3
1979	5.8	7.5	2.1	6.1	3.0	3.9	5.7
1980	7.1	7.5	2.0	6.5	3.0	3.9	7.3
1981	7.6	7.6	2.2	7.7	4.2	4.2	11.3
1982	9.7	11.0				4.6	
1981:							
I	7.4	7.3	2.2	7.0	3.5	3.9	10.3
II	7.4	7.2	2.4	7.7	3.9	4.3	11.1
III	7.4	7.6	2.2	7.9	4.4	4.1	11.5
IV	8.3	8.4	2.2	7.9	4.9	4.5	12.5
1982:							
I	8.8	8.6	2.3	8.3	5.3	4.6	12.8
II	9.4	10.2	2.4	8.6	5.8	4.6	12.9
III	10.0	12.1	2.4	8.7	6.2	4.5	13.0
IV	10.7	12.7				4.5	
	Hourly compensation (1977=100)[2]						
1960	36.7	29.9	6.6	16.2	10.5	11.9	24.9
1961	37.7	29.4	7.7	17.8	12.3	13.1	26.8
1962	39.1	28.7	8.8	19.6	13.9	15.5	28.3
1963	40.3	29.4	9.8	21.7	14.9	18.3	29.5
1964	42.0	30.6	11.0	23.3	16.1	20.4	31.6
1965	42.8	32.1	12.4	25.1	17.6	21.8	34.7
1966	44.8	34.6	13.6	26.7	19.0	22.8	37.6
1967	47.0	37.3	15.3	28.9	20.1	25.4	38.2
1968	50.4	40.0	17.9	32.6	21.3	27.1	35.6
1969	53.9	43.0	21.3	32.3	23.6	30.7	38.8
1970	57.6	47.8	25.4	33.9	29.5	36.8	44.3
1971	61.1	53.1	30.3	38.0	34.7	43.1	51.8
1972	64.4	58.1	40.1	46.2	42.0	52.3	60.0
1973	69.0	63.4	55.0	60.0	56.9	66.4	65.5
1974	76.3	75.0	67.1	66.2	67.1	74.0	78.2
1975	85.4	82.4	77.1	88.5	79.4	95.0	96.5
1976	92.3	97.1	82.3	90.6	83.5	89.5	91.8
1977	100.0	100.0	100.0	100.0	100.0	100.0	100.0
1978	108.3	99.4	136.1	123.1	125.6	119.1	128.1
1979	118.9	106.6	138.5	148.2	147.5	143.1	168.5
1980	132.8	116.4	142.6	174.2	161.7	164.8	228.2
1981	146.4	126.1	157.0	158.3	139.9	152.4	230.8
1982	158.8						

[1] Unemployment rates, approximating U.S. concepts. Data for United Kingdom exclude Northern Ireland. Quarterly data for France, West Germany, and United Kingdom should be viewed as less precise indicators of unemployment under U.S. concepts than the annual data. Beginning 1977, changes in the Italian survey resulted in a large increase in persons enumerated as unemployed. However, many also reported that they had not actively sought work in the past 30 days. Such persons have been provisionally excluded for comparability with U.S. concepts; their inclusion would more than double the rates shown for Italy.

[2] Hourly compensation in manufacturing, U.S. dollar basis. Data relate to all employed persons (wage and salary earners and the self-employed) in the United States and Canada, and to all employees (wage and salary earners) in the other countries. For France and United Kingdom compensation adjusted to include changes in employment taxes that are not compensation to employees, but are labor costs to employers.

Source: Department of Labor, Bureau of Labor Statistics.

21 / 27 / 46 / 53 / 57 / 58 / 64 / 65 / 66 / 70-1 / 74 / 78 / 79 / 84 / 86 / 106 / 136

Recorder [illegible] Nie's / , ages perspective 60's.